The Goebbels Diaries

Dr. Joseph Goebbels being interviewed in Berlin
by Louis P. Lochner, editor and translator of the diaries.

The Goebbels Diaries

1942 - 1943

EDITED, TRANSLATED

AND WITH AN INTRODUCTION BY

Louis P. Lochner

Doubleday & Company, Inc.

Garden City   1948   New York

Publisher's Note

When the Russians occupied Berlin in 1945 they went through the German official archives with more vigor than discrimination, shipped some material to Russia, destroyed some, and left the rest scattered underfoot. They often followed a system that is difficult to understand —emptying papers on the floor and shipping to Russia the filing cabinets that had contained them.

Considerable fragments of Dr. Goebbels's diaries, from which the following pages were selected, were found in the courtyard of his ministry, where they had evidently narrowly escaped burning, many of the pages being singed and all smelling of smoke. Apparently they were originally bound in the German type of office folder. Thin metal strips in the salmon-colored binders were run through holes punched in the paper, bent over, and locked into place.

At that time all Berlin was one great junk yard, with desperate people laying hands on anything tangible and movable that could be used for barter. The unburned papers were taken away by one of these amateur junk dealers, who carefully salvaged the binders and discarded the contents—leaving more than 7,000 sheets of loose paper. A few binders had not been removed but most of the pages were tied up in bundles as wastepaper. It later proved a considerable task to put them together again in the right sequence, as they were not numbered.

In the same batch were found a number of odds and ends from Goebbels's private files. Many of the papers were water-soaked and showed signs of dirt and the imprint of nails where they had been walked on. The edges of some were scorched, showing that attempts to burn them had failed.

Among the papers in this miscellaneous batch were found the following:

The rough draft, headed *Entwurf*, of a message to Hermann Goering congratulating him on his fiftieth birthday.

A receipted bill from a jeweler for repairs to a Nazi party emblem —seventy-five pfennigs, dated June 20, 1939.

A six-page radio address, corrected by Goebbels in blue pencil, dated October 3, 1944.

A list of fifteen articles of old clothing, dated June 10, 1942, given by Goebbels to a charity collection. A note was appended that Mrs. Goebbels could do nothing about getting her donation together until she had talked with her husband.

An expense account, taking up five sheets of paper, for Goebbels's trip on March 8, 1943, by airplane from Berlin to Hitler's GHQ, where Goebbels remained one day and then flew back to Berlin after a conference with Hitler. Expenses totaled 85 marks.

A letter dated June 2, 1931, signed by two women, in response to a request published by Goebbels in the newspaper, *Angriff*, asking for witnesses to an incident on June 1, 1931 (before Hitler came to power). The letter is notarized:

"Dr. Goebbels and another came out of the police station in the Maikaeferkaserne with the Fuehrer. As he came through the door, the police brought one of our brown shirts (S.A. Maenner) by force up the steps to the entrance. Dr. Goebbels, who stood in their way at the door, was hit on the shoulder by one of the police officials and pushed out of the way so that he fell down the steps. The handling of our Fuehrer started a demonstration on the part of the crowd, which hooted at the police, and *Heils* for the Fuehrer broke out. Then the police attacked the crowd with blackjacks and we were driven off."

A letter of January 26, 1939, notifying Goebbels that the taxes on his Schwanenwerder property had been increased and that he owed some back taxes for the previous year.

A report by one of Goebbels's subordinates on the moving of Goebbels's property from his Schwanenwerder home to a safe place: some to Lanke, and some into the air-raid shelter in the Hermann Goeringstrasse. The inventory includes oriental rugs, furniture, Gobelin tapestries, lamps, cut glass, silver, porcelain, linen, et cetera. The report concludes that Goebbels's valet, Emil, would be responsible for taking Goebbels's pistols into the Hermann Goeringstrasse shelter during an alarm. And *"Pistole"* was underlined in the original.

A letter dated January 2, 1933 (about four weeks before Hitler took over), showing that Goebbels was in trouble about his income tax. The letter was written by a Nazi tax consultant, who reported that in dealing with the tax people he "registered a complaint on the ground that such a payment is impossible and would result in the destruction of your economic independence." A subsequent letter, dated March 28, 1933 (two months after the Nazis were in power), indicated that the tax specialist, Schuler, had been able to fix up the matter of the back taxes satisfactorily.

A telegram sent by Goebbels one month before his death (March 13, 1945) to Colonel Berger, thanking the German troops at the Neisse River bridgehead for their collection and the donation of more than a quarter of a million marks for Winter Relief.

There was also a typewritten undated balance sheet showing Goebbels's income, the allowance he made to Frau Goebbels, et cetera. For income-tax purposes he declared a total income of 10,281.55 marks, of which he paid 6,481.55 to his wife, leaving 3,800 for himself.

There was a handwritten analysis of Goebbels's income for the years 1933 through 1937 inclusive. It was done in thirteen columns, showing income from book royalties, salary, interest, deductions for various taxes, et cetera. His total income before taxes and deductions was:

1933	34,376 marks
1934	134,423
1935	62,190
1936	63,654
1937	66,905

One sheet of paper, handwritten, but not in Goebbels's writing, was headed: Account with Central Publishing Company of the National Socialist party. From December 16, 1935, to December 23, 1936, he drew advances amounting to 290,000 marks against future royalties. His book royalties from December 31, 1935, to December 31, 1936, amounted to 63,416.31 marks. So he was in debt to the Nazi Publishing Company (*Centralverlag der NSDAP*) to the amount of 226,583.69 marks.

It is an interesting side light on Goebbels's financial methods that whereas in 1936 he declared a total income of 63,654 marks, his income from book royalties alone amounted to approximately the same—63,-416.31 marks.

An account for the purchase of paintings showed that 154,000 marks' worth of paintings were bought, on which a 5 per cent commission was paid for purchase or handling. This was dated January 30, 1945—three months before Berlin fell. The paintings, with a few exceptions, were all by German artists. Six gifts of paintings were noted, with dates of gift to:

Sauckel, on his fiftieth birthday, October 27, 1944.

Gauleiter Streicher, on his sixtieth birthday, February 12, 1945.

Dr. Ley, on his fifty-fifth birthday, February 15, 1945.

Dr. Hierl, on his seventieth birthday, February 24, 1945.

Schaub, on his birthday, August 10, 1944.

Minister Dr. Meissner, on his sixty-fifth birthday, March 13, 1945.

There are a number of drafts of birthday telegrams. Apparently Goebbels had a system whereby his office automatically laid before him drafts of birthday greetings which he, Goebbels, then corrected.

A memorandum dated June 4, 1942, to Goebbels, called attention to four birthdays coming in the following week.

In red crayon was a notation, *erledigt,* or taken care of, about the birthday of the Minister of Posts, Dr. Ohnesorge, aged 70.

Beside the name of Professor Paul Schultze Naumburg, aged 73, Goebbels wrote *Nein.*

Beside the name of Richard Strauss, Garmisch-Partenkirchen, aged 78, on Thursday, June 11, Goebbels also wrote *Nein.*

Beside the name of Jenny Jugo, Goebbels wrote *Blumen/Karte* (flowers and card).

There was a file on Goebbels's mortgage of 100,000 marks on the Schwanenwerder place, which he apparently bought after the outbreak of war in 1939.

The diaries were typed on fine water-marked paper, which was rare in wartime Germany and available only to high government officials. In looking over the material offered for sale or barter, a customer was struck by the impressive quality of the paper and sensed that he must have fallen on something of interest and importance. He acquired the lot for its value as scrap paper. The bundles, roughly roped together, passed through several hands, and eventually came into the possession of Mr. Frank E. Mason, who has made a number of visits to Germany since the war. Mr. Mason has had long experience in Germany, first as Military Attaché at the American Embassy in Berlin at the end of World War I and later as a correspondent. It was obvious to him that the material consisted of fragments of Dr. Goebbels's diaries. An examination by Louis P. Lochner, former chief of the Berlin bureau of the Associated Press, revealed the authenticity of the documents, as Mr. Lochner himself explains in detail in his introduction to this volume. Publication was decided on only after this had been clearly established.

Goebbels indulged in free-and-easy abuse of everybody who disagreed with him. His entries are given as he wrote them, with the gutter language into which he frequently lapsed. This was essential to a faithful presentation, although the publishers obviously share neither his views nor his expression of them.

The selections reveal Goebbels as the unflagging motive force behind the vicious anti-Semitism of the Nazi regime. His aim was the extermination of all Jews. Hitler was in complete sympathy with this infamous project, as were his henchmen. Goebbels's role was to keep Hitler's mind inflamed and obtain authority to carry out specific measures against the Jews. He thus reveals himself as having a major share of responsibility for the atrocities that shocked the world. A number of examples of this distasteful material have been reproduced, not only because they reflected Goebbels's mentality, but more particularly because his views were translated into action and are therefore of vital significance. Goebbels also reveals himself as violently opposed to the Christian churches. He makes it clear that while he wants to devote himself to the extermination of the Jews during the war, he plans to deal with the churches after the war and reduce them to impotence.

The task of selecting, editing, and translating the text of this important document was exacting. It called for a man with knowledge and scholarly background. It is fortunate that Mr. Lochner was available for this work. He brought to it long experience, knowledge of European politics, wide acquaintance among political figures under the Weimar Republic and the Nazi regime, and complete command of the German language. For more than twenty years he was chief of the Berlin bureau of The Associated Press, and on his return to this country in 1942 he wrote *What About Germany?*—a book that has had considerable success. He had unique standing in Berlin, as is shown by the fact that for many years he was president of the Foreign Press Association and for six years president of the American Chamber of Commerce.

The publishers regret that it was possible to make use of only a small part of the original material in a single volume. The level of interest could have been maintained if far more space had been available. The original diaries will serve as source material for many future writers, and to this end they are to be deposited in the Hoover War Library at Stanford University where they will be accessible to the public. It is hoped that this will result in further translations and publications.

HUGH GIBSON

The Office of Alien Property has granted permission to publish a translation of selections from the manuscript purporting to be the 1942–43 diary of Paul Joseph Goebbels. No representative of the interested agencies of the United States Government has read the original manuscript or the translation of excerpts therefrom. The Department of State desires, as a matter of policy, to encourage widespread publication of documents such as this purports to be, of significance in the field of foreign policy, and has therefore not objected to the publication. The United States Government, however, neither warrants nor disclaims the authenticity of the manuscript upon which this publication is based, and neither approves nor disapproves of the translation, selection of material, annotation, or other editorial comment contained herein. It is proposed that the manuscript will be made available to all those who are interested in studying it or in translating all or part of it.

Introduction

Introduction

BY LOUIS P. LOCHNER

I went at the task of selecting representative material for this book with a good deal of trepidation. Here were some 7,100 pages (approximately 750,000 words) of German copy to select from, yet the book was to be limited to about five hundred printed pages. It was much the same sort of situation I faced constantly during my years of newspaper service as chief of the Berlin Bureau of The Associated Press of America: whenever Adolf Hitler delivered one of his addresses to the German Reichstag, which often lasted for two hours, I was faced with the problem of remaining within the number of words that the newspapers having membership in The Associated Press could absorb, yet missing nothing of importance to the reader.

The Goebbels diaries, from which representative sections have been selected for this book, cover the following periods:

January 21 to May 23, 1942, with the entries for March 22 to March 25 and April 10 missing.

December 7 to December 20, 1942.

March 1 to March 20, 1943.

April 9 to May 28, 1943, with the entries for May 2 to May 6 missing.

July 25 to July 30, 1943.

September 8 to September 30, 1943.

November 1 to November 30, 1943, with the entries for November 5 and November 23 missing.

December 4 to December 9, 1943.

No doubt some of the missing pages went up in flames, for there is a smell of burnt paper to the whole collection, and some pages are singed.

It is also likely that large sections of the diaries, indeed whole volumes, were destroyed in ignorance of their content and importance. If this be true, the world has lost documents of inestimable value.

Each day Joseph Goebbels dictated at great length an account of what transpired the previous day. This fact should be kept in mind by the reader, who may occasionally be puzzled to find the Propaganda Minister referring to an event as having occurred on one day when obviously it must have transpired the day before.

For his diaries he used an especially heavy watermarked paper and large German-Gothic script of a sort one seldom finds on typewriters. There was triple spacing between the lines, and the margins were wide. No ordinary mortal in those days could have commanded such paper or permitted himself the luxury of such large type and generous spacing.

Although Goebbels seems never to have failed to record his daily observations, which in some cases took up as many as eighty-five typewritten pages, he apparently seldom, if ever, took the time to read over what he had previously written. It thus happened that he was frequently repetitious; in fact, at times he used virtually the same words on two consecutive days to describe the same event.

Every day's entry began with *Die Lage* (The Situation). It was virtually a recapitulation of the daily military communiqué—the confidential and complete communiqué to which only privileged persons had access. In a few cases *Die Lage* is followed by the words "To be inserted later." The little doctor's busy life was such, however, that he never seems to have bothered to have this material inserted later.

(Paul) Joseph Goebbels was born October 29, 1897, in the smoky factory town of Rheydt in the Rhineland. He was the son of a factory foreman, Fritz Goebbels, and his wife, Maria Odenhausen, a blacksmith's daughter. His parents were devout Roman Catholics, as were his various relations.

The boy Joseph—or, as he was nicknamed, Jupp (pronounced Youp) —attended one of the Catholic grade schools of this textile center of 30,000 inhabitants, and also went through the Gymnasium, or high school, of his native city. He was rejected for military service during World War I because of a deformed foot.

He managed to secure a number of Catholic scholarships and attended eight famous German universities—Bonn, Freiburg, Wuerzburg, Munich, Cologne, Frankfurt, Berlin, and finally Heidelberg, where he took his Ph.D. degree in 1921 at the age of twenty-four. He studied history, philology, and the history of art and literature.

His ambition was to be a writer. The year of his graduation at Heidelberg he wrote an unsuccessful novel, *Michael,* and followed it by two plays, *Blood Seed* (*Blutsaat*) and *The Wanderer* (*Der Wanderer*), which no producer would accept. He also applied, unsuccessfully, for a reporter's job on the *Berliner Tageblatt,* internationally famed liberal daily.

All these experiences, together with the loss of the war and the collapse of the German Empire, embittered him and kept him restlessly wandering from Rheydt to Cologne, Berlin, and Munich, until, rather by accident, he heard Adolf Hitler speak at Munich in 1922.

Young Joseph Goebbels first tried to interest university students in Hitler's message and thereby discovered that he had the gift of eloquence. That was just the sort of man Hitler needed. The Fuehrer tested his disciple's abilities in the Rhine and Ruhr, then under Allied occupation. Working under an assumed name, Goebbels managed to win converts to Nazism and located his office at Hattingen in the Ruhr Valley. In 1924 the French occupation authorities ejected him.

Goebbels then drifted to Elberfeld, where he became editor of a Nazi organ, *Voelkische Freiheit* (Racist Freedom). His articles against the French Negro troops of occupation were especially vitriolic. That same year he was appointed business manager for the Nazi gau, or district, of Rhine-Ruhr.

I have been fortunate in having access to an important document dealing with this period of Goebbels's life. Former President Hoover, during a visit to Germany in 1946, was given a hand-written diary kept by Dr. Goebbels from August 12, 1925, to October 16, 1926, which he has kindly placed at my disposal. This diary is important in its revelation of a little scoundrel in training to become a great scoundrel. In addition, it gives valuable evidence of the authenticity of the later diaries.

The accounts of those days are replete with references to beer-hall fights, street brawls, and encounters with the police. Goebbels turned his back completely upon the church in which he was raised, and abandoned the faith of his fathers.

Father and Mother Goebbels were greatly displeased at their son's apostasy. He complains, on the occasion of a visit to his parents at Rheydt, September 11, 1925: "Father is serious and uncommunicative. That depresses me." He writes on the occasion of his twenty-eighth birthday at Elberfeld: "Not a word from home. How hurt I feel!" Two days later he observes: "Not a word from home for my birthday, nor anything else. That rather pains me. I am gradually losing contact.

And yet I think so often and with such love of home. Why do I have to lose everything, yes, everything?"

In speaking of his visits he occasionally refers to his much younger brother, Konrad. He does not mention his brother Hans, his senior by two years, probably because Hans no longer lived at home in 1925-26. He did manage, however, in 1933 to secure a lucrative position for Hans as Director General of the Provincial Fire and Life Insurance Companies of the Rhine Province. He seemed especially attached to his only sister Maria.

I cite a few examples from the handwritten earlier diaries:

September 30, 1925: "Dr. Ley is a fool and possibly an intriguer."

October 2, 1925: "Stresemann has started for the Locarno Conference, to sell Germany out to capitalism. That fat, complacent swine!"

October 12, 1925: "In Munich [Nazi] scoundrels are at work—nitwits who won't tolerate real brains. . . . That's the reason for the opposition to Strasser and me."

October 26, 1925: "Streicher spoke. Like a pig."

January 26, 1926: "Kaufmann arrived with Lucas. I don't like it. Lucas is a stupid camel. Likes to show off. But there's nothing to him."

March 27, 1926: "Went to the office for a moment. Found that camel, Dr. Ziegler, there. He had been saying bad things about me. Defamed me. I can tell it by the looks of the scoundrel."

These examples are sufficient to establish a similarity of vituperative expressions between both sets of diaries, and to indicate that the later diaries, although typewritten, chronicled Goebbels's real thoughts.

This is true also of Goebbels's commentaries on Hitler. If one had only the typewritten diaries to go by, one might conclude from the adulation amounting almost to deification of the Fuehrer that Goebbels was writing with a view to expediency rather than from conviction —witness an entry like that of March 19, 1942: "As long as he [the Fuehrer] lives and is among us in good health, as long as he can give us the strength of his spirit and the power of his manliness, no evil can touch us." Could such an apotheosis have been written in sincerity by as coldly calculating a realist as Joseph Goebbels, by a man who from time to time even disagreed with the leader?

Here again the earlier diaries furnish corroborative evidence. They prove that Joseph Goebbels, who otherwise seemed to love no one but himself and his children, did indeed adore Adolf Hitler.

I quote a few significant entries:

November 6, 1925: "Brunswick. We drove to see Hitler. He was just eating his dinner. Immediately he jumped up and stood facing us. He squeezed my hand. Like an old friend.

"And these large blue eyes! Like stars. He is happy to see me. I am supremely happy. . . .

"Later I drove to the meeting and talked for two hours. Tremendous applause. Then *heils* and hand-clapping. He has arrived. He shakes my hand. He is completely exhausted from his great speech [delivered elsewhere]. Then he took the floor here for half an hour.

"Wit, irony, humor, sarcasm, earnestness, passion, white heat—all this is contained in his speech. This man has everything it takes to be king. The great tribune of the people. The coming dictator."

November 23, 1925: "Plauen. I arrive. Hitler is there. My joy is great. He greets me like an old friend. And lavishes attention on me. I have him all to myself. What a guy (*So ein Kerl!*).

"And then he speaks. How small I am!

"He gives me his picture. With a greeting to the Rhineland.

"Heil Hitler. . . .

"I want Hitler to be my friend. His picture is standing on my table. I simply could not bear it if I ever had to despair of this man."

December 29, 1925: "Rheydt. Awakened early in the morning. Schmitz brought me a package. A Christmas greeting from Hitler. His book, bound in leather, with a dedication, 'In recognition of the exemplary manner of your fighting.' I am happy!"

April 13, 1926: "Munich. At 8 P.M. by car to the Buergerbraeu. Hitler is already there. My heart beats as though it were about to burst (*zum Zerspringen*). Into the hall. Frenzied greetings. Man after man, the house jam-packed. Streicher opens the proceedings. Then I speak for two and a half hours. I give everything there is in me. The people simply rave. They applaud noisily. As I conclude, Hitler embraces me. His eyes are filled with tears. I am happy."

April 19, 1926: "Stuttgart. Hitler embraces me when he sees me. He lavishes a lot of praise on me. I believe he has taken me to his heart as no one else."

June 14, 1926: "Elberfeld. I am so happy Hitler is coming. I venerate and love him."

June 16, 1926: "Duesseldorf. Hitler has been here for two days. . . . Hitler, the dear old comrade. One cannot but like him as a person. In addition he is an outstanding personality. One always learns something new from this obstinate man. As a speaker he combines gesture, mimicry, and language in great harmony. The born agitator. With that man one can conquer the world. Unleash him and he makes the whole corrupt republic totter. His most beautiful words yesterday: 'God showed us mercy beyond measure in our struggle. His most beautiful gift to us is the hatred of our enemies, whom we in turn hate with all our hearts.'"

July 6, 1926: "Weimar. Hitler spoke. About politics, the Idea, and organization. Deep and mystical. Almost like a gospel. One shudders as one skirts the abyss of life with him. I thank Fate which gave us this man."

When one reads these earlier diary entries, one cannot but conclude that the diaries of 1942 and 1943 are sincere in their portrayal of a very close relationship of mutual trust between Hitler and Goebbels. The sequel to the diaries, too, bears testimony to the sincerity of Goebbels's adoration of his Fuehrer and to the sincerity of the diaries: he committed suicide immediately after Hitler passed out of his life!

Unfortunately space does not permit the systematic inclusion of excerpts from the earlier handwritten diaries. Nevertheless, some sections of them seem to me essential for a proper understanding of Goebbels and his time.

There is, first of all, Goebbels's revelation of his attitude toward his fellow men. The diaries for 1942–43 convey this only by inference. On August 12, 1925, however, he put down in black and white: "As soon as I am with a person for three days, I don't like him any longer; and if I am with him for a whole week, I hate him like the plague."

On October 15, 1925, he observed, "I have learned to despise the human being from the bottom of my soul. He makes me sick in my stomach. Phooey!"

On April 24, 1926, he had occasion to write: "Much dirt and many intrigues. The human being is a *canaille*."

On August 9, 1926, he found that "The only real friend one has in the end is the dog." This was followed on August 17 with a further tribute to his dog Benno: "The more I get to know the human species, the more I care for my Benno."

The earlier diaries further reveal, as already pointed out, that Goebbels's parents by no means approved of his conversion from Catholicism to Nazism.

Apparently son Joseph attempted occasionally to argue things out, for I find the laconic entries, *Krach mit Vater* (set-to with Father), and *Krach zu Hause* (family fight) recurring from time to time. On January 20, 1926, he wrote: "For a long time no word from home. They are angry with me. I am an apostate."

The earlier diaries afford insight into the little doctor's personal habits for which one looks in vain in the 1942–43 versions: his love life. Goebbels's amours were a matter of notoriety throughout Germany. His philandering even after he had become a Reich Minister was so well known and so scandalous that his wife, Magda, would on more than one occasion have sued for divorce had not Hitler insisted that he would stand for no marital scandal in the case of a person so highly placed as Dr. Goebbels.

In the diaries here offered, however, the chronicler of his life and work, otherwise so candid, chooses to be silent on this much-commented phase of extracurricular activities.

The Goebbels diaries for 1925 and 1926 make spicy reading for anybody interested in the amours of men of affairs. His loves in those years were Alma, Else, Anke, an unnamed Franconian, and a Munich girl—not successively but simultaneously.

Here are some entries:

August 14, 1925: "Alma wrote me a postcard from Bad Harzburg. The first sign of her since that night. This teasing, charming Alma! I rather like the kid.

"Received first letter from Else in Switzerland. Only Else dear can write like that. . . . Soon I'm going to the Rhine for a week, to be quite alone. Then Else will come to call for me. How happy I am in anticipation!"

August 15, 1925: "In these days I must think so often of Anke. Why just now? Because it is travel time? How wonderful it was to travel with her! This wonderful wench!

"I am yearning for Else. When shall I have her in my arms again? . . .

"Else dear, when shall I see you again?

"Alma, you dear featherweight!

"Anke, never can I forget you!

"And now I am, oh, so lonesome!"

August 27, 1925: "Three days on the Rhine. I am lazy, go hiking, and sleep. . . .

"Not a word from Else. Did she fail to receive my postcard? Or is she angry with me? How I pine for her!

"I am living in the same room as I did with her last Whitsuntide. What thoughts! What feeling! Why doesn't she come?

"I am standing at the Rhine waiting for you. Come, oh come, you kindly one, and bless me!"

August 30, 1925: "I received an invitation to give an address in Recklinghausen. How peculiarly that strikes me! I should like to speak there provided I knew Anke to be sitting among the listeners."

September 3, 1925: "Else is here! On Tuesday she returned jubilantly from Switzerland—fat, buxom, healthy, gay, only slightly tanned. She is very happy and in the best of spirits. She is good to me and gives me much joy."

October 14, 1925: "Why did Anke have to leave me quite alone? Was it a case of a broken pledge? On her part or mine? I just mustn't think about these things. Work alone can relieve me. . . . Probably that is best, after all!"

October 29, 1925: "Birthday! Twenty-eight years old. . . .

"I am getting old. I notice that today with a shudder. My hair is thinning out. On the way to baldness.

"But I want in all eternity to remain young at heart!"

December 21, 1925: "There is a curse on me and the women. Woe to those who love me! What a painful thought! It makes one despair."

December 29, 1925: "To Crefeld last night with Hess. Christmas celebration. A delightful, beautiful girl from Franconia. She's my type. Home with her through rain and storm. *Au revoir!*

"Else arrived."

January 20, 1926: "I yearn for the loving hands of a kindly woman."

January 31, 1926: "Missed the train. Swore and cursed. But charming chambermaid from Munich!"

February 6, 1926: "I yearn for a sweet woman! Oh, torturing pain! Do you call that life?"

Elsewhere in this introduction I have referred to Goebbels's radicalism. Two entries (among others) in the earlier diaries show how close the then young agitator felt to the Communists:

October 23, 1925: "In the final analysis it would be better for us to end our existence under Bolshevism than to endure slavery under capitalism."

January 31, 1926: "I think it is terrible that we and the Communists are bashing in each other's heads. . . . Where can we get together sometime with the leading Communists?"

It was over the issue of radicalism, in fact, that Goebbels in 1926 for a while entertained grave doubts about Adolf Hitler.

On February 15, 1926, Goebbels heard the Fuehrer speak at Bamberg. The little doctor wrote:

"Hitler talked for two hours. I feel as though someone had beaten me. What sort of a Hitler is this? A reactionary? Extremely lacking in poise and assuredness. Russian question: quite off the beam. Italy and England our natural allies! Terrible! Our task, he says, is the destruction of Bolshevism. Bolshevism is a Jewish creation. We must break Russia. Two hundred and eighty millions! . . .

"I am unable to say a word. I feel as though someone had hit me over the head. . . . How my heart hurts! . . . I should like to cry. . . .

"Certainly one of the greatest disappointments of my life. I no longer have complete faith in Hitler. That is the terrible thing about it: my props have been taken from under me. I am only half a person."

A month later, however, Goebbels begins to regain confidence that Hitler, after all, is right. On March 13 he wrote:

"I read Adolf Hitler's *The South Tyrol Question and the Problem of Germany's Alliances,* a wonderfully clear and broad-minded brochure. He's a great guy, all right—our chief."

His last doubts were dispelled when he heard Hitler speak in Munich on April 13. Here is the story of his capitulation:

"Hitler arrived. . . . He spoke for three hours. Brilliantly. He can make you doubt your own views. Italy and England our allies. Russia wants to devour us. All that is contained in his brochure and in the second volume of *Mein Kampf* which is to appear soon.

"We disagree. We ask questions. He gives brilliant replies. I love him. The social question: he opens great new vistas. He has thought everything through. His ideal: a just collectivism and individualism. As to soil—everything on and under it belongs to the people. Production to be creative and individualistic. Trusts, transportation, et cetera, to be socialized. That's something! He has thought it all through. I am now at ease about him. He is a he-man. He takes everything into account. A hothead like that can be my leader. I bow to the greater man, to the political genius."

Goebbels's script is one of the most difficult I have ever deciphered. Ordinarily German handwriting does not bother me in the least. When I first looked at the handwritten diaries of Joseph Goebbels cursorily I thought, "What regular, clear writing!" On closer inspection, however, the Goebbels calligraphy proved anything but easy to read.

It seemed, indeed, like a mirror of the man Goebbels as I knew him: apparently frank and straightforward, with a disarming smile and ingratiating voice, he was in reality a master at hiding his real thoughts behind a mask of urbanity.

In his handwriting, too, he evidently tried to hide something.

More difficult even than deciphering Goebbels's writing, however, was the translation of his innumerable German colloquial and slang expressions. I could meet the problem only by using equivalent American slang.

From the beginning of his career as a National Socialist Goebbels was a glutton for work. He spoke night after night, edited his paper, attended to a multitude of details of political organization, and still found time with Gregor Strasser to start the *National-Sozialistische Briefe* (National Socialist Letters) which were soon eagerly read by German workers. Goebbels could truly claim that he and Strasser secured Hitler his working-class following—Hitler himself had appealed mainly to the middle class, the petty bourgeoisie, as well as to ardent nationalists of every persuasion.

These *Briefe* were also a powerful weapon in the Goebbels-Strasser fight within the young and uproarious Nazi party against the "conservatives" such as Gottfried Feder, Hermann Esser, and, strangely enough, Julius Streicher. Goebbels was always to be found on the side of the radicals.

The Goebbels-Strasser duumvirate did not last long. At the Nazi party convention of 1926 at Bamberg, Bavaria, Goebbels soon sensed that Strasser and the Fuehrer did not see eye to eye, and decided his bread was buttered on the Hitler side. He sided with his idol against his friend. Hitler rewarded him on November 9, the anniversary of the ill-fated beer-cellar putsch of 1923, by making him Gauleiter for Greater Berlin, a task well calculated to test to the full the abilities of the little doctor, as an organizer, writer, strategist, and political leader.

The capital in those days was known as *das rote Berlin* (Red Berlin). It polled a large Communist vote, and the Socialists were the dominating party. That was grist for the fiery doctor's mill. Street brawls and beer-hall fights were the order of the day. In 1927 Goebbels founded a weekly paper, *Der Angriff* (The Attack), which by 1929 became a biweekly and from 1930 on a daily. If the Communists hitherto held a monopoly on guttersnipe vituperative language, they now had a thing or two to learn from the venomous Nazi editor.

Goebbels's career as a parliamentarian began in 1928, when he was elected to the German Reichstag. A year later he also became a town councillor of Berlin.

Time and again the Nazi organization of Berlin came into conflict with the police and was forbidden. Nevertheless Goebbels managed in 1927 to show up at the Nuremberg party convention with 700 Berlin SA Brown Shirts.

Adolf Hitler was much impressed with *der gescheite Dr. Goebbels* (the cleverly intelligent Dr. Goebbels), as I once heard him call his Propaganda Minister in a Reichstag speech. This young man showed that he possessed something which many an older politician could well envy him: an uncanny understanding of the psychology of the German people. Goebbels was very often way off in his estimate of foreign nations; however, he did know his fellow Germans.

In 1929 Hitler made the then thirty-two-year-old Goebbels Reich Propaganda Leader of the Nazi party. "Propaganda has only one object," the new Reichsleiter said on one occasion—"to conquer the masses. Every means that furthers this aim is good; every means that hinders it is bad." He had already given samples of his skill at propaganda not only by his articles and the innumerable handbills and posters he designed, but also in the books, all written before 1930, *The Unknown SA Man, Lenin or Hitler? The Second Revolution, Buch Isidor,* and *Knorke.*

Goebbels was quite willing to admit that his speeches and writings were usually on the "primitive" side. "Our propaganda is primitive," The Associated Press reported him as saying, "because the people think primitively. We speak the language the people understand."

In his *Battle for Berlin* (*Kampf um Berlin*), written in 1934, after he had already become Reich Propaganda Minister but dealing with his years as Gauleiter of Berlin from 1929 on, he wrote: "Masses are unformed stuff. Only in the hands of the political artists do the masses become a people and the people a nation."

Goebbels proved to be a wizard at demagoguery. He mixed satire with humor, irony with somberness, quips in the vernacular with pontifical adjurations. His dark piercing eyes, his straight black hair brushed back, his taut skin, made one think of certain representations of Mephistopheles.

January 30, 1933, brought the accession of Adolf Hitler to undreamed-of power. In the first official announcements the name of Dr. Goebbels was conspicuously absent. Hermann Goering and Wilhelm Frick were the only two National Socialists besides Adolf Hitler in the first Hitler cabinet.

Goebbels could well afford to wait. Hitler had great plans for him. On June 30, 1933, he decreed the establishment of a new cabinet office, that of Reich Ministry for Public Enlightenment and Propaganda, with Joseph Goebbels as its head, stating that the new venture would be "responsible for all tasks having to do with influencing the mental and spiritual life of the nation, for winning allegiance to the state, its culture and economy, for informing the public at home and abroad about the nation, and for administering all institutions and installations contributing to these ends."

Decree followed decree, expanding his powers and functions. There was the Reich Culture Chamber Law of September 22, 1933, channeling all intellectual and cultural life into this one chamber with its six sub-chambers (Reich Radio Chamber, Reich Theater Chamber, Reich Press Chamber, et cetera) and appointing Goebbels as president which, under Nazism, meant dictator. There was the Journalists' Law of October 4, 1933, which made all newsmen servants of the state and subject to license by Goebbels. There was the decree of November 26, 1936, forbidding all artistic criticism.

Soon Goebbels unblushingly forbade the publication of speeches by cabinet members. He even decreed that nobody could quote past utterances of the Fuehrer without the approval of his Propaganda Ministry.

Goebbels unscrupulously used his vast powers to foster anti-Semitism by fabricating stories about atrocities allegedly committed by the Jews. As World War II loomed on the horizon—and no Nazi besides Hitler himself knew better than Goebbels how certain it was to come —he kept up a constant barrage of stories alleging maltreatment and even torture of German nationals by the populations of neighboring states.

He thus prepared the ground well for Hitler's war on civilization.

Even after his phenomenal rise to power Goebbels never lost sight of the desirability of making himself *persona gratissima* to Adolf Hitler. He could not impress Hitler with a war record like that of Hermann Goering, the *Pour le Mérite* aviation ace of World War I, as he was physically incapacitated for military service. The Fuehrer, however, laid great stress upon large families.

Goebbels had married the comely and socially presentable Magda, a woman who in her first marriage to a German industrialist named Quandt already had one son, Harald. It was a matter of common gossip in Berlin society circles that Joseph Goebbels insisted that his wife deliver one baby a year. His offspring consisted of six children at the end of the Hitler regime. Goebbels, coldly calculating that these children would probably not have much of a chance in a world to which Nazism was anathema, poisoned them all and prevailed upon Magda likewise to take poison.

Before the war, however, the wife and children were quite an asset in Goebbels's bid for Hitler's affection. The children were taught to say nice things to "Onkel Adolf." Goebbels records with pride that the Fuehrer during his private talks usually inquired about Hilde, Holde, and Helga. He apparently knew the three younger children, Heide, Hedda, and Helmuth less well. Also, he vowed that after the war he would see to it that his family devote itself to his idol even more than before the great conflict.

Such was the Joseph Goebbels of pre-World War II days, such were his powers. The diaries will show that even these powers did not satiate his inordinate ambition, but that he used the Fuehrer's absence at the military front virtually to set himself up as dictator in domestic affairs.

I saw Dr. Joseph Goebbels for the first time in 1932 during the brief chancellorship of Franz von Papen, when the ban on Nazi party public meetings in Prussia and on the wearing of Party uniforms was lifted by this wily diplomat and politician, who told me he permitted the Nazis to meet freely "so that they might hang themselves by their own words."

The Nazis immediately staged a series of demonstrations all over Greater Berlin, among them one in the famed Sports Palace, Berlin's Madison Square Garden. In those days the Nazis craved international attention, and the foreign press was assigned choice seats on the huge platform, near the speaker's lectern.

What struck me as I heard Dr. Goebbels that first time, and what made me watch him closely thereafter, was the fact that this diminutive man, one of the most versatile spellbinders Germany has had in generations, was absolutely cool and self-possessed while at the same time he gave the impression of being deeply stirred and carried away by his own eloquence.

His voice, of a deeply resonant quality, seemed to quiver with emotion. His gestures seemed passionate. His general attitude seemed to be that of a man so wrapped up in his fanaticism that time meant nothing so long as he had a message to deliver.

I noticed something else, however: his fascinatingly delicate hands moved in powerful gestures without the slightest trembling and belied the quiver in his voice. His gestures, although seemingly spontaneous, indicated careful planning, for he always threw himself into position for a particular gesture before actually beginning to execute it. Beside him lay a watch which he consulted from time to time by a stealthy glance, clearly showing that he was well aware of the passage of time.

In short, here was a showman who knew exactly what he was doing every moment and who calculated in advance the effect of every spoken word and every gesture. Disgustingly grating though the raucous voice of Adolf Hitler was and disturbing though the frequent breaks in his voice were as he talked himself into a high pitch of frenzied exaltation, the hearer nevertheless had the impression that here was a man who believed what he said or at least intoxicated himself into this belief on hearing his own fulminations. With Goebbels I had the feeling that he would have defended Communism, monarchy, or even democracy with the same pathos and emotion, yes, even the same fanaticism, had his idol, Hitler, chosen to sponsor any of these.

About three years later a German friend told me of attending a party at which Goebbels amused all present by successively delivering a speech on behalf of the restoration of the monarchy, the re-establishment of the Weimar Republic, the introduction of Communism in the German Reich, and, finally, on behalf of National Socialism.

"I assure you," this friend said, "that I was ready at the end of each speech to join the particular cause Goebbels had just advocated. He had compelling and convincing arguments for each of the four forms of government."

A striking example of Goebbels's capacity for unabashed prevarication was given the foreign correspondents accredited at Berlin on November 10, 1938, the day after Hitler had given the "go" sign to his hordes to loot Jewish shops, demolish Jewish property, set fire to synagogues, and arrest innocent Jews. We were asked to come to the Propaganda Ministry late that forenoon, as Dr. Goebbels wished to make a statement.

Ordinarily at our daily press conference, which was usually conducted by the section chief in charge of foreign press matters of the Propaganda Ministry, we sat in armchairs on which one could easily write. Also, there was always ample opportunity for asking questions. This time we were led into the so-called "Throne Room," a large, ceremonial hall of the Leopold Palace, housing the Propaganda Ministry. There were no seats. We stood around until it was time for the Minister to appear.

Suddenly he entered with quick, nervous steps, invited us to stand in a semicircle about him, and then delivered a declaration to the effect that "all the accounts that have come to your ears about alleged looting and destruction of Jewish property are a stinking lie (*sind erstunken und erlogen*). Not a hair of a Jew was disturbed (*den Juden ist kein Haar gekruemmt worden*)."

We looked at one another in amazement. In all our journalistic careers no one among us had experienced anything like it.

Only three minutes from the Wilhelmplatz, on which the Propaganda Ministry was located, was Berlin's famous shopping street, the Leipziger Strasse, at the head of which was Wertheim's internationally known department store, its great show windows broken, its celebrated displays a pile of rubble. Yet Goebbels dared tell us that what we had seen with our own eyes was a "stinking lie."

After a few paralyzing moments we had recovered sufficiently from this shock to want to press Dr. Goebbels with questions. He had disappeared. He had cleverly used the moment of our consternation to eliminate any possibility of our asking him embarrassing questions.

What Goebbels failed to include in his calculations when he launched this coup was that while all of us truthfully reported his words and, in order to be able to remain at our posts in Germany, refrained from tearing his statement to pieces, we had the previous day sent long eyewitness accounts of burning synagogues, demolished show windows, beaten Jews, and Nazi gangsters moving through the streets and shouting "*Juda Verrecke* [Croak the Jews]!"

My wife and I had spent hours the night before watching frenzied Nazis at their work of destruction. Also, some of us had filed stories just before the Goebbels news conference began, describing how we had picked our way to the Wilhelmplatz by making many a detour in order not to cut our tires on the smashed glass of costly display windows that littered the main thoroughfares.

The effect, therefore, of our truthful reporting of Goebbels's statement was quite different from what Hitler's Propaganda Minister had expected.

The whole civilized world was shocked when on the evening of May 10, 1933, the books of authors displeasing to the Nazis, including even those of our own Helen Keller, were solemnly burned on the immense Franz Joseph Platz between the University of Berlin and the State Opera on Unter den Linden. I was a witness to the scene.

All afternoon Nazi raiding parties had gone into public and private libraries, throwing onto the streets such books as Dr. Goebbels in his supreme wisdom had decided were unfit for Nazi Germany. From the streets Nazi columns of beer-hall fighters had picked up these discarded volumes and taken them to the square above referred to.

Here the heap grew higher and higher, and every few minutes another howling mob arrived, adding more books to the impressive pyre.

Then, as night fell, students from the university, mobilized by the little doctor, performed veritable Indian dances and incantations as the flames began to soar skyward.

When the orgy was at its height, a cavalcade of cars hove into sight. It was the Propaganda Minister himself, accompanied by his body-guard and a number of fellow torch bearers of the new Nazi *Kultur*.

"Fellow students, German men and women!" he said as he stepped before a microphone for all Germany to hear him. "The age of extreme Jewish intellectualism has now ended, and the success of the German revolution has again given the right of way to the German spirit. . . .

"You are doing the right thing in committing the evil spirit of the past to the flames at this late hour of the night. It is a strong, great, and symbolic act—an act that is to bear witness before all the world to the fact that the spiritual foundation of the November Republic has disappeared. From these ashes there will rise the phoenix of a new spirit. . . .

"The past is lying in flames. The future will rise from the flames within our own hearts. . . . Brightened by these flames our vow shall be: The Reich and the Nation and our Fuehrer Adolf Hitler: *Heil! Heil! Heil!*"

The few foreign correspondents who had taken the trouble to view this "symbolic act" were stunned. What had happened to the "Land of Thinkers and Poets?" they wondered.

Goebbels always played the double role of living a luxurious life but pretending to be simple—the true representative of the common man in Germany. It would not do for the people to read what a gay party he was giving—the drab enumeration of prominent people who attended gave his communiqué the flavor of a stilted official reception.

It is true that at the very beginning of his career as a cabinet minister, he forgot for a short while that he had chosen to pose as the outstanding exponent of the proletarian sector of the Nazi movement. A newsreel, *Daddy's Birthday*, was released showing the private life of the Goebbels family. The Minister made the psychological mistake of permitting a scene to be filmed which showed his children, each with a groom for his pony. At some of the showings the audience booed and whistled, and within a few days the newsreel was withdrawn.

He also made a psychological mistake when he prevailed upon his wife, Magda, to become head of a Nazi fashion center in July 1933. Public ridicule resulted in the complete closing down of this venture.

Goebbels was quick to profit from these two mistakes. From then on he was the simple man who contrasted sharply with his then closest rival, the pleasure-loving, epicurean, spendthrift Hermann Goering. In fact Goebbels even made use of his prerogatives as Minister of Propaganda to forbid the publication of certain pictures of Goering's costly Opera Ball on January 12, 1936. For purposes of window dressing the bemedaled Minister of Aviation had invited to this ball such social luminaries as Ex-Czar Ferdinand of Bulgaria, the former German Crown Prince Frederick Wilhelm and his family (one son, Prince Louis Ferdinand, however, refused to attend, as he saw through the maneuver), Duke Charles Edward of Coburg and Gotha, Krupp von Bohlen und Halbach, Werner von Siemens, and others. Goebbels did not want the German public to know that any top Nazi was consorting with the former German aristocracy and plutocracy. Nor did he want the public to know that the vast Opera House was redecorated in white satin and that more than a million marks had been spent to give luster to the occasion.

In that connection I recall a so-called *Bierabend* (in other words, a buffet supper with beer, sandwiches, and salads) given in the Propaganda Ministry in honor of provincial journalists from all over Germany who had come to Berlin for what was called a convention, but in reality was an indoctrination week in Nazi news policies. The vice-president, the secretary, and I were invited as representatives of the Foreign Press Association and were the only foreigners present.

We were asked to take seats informally. A functionary of the Propaganda Ministry presided at each round table for eight to ten persons. Fortunately for me I happened to sit down at a table over which someone from the moving-picture division of the Ministry presided; in other words, a man who did not know the newsmen. I was careful not to pronounce my name distinctly when all of us in that group mutually introduced ourselves, and was happy to note that the Propaganda Ministry representative regarded me as just another provincial correspondent.

It was not long before he delivered himself of something which, by comparing notes with my other colleagues, was being said in almost the same words at all the other tables.

"Our Minister, Dr. Goebbels, is one of the most modest men I ever knew," quoth his handy man. "He hates all pomp and luxury. He is therefore very much embarrassed that he has had to move into a large villa at Schwanenwerder on the Wannsee. But he realizes that as

Minister of the Reich he owes something to his official position. After all, he can't receive a distinguished guest like Count Ciano in a five-room apartment! So he is putting up with the inconvenience of a rather swanky villa as a national duty."

Goebbels was clever enough to have learned from the newsreel fiasco that a luxurious suburban estate would draw unfavorable comment. What better way of forestalling criticism than letting the men throughout Germany who controlled public opinion through their newspapers know how chagrined he was at having to live in luxury?

Costly parties were the order of the day in Hitler's Third Reich. The beer-hall fighters who had won their way to power and position by brute force considered themselves entitled to the spoils of war, and Hitler approved. One high-water mark of such festivities had been the Goering Opera Ball. It would lead too far afield to describe it in a book devoted to Goebbels.

Even this sumptuous ball, however, was nothing compared with the Venetian Night given by the man of the people, Joseph Goebbels, in July 1937 in honor of the delegates to the convention of the International Chamber of Commerce.

Peacock Island, charmingly located in idyllic Wannsee, some fifteen miles outside of Berlin on the way to Potsdam, with its romantic castle erected in 1794 for Frederick Wilhelm III, had been converted into a scene from the Arabian Nights. As we crossed over from the mainland on a pontoon bridge, the path leading to where Dr. and Mrs. Goebbels waited to receive their guests was lined on both sides with hundreds of the prettiest girls from Berlin's numerous higher schools. All of them were dressed in white silk breeches and blouses, white silk stockings, and white leather slippers. Each held a white wand. They bowed as the guests slowly walked several hundred yards to the reception line.

On a beautiful greensward tables had been set for groups of twelve, ten, eight, and smaller parties. We were some three thousand guests. A sumptuous dinner was served the like of which we had not eaten in Berlin for years, for Rudolf Hess had already delivered himself of the slogan, "Guns instead of butter." Fringing the greensward on one side was the longest bar I have ever seen, with eighty attendants at our service to concoct any drink that might be wanted, or to serve champagne without limit. Every lady guest was presented with an artistic figurine from the Prussian State Porcelain Factory.

In another part of the island a gigantic rotunda had been constructed in which the guests could dance, and on which, later in the

evening the ensemble of the Civic Opera performed a charming ballet
and other members of Berlin's artist colony put on a floor show.

All for the glory of the Third Reich! But the official communiqué
for the German press was stilted and drab. The common people were
not to know that the days of Augustus the Strong of Saxony and
Poland had returned to Germany under the auspices of the tribune of
the people, Joseph Goebbels.

During the first year of the Nazi regime the foreign correspondents
had virtually no contact with the newly created Propaganda Ministry.
Goebbels ignored the foreign press (except for certain satellite journalists), since the overwhelming majority of the newsmen from other
countries on duty in Berlin were critical, to say the least, of Nazism.

Gradually Goebbels realized that such a condition of affairs was
untenable; that so long as foreign correspondents were tolerated
there must also be some official contact between them and the German
authorities. Even unfavorable publicity would be better than no
publicity at all. Besides, Hitler might at any time accuse him of
having failed even to try to win over the foreign correspondents to
an understanding of what he and his movement were attempting
to do.

In the spring of 1934, therefore, Goebbels reversed himself and
invited the foreign correspondents as well as the diplomatic corps
to a tea party in Leopold Palace.

Shortly afterward the Foreign Press Association gave its traditional
annual banquet in honor of the German Government, the diplomatic
corps, and leaders of German thought. In the Republican days most
members of the cabinet had attended. The German Chancellor or the
Foreign Minister had always delivered a major speech. The Nazis
snubbed us. No cabinet member came—only a few minor officials.

In the years of the Weimar Republic it had not been difficult for me
to find appropriate words of welcome to our German and foreign diplomatic guests. The leaders of the short-lived German republic were anxious to fit themselves into the pattern of a co-operative, peaceful world.

But to speak on an occasion like this, when the Nazi Government deliberately snubbed us, and yet not risk deportation, was far more difficult. Unwittingly the absent Dr. Goebbels came to my rescue.

Some days before our banquet a representative of *Der Angriff* had
been ejected from Rumania. That, of course, was before Ion Antonescu.
I cannot remember what the specific charges were. In general they
were the same as those made—and rightly so—against so many German

correspondents abroad after the Nazis took over. Most of these men were now no longer reporters; they were political agents of the Nazi regime.

Goebbels seized upon the occasion to write a scathing editorial protesting against the eviction. He posed as a champion of free speech and untrammeled inquiry into facts. The foreign correspondent, he held, must be permitted to contact not only the government but also the opposition, must have the privilege of writing both complimentary and uncomplimentary things about the country of which he is a guest. In short, Goebbels advocated for his correspondents abroad all those things that we had been permitted to do under the Weimar Republic but were being reprimanded and even threatened for doing in the Third Reich.

My speech on this occasion was, for once, "Made in Germany." I stated that it was a comforting thing for a foreign correspondent to find that his conception of his duties coincided with that of the country to which he was assigned. I therefore took pleasure in quoting the official German position on this matter.

After concluding the reading of the Goebbels editorial, I said that every foreign correspondent present no doubt agreed with this official Nazi view as expressed by Dr. Goebbels, wherefore I raised my glass to that freedom of the press on which we were all agreed, and which had been aptly defined in *Der Angriff*.

If I ever saw silly faces, it was those of the few Nazis present.

Quite by accident I came to hear Goebbels make a pronouncement which put the final touch on Nazi regimentation of the German mind. Among the numerous invitations to public ceremonies which constantly passed over my desk in The Associated Press Bureau at Berlin there was one asking me to attend a meeting of the *Reichskulturkamm..r* (Reich Chamber of Culture) in Philharmonic Hall at noon, November 29, 1936. Goebbels was to be the speaker. That meant we would receive the text of his address via the German News Bureau soon after he had finished. Therefore, why bother to go to the meeting?

Preceding and following the address, however, Berlin's Philharmonic Orchestra was to play. I was willing even to listen to a tirade by Goebbels if I could hear Beethoven and Schubert performed by the Berlin Philharmonic. I hastened to the nearby hall.

Goebbels arose and, in cold, biting language, and without his usual effort to ingratiate himself with his listeners, calmly announced that musical, theatrical, literary, and artistic critic..sm was hereafter forbidden. The professional press and radio critics were ordered to limit themselves to *Betrachtungen* (reflections or contemplations), which meant that they might write something about the artist himself and his method of work, possibly even a word or two as to how the musical composition or the play had originated, but nothing to indicate a critical attitude toward either the performer or his work.

The representatives of every sector of German art present looked at one another in amazement. The newspaper critics bit their lips in livid rage. The last vestige of relative freedom of the press was thus eliminated by the dictum of the Propaganda Minister.

I was glad I had gone. To observe the smugness with which Goebbels addressed the leaders of art and culture in Germany, to catch the malicious glint in his eye as he noted the helpless consternation of his listeners, and to hear the raucous applause of the Nazi party leaders of the beer-hall roustabout type who were sprinkled among the writers, musicians, painters, sculptors, and other artists—that was worth coming for.

Strangely enough, my last experience as a free man in Germany had to do with Joseph Goebbels. Stranger still, although Goebbels and I had a mutual aversion toward each other—Goebbels said in his diary entry for May 19, 1942, what he thought of me—my last experience was a gratifying one.

Here is the unusual story: At Hanover there was a dear friend of our family, Frau Lotte B, a Jewess. She was arrested and ordered deported to the Baltic States, then under German occupation.

Her husband had been a naval captain in World War I and had a distinguished record. He had taken his son to the United States where news reached him of the November 1938 pogrom. He saw that a return to Germany meant disaster. Therefore he moved heaven and earth to have his wife join him, and actually secured a visa to Cuba for her. Friends in Germany were instrumental in obtaining transit visas through France and Spain.

Despite Frau B's possessing the necessary papers for emigration, the Nazis placed her on one of the cattle trains filled with Jews who were to be shipped to some Baltic ghetto—Riga, if I remember correctly.

It was at this stage of events that mutual friends acquainted me with the situation. I ran from office to office, only to learn that, in the last analysis, Jewish affairs were in the hands of none other than Joseph Goebbels.

If ever it was difficult for me to become a petitioner it was now. I loathed Dr. Goebbels. I hated to ask him for anything. I feared he might ask something of me in return which my conscience would forbid me to do. Yet the thought of this splendid woman being permanently separated from her husband and child, left to perish miserably in a concentration camp, would not let me sleep.

For the first and only time in my life I therefore asked a favor of Dr. Goebbels. I reminded him that in the first place the Nazis on assuming power had specifically stated they would treat Jews with a distinguished war record differently from others of their race or religion. Herr B's record as a naval hero was beyond challenge. Therefore he was—so I argued—entitled to special consideration.

Secondly, I argued that the purpose of the evacuations obviously was to drive all Jews out of Germany. Then what objection could there be to letting Frau B start westward for America instead of eastward to the Baltic States? In either case Nazi Germany would be rid of her.

On more than one occasion I have been baffled by the unpredictable workings of the Nazi mind. To my surprise Goebbels sent me word through Dr. Rudolf Semler of the Propaganda Ministry, who had been very helpful to me in this matter, that he would see to it that Frau B was taken off the ghetto train and allowed to proceed to Spain. He attached no conditions. He did not try to make a deal with me. Dr. Semler told me privately, however, that I had "shamed" him into taking favorable action by my reference to Herr B's war record.

Pearl Harbor followed soon thereafter, and four days later, on December 11, 1941, Adolf Hitler declared war on the United States. We journalists were permitted to join the embassy and consulate staffs for internment at Bad Nauheim where we had to wait five months before being allowed to proceed to Lisbon and there board the New York-bound SS *Drottningholm* which had just brought the Axis diplomats and journalists to Portugal.

On the morning of December 14, just as Mrs. Lochner and I were about to drive to the American Embassy to join the rest of the internees, the telephone rang. It was the Postal Ministry which read a telegram to me from Frau B stating that she had arrived safely in Madrid.

What was Goebbels's place in the Nazi scheme of things? I remember a talk I had back in 1930 with Ernst Roehm, the only man in the Nazi hierarchy who addressed Adolf Hitler by the familiar German "*Du.*" He was brought to my office by a Bolivian diplomat, Federico

Nielsen-Reyes, who thought it high time an Associated Press representative knew some of the men of the coming regime in Germany. Roehm in turn introduced me to Hitler several months later.

Discussing the various leaders of the Nazi movement, Roehm pointed out that Goebbels often annoyed Hitler by the guttersnipe language used in the *Angriff*, the Berlin organ of the Nazi party of which Goebbels was editor in chief. "Goebbels is a special case, and the Fuehrer at first did not know what to do with him," Roehm told me. "He finally decided that, since Berlin was so 'red,' Goebbels might well work off his energies there."

Step by step, moving rather cautiously at first, Goebbels entrenched himself. He took sides against Roehm and was in Hitler's immediate entourage during the crisis of June 30, 1934, when the fate of the regime seemed to hang in the balance. At the same time he seems to have looked out for a possibility of securing a berth elsewhere in case the repercussions of the Roehm revolt and the attendant wholesale purges proved too great for Hitler to retain his dictatorship. Coming to Prague soon after to cover a story there, I received an unexpected visit from Otto Strasser, leader of the "Black Front" which for a while played with Hitler and had then broken away from him because he was not radical enough. Strasser at that time claimed that Goebbels was in contact with him and was ready to join the Strasser forces in case Hitler were overthrown.

I believe it is no exaggeration to say that at the time when the Goebbels diaries were written the little doctor was the most important and influential man after Hitler, not even excepting the seemingly all-powerful Heinrich Himmler. Goering, the successor-designate to Hitler, was already in eclipse. Himmler had only brute force at his command. He was not a man of exceptional intellect. Nor was he powerful in his own right. His power, like that of Martin Bormann, depended upon Adolf Hitler. His clumsiness in trying to negotiate a separate peace in the closing days of the war shows what was bound to happen to him once he failed to act on directives from Hitler.

Goebbels, on the other hand, undoubtedly had brains. He was vested with more and more authority as time went on, until by 1943 he was virtually running the country while Hitler was running the war.

One indication of the power exerted by Goebbels is his repeated mention that he issued orders to arrest this or that person. The following entry, under date of November 19, 1943, illustrates what I mean:

"There is some complaint about the attitude of certain classes of our population toward English prisoners of war. . . . I have given orders that people who are so unmindful of their honor as to behave thus be summoned into court and given heavy penitentiary sentences."

In fact, a careful reading of the diaries makes one feel that Goebbels was a law unto himself, barring only his respect for Adolf Hitler, whose will he, in the last analysis, obeyed, even though he by no means meekly accepted an adverse decision but kept reverting to the subject until he had either changed the Fuehrer's mind or found him adamant in his decision.

What, then, are some of the other characteristics of Goebbels as he reveals himself in his diaries for 1942–43?

Overshadowing all other characteristics was his inordinate ambition. Obsessed with ambition, he became a glutton for work—not because he was overconscientious, but because he was driven on by an almost psychopathic lust for power.

To achieve power he needed to be in the know on what was going on around about him. Accordingly we find him listening by the hour to the gossip of men who could inform him on the foibles and weaknesses of possible rivals. We find him sticking his nose into everything, even in matters which in nowise concerned him.

I could turn to almost any page of his diaries and find him occupying his mind with such matters as potato rations, hair-dos for women in wartime, Nazi terminology in foreign-language dictionaries, griping by the average citizen, requisitioning of copper and pewter ware, the administration of justice, new taxes, houses of ill fame for foreign slave workers, fees for troop entertainers, diet for dancing girls, women in industry, experiments in artificial insemination, itinerary for Countess Ciano, civilian behavior in wartime, character of radio shows, German foreign policy, attitude toward occupied countries, corruption in high places—just to mention a few topics at random.

So ambitious was Goebbels that he refused to take out time for necessary rest. Apparently he feared that by being away from his duties for even a fortnight he might miss something of importance in the determining of which he should have a hand.

He writes about trouble with his nerves, about an itch that has become unbearable, about being very tired and badly in need of rest, about the terrible pain caused by a bad kidney attack, et cetera. Yet such is his ambition and jealous concern for keeping power in his hands that he refuses consistently to heed his doctor's orders to go to Karlsbad for a cure.

Hand in hand with his overweening ambition went a colossal vanity.

"The Fuehrer told Speer he never once discovered a psychological error in my propaganda," he wrote jubilantly on April 24, 1943. "The Fuehrer said if he had a dozen persons like myself he would appoint me," he wrote complacently in connection with filling a post of gauleiter.

"I was in top form and used persuasive and pointed arguments," he exclaimed on February 7, 1942. "My articles are so fascinating both for the German and the international readers," was his comment on April 6, 1942.

A little flattery—and Goebbels was ready to change his opinion about a person. This is strikingly illustrated in the case of King Boris of Bulgaria. Goebbels hated royalty and aristocracy. The Hohenzollerns weren't "worth a hoot," the Italian royal house was "despicable," Queen Wilhelmina of the Netherlands "surely a sad sight." Quite in keeping with this general estimate of blue bloods was his opinion of King Boris as expressed in his diary for January 25, 1942: "a sly, crafty fellow," who "is said to be playing a somewhat double-faced game."

Then Boris did him the honor of summoning him for a private audience which, although scheduled to last only twenty minutes, stretched out for more than an hour.

Goebbels hears that his articles are "required reading" for the Bulgarian monarch, that he uses Goebbels's arguments in talking to his military staff, that Goebbels would have prevented German defeat in 1918 had he then been Minister for Propaganda.

Suddenly Goebbels reversed himself; he now wrote of Boris (see diary entry for March 28, 1942): "He is a real people's king . . . an impassioned devotee of Hitler's genius as a leader . . . sympathetic."

Goebbels was undoubtedly one of the most radical of the Nazi leaders. His early doubt about Hitler, as I have pointed out previously, revolved about the question whether the Fuehrer saw social and economic problems radically enough.

But this radicalism extends to all fields other than the social-economic. He insists upon a fundamental change in the administration of justice, even to the extent of throwing overboard existing legal concepts and substituting Hitler's supreme will and the "sound common sense of the people" as the basis for legal findings. It is he who suggests to Hitler that he should have the sham Reichstag expressly confer upon the Fuehrer the right to dismiss from office anybody he pleases without a hearing. He wants Hitler to authorize the shooting of enemy parachutists and is disappointed that the Fuehrer does not agree with him.

Above all, Goebbels's radicalism was attested by the fact that he, more conspicuously than any other Nazi leader, advocated "total war." The whole nation must take part in this war, he felt. He therefore opposed so-called "soup money" for civil servants when they had to work longer hours, insisting that the civilian should fare no better than the soldier. He advocated the drafting of women into important war industries—again on the theory that the entire nation must wage this war.

With Goebbels, only a Nazi was a full-fledged human being. However often he may lose his temper over the shortcomings of his fellow leaders, in the last analysis they rank higher with him than non-Nazis. To him the Waffen-SS is a military element far superior to the regular army. General Sepp Dietrich is admirable because he is the leading general of the SS troops. Next come Field Marshal Erwin Rommel, Colonel General Eduard Dietl, and Colonel General Heinz Guderian, all of them ardent Nazis. The leftovers from imperial and republican days, men such as Brauchitsch, Manstein, Bock, Busch, Kuechler, List, Halder, Fromm, Stuelpnagel, are either not to be trusted or are inept or lacking in imagination.

Even Party considerations failed to count with him, however, when the interests of his own Propaganda Ministry were involved. He will not stand for having the Party establish a general news service of its own. He intervenes when Gauleiter Joseph Buerckel tries to set up an independent cultural office. He resents any attempt by the Ministry of the Interior, which is technically in charge of civil-service appointments and at the head of which is one of Hitler's oldest collaborators, Dr. Wilhelm Frick, to have any say about appointments to the Propaganda Ministry, and denies the Finance Ministry its right to be consulted on these appointments on the ground that the budget is involved.

Goebbels was a peculiar mixture of realist and wishful thinker. Despite his vanity he often viewed situations with a greater sense of realism than did some of his co-leaders. He saw, for instance, how wrong it was for the Nazi regime not to drive a wedge between the conquered peoples of the East and the Bolsheviks by promising the Ukrainians, White Russians, and others land for the peasants and religious freedom.

Ardent Nazi though he was, he was acutely aware of the danger to the regime inherent in the love for good living, even in wartime, by leaders of the regime.

Not because he was humane, but because he was a realist, Goebbels advocated decent food and pay for slave labor. Only by offering food and monetary inducements, he felt, would these forced laborers step up production.

Parenthetically I may add that he was an extreme realist when it came to his own health. When he had the violent kidney attack he preferred to entrust his precious body to the care of Catholic nuns as nurses, spurning the much-advertised "Brown Sisters" of the Nazi regime.

On the other hand Goebbels frequently shows that wishful thinking could easily sidetrack his innate sense of realism. He refused to believe, for instance, because he did not want to believe, that America really had great potentialities for war production. Instead, he poohpoohed American claims and accused President Roosevelt, General Marshall, Secretary of the Navy Knox, and Harry Hopkins of exaggerating American production.

Wishful thinking led him to prophesy that the Allies, on reaching Italy, would indulge in wholesale looting of art treasures, that Italy would never declare war on Germany, that Sir Stafford Cripps would not accept an appointment to go to India, that President Roosevelt was trying to seize India and the French colonial empire, and that Germany proper could never be invaded.

The diaries become almost humorous reading in those passages in which Goebbels feigns moral indignation at certain occurrences in the Allied camp. For instance, he pretends to be sickened on reading about the telegrams sent to Stalin by the "plutocracies" on the occasion of Red Army day—as though this were any different from what the Nazis did during their brief marriage of convenience with the Bolsheviks from the autumn of 1939 until June 22, 1941.

Time and again he assumes a holier-than-thou attitude toward the Western Powers as regards the alleged falsification or withholding of news. Yet his diaries are replete with cynical admissions that he has doctored the news and kept the German public in ignorance of important developments.

In this introduction space forbids dealing with numerous other aspects of the diaries which make them a veritable Book of Revelations on the Nazi regime. Suffice it merely to indicate some of them. Totalitarianism is revealed as amazingly inept and bungling, quite in contrast to the popular notion that authoritarian regimes at least are efficient, however brutal they may be.

The vaunted German Luftwaffe is shown to have been far weaker in the years under discussion than the outside world assumed it to be. The aims and methods of Nazi foreign policy are disclosed with a frankness and cynicism that makes National Socialism stand forth as absolutely amoral and immoral, as ready to cheat friend, foe, and neutral alike. Hitler's and Goebbels's contempt for other nations and their public men was abysmal. Goebbels gloatingly planned the extermination of all Jews, and the reduction of the Christian churches to impotence.

Also the Goebbels diaries are calculated to cause wide discussion as to whether Allied psychological warfare was waged with the necessary acumen, and whether Unconditional Surrender did not needlessly prolong the war.

The Goebbels diaries are by no means merely a vain public official's reflections on his own importance and his non-authoritative interpretations of contemporaneous events. They are the day-by-day record of occurrences in Germany and the world, written by one of the three top men in the Nazi hierarchy, who in the early days of the regime were often called "the Nazi trinity."

Adolf Hitler, of course, was the Number One man. If any further evidence of this is needed, the Goebbels diaries clearly establish this fact.

Next there was Hermann Goering, designated by Hitler as his successor in the event of his death or incapacity.

And finally there was the little doctor, Joseph Goebbels, the third man of the trinity, whose story is told in the following pages in his own words.

1942

January 1942

The Goebbels diaries begin six weeks after Pearl Harbor. On December 7, 1941, the Japanese had made their sneak attack; four days later Adolf Hitler, to the surprise even of many of his most intimate followers, declared war on the United States.

Shortly before, the German armies for the first time had met with major reverses. A winter of unexampled severity had come so rapidly in Russia that the German drive on Moscow was abruptly stopped.

Not only did a German Government spokesman have to admit in a press conference on December 8, 1941, that it was now out of the question to reach Moscow, but Dr. Goebbels took the unusual step of making a radio appeal to the German nation on December 20 to donate furs, woolens, anything warm available for the soldiers at the front.

Hitler further astounded the world by announcing on December 21 that Field Marshal Walther von Brauchitsch had been removed as Generalissimo of the Army and that the Fuehrer had taken personal command. In a New Year's message to the German people Hitler further warned that hard fighting was ahead in 1942.

On the Allied side, four major events took place after Pearl Harbor and before the date of the first entry in the diaries:

1. Winston Churchill, it was announced on December 22, flew to Washington for a conference with President Roosevelt;

2. British Foreign Minister Anthony Eden, it was revealed December 28, went to Moscow to confer with Stalin and Molotov;

3. Representatives of all twenty-six nations then at war with the Axis issued a "Declaration of the United Nations" on January 1, 1942, in which each pledged not to make a separate peace with the enemy;

4. United States Undersecretary of State Sumner Welles on January 15, at the opening session of the Rio de Janeiro conference, urged that the Latin-American countries sever all ties with the Axis.

January 21, 1942

Japan has notified us that it has requested Thailand not to declare war on England for the present, nor to adhere to the Three-Power Pact, since the Japanese desire to use Thailand as much as possible for assembling their forces against Burma unhindered without being disturbed by enemy air raids.

Immediately upon my return to Berlin I gave the cabinet a detailed report on the over-all situation, based on my discussions with the Fuehrer.

I gave a rather long report and supplied a considerable number of details, but pledged all participants to strictest secrecy.

[Goebbels was summoned to Hitler's headquarters in East Prussia from time to time. Cabinet meetings were practically a thing of the past, at least as far as Hitler himself was concerned. This was a rare occasion.]

After that I talked at length with Martin. I tried to persuade him to tell me the names of all officers in the OKW and the OKH who are guilty of fostering defeatism, and to make a written report on them. The Fuehrer has called for such a written report from me so that he may take proper measures.

[OKW stands for *Ober-Kommando der Wehrmacht,* or Supreme Command of the Armed Forces. OKH stands for *Ober-Kommando des Heeres,* or Supreme Command of the Army.

Lieutenant Colonel Martin was the liaison officer of the Wehrmacht to the Propaganda Ministry.]

I told Martin it wasn't right for him to spare these people, but that on the contrary he must stand by his oath of allegiance to the Fuehrer. He agreed with me absolutely and declared himself willing to proceed in accordance with my proposals. That won't make his colleagues love him, but the Fuehrer has expressly guaranteed to take him under his personal protection if he makes such a report. That should be sufficient for an officer, aside from the fact that he must summon enough courage to report defeatist currents to the top level. At the end of World War I all responsible men stated in their memoirs what they thought and what they really ought to have done, but nobody had done it. Now we don't want to do so much thinking, but rather act and do what our conscience commands us to do. Martin is quite open-minded toward my line of reasoning . . .

[In view of later developments, which culminated in the attempt on Hitler's life on July 20, 1944, it is interesting to note that certain officers were spreading defeatist propaganda more than two years before this attempt. After Stalingrad, as a matter of fact, few responsible officers believed in victory.]

With Gutterer I discuss our tactics with reference to other ministries. I consider it my duty not only to keep my own Ministry in order, but also to proceed generally against the defeatism prevalent in Berlin Government quarters. I won't shirk this duty, no matter what the consequences. I fear neither a fact nor a person, but only the possibility of losing the war. In times of crisis fear of persons is a most dangerous thing and there is but one sin, as Nietzsche put it; namely, that of cowardice. It is sometimes much more difficult to be courageous in civilian than in military life. That sort of courage is now *à propos* and necessary.

[Leopold Gutterer was under-secretary in Goebbels's Propaganda Ministry and ranked directly behind the minister. In this first available diary entry Goebbels already stands revealed as a ruthless radical who considered it his duty to act as Hitler's deputy in domestic matters. The impression given by the Goebbels diary throughout is that Hitler ran the war while Goebbels ran the country.]

We are receiving reports about the extraordinarily low morale of the Bolshevik troops along the border of Manchukuo. But I prevent publication of such information because it might awaken too great hopes in the German people. I am very keen about holding such reports back. The German people must face the hard facts of war and must not nurture empty hopes.

An American newspaper [*sic*], *The Reader's Digest,* with a circulation of 5,300,000, has published a sensational article which asserts that the United States in the last analysis is unable to undertake anything against the armed forces of the Axis. America's war was a hopeless undertaking and could only result in bleeding the nations white. At least one voice in the wilderness! It remains to be seen, however, whether this viewpoint will make headway.[1]

Heydrich has now installed his new Government of the Protectorate. Hacha has made the declaration of solidarity with the Reich that was requested of him. Heydrich's policy in the Protectorate is truly a model one. He mastered the crisis there with ease. As a result the Protectorate is now in the best of spirits, quite in contrast to other occupied or annexed areas.

[Reinhard Heydrich, known as The Hangman, was Heinrich Himmler's right-hand man as chief of the Security Police of the Gestapo until his appointment as Protector of Bohemia-Moravia, succeeding Baron Konstantin von Neurath, who was considered too mild. Heydrich was notorious for his ruthless methods. Goebbels was wrong in characterizing Heydrich's administration as a "model" one under which the Czechs were happy, for Heydrich was later assassinated at Prague in May 1942 by a group of exasperated Czechs.

[1]No such assertion was ever made in any article in *The Reader's Digest.* Like most American magazines, prior to Pearl Harbor, *The Reader's Digest* published articles pro and con America's participation in the war, some of which were seized upon by Goebbels and distorted for his own purposes.

Former Supreme Court Judge Emil Hacha became Hitler's satellite "president" of the Protectorate after the partition of the Czechoslovak Republic in 1938 and the flight of its president, Eduard Beneš.]

I have ordered my men to proceed rigorously against Berlin defeatism and if necessary box the ears of some sourpuss, thereby creating a *fait accompli* and teaching all potential defeatists a lesson. We are living in extremely tough times, and tough measures are necessary.

[Goebbels never hesitated to invoke rowdy measures. About a year before the Nazis took Germany over, he had his henchmen release mice during a Berlin performance of the motion-picture version of Erich Maria Remarque's *All Quiet on the Western Front*. The panic which ensued resulted in the cancellation of later showings.]

My visit to the Fuehrer's GHQ has had the most beneficent consequences for me personally. Not that I needed to be buoyed up by the Fuehrer, but, thank God, the Fuehrer absolutely approved the course on which I have embarked. That is both reassuring and inspiring. I now feel secure and can approach the solution of the difficult problems in store for us in the immediate future with sovereign certainty.

January 22, 1942

The Japanese Foreign Minister, Togo, delivered an extraordinarily firm, manly, and diplomatically clever speech in Parliament. He rejected the theory of race struggle, stretched out the hand of peace to the South American states, and above all handled the peoples in East Asia, who are oppressed by the English and Americans, with exceptional psychological skill. The Japanese are pursuing a tactical course fraught with extraordinary danger both for England and the United States. It is evident that the Japanese have had considerable political and diplomatic experience. Added to their great military powers this experience is calculated to achieve corresponding successes.

[Shigenori Togo, born, 1882, was Japanese Minister for Foreign Affairs in 1941–42 and Minister of Education in 1943. He had previously been Secretary of Embassy in Berlin and Washington, Counsellor of Embassy in Berlin, Director of European and West Asiatic Affairs of the Japanese Foreign Office in 1933–36, and Ambassador to Germany in 1937–39, to Russia in 1939–40.]

The debate in England still revolves around the argument that a victory must be won at least in one theater of war, and that this theater is Libya. Churchill has become a collector of deserts—an activity into which England only a few years ago tried to force Mussolini.

Our relations with France are being subjected to severe strain. I discussed this subject at length with the Fuehrer during my last visit to GHQ. The Fuehrer doesn't want any preliminary peace. Nor does he believe that France is in any way ready to help us create the new order in Europe. Even Pétain wants to bide his time and seize upon an auspicious moment for restoring France to the position of a Great Power. The French could render us some service in North Africa, but it isn't sufficiently important for us to meet their wishes. The French Fleet, too, can't be placed at our service at present since it lacks the necessary fuel.

The Fuehrer has become somewhat suspicious of Abetz. However great Abetz's achievements may have been in the question of German-French relations, the fact must not be overlooked that he has a French wife and that he will therefore always be under a severe psychological strain.

[Otto Abetz, a former member of the German Democratic party and in his younger years an ardent pacifist, became a member of the French section of Joachim von Ribbentrop's Intelligence Bureau soon after Hitler's accession to power in Germany. From 1935 until 1939 he was a professional propagandist for the Nazis in France, but was expelled in 1939, some months before World War II began.

The German Foreign Office sent him back to France in June 1940 as plenipotentiary to the Army of Occupation in France. From August 1940 until 1944 he was German envoy to the Military Administration in Paris.]

Lieutenant Colonel Martin has handed me his written declaration for the Fuehrer. His doing so was an act of extraordinary courage, which I value highly in him. The Fuehrer now certainly has the data for proceeding energetically against defeatist tendencies in the OKW and especially in the OKH. An example must be made here, for if such tendencies exist among officers, how can one blame the common man for gradually losing courage and getting the blues?

The reports of the SD reveal the following:

The anxiety of the German people about the Eastern Front is increasing. Deaths owing to freezing are an especially important factor in this connection. The number of cases of freezing revealed by transports from the Eastern Front back home is so enormous as to cause great indignation here and there. Unrest is, however, not sufficiently great to constitute a threat. People continue to criticize the OKW communiqué because it gives no clear picture of the situation. Soldiers' mail, too, has a devastating effect. Words cannot describe what our soldiers are writing back home from the front. This is in part because every individual wants to appear important. The passion for showing off here plays a considerable role. When the soldier writes and exaggerates he doesn't stop to think that he may be causing his family and his relatives a lot of worry. I suggest once more that the OKW indoctrinate the soldiers on this point, but I don't expect much. It is a question of a human weakness against which one is powerless.

[The SD—*Sicherheits-Dienst* or Security Service—was a special section of the Gestapo and was especially responsible for the security of the Nazi leaders. It undertook constant opinion samplings.]

Movie production is flourishing almost unbelievably despite the war. What a good idea of mine it was to have taken possession of the films on behalf of the Reich several years ago! It would be terrible if the high profits now being earned by the motion-picture industry were to flow into private hands.

I talked with Stephan about the question of buying up news concerns abroad. I believe we should continue to do so, for the greater the number of news outlets, especially newspapers, we own abroad, the better will this be for our future role of leadership in Europe.

[Dr. Werner Stephan was secretary of the Democratic party before the Nazis took over, but changed his politics quickly and became the right-hand man of Dr. Otto Dietrich, undersecretary in the Propaganda Ministry. He was later taken over directly by Goebbels, who entrusted him with the task of quietly buying up newspapers, news agencies, movie houses, and other facilities for German propaganda in foreign countries.]

I saw the new American propaganda movie, *The Foreign Correspondent.* It is a first-class production, a criminological bang-up hit, which no doubt will make a certain impression upon the broad masses of the people in enemy countries. Significantly enough this film, with its absolutely anti-German tendency, was allowed to run for months in Sweden. The Swedes and the Swiss are playing with fire. Let us hope they will burn their fingers before this war is over.

January 23, 1942

Rommel's boldly conceived attack in North Africa is extremely gratifying. The English are again trying to alibi with weather difficulties. In the course of the day, however, they must nevertheless admit being pushed back quite a distance. Rommel is praised highly by the English press. He is altogether one of our most popular generals. We could well use a few more such big shots.

[Field Marshal Erwin Rommel, born in 1891, a product of Tuebingen University, received Imperial Germany's highest decoration, the *Pour le Mérite,* for bravery in the Isonzo battle in 1917. After the war he became a teacher in the Dresden Military Academy. An early Nazi, he was attached to Hitler's bodyguard, and commanded the Fuehrer's headquarters in the Austrian, Sudetenland,

and Czech occupations, and during the Polish campaign of 1939. During the 1940 campaign in France he commanded a Panzer division, and in 1941 was transferred to North Africa, where he acquired the sobriquet of "Desert Fox" as commanding general of the Afrika Korps. In 1943 he was put in charge of northern Italy as commander in chief, and in 1944 placed in command of an army corps in France. He finally lost faith in Hitler and joined the opposition. After the great purge following the attack on Hitler's life on July 20, 1944, Rommel was visited by two high brother officers who had orders to take him along. On the way he was handed poison and told he had the choice of committing suicide, whereupon his name would remain an honored one and he be given a military funeral, or he would be tried for treason and executed, whereupon all his possessions would be confiscated and his family rendered penniless. He chose suicide and swallowed the poison while in the car—hence the legend of an "automobile accident." (See the *Von Hassell Diaries* for interesting additional information.)]

Negotiations in Rio are continuing. Argentina is resisting pressure by the United States in every way possible. . . .

Sumner Welles is trying very hard to obtain results, but the South American states, I suppose, would first like to see some military successes by the Americans before they jump into the war. One can hardly expect them to engage themselves on the side of so undependable a partner. Roosevelt no longer enjoys the reputation and prestige that he had even a few months ago.

Once again I must concern myself with OFI-Havas. The French have a truly detestable news policy, especially as regards conditions in the East. I demanded that the Foreign Office launch an energetic protest in Vichy and, if necessary, threaten and apply reprisals. What an idea, to let defeated and conquered nations create difficulties for us with news! But that's what happens when you show too conciliatory an attitude toward the defeated enemy. Our policies toward France have, in my opinion, just about failed. We have made peace without concluding peace [*Wir haben Frieden gemacht, ohne Frieden abzuschliessen*] and are beginning to feel the results more and more.

[Before the war, the semi-official French news agency was the *Agence Havas*. Its assets were taken over by the Vichy government of France, and the name changed to *Office Francaise d'Information*, or OFI for short.]

In view of this situation between ourselves and France I have declined a request to raise the ban on French literature and music in the German Reich. There is no reason why I should. We are still in a state of war with France. I don't know whether tomorrow or the day after tomorrow open war won't break out again. It is wise, therefore, for the intellectual and cultural leadership of the nation to take this possibility into account.

I am about to release some three hundred officials of my Ministry to the Army and the munitions industry and to replace them by women. That involves some difficulties, but these will be gradually overcome. The Party, especially, will have to help me with this. I should like also to force society ladies and women from our better strata into this work. I therefore had a long discussion about this with Frau von Dirksen who is very enthusiastic about my plan and who has promised to support me in a big way.

[Ella von Dirksen, mother of the former German Ambassador to Japan and Great Britain, Herbert von Dirksen, was one of the first blue bloods to embrace the Nazi faith. Once a week she held open house in her spacious Berlin residence, and Goebbels was a regular caller. At Frau von Dirksen's home he was introduced to many men and women prominent in society, and it is claimed he also was taught proper table manners there.]

Geheimrat Opel of the Opel Works came to me to complain of the great number of "confidential," "strictly confidential," and "secret" reports and news services emanating from different Reich offices and organizations. That has gradually become a cancerous growth. I am going to put an end to this nonsense and will replace this super-production of confidential reports by one single news service to be issued by the Ministry itself. In excited and strained times the hunger for news must somehow be satisfied. If that isn't done, conditions such as those here referred to arise which can be remedied only by great effort.

[Wilhelm von Opel, head of the Adam Opel automobile works, was an ardent nationalist who in this editor's presence delivered a super-patriotic speech during an international automobile fair in Berlin in the days of the Weimar Republic, claiming that the German automobile industry, hard pressed though it might be for lack of capital, would never sell out to any foreign interests. Only a few years later, in 1929, General Motors of New York absorbed the Opel plants.]

At last all government departments are in accord about regulating the question of listening to foreign broadcasts. I have arrived at an agreement even with the Foreign Office. Lammers has meanwhile issued a circular letter to the highest functionaries of the Reich. It is therefore to be expected that order will gradually be established in this sector also, and that rumor mongering will be stopped by and by, especially in Berlin Government quarters. That is imperative, for especially in the so-called government circles the number of defeatists and gripers is legion. It is not true that these circles can take it when unpleasant news reaches them. They are the very ones who are most susceptible; therefore it is they who must be especially protected against defeatist tendencies or rumors. This can best be done by referring them for their reading to the regular news sources and by not letting them have any secret information at all. That goes even for a

large number of ministers of the Reich who have no general conception
of the over-all picture but have only to administer their own departments. They really don't have to know anything more than what is
necessary for their department. It wouldn't hurt if they could be correctly informed about the over-all situation. It is half-knowledge that
is always most dangerous.

[Dr. Hans Heinrich Lammers had slowly climbed the ladder of German bureaucracy as an administrative official under the aegis of the German Nationalist
party until Adolf Hitler loomed large on the political horizon. Lammers then
joined the Nazi party. When Hitler became Chancellor in 1933, he needed someone with long administrative experience to organize and run his chancellery.
Lammers was given the post. By the time World War II started he had risen to
the rank of a Reich or cabinet minister although his job was still that of Chief
of the Chancellery. He was exceedingly fond of decorations, and his uniform of
an *Obergruppen-fuehrer* of the SS (with general's rank) was almost as spectacu-
larly studded with decorations as was Hermann Goering's Luftwaffe uniform.
Friction arose between Goebbels and Goering on the one hand and Lammers
on the other over Lammers's considering himself as a sort of acting chancellor
while the Fuehrer was at the front running the war. This whole conflict is described dramatically later, when Goering, Goebbels, Ley, Funk, and Speer "ganged
up" against Lammers, Bormann, and Keitel. See especially the diary entry for
March 2, 1943.]

January 24, 1942

OFI-Havas still continues to issue tendentious and insolent reports
about the Eastern Front. Following my suggestion, the Foreign Office
has now drafted a note of protest for Vichy. It will be delivered during
the next few days. We shall possibly cut the Frenchmen off from their
teletypes and veto the establishment of an OFI office in Paris and in
Berlin unless they accustom themselves to reporting quite differently.

Rommel's latest success is wonderful. To be sure the English blame
bad weather; nevertheless they must admit that our Afrika Korps has
once again surprised and outguessed them by all rules of the game.
The English press calls Rommel a rascal who has once again pulled a
rabbit out of the hat. The propaganda which the English are carrying
on for Rommel is exceedingly nearsighted from their viewpoint. They
are making him one of the most popular generals in the entire world.
That's perfectly okay with us, for in the first place Rommel deserves it,
and second he is such an exemplary character and outstanding soldier
that propaganda on his behalf can do no harm. For once propaganda
is being done for the right person.

The Americans are so helpless that they must fall back again and
again upon boasting about their matériel. Their loud mouths produce
a thousand airplanes and tanks almost daily, but when they need them

in eastern Asia they haven't got them and are therefore taking one beating after another.

The Rio conference has entered upon a serious crisis. Argentina is rearing on her hind legs, and Chile is now taking her side. Despite all his eloquence Sumner Welles has until this moment not attained his goal, and it is very questionable whether he will ever reach it. Argentina and Chile at the last moment refused to agree to a common formula and negotiations are beginning all over again. Roosevelt has played a somewhat unlucky hand in recent weeks. The chief reason is that he can't produce any military victories. If it is true that nothing succeeds like success, it is also true that nothing defeats like defeat.

[The Pan-American Conference for Foreign Ministers opened in Rio de Janeiro on January 15, 1942, with an appeal by United States Undersecretary of State Sumner Welles for unity in breaking away from the Axis. It ended January 28, and Mr. Welles was able to state that the delegates of twenty-one American republics "officially and unanimously proclaimed that they jointly recommended the severance of diplomatic relations between all the American republics and the governments of Japan, Germany, and Italy, because of the aggression committed by a member of the Tripartite Pact against one of the American family of nations; namely, the United States."]

In London, too, things look none too good. Even though, in my opinion, the recurring rumors of a government crisis are grossly exaggerated, nevertheless one cannot overlook the fact that the English people are very restive and apprehensive, and that Churchill must work very hard to dispel this unrest and worry. But I suppose he will succeed once again, all the more so since England has nobody to put in his place.

I have received a confidential report about a talk which one of our special informants had with Pétain. The situation at Vichy, according to this report, is exactly as it was characterized in my recent entry. Vichy desires neither a Bolshevik nor a complete German victory. Pétain, according to our informant, is absolutely vigorous in mind and body. He is the real force behind the policy of watchful waiting. He would far prefer to have Germany and the Soviet Union grind each other to pieces and bleed each other white, thereby enabling France to resume the status of a Great Power, at least to a certain extent. The French are certainly cutting into their own flesh and, when the war is ended, will have to pay the piper for having maintained a waiting attitude far too long.

[Marshal Henri-Philippe Pétain, who became Chief of State of the Vichy Government after the collapse of France in 1940, was condemned to death on August 14, 1945, for collaboration with the enemy, but in view of his advanced age of eighty-nine years his sentence was commuted to life imprisonment.]

I had a long talk with General Schmundt concerning conditions in the OKW. The Fuehrer sent him to Berlin expressly to remedy the situation.

[Major General Rudolf Schmundt was chief Wehrmacht adjutant to the Fuehrer, who, in addition, had five personal adjutants taken from Nazi party formations. Schmundt kept the official military diary of Hitler's GHQ. He was killed when the bomb that was to end Hitler's life went off on July 20, 1944.]

To a great degree the defeatist tendencies in the OKW and the OKH arise from the altogether too irresponsible distribution of news material, especially on the part of the Seehaus. I am going to put my foot down and see to it that our own departments do not engage in defeatist propaganda. Admiral Canaris has given me quite a number of hair-raising examples showing the irresponsible handling of confidential material. These examples suit me fine. They furnish the basis for taking exceedingly severe and radical measures.

[The so-called Seehaus Service was a thorn in Goebbels's flesh, and with reason. This monitoring service, which issued a daily news letter, derived its name from the fact that it was located in what was once a very popular Berlin suburban restaurant, the Seehaus (House on the Lake), romantically situated on the Wannsee halfway between Berlin and Potsdam.

To workers in the German Underground it was known that the men and women who were responsible for this monitoring service of the German Foreign Office were for the most part anti-Hitlerites who did much to stir up defeatism in Germany. They were even called the "Sabotage Club" by people in the know.

While their job was the strictly technical one of listening to and taking down informative broadcasts throughout the world, the responsible officials of this service cleverly put the material together in such a manner as to raise doubts in the authenticity of news distributed by Goebbels's Propaganda Ministry. If, say, Goebbels kept from the public some defeat on the Eastern Front, the Seehaus people would spread news of the defeat to the various government departments by simply copying down what the BBC of London reported about it. When later developments showed that the BBC report was right and Goebbels wrong, readers of the Seehaus service became more skeptical of Goebbels's news reports.

Admiral Wilhelm Canaris, chief of German Intelligence, was a bitter enemy of the Nazi regime. He played his part so cleverly, however, that the Nazis did not become aware of his subversive activities until 1944.

Even as sophisticated a man as Goebbels evidently did not see through him, but felt so flattered that Canaris paid him a visit that he took a liking to the admiral. When the Nazis finally found out that he had been one of the main conspirators of the group which on July 20, 1944, attempted to assassinate Hitler, they were so enraged that the admiral was tortured, hanged, revived, and hanged again.]

From Upper Silesia I received information to the effect that wounded soldiers are still being transported in unheated boxcars, and that the soldiers are lying, some with frozen limbs, in these trains, without blankets, neglected, and unfed for seventy or eighty hours. I am raising Cain with the hospital echelons of the Army and am arranging for the Party to take over in order that at least this extremely difficult and embarrassing problem may be solved.

The Red Cross will send its advance columns also into the occupied areas close to the front so that everything possible may be done to guarantee competent care for the wounded. This shows once more that the various departments of the Wehrmacht are not in a position to meet a really difficult problem by clever improvisation. Trains of boxcars for wounded are not mentioned in the *Mob.-Calendar,* hence they don't exist.

[The *Mob.-Calendar* was a book of instructions as to what was to be done in the event of mobilization.]

Morale among the people is so-so. There is still a lot of talk about the dismissal of Brauchitsch. People haven't quite made up their minds whether he left because he wanted to or not. It certainly isn't true that this incident has already dropped out completely in public discussions.

[Field Marshal Walther von Brauchitsch succeeded Colonel General Werner von Fritsch in 1938 as commander in chief of the German Army. Hitler soon won him over by quietly arranging for his divorce and giving him an estate. The two clicked well at first. In his famous speech to the generals at Berchtesgaden on August 22, 1939, a week before World War II broke out, Hitler said: "Colonel General von Brauchitsch has promised me to finish the war in Poland in a few weeks. Had he reported that I need two years or even only one year to do it, I should not have issued the order to march but should have allied myself temporarily with England instead of with Russia. For we are not in a position to carry on a long war." After the conclusion of the campaign in France in June 1940, Hitler in his Reichstag speech of July 19 gave unstinted praise to Brauchitsch.]

I also have the impression that foreign broadcasts are again being listened to more extensively. About this, too, the right word must be said at an early opportunity.

The Reich Food Ministry is insistent that the price of potatoes be raised. I am against that. While it is true that the farmers must get better prices as an incentive for increasing the crop acreage, on the other hand one cannot overlook the fact that a raise in the price of potatoes chiefly affects the masses, for in the budget of the common man the price of potatoes plays quite a different role from that in the budget of the wealthier classes. I therefore favor a policy of premiums financed by the state.

At noon the state funeral of Field Marshal General von Reichenau was held. The ceremony was planned by the OKH. It is unbelievably bad, psychologically clumsy, and the music absolutely amateurish. Following the national anthems the first movement from the Fifth Symphony was played by pupils of the Army Music School; well, what can you expect? I arranged with General Schmundt that in future the state ceremonies of the Wehrmacht, too, be turned over to our Ministry, since we alone can guarantee that they will come off in a manner worthy of the state.

[Field Marshal Walter von Reichenau (1884–1942) was one of the first high officers to embrace the Nazi faith. As chief of the Wehrmacht chancellery he exercised considerable influence, but apparently feared that such swivel-chair activity might condemn him to home duty in the event of war. He therefore requested Hitler to let him have an active command. In 1935 he was appointed commanding general of the Seventh Army Corps, with headquarters at Munich.

He distinguished himself during the brief war against Poland in 1939 as commander of Army Group South. Always devoted to sports, he swam across the Vistula at the head of his troops. When the war in the West started, Von Reichenau, now a colonel general, commanded the Sixth Army, with headquarters in Belgium. At the conclusion of the campaign against France and the Lowlands in 1940, Hitler promoted him to field marshal. Hitler replaced Field Marshal Von Rundstedt with Von Reichenau in December 1941.

He died January 17, 1942, so far as this editor has been able to learn, from an infection suffered in the campaign against Russia. There have, however, also been rumors that Von Reichenau met a violent death. The *Von Hassell Diaries* interestingly relate how "Hitler exploited it (the death) from the Party point of view."]

January 25, 1942

We have issued a special communiqué to the effect that German submarines have succeeded in sinking 125,000 tons of enemy shipping off the American Atlantic coast. That is an exceedingly good piece of news for the German people. It bears testimony to the tremendous activity of our submarines and their widely extended radius of action, as well as to the fact that German heroism conquers even the widest oceans. At last a special bulletin! We certainly needed it, and it acts like rain on parched land. Everybody regards the communiqué as a very effective answer to the warmonger Roosevelt, whom the whole German people curse. Many people are in a quandary as to whether they ought to hate him or Churchill more.

I talked with Sepp Dietrich, who has just returned from the southern front to get married in Berlin. He gives me a briefing on the situation along his sector of the front. He is very optimistic. In sharp contrast to the leading gentlemen of the Army, the leaders of the Waffen-SS have had National Socialist training. For them difficulties exist only to be overcome.

[General Joseph (Sepp) Dietrich was commander of the *Leibstandarte Adolf Hitler*. Among the various formations of the Nazi SS there was a division, or

Standarte, assigned especially to the duty of protecting the life of the Fuehrer. This bodyguard bore the name of Leibstandarte Adolf Hitler. It was armed better than any other military formation. During the war it was given precedence over other divisions, especially when it came to entering conquered cities triumphantly. Much to the chagrin of the regular Army, the seizure of a city was often postponed until the Leibstandarte could come to the scene of action for the final kill. Dietrich had been Hitler's personal chauffeur for many years. When Hitler appeared at Wiessee, Bavaria, on June 30, 1934, to arrest the rebellious Ernst Roehm, chief of staff of the SA, and his accomplices, one of Roehm's men aimed a revolver at Hitler. He was overpowered by Sepp Dietrich. From then on his rise in the Nazi hierarchy was rapid.]

Rommel is generally feared in London. He is already regarded as a sort of legendary figure. It seems like a miracle that he succeeded in almost surrounding a part of the British forces. That shows what the initiative, courage, and imagination of a real soldier can do, even under the most unfavorable circumstances. In Rommel's favor is, of course, the fact that he is still very young and can stand punishment.

The Australians are extremely angry because English aid for Australia is so long in coming; at present not even the initial stages of it are discernible anywhere. The Australian Government has therefore bypassed Churchill and turned to the English people with a most urgent appeal for help. This problem may become pretty precarious for England. I issue orders to continue to probe this open wound and to rub salt into it.

The Rio conference seems to end in a compromise formula. Despite the energetic exertions of Sumner Welles, no unanimous resolution to declare war on Germany was passed. It was finally agreed to recommend the severance of diplomatic relations with the Axis Powers. Argentina prevailed with her obstinacy and finally prevented a complete solution, despite continuous North American pressure.

I have received confidential information concerning the probable successor to the Archbishop of Canterbury. He will be Bishop Temple, who is much more dangerous than the old Canterbury gentleman. Temple is close to the Labor party, was formerly a moderate friend of Germany, and is now a real German hater. He stands 100 per cent behind Churchill, is clever at dialectics and, because of that fact, extremely dangerous. That means we may expect a number of severe attacks from the English clergy. But for the moment I see no special danger in this fact.

[The Rt. Hon. Most Rev. William Temple, born, 1881, was educated at Rugby and Balliol colleges, Oxford, and became a priest in 1909. He was Bishop of Manchester, 1921–29, Archbishop of York and Primate of England, 1929–42, and in 1942 became Archbishop of Canterbury and Primate of all England.]

Our adversaries lament the fact that they have no compelling peace slogan. Quite obviously they would like to use it to deceive the German people. I won't permit this theme to be discussed by our writers because I am convinced that so delicate a problem had best be put on ice and killed by silence. We can surely congratulate ourselves that our enemies have no Wilson Fourteen Points. Of course, if they had them, we wouldn't be duped by them as were the German people of 1917 and 1918.

Several reports indicate that anti-German sentiment in certain Bulgarian Government circles is slightly on the increase. Especially Czar Boris is said to be playing a somewhat double-faced game. He is a sly, crafty fellow, who, obviously impressed by the severity of the defensive battles on the Eastern Front, is looking for some back door by which he might eventually escape. This is a very shortsighted policy which will, of course, immediately be reversed, once our offensive has started again. . . .

[King Boris, born, 1894, of the House of Saxe-Coburg-Gotha, succeeded his father, Ferdinand, to the throne of Bulgaria in 1918, when the defeated country and ally of Germany insisted upon the latter's abdication. Boris was very fond of driving locomotives. He died under rather mysterious circumstances in 1943.]

The Fuehrer sent word to me that he does not desire the circulation of the *Stuermer* reduced or that it cease publication altogether. I am very happy about this decision. The Fuehrer stands by his old Party members and fellow fighters and won't let occasional trouble and differences affect him. Because he is so loyal to his co-workers, these, in turn, are equally faithful to him.

[The *Stuermer* (The Stormer) was a pornographic anti-Semitic weekly published by Julius Streicher, Gauleiter of Nuremberg, and one of the most disreputable, repulsive, and criminal characters in the Nazi hierarchy. Streicher's debaucheries and graft became so scandalous that Hitler had finally to relieve him of his Gauleiter job. But he permitted him to continue publication of the *Stuermer*. All over Germany there were glass-covered bulletin boards for exhibiting the current editions of this publication. Parents protested vigorously that their children were being corrupted by reading the filthy and sexy accounts and seeing the pornographic cartoons in the *Stuermer*. Streicher was hanged as a major war criminal.]

I, too, believe that our propaganda on the Jewish question must continue undiminished. How much is still to be done about this can be seen from the following: in connection with the evacuation of a prominent Berlin Jew, an examination of his personal papers and effects revealed that as late as the middle of 1941 the German Crown Prince wrote this Jew very cordial letters and presented him with photographs with exceedingly friendly inscriptions. The House of Hohenzollern of today isn't worth a tinker's damn.

[Goebbels had no use for members of the House of Hohenzollern, whereas Goering was always proud of his friendship with Crown Prince Frederick Wilhelm. The former Crown Prince had many friends among the Jews.]

The problem of sexual activities of the numerous foreign workers now on German soil is a difficult one. This situation in some cases is absolutely grotesque. I suppose the final solution lies in a liberal policy of establishing houses of ill fame. But that is a rather delicate matter which must be dealt with carefully.

I had a long talk with Admiral Canaris concerning the reprehensible attitude of a number of OKW and OKH officers. In his opinion one of the chief reasons is because the Seehaus Service is being distributed so widely among officers and officials. I had a list of subscribers furnished me from which it appears that the Seehaus Service has become a veritable fountainhead of defeatism. The Fuehrer has urgently requested that the list be submitted to him. He won't be very happy when he sees that one hundred and eighty officials of the Foreign Office alone are daily subscribers to the Seehaus Service.

I immediately put an end to this nuisance as far as the OKW is concerned. I am permitting only two copies of the Seehaus Service to go to the OKW. At the Foreign Office, too, vigorous steps will have to be taken. In my opinion only such persons as received permission from the Fuehrer to listen to foreign broadcasts should also receive the Seehaus Service. Their number is very limited and I see no real danger there.

[Reference is here made to the fact that it was generally forbidden in Nazi Germany to listen to foreign broadcasts. Special permits were issued to a few persons in official positions who were dependent upon these broadcasts for their work. The foreign correspondents accredited in Berlin also received the special permit. In signing a receipt for it they had to pledge themselves to silence about what they heard.]

The officials of the Propaganda Ministry, especially the editors of the foreign-language broadcasts, must, of course, for the most part receive the Seehaus Service. But that is nothing to worry about, since I indoctrinate them daily and there is no possibility of their becoming gradually infected. Admiral Canaris fully agrees with me in this matter and promises to see to it that the sources of defeatism be stopped up in the OKW and the OKH.

Officials are now to work fifty-eight hours per week instead of forty-six. The Ministry of the Interior immediately proposed that twenty-five marks per month be paid them as so-called "soup money." I regard that as wrong. Officialdom should do its duty. If it is demanded of officials that they work a few hours more in wartime than under normal peace conditions, they ought to look upon that as a sort of service of honor.

January 26, 1942

I have received a report from a commanding general at the northern front which is extraordinarily favorable. The general says the Russian forces there are very weak and are being bled white. He believes the Soviet Union will collapse in the spring, provided we are in a position to deliver a few decisive blows. Even though I am not able as yet to share this optimism I nevertheless believe he has something. It may well be that the times through which we now are passing will later be regarded as the most advantageous in the entire history of this war; possibly it is actually true that the Bolsheviks are now using up their last resources and will break down under a severe blow.

But let us not cling too much to such hopes. Our preparations for the coming spring and summer must be made just as though the Bolsheviks still had very great reserves. That will make us immune to surprises and we won't have moral setbacks like those of last summer and autumn. The more difficult we imagine war to be, the easier it will prove in the end.

Roosevelt has nothing positive to report in the way of victories. His loud-mouthed speeches before the war are still remembered by everybody. The discrepancy between what he prophesied and what has actually happened is so obvious that he can get out of this dangerous scrape only by lies and rumors.

Churchill, on the other hand, continues merrily to prevaricate. He must, for opposition against him, and especially against his co-workers, is constantly growing.

Thailand has now officially declared war against England and the United States. That is no doubt a great help for Japan, even though the striking power of the Siamese armed forces must not be overestimated.

A moral breakdown such as we experienced in November 1918 can be brought about in England only with great difficulty, if at all. We should have no illusions in this respect and should not place hopes in a type of warfare that was once successful in the case of the German people, but in all likelihood will never succeed with the English.

I spent considerable time today looking into the so-called Seehaus Service, and carefully studied one day's output of this subversive office, which is being financed out of funds of its own. I have arrived at the conclusion that this service must be limited as much as possible. I hope the Fuehrer will confer the necessary powers on me to enable me to intervene rigorously. Everybody who counts now agrees with me that the dangerous manipulations of this service must be curbed to prevent a collapse of morale among the leaders of the state and the Wehrmacht.

January 27, 1942

I have again spent a lot of time trying to limit the distribution of the Seehaus Service to a minimum. But I must overcome resistance after resistance because all departments of the Reich and all allegedly prominent persons are very anxious to continue to receive this material on the wrong assumption that it will give them a picture of the over-all situation. That is not at all true. The Fuehrer shares my point of view completely. He goes even further. He believes the Seehaus Service should be distributed to only a few persons in the entire country.

I talked about this at length to General Schmundt. The Foreign Office is trying very hard at GHQ to place the blame for the failure of the Seehaus Service on the Propaganda Ministry. But it can't put this over, for after all the Seehaus Service was founded by the Foreign Office and could develop into such a mammoth concern for the spread of tendentious news only by competition with the Propaganda Ministry.

Whether or not I already have full authority for so doing, I am intervening vigorously and have especially forbidden the distribution of material to higher officials and officers since they are most easily demoralized by such a news service.

Gradually all other important Reich ministers are beginning to realize that my standpoint is right, that we have been altogether too lax in this matter, and that we must pay for our negligence, as sentiment in Berlin government and military circles is essentially different from that among the masses of the people. The reason for this is that these leadership positions have depended solely upon this defeatist material and received no objective reports on the real condition of things. It is self-evident that people who are supplied daily with such material must at the same time be told how to interpret it. That's what is happening in our Ministry but not in the other ministries and departments. . . .

The United States is trying desperately to drag us into a discussion of racial questions, especially in regard to Japan. The American press has launched impassioned articles against the yellow race and is trying, via Stockholm, to get them published all over the world. Several Stockholm newspapers have fallen for this palpable propaganda. I suppose the Americans believe we can be persuaded to reply to this propaganda and get dragged into the discussion. That's where they are mistaken. I have forbidden the German news services even to mention these somewhat ticklish and delicate problems, as I am convinced we can't win any laurels here. As a matter of fact our position regarding Japan and the problems of eastern Asia is rather precarious, since we are uncompromising in our racial views. It is best to overcome this difficulty by silence.

I have received a report from Croatia. Sentiment toward us there is getting worse all the time. There are many reasons for it, chiefly the fact that the Poglavnik [Fuehrer] has by no means firmly established himself. His pro-Italian policy, especially, finds no echo among the Croatian people. At first the attitude toward us was very friendly, but as no help is to be expected from us against the Italians, anger at the Italians is extended to us also. The Italians have already cost us considerable sympathy in the world.

[Ante Pavelič, born in 1869, the self-appointed dictator (Poglavnik) of the Axis puppet state of Croatia, lived in Italy for many years as an exile and was there given much aid by Mussolini. When he assumed power, he had as his praetorian guard, just as Hitler had the SA and SS, the Croatian "Ustachi" organization. He embarked upon a pro-Italian policy. The Croatian people, however, have always hated their next-door neighbor Italy, with its aspirations for the port of Susac and the Dalmatian coast, while they tolerated the Germans, who were formidable supporters of Croatian tourist trade.]

Knothe reported to me on the results of his purchasing activities in the southeast. He has bought up a large number of movie houses. They give us certain outlets for our film distribution in the Balkans. The German motion picture now completely dominates the Balkans, and American films have been pushed back more and more. I am trying most earnestly to expand our holdings still further in the southeast so that, when peace comes, we may be so firmly entrenched there that nobody can dislodge us again.

[Knothe was one of Goebbels's numerous handy men in the Propaganda Ministry.]

Sepp Dietrich is a real trouper and makes one think of a Napoleonic general. If we had twenty men like that as divisional commanders we wouldn't have to worry at all about the Eastern Front. He told me in detail how the bourgeois generals on the southern front lost their nerve and how this weakness of character naturally communicated itself to the troops. For the troops are always like their leaders, both in a good and a bad sense.

The incidents that Sepp Dietrich related to me about the Russian people in the occupied areas are simply hair-raising. They are not a people, but a conglomeration of animals. The greatest danger threatening us in the East is the stolid dullness of this mass. That applies both to the civilian population and to the soldiers. The soldiers won't surrender, as is the fashion in western Europe, when completely surrounded, but continue to fight until they are beaten to death. Bolshevism has merely accentuated this racial propensity of the Russian people. In other words, we are facing an adversary about whom we must be careful. The human mind cannot possibly imagine what it would mean if this opponent were to pour into western Europe like a flood.

Terboven intends to deliver a radio address bitterly attacking the Bishop of Norway, who has acquired notoriety because of a number of stupid remarks. I advised him most urgently to keep hands off. I consider it beneath our dignity and harmful to our authority for a Reich commissioner in an area occupied by us to attack a public personage without, at the same time, saying how he will punish him. You attack without punishing only when you have no power. If you have power, you arrest or punish and give the reason why.

[Josef Terboven, Gauleiter for the Essen area, was appointed Reich Commissioner for occupied Norway by Hitler in 1940. He was sent to Norway because he was regarded as particularly "tough." Soon it became evident, however, that he was too robust after all. Goebbels later speaks of him as "the most hated man in Norway" or "a bull in a China shop." (See also diary entries of December 5 and 6, 1943.)
Dr. Eivind Josef Berggraf, born in 1884, was at that time Lutheran Bishop of Oslo. He resigned in 1942 in protest against Nazi persecution of the church and was arrested in March 1943. He was a member of the Norwegian Academy of Science and Letters.]

During an alert tonight I was able to sit down with a number of my old co-workers. We discussed the situation in general and in particular. I was happy to observe that my collaborators, no matter where they may be or in what office or army outfit are doing their duty, have very clear and uncompromising views. All the good training I gave them over a period of years is yielding results. I don't believe there is a single person who "graduated" under me who will lose his nerve easily.

January 28, 1942

Churchill has spoken at last. . . . The tenor of his speech is extremely gloomy and pessimistic. He must admit that Rommel is undefeated. He compares the position of England with that of a drowning man who has only his head above water. He admits very serious losses in North Africa. But he cleverly assumes responsibility for them so as not to have to kick anybody out. The fact that he defends his co-workers awakens sympathy for him. I shall not have this section of his speech released for the German press and radio.

Stalin's bust has been unveiled in the London Exchange. That's where it belongs. The collaboration between Bolshevism and super-capitalism is thereby publicly symbolized. England has sunk low. She is facing difficult times. She can thank Churchill. . . .

Churchill hasn't the faintest intention of permitting truthful news reporting. He always admits only what he can't avoid admitting or what can't be denied. . . .

I had the Foreign Office give me a report on our relations to Sweden. Sweden has, after all, done more for the German war effort than is generally assumed. More particularly, Sweden has given us valuable support in our fight against the Soviet Union. While she insists on remaining neutral, that after all is very much in our favor. There can be no doubt but that she would defend her neutrality by force of arms in case we tried to put her under pressure.

It isn't possible in Sweden to get after Professor Segerstedt, publisher of *Goeteborg's Handels-och Sjoefahrtstidning*. His paper is most embarrassing to the Swedish Government, but it must be permitted to continue publication because of English pressure.

[Torgny Karl Segerstedt, D.D., former professor of the history of religion at Stockholm University, became editor in chief of the *Goeteborg Trade and Shipping News*, one of the best-known dailies in the Scandinavian peninsula, in 1917. He was an outspoken opponent of Nazism.]

The King and the Crown Prince are undoubtedly on our side. The King has already once offered his abdication when a decisive question was at issue. The abdication was to become effective in case his government did not concede him such support of the German-Finnish war effort as he desired. We must therefore be satisfied with Sweden's contribution to the German-Finnish war effort, meager though it is, despite the provocative and insolent attitude of a part of the Swedish press, and not talk out of turn.

[Dr. Goebbels certainly seems muddled in his own mind about Sweden's position. In this day's entry he draws comfort from the fact that Sweden is neutral and regards this as an indication that Sweden is helping Germany and is on her side. In the very next sentence, however, he states that Sweden would not hesitate to take up arms against Germany if her neutrality were threatened.

Goebbels further makes the mistake of interpreting the Swedish King's offer to abdicate as a sign that he is "undoubtedly" on the German side when in fact this was a gesture to his own people to prevent Sweden's involvement in the war; in other words, a purely pro-Swedish attitude.

Later references in the diaries teem with accusations about Sweden, the "state which has no right to existence anyway," the "Germanic renegade," which is "playing with fire"; the country which refused to join the International Film Chamber created by Goebbels; the nation that becomes more insolent every time Germany suffers a reverse.

His contempt for Sweden is expressed on April 15, 1942: "It would have been better if we had also taken Sweden during our campaign in the north."]

Just now a hot fight is on in Sweden for control of the press—a fight between Bonnier and Kreuger. Kreuger is trying desperately to retain control of the nationalistic section of the press, which in a great measure is on our side. Bonnier, however, is doing everything possible to destroy this last remnant of national press freedom in Sweden and to get the nationalistic press of Sweden into Jewish, that is pro-English, hands.

I hope that the severe frost of the last fourteen days will gradually let up. At the moment, it is true, no improvement is noticeable, and it would be terrible if we had to live through another winter like that at the beginning of 1940. But we shall find some way out; if necessary, the people at home will have to assume added burdens. The front suffers so many trials and tribulations that it is certainly reasonable to ask the people at home to contribute their share to the war effort.

I authorize Seyss-Inquart to open a theater in the Hague in which opera, comic opera, and drama are to be produced. I do this with one weeping and one laughing eye for, really, the Dutch don't deserve such great cultural support. Perhaps they don't even have the proper appreciation for it. But Seyss-Inquart is very insistent, and after all the Germans in Holland have some right to such a theater.

[Artur Seyss-Inquart, more than any other Austrian, was responsible for the Anschluss to Germany. Misusing his personal friendship with Chancellor Kurt von Schuschnigg, he managed to become Minister of the Interior and Security in February 1938 in the last Schuschnigg cabinet. That gave him, an ardent Nazi, control of the police and of Austrian officialdom. He reassured Schuschnigg again and again that he would live up to the Austrian constitution, but secretly made all preparations for Hitler's coup of a month later. The Fuehrer then appointed him Austrian Chancellor and Minister of Defense. After the integration of Austria into the Reich and its subdivision into several gaus, Seyss-Inquart in 1939 became a minister without portfolio in Hitler's so-called cabinet (which, however, never met), until World War II broke out, when he was appointed deputy governor of occupied Poland late in 1939, and Reich Commissioner for the Netherlands in 1940. He was tried as a major war criminal by the International Military Tribunal in Nuremberg and hanged.]

January 29, 1942

Rosenberg's office has worked out an agrarian reform for the occupied areas which envisages the gradual elimination of the *kolchose* [collective community farm] and the return of land to private ownership. I expect very much from this reform when brought to the attention of the broad masses of the farmers. If we should be in a position actually to give the farmers land, they would look forward to an eventual return of the Bolsheviks with decidedly mixed feelings.

[Alfred Rosenberg, Nazi party *Reichsleiter* for ideological indoctrination and editor of the official Party organ, the *Voelkischer Beobachter* (Racist Observer), was one of Hitler's earliest followers and author of an exceedingly abstruse and involved book, the *Myth of the Twentieth Century*. He was one of the bitterest opponents of Christianity and worked for its complete abolition in Germany.

Born in the Baltic States and educated in the University of Riga, he always sidestepped the question of his opponents as to what he had done during World War I.

As the German armies swept eastward in 1941 after Germany's declaration of war on Soviet Russia, Hitler appointed Rosenberg Reich Minister for the Eastern Occupied Areas. The appointment was made purely on the basis of personal loyalty to an old fellow Nazi and because Rosenberg knew the Russian language. He was a notoriously poor administrator, however. Throughout the Goebbels diary this inefficiency of Rosenberg's is harped upon. Rosenberg was hanged in Nuremberg after the International Military Tribunal found him guilty of having committed major war crimes.]

The landing of American troops in northern Ireland created a great sensation. Although southern Irish territory is not involved, De Valera protested vigorously. Possibly the Americans, acting on behalf of the English, merely wanted to try out how the Irish Government would react. This reaction was probably stronger than was anticipated in London, and I suppose there is momentarily no danger that the English will occupy Ireland proper. In the United States De Valera's reaction meets with feigned astonishment. But this pretended surprise offends the Irish more than it enlightens them.

[Eamon De Valera was President of the Irish Republic from 1919–22, and has been Prime Minister and Minister for External Affairs since 1937. He was president of the League of Nations Assembly in 1938.]

Terboven called me from Oslo. He intends to proceed against the Bishop of Norway, in whose home papers of an extremely compromising nature have been found concerning his collaboration with the English. I deny his request to have the controversy aired in the Reich. He will start things in Norway alone, where it is fitting and proper.

I had to clear up a number of domestic questions, especially the problem of allocating paper for the production of books. The Eher Verlag is making unjustifiable claims which must be rejected. On the other hand it is true that naturally the official publishing house of the Party deserves a higher priority than any other firm. My task consists in finding the right balance.

[The Eher Verlag, or publishing house, also known as "Amann's Octopus," was the official publications establishment of the Nazi party. Hitler's *Mein Kampf*, Rosenberg's *Myth of the Twentieth Century*, the daily *Voelkischer Beobachter*, and countless other books, pamphlets, and periodicals were published there. Hitler was generally believed to be one of the main stockholders, while the Party owned the rest. Its general manager was Max Amann, who had been the drill sergeant of Hitler's company in World War I. Like all the other "empire builders" of the Party, Amann kept increasing the holdings of the Eher Verlag by placing so many difficulties in the way of non-Party bourgeois newspapers, even though they all now supported the Nazi regime, that they sold out on terms decidedly favorable to Amann—hence the name "Amann's Octopus," which stretched out its tentacles in every direction in the publishing world. Amann had the title of Reichsleiter of the Nazi party, in charge of the press and publications. This gave him cabinet rank.]

Snow has enveloped all Berlin in a white garment. It's no fun, however, to contemplate this beautiful spectacle of nature, since every change in weather creates a whole series of new problems. One can hardly conceive of weather ideal to meet all demands. . . .

In the evening I had a long talk with my mother who, to me, always represents the voice of the people. She knows the sentiments of the people better than most experts who judge from the ivory tower of scientific inquiry, as in her case the voice of the people itself speaks. Again I learned a lot; especially that the rank and file are usually much more primitive than we imagine. Propaganda must therefore always be essentially simple and repetitious. In the long run only he will achieve basic results in influencing public opinion who is able to reduce problems to the simplest terms and who has the courage to keep forever repeating them in this simplified form despite the objections of the intellectuals.

January 30, 1942

It is interesting to observe what importance the clever exploitation of religion can assume. The Tartars at first had a none-too-gratifying attitude toward the German Wehrmacht. But they changed about

completely when permitted to sing their religious chants from the
tops of minarets. Their change of attitude went so far that Tartar
auxiliary companies which fought actively against the Bolsheviks
could be formed. Our efforts there were supported by our propaganda
companies who distributed a picture showing the Grand Mufti of
Jerusalem visiting the Fuehrer. That was extremely successful.

[Haj Amin el Hussein was the Grand Mufti. He visited Germany early in
November 1941, then went to Italy for about a month, and on his return to Berlin
was received by Hitler on December 8, 1941. In August 1946 the British Government refused to have him come to London as a member of the Arab delegation
because of his pro-Axis activities.]

Churchill's stock is beginning to rise again. Although opposition to
him in the Lower House is apparently strong, nobody dares propose
a vote of no confidence. He had, however, to stand for some pretty
outspoken criticism. On the whole this criticism was more moderate
than might have been expected, after the attacks in the press these
last weeks.

Rommel has marched into Bengasi again and found an unbelievable amount of booty. This is a wonderful piece of news which comes
extremely handy in this period of stagnation. The Fuehrer is very
happy about it. He promoted Rommel to colonel general.

[In the German Army generals ranked as follows: major general (there was no
brigadier), lieutenant general, general, colonel general, field marshal general.
Also, there was the special title of Reich Marshal given to Hermann Goering by
Hitler. That gave Goering a unique rank and raised him ahead of all field marshals.]

The United States newspapers are asking anxiously what has happened to their Pacific Fleet. For the most part the fleet is lying at the
bottom of the ocean.

[Goebbels at first believed Japanese news reports implicitly. Only much later
his diary entries indicate doubt in their veracity.]

Knox delivered a very pusillanimous speech. While claiming that
the Japanese have become very jumpy and nervous, he tried to get
himself out of his rather precarious psychological fix by telling lies.
He who before the outbreak of war had been the principal spokesman,
in fact the megaphone of the Roosevelt government, is now a sorry
sight indeed. Apparently he feels subconsciously that, in case America
were faced with a crisis, he would be made partly responsible for it,
as he was one of the chief warmongers.

[Secretary of the Navy Frank E. Knox during the first months after America's
participation in the war was a favorite target for Goebbels's jibes. The little doc-

tor was especially fond of reminding Knox of statements made before America's entry into the war.]

In the Anglo-Saxon countries a bitter fight is still going on about the relative order of importance of the theaters of war. Whenever the English sustain losses in North Africa they say the European theater of war is more important; whenever they have reverses in Europe they claim the East Asia theater has precedence; but when they are defeated in East Asia the North African theater again holds higher rank. In short, precedence is always enjoyed by the theater of war in which they aren't getting a drubbing, whereas the theater in which at that time they are having reverses is always far less important.

I have received pitiful reports about the situation in Greece. Hunger there has become an epidemic affecting the entire population. People are dying from undernourishment on the streets of Athens by the thousands—a result of the brutal British blockade and that, too, a blockade against a people who foolishly wanted to pull the chestnuts out of the fire for the English. That's how London thanks them.

In Finland, too, food conditions are horrible. The Finnish people this winter are showing a heroism worthy of greatest admiration. We could use more such allies. The German people won't find it too difficult to give up part of their bread ration in favor of Finland.

Lammers told me a lot about certain goings-on in top government departments. In the Ministry for Eastern Affairs, for instance, things don't seem to click at all. Rosenberg, after all, is more of a theoretician than a practical organizer. . . . Everywhere he is building up a gigantic apparatus of which, in the end, he loses all control.

Lammers also argued that something must be done for the government officials. He mentioned an article in the *National Zeitung* of Essen which criticized officialdom severely. I gave orders forbidding all such attacks in the future. It won't do to have two professions in Germany, namely, that of the teacher and the government official, subjected to public criticism, whereas an editor would of course not dare to tangle with a leading Party member or a prominent military officer.

I had a long talk with Viktor Lutze who told me of a number of complaints of the SA. He also wanted to get a general briefing on the situation. Apparently his conscience isn't very clear. Most likely he has again been shooting off his mouth and is looking for an alibi. I warned him earnestly to restrain himself in the future and in no way to criticize or cast doubt on the political or military conduct of the war. I told him emphatically that the Fuehrer will stand for no monkey business. He seemed to get the point, and I believe he will hold himself in better check hereafter. Considering his disposition, however, I doubt whether he will be able to keep this up long.

[Viktor Lutze became supreme commander of Hitler's Brown Shirts, the SA (*Sturmabteilung*—Storm Troops) after Ernst Roehm, one of Hitler's closest friends, had been executed on the Fuehrer's personal orders during the blood purge of June 30, 1934, for allegedly plotting the overthrow of the regime. Under Lutze the SA became a negligible quantity. This entry in the diary would seem to indicate that Goebbels did not have very high regard for Lutze. In an entry on April 15, 1942, he criticizes Lutze even more severely. When the SA chieftain was killed in a motor accident in May 1943, however, and given the most pompous state funeral accorded any follower of Hitler, Goebbels sang Lutze's praises in highest terms in his diary entry of May 8, 1943.]

The Fuehrer returned from his GHQ to Berlin at noon. I immediately had a long talk with him which was extraordinarily favorable and satisfactory. It fills me with joy to note how well he looks and how splendid is his spiritual and physical condition. He started right in on the Churchill speech, which the Fuehrer regards as exceptionally weak and wearisome. He, too, does not believe that Churchill is any longer sitting on top of the world, but on the other hand he sees no possibility of an early collapse of the Churchill regime. . . .

Churchill, by the way, remarked in his speech that Hess had really flown to England in order to unseat Churchill and bring about a suitable peace. That he made this remark is a proof of his nervousness, for it is certainly exceptionally shortsighted and is grist for the mill of those who are ready for an understanding with us.

[Rudolf Hess, born in 1894, Hitler's shadow until his sensational flight to England in 1941, joined the Nazi party as early as 1920 and became the Fuehrer's private secretary. He was arrested, tried, and sentenced with Hitler to imprisonment at Landsberg, Bavaria, where Hitler wrote *Mein Kampf*, dictating most passages to his faithful disciple, Hess. The Nazi prisoners at that time were allowed to gather together in an anteroom to Hitler's prison cell and had a good time, generally speaking.

On taking over the government of Germany in 1933, Hitler made Hess a minister without portfolio and appointed him his deputy for Party matters. It is not surprising, in view of the constant intrigues among Nazis sparring for position, that Hess was unpopular with the Party membership. Trouble-shooters seldom are popular. Recalling that he had been born in Egypt of German parents, they nicknamed him *der hinterhaeltige Aegypter* ("the treacherous Egyptian"). Also, in view of his unctuous manner of speaking, he was called *der Prediger* ("the Preacher"). It was his task every year to open the Party convention at Nuremberg and to preside over the plenary sessions. He was an extremely dull speaker, but his slogan, "Guns instead of butter," became internationally notorious.

In 1941 he flew to the British Isles, thinking he could persuade the British people and leading politicians to make peace with Nazi Germany and join with the Germans in fighting the Soviet Russians. (See also the entry under date of February 13, 1942, last paragraph.)]

The Tories are no doubt playing a decisive role behind the scenes in England. Churchill has never been a friend of the Tories. He was always an outsider, and before the war was regarded as half crazy. Nobody took him seriously.

The Fuehrer profoundly regrets the heavy losses sustained by the white race in East Asia, but that isn't our fault.

[The Nazi alliance with the Japanese was never popular in Germany. A nation which was so indoctrinated with the conception of Nordic racial supremacy found it difficult to understand why the Japanese should be considered the racial equals of the Teutons, and why intimate relations with Jews should be punished by death whereas similar relations with the Japanese met with no official disapproval.]

January 31, 1942

Churchill's closing speech in the House of Commons before the ballot on the vote of confidence was a collection of demagogic utterances. The ovation given him at the close of the session by the members was naturally a show put on for the world and has no political significance.

Rommel's advance produced a veritable shock in London. There is embarrassed stammering about the recapture of Bengasi. The Reuter Agency up to this hour has not been able to offer any plausible explanation. By way of providing a good out, however, Rommel is praised beyond measure. No doubt he deserves it and nobody begrudges it to him, but on the other hand one must not overlook the fact that the English pour out this praise only in order to present themselves to the world as polished gentlemen, who are fair and more than fair to the enemy even in defeat. We know these English tactics and are no longer taken in by them.

I continue to receive an enormous number of letters which on the whole are very favorable. Above all there is praise for my articles in the *Reich*, which apparently are exerting the greatest influence upon public opinion.

At noon I attended a reception at the Fuehrer's in honor of a delegation of Italian party members who came to Berlin for the celebration of our accession to power. The Fuehrer was in an exceptionally good mood, and talked very animatedly and convincingly to the Italian Gauleiters. The most impressive thing is his absolute and firm conviction that victory is ours, which he expressed so clearly and irrefutably that it made the deepest impression upon the Italian gentlemen. Our guests waxed enthusiastic about the fascinating personality of the Fuehrer, and especially at the youthfulness and poise of his behavior. Most of the Italian gentlemen had never before seen the Fuehrer and the impression he made on them is therefore all the more profound.

[January 30, 1933, was the *Tag der Machtergreifung* (Day of Seizure of Power). Its anniversary was declared a legal holiday, and Hitler usually addressed the nation on January 30 in a Reichstag session or at the Sports Palace.
    The *Sport-Palast*, with a capacity of about 25,000, was Berlin's counterpart of Madison Square Garden of New York.]

Later the Italians were received for lunch in my Ministry. Most members of the cabinet also attended. I could now converse at length with these gentlemen. They are an impressive elite of leaders, comparable to the best of our own Gauleiters. There isn't a single one among them who isn't full of enthusiasm for the Axis. Mussolini appears gradually to have eliminated from party leadership all elements which tried, even though only passively, to oppose his course. I received the very best impression of these Italians.

After dinner there was an exchange of speeches. I talked briefly to the delegation. Alfieri and the leader of the Italian delegation also spoke. Both events, at the Fuehrer's and in the Ministry, are evidence of the cordial friendship which binds the two Axis powers together.

[Dino Alfieri was Italian Ambassador in Germany at that time. He had been Goebbels's opposite number for a while as Italian Minister of Propaganda. The two men never got along very well.]

Very drastic and explosive expression was given to this friendship at the afternoon mass meeting in the Sports Palace, in the course of which the Fuehrer spoke. The Sports Palace was, as usual, filled to the rafters, and turbulent enthusiasm was manifested. It reminded me of the old days during our struggle for power. The meeting came off in the manner of 1930, 1931 and 1932.

When I extended words of greeting to the Fuehrer I could hardly finish any sentence, because the audience interrupted me again and again with stormy applause. I welcomed the Italian party delegation and this welcome, too, was greeted with salvos of applause by the politically alert Berliners. That was clever of them. The Berliners know the score and realize that the main problem of the moment is to keep the ally on our side. That is of course more difficult in winter than in summer, for in summertime our victories prevent our allies from becoming uncertain factors.

Thereupon the Fuehrer spoke. . . . The general purport of his speech was to strengthen morale at home and to educate the people to become tough politically.

The address made a tremendous impression both upon those present at the meeting and on the entire German nation. We may now rest assured that the main psychological difficulties have been overcome. We are now standing with both feet on the ground again. . . . The enthusiasm of the audience exceeded anything that the human mind can imagine. . . . The Fuehrer has charged the entire nation as though it were a storage battery.

As always, the Fuehrer is at his post. . . . As long as he is there, one need not worry about the future. My assertion that the Fuehrer is in good health created the deepest impression. As long as he lives in our midst in good health, as long as he can give us the strength of his spirit and the power of his manliness, no evil can touch us. The entire people became convinced of this anew today.

February 1942

QUISLING IS PROCLAIMED NORWEGIAN PREMIER. JAPANESE BOMB SURA-
BAYA. ROMMEL'S TROOPS RECAPTURE DERNA. LORD BEAVERBROOK BECOMES
MINISTER OF WAR PRODUCTION. MUSTAFA NAHAS PASHA BECOMES EGYP-
TIAN PREMIER. JAPANESE LAND AT SINGAPORE. THREE GERMAN MEN-OF-WAR
SLIP OUT OF BREST AND HEAD FOR HOME. SINGAPORE SURRENDERS.
JAPANESE CAPTURE PALEMBORG, SUMATRA OIL CENTER. CRIPPS ENTERS
CHURCHILL'S WAR CABINET. RIOM TRIAL OPENS. WILLIAM TEMPLE AP-
POINTED ARCHBISHOP OF CANTERBURY. JAPANESE OVERRUN BALI. BRITISH
APPLY "SCORCHED-EARTH" POLICY IN RANGOON. BATTLE OF JAVA SEA.
PÉTAIN PROMISES UNITED STATES TO KEEP FRENCH FLEET OUT OF NAZI
HANDS.

February 1, 1942

Japan acts with great self-assurance. Indeed the Japanese propagandists, in my opinion, often overshoot the mark.

Nothing of importance has happened internationally except that
Franco has delivered a speech, intended chiefly for home consumption, in which he declared that the Spaniards are God's chosen people
and will remain faithful to the Catholic Church. It would be far
more fitting for Spain to remain faithful to the Axis, for no special
laurels are to be had from the Catholic Church. Franco, as we know,
is a bigoted churchgoer. He permits Spain today to be practically
governed, not by himself, but by his wife and her father confessor.
That's a nice revolutionist we placed on the throne! But after all it
is better for him to sit there than for any old Bolshevik who would
undoubtedly be on the side of our enemies.

[Francisco Franco Bahamonde, born in 1892, the *Caudillo*, is head of the Spanish state. From 1936–39 he commanded the Nationalist troops which ousted the

Republican regime and had himself appointed "head of state and generalissimo." Since 1942 he also has had the title of President of the Political Junta of the Falange.]

The German people ought not to do any griping. They still have a standard of living that is impossible in any other country of Europe, whether in the war or not. The home folk have thus far felt the war but very little, so that one need shed no tears if somewhat heavier sacrifices are now placed on their shoulders.

I had reports submitted to me about a number of deficiencies. The coal situation is critical in Berlin, and if we don't adopt proper measures, it will undoubtedly become very serious in the second half of February. We shall then be forced to close the schools and even to stop production in some sections of the munitions industry. I don't want things to go that far.

I spent a lot of time on the problem of increasing production. I don't believe that it can be solved by laws. I incline to the belief that something can be accomplished only by appealing to national discipline and to a sense of national duty. Also, premiums must be offered. Factories that produce especially well should receive special rations of cigarettes and alcohol. I therefore forbade the general distribution in Berlin of such alcohol as is available, and insisted that available liquor be used as rewards for special performance in the factories.

February 2, 1942

The English have become decidedly more modest since the Fuehrer's speech. . . . One really wonders on what grounds the English had the insolence to declare war on the Axis Powers. Either they must not have known our superiority and their inferiority, or else—and this seems more plausible—they intended from the very beginning to have other countries and peoples do their fighting for them. At any rate, that's where I attack the English vigorously in the German press and also in our foreign-language broadcasts. But the English won't let themselves be disturbed in the complacency of their arguments. They are a very peculiar people with whom it is difficult to have an argument. They are obdurate to a degree that gets on one's nerves in the long run. But possibly that is a national advantage rather than a disadvantage.

February 3, 1942

A number of developments that, according to the maps, seem unfavorable to us have led the Bolsheviks once again to utter cries of triumph. They now declare that Kharkov is in immediate danger and that this enables them to strike at the very heart of our troops. Well, we shall see! . . . The Bolsheviks don't seem to have confidence in their own strength any more. Even their loudest reports of victory indicate that they have their secret doubts. Certainly their special bulletins don't have the same assurance as those in mid-December.

The Japanese are so cocksure and positive about their prognoses that one can hardly doubt their successes. On the other hand, of course, one must not fail to observe that the Japanese now and then exaggerate grossly and that their propaganda is very juvenile. Thus, for instance, the navy spokesman declared at Tokyo that the Japanese intend to land on the American continent and march into Washington. I call that pretty strong medicine and claim the Japanese are only hurting their cause by such pronouncements. I therefore gave orders that grossly exaggerated Japanese news items must not be published in the German press. Mistakes of this type usually occur only at the beginning of a war when the tricks of the trade have not yet been mastered.

The English boast that General Auchinleck is about to start a counteroffensive [in North Africa]. That is something, however, that the English always do when things are in bad shape. Anyway, their news policy is something that we could never afford to imitate. Apparently the English people don't make their government responsible tomorrow for what it said today. It is extremely easy to lead the English people. The German people are much more sensitive about these matters. Even today utterances of leading men of the Reich dating back to September and October 1939 are still thrown up to us if things have not come off as prophesied.

[Sir Claude J. E. Auchinleck, born, 1884 and educated in Wellington College, was deputy chief of General Staff Army Headquarters, India, 1936–38; served in Norway in 1940; became commander in chief of the Southern Command in 1940, of India, 1941, of the Middle East, 1941–42, and of India, 1943. President Truman awarded him the Legion of Merit in 1945.]

In the United States there has been a noticeable letdown. Boastful figures concerning the potentialities of American arms production are no longer published. My attention has been called to the fact that the American war industry would of course be able to manufacture enormous quantities of matériel if life in America were slanted completely in the direction of war. So far there are no signs of this. But of course that may come more quickly than people imagine. We see by the example of the Soviet Union what a big people are able to do along that line. Public and private life there has for a quarter century been geared solely to war. The success is enormous.

Quisling's appointment as premier has created a sensation in the countries at war with us and has drawn in its wake great waves of angry commentary. Quisling is hated violently in the entire enemy world and is now the target for vile calumniation. He has actually succeeded in becoming a symbol, although he doesn't really deserve it. But the more he is attacked abroad, the more it becomes our duty to support him. I therefore gave the German press instructions to give his appointment a good build-up and to see to it that with us, at least, he receives favorable publicity. On the other hand I forbid using the word "Fuehrer" in the German press when applied to Quisling. Even if he calls himself *Foerer* in Norway, and even if the word Foerer can easily be translated as Fuehrer, I nevertheless don't consider it right that the term Fuehrer be applied to any other person than the Fuehrer himself. There are certain terms that we must absolutely reserve to ourselves, among them also the word Reich. We must not tolerate any other state to call its confines a Reich. The whole world must in future understand that by Reich is meant only the German Reich.

[Vidkun Quisling, born in 1887, was educated in the Royal Norwegian Officers' School and Military Academy. He was an officer of the Norwegian General Staff, 1911–23; Military Attaché in Petrograd, 1918–19; and was charged with the care of British interests in Russia during the interruption of diplomatic relationships, 1927–29. He was Norwegian Minister of Defense, 1931–33, and then became leader of the Norwegian Nationalist movement which made the entry of German troops into Norway in April 1940 easy. He became head of the German-controlled Norwegian Government in April 1940 and was appointed Premier in 1942. On October 24, 1945, he was executed for treason. King Haakon denied his wife's petition for clemency.]

Seyss-Inquart wrote me a letter importuning me to include the wild purchases by German officials in the occupied areas in my campaign against the black market. These purchases have become a veritable pest. Heydrich punished them severely in the Protectorate. In the long run similar measures can probably not be avoided in other areas. Various departments of the Reich Government have acted very shamelessly in this matter. They did tremendous harm to the German name and it will take some time before we regain the respect of the peoples in the occupied areas.

I received word from the western part of the Reich that eleven clergymen who are under indictment for listening to English broadcasts are soon to be tried. I informed the Fuehrer, since this trial will undoubtedly assume a pronouncedly political character. If things went my way, I would inflict the heaviest punishment on these "skypilots" [*Pfaffen*] and would possibly even condemn them to death for doing such damage to the Reich. But of course such a question cannot be handled by itself but must be viewed as part of a larger picture, and it is up to the Fuehrer whether or not he considers such a trial desirable at this moment.

Owing to the absence of Hinkel the radio programs have deteriorated very much. During the hours set aside for entertainment almost nothing but symphonic music is offered. That's what we get for letting Glasmeier appoint a musical director general, Schulz-Dornburg, to be responsible for the entertainment program. People of this type usually sit in an ivory tower and don't know what the common man wants and what he needs most. . . . It is wrong to appoint a musical expert for so difficult a task. Experts are always handicapped in their relation to the common people. They lack the necessary instinct for realizing what the people are thinking.

[Hans Hinkel, who was on leave for a special mission at the time of this entry, was one of the Nazi "Old Guard" who took part in Hitler's ill-fated beer-cellar putsch in Munich in 1923. He became state commissioner for the Prussian Ministry of Science, Arts, and Education in 1933, and supervisor of Jewish cultural activity in 1935. Later he joined Goebbels's Propaganda Ministry and was put in charge of its radio section.

Dr. Heinrich Glasmeier was superintendent of broadcasts and deputy to Hinkel. He was also used in other capacities by Goebbels. (See, for instance, the diary entry for November 13, 1943.) When the Nazis came into power in 1933 he was appointed general manager of the Cologne Radio Station. He was on the executive board of the Reich Radio Chamber. Rudolf Schulz-Dornburg was one of innumerable German *Kapellmeisters*.]

February 4, 1942

In the United States people are extremely concerned about the situation in the Pacific. Even that big mouth and tall talker, Knox, delivered a speech which was diametrically opposed to his emanations before the outbreak of the war. He who previously always boasted that the United States Fleet was big enough to conduct a two-ocean war must now suddenly admit very modestly that the American Fleet is hardly big enough for one ocean, that it cannot fight a two-ocean war, that the necessary labor is lacking to increase the fleet and especially the air force, that one must envisage a war of long duration, that the workers don't want to do any night-shift work, et cetera.

All this gives one the impression that the United States is for the first time seriously facing the problems of the war. They could have done that at less cost if they had studied developments in Germany. Had they done so, however, they would, in all likelihood, not have entered the war. It's great fun to observe how the big mouths on the other side, who three months ago boasted how they would polish off Japan in six or eight weeks, now suddenly hem and haw and are compelled to face the facts. I permitted the release of the Knox speech to the German press and news services so they could pick it to pieces. It is excellently suited for polemics, all the more so as we can also use this occasion to refute the pompous array of figures with which Roosevelt tried to bluff the world in his last speech.

Quisling gave the DNB representative a long interview about his policies. He makes the somewhat grotesque claim that in his hands as premier is concentrated all the power formerly held by the King, the Parliament, and the Prime Minister. That's laying it on a bit thick, for after all there is a Reich commissioner standing beside him! Nevertheless we release this version, since naturally we are highly interested in letting the Norwegian Government appear as big and independent as possible.

[DNB stands for *Deutsches Nachrichten-Buero* (German News Bureau), the official news agency of the Nazi regime.]

News comes from Budapest that Horthy intends to make his eldest son his presumptive successor. That would be a great misfortune, for this son is even more friendly to the Jews than Horthy himself. I hear, however, that Horthy is again in excellent health, so that the problem of his successor for the present is purely theoretical.

[The son of Nicholas Horthy, Regent of Hungary, was married to a Jewess. Horthy, on being taken prisoner by the Americans in May 1945, tearfully told a group of American correspondents in Bavaria that his son was a victim of the Nazi war.

Nicholas Horthy de Nagybanya, admiral of a country which has no navy and head of a kingdom which has no king, was born in 1868 in Kenderes, Hungary, the fourth son of a member of the House of Magnates. He was educated in the Imperial Austrian Naval Academy in Fiume. During World War I he commanded the battleship *Hapsburg* for ten months with the rank of captain, and then the cruiser *Novara*. Later he became a hero overnight by breaking through the Allied blockade in the Straits of Otranto. Emperor Charles I promoted him to rear admiral in command of the Austro-Hungarian fleet over the heads of older officers. The next year he was made vice-admiral. He crushed the Communist Revolution of Bela Khun in 1919, and in 1920 was elected Regent Governor of Hungary by the Hungarian National Assembly. His word was law from then on.]

February 5, 1942

Figures are now available concerning casualties because of freezing. We must differentiate between injuries of the first, second, and third degrees. First-degree frostbite comprises the light cases. Generally speaking, the soldier remains with his outfit and is treated there. Up to January 20 there were 4,000 third-degree frostbite cases, in other words, most serious cases. These 4,000 cases include 1,856 necessitating amputations of a more serious nature. . . . Besides these 4,000 third-degree cases, 46,000 cases were recorded of first and second degree, that is, injuries of a lighter or medium nature.

Churchill's preparations for the East Asia conflict are being revealed more and more as amateurish. Parliament would undoubtedly have sent him flying long ago if there were an adequate successor. But look as you will far and wide, he is nowhere to be discovered.

The fact that the Fuehrer in his Sports Palace address spoke such exceptionally appreciative words about the Party made a very favorable impression on the Party.

The Brauchitsch question may now be regarded as settled by the Fuehrer's speech, but a last remnant of suspicion still remains with the German people. The fact that the Fuehrer himself has taken over the active command of the Army is having a wonderful effect. Recent German successes in the East are credited to him, and rightly so. He has actually saved the Eastern Front.

The Jewish question is again giving us a headache; this time, however, not because we have gone too far, but because we are not going far enough. Among large sections of the German people the idea is gaining headway that the Jewish question cannot be regarded as solved until all Jews have left the Reich.

Some difficulties arise for us from the fact that the churches, especially the Catholic Church, are trying to use our seizure of church bells for war purposes as an excuse for unrestrained propaganda against National Socialism. I have therefore given orders that bells be taken away only after the population has been adequately informed by the Party of the reasons for so doing.

A confidential report concerning internal conditions in Hungary indicates . . . that the Hungarians are actually ready to risk more lives [in the war effort]. It is gradually dawning upon them that they can't just sit in club chairs while the new Europe is being shaped, and later share in the successes. The Hungarians must risk blood if they want to get more territory.

I wrote an article about increased production and courtesy which undoubtedly will prove a major sensation on publication. I chose my arguments very carefully and believe they will dominate public discussion. I may possibly put this exposé of mine through the entire German press in order to acquaint all the people with the ideas and arguments there laid down.

February 6, 1942

One of the armies [in the East] has reported that marching orders can't be carried out because there is no gasoline.

Moscow is exceedingly dissatisfied with the British contribution in other theaters of war. The Bolsheviks are gradually beginning to understand what a ball and chain they tied to their feet by allying themselves with the British Empire. They admit that our troops offer great resistance and that it is difficult to attain objectives when facing them. . . . Generally speaking one can say that the Eastern Front is no longer under severe strain.

Despite Wavell's appeal to the troops in Singapore to hold out, there is almost no hope of further resistance by the island fortress. The position has become untenable chiefly because there isn't sufficient fighter-plane protection. Those 100,000 planes that Mr. Roosevelt was going to build are not yet ready; there aren't even enough ready adequately to defend a relatively small space. . . . I am convinced that no matter how nonchalant they may act about Singapore, its loss will be a real shock to the English people. Churchill is already having a hard time calming public opinion.

[Viscount Field Marshal Wavell, born, 1883 had been commander in chief of the British Middle East Command, 1940–41, but was at this time Commander in Chief, India. In 1943 he was made Viceroy of India.]

Most [British] newspapers think Churchill hasn't gone nearly far enough in reshuffling his Cabinet. People thought a number of strong men would be included; instead, Churchill got stuck with Beaverbrook. Beaverbrook seems to have obtained pretty far-reaching powers. But no man with imagination, or a strong character, can maintain his position long beside Churchill. Churchill delivered a very thin and pretty confused speech in the House, explaining the reconstruction of his Cabinet. He dwelt especially on the difficulties the British Empire faces in its relations with Australia. Australia is becoming more and more obstinate and the English world empire faces the danger that, if the crisis within the Commonwealth should develop, Australia may someday incline more toward the United States.

[Goebbels's estimate of Lord Beaverbrook underwent quick changes. Here he is represented as a strong character; on September 26, 1943, he is depicted as a great enemy of Sovietism; on September 29, 1943, as a man who favored an understanding with the Soviets.
Lord Beaverbrook, the former Rt. Hon. William Maxwell Aitken, born in 1879, is a British newspaper magnate and chief stockholder of the London *Daily Express.* He sponsored the Empire Free Trade Movement. During the war he was successively Minister for Aircraft Production, Minister of State, of Supply, of War Production, and Lord Privy Seal.]

Had a minor set-to with Rosenberg about the manner of conducting our ideological celebrations. He knows nothing about organization, that's why he is monkeying so much with it. I will hold my own against him, however.

In the evening I was able to be with the children for an hour. After that I took a look at the Italian Gigli motion picture *The Tragedy of Love,* the artistic level of which is so far below the normal that it really ought to be prohibited. The Italians are not only not doing anything about the war effort, but they are hardly producing anything worth while in the realm of the arts. One might almost say that fascism has reacted upon the creative life of the Italian people somewhat like sterilization. It is, after all, nothing like National Socialism. While the latter goes deep down to the roots, fascism is only a superficial thing. That is regrettable, but one must recognize it clearly. National Socialism is really a way of life [*eine Weltanschauung*]. It always begins at the beginning and lays new foundations for life. That's why our task is so difficult, but also so beautiful, and the goal ahead is well worth our best effort.

[Beniamino Gigli was Italy's best-known operatic tenor after the late Enrico Caruso.]

February 7, 1942

Rommel continues to be the pronounced favorite even of the enemy news services. He has succeeded in becoming a real phantom general. He is just as popular today in the United States as in London and Berlin, and one of the few figures in the German Army with a world reputation.

We got hold of a secret message of the [British] Foreign Office to its embassies and legations. It is a warning not to be optimistic about the situation in the East; the German Army was by no means defeated; its power to resist was unbroken; and, as the weather improves, it must be expected to start new offensives.

Nahas Pasha has issued a pro-British declaration, stating that the Anglo-Egyptian treaty will be carried out both in letter and in spirit. We don't place too great hopes in Nahas Pasha; nevertheless one must not forget that he simply had to make such a declaration because he and his government are under the thumb of the English and he can't afford in any way to oppose the pro-British course.

[Mustafa El Nahas Pasha was Egyptian Prime Minister and chairman of the Wafd party. He was born in 1876 and educated at Cairo College.]

A number of minor bomb explosions reported as having occurred in the baggage rooms of Berlin railway stations, among them the Anhalter and Stettiner stations. I sense a certain danger in this. Any rowdy can hand in his suitcase with a time bomb at the baggage-checking counter, and two or three hours later a part of the railway station is blown up. I am having an inquiry made as to whether baggage can't be controlled more effectively. But here, as everywhere else, we lack man power necessary for work like this. Lack of labor here, as everywhere, is the greatest problem with which we are faced at present.

At noon I received the representatives of the Auslands Organisation who have come to Berlin from all European and overseas countries, and gave them a comprehensive survey of the military and political situation. I was in top form, used persuasive and pointed arguments, and won fervent applause from the representatives of the AO. I am sure they will return to their heavy labors spiritually elated.

[The Auslands Organisation or AO (federation of Germans living abroad) was the contact organization for the Nazi regime to keep up its connection with and to indoctrinate Germans who emigrated to foreign countries or were in these countries on duty. As the Nazis became more powerful and efficient, the AO developed into both a propaganda and an espionage organization, the latter not so much in a technical sense, perhaps. That is, many of the rank and file of the membership probably did not realize that they were being used for espionage purposes; they merely thought they were giving information useful to the leaders of the AO in the discharge of their duties.]

February 8, 1942

The reconstruction of the Egyptian Government has brought no sensational changes. Nahas Pasha declared that he intended to carry out the treaty with England without any reservation. He was clever enough, however, to obtain authority to dissolve Parliament. That, undoubtedly, is right. We did the same thing in February 1933. He must first get parliamentary backing before he can bring about fundamental changes. I still hope that he may act more favorably for us than we are inclined for the present to assume.

[The dissolution of the German Reichstag early in February 1933 enabled the Nazis to terrorize the population during the campaign for new elections, start the Reichstag fire, and use alleged Communist incendiarism as an excuse for outlawing the Communist party and fully entrenching themselves.]

Anglo-American collaboration is the principal theme of the Anglo-Saxon press. There seem to be all sorts of difficulties about it. That's owing to the fact that in the much-advertised democracies nobody knows who is to give orders and who is to obey. Undoubtedly, too, the personal vanities and rivalries between Churchill and Roosevelt play an important role. We may certainly consider ourselves lucky not to be opposed by a front that is united ideologically. Lack of organization results in many a chance being missed, especially in this war, where everything depends upon who strikes first and most devastatingly.

Rosenberg wrote me a letter stating that he intends to oppose the idea of a fight against the religious denominations. That's just too funny! Now, when we are in a tight pinch, everybody poses as a champion who fights against the very things that he himself started. I suppose the final result will be that we who have for years opposed the folly of our pronouncements on the religious question and similar things will be regarded as the real originators of the difficulties resulting from this folly!

I consider it absolutely essential that the news bureaus be owned by the Reich. News policy is a sovereign function of the state, which the state can never renounce. News policy is a cardinal political affair, and political matters of this character must be in the hands of the Reich and not the Party. The Party is in no position to establish a real news service. In a news service 99.9 per cent of the items deal with news about the state leadership and only the remaining small percentage deals with the work of the Party. There will be some fights about this, but I won't give in.

February 9, 1942

A serious explosion has occurred in Tangiers. The Secret Service is badly compromised. The Spaniards are raising a hell of a row. Tangiers last Saturday evening teemed with giant demonstrations against the English. Reuter is spreading the most insolent lies, claiming that it was a question of a bombing attempt by the Axis Powers.

In the course of the day a shattering piece of news reached me. Dr. Todt crashed and was killed on leaving the airport of Rastenburg this morning following a visit at GHQ. The plane dropped from a height of four hundred meters and exploded on the ground. The passengers were so badly burned that it was hardly possible to gather up the corpses. This loss is absolutely overwhelming. Todt was one of the really great figures of the National Socialist regime. A product of the Party, he fulfilled a number of historic tasks, the effects of which cannot even be estimated at the moment. With the genial, spark-plug power of his personality he combined an extremely pleasing simplicity of behavior and an objectivity in his approach to his work in so compelling a form that everybody could not but esteem and love him. The ensuing months will show what we have lost in him. The Fuehrer, too, is hard hit by this loss. We have recently had to endure such heavy personnel losses that one really begins to believe that troubles never come singly.

[Dr. Fritz Todt, born September 4, 1891, Minister of Munitions, was one of the top Nazis whom foreigners liked. He had none of the strutting, arrogant mannerisms of the typical Party brass hats. Modest and unassuming, he made many a foreign visitor wonder how he ever got mixed up with Nazism. His first outstanding achievement was the construction of the *Reichsautobahnen*, or super-highways, that proved so advantageous to the Allied armies as they swept through Germany. Next he constructed the gigantic Siegfried Line, or *Westwall*, opposite the Maginot Line, and later started the *Ostwall* as an opposite number to the Stalin Line to the east. In 1941 Hitler created a new Ministry of Munitions and appointed Todt to head it. The labor battalions which built the fortifications and followed directly behind the combat elements of the German Army to repair bridges and roads were called the *Organisation Todt*, or OT for short.]

I spent the entire day preparing the funeral ceremony for Todt. A solemn state funeral in Berlin is to honor him before the entire world. The Fuehrer wants personally to come to Berlin to pay him a tribute on behalf of our nation and thereby to confer the last and highest honors on him.

Throughout the day I feel numb over this loss. I hardly have time to think. There are so many people in public life who are as superfluous as a goiter. Death does not dare touch them. But when there is someone among them who has the ability to help make history, a senseless and cruel fate tears him from our ranks and he leaves a void that simply cannot be filled.

February 10, 1942

Generally speaking, Dr. Todt's fatal crash is regretted throughout the world. Even the English feel they must pay a tribute to his great talent for organization. Of course there are also a few English voices stupid enough to doubt the official version of the cause of Todt's death. That's the way English gentlemen are: they are nonchalant and polite as long as everything is well with them, but they cast off their masks and reveal themselves as brutal world oppressors the moment one trespasses on their preserves or a man appears on the scene with whom they must reckon.

Beginning April 6, food rations must be reduced. Emphasis is laid upon the fact, however, that the workers performing hardest labor and the children are not to be affected too much. That is important, especially so far as the children are concerned.

There can be no doubt that the rations in force after April 6 will no longer be sufficient to guarantee health and the maintenance of reserves of human labor power. We must therefore expect a number of developments which we have hitherto been in a position to avoid.

We are now gradually entering upon conditions that in some ways resemble those of World War I during its third year. It is quite obvious that a war which extends over so long a period of time, and encompasses such tremendous spaces of earth, cannot but make a dent in the food economy of a people. It is satisfying and comforting, however, to know that similar conditions obtain in England also, so that our difficulties are not because of the blockade but rather because of the long duration of the war.

Hinkel reported to me about his experiences during a trip to Bavaria. Conditions in certain parts there are nothing to be proud of. Some of the Bavarian leaders, including those of the Party, are trying in every way possible to escape war duty. After all, they aren't Prussians!

[Goebbels was a Westphalian, hence a citizen of the state of Prussia, of which Westphalia was a province.]

Once English world domination has been broken, one element of constant unrest and nervousness in world politics will no doubt have disappeared. The English succeeded in conquering one sixth of the earth by their methods. But that was during an epoch when the great national states were not yet ready. Now, however, Germany is ready, Italy is trying hard to get ready, and Japan is just at the point of being ready. England will have to reckon with these three new world powers.

It's a fight for the highest stakes. No matter how long it lasts, we shall have to see it through. For if we don't succeed in shattering English domination in the world, all sacrifices of World War I and World War II will have been in vain.

[The idea of putting an end to British world domination obsessed the Nazis. This editor recalls meeting one of the best-known and best-informed Nazi editors on the day England and France declared war on Germany because of the invasion of Poland. His first words were, "No matter what happens—this is the end of the British Empire."]

February 11, 1942

In conservative English circles opposition to Cripps is beginning to grow. He has a disquieting way of warning and admonishing, so that they'd like to banish him to some distant diplomatic post. Cripps, however, shows no inclination to accept such a post. He is a simon-pure parlor Bolshevik and believes his hour has come. Undoubtedly Bolshevism is making progress among the English people and it is quite possible that at some future time a prophecy of the Fuehrer's may find its fulfillment, in the effect that it will not be Europe that will be corrupted by Bolshevism, but rather England and the United States.

The English press hasn't yet made up its mind on which side to array itself, whether Cripps's or Churchill's, who hasn't yet publicly committed himself. One section of the English press enthusiastically praises Cripps, another section denounces him just as vigorously. All these happenings are extraordinarily full of meaning for us and are excellently suited to commentary in the German press.

The fact that Cripps proclaimed Berlin as the future capital of Bolshevism is, of course, grist for our mill. The German public likes to read that sort of thing. There are always nitwits on the other side who throw us the ball whenever we want it. All we have to do is to hold up our hand and a propaganda ball flies into it from the enemy side.

[Goebbels at first placed great hopes in Sir Stafford Cripps, who, he expected, would bring about a cleavage in Great Britain. In his first references to him he is full of praise for "this fair-haired boy and parlor Bolshevik." He changed his tune, however, when to his great surprise the British statesman accepted the mission to India. From then on he was "a greatly overrated man!"
The Rt. Hon. Sir Stafford Cripps, son of Lord Parmoor, entered politics in 1931 when he became a Labor MP for Bristol East. He opposed the formation of the National Government. He was Ambassador to Soviet Russia, 1940–42, Lord Privy Seal and leader of the House of Commons, and subsequently, in November 1942, Minister of Aircraft Production.]

Because of transportation and material shortages we are compelled to cut out all fairs for 1942. This was a difficult decision to make but one that was inevitable. In Leipzig, especially, there is great lamentation, as the fair had been almost entirely prepared. But there is nothing to be done about it. The needs which we must obey are more compelling.

[Of all German expositions, the autumn and spring fairs at Leipzig, dating back to the Middle Ages, were the most important.]

The fall of Singapore has made a very deep impression on the German public. The Japanese rate exceptionally high with us. They are regarded as an ally worthy of fighting on our side.

Morale in the Ukraine is none too good. It would be a great help if we could promise land to the peasants. But as things are this is impossible. The intelligentsia is solidly on our side. The Ukrainian intellectuals know perfectly well what Bolshevism would do to them if it should return. For that reason they regard National Socialism and the German occupation as the lesser of two evils.

How profound the English crisis is may be seen from the fact that Hore-Belisha, the former Jewish Minister of War, has deserted the Liberal party with two other members. Rumor has it he intends to form a new anti-Churchill party with Cripps.

A number of domestic problems demand solution. Administrative reform is under discussion. Frick is trying to inject himself into the work started by Dr. Lammers, but he is only partially successful in this. The Ministry of the Interior as a simplifier of administration is a real joke.

[Wilhelm Frick, the first Nazi to attain high political office in Germany as Thuringian Minister of the Interior, was floor leader of the Nazis in the Reichstag and became Reich's Minister of the Interior on Hitler's assumption of power in 1933. Through Goebbels's intrigues Frick was eased out of his office in 1942 and appointed Protector of Bohemia-Moravia. He was hanged in Nuremberg.

The feud between Goebbels and Dr. Frick was particularly bitter, even for a regime in which fights and jealousies among the leaders were the order of the day.

Goebbels was an ultra-radical; Frick, a bureaucrat by training and profession, was averse to extreme measures. Goebbels was aggressive and ruthless; Frick rather mild-mannered and at times even timid.

But there was also a personal reason for their enmity. Goebbels as Minister of Propaganda was also president of the Reich Culture Chamber and as such controlled the cultural and artistic life of the nation. He therefore resented it very much that Frick from time to time invited friends and associates to an evening of music in his home. Both Frick and his wife were very fond of the fine arts. Goebbels did not like this "competition."]

It is disgusting how many big shots are now trying to prove to me that they can't continue their work unless they receive permission to listen to foreign radio broadcasts. In almost all cases I deny their requests. I agree to place at the disposal of every individual only such material as is essential for his special work. The task and duty of listening to foreign broadcasts must devolve on the political offices created for this purpose. Administrative offices have nothing whatever to do with it.

Diewerge returned from Paris and gave me a detailed report on conditions there. He has spoken to Bonnet, who is ready to testify in the murder trial of the Jew Grynzpan which is to take place soon. Bonnet is ready to testify that he opposed the declaration of war against Germany, but that the French Government was put under such heavy pressure by the Jews that it could not avoid declaring war. This shows in what an irresponsible way this war was started and how heavily those must be punished who acted so rashly.

[Diewerge was a member of Goebbels's staff in the Propaganda Ministry.
Georges Bonnet was Minister for Foreign Affairs in the Daladier cabinet at the time of the outbreak of World War II. In September 1939 he became Minister of Justice, a portfolio which he held until March 1940. In 1941 he became a member of the National Council.
Herschel Grynzpan was a Polish Jew who came to the German Embassy on November 9, 1938, and killed his friend, Ernst vom Rath, in what was described by the Nazis at the time as a fit of homosexual jealousy. When Hitler was informed of the incident in Munich, where he and his Old Guard were celebrating the anniversary of the 1923 beer-cellar *putsch*, he gave orders, in a fit of rage, for a general pogrom of the Jews. This was followed later by a terrific money fine on all Jews within the Reich.]

The Fuehrer returned to Berlin for the funeral ceremony in honor of Reich Minister Dr. Todt. I went to see him immediately at noon and noted that the loss of Dr. Todt has shaken him badly. . . . Todt was one of the men closest to the Fuehrer. . . . The Fuehrer told me privately how hard this loss had struck him and how sad he was at the idea of one friend after another gradually leaving our group.

The general situation gives the Fuehrer every reason to be satisfied with developments. He is somewhat worried about our three men-of-war, the *Gneisenau, Scharnhorst,* and *Prinz Eugen,* which have left Brest to seek a safe harbor. They are on their way, and we are all trembling lest something happen to them. It would be terrible if even one of these three ships were to share the fate of the *Bismarck.* Up to this hour the English haven't noticed anything, but undoubtedly they will attempt to attack the ships, as they are sure to be informed of their departure by spies. The Channel passage will be difficult but the attempt must be risked, so that the ships may at least reach a secure haven. Foreign countries will no doubt be alarmed to realize that these three ships, which have been reported sunk so often, are now majestically sailing the seas.

[On May 27, 1941, the German battleship *Bismarck* was sunk four hundred miles off the French coast after a running sea battle with the British Navy. Goebbels naturally feared the *Gneisenau*, *Scharnhorst*, and *Prinz Eugen* might share her fate.]

The Fuehrer regards the fall of Singapore as a very serious thing for the English. He believes a crisis may possibly arise for the British Empire. Churchill's position may be badly shaken. I am not prepared as yet to believe it. Churchill is already trying to minimize these events, and as the English know very well that Churchill's fall would provoke a most serious crisis for the British war spirit, they will shrink from this last measure for settling scores with the arch liar.

Week by week the Tories are becoming more and more distrustful of the Churchill policies. This distrust has been especially fed by the silly declarations of Cripps. His latest effusions have created such a sensation in neutral countries that we may in future expect all sorts of good things from this fair-haired boy [*Edelknabe*].

The Fuehrer has the greatest respect and highest praise for the way the Japanese are conducting the war. The Japanese deserve this. They are fighting so bravely and with such an enviable national idealism that one could only wish we had more such allies.

The Fuehrer's extreme confidence and his firm grasp of all domestic, foreign, and military problems are truly wonderful. He won't let anything confound or mislead him. He believes in victory more firmly than ever, and of course he has every reason to do so. We shall achieve victory provided we continue to fight for it with the same energy and with the same selflessness.

At 3 P.M. the state funeral for Dr. Todt was held in the Mosaic Hall of the Reich Chancellery. It was profoundly touching. Every person of prominence in the state, Party, and Wehrmacht attended. One could weep at the thought that so valuable and indispensable a collaborator has been taken from our ranks in such a senseless way. The Fuehrer gave most eloquent expression to this idea in his address. As he spoke the Fuehrer was at times so deeply moved that he could hardly continue. But that made all the deeper impression upon those present and no doubt upon the public as well. We all have the distressing feeling of taking leave of a man who belonged to us as though he were a part of us.

[The Mosaic Hall (*Mosaik-Saal*) was so named because the floor, walls, and ceiling of one of the large reception halls in Hitler's gaudy New Chancellery

(*Neue Reichskanzlei*) were covered with small stones set in artistic patterns, i.e., mosaics.]

The Fuehrer once more described all the achievements of the deceased in detail and said he had at first intended to confer the Knight's Cross upon him, but that he had abandoned this idea because the Knight's Cross, despite its high rank, did not do justice to Todt's meritorious service. He therefore conferred upon Todt, as the first to be thus honored, the highest class of the new German Order created by himself. Todt certainly deserved this. If anybody had a right to be awarded posthumously the highest honors that the Reich can confer, it was he.

The ceremony was sad and sorrowful. When the remains of Todt were carried out of the Reich Chancellery it seemed to all of us that a brother was leaving us.

On this day I was not really in the mood to attend to all sorts of petty details. The Fuehrer, too, retired. I occupied my mind with a number of problems that will assume importance only in the distant future. Work is always the best antidote to attacks on the soul and spirit. I passed the evening in a melancholy mood. I had a growing feeling of loneliness. It is terrible even to imagine that the men who embarked upon this gigantic struggle and are responsible for so doing might be removed from their work before the conclusion of the war. Just as we won a revolution together, so we want also to win a war together. Reconstruction after the war won't be so difficult as winning victory. That's why we must now concentrate all energies upon the achievement of victory.

February 12, 1942

After Singapore, Moscow is the principal theme of international discussion. Cripps's speech met with the sharpest criticism in the neutral countries. Individual English papers, too, object to his statements. But I give hardly any publicity to these voices, for it is not in our interest to classify Cripps as an outsider. On the contrary, he is to be, so to speak, the mouthpiece of the group in power in England. That gives us a much better basis for arguing against him.

I have given instructions for our Ministry to prepare dictionaries for the occupied areas in which the German language is to be taught. They are, above all, to use a terminology that conforms to our modern conception of the state. Especially those expressions are to be translated that stem from our political dogmatism. That is an indirect form of propaganda from which I expect rather good results in the long run.

In our propaganda we must take into consideration the impending reduction of food rations, the reasons for which must be given to the population in detail. I am having all arguments put together with which the reduction can be explained effectively. While they are very convincing, I am somewhat inclined to doubt whether they will be fully effective, for no one will listen to well-reasoned arguments if butter and meat are taken away from him.

If I were an Englishman I would tremble for the fate of the Empire. But as I am not an Englishman and as I am convinced that our victory can be attained only through the collapse of the British world empire, I view developments with firm confidence. There was a time when we considered the existence of the British world empire a necessity for the welfare of Europe. This time is past. . . . Churchill gambled away the chance we gave England. England will have to pay very dearly for this statesman. But that isn't our worry. Our worry is so to wage war that the Axis Powers will soon attain complete victory.

February 13, 1942

What disappointments the American people must experience these days! All hopes awakened in them seem to prove false. I am convinced that the American statesmen themselves believed what they prophesied. The United Press, for instance, reports that Hull is very much depressed over American failures to date and is thinking of resigning.

Cripps continues to carry on agitation on behalf of the Bolsheviks. For us he is a propagandist whom we simply could not pay with money. I therefore ordered the press not to picture him as an outsider. On the contrary, we must represent him as a sort of mouthpiece for Churchill. Of course he isn't that actually, but he is most useful to us that way.

It is claimed that Hore-Belisha and Cripps intend to found a new anti-Churchill party. It remains to be seen whether they will actually succeed in this. It would be best, of course, if Churchill were defeated and Hore-Belisha took his place. Today we would most heartily welcome a Jew as Prime Minister.

Lieutenant Colonel Hermann, Dietl's adjutant, gave our ministerial conference a survey of the present situation on the northern sector of the Eastern Front. Conditions at times are really gruesome there.

Some of the mountain troops have not had a furlough since the beginning of the campaign in Norway. They are exceedingly homesick and their morale is kept up only by the challenging example of Dietl. He is a true people's general. He is constantly with his troops and has achieved a popularity that is indescribable.

[Colonel General Eduard Dietl, commander of the German forces in the extreme north, was a Bavarian mountaineer who distinguished himself by boldness and bravery during the Norwegian campaign in April 1940. He was a member of the *Epp Freikorps* in 1919, joined the Nazi party in 1920, and participated in the Hitler *putsch* in 1923. As a colonel he commanded the Ninety-ninth Alpine Regiment at Kempten. He participated in the occupation of Austria in 1938, and was commander of an Alpine division in Poland in 1939.]

Despite their depressing surroundings, the troops themselves are in good spirits. They have gone through several crises which, however, could be overcome by joint effort. The way our people at home are taking care of these troops is most praiseworthy, Lieutenant Colonel Hermann told me. I did something extra for them and assigned a three-quarter liter bottle of schnapps to every soldier at the northern front. That means I am diverting 150,000 bottles intended for the Berlin population. The Berliner will have to get along without this schnapps; the soldiers in the north need it more.

I discussed the present position of economy and foreign exchange with Funk. He is having great difficulties with Rumania. Antonescu does not deliver what he promised. To some extent he isn't in a position to do so. The dilatoriness of the Rumanians isn't so much the fault of the marshal as it is of young Mihai Antonescu, who is playing a rather disastrous role in the economic life of his country.

[Walter Funk, born in 1890, was Nazi Minister of Economics and President of the Reichsbank, and was sentenced for life at Nuremberg, having been found guilty of major crimes against humanity. Funk himself exclaimed in this editor's presence, shortly after his appointment to the Economics Ministry in 1938, "Who would ever have thought I'd land up here!" For he started as an obscure journalist when his dream of becoming a musician did not materialize. He finally rose to the position of financial editor for the conservative *Berliner Boersenzeitung*, the organ of the capital's "Wall Street," and joined the Nazi party early. Goebbels first took him into his Propaganda Ministry as chief of the press section and with the rank of *Staatssekretaer* (equivalent to our undersecretary). There he had to give Hitler a daily review of press commentary. Hitler liked him so well that he promoted him to a cabinet post when Dr. Hjalmar Schacht's "orthodox" financing no longer suited the Nazis.

Ion Antonescu was Rumanian dictator from 1940 to 1944. He had been one of the leaders of the Iron Guard. King Mihai dismissed him and he was classified as a war criminal by the Allies upon his arrest. Mihai Antonescu was deputy Prime Minister and president of the Liberal Youth Association. He, too, was arrested in 1944 and classified as a war criminal. Both Antonescus were executed June 1, 1946, at Bucharest.]

It is a grotesque thing that neither the Italians nor the Spaniards are willing to have the war matériel which we furnish them credited to the deliveries they are to make to us. They demand that this be postponed until after the war. In other words, we are furnishing the Italians war matériel but must make separate payment for the goods the Italians furnish us. It is surely a headache. [*Es ist schon ein wahres Kreuz.*] We are waging this war not only by shedding our blood but also by supplying the materials and the labor. It is only right and just that we take the leadership of Europe definitely into our hands after the war and not let ourselves be pushed off our course by any other state, no matter how big it may be or what exaggerated claims it may put in. The German people must suffer and stand for so much; they have actually won the hegemony of Europe and have a moral right to it.

At noon I was a guest at the Fuehrer's. He gave a small luncheon in honor of Quisling who is in Berlin at present and conversed at length with the Fuehrer. The Fuehrer is naturally very happy that our warships succeeded in breaking through. He believes we gained enormously in prestige while the British lost prestige correspondingly. He is still of the opinion that Churchill has been maneuvered into a dangerous position and that his fall may possibly be expected.

[This refers to the *Gneisenau, Scharnhorst,* and *Prinz Eugen* which left the French harbor of Brest (see February 11, 1942), sailed through the English Channel unmolested, and arrived in a northern port.]

Singapore, too, has weakened his position very much. As the crisis extended it would exhaust the energies of the English public more and more and someday a catastrophe would result. Although I am not so optimistic in these matters as the Fuehrer, I believe, nevertheless, it may be assumed that Churchill's position has been weakened, and that he must watch his step. . . .

As to Quisling, he developed very naïve ideas in his talk with the Fuehrer, as the latter confided to me. He thinks he will be permitted to build up a new Norwegian Army, protect the Norwegian harbors himself, and finally create an entirely free Norway. That, of course, is very childish. The Fuehrer replied evasively to these claims.

As for myself, I have the impression that Quisling is in fact nothing but a Quisling. I can't feel any sympathy for him. He is a dogmatist and theoretician whom one can evidently not expect to develop great statesmanlike qualities.

I discussed a number of internal Party measures with Bormann.

He is very critical of Dr. Ley, who is smashing a lot of china with his hysterical articles. The Fuehrer has had to scold him hard because of his articles on increased production, since they contained veiled attacks against the Ministry of Munitions. In my presence the Fuehrer gave Ley a tongue-lashing and, when the latter tried to reply, told him that it just won't do for anybody to start things on his own at a time when other departments and other personalities are concerning themselves with the same problem. He gave orders that nothing be done in the matter of increased production without the permission of the Ministry of Munitions.

[Reichsleiter Martin Bormann became Rudolf Hess's successor as Hitler's deputy in party matters after Hess's sensational flight to England in 1941. He proved to be one of the most radical and uncompromising Nazis, filled with a hatred for the Church. He was tried *in absentia* at Nuremberg, but no definite proof of his death was produced. He was with Hitler in his bunker almost to the last.

Dr. Robert Ley, who committed suicide at Nuremberg shortly before the big war crimes trial began, was head of the German Labor Front, besides being Reichsleiter, with cabinet rank, of the political division of the Nazi party. In the early days of the Nazi regime Robert Ley was Gauleiter for Cologne-Aachen. In May 1933 he engineered a *coup d'état* against the German trade unions which at that time were still a power. The trade unions, not fully realizing the revolutionary character of Nazism, thought they could best overcome Nazism by seeming to play with it, but actually boring from within, and therefore agreed to participate in the annual demonstrations on Europe's Labor Day, May 1. While Hitler was haranguing them on Tempelhof Field, Berlin, and the workers throughout the Reich were assembled at their customary demonstration centers to listen to the broadcasts of the speech, Ley and the SA invaded trade-union headquarters everywhere, seized the books and funds, and wrote "finis" to the German organized labor movement. Instead, Hitler commissioned Ley to organize the German Labor Front which both workers and employers were compelled to join.]

Increased production, in any case, isn't a question that everybody can solve for himself, but an enormous problem that can be tackled only by common effort. The Fuehrer believes that rigorous measures must be taken, that the entire process of production must be examined anew, and that the captains of industry who are unwilling to follow the directives given by us must lose their factories, no matter whether that means their economic ruin or not. After all, nobody cares whether a soldier goes to pieces economically or even physically when he goes to war, and the soldier certainly does as much personally for the war effort, if not more, than the industrialist who manufactures arms and munitions. The Fuehrer has ordered the munitions producers to come to him in the afternoon, when he will give them instructions and tell them off.

Bormann complained bitterly about Rosenberg, who has managed to create a veritable chaos in his Ministry and is picking a quarrel with every Tom, Dick, and Harry. Rosenberg, too, is a sort of Quisling type. A good theoretician but no practitioner, he is completely at sea as far as organization is concerned, besides having rather childish ideas.

Hess has written a letter to his wife. It is disarmingly naïve. He still thinks he has done a great thing for the war effort and declares he believes the dream of Professor Haushofer, that he will someday return home with peace in his hands, will yet come true. As for the rest, he is chiefly concerned about his health. In other words, he hasn't stopped his quackery. He is certainly not in the condition in which we thought him to be. He is past hope of redemption. [*An ihm ist Hopfen und Malz verloren.*]

[The reference to Hess's "quackery" recalls the fact that Hess did not believe in orthodox medicine but supported all sorts of "nature fakers" and prevailed upon Hitler to have them licensed as practitioners on a par with regular medical men.]

February 14, 1942

The fact that we sailed through the Channel with our three big ships is today's great sensation in London. People act as though they were stunned. There is talk of a great sea battle, and an effort to prove that the German squadron sustained heavy losses. There isn't a word of truth to that. Meanwhile the facts are seeping through.

It is a characteristic fact that the French on the Eastern Front are not giving a good account of themselves. These people are no longer worth anything. They have lost their military punch. A macabre nation, bent upon pleasure, which has rightfully suffered a catastrophe. We need no longer have any fears—the French won't cross our path for a long time to come.

The Spaniards are extraordinarily courageous, but have military peculiarities which we simply cannot understand. For example, they just can't comprehend that horses must be looked after and fed. On the other hand, however, they go after the enemy like Bluecher. They have thought out a new system of defense in which the Soviet population must help, and the Russian peasants stand for this without raising an eyebrow.

In that connection it is significant that most of the local population leave with us wherever our troops are compelled to withdraw. Bolshevism is a doctrine of the devil, and anybody who has once suffered from this scourge doesn't want to have anything to do with it again.

The sufferings of the Russian people under Bolshevism are indescribable. This Jewish terrorism must be radically eliminated from all of Europe. That is our historic task.

[It was a dogma with the Nazis that Bolshevism was a Jewish invention.]

World Jewry will suffer a great catastrophe at the same time as Bolshevism. The Fuehrer once more expressed his determination to clean up the Jews in Europe pitilessly. There must be no squeamish sentimentalism about it. The Jews have deserved the catastrophe that has now overtaken them. Their destruction will go hand in hand with the destruction of our enemies. We must hasten this process with cold ruthlessness. We shall thereby render an inestimable service to a humanity tormented for thousands of years by the Jews. This uncompromising anti-Semitic attitude must prevail among our own people despite all objectors. The Fuehrer expressed this idea vigorously and repeated it afterward to a group of officers who can put that in their pipes and smoke it.

[Inasmuch as pages 9–36 of this day's diary entry are missing, it is not apparent what the occasion was for this diatribe of Hitler's against the Jews. The Fuehrer remained in Berlin for some days following the funeral of Dr. Fritz Todt, Minister of Munitions, and constantly received his underlings. It is probably not wrong to assume that this was one of Hitler's conversations "unter vier Augen" (literally under four eyes) with Goebbels alone, of which the little doctor was so proud.]

The Fuehrer realizes the full implications of the great opportunities offered by this war. He is conscious of the fact that he is fighting a battle of gigantic dimensions and that the fate of the entire civilized world depends upon its issue.

The Fuehrer continues to have the greatest admiration for the Japs. They prepared everything secretly. We have now heard that Kurusu and Nomura negotiated in Washington without having the faintest idea as to what the Japanese war leaders were planning. That's a good thing. When you are gambling for the existence of your own people you should employ all methods of a tricky and superior war strategy. It means, of course, that Kurusu and Nomura played an exceedingly ludicrous role, but that is of less importance. They deserved making fools of themselves, for these two diplomats had always been the representatives of Japanese appeasement, which has now proven entirely senseless and inimical to Japan.

[This entry in Goebbels's diary makes special Ambassador Saburu Kurusu and regular Ambassador Admiral Kichisaburo Nomura appear in a more favorable light. According to Goebbels they did not know what they were doing. Goebbels knew Kurusu well because he had been Japanese Ambassador to Germany preceding his mission to Washington. It was he who signed the pact of alliance in Hitler's chancellery on September 27, 1940. Berlin society at the time was agog with the rumor that Kurusu, forgetting that he was surrounded by agents of Hitler who understood Japanese, turned to his counsellor of embassy as he sat down to sign the pact and said, "I don't think I am rendering my country a service with this signature." At any rate Kurusu was recalled soon thereafter, allegedly because the remark was promptly relayed to the Fuehrer. Kurusu had an American wife and two daughters who spoke English perfectly and were very American in their outlook and behavior.]

We, too, have employed such methods again and again. Our Ambassador in Moscow, Count von der Schulenburg, also hadn't the faintest idea that the Reich was determined to attack. He kept insisting that our best policy would be to make Stalin our friend and ally. He also refused to believe that the Soviet Union was making tremendous military preparations against the Reich. There is no doubt that one does best if one keeps the diplomats uninformed about the background of politics. They must sometimes play a role for which they don't have the necessary theatrical abilities, and even if they did possess them, they would undoubtedly act an appeasement role more convincingly and play the finer nuances more genuinely, if they themselves were believers in appeasement. Genuineness in playing an appeasement role is sometimes the most convincing argument for their political trustworthiness.

[Count von der Schulenburg was purged in connection with the mass executions of leading Germans implicated in the plot which culminated in the abortive attempt on Hitler's life, July 20, 1944. He is frequently referred to in the *Von Hassell Diaries*. Count Friedrich Werner von der Schulenburg, born, November 20, 1875, was a German diplomat with a long career of service, his last posts having been Minister to Iran, Minister to Rumania, and Ambassador to Russia.]

How stupidly diplomacy sometimes does these things was illustrated by the Fuehrer in an incident before the offensive in the West. At that time there was at our Legation in the Hague an obvious traitor, a certain attaché Von Prittwitz, who collaborated with the [British] Secret Service. The attention of our Legation was called to this fact. The minister thereupon very cleverly called the entire staff together, explained the situation, and thereby gave the traitor a chance to escape to England just in time. With that kind of diplomacy you naturally can't steal horses! It is therefore better if the diplomats know nothing, neither a part nor the whole thing. They will then do stupid things, to be sure, but they won't do any harm.

The weakness of diplomacy is its social ties. These can never be quite overcome, and one must therefore be conscious of this weakness when determining one's policies. One must not stick to old methods that have long been outmoded but must play politics and conduct war with modern methods.

February 15, 1942

When one surveys the over-all situation critically one becomes convinced that there is a deep moral and political depression in London as well as in Washington. This should not be overestimated for it can naturally still be overcome. Nevertheless the Anglo-Saxons have taken such heavy blows during the last week that their knees are beginning to tremble.

What I do personally continues to meet with general approval. What I've done with the radio as well as the newsreel is lauded in terms of highest praise. My articles are having the greatest effect throughout the world, nor need I complain of their echo among the German people.

The hundreds of thousands of foreign workers now employed in the Reich are a headache. The danger exists that intercourse between these workers and German women will cause a gradual deterioration of our race. This danger must be checked by every possible means. But it is difficult to discuss such a question in public because the peoples and nations affected immediately take offense. For example, the Italians fight tooth and nail against being regarded as racially inferior to, or even different from, ourselves.

I had a long talk with Heydrich about conditions in the Protectorate. Sentiment there is now much more favorable to us. Heydrich's measures are producing good results. It is true that the intelligentsia is still hostile to us. But we must rally the rank and file of the people to our side and against them. The danger to German security from Czech elements in the Protectorate has been completely overcome. Heydrich operates successfully.

He plays cat and mouse with the Czechs and they swallow everything he places before them. He has carried out a number of extremely popular measures, among them first and foremost the practically complete conquest of the black market. . . . Slavs, he emphasized, cannot be educated as one educates a Germanic people. One must either break them or humble them constantly. At present he does the latter. Our task in the Protectorate is perfectly clear.

Neurath completely misjudged it, and that's how the first crisis in Prague arose.

[Baron Konstantin von Neurath, former German Foreign Minister, was too old and easy-going as first Protector of Bohemia-Moravia to suit Hitler. He was persuaded to resign for reasons of health, and Heydrich was put in his place. The whole world was shocked when, in April 1942, the Nazis completely wiped out the Czech town of Lidice as a reprisal for the assassination of Heydrich.

When President Von Hindenburg appointed Hitler Chancellor on January 30, 1933, he stipulated that Foreign Minister von Neurath be retained. Hitler agreed, but on Von Neurath's sixty-fifth birthday, on February 2, 1938, relieved him of his duties and replaced him with the more robust and unscrupulous Joachim von Ribbentrop. Soon thereafter he appointed him Protector of Bohemia-Moravia at Prague. Von Neurath was condemned to fifteen years' imprisonment as a major offender in the Nuremberg War Crimes Trial in 1946.]

Seyss-Inquart gave me a survey of the present situation in Holland. . . .

The Dutchman is, generally speaking, an unpolitical individual. Calvinism and the materialistic love of good living have made him very individualistic. His character is in many respects quite strange to us. You therefore can't do very much in Holland with cultural institutions, since the Dutchman is not used to them and, in fact, hardly knows them. His pigheadedness can't be beaten. Nevertheless I believe that further developments will improve sentiment toward us in the Netherlands. Seyss-Inquart is pursuing a policy of restraint which, though not altogether National Socialistic, is nevertheless purposeful.

Sentiment in Paris is not hostile to us. However, the critical food situation does stand between us and the French people. If we were in a position today to supply sufficient food to the occupied areas, we could win countless moral victories. Cultural propaganda is still the best propaganda in dealing with the French. I shall therefore increase it even more.

[It is interesting to observe that the French Army of Occupation and French Military Government in Germany are now stressing cultural propaganda more than the other three occupying countries do in their respective zones.]

It is, by the way, a significant thing that our front-line soldiers are always missionaries for German prestige. The soldiers of the third and fourth line, however, i.e., the military bureaucracy, merely disgust a people that attaches such importance to personal bearing. But there isn't much we can do about it. Our man power is limited, and our men are now more necessary for fighting the war than for making a favorable impression by their appearance in Paris.

February 16, 1942

Singapore this afternoon offered to capitulate after having fought desperately. For the first time in this war the English are obliged to hoist the white flag in grand style. That is certainly a blow to English prestige. That fact finds expression in the British press. A feeling of deep shame permeates the entire world empire.

The differences between England and the United States are growing quite naturally and so quickly that we shall desist from trying to increase them by our commentary. The English might otherwise take up some of our comments and use them to prove to the Americans how undesirable such conflicts are. A precious plant like this must be allowed to grow with the aid of natural rain and natural sun under God's free sky. I expect a lot from these differences of opinion, but the time has not yet come for making them grow by artificial means.

Franco delivered a very aggressive speech against Bolshevism. It would be far better if he declared war on Bolshevism. But what can you expect from that sort of general?

Late at night Churchill spoke. The same old stuff. A certain hopelessness finds expression. . . . But his slogan of "Blood, Sweat, and Tears" has entrenched him in a position that makes him totally immune from attack. He is like a doctor who prophesies that his patient will die and who, every time the patient's condition worsens, smugly explains that, after all, he prophesied it.

February 17, 1942

For the further progress of the war we cannot possibly think of a prime minister who would be better for us than Churchill. Aside from the fact that we are accustomed to his personality and his policies, it must not be overlooked that Churchill's strategy is so short-sighted that he will certainly lead the empire from one reverse into another. Let us therefore rejoice that he continues at the head of the world empire. If the empire is to be laid to eternal rest anyway, it is comforting to have an experienced gravedigger at hand.

[This is a clear case of "sour grapes" to hide Goebbels's chagrin at Churchill's latest victory in Parliament. Both Goebbels and Hitler, it will be recalled, considered the parliamentary crisis in London as very grave.]

Roosevelt radioed a speech to Canada urging subscription to the war loan. Like his little handyman [*sein kleiner Moritz*] Knox, he has become extremely modest. I have the impression that the leaders in the Anglo-Saxon camp are imbued with a spirit of deep resignation. Hull is again reported to have spoken very pessimistically to the men around him. In other words, conditions in the enemy camp are not as the somewhat frivolous commentaries in the press would have us believe them.

I am having some trouble with the press because it doesn't take to my suggestions as I should like. Unfortunately Fritzsche is altogether too much on the side of the press. Why, the press ought to howl with joy [*wiehern vor Freude*] at being given such excellent material for commentary. Instead, the bourgeois papers especially seem to be so tired of using this material that I could burst with anger. I therefore consider it my duty to keep exhorting and goading them on. If you don't constantly build a fire under the people responsible for informing the public, and if you don't constantly push them on, they gradually become dull and tired.

[Hans Fritzsche was Goebbels's top radio commentator and his deputy for news handouts to the German press. He was indicted as a major war criminal and tried at Nuremberg by the International Military Tribunal. He was acquitted but rearrested by the Germans and tried under the de-Nazification law. The German court condemned him to nine years' imprisonment.

An interesting admission that the non-Nazi editors were not so gullible and tractable as Goebbels wanted them to be.]

Statistics on suicides show a decreasing curve. It looks indeed as though nobody wants voluntarily to depart this life. Everybody wants to live to see the end of the war, and rightly so, for it will surely be a joyful occasion for the entire people.

February 18, 1942

The participation of the Japanese in this war is a real gift from the gods for us. They have changed the situation fundamentally during this fateful winter. Thanks chiefly to them we have survived the greatest crisis.

Churchill was forced to justify himself in a brief declaration in the House of Commons. His declaration is about the limit of anything he has so far done. He admits that the German Fleet succeeded in forcing its way through the Channel, but now suddenly claims that when you consider it in the right light, this is a tremendous advantage for England. The R.A.F. no longer needs to fly attacks on Brest but can now concentrate on air raids against the Reich. Besides, the

German Fleet at Brest had been a constant threat to the home fleet. This threat was now practically eliminated. . . .

During the forty-minute debate in the House so much dirty linen was washed that we can only be very happy about it.

In the evening I had a look at the Polish-Yiddish motion picture, *The Dybuk*. This film is intended to be a Jewish propaganda picture. Its effect, however, is so anti-Semitic that one can only be surprised to note how little the Jews know about themselves and how little they realize what is repulsive to a non-Jewish person and what is not. Looking at this film I realized once again that the Jewish race is the most dangerous one that inhabits the globe, and that we must show them no mercy and no indulgence. This riffraff must be eliminated and destroyed. Otherwise it won't be possible to bring peace to the world.

February 19, 1942

It is typical for the English to try to relieve their feelings by announcing abnormal war aims. The fact that in their periodicals they are letting their imagination run wild with plans for revenge shows how furious they are with us. The worse their military situation becomes, the more they blow themselves up. But that has always been a national disease of the British and one need not take it too seriously.

These press commentaries suit us exactly. Nothing better could happen to us than to have the English at this very moment openly proclaim their intention to destroy Germany completely, that is, not only the Nazi regime, but the entire German people.

American newspapers claim that Stalin has been preordained to save Christianity. What queer intellectual jumps the plutocratic spokesmen make in their present distress! Nothing is too nonsensical to be thought, said, printed, or written during this war.

I am having the question investigated as to how we may in future obtain authentic news from the United States. We have established a number of news bridgeheads in South America. For the present they still function, but of course we don't know how long that will continue. The situation in the South American countries is becoming more difficult from week to week, and possibly we shall have to expect a number of declarations of war there also. As far as the military situation is concerned, they are only of secondary importance.

We have published a diplomatic report sent to Daladier by the former French Minister in the Hague. It claims that the former Dutch Foreign Minister, Kleffens, at the end of 1939 suggested a plan for an attempt on the Fuehrer and Ribbentrop. There is no exact proof of this, however, as the language of the report is somewhat obscure.

[Edouard Daladier, born in 1884, was French Prime Minister and Minister of National Defense, 1938–40, in other words, both during the "appeasement" negotiations at Munich on September 30, 1938, when Czechoslovakia was compelled to cede the Sudetenland to Hitler, and at the outbreak of World War II. He was arrested in June 1940, on the charge of "war responsibility."
Eelco Nicolaas van Kleffens, born, 1894, and educated at Leyden University, is a Dutch diplomat and politician, who, after having held numerous diplomatic posts, became Minister for Foreign Affairs in 1939.
Joachim von Ribbentrop, born May 30, 1893, a former champagne merchant whose title of nobility (von) was obtained irregularly through adoption by an uncle who had only a personal but not a hereditary title, was picked by Hitler because of his glib tongue and seeming knowledge of foreign affairs. He was at first a personal agent of the Fuehrer, but in 1938 was appointed Foreign Minister. He was hanged at Nuremberg.]

Personally I should have preferred to hold back things like that. In wartime one should not speak of assassination either in a negative or an affirmative sense. There are certain words from which we should shrink as the devil does from Holy Water; among these are, for instance, the words "sabotage" and "assassination." One must not permit such terms to become part and parcel of everyday slang.

The food difficulties in all occupied areas are enormous. For some time to come we shall not be able to overcome them. The wonder to me is that the peoples in the occupied areas are remaining so quiet.

The Catholic Church continues to act in a dastardly way. A number of pastoral letters have been laid before me which are so unrealistic [weltfremd] and treacherous that nothing need be added. Nevertheless we shall not proceed against them. Let the "skypilots" [Pfaffen] have their say; we'll present our bill to them after the war.

Complaint has been made about the behavior of French prisoners of war, who evidently don't appreciate their relative freedom. We shall watch this carefully and possibly take away their privileges.

February 20, 1942

In the United States a lot of criticism is at present directed against Churchill. We take no note of this criticism because we don't want this tender plant of disagreement between the two allies to die prematurely.

Vansittart has aligned himself with the periodical, *John Bull,* and has declared that the German people must be completely disarmed for an entire generation and re-educated. We know that type of education by English capitalists and hard-boiled brutalists [*sic*]! It's a good thing, however, that the English are now letting the cat out of the bag. That can only help our domestic propaganda.

Although England is fighting at present against tremendous obstacles it cannot be said that morale among the common people is low. The English people are used to hard blows, and to a certain extent the way they take it compels admiration. In times of crisis the British Government profits by the pigheadedness of the British national character but someday, somehow, this pigheadedness will end; namely, when the blows begin to be staggering and deadly.

Nobody in all Europe wants to have anything to do with Bolshevism. Even from the viewpoint of foreign policy it suits us exactly for Cripps to continue his activity. Yes, we really ought to wish that Churchill would take him into his government, a thing that according to latest reports is by no means outside the range of possibility.

The Riom trial of French war criminals has begun. Daladier, Gamelin, and Blum are the chief defendants in the dock. It does not look as though there will be a real squaring of accounts. The whole trial will probably be conducted according to the principle, "Wash my skin but don't make me wet." Besides, the court is to sit only three days a week, and for only a few hours per session, so that we must count upon a long duration of the trial, especially considering the maze of material that must be gone through. The defendants began immediately to defend themselves vigorously. It remains to be seen whether political sensations will develop. We had really thought the causes of the war would be gone into. Instead, the intention is to determine the causes for the French defeat. We are certainly not particularly interested in that.

[General Maurice Gustave Gamelin, born, 1872, was chief of staff to General Joffre in World War I. He was chief of the General Staff of the French Army in 1931–35, Inspector-General, 1935–37, and vice-president of the Higher Council of War, 1935–40. When World War II broke out he became Allied Commander in Chief for France in September 1939 but was relieved in May 1940. After the French defeat he was arrested and detained at Fort Portalet.

Léon Blum, leader of the French Socialist party, was Prime Minister, 1936–37 and vice-president of the Cabinet, 1937–38. He, too, was arrested in 1940 and taken to Fort Portalet.]

In Brazil they are wondering whether they ought not to declare war on us on account of torpedoings by our submarines. For the moment, however, everybody is extremely careful in this respect. The South American nations know perfectly well that war can no longer remain a pure theory for them, but that they will at least have to count on German torpedoes in the event of war. That is something which, after all, might give some trouble to the corrupt characters that are now governing the South American nations.

The Italians are causing us difficulties in various ways. Now they are trying to horn in on the newly founded movie industry at Bucharest, which was really to be our field. Of course they are doing it with insufficient means, but nevertheless they would like to keep their fingers in the pie. There isn't much to be done about it for the moment.

They also proposed that we buy the Berlin exhibition of Italian books at a price of 400,000 marks. It is worth about 50,000 marks. This is a very touchy subject which I am referring to the Foreign Office for disposal, for German foreign policy and especially relations with our allies are chiefly its concern, and I don't see why I should spend such sums out of my budget for such trifles.

The eldest son of Horthy has been designated as his [father's] deputy by acclamation of the Hungarian House of Representatives. This is a piece of first rate political skulduggery. But we are keeping hands off. . . . Horthy's son is a pronounced Jew-lover, an Anglophile to the bones, a man without any profound education and without broad political comprehension; in short, a personality with whom, if he were Regent of Hungary, we would have some difficulties to iron out. But this isn't the time to bother about such delicate questions. When in need the devil will eat flies, and in wartime we will stand even for an objectionable deputy regent of Hungary. After all, we must have something left to do after the war!

By a decree of the Fuehrer all intercourse with Polish girls by soldiers stationed in Poland is forbidden and punishable. I doubt very much whether this decree is practical. Experience points to the contrary. The question of intercourse of German soldiers and officials in occupied areas with the female population there is exceedingly difficult and delicate. As long as German women are forbidden to follow the armies in these areas one can't be too severe, for somehow nature will claim its rights after all.

It is really amusing to see how all ministers now approach the Fuehrer, asking his permission to listen to foreign radio stations. The reason they assign is nothing short of grotesque. For example, the

Minister of Education declared he must know what our enemies are supplying in the way of anti-German news in order that he may indoctrinate youth against such reports! The Fuehrer rejects all such requests brusquely and encourages my efforts to keep news distribution as restricted and limited as possible.

During the night the news reached us that Churchill, under pressure of public opinion, was forced to reshuffle his Cabinet. The most outstanding characteristic of this reconstruction to me seems to be the fact that Cripps has been taken into the Government. We really ought to celebrate. We could not possibly have expected anything more favorable to us.

February 21, 1942

The appointment of Cripps has placed in our hands a propaganda argument that could not possibly be more favorable. It is effective for domestic as well as for foreign and also for military politics. It is good for our people, it is good for our allies, it is good for the neutrals, and it is fateful for our enemies. What better thing could we wish for or imagine?

The trial at Riom is going its prescribed slow course. Gamelin, Blum, and Daladier are quite insolent in court. They act as though they were the prosecution and, as has always been the case with us, too, under similar circumstances, the judges are impressed. I suppose it won't be long before Pétain and his men will be sitting in the defendants' dock instead of the warmongers and the defeatist clique.

Bishop Preysing of Berlin continues to criticize the German war leaders. I had at first intended to order him to come to see me personally and then to tell him off, but I got away from that idea because I am convinced this would lead to nothing. He would in all likelihood present me with a list of his complaints and then either deny his misdeeds or else hypocritically promise improvement. It is best not to touch on this theme at all but rather to postpone it to the end of the war.

[Count Konrad von Preysing, Catholic bishop of Berlin, was one of the cleverest men in the hierarchy of the Church of Rome, as was indicated by his elevation to cardinal in 1945. The real reason, it is safe to assume, why Goebbels did not summon the bishop was that he feared this prince of the Catholic Church, who would probably have come out on top in any argument.]

There is complaint about too much gabbing by the people, especially by men in uniform. Our soldiers are boasting too much. They try to make an impression upon the civilians, especially upon the women, and thereby merely create unrest and mischief. But there isn't much one can do about it. We have warned so frequently that we almost feel ashamed to raise the issue again. Human beings, especially the Germans, are talkative. You can't change them. You must take them as they are, and must put up with the deplorable consequences.

In the afternoon Magda returned from her cure at Dresden. She brought Harald with her and our family is now complete again. The children are very happy to have their mother with them again.

Magda told me about a number of incidents in Saxony that are nothing to be very proud of. Political conditions there are deplorable. It is a great pity that overwork prevents me from attending to all these details. The little kings throughout the land naturally make good use of such a situation.

[Goebbels at this time considered himself a sort of deputy to Hitler. It was really none of his business as Minister of Propaganda to take a hand in the political situation in the various gaus.

Magda was the given name of Goebbels's wife. The couple were at various times at the point of divorce, chiefly because of Goebbels's philandering, but Hitler wanted no scandal about the men closest to him and therefore repeatedly asked the couple to patch up their differences. Despite their disharmony Goebbels insisted that his wife bear him a child a year, since Hitler laid great stress on large families. Relations between the two apparently improved very much during the war, although Goebbels never speaks of his wife in the same terms of affection as he does of his children.

From her first husband, a rich industrialist named Quandt, Magda Goebbels had one son, Harald. From her marriage with the Propaganda Minister resulted Helga, Hilde, Holde, and three more children.]

February 22, 1942

The situation on the Eastern Front has become somewhat more critical. Here and there conditions are developing that are not exactly a cause for joy. It looks as though Stalin were making a special effort to achieve a number of noteworthy victories so that he might report them during the exercises of February 23, the Day of the Red Army. As a result the Bolsheviks attacked with unheard-of fury. They succeeded here and there in attaining isolated tactical results. Although the situation is not too critical, nevertheless it may cause us some trouble. . . .

Our troops are pretty well knocked out by the continuous hard fighting. At many points, too, the supply lines are not functioning. The troops don't think it funny to be sent now here, now there. Hardly have the soldiers dug themselves in when they must start moving again. The distances they must cover are pretty big but the speed with which these are negotiated is very slow indeed.

We can certainly thank God that we have an equivalent for the Eastern Front in East Asia and especially in the Atlantic. Our latest news flash reporting the sinking of additional 100,000 tons off the American coast gives a mighty fillip to morale at home.

A confidential report is presented to me giving me the real background to Cripps's policies. It appears that Cripps desires the Sovietization of English industry and, especially, greater participation of British production in the war. But he certainly does not desire to Bolshevize the country. That, of course, is no good for our propaganda. For us Cripps is the prototype of the Bolshevik in England. Whether he actually wants Bolshevism or not is really beside the point. It all depends on the effect.

Bormann issued a decree to the Party demanding greater simplicity during appearances of leading personalities and simpler banquets; also an admonition to the Party to set a good example for the people. This decree is very commendable. Let's hope it will be observed.

I talked to Hinkel about checking up on the teachers of dramatic schools. In that sector you find a crowd that had better be locked up in a concentration camp.

Our enemies abroad have unfortunately gained possession of a circular letter by Bormann concerning the church question. Why does Bormann at this time have to let loose a pronouncement on the church question anyway? The church question is no problem that has any decisive importance for the winning of the war.

February 23, 1942

Stalin issued [a program of] thirty points to his army. These points are about as naïve as can be imagined. But I suppose he knows how to treat his Russian people. They are as primitive as the language he uses to talk to them.

February 24, 1942

I have issued orders to the German press to handle the situation in the East favorably, but not too optimistically. Otherwise we might go to the opposite extreme from the preceding weeks. Our people would cease to worry at all about the situation in the East. That would be most unfortunate at this moment.

Temple is to be the new Archbishop of Canterbury. He, too, is under suspicion of favoring Socialist-Bolshevik ideas. We therefore note the same development there [in the church] that we have been able to diagnose in the reshuffling of the Cabinet.

The whole tendency in England now gives us an opportunity for starting a broad-scale discussion along lines which enable us more and more to appeal to conservative circles [in England] in effective terms and especially to work on the neutrals. Until now I never expected the English people would offer us a special opportunity for effective propaganda. Now, however, a little door seems to have opened for the first time by which we can slip in.

Stalin addressed an appeal to the Bolsheviks and the world. While his appeal is replete with misrepresentations and false news of victories, it is, on the other hand, characterized by an impressive realism. Stalin declared the German Army by no means defeated and that it would be unworthy of a Soviet soldier to underestimate the enemy. The German Army would surely be beaten in the end, but that time was still a long way off.

Stalin received a great many telegrams of congratulation from the plutocracies. No billionaire from Wall Street missed the chance to transmit his best wishes. This whole business looks like a complete perversity of political thought and conception. Moscow is today the last hope of capitalism. What we have prophesied for many years is coming true in a most dreadful manner. The Bolsheviks no doubt are none too elated over the plutocratic congratulations. England and the United States send telegrams of homage but no arms. Stalin could certainly use weapons much better than homage.

The official Turkish news agency has issued a somewhat insolent declaration about a démarche of Von Papen which, however, is of no special importance. Turkey, after all, is compelled, in the interests of her neutrality, to have the pendulum swing now to this side, now to that. One need not take this too seriously.

[Ambassador Franz von Papen was apparently greatly overrated by foreign countries. At this time he had very little influence on German foreign policy. But every time he moved, some paper or news agency claimed he was engaged in a new peace move. He was, however, one of the men in high places who bears chief responsibility for Hitler's rise to power. He first intrigued against the last

Republic Cabinet, that of Chancellor Heinrich Bruening, then had himself appointed Chancellor by the rather senile Von Hindenburg. When the funds of the
Nazi party ran out, Von Papen arranged for a meeting of Hitler with the big industrialists of the Rhine and Ruhr at the home of Baron von Schroeder in Cologne,
and later agreed to be Vice-Chancellor in Hitler's first cabinet. In 1934 he accepted appointment as Special Minister to Austria, where he prepared the
Anschluss. He was tried at Nuremberg in 1945–46 and acquitted. Then the Germans themselves tried him and condemned him to eight years' hard labor.]

We shall have to change our propaganda and our policies in the
East, as already arranged with the Fuehrer. These were hitherto based
on the assumption that we would take possession of the East very
quickly. This hope, however, has not been realized. We must therefore
envisage a longer duration and are accordingly compelled to change
our slogans and our policies fundamentally. It may even become necessary to set up sham governments in the occupied countries.

[Hitler's whole conception of the war he planned and unloosed upon the world
was that it would be a *Blitzkrieg* of short duration.]

February 25, 1942

Roosevelt has spoken. His address is nothing but a bluff. He advised
all his listeners to arm themselves with a globe as they might not otherwise understand him, but we recommend to his listeners that when
they read his speech they had better arm themselves with the addresses
Roosevelt delivered before his election, since such a comparison would
undoubtedly be much better than a comparison of his somewhat
jumbled prognoses with the real situation on the globe.

The English people seem to me to be rather constipated. Things
must come to a pretty bad pass before they lose their nerve. We must
handle them much more carefully. The German people remind us
even today of careless turns of speech used during the first weeks of the
war. They have a good memory in that regard. The English sometimes
give you the impression that they haven't any memory at all.

[British doggedness in seeing the war through always puzzled the Hitlerites.]

The United States boasts of a gigantic victory in the fight for Bali.
They claim to have sunk all Japanese ships, but unfortunately the
Japanese nevertheless landed on Bali. In the Anglo-Saxon countries
you can mislead the people with tall tales like that. We wouldn't dare
claim anything of the sort. The German people would box our ears
right and left at such news.

Arrived in Munich early, and immediately had a number of talks.

[It must be remembered that Goebbels always wrote his diary on the following day. In other words, he really arrived at Munich February 24, the anniversary of Hitler's proclamation in 1920 of the Nazi party's program of twenty-five
points which, he held, were unchangeable and could not be amended. Usually on
February 24 the Gauleiters and other high functionaries of the Party assembled
at Munich.]

It looks as though we shall have to take very draconian measures.
All building activity in the entire Reich is to stop completely. The
Gauleiters have been ordered to watch this situation personally.

Reinhardt gave a survey of the finances of the Reich. . . . He proved
in detail that there is no possibility of an inflation either now or after
the war.

[Fritz Reinhardt was undersecretary in the Reich Finance Ministry. An ardent
Nazi and a very aggressive personality with a strident, loud voice, he completely
eclipsed the Finance Minister, mild-mannered Count Lutz von Schwerin Krosigk,
a hold-over from the last cabinet of the Weimar Republic and a former Rhodes
scholar. Reinhardt insisted in every public speech that the German reichsmark
was more solidly founded than any other currency in the world, as it was based
on the personal integrity of Adolf Hitler and the working capacity of the German
people, and not on any gold or other medium of value. He never mentioned that
the reichsmark was pegged, and that it was obtainable in the black market even
before the outbreak of the war at one tenth its official value and even less. Even
the Reichsbank made deals in which the reichsmark was given a much lower
value than the official rate.]

I discussed the Fischer case with Schwarz. Schwarz, too, believes
Fischer should not be put on trial, either in an ordinary or a Party
court, but should gradually be eliminated from office and given a business sinecure. I agreed to get it for him.

[Erich Fischer was chief of the political division of the press section of the
Nazi party. He evidently committed an offense so grave that he should have been
indicted and tried. But the Nazis hushed up cases of corruption involving Party
members. Fischer, on the advice of Goebbels and with the acquiescence of Xaver
Schwarz, was given a soft berth in some business or industrial concern.

Xaver Schwarz was one of the oldest of the Nazis, and held the post of treasurer
of the Party throughout. He was fond of distributing signed photographs of himself
to deserving comrades and visitors.

No sooner had the Nazis come into their own than he "acquired" an estate on
one of the enchanting lakes of Upper Bavaria and personally supervised the construction of a sumptuous residence which, it was generally rumored, was to cost
50,000 marks (then worth $20,000).

He proved such a slave driver, however, that the workers became incensed and
one day put up a sign: "Xaver Schwarz! Where did you get the 50,000 marks?"

When Schwarz arrived on the premises he saw the sign and fell into a rage. He
telephoned the Gestapo and had Himmler's minions put every worker "through
the wringer." But nobody revealed who had painted and put up the sign.

Schwarz then decided to play upon human avarice. He put up a sign of his own:

"Five thousand marks' reward to anyone who will reveal the perpetrators of the sign."

The response came promptly the next morning in the form of a new sign: "Xaver Schwarz! Where did you get the 55,000 marks?"]

Ley, of course, is very sad that the campaign for increasing production was wrested from him by Speer. But there is nothing to be done about it.

[Prof. Albert Speer, born, 1905, an architect by profession, joined the Nazi party early—in 1933—and met with Hitler's favor, who had very decided views on architecture and permitted no ideas except those which accorded with his own views to find expression in public buildings. Speer rebuilt the Reich Chancellery at Berlin into the gaudy edifice it later became, and erected the Party buildings at Nuremberg. After the death in an airplane accident of Minister of Munitions Fritz Todt, Hitler, in 1942, appointed him in Todt's place. Among added duties gradually heaped upon him were those of Director of War Production, Director of Roads, Water and Power, and Plenary General for the Supervision and Reconstruction of Bombed Cities. Speer was indicted at Nuremberg as a major war criminal and sentenced to twenty years' imprisonment.]

The Fuehrer has issued a decree by which members of the SS who violate Article 175 will in future be punished by death. This is a very wholesome decree which will render the elite organization of the Party immune to this cancer.

[Article 175 in the German criminal code dealt with homosexuality. The number of the article was so well known that Germans spoke of homosexual persons as "Hundred seventy-fivers."]

February 26, 1942

Churchill's last speech is the chief topic of discussion. It is a speech of deep pessimism. Seldom has Churchill painted the situation in such somber colors. Fate is gradually catching up with him. He admits that England drove the United States into the war; he had hoped, however, that Japan would not be an enemy. That, of course, is an insolent lie, for Churchill was well aware that Japan was compelled by the Three-Power Pact to take active part in the war from the moment the United States attacked the Axis Powers.

[The Three-Power Pact was the alliance between Germany, Italy, and Japan signed in Hitler's Reich Chancellery on September 27, 1940. Germany and Italy declared war on the United States and not vice versa.]

An attempt was made at Ankara to assassinate Ambassador von Papen and his wife. The man who threw the bomb was torn to pieces by it whereas Papen and his wife remained unhurt. The origin of this attempt is perfectly clear. It was without a doubt prepared by the

[British] Secret Service in collaboration with the [Russian] GPU.
. . . We are publishing the news of the attempt with the proper commentary. But we avoid playing it up too much because lavish publicity
about such attempts may serve as an encouragement.

[Several times in this diary Goebbels testifies to his awareness of the danger of
attempts on the lives of men of the regime.]

Publication of the plan for murdering the Fuehrer at first shocked
the people, then angered them. The people don't want news of that
sort. There are certain things that should not be discussed too publicly. Among these are the life and health of the Fuehrer.

I talked to Hinkel about reducing considerably the fees for entertainers of the troops. A sort of war profiteering has developed among
the artists which must be eliminated at all costs. We surely can't stand
for having artists act at the front as though they were the great spiritual
mentors of the soldiers and then pay them three, four, or five hundred
marks per evening just for reading a poem! If our soldiers were aware
of that they would in all likelihood treat the artists quite differently.

[The Germans had an organization similar to the USO. For Hans Hinkel, see
diary entry of February 3. Evidently the matter of providing entertainment for
the troops was placed in Hinkel's hands after his return to office.]

February 27, 1942

Cripps delivered his maiden speech in the House of Commons. It
was cleverly done and he wove into it a number of arguments which
are somewhat dangerous for us. For instance, he berated the plutocrats
and the parasites who are not taking part in the war, et cetera. One
can see where he is headed.

I gave orders to the German news and propaganda services for the
present not to report such utterances of Cripps. . . . We must not present Cripps as the representative of a new, socially conscious group
with pietistic background which espouses a sort of cleansed form of
Bolshevism, quite different from the one sponsored in Moscow. A situation might arise by which certain elements in Germany which are somewhat inclined toward Communism might look upon him as a sort of
savior of the idea of Bolshevism. That must not happen under any
circumstances. . . . Cripps must be presented to the German people, and
especially to the neutral world, as the man who is carrying forward the
Bolshevization of Europe on the orders of Stalin and Moscow. There
mustn't be a word about social arguments.

I read a detailed report on the real condition of American war industry. For the moment we need have no fear.

[The Nazis simply would not believe that America could develop a gigantic war industry within an incredibly short time.]

The inhabitants of the occupied areas have their fill of material worries. Hunger and cold are the order of the day. People who have been thus hard hit by fate, generally speaking, don't make revolutions.

I have started looking after the submarines in a big way. The U-boat men deserve it. I am especially concerned that they should receive light, relaxing literature. I ordered all my collaborators to let practical rather than theoretical considerations determine what they will furnish the troops and the German people for their uplift and entertainment.

There are always ideologists in our midst who believe a man of the submarine crews on emerging from the machinery compartment dirty and oil-bespattered would like nothing better than to read the *Myth of the Twentieth Century*. That, of course, is sheer nonsense. This man is in no mood for such a thing and has no intention of letting himself be taught a way of life. He is living our way of life and doesn't have to be taught it. He is anxious to relax and we must make it possible for him to do so by furnishing him literature of a lighter nature, light radio music, and similar things. I am pursuing this policy in our broadcasts, our motion-picture programs, and also our literature. After the war we can talk again about ideological education. At present we are living our ideology and don't have to be taught it.

February 28, 1942

The would-be murderers of Papen have been found. They are said to be Poles. Nevertheless England's hand can't be denied. The English, of course, would not hire one of their own people to make an attempt on Papen's life.

The epidemic of assassination is spreading alarmingly in French cities. Our Wehrmacht commands there are not energetic enough in trying to stop it. General Stuelpnagel in Paris has been relieved; his successor is again a Stuelpnagel. It looks as though our military administration in Paris were to go to pieces because of the Stuelpnagels.

[The two Stuelpnagels he referred to are General Otto von Stuelpnagel, born, 1878, who was military commander of France, 1940–42, and General Heinrich von Stuelpnagel (1886–1944), an infantry general who succeeded his namesake

Otto, 1942–44. He was arrested and tortured to death by the Nazis after the July 20, 1944, attempt on Hitler's life.]

Hadamovsky vigorously denies that Paris is hungry. The reports coming from there have been exaggerated. It is true that the food rations regularly allotted to the French are none too high, but everybody gets something in a roundabout way. The food is not rationed so effectively there as with us. One therefore must not judge by normal rations but take into account the rations that individuals secure for themselves privately.

[Eugen Hadamovsky was the Nazi party's radio expert. Born on December 14, 1904, in Berlin, he joined the Nazi movement early and was appointed head of the Radio Section of the Berlin gau in 1931 by Goebbels, the Gauleiter of Berlin. Later he was made director of the *Reichs-Rundfunk-Gesellschaft* (Reich Broadcasting Company).]

The Paris Embassy complains about the lack of clarity in the German policy toward France. It is true that we are steering a zigzag course. One ought to deal differently with the Frenchmen—either make peace or wage war. This constant oscillation, however, between severity and appeasement is an evil thing.

The Philharmonic Orchestra has attained splendid heights. Its entire membership has been excused from army service, because it has important tasks to fulfill at home and because, besides, as an ensemble it has so high a value that it must not be torn asunder.

March 1942

JAPANESE POUR INTO JAVA. WAVELL APPOINTED COMMANDER IN CHIEF OF INDIA AND BURMA. RENAULT FACTORIES AT BRILLANCOURT BOMBED BY R.A.F. JAPANESE LAND ON SALAMAUA; CAPTURE RANGOON. ESSEN HEAVILY BOMBED. TWENTY FRENCH HOSTAGES SHOT. VON KALLAY HEADS NEW HUNGARIAN CABINET. CHURCHILL ANNOUNCES CRIPPS WILL GO TO INDIA. HITLER PREDICTS TOTAL DESTRUCTION OF RUSSIA'S "BOLSHEVIK HORDES" BY SUMMER 1942. MACARTHUR REACHES AUSTRALIA. GERMANY CLOSES ALL NORWEGIAN PORTS. BRITISH COMMANDOS RAID NAZI SUBMARINE BASE AT ST. NAZAIRE, FRANCE. ROOSEVELT ANNOUNCES CREATION OF PACIFIC WAR COUNCIL.

March 1, 1942

The English parachute raid [at Le Havre] is of course of quite secondary importance militarily. Merely the loss of our "Wuerzburg gadget" may bring us some trouble. Undoubtedly the defenses along the French coast did not function properly. Apparently our men have been asleep. I suspect the Fuehrer will take care of that situation.

[Goebbels does not explain what the Wuerzburg gadget (*Wuerzburg Geraet*) is.]

The fact is that living in France has never yet been a good thing for occupation troops. I hear things about our occupation forces there that are anything but flattering. It would be a good thing soon to replace the troop elements stationed there by others, and to have these replacements take place more frequently. Unfortunately this is impossible chiefly on account of the transportation problem.

In any case, we have now been warned. If the English should undertake similar raids in the future, we would know how to meet them with the proper countermeasures. Undoubtedly the English made this sally only for reasons of prestige. Mr. Churchill needs a victory and of course is going to make a terrific sensation of the parachute landing.

Stafford Cripps is making himself more conspicuous. In a radio broadcast he appealed to the workers of Europe to go slow on their work. We don't take any notice of it. It is difficult to pose a counter-slogan to such a slogan, for the slogan of "go slow" is always much more effective than that of "work fast." It is best to kill such a thing with silence.

The *Manchester Guardian* now admits that morale in England was about the lowest possible before the reshuffling of the Cabinet. I am now convinced that a crisis of dangerous proportions existed during these days in London. One never learns about such things until much later. That's the way it was, too, during World War I. The English people show fantastic national discipline, especially in wartime. Anything they want to keep to themselves simply doesn't get out.

The Indian crisis is on the upgrade. We have succeeded in prevailing upon the Indian nationalist leader, Bose, to issue an imposing declaration of war against England. It will be published most prominently in the German press and commented upon. In that way we shall now begin our official fight on behalf of India, even though we don't as yet admit it openly.

[Subhas Chandra Bose was head of the *Zentrale freies Indien* (Central Bureau for a Free India), which had its Berlin office at No. 2 Lichtenstein Allee. With Pandit K. A. Bhatta as editor, he brought out a monthly magazine, *Azad Hind,* with Nazi money. It was published with the English text on the right side, the German on the left. Later he left for Japan and, according to reports, was seized there by the Americans, tried, and executed for treason.]

We have held back for a very long time, for the simple reason that things had not advanced far enough as yet in India and that one must not waste one's powder as long as the enemy is near.

Listening to enemy and neutral broadcasts in Italy has been forbidden. At last! At last! It might just as well have been done immediately upon Italy's entry into the war. As it was, the enemy stations did lots of harm in Italy.

As soon as the transportation situation has improved, we shall be able to ship potatoes into the big cities again. The potato supplies themselves are quite sufficient. We must, however, make rather big preparations for the new harvest. We are in a dilemma in as much as farmers' wives whose husbands are in the services receive such high allotments that they don't care to work. They would rather go to the nearest larger town and get themselves a hairdo. I therefore propose that, while continuing allotments to the wives of servicemen, we do not pay them out, but deposit them in savings accounts which can't be touched until after the war. Anyway, these women, who never had much money in their hands before, are simply being spoiled by what they now receive. They are getting used to a standard of living that they won't be able to keep up after the war. That will only make them dissatisfied. They must be kept to their work. We can't lick our food situation if the hands that hitherto worked on the soil don't continue to do their part.

Our giving several weeks' home leave to Polish farm and factory hands, which stirred up such a rumpus, has been an extraordinary success from a propaganda viewpoint. The Polish laborers who worked in the Reich talked big when they got home. They described the Reich as a veritable paradise. It isn't so difficult any more to hire new hands. Labor is what we need most urgently today.

March 2, 1942

Bose's appeal has made a deep impression on world public opinion. The crisis in India can no longer be denied. We are doing everything possible to pour oil on the fire without being caught at it. Things aren't yet far enough along for us to incite the peoples of India to open rebellion. The Japs must win some more victories before things are far enough along.

This morning the British still declared with sonorous confidence that Java was to be held. In the evening they had modestly to admit that the Japanese had succeeded in landing. The communiqués both in London and Washington are becoming more restrained from hour to hour. The situation in Burma, too, is regarded as exceptionally serious. The Americans are now straining at the leash. They demand energetically that the English open a second front and start an offensive. But nobody seems to know quite where the English are to attack. Some plead in favor of attempting an invasion in the west, others are for an attack on Italy. All these possibilities have naturally been taken into consideration by our war leaders, and we would give the English a warm reception were they to come.

Chile sent a note warning the Axis Powers about further torpedo-ings. The South American states are now gradually awakening from the doped state into which the United States put them and are now viewing the general situation with perceptibly greater realism. They probably thought they could fulfill their obligations toward the Anglo-Saxons by issuing empty threats. Now, however, they see German submarines everywhere off the North and South American coasts, and must pay in blood and treasure for the Anglo-American war. That is somewhat more expensive than merely issuing bombastic declarations. This war has developed from a European war into a real world war. Anybody who places his hand in the fire must expect to get burned.

March 3, 1942

In the course of the afternoon the Japanese announced the sinking of a heavy British cruiser and two British destroyers. The Japanese are gradually inflicting mortal wounds upon the enemy fleets in East Asia. Once they have gained absolute superiority in the air and on the sea in this entire area, neither the British nor the American world empire can be saved.

I have received a secret report on the situation in London, from which it appears beyond doubt that a large section of the Tories is working for a separate peace with Germany. Only nobody knows as yet how to do that practically. Churchill, of course, isn't thinking of entering into any sort of discussion with us. He can fight the rebellious factions of the Tories with the dangerous weapon of Parliamentary dissolution. Undoubtedly Churchill would come out on top in an election since it would be impossible for reasons of national policy to conduct a rigorous election campaign against him. But this may change overnight. The situation in England has become so fluid that one cannot prophesy anything about the future.

De Gaulle has been recognized by Roosevelt. The operatic general has for a long time fought for this distinction. It is most revealing, however, and indicative of the weak position in which the United States finds itself that it must publicly link itself up with this character.

[General Charles de Gaulle was the leader of the French Resistance Movement and the first chief of state after France's liberation in 1944.]

In Oslo, Bishop Berggraf and the other bishops have resigned. The chief reason for this lies in the fact that Quisling has issued a number of decrees by which Norwegian youth has been placed under the aegis of *Nasjonal Samling*. This whole affair is still somewhat obscure. In any case a new problem has arisen that is certainly going to cause us some trouble during the next few weeks, especially in the Scandinavian countries. But nowadays developments race along so fast that time will soon pass over these also.

[Vidkun Quisling tried to absorb Norwegian youth in his fascist party, the Nasjonal Samling, just as Hitler virtually compelled all German children to join the Hitler Youth.]

Here at home we are face to face with new shortages. We shall have to collect copper and pewter ware on a large scale since our war industry is in dire need of these raw materials. Unfortunately we can give only a limited number of substitutes for the requisitioned and collected utensils. How, for instance, are housewives to do their washing if they haven't any laundry equipment? The Ministry of Economic Affairs declares it is powerless in this matter. Nevertheless we must try to get hold of these raw materials because otherwise arms and munitions production will receive a serious setback.

The forged Moelders letter to a [Catholic] dean in Stettin is being passed around secretly in the entire Catholic and Protestant world. I am going to see to it that one of the clergymen who circulated this letter be summoned into court and that the dean be made to say under oath that he never received such a letter from Moelders. . . .

The means the churches are trying to employ are truly an effrontery. But one can see that they really have no telling arguments and must resort to lies and calumny to make any impression on the public.

[The so-called forged letter of Moelders played quite a role in Germany at this time. Werner Moelders (1913–41) was the No. 1 ace of the Luftwaffe of World War II. An ardent Catholic, he protested violently when the Nazi party, after the great raid of Muenster in 1941, seized a convent in which his sister was a nun. On another occasion he was reported to have entered his name in the guest book of some prominent club and to have written in the space for profession or business, "Night pirate." When urged to change this, he is said to have replied: "You always call the R.A.F. fliers 'night pirates' in the official communiqués— isn't that what I am when I fly to England?"

The "forged letter" was a document purported to have been written to his confessor, in which, it was claimed, he severely criticized the government.

Moelders died in an airplane accident over Breslau on November 22, 1941, and there were many rumors that his death was not accidental. One credible version had it, however, that the transport plane in which he traveled was mistaken for a Russian bomber by the German Luftwaffe and that Moelders was shot down by his own comrades. He was at that time colonel and inspector of pursuit planes.]

March 4, 1942

Reuter has practically given up the Burma Road as lost. It is hard to understand why the English are so wedded to an ideology of retreat and why they have so little appreciation of the precarious situation in which their world empire finds itself.

In London there is boundless wrath about the appeal of Bose, whose present abode is fortunately not known. At the last moment I prevented the Foreign Office from revealing it prematurely. For the present it is a good thing to have Bose do his stuff from an anonymous center. There will always come some proper moment for us to reveal that he is in our midst.

The situation in Oslo is heading for a crisis. The question of the bishops continues to give trouble. A large number of teachers have identified themselves with the rebellious bishops. They have therefore been told either to resume their work immediately or be sent to northern Norway as forced labor. That is a very practical threat, for in that way we get rid of a part of the opposition, and we obtain the necessary man power for northern Norway. There must be no sentimentality in this matter. We are fighting for our lives and whoever crosses our path must pay for it.

Again there has been an assassination in Paris. A German guard was shot to death right on the street. The new military commander, also a Stuelpnagel, but apparently a better one than the first Stuelpnagel, had twenty Communists shot immediately and threatened to have an additional twenty Communists and Jews, whose names are published, executed if the culprit is not found. That's the method I proposed. If rigorously applied it will lead to visible results.

March 5, 1942

Bose is trying to organize Indian resistance from Berlin. . . . At present they don't know in London where Bose is really keeping himself. I am quite glad that I prevented his whereabouts being revealed. I shall see to it that Bose continues to remain camouflaged. He is to be uncovered only after he has been received by the Fuehrer.

Queen Wilhelmina has issued an appeal to Java that puts in the shade everything that has hitherto emanated from her. This Wilhelmina surely is a sad sight. [*Diese Wilhelmine ist in der Tat ein Stueckchen Malheur.*] One can see what happens if women have a decisive word to say in politics.

The bomb raid on Paris is the most sensational event of the day. Its extent was far greater than at first imagined. The number of casualties is given differently by different sources, but it is certain that there are at least six hundred dead. There is even talk of one thousand dead and several thousand injured. The Vichy Government says the DeGaullists are responsible for this crime. We are exploiting this incident in a big way in our propaganda in France, especially in the areas occupied by us. . . . Pétain has issued a few tear-jerking, sentimental communiqués, but they show that he is a thoroughly worn-out old man who knows as much about politics as a cow knows about the Spanish language.

It is reported to me that emotions have reached the boiling point in Paris. I gave our propaganda offices there exact instructions as to how to make use of the incident. How I would like to be chief of propaganda in Paris for a fortnight! With this material one could with little effort make the Paris population raving mad.

It cannot be denied that we are facing far more difficult problems during the third year of war than we could even conceive of during the first year.

The purchasing power that is straying about the country without being invested is giving us a big headache. I shall persuade the Fuehrer to talk about this problem in his next speech on winter relief. Nobody but the Fuehrer today has sufficient authority to dispel the fear and worry of our people about a coming inflation.

I have received a report about the fate of the German minorities in Hungary. The Hungarians still dare to commit acts of effrontery toward us that go far beyond what we can stand for. I suppose, however, we must keep quiet for the moment. We are dependent upon them. But every one of us is yearning for the moment when we can really talk turkey to the Hungarians [wenn wir einmal Fraktur reden koennen].

March 6, 1942

Our losses in the East for the period of June 22, 1941, to February 20, 1942, were 199,448 dead (including 7,879 officers), 708,351 wounded (including 20,992 officers), 44,342 missing (including 701 officers)—a total of 952,141 (including 29,572 officers).

Until February 20, 112,627 cases of freezing or frostbite were reported, including 14,357 third-degree and 62,000 second-degree cases. . . .

According to these figures it appears we had almost one million casualties in our entire campaign in the East, among them about 200,000 fatalities. That is, of course, quite a number. Nevertheless it cannot be compared with the figures of World War I.

The number of those who suffered from freezing is considerably higher than we had at first imagined. The number given us at the beginning of February did indeed seem rather unlikely. The higher number is chiefly owing to the fact that the earlier figure was based solely on individual reports. Even as it is, the final figure is only a small fraction of what is being spread around among the people in the form of rumors. . . .

As things stand today, I do not feel it opportune to make these figures public now. One must wait for a more favorable moment. The most suitable time for publication will come when we can claim new military victories.

There is a lot of *sub rosa* talk in the neutral countries about the possibilities of a separate peace with the Soviet Union. In London they are already scared about it. Such fear, however, is unwarranted. The Soviet Union will and must be knocked out, no matter how long that may take. The situation is ripe for putting an end to Bolshevism in all Europe, and considering our position we can't give up that aim.

A frontal attack on black markets was made in the House of Commons. No bones are made about the fact that Jews were chiefly implicated in profiteering in the food market. Heading the procession were the Jewish immigrants who went from Germany to England. Jews always remain the same. You must either stigmatize them with a yellow star, or put them in concentration camps, or shoot them, or else let them saturate all public life with corruption, especially during a war. There is no halfway measure.

In London they are at present busy threatening further air attacks on the Reich. That has now happened so often that we don't have to take it seriously. Nevertheless I won't let reports of that kind get into the German press, because there are still dumbbells among us who fall for such threats.

The extraordinarily unfavorable effect on public opinion of the English air raids on Paris has put London decidedly on the defensive. The latest estimate in Paris is between eight hundred and one thousand dead; exact figures are still not obtainable. Feelings in France have reached the boiling point. At present the English are not at all popular with the French people. How well they are aware of this can be seen from the fact that their broadcasts stammer new but untenable excuses practically every hour. The British Government has even felt impelled to express its sympathies to the French people. Such expressions of sympathy are of so hair-raising a cynicism that we can well claim nothing like it would be possible anywhere else in the world. The style of the message [of condolence] is so typically Churchillian that it is not difficult to discover his hand in it.

Information from Paris indicates that sentiment there has become more anti-British than it has ever been before. To intensify this condition, I now propose a gigantic state funeral for those killed in the bomb raid. I planned this state funeral down to the smallest details, and the agreement of the French authorities is to be sought. I am sending Waechter to Paris to arrange everything. It is to be very demonstrative and to be so staged that no Frenchman with any heart can fail to be impressed by this ceremony. In addition I am having bill posters put up in Paris quoting especially provocative statements by the DeGaullists in London.

[To Goebbels a message of condolence is evidence of "hair-raising cynicism"; a state funeral for the victims for purposes of propaganda, when arranged by the Nazi regime, is a virtue!

Werner Waechter was head of the propaganda section in the national propaganda office of the Nazi party. There were various departments, such as culture, film, radio, et cetera.]

The Americans had hoped that Eire would, without further ado, join their side as soon as troops landed in the English part of Ireland. They obviously overestimated the ties of the Irish to the Irishmen in America. De Valera isn't thinking of yielding to such a psychological squeeze.

An SD report informed me about the situation in occupied Russia. It is, after all, more unstable than was generally assumed. The Partisan danger is increasing week by week. The Partisans are in command of large areas in occupied Russia and are conducting a regime of terror there. The national movements, too, have become more insolent than was at first imagined. That applies as well to the Baltic States as to the Ukraine. Everywhere the Jews are busy inciting and stirring up trouble. It is therefore understandable that many of them must pay with their lives for this. Anyway, I am of the opinion that the greater the number of Jews liquidated, the more consolidated will the situation in Europe be after this war. One must have no mistaken sentimentality about it. The Jews are Europe's misfortune. They must somehow be eliminated, otherwise we are in danger of being eliminated by them.

The food situation in the occupied eastern areas is exceptionally precarious. Thousands and tens of thousands of people are dying of hunger without anybody even raising a finger. We shall undoubtedly face exceptional difficulties and problems there for a number of years to come. Very much water will still have to flow down the Rhine before this area has been integrated into the European economy and its rich products made available to our section of the globe.

Seldom, I believe, in our generation has spring been awaited so fervently as the one now in the offing. We Germans and untold millions of human beings in the rest of the world expect the decision to come during this spring and summer. We shall do everything possible to fulfill this expectation. I do not dare to prophesy whether we shall succeed. The imponderables involved are so manifold that one can hardly include them as stable factors in a political and military estimate. One must therefore take this standpoint: Do everything that can be done, miss nothing in the way of preparations, do one's duty wherever necessary, but for the rest enter upon one's work with firm trust in one's own strength. Then success is assured.

March 7, 1942

The Foreign Office gave me a report on our relations with Vichy France. Before the entry of the United States into the war we believed a bridge to European peace might be built starting from Vichy. This hope is now gone for good. The Vichy Frenchmen would be ready under certain circumstances not only to give up their neutrality, but also to take an active hand in the war if we now offered them an acceptable peace. That, however, is something the Fuehrer does not want to do. And he is right. For the situation isn't such that we are in any way dependent upon France's military support, which would always be limited anyway. We should not give our trump cards away too early. Above all, the war against France must have an historic result. While France still has even a breath of life she will always remain our enemy. We must definitely eliminate France's military and political power from a future European interplay of forces. The Fuehrer is here following a very delicately attuned [*fein reagierenden*] national-political instinct, even though many members of the Foreign Office are of a different opinion.

I read a detailed report from the SD and police regarding a final solution of the Jewish question. Any final solution involves a tremendous number of new viewpoints. The Jewish question must be solved within a pan-European frame. There are 11,000,000 Jews still in Europe. They will have to be concentrated later, to begin with, in the East; possibly an island, such as Madagascar, can be assigned to them after the war. In any case there can be no peace in Europe until the last Jews are eliminated from the continent.

That, of course, raises a large number of exceedingly delicate questions. What is to be done with the half-Jews? What with those related to Jews? In-laws of Jews? Persons married to Jews? Evidently we still have quite a lot to do and undoubtedly a multitude of personal tragedies will ensue within the framework of the solution of this problem. But that is unavoidable. The situation is now ripe for a final settlement of the Jewish question. Later generations will no longer have the will power or the instinctive alertness. That's why we are doing a good work in proceeding radically and consistently. The task we are assuming today will be an advantage and a boon to our descendants.

[No better admission of the injustice of the Nazi attitude toward the Jewish problem could be made than the statement that later generations will not act as the Nazis did.]

The Ministry of Justice must admit to its disgrace that it sees no possibility of taking effective steps against the reading of the forged Moelders letter; there's no law which applies [unsere Gesetzgebung biete dafuer keine Handhabe]. That means it is no insult to say of a man, even though he is a popular hero, that he was a Catholic and practically an enemy of the state. That kind of justice isn't worth a hoot [ist keinen Schuss Pulver wert]. I am now going to have a number of clergymen, who read the Moelders letter from their pulpits and who decline to publish a denial despite being taught the facts, taken into a concentration camp and will then publish a bulletin about it. If I were Minister of Justice I would find some passage among the thousands of paragraphs which would enable me to fight such an infamous undertaking by the Church. But our justice is being administered, not in a National Socialist, but in a bourgeois manner.

[The lawlessness of the Nazi regime is well illustrated by the fact that Goebbels evidently had enough power to send priests to concentration camps even though the Ministry of Justice declared there was nothing illegal about their action. All that Goebbels had to do was to ask his friend Himmler to arrest anybody he chose. Himmler was responsible to Hitler alone, and not under the jurisdiction of the Ministry of Justice.]

March 8, 1942

We are having great difficulties everywhere. For instance, in one army corps alone 18,000 horses fell during February, 795 of them from exhaustion.

Stalin continues to fabricate pompous and mendacious reports of victories. He has once again encircled our 16th Army and destroyed nineteen German divisions. If all had been killed, taken prisoner, or been destroyed whom Stalin claims to have killed, taken prisoner, and destroyed, since the middle of November of last year, not a single German soldier would be left on Russian territory today.

The reaction of world public opinion to the happenings in Paris is extremely embarrassing to the English. Pétain issued a proclamation that is neither flesh, fish, nor fowl. It is somewhat tearful and shows that the marshal has grown very old, and above all, that he wishes in no way to commit himself to an anti-English policy, which of course is understandable. While he used a few strong words against the English crime, they are undoubtedly not to be understood in a political sense.

The Vichy people, incidentally, are seeing to it that the victims of the English bomb raid are buried as quickly as possible. They are being interred in the various cemeteries in the early morning hours. Attendance, I am told, is very small because nothing is said about the place and time of burial.

[In other words, Goebbels's grandly planned state funeral fizzled out, despite the glowing description in the diary entry for March 10.]

I find it necessary to take further measures against the "Yellow Peril" propaganda which certain anonymous circles in the Reich are spreading. They are thereby torpedoing our foreign and military policy. That's a typical example showing how little we Germans know about politics. We are altogether too easily inclined to judge foreign and military questions by our feelings and sentiments, and not to think them through realistically. I am now mobilizing our Party against such nonsense.

March 9, 1942

The Dutch communiqué [concerning Java] is, so to speak, a final epilogue. It criticizes the English severely for their lack of readiness to help and asserts that the Dutch risked all their armed forces to save Malaya, whereas now they themselves are being left pretty well in the lurch by the English and the Americans. . . . Their communiqué strikes one as partly tragic, partly comic. No sympathy need be wasted on such weak peoples. It is bad and regrettable for Europe that Holland loses her colonial possessions, but in the last analysis so small a people has no right to any overseas possessions so long as a nation of the rank of Germany hasn't any at all.

We are faced with the difficult task of making clear to the German people that in case Churchill falls this does not mean a possible collapse of England, but, on the contrary, an even more vigorous and energetic prosecution of the war. This, of course, cannot hurt us much in the long run, but it might cause us all sorts of temporary trouble.

[The Nazis evidently felt sure Sir Stafford Cripps would replace Winston Churchill as Prime Minister.]

The *Times* has become the loud-speaker for English-Bolshevik collaboration. What has become of this serious paper of the London gentry anyway? It now demands a three-power pact between England, the United States, and the Soviet Union. As it makes this cynical demand, it does not seem to have the slightest inhibition of an ideological nature.   •

In late evening came the news, unconfirmed for the present, that Rangoon had fallen. If it proves true, that means the Anglo-American war leaders have once again suffered a blow from which they cannot soon recover. England is on the toboggan. The misfortune which has overtaken her in these weeks is like an avalanche that begins with small snowflakes and later, with thunderous noise, rolls irresistibly down into the valley.

March 10, 1942

Cries of distress are heard from Australia. The possibility of a separate peace with Japan is already being discussed between the lines. The Japanese have come so close to Australia that it seems to lie directly before their eyes as willing and enticing booty. It has ever been the territorial aspiration of Tokyo to possess this fifth continent as territory for emigration. The shortsighted and foolish policies and the war conduct of the English and the Americans have brought the Japanese a good deal nearer to their goal.

Cripps is endeavoring to push the India problem into the foreground anew. There seems to be an embittered fight backstage about India.

Churchill doesn't want to yield, but Cripps believes that he can mobilize the Indian people for the British war effort by relaxing the bonds of India. I believe it is too late for that.

Our funeral ceremony at the Place de la Concorde [in Paris] seems to have been tremendously impressive. On Sunday hundreds of thousands of people filed by the catafalque erected there.

Nevertheless we don't make much of this event in the German press, considering the fact that heavy air raids were also made on the Ruhr region which, however, we cannot set out prominently in the German press. The German people would consider it an insult and find it hard to understand if the German press were to shed tears for the Parisians but took note of our own losses in only a few lines.

I received a report from Spain. Franco has paid a visit to Catalonia. He must have been relatively clever about it. His clerical ties have been strengthened. German observers also accuse him of monarchistic tendencies. Germany and Italy were not mentioned in his speech. Franco is only mediocre. One must not expect too much from him.

To think what questions of domestic politics are laid before one in the course of a day! Should dancing girls be inducted into the Women's Labor Service? If one doesn't do it, they fail to get the necessary Nazi indoctrination; if one does, they become fat and ungainly and unfit for the dancing profession. We are now trying to put the dancing girls through special courses, and while organizing them as in labor service, to give them a type of work to do that will not disqualify them for their profession.

March 11, 1942

Van Mook upon his arrival in Australia gave an exceptionally pessimistic interview in which he expressed quite clearly and without beating about the bush that he expected greater help from the Allies. The fact that he did not say more is, I suppose, because he was given a sizable check.

[Hubertus Johannes van Mook, born, 1894, was a Dutch economist and administrator educated at Surabaya College and Amsterdam, Delft, and Leyden universities. At this time he was Lieutenant Governor General in the East Indies. He was later appointed Minister of Colonies in the Netherlands Government-in-exile at London. Goebbels was obsessed with the idea that the statesmen of small nations were in the pay of Great Britain.]

Cripps expressed his unqualified admiration for Stalin and predicted certain victory for 1942. Cripps published these statements in a series of replies to twenty questions laid before him by the American periodical *Life*. He expressed himself somewhat more carefully with reference to the Bolshevization of Europe. Nevertheless he indulged in a few turns of speech which, with minor corrections, we can use for exceptionally effective propaganda. . . .

I don't believe Churchill will succeed in sending Cripps to India. Cripps will be careful not to give up the favorable position he now holds in London by absenting himself for a long time.

For the present we have no possibility whatever of exerting any influence upon the formation of the Hungarian Cabinet, since we must ask a great deal of the Hungarians during the next weeks and months and therefore keep them in good humor. But we can later catch up with what we are neglecting to do today.

I took energetic measures to stop the discussion about the "Yellow Peril." It isn't possible to discuss this theme at all today, either in a positive or negative sense. The excellent reasons which we can give for our present attitude cannot be discussed in public because they would undoubtedly insult the Japanese and furnish the English valuable material for argument against the Axis. Other reasons, however, be they of a historic or contemplative nature, are not convincing. We must therefore try to carry the real reasons to the people by a word-of-mouth propaganda, but refrain from public discussion of this problem.

As a result of a pastoral letter by Bishop Preysing concerning the religious question, we find ourselves in a somewhat precarious situation in Berlin. Unfortunately a number of church buildings were requisitioned by the Party and the Gestapo without my knowledge. Although I had forbidden this in the strongest terms, a couple of smart alecks [*Besserwisser*, literally better-knowers] have been at work, with the result that we have now conjured up a church conflict in Berlin which I did not desire at all but tried under all circumstances to avoid. I am now going to pound the table [*mit der Faust dreinschlagen*]. Here I try in every way possible to keep controversial matters away at least from my district, but now the rowdies and beer-hall fighters come and make a mess for me [*bereiten mir noch Unrat*] even in the Reich capital. The church question is as far as possible not to be discussed at all during the entire war, no matter how recalcitrant the "skypilots" may prove to be in this or that matter.

After the war we shall certainly have other possibilities of making them see the light.

I had a few hours' time tonight to read Wirsing's new book, *The Continent Without Limit*. Wirsing gives us a picture of American life, American business, culture, and politics. The material he has assembled is truly shattering. Roosevelt is one of the worst enemies of modern culture and civilization. If we do not succeed in definitely defeating the enemy, made up of Bolshevism, plutocracy, and lack of culture, the world will be headed for densest darkness. That is the reason why we must courageously and uncompromisingly take all inconveniences and hardships upon ourselves. We are actually carrying in our hands the torch that brings light to humanity.

[Giselher Wirsing was editor of one of the large Munich dailies, the *Muenchner Neueste Nachrichten*. Foreign policy was his specialty.]

March 12, 1942

Eden delivered a speech in the House of Commons in which he accused the Japanese of frightful atrocities committed against the English prisoners of war in Hong Kong. We know his line. It is above all an eloquent sign that things are exceedingly bad with the English. Every time they encounter defeat after defeat they begin to deal in sentimentality and to weep crocodile tears. The Japanese immediately gave a tart and convincing answer. For reasons of courtesy we are displaying this reply prominently.

The House of Lords has once again taken a stand against the Arabs and for the Jews. It is surprising how much Jewish influence there is among the English people, especially the upper crust, which is hardly English in character any longer. The chief reason is no doubt the fact that these Upper Ten Thousand have become so infested with the Jewish virus by Jewish marriages that they can hardly think in English.

The problem of the "Yellow Peril" is assuming more and more dangerous forms in the popular discussion. I am now trying to get Ambassador General Oshima to give us a detailed interview in which he will above all indicate Japan's readiness to let the Axis Powers participate in the tremendous wealth and raw-material sources of which they have gained possession.

[General Hirosi Oshima was the Japanese Ambassador to Germany at that time. He had been military attaché in Berlin at an earlier period. The Nazis kept him under the influence of alcohol most of the time.]

Embarrassing consequences have resulted from the irresponsible and unpsychological publication of various court decisions. Hereafter I am having all court verdicts of any national importance released jointly by the Ministry of Justice and ourselves. Our courthouse reporters don't have the necessary feel for selecting and publishing verdicts according to psychological considerations. The publication of court decisions is not a question of mere publicity but of public education. In connection with every verdict we must ask ourselves whether publication at this moment will have a favorable or unfavorable effect. That is a matter which only our Ministry can decide in the end.

[Nobody who has not lived under Nazism can grasp how absolute was Goebbels's control of the German mind. But incidents like the above at least will give the average American an inkling.]

In the evening I started on a trip that is to take me first to the Ostmark [Austria] and then to Munich. Tomorrow I am to speak in Graz for the first time in my life. I am already happy in anticipation.

[Graz is the capital of the Austrian province of Styria, or *Steiermark*. The Styrians are a mountaineer people, hardy and frugal.]

March 13, 1942

Naumann has already mastered his tasks very well, and is an indispensable assistant to me. He has taken hold energetically of my prospective purchase of land in the neighborhood of Berlin. I should very much like to have some estate that belongs to me and that I earn by my own labors. It is, of course, very difficult at the moment to buy land because nobody wants to sell. But I will continue to pursue this aim. It is especially desirable for the sake of the family to own something that is stable, keeps its value, and that one can later pass on as an inheritance.

[Dr. Werner Naumann held a position similar to that of an executive assistant to the president of an American corporation. He was Goebbels's right-hand man in the little doctor's capacity of *Reichspropagandaleiter* of the Nazi party. Goebbels, it will be recalled, was not only Minister of Propaganda—in other words, a state official and member of the cabinet—but also head of the propaganda department of the Nazi party and Gauleiter for Berlin. Naumann had the rank of *Ministerialdirigent* and was paid by the public exchequer. Goebbels, who always assumed a holier-than-thou attitude toward Goering and other open-and-aboveboard "grafters," saw nothing unethical in having Dr. Naumann take time out to act as his personal real-estate agent. Goebbels, while playing the role of the simple man of the people, was a shrewd real-estate speculator.]

The reception in Graz was very large and warmhearted. The Styrians are a wonderful tribe. The young people, especially, have a capacity for enthusiasm which indicates they are anything but blasé.

In the evening I spoke in the new Volkshalle to more than 25,000 people and tried to outline the prospects for the future on a somewhat higher plane. The people followed me wonderfully, and the meeting was a great success.

Tojo has delivered a speech. It is noteworthy in that he gives unmistakable hints to Australia as well as India and China. He offered separate negotiations to Australia and threatened that Australia would suffer the same fate as Java in case the offer were not accepted.

[General Hideki Tojo was Japanese Minister of War in the Konoye Cabinet, July to October 1941, and then succeeded Prince Konoye as Prime Minister, at the same time retaining the portfolio of Minister of War. He was indicted as a major war criminal.]

Cripps's mission to India is a great world sensation. The English are placing high hopes on it. But these will presumably not be fulfilled in the way the English think. One has the impression that the British are letting the pound sterling play an important role. The Indian princes, of course, are all corruptible and being paid by England.

[Goebbels's obsession that all British satellites were paid creatures was so great that he apparently even forgot that "the wealth of Ormuz and of Ind" was concentrated in the hands of Indian princes.]

Whether the Indians will take their fate into their own hands is very much to be doubted. This people is divided by so many religious sects and so many racial elements that it is scarcely capable of a unified and energetic expression of will.

March 14, 1942

Bose has issued a new proclamation. We are pumping it into India. Bose is an excellent worker and I am happy that I did not permit his whereabouts to be revealed for the present.

There are rumors to the effect that armed conflicts have already broken out in Calcutta. Unfortunately they are not confirmed; neither has there been any confirmation that important circles in Australia favor a separate peace.

We left Graz in the morning. The population gave us a very cordial and touching farewell. I am most deeply impressed with my visit to

Graz, which for the first time brought me into closer contact with the population of Styria. The leadership of the gau is splendid. The population is showing a spirit that deserves admiration. One can work excellently with Uiberreither. He enjoys the greatest confidence throughout the gau. Here we have a Gauleiter with whom we can do something. . . . In the afternoon we arrived in Vienna. . . .

[Dr. Siegfried Uiberreither was the Gauleiter for Styria.]

In the late afternoon the great Anschluss celebration took place on Hero's Square, with about 100,000 people participating. The enthusiasm was indescribable. Schirach spoke first, after which I was given the floor. In a few monumental sentences I gave a picture of the present situation which drew veritable storms of applause. The Viennese seem to have the ambition of putting their best foot forward . . .

[Baldur von Schirach, former Reich Youth leader, was Gauleiter for Vienna.]

One need have no fears about Vienna. The passages of my address that drew the wildest applause were the ones in which I spoke of the insoluble union of this city with the Reich. Vienna has indeed become a Reich city.

March 15, 1942

There were raids on the Reich with Cologne as the principal target. Five major, twenty medium, and thirty-five smaller fires. The country around about was hit by phosphorous bombs. Several railway lines are temporarily out of commission. One cable factory was heavily damaged. To date five dead and twenty-nine wounded. An enemy plane was shot down by night fighters. A bomb struck the bridge across the Rhine at Muehlheim; traffic there has been interrupted. The moving-picture office of the gau has been completely destroyed. One department store burned out.

My speech and my last article concerning the "Sneaking Crisis" of the British Empire commanded much attention abroad, especially in Spain, Portugal, and with the Axis Powers.

I believe it is very useful for our German propaganda to have German opinion channeled through the neutral press practically every week end by quotations from my weekly contribution. In this way the German standpoint is made known in a manner that must not be underestimated.

The Fuehrer has offered a reward of 100,000 marks for the apprehension of the author of the falsified Moelders letter. Through Schirach I learned that this letter was distributed very widely in Vienna by officers of the Wehrmacht. Among others even General Streccius personally participated in the distribution, believing the letter to be genuine. When Schirach challenged him and proved the forgery, he had to admit that the letter was sent him by Field Marshal General von Mackensen. This old gentleman, who knows pitifully little about politics, has for years busied himself with the church question. Unfortunately one cannot do much against him on account of the importance of his personality. Nevertheless I shall have to call the Fuehrer's attention to the disloyalty of his procedure.

[Field Marshal August von Mackensen, last of the remaining German field marshals of World War I, was a Nazi showpiece like Gerhart Hauptmann and Richard Strauss. He was a staunch member of the Lutheran Confessional Synod, however, and therefore opposed the anti-Christian tendencies of Nazism. He often intervened with Hitler and other top Nazis on behalf of Protestant clergymen, among them Pastor Martin Niemoeller.

General Streccius was the military commander of Vienna.]

Waechter returned from Paris. He reported that sentiment among the Parisians is by no means so anti-English as we here imagined. The Parisians are a peculiar people. At first they rejoiced that the English had inflicted damage upon the Germans with their bombs. Then, when they learned that hardly a German died, but that casualties occurred only among the Frenchmen, they suddenly griped that Paris had not been protected sufficiently by anti-aircraft guns and that no alert had been sounded. You can't do much with the Frenchmen of today. As a whole they are a macabre people, evidently doomed to national-political destruction.

March 16, 1942

The Moelders letter is now making its rounds [*geistert herum*] in foreign countries. Radio London has seized upon this forgery to argue against the National Socialist regime. In view of the communiqué we issued this can no longer do us any real damage. Nevertheless it is interesting to note to what defeatist work the German generals, headed by Field Marshal von Mackensen, have lent themselves, even though unwittingly. Either these gentlemen are too foolish to discern the motives behind a procedure launched very cleverly by the Church, or they are knowingly siding with the enemies of the state—a thing that I should not like to assume for the present. In any case I believe I must report this whole matter to the Fuehrer, and I shall do that on my next visit to GHQ.

I read a report of the SD about the situation in the occupied East. The activity of Partisans has increased noticeably during recent weeks. They are conducting a well-organized guerrilla war. It is very difficult to get at them because they are using such terrorist methods in the areas occupied by us that the population is afraid of collaborating with us loyally any longer. The spearheads of this whole Partisan activity are the political commissars and especially the Jews. It has therefore proven necessary once again to shoot more Jews. There won't be any peace in these areas as long as any Jews are active there. Sentimentality is out of place here. Either we must renounce the lives of our own soldiers, or we must uncompromisingly prevent further propaganda by criminal and chaotic elements in the hinterland.

In the East, nationalistic currents are increasingly observable in all former Baltic States. The populations there apparently imagined that the German Wehrmacht would shed its blood to set up new governments in these midget states, which at the end of the war, or possibly even during the war, would veer over to the side of our enemies. That is a childish, naïve bit of imagination which makes no impression upon us. One would have to take the imperial regime of Kaiser Wilhelm as a model if one were to inaugurate so shortsighted a policy. National Socialism is much more cold-blooded and much more realistic in all these questions. It does only what is useful for its own people, and in this instance the interest of our people undoubtedly lies in the rigorous establishment of German order within this area without paying any attention to the claims, more or less justified, of the small nationalities living there.

The enemy is now making use of horoscopes in the form of hand-bills dropped from planes, in which a terrible future is prophesied for the German people. But we know something about this ourselves! I am having counter-horoscopes worked up which we are going to distribute, especially in the occupied areas.

March 17, 1942

The Fuehrer spoke on Memorial Day in Berlin. It was an excellent, indeed a classical speech both in style and content. . . . He gave expression to his absolute confidence that the Soviets would be completely destroyed during the ensuing summer. There was no hope for them any longer. The summer would therefore be the decisive point of the conflict. . . . The Bolsheviks would be thrown back so far that they could never again touch the cultured soil of Europe. The Bolshevik danger would thereby be eliminated for our continent.

[The *Heldengedenktag*, literally Heroes' Memorial Day, was celebrated on the third Sunday in March. Whenever possible Hitler himself delivered the address.]

The Viceroy of India assembled the Indian princes about him and adjured them most solemnly to rally to and remain on the side of England. The Indian people haven't much to expect of these princes. They are, for the most part, corrupt and bribed characters, who will go with the English as long as they receive money there. The Indian people will have to look to other quarters for their liberation.

The Japanese have become somewhat insolent and overconfident. Their new ambassador to the Soviet Union at Kuibyshev has rashly declared that a naval parade of the Axis Powers before London or New York following victory by no means belonged to the realm of dreams and fantasies, but would become a reality. Would to God it were true! [Literally: His word in God's ear!]

My insistence on central direction of the reporting on trials was not intended to support verdicts that are out of accord with public sentiment and not let the public know about them. That wasn't my purpose. My attention has been called to this danger and I am wondering whether I ought not to send Party comrades as observers into the various courts so that they may quietly inform me and enable me to take measures against verdicts that do not correspond to the times.

March 18, 1942

Sumner Welles has spoken most insulting and vulgar words against the Fuehrer because of his speech on Memorial Day. His invective fairly bursts with insults and is the best proof that things are going badly on the enemy side.

Lord Halifax is much more modest in his utterances. This bigoted itinerant preacher, who, after the western offensive, declined the hand of the Fuehrer stretched out to him on behalf of peace, is now able to prophesy nothing but dark and difficult times. No doubt he would now think twice if he had the same opportunity offered again.

[Viscount Halifax, the former Edward Frederick Lindley Wood, after a long and varied diplomatic career, became British Secretary of State for Foreign Affairs in 1938 and in this capacity visited Adolf Hitler in Berchtesgaden the

same year. His term as Foreign Minister came to an end in 1940, and in 1941 he
was appointed Ambassador to the United States. President Roosevelt took the
unusual step of personally welcoming him on January 24, 1941, on his arrival.]

March 19, 1942

In Australia they are playing with the slogan of the scorched earth.
These states and countries that are tied to the apron strings of the
English will never grow up. One can explain their attitude only on the
ground that they are rewarded with good checks.

The Turkish Foreign Minister, Saracoglu, has given an interview to
an Italian newspaper in which he favors absolute neutrality toward
the Axis as well as the Anglo-Saxon powers, but nevertheless uses turns
of speech to which we haven't been used hitherto. His attitude is
typical for Turkey. Ankara no doubt has the intention of deciding in
favor of one side or the other only when victory for that side is absolutely sure.

[Skukri Saracoglu (or Sarajoglu) was Turkish Minister of Foreign Affairs from
1938–42 and again from 1944 on. In 1942 he was Prime Minister for a short time.
The Nazis had placed great hopes in Ambassador Franz von Papen's diplomatic
ability to draw Turkey into the Axis camp, or at least to prevent her from joining
the Allies.]

In the Ministry of Justice they don't really know what to do about
the war. Since Guertner's death the Ministry of Justice has become an
orphan so far as leadership is concerned. I shall suggest a change of
personnel to the Fuehrer. We shall otherwise be working in a vacuum.
We propose a multitude of reforms, improvements, and drafts of laws,
but they don't have the right effect because a sort of quiet sabotage
is going on in the central offices. The bourgeois elements dominate
there, and as the sky is high and the Fuehrer far away, it is very
difficult indeed to prevail against this tough and solid bureaucracy.
But I won't desist. I am convinced we shall have to adopt much more
stringent measures in our conduct of the war.

[Dr. Franz Guertner, former Bavarian Minister of Justice, was Reich Minister
of Justice in the Von Papen Cabinet of 1932 and the short-lived Kurt von
Schleicher Cabinet of 1932–33. In 1933 Hindenburg insisted that Hitler keep him
on as Minister of Justice. The Fuehrer was able to bypass Guertner, however, by
making the SS independent of the Judiciary and vesting in it powers of arrest
without warrant and detention in concentration camps without trial. Guertner,
instead of resigning in protest, meekly accepted the situation. Guertner proved a
relatively mild-mannered Minister of Justice, and the Nazis heaved a sigh of relief when he died a natural death in 1941.]

The slogan of increasing production won't prove very effective
when the decrease in food rations becomes known. I have given

orders to distribute the announcement about the decrease here and there quietly, so that no severe shock may result at the time of their actual publication. Also, the German press has been ordered to report on the difficulties of the English food situation, so that the German public may deduce from it that our shortages are not a result of the English blockade but merely a result of the general war situation.

Goering has now signed the law to combat profiteering and black marketeering. However, the text presented to him by the Reich Economic Minister was a drastically amended one which was much milder at decisive points than the original. Now it will certainly not fully achieve its purpose. I shall have to report this matter once more to the Fuehrer, and I expect to be supported by Bormann and the Party. It really makes one despair how the ministerial bureaucracy tries again and again to hinder [cramp the style of] those who favor a radical conduct of the war, and to create one difficulty after another for them. This bureaucracy always rests its case on so-called common sense and the wisdom of experience. Now, the point is that our great successes in the past were achieved neither by so-called sound common sense nor through the wisdom of experience. They were the result of clever psychology and a pronounced ability to sense the thinking processes of the broad masses of the population.

In Paris the bomb damage was not so bad as it had at first been supposed. The population has long forgotten it. The Frenchmen will never learn. Besides, they have in part already become very insolent. But we'll polish them off at the right time. By being arrogant they would like to compel us to make a preliminary peace with them. That will never do, for once they find out what the Fuehrer really demands of them, the game is up anyway. It is best to let the whole thing hang fire for the present. . . .

Whether we shall succeed during the coming spring and summer in defeating the Bolsheviks—this no man can say. We know what we have and what we must risk, but we don't know what the Bolsheviks have and what they can risk. One might conjecture that they risked everything this winter, but one can't claim it with certainty. We must in part rely upon our good luck, and fight. Many situations like that arise in the course of a war. The victor will always be the one who has the greater amount of courage and the stronger nerves. It is we without a doubt who have both.

March 20, 1942

Will this winter never end? Is a new glacial age in the offing? Certainly one is inclined at times to yield to this suspicion when one contemplates the constant, repeated attacks by winter weather.

Through snow and frost we drove directly to GHQ. Morale there is extraordinarily good, although the endless winter has a somewhat depressing effect. But hope rightly prevails that the winter will have to end soon and then all the worries that torment us today will be over.

My work in Berlin is praised by everybody. My decision to conduct our propaganda along severer lines now meets with full approval at GHQ. . . .

The Fuehrer, thank God, appears to be in good health. He has gone through exceedingly difficult days, and his whole bearing shows it. The Fuehrer is really to be pitied. He must take the entire burden of the war upon his shoulders, and nobody can relieve him of the responsibility for all the decisions that must be made.

I became especially conscious of this during a talk with Schaub. He told me that the Fuehrer had recently been somewhat ailing. One can understand this, for even physically it is impossible for one person to carry such a gigantic load over an extended period. Added to this is the fact that the Fuehrer practically lives in a concentration camp. Whether the guards before his GHQ are furnished by the SS or by some PW camp—the effect is the same. The loneliness of GHQ and the whole method of working there naturally have at long last an extraordinarily depressing effect upon the Fuehrer. He hasn't the slightest opportunity for relaxation, and as long as he is awake is surrounded by work and responsibility. The solitude in which he is compelled to perform his duties must sooner or later affect him deeply and gnaw at his vitals.

[SS Group Leader Julius Schaub was Hitler's personal adjutant. He had been with him for many years.]

If during the past winter, which is still loath to take leave, he managed to pull through relatively well, that is proof of his truly bearlike nature. The generals, for the most part, have not helped matters either. Opinions about the leadership of the German Wehrmacht are quite different today from what they were, for instance, after the offensive in France. High general staff officers are in no way able to stand severe strain or cope with heavy spiritual crises. That's something they haven't learned. They were not taught sufficiently to emulate the example of

Prussian generals. Besides, the initial successes in this war have filled them too much with the idea that everything can succeed at first try and that serious difficulties cannot possibly arise anywhere.

The Fuehrer alone saved the front during the past winter. The fact that he would not yield and gave no sign of weakness whatever was the real reason that the front did not become shaky but stood firm on the whole.

Realizing this situation, I consider it all the more my duty to let the Fuehrer now and then have reports, news, and items that will distract him somewhat from his immediate war tasks. It must be done adroitly, so that he won't notice it, for as soon as he does, he resents all such attempts. I am glad that during the past weeks I always sent material to GHQ that interested the Fuehrer from the purely human side, especially items about art and cultural life from which he is completely cut off, although in normal times they quite preoccupy him.

Toward noon I had my first, and in the afternoon my second, talk of several hours with the Fuehrer. They touched me deeply and enabled me to realize that the work I have thus far done in Berlin corresponds in every respect to what the Fuehrer envisages as civilian war conduct.

Our greeting was extremely cordial. One cannot but notice that the Fuehrer is happy to welcome one of his old co-fighters and especially to be able to say in complete privacy all those things that he can't tell to a larger circle.

The Fuehrer's appearance of being healthy is somewhat misleading. The superficial impression is that he is in the very best physical shape. In reality that is not the case, however. In our intimate talk he told me that recently he has been somewhat ailing. From time to time he has had to fight off severe attacks of giddiness. The long winter has affected his spiritual condition in a way that has left its mark.

The Fuehrer, I recall, never cared very much for winter. In the old days we used sometimes to laugh at his physical revulsion against frost and snow. For instance, he could never understand how some people in spring could look for altitudes where there was still snow for skiing! Now his aversion to winter has received cruel and terrible vindication. He certainly never imagined that a time would come when winter would so unrelentingly take advantage of his instinctive antipathy and inflict such suffering upon German troops. All this happened to a degree hitherto considered unbelievable. This long, hard, cruel winter be damned! It has confronted us with problems that we should not have thought possible. This winter put not only the German Wehrmacht but especially its Supreme Commander under a cruel strain. It is nothing short of a miracle that we stood it. It is too early as yet to appreciate fully what the Fuehrer suffered during these months. He told me he would later have occasion to talk and possibly write about all this.

The war reached its highest intensity during the period since the end of November. Sometimes, the Fuehrer said, he feared it simply would not be possible to survive. Invariably, however, he fought off the assaults of the enemy with his last ounce of will and thus always succeeded in coming out on top. Thank God the German people learned about only a fraction of all this. This shows how right it is to spare the people the heaviest burdens of the war, especially those of a spiritual nature. . . . What worries and torments the Fuehrer most is the fact that the country is still covered with snow, and that frost and cold are still stalking through field and forest. Although he doesn't talk much about it one can feel how unhappy he is about the long duration of the winter—a winter that came so suddenly and is departing so unwillingly.

I told him about my experiences in Vienna, Graz, and Linz. He asked me about the smallest details and admitted his deep yearning to return to these beautiful spots that are so dear to his heart.

The Fuehrer has no misgivings about sentiment at home. He is well aware that the German people, if correctly led, will survive the severe strains of this war. I described to him in detail how difficult it will be in the next few days to make the German people understand why food rations must be reduced, and how hard it will be to put these reductions into effect. The Fuehrer has done everything possible to avoid them. Even now he will make every effort to insure greater supplies of food, especially from the Ukraine. For the moment, however, this is utterly impossible in view of the exceptionally strained transport situation. . . . I don't share the Fuehrer's optimism that we shall succeed within a reasonable time in getting worth-while supplies out of the Ukraine. We lack the man power, the organization, and especially the transportation to do this. It is very doubtful whether the food situation will be any better this summer than at present. . . .

This damned long winter still prevents our opening the potato dugouts with their vast supplies of potatoes. Here we are at the beginning of spring, and still we are struggling with problems of the winter as though it were only the turn of the year! As soon as these dugouts can be opened, the Fuehrer approves of speeding up potato transport as much as possible.

Unfortunately the Ministry of Transport has failed again. The necessary number of locomotives is lacking. We sold locomotives to foreign countries in peacetime instead of stock-piling them for the time of need. The old-fogey ministerial directors in the Reich Ministry of Transport fumbled the ball so criminally that an example ought to be made of them.

The Fuehrer has decided to rule with a heavier hand henceforth. I told him of individual cases of miscarriages of justice. They paralleled his own observations. He is now determined to invoke the most radical measures.

I proposed a law to the effect that whoever violates the commonly known principles of National Socialistic leadership is to be punished with imprisonment and in very serious cases even with death. Such a law would enable us to place our domestic war effort on an entirely new basis and especially to lay our hands on those who have hitherto eluded us. Schlegelberger, the undersecretary in the Ministry of Justice, who since the death of Guertner has headed German justice, always refuses my requests on the grounds that there is no legal basis for action. That basis could be created by the proposed law. Beyond that, the failure of justice is of course a question of personalities and not of lack of laws. It is essential that the Ministry of Justice, which has been orphaned since the death of Guertner, be placed in new hands. I proposed the president of the People's Court, Thierack, who is a real National Socialist and certainly won't stumble over a thread. . . . Justice must not become the mistress of the state, but must be the servant of state policy.

[Franz Schlegelberger was a holdover from the days of the Weimar Republic, where he had gradually advanced to the position of undersecretary in the Ministry of Justice by 1931. When Dr. Franz Guertner died in 1941 no successor was appointed, but Schlegelberger became Acting Minister of Justice.

SS Group Leader Otto Georg Thierack was vice-president of the German Supreme Court during the first years of Nazism, but in 1939 became presiding judge of the notorious star-chamber People's Court (*Volksgerichtshof*). In recognition of his radical Nazi practices there, Hitler now followed Goebbels's suggestion and appointed him Reich Minister of Justice. He was instructed by Hitler to make German justice, which still rested on Roman law, conform to the Nazi principle that "right consists in whatever is of service to the National Socialist State" (*Recht ist was dem National-Sozialistischen Staat nuetzt*).]

The Fuehrer would like to have the Reichstag vote him special powers for a thorough political and military housecleaning, so as to let the evildoers know that he is fully backed by the entire people. He

intends to summon the Reichstag soon and have it vote him blanket
powers for proceeding against saboteurs and especially against officials
derelict in their duties. . . .

[The Reichstag was the counterpart of the American Congress. It enjoyed somewhat limited powers during the imperial regime, became much like Congress or
the English Parliament during the Weimer Republic of 1918–33, only to be
reduced to a sounding board for Adolf Hitler during the Nazi regime. During
Nazism it was jokingly called the "world's best-paid singing society," for its members assembled once or twice a year to listen to Hitler, then stood up lustily to
sing "Deutschland ueber Alles" and the "Horst Wessel Lied," and drew about two
hundred and fifty dollars a month year in, year out, for this manifestation of
lung power.]

The mere existence of blanket powers for the Fuehrer, authorizing
him not only to fire from their jobs officers who fail to do their duty,
but to discharge them dishonorably, would work wonders. All you
need to do is to select some single case and make an example of it.
That clears the atmosphere. The same thing should be done on the
civilian sector, for in civilian jobs, too, there are officials who in no
wise perform their duties as demanded by the exigencies of war. Men
in public life, no matter what their field, who are guilty of gross neglect
of duty should be punished, possibly even shot; men who are not equal
to their tasks because they lack intelligence or leadership qualities
should be subject to dismissal without pension. . . . The Fuehrer was
in a frame of mind that caused my proposals for conducting our war
in a more radical manner to meet with an absolutely favorable response
on his part. I needed merely to touch a theme lightly, and already I
had gained my point. Everything I proposed was accepted item by
item and without objection by the Fuehrer.

I told the Fuehrer about Streccius of Vienna in connection with the
forged Moelders letter. He simply fumed with anger. He asked me to
prepare a written report for him, whereupon he will throw Streccius
out without warning. As a matter of fact he did not even know this
ludicrous general. . . . Unfortunately nothing can be undertaken against
Mackensen. But the Fuehrer formed his opinion of the old field marshal
general in political matters long ago.

His opinion about various leaders of the Wehrmacht has changed
fundamentally during the past winter. He does not think so much of
the generals as he used to. He has nothing but contempt for many of
them.

I reported to the Fuehrer about the disgusting incidents at German
railway stations and in German express trains, and explained that bet-

ter-situated people simply will not heed our advice and our requests. He authorized me to invoke concentration-camp punishment to put an end to this nuisance.

[Goebbels refers to the fact that society women and people of wealth were able to secure sleepers and first-class seats, whereas German servicemen had to put up with inconveniences of every sort. Goebbels on one occasion, on arriving from outside Berlin, tried to argue with the better-situated to make room for servicemen, but was snubbed.]

Unfortunately I must complain about Dr. Ley. He is conducting a propaganda for increasing production that is most inopportune, especially now, at a time of reduced food rations. The Fuehrer recommends that I talk personally to Ley and point out his mistake.

We got to talking about political matters. The Fuehrer is very much attached to Mussolini and regards him as the only guarantor of German-Italian collaboration. The Italian people and Fascism will stick to our side as long as Mussolini is there. . . . The Fuehrer really intended to present him with a new Condor plane, but will refrain from so doing because he knows that Mussolini will immediately take the stick, and in case anything were to happen to him, he [Hitler] would never forgive himself. . . . Flying is Mussolini's great passion. During a war, however, a statesman in such a position has something else to do than to indulge in aviation sports. The Fuehrer spoke about Mussolini only in terms of greatest respect. He has made of the Italian people whatever it was possible to make of them. If here and there German-Italian collaboration doesn't function, that isn't Mussolini's fault, but is rather because of the lack of military qualities in the Italian people themselves.

Then the Fuehrer came to talk about himself. It is truly touching to hear him complain about the winter that has caused him such terrific worries and difficulties. I noted that he has already become quite gray and that merely telling about the cares of the winter makes him seem to have aged very much. . . .

The Fuehrer described to me how close we were during the past months to a Napoleonic winter. Had he weakened for only one moment, the front would have caved in and a catastrophe ensued that would have put the Napoleonic disaster far into the shade. Millions of fine soldiers would have been exposed to death by hunger and cold, and in all likelihood our workers—not to mention the intelligentsia—would have been led into slavery. Brauchitsch bears a great deal of responsibility for this eventuality. The Fuehrer spoke of him only in terms of contempt. A vain, cowardly wretch who could not even appraise the situation, much less master it. By his constant interference and consistent disobedience he completely spoiled the entire plan for the eastern campaign as it was designed with crystal clarity by the Fuehrer. The Fuehrer had a plan that was bound to lead to victory. Had Brauchitsch done what was asked of him and what he really should have done, our position in the East today would be entirely different from what it is.

The Fuehrer had no intention whatever of going to Moscow. He wanted to cut off the Caucasus and thereby strike the Soviet system at its most vulnerable point. But Brauchitsch and his general staff knew better. Brauchitsch always urged going to Moscow. He wanted prestige successes instead of factual successes. The Fuehrer described him as a coward and a nincompoop. He also had tried to weaken the plan of campaign for the West. But here the Fuehrer was able to take a hand in time. . . .

The Fuehrer again has a perfectly clear plan for the coming spring and summer. He does not want to overextend the war. His aims are the Caucasus, Leningrad, and Moscow. If these aims are attained by us, he is determined under all circumstances to end the campaign at the beginning of next October and to go into winter quarters early. He intends possibly to construct a gigantic line of defense and to let the eastern campaign rest there. A winter like the past can never again surprise us. Possibly this may mean a hundred years' war in the East, but that need not worry us. Our position toward what remains of Russia would then be like that of England toward India.

Our offensive will in all likelihood not begin before the end of May or the beginning of June. It will then, however, start out with a devastating impact. The Fuehrer has no intention of attacking along the whole front, but rather to launch assaults on one sector at a time and there to undertake advances of really decisive importance. The first advance against the Bolsheviks will start in a couple of days in the Crimea, which the Fuehrer desires to clear completely of the enemy.

The Fuehrer, incidentally, has rather high regard for the Soviet war leadership. Stalin's brutal hand has saved the Russian front. To hold our own we shall have to apply similar methods on our side. This toughness has sometimes been wanting with us and we must try to find an equivalent.

It is not difficult for me to gather from this whole presentation of the situation that the Fuehrer alone saved the Eastern Front this winter. His determination and firmness have put everything back in shape again. If today he is a sick and ailing man, that was a high price to pay, but it is worth it.

I can only hope that when spring comes the Fuehrer will soon be at the peak of health again. What he now needs is air, sunshine, spring, and the prospect of good weather. The whole atmosphere at GHQ is a truly depressing one. Ever to be surrounded by snow, ice, and frost allows no man to live there happily, even though he be a superman.

The Fuehrer this time truly worries me. I have never seen him so serious and grave as today. I told him that I, too, was not in the best of health. We spoke intimately as man to man. War takes a severe toll on the nerves of all of us. But that can't be helped. I hope when the war is over only a memory of it will remain.

My work meets with the Fuehrer's highest approval and gives him great satisfaction. It is wonderful for me to be able to chat at length with the Fuehrer about all sorts of personal things. He has the effect of a dynamo. After spending an afternoon with him, one feels like a storage battery that has just been charged anew.

Our discussion turned to England. The Fuehrer regards the English crisis as more profound than I had assumed. He believes there will be a sharp movement either to the right or to the left. Either Cripps will Bolshevize England, or the Tories will take control again. At present the Fuehrer is more inclined toward the latter possibility. He believes England is about to face a situation that will no longer permit the Tories merely to look on. For the moment they are letting things drift, but undoubtedly they will be heard from when the crisis has reached its climax.

The Fuehrer is rather disposed to believe that the United States will be ripe for Bolshevism at a certain moment, but today nobody can say just when that will happen.

According to the briefing given the Fuehrer, Japanese aspirations are approximately these: Tokyo intends at first to gain a foothold at various points in Australia without trying to take possession of the entire Australian continent, and then to advance upon India. At first Ceylon is to be overrun, so as to paralyze all shipping around India. That will strike at one of England's main arteries. The British Empire can't stand such a strain for long. That will be our best chance for finally knocking out England. But it will take time, and you can't measure such a development with a yardstick. It is, of course, possible that England's collapse will occur quite suddenly, but one should not count too much on it and not rest one's chances solely on such a possibility.

I told the Fuehrer how wonderful it is to imagine peacetime again. He feels the same way. We all long for the day when we can take part in reconstruction and not experience only the seamy side of this tremendous revolution. Every one of us has a strong yearning for life per se—for a life such as nobody can lead during the war.

The Fuehrer inquired solicitously about everybody at home—how Helga, Hilde, and especially Holge were, how the entire family was, and how and what it was doing. He remembers everyone, but regrets that he can pay so little attention to matters of this kind. I decided then and there that my family and I must look after him more after this war, especially since we can't do it now that the war is on.

[Helga, Hilde and Holge were three of Goebbels's children.]

Finally we talked about the Jewish question. Here the Fuehrer is as uncompromising as ever. The Jews must be got out of Europe, if necessary by applying most brutal methods.

For the present he does not want to become very active in the church question. He would like to save that up for the end of the war. . . .

Our whole conversation was conducted in the most cordial and intimate manner. I was happy to be with the Fuehrer again. The Fuehrer was happy to be able to talk in so personal a manner in absolute privacy. His devotion and meticulous care are touching. He inquired into all sorts of details that interest him, both of a personal and factual nature.

A little dog that was presented to him now plays about in his room. His whole heart belongs to that dog. The canine may do anything it wants in his bunker. At present it is the object closest to the Fuehrer's heart.

The Fuehrer had dinner served somewhat earlier than usual to enable me to share it before my departure. We talked at length about the gigantic military successes achieved by the Japanese. The Fuehrer is full of admiration for the Japanese Army. Aside from that, however, he naturally views the strong ascendancy of the Japanese in eastern Asia and the recession of the white man with certain misgivings. But there is nothing to be done about it. The English didn't want it otherwise. . . .

The Fuehrer regretted that Antonescu did not succeed in collaborating with the Iron Guard. A stagnant condition obtains in Rumania as a result. The [political] parties are gone and Antonescu has no political group on which he can lean for support. He will have to pay dearly for it someday.

But we, too, must realize that we shall have to fill with human beings such wide spaces in the East as we shall conquer. In geography there can be no spaces without human beings, just as in politics there can be no vacuums. Every space must be filled, and if we don't fill those that we control, someone else will do it. Hence our chief task will consist in filling up the areas in the East and in creating human beings to take possession of these spaces and establish their homes there. That is the question that the Japanese, too, are facing. To conquer Australia won't be hard, but to fill up Australia will be a difficult task. The English didn't succeed and that's why they are going to lose Australia.

At 8:30 P.M. I had to leave. The Fuehrer was very much touched when I left. He wishes me to visit him again soon. I am almost benumbed at having to leave him. . . .

A long, dreamless sleep. When we arrived in Berlin toward noon, the capital was again enveloped in a white robe of snow. Not a sign of spring anywhere. Winter has again returned.

March 21, 1942

General Schmundt complained bitterly about the indolence of a number of higher officers who either do not want to understand the Fuehrer or in some cases are not able to. They are thereby robbing themselves, as General Schmundt put it, of the greatest happiness that a contemporary can today experience; namely, that of serving a genius.

Vansittart delivered his maiden speech in the House of Lords. He directed a sharp attack against the German emigrés who are active in London and who are against the Nazis but not against the Germans. He demands a propaganda directed against Germany as such and not against National Socialism. He wants to destroy Germany, not the National Socialist movement. That's music for our ears. Let Vansittart carry on. He is merely supplying grist for our propaganda mill.

[Lord Vansittart was the English mouthpiece of anti-German bitter-enders. Goebbels consistently held that it was a psychological mistake for Vansittart and his followers to make no distinction between the Nazis and other Germans.]

Rumors of peace have once again cropped up, especially in connection with Papen's trip to Berlin. Papen is always described by our adversaries as a great poisoner which in reality he isn't at all. Allegedly he is now to inquire into the possibilities of peace, especially a separate peace with the Soviet Union. That, of course, is stuff and nonsense.

I received a report about the latest developments in German science. Research in the realm of atomic destruction has now proceeded to a point where its results may possibly be made use of in the conduct of this war. Tremendous destruction, it is claimed, can be wrought with a minimum of effort so that the prospects for a longer duration of the war and for a later war are terrifying. Modern technic places in the hands of human beings means of destruction that are simply incredible. German science is at its peak in this matter. It is essential that we be ahead of everybody, for whoever introduces a revolutionary novelty into this war has the greater chance of winning it.

[This entry is significant both because Goebbels claims that the Germans were close to perfecting the atomic bomb and because of his prophetic statement, proven at Hiroshima to have been realistic, that "whoever introduces a revolutionary novelty into this war has the greater chance of winning it."]

Hilgenfeldt reported to me about his difficulties with Wehrmacht officers in taking care of the wounded who return from the East. Here jurisdictional fights are being fought at a time when our wounded are in most urgent need of aid. I pounded on the table energetically. The Wehrmacht has proven unable to solve these problems; it should at least let other competent and willing departments go to work and not hinder them constantly with childish jurisdictional objections. The Wehrmacht leadership has failed so generally during this winter that it must be relieved of many tasks for which it was hitherto responsible, especially tasks for ameliorating the effects of war that can be accomplished only by improvisation. There are other offices, especially in the Party and its sub-organizations, that handle such matters better, especially because they know how to improvise and, so to speak, to stamp results out of the ground.

[Erich Hilgenfeldt was head of the Nazi Social Welfare Organization known as the NSV (National-Sozialistische Volkswohlfahrt). Goebbels, a Nazi first, last, and all the time, seized upon every opportunity to take jobs away from non-Nazi offices and put them into Nazi hands. Here he is seen taking work away from the Wehrmacht.]

In the afternoon I had a more than three-hour talk with Goering, which came off in an atmosphere of the greatest friendliness and cordiality. I was happy we could let our hair down. We surveyed the overall situation, and I was gratified to note that we agree 100 per cent on all important problems. Without having consulted each other we have arrived at almost exactly the same appraisal of the situation.

Goering is in exceptionally good condition physically. He works hard, achieves enormous successes, tackles problems with a healthy common sense, without much theorizing, and for this reason is pretty skeptical about certain trends in the Party. I can't blame him for this. He has the rare good fortune of not being dependent on the Party in his work, so that he can risk being more independent. In many respects he is to be envied.

We start with the transportation problem. . . . Then we talk in detail about the forged letter of Moelders. Goering already knew that this letter had been distributed chiefly by Mackensen. . . . He has been ordered by the Fuehrer to ask Field Marshal von Mackensen to come to see him and give him a piece of his mind. Mackensen has for some time been active as a sort of granddaddy of the Christian churches. Shortsighted as he is, he assumed that Moelders had spoken on behalf of the Protestant Church, because he believed that only Protestantism had a dean. As a matter of fact the forged Moelders letter was addressed to the only Catholic dean in Germany; namely, the one at Stettin. So here Mackensen stepped into something.

Now that Hindenburg is no longer alive the old gentleman is being used a little too much by subversive elements for their propaganda. But we won't stand for that. Goering will give him an unequivocal piece of his mind. Goering also addressed a sharp letter to Bishops Galen of Muenster and Berning of Osnabrueck. He reminded them of their oath, pledged to him, of fidelity to the state and reprimanded them severely for their treasonable attitude.

[Bishop Count Clemens von Galen of Muenster belonged to one of the oldest families in Germany, whose title of nobility dated from the ninth century. He was a bold opponent of Nazism and one of the most colorful men in the Catholic hierarchy of Germany. He received the cardinal's hat in 1946, but died of exhaustion on his way home from Rome. His colleague, Bishop Berning of Osnabrueck, was another doughty fighter against Nazism.]

While I was with him, the answers to this letter happened to arrive. They are relatively meek. The bishops try to alibi and with involved turns of speech to prove that they kept their oath. Goering naturally won't accept that. I suggest to Goering that he write another letter, especially to Galen, charging him to his face with having created the greatest unrest in the Reich by his claim that seriously wounded soldiers were being liquidated, and pointing out that his utterances are being used by the English propaganda services against the National Socialist regime.

On the one hand it can't be denied that certain measures of the Party, especially the decree about crucifixes, have made it altogether too easy for the bishops to rant against the state. Goering, too, is very much put out about it. His whole attitude toward the Christian denominations is quite open and aboveboard. He sees through them, and has no intention whatever of taking them under his protection. On the other hand he agrees with me completely that it won't do to get started now, in wartime, on so difficult and far-reaching a problem. The Fuehrer, too, expressed that viewpoint to him as he has often expressed it to me. In this connection the Fuehrer declared that if his mother still lived, she would undoubtedly go to church today, and he could and would not hinder her. . . .

[The Nazis insisted upon the removal of crucifixes from schools and hospitals.]

We are in complete agreement about the Wehrmacht. Goering has nothing but abysmal contempt for the cowardly generals. . . . Field Marshal General Keitel, he said, was not tough enough. He was probably responsible for the fact that the plan of campaign in the East did not function properly. He carried the Fuehrer's commands to the OKH with trembling knees. Brauchitsch was not alone at fault. While he bore a great part of the responsibility he was not told sufficiently plainly [by Keitel] that he must obey the Fuehrer, and that if he did not do so, he would soon feel the consequences. . . .

[Field Marshal Wilhelm Keitel, born, 1882, an officer from World War I, became chief of the Wehrmacht office of the Minister of War in 1935, succeeding General Walter von Reichenau, who had applied for an active command. Throughout World War II Keitel was chief of the Supreme Command of the German armed forces, an imposing title which in reality was nothing but a rubber-stamp position under Hitler. He was hanged in Nuremberg in 1946 as a major war criminal.]

Goering, too, is not yet clear in his own mind whether the pending spring and summer offensive will succeed in smashing the Russians. He hopes for it, but so little is known about the preparations of the Bolsheviks that an exact prognosis is impossible. If we succeed in beating the Bolsheviks militarily, everything will be fine. If we fail, we shall have to face a period during which extraordinarily sharp inroads on the life of every individual will be necessary in order to render the nation secure against the impending storms.

In southern Italy a number of embarrassing incidents occurred between the Luftwaffe and the female population. Goering, however, succeeded in getting things straightened out during his last visit to the Duce.

We talked at some length about Hess. Goering has nothing but contempt for him. Undoubtedly he brought us into a position last summer in which we were pretty close to ruin. Had Churchill actually succeeded in discrediting our fidelity to our Allies, the war might conceivably have taken an entirely different turn. All of us were quite justified in being extremely worried at the time and having gravest doubts about the immediate future. But a kind fate held its protecting hand over us.

Goering told me of his exceedingly funny and humorous experiences when last he visited the ministries along Wilhemstrasse and Unter den Linden on the Sunday on which his birthday fell. Nowhere could he find anybody. Everybody had taken the Sunday off. That is a situation I have criticized and complained about throughout this entire war. An emergency service has at last been established in one of the ministries.

[Hermann Goering was born January 12, 1893.]

Goering spoke of Frick as a complete nincompoop. He's right about that. He criticized Darré very sharply because he does nothing but write letters and memoranda. . . . He expressed most serious doubts that Rosenberg will measure up in the long run to his tremendous task. We all know, of course, that he just can't organize. He is a pure theoretician. How, then, can he be expected to be a practical organizer and administrator of a stupendous area almost as large as a continent?

[Walther Darré was Minister of Food and Agriculture. Goebbels himself speaks again of him in an interesting way in the entries for May 19 and May 21.]

Actually Russia is a land of unlimited possibilities. The dividing line between Asia and Europe has been drawn quite arbitrarily. Maybe a large part of Asia will at some time be joined to Europe, and we can then form a sort of Eurasia. That continent will then possibly have to settle scores with the United States who also represent a real continent. But that is something to worry about later. For the present we must bring the war to a victorious conclusion. Nobody knows just when we shall succeed. Goering, too, is exceedingly cautious in his prognosis. Perhaps we shall reach our goal sooner than any of us think; possibly, however, it may take a very long time still. We must fortify ourselves with strength and fortitude and view the things that are to come with great optimism. . . .

Goering spoke in terms of highest praise about our work. We resolve to meet more frequently and have frank talks about everything. In these times it is especially necessary that the leading men about the Fuehrer understand each other well, know exactly what they want, and permit no differences to arise between them. The result of my talk with Goering is exceptionally satisfactory and favorable. To think of all one can clarify and settle in three hours like these! . . .

In the evening I viewed the Russian Bolshevik movie, *Suvarov*. It is a decidedly nationalistic film, in which the Bolsheviks try to establish a connection between the Russia of today and the old heroic history of the country. Certain passages in the film are childishly naïve, as though a twelve-year-old had shot the scenes. Other passages, again, are of extraordinary vitality. There are lots of possibilities latent in the Russians. If they were really to be organized thoroughly as a people they would undoubtedly represent the most tremendous danger possible for Europe. That must be prevented, and that is one of the objectives we must attain during the pending offensive. May God grant us success!

March 26, 1942

Fear of an offensive is the absolutely dominating factor on the other side. The loud noise about victories and triumphant successes is over. Harsh reality again asserts itself. Churchill's phrases have proven barren.

Bose's propaganda, conducted from Berlin, is extremely embarrassing to the English. It is being heard more widely than I at first thought possible. All the better that we have not yet revealed where he is staying! His propaganda can take effect more easily thus.

Vernon Bartlett has written an article concerning British propaganda for Germany, which he considers absolutely wrong. He said Vansittart's latest speech had merely been grist for my mill, which in fact it was.

[Vernon Bartlett, M.P., was at this time diplomatic adviser to the London *News Chronicle*.]

The more radical the English are in prophesying a disgraceful peace for Germany, the more easily I succeed in toughening and hardening German resistance. We'd be in a dangerous fix now if British propaganda from the beginning of the war to this hour had respected the German will to live and the German conception of honor. That's how Chamberlain began on the first day of the war. Thank God, the English did not continue along that line. Even though we would always try to discredit them by citing 1918 as an example, they would nevertheless find foolish adherents here and there, especially since the domestic situation always becomes more strained the longer the war lasts.

[Goebbels, as already pointed out previously, was convinced that a propaganda policy of the Allies by which a differentiation was made between the Nazi regime and its crimes on the one hand and the decent element of Germany and its feeling for honor on the other, would have torn Germany asunder and caused great difficulties for the regime. The historian of the future will probably have to re-evaluate the wisdom of the Allied insistence upon unconditional surrender which was predicated on the assumption that all Germans were alike. Goebbels, after all, knew something about propaganda and the psychology of the German people.]

The same thing would, of course, be true in the case of Italy. There, however, the English are proceeding somewhat more cleverly. The United States has now proclaimed Sforza as the standard bearer of a future Italian regime. He is the spokesman of a so-called "Free Italy." For the present such nonsense is ineffective.

[Count Carlo Sforza, Italian statesman and diplomat, former Foreign Minister, was the "grand old man" of the Italian anti-Fascist emigrants. In 1920–21 he was Italian Foreign Minister. He resigned as Ambassador to France on the advent of the Fascists to power late in 1922 and was leader of the democratic opposition until the suppression of opposition parties in 1926. He went into exile and lectured at many foreign universities, including some in the United States. He returned to Italy at the age of seventy-one to become a member of the Badoglio cabinet in April 1944, and was president of the Italian Consultative Assembly in 1945.]

The Foreign Office has briefed me on the situation in Brazil. There a bitter fight is on between President Vargas, who is pretty much on our side, and Foreign Minister Aranha, who is evidently a character bought by Roosevelt and is apparently doing everything possible to provoke a conflict with the Reich and the Axis Powers.

[Getulio Dornelles Vargas, born, 1882, educated at Rio Parde Military School, became President of the Brazilian Republic in 1930, after having previously served as President of the State of Rio Grande do Sul. He resigned in 1945.
Oswaldo Aranha, born, 1894, Brazilian diplomat, became Minister for Foreign Affairs in 1938, after having been Ambassador to the United States, 1934–38. He has more recently been playing a leading role in the United Nations.]

We have, alas, no facilities for reprisal. We have about six hundred Brazilians in our hands whereas in Brazil alone there are 150,000 Germans. The economic possibilities of striking back are also extraordinarily limited with us, as we don't own one tenth as much Brazilian capital as the Brazilians possess of German capital. So we have to be rather careful.

The SD report paints the situation in rather somber colors [*grau in grau*]. It declares no news during the entire war has had as depressing an effect as this [the shortening of food rations], and that morale has thereby reached a low never before attained. I think that is seeing things somewhat too pessimistically.

It's a dirty, low thing for the Catholic Church to continue its subversive activity in every way possible and now even to extend its propaganda to Protestant children evacuated from regions threatened by air raids. Next to the Jews these politico-divines [*politisierenden Pfaffen*] are about the most loathsome riffraff that we are still sheltering in the Reich. The time will come after the war for an over-all solution of this problem. Only one can be the master in the state, either the Church or the state itself. National Socialism is faced with the task of establishing supremacy uncompromisingly over the political claims of the Church.

The Metropole Theater folk are very grateful that I can devote a few late hours to them. For my work, however, that isn't very good; it distracts me. It engenders too deep a yearning for peace, and that won't do in wartime. Just as a wanderer in the desert shouldn't forever think of water, so a man who helps run a war must never think of peace. If and when peace comes, there is plenty of time to think of it; if it doesn't come, then there is but one task; namely, to wage war.

[Goebbels's fondness for theatrical people, especially pretty actresses, was proverbial. It is not difficult to understand this nostalgic reference. The Metropole Theater specialized in musical comedies.]

March 27, 1942

Nothing of importance has been reported from East Asia. The American and British press is gabbing about an offensive in Australia that the Allies have allegedly begun. Their claims are now so modest that they even regard the mere presence of a better-known general in a certain country as an offensive.

[Goebbels obviously refers to General Douglas MacArthur.]

Cripps is evidently trying to force a decision [in India], for not only does he want to achieve a practical result, but success is exceedingly important to him personally. He received the journalists and cracked foolish, typically English jokes. He wouldn't commit himself. It seems quite clear that the English will try to promise the Indians dominion status after the war—a promise that they certainly wouldn't keep if England were to win the war and could further expand her imperial might.

Churchill, incidentally, took the floor himself in the House of Commons. His speech bubbled over with obscure phrases. He speaks in generalities, declaring the position has improved tremendously. It hardly pays to argue with him.

The German Embassy in Rome sent me a speech by Mussolini which was delivered January 3 before the Party leaders. This speech is exceptionally caustic and is directed especially against the defeatist bourgeois circles that criticize the war effort. In this confidential address Mussolini declared his unalterable determination to continue to march to the end with Germany and the Fuehrer.... He really deserves a better people than the one he now leads.

A much more clever form of propaganda against the Reich has been proposed in the United States. The idea is not to go against the German people but against Nazism. I sense a certain danger. Fortunately the enemy propaganda is not so unified and consistent as to be able to stick to such a propaganda slogan for a period of years. If this were the case we would face great difficulties every time we were under a new, heavy strain.

If I were on the enemy side, I should from the very first day on have adopted the slogan of fighting against Nazism, but not against the German people. That's how Chamberlain began on the first day of the war, but, thank God, the English didn't follow through. I gave orders that the German press is not to publish or discuss turns of speech such as are being used increasingly in the American press. One should simply not talk about these things. Even if you argue about them you nevertheless spread them.

The German people must remain convinced—as indeed the facts warrant—that this war strikes at their very lives and their national possibilities of development, and that they must fight it with their entire strength.

The Wafd party has achieved a glorious victory; let's not question with what means, but it did gain 216 out of 264 seats. That makes it possible for Nahas Pasha to act. Of course not much is to be expected of him, as he has probably been a satellite of the English for some time already.

Beginning with Lublin, the Jews in the General Government are now being evacuated eastward. The procedure is a pretty barbaric one and not to be described here more definitely. Not much will remain of the Jews. On the whole it can be said that about 60 per cent of them will have to be liquidated whereas only about 40 per cent can be used for forced labor.

[By General Government is meant German-occupied Poland. It is obvious from this entry that Goebbels knew of the gas-chamber atrocities, but it is significant that there was any form of human depravity which he would recognize as barbaric when resorted to by Nazis.]

The former Gauleiter of Vienna, who is to carry this measure through, is doing it with considerable circumspection and according to a method that does not attract too much attention. A judgment is being visited upon the Jews that, while barbaric, is fully deserved by them. The prophesy which the Fuehrer made about them for having brought on a new world war is beginning to come true in a most terrible manner. One must not be sentimental in these matters. If we did not fight the Jews, they would destroy us. It's a life-and-death struggle between the Aryan race and the Jewish bacillus. No other government and no other regime would have the strength for such a global solution of this question. Here, too, the Fuehrer is the undismayed champion of a radical solution necessitated by conditions and therefore inexorable. Fortunately a whole series of possibilities presents itself for us in wartime that would be denied us in peacetime. We shall have to profit by this.

[Hitler in a Reichstag speech on January 30, 1939, prophesied that the outbreak of another world war would mean the end of the Jews in Europe. He then said: "I want today once again to make a prophecy: In case the international Jewish financiers within and outside Europe succeed once more in hurling the peoples into a world war, the result will be, not the Bolshevization of the world and with it a victory of Jewry, but the annihilation of the Jewish race in Europe."]

The ghettos that will be emptied in the cities of the General Government will now be refilled with Jews thrown out of the Reich. This process is to be repeated from time to time. There is nothing funny in it for the Jews, and the fact that Jewry's representatives in England and America are today organizing and sponsoring the war against Germany must be paid for dearly by its representatives in Europe— and that's only right.

Commander Hartenstein reported to me about a submarine trip into the Caribbean Sea. Our submarines are finding fat booty there. The Americans are not at all prepared and have almost no defense against submarine attacks. The submarines are at sea for about sixty days all told. They keep shooting until their last torpedo is gone and on their return try, if possible, to destroy transports they meet by artillery fire. Morale among the submarine men is splendid, especially since their last great successes. It is astonishing how combat transforms young men into genuine leaders within a short time. This particular submarine commander, who almost strikes you as a teen-ager, is a real man and a leader from head to foot.

March 28, 1942

Things are relatively quiet in East Asia. The Japanese seem to be catching their breath and accumulating strength for their next blow. Australia is raising a hell of a row [*einen Mordskrach*]. It is arguing with everybody all around. Behind it all, however, there is no military power whatever. MacArthur has no easy task so far as Australia is concerned. Those in power in Australia at present are descendants of the former British penal colony. They don't mince words. They would be pretty surprised, however, if one of these days the Japanese established bases on their continent.

Churchill's last speech is being debated in London. Churchill in reality spoke much more pessimistically than at first appeared. The gloomy beginning of his speech was forbidden for Reuters foreign service and was quoted only in the domestic English service. We nevertheless got hold of it and can now contrast the Churchill who strikes a note of relative optimism for the countries abroad with the Churchill who describes the situation exactly as it is for the home folk. The London propaganda offices claim Churchill has spoken the simple truth. In other words, there are two kinds of truth for this British Premier, one for foreign countries and one for home consumption.

Hamsun wrote a very witty and exceptionally biting article against Roosevelt. Hamsun, one of the most outstanding intellectuals of modern Europe, has, until now, always stood by the flag of the New Order.

[Goebbels here refers to the celebrated Norwegian novelist and Nobel Literature Prize winner, Knut Hamsun, whose novels, *The Growth of the Soil, Hunger, Vagabonds, Mysteries,* and *The Last Chapter*—to mention the best known—have been translated into the English language. The visit of Hamsun at the official Goebbels home on May 18, 1943, is described in detail under date of May 19.]

The English are about to introduce their super-summertime. That again creates the problem for us of interrupting our entertainment broadcasts to make room for the news service in the English language. I am trying to persuade the Luftwaffe to give me one of the broadcasting stations in occupied France, for at present we can hardly afford to have the general entertainment program interrupted.

Sauckel has been appointed Reich Plenipotentiary for man power. When he comes to Berlin the next time I am going to talk to him and present my wishes. Undoubtedly his strong National Socialist hand will achieve miracles. It should not be difficult to mobilize at least a million additional workers from among the German people; one must merely go at it energetically and not be scared by ever-recurring difficulties.

[Fritz Sauckel, Gauleiter for Thuringia, was regarded as one of the toughest of the Old Guard Nazis, and was put in charge of the whole problem of forced labor. The Nuremberg International Military Tribunal found him guilty of crimes against humanity because of his ruthless treatment of slave laborers from all occupied countries, and had him hanged. In a number of later entries Goebbels speaks very disparagingly of him.

Sauckel was the man who had the sarcophagi of Goethe and Schiller removed from their resting place in the royal mausoleum of Weimar and taken to Jena to an air-raid bunker, and then ordered that the bodies of these two titans of German culture be blown to bits in the event of an American advance into Thuringia. The workers of Jena considered this sacrilege, however, and hid the two coffins. They informed Major William M. Brown, American military governor of Weimar, of what they had done, and Brown ceremoniously brought the remains back to Weimar, where he restored them to their original resting place.]

I have ordered an investigation into the nuisance of questionnaires. That has really become a public scandal. One can hardly buy an orange today without answering a questionnaire with the most ludicrous questions. It is high time that this nuisance be stopped. If I succeed in this I shall undoubtedly render a great service on behalf of domestic tranquility.

The leadership of the Waffen-SS looks after its members materially and spiritually in a model way. That means, of course, that new conflicts constantly arise between the Waffen-SS and the Army, which is very lax in these matters. But, after all, the Waffen-SS cannot stop looking after its troops merely because the Army is inactive in that respect! Quite a number of cases are reported to me that are simply hair-raising. One can hardly put into words what the Army neglects to do in the way of taking care of the troops and supplying them with munitions and weapons. The gentlemen of the OKH are nothing but frustrated German National or People's party bureaucrats. If National Socialism hadn't come they would in all likelihood sit somewhere in an inconspicuous place as obscure attorneys or ward heelers for the bourgeois parties. Now they are show-offs pretending to be top brass hats. They are entirely unfit for any leadership role, especially because they have no initiative and cannot improvise. Their chief task con-

sists in creating difficulties for people who do something and who
know something. But the SS won't have anybody scratch the butter
off its bread, and that is fine. . . .

[Goebbels here refers to the fact that many of the older officers had taken their
discharge at the end of World War I, since Germany was permitted to have only
a professional army of 100,000 men, and found berths as attorneys or low-ranking
officials of the ultra-conservative German National party and of the late Gustav
Stresemann's People's party. Goebbels despised bourgeois society, and felt much
closer to the Communists than to former members of the defunct middle-class and
conservative parties.]

The London press has started a major press campaign against
Bulgaria, especially on the question of whether Bulgaria wants to
attack Turkey. That, of course, is utter nonsense; nevertheless London
tries thereby to torpedo King Boris's trip to Germany.

King Boris expressed the wish of talking with me at leisure. I
visited him at Bellevue Castle where he is residing for a few days. Our
talk, which was really to take up only twenty minutes, stretched out for
more than two hours. The King is extraordinarily charming and has
returned from the Fuehrer full of new ideas, suggestions and initia-
tives. The Fuehrer has this time given him a complete briefing on all
matters that concern him. Boris is an impassioned devotee of Hitler's
genius as a leader; he really looks upon him as a sort of emissary of
God.

He shows the greatest understanding for my work. He follows what
I do with such alert interest that I am simply surprised at what he
knows and what he asks about. My articles in the *Reich* are part of
his required reading. Yes, he told me he even uses the arguments
advanced in these articles in all his diplomatic negotiations. He is full
of admiration for the sensitiveness of our psychological approach in
leading the German people which, he claims, differs most strikingly
from that of World War I.

He is a real people's king. He describes to me how he travels incognito through Bulgarian villages to learn about the sentiment of the
people. Undoubtedly sentiment was pro-Russian even a short time
ago, but under the impact of the presence of German troops it has
veered over noticeably to our side. The King has observed marked
friendliness to Germany even in such sections of the country as were
hitherto known for their pro-Russian sympathies. He is very happy that
the Fuehrer does not expect more of him than that he be a stabilizing
factor in the Balkans.

The Fuehrer is showing himself extremely liberal toward Bulgaria.
Bulgaria, after all, cannot easily take an active part in the war, since

it has almost never lived in peace throughout its young national history. It can, however, supply auxiliary troops here and there, as indeed it has done, for example, in Serbia. For this we can only be thankful to the King.

Bulgaria's national aspirations have for the most part been satisfied. The King, of course, is not thinking of fighting Turkey. . . .

It is truly astonishing with what love and devotion he stands behind the Fuehrer. If all our allies were like that, we could be satisfied. The King has made intensive studies about German morale and is very well satisfied by the results. He knows conditions exactly as they were during World War I and realizes that they are in sharpest contrast with those of today. He is surprised at the quiet composure, especially of the Berlin population, and praises it highly.

It was late in the night when we parted from each other in the most cordial spirit. One cannot but find this king sympathetic. If all heads of states in Europe were as open-minded and ready to support the New Order, hardly an obstacle could be placed in the way of the future Europe.

[The reader will no doubt be struck, as this editor was, by Goebbels's complete reversal of opinion regarding Czar Boris of Bulgaria. In his diary entry for January 25, 1942, he describes him as a "sly, crafty fellow" who was "playing a double-faced game." The reader is again referred to the Boris-Von Hassell conversation recorded in the *Von Hassell Diaries*.]

March 29, 1942

The English are continuing their infamous and infernal campaign against Czar Boris, claiming he had mobilized in order to take a hand in the campaign in the East. Not a word of this is true. On the contrary, as I gather from a confidential report, the situation in Bulgaria is quite muddled. It isn't at all true that only elements friendly to the Axis are dominant there. There are also quite a number of pro-Russians, besides Free Masons, who are by no means ready to yield the field without challenge and resistance. Czar Boris has a lot of difficulties to overcome before he can bring the political situation at home into a state of absolute balance. In any case the English are groping in the dark completely if they believe the Bulgarians will attack Turkey. As a matter of fact they don't seem really to believe it themselves, but merely claim it.

The Bolshevizing process to which England is now subjected is gradually extending to the United States. While this is happening only very slowly, it is nevertheless quite visible to the eye of any informed person and is continuing with frightening consistency. If this war lasts much longer, certainly the prophecy of the Fuehrer will be fulfilled according to which the states that have sicked Bolshevism on to us will themselves be devoured by it.

There are rumors that Pétain wants to take Laval back into his government. Of course these rumors are as yet entirely unconfirmed. In any case Pétain had a secret talk with Laval, the results of which are as yet unknown.

[Pierre Laval, Premier of France in the days shortly before Nazi accession to power in Germany in 1933, became Minister for Foreign Affairs in Pétain's collaborationist cabinet of 1940, but soon had a quarrel with the chief of state whose functions he was trying gradually to take over. In 1942 Pétain invited him to join the cabinet again, this time as Premier. Laval accepted. He was found guilty of treason by a Paris court in 1946 and, after trying in vain to commit suicide by swallowing poison, was executed by a firing squad in Fresnes Prison on October 15, 1945.]

Our navy journals have asked me to let them have my editorials a little sooner. They are published in all the navy papers. The members of the Navy are extremely interested in them and agree with them completely. I am happy that my editorials are held in such high esteem by the fighting forces. It proves that I have found a method of argumentation that is very effective both at home and at the front.

For the first time the Wehrmacht communiqué points out that winter may be regarded as having ended. When I hear this sentence I grow quite hot under the collar, so excited am I. Just to think of what this winter brought us in the way of sacrifices, worries, and spiritual and material torment! How long have we waited for this hour! Now it has come at last.

March 30, 1942

MacArthur is being praised more and more in the United States like a general of the movies. I am having this gentleman taken down a few pegs in our propaganda services. The Americans are trying to blow him up into the greatest general of this war. After all, he has in reality nothing to show in the way of heroic deeds or achievements except his relatively brief resistance on Corregidor. Imagine what the Americans would do if they had a Dietl or a Rommel! This shows how modest we really are in our propaganda.

Cripps is hoping for success in India within about a fortnight. He is proceeding rather cleverly, and there is danger that he may actually succeed in attaching India once more to England's apron strings. He still has some resistance to overcome, but one never knows to what extent English pounds sterling are brought into play at the decisive hour. I therefore order our propaganda to be reversed somewhat; namely, to the effect that the German people won't be greatly disappointed if a compromise is worked out in India.

This Sunday is thoroughly spoiled by an exceptionally heavy air raid by the RAF on Luebeck. In the morning I had already received a very alarming report from our propaganda office there, which I at first assumed to be exaggerated. In the course of the evening, however, I was informed of the seriousness of the situation by a long-distance call from Kaufmann. Kaufmann believes that no German city has ever before been attacked so severely from the air. Conditions in Luebeck are in part chaotic. Kaufmann took a hand with great energy and started the necessary rescue measures, but he isn't being given the proper support from Berlin.

[Karl Kaufmann, one of the Nazi Old Guard, was Gauleiter of the Hamburg area which included the Hanseatic City of Luebeck.]

Immediately after that the Fuehrer called me from GHQ and was very much put out about the negligence of the Ministry of the Interior, which did not even succeed in calling the departmental heads together on Sunday evening to discuss the necessary relief measures. The Fuehrer therefore took the matter of caring for bomb-damaged areas out of the hands of the Ministry of the Interior and transferred blanket powers to me. . . . By midnight everything was arranged that could possibly be done. The Ministry of the Interior has once again fizzled out completely. But that's okay with me. In that way I at least have been given plenary powers to do something without being constantly hindered by the bureaucracy.

[This was probably one of Goebbels's happiest days of the year. Dr. Wilhelm Frick, as already pointed out, was his "bête noire" in the Nazi hierarchy. Goebbels now not only received additional plenary powers—and no Nazi was hungrier for power than was the little doctor—but the man from whom this particular power was taken was none other than Dr. Frick.]

March 31, 1942

The situation at Luebeck is anything but pleasant. I telephoned several times to Kaufmann, who gave me a picture of the destruction. Eighty per cent of the old part of the city must be considered lost. Stupendous numbers of works of art have fallen victim to the British craze for destruction. . . .

April 1942

ELEVEN HUNDRED NORSE CLERICS RESIGN IN PROTEST AGAINST QUISLING RULE. GENERAL MARSHALL AND HARRY HOPKINS CONFER IN LONDON WITH BRITISH OFFICIALS. JAPANESE OVERRUN BATAAN. JAPANESE TROOPS LAND ON CEBU, P.I. QUISLING ASSUMES CONTROL OF NORWAY'S CHURCHES. LAVAL RETURNS TO POWER AS FRENCH PREMIER. RUNDSTEDT ASSUMES COMMAND OF GERMAN DEFENSES ALONG ENTIRE ATLANTIC COAST. AMBASSADOR LEAHY RECALLED FROM VICHY. JAPANESE MAINLAND BOMBED FOR FIRST TIME. GENERAL GIRAUD ESCAPES FROM GERMAN PRISON CAMP. STALIN ASSERTS SOVIET UNION HAS NO TERRITORIAL AMBITIONS IN FOREIGN COUNTRIES. GERMANS SLAY EIGHTEEN NORWEGIAN HOSTAGES. HITLER AND MUSSOLINI CONFER AT SALZBURG.

April 1, 1942

Commander Endrass has failed to return from a mission. The German submarine force has thereby lost one of its ablest commanders and I a good, sympathetic, charming acquaintance with whom I was on most cordial terms. I still think with sorrow of the splendid evening I spent with Endrass at Schwanenwerder. All this young blood must now be shed for the Fatherland. War is a negative selection. It would be much better if a couple of hundred idle plutocrats at home had to walk the plank [*verschuett gingen*]. As it is, however, the very best that we have are lost to us.

[Schwanenwerder is a charming island in the Wannsee, a lake between Berlin and Potsdam on which thousands of Berliners spent their Sundays. Goebbels had a swanky home on Schwanenwerder, which is connected with the mainland by a small bridge. The Goebbels house was destroyed completely by Anglo-American air action. Besides his official Berlin residence, next to the American Embassy, Goebbels also had another country home; namely, in Lanke, a village about twenty-five miles north of the capital.]

We shall naturally prepare much better for the next winter than we did for the last. The difficulties of the past winter were owing mainly to the fact that we had had no real experience in an eastern campaign. Now, however, we know the difficulties that confront us, and we shall take the necessary countermeasures in the course of the summer and early autumn.

I cannot imagine that Churchill expected a real operational success at St. Nazaire. He owed an offensive undertaking of some sort to the man on the street and started it, although most serious sacrifices were involved, in order to make it a propaganda affair. As the English were chased home, however, with bloody heads (in so far as they got home at all), it is to be assumed that Mister Churchill will think twice in the future before he goes on such ventures.

I have received a report on the internal situation in Hungary according to which that country is in the midst of a sort of state crisis. Kállay, the new Prime Minister, has long been known as hostile to Germany. Also, he was involved in rather shady deals when he was Minister of Agriculture. Bárdossy resigned, as I suspected right away, because he violently opposed the appointment of the Regent's son as Deputy Regent. Young Horthy is a pronounced friend of the Jews and does not want to have much to do with the Axis Powers. . . .

[Dr. Miklos Kállay de Nagy Kálló was Hungarian Prime Minister from 1942–44, after having served as Minister of Agriculture in the Fascist cabinet of Goemboes from 1932–35. He was arrested and sent to Dachau concentration camp in 1944.]

Fortunately we never had any illusions about the Hungarians, so that now we are not disappointed. We shall be on the lookout so no harm can be done. . . . There certainly can no longer be any talk of a comradeship in arms, about which the Hungarians love to prate in their official speeches and when they extend their personal greetings officially.

It is small comfort for me that everything I proposed in time is now being done somewhat too late. Just as it was with the collection of woollen goods, so it is now with man power. Now suddenly all influential officials are much more open-minded regarding the question of drafting women for labor. The Russian civilian population, too, is to be drafted on a very large scale for work in Germany. That means, of course, they must be fed better than the Russian prisoners thus far. Also, of course, they must be given certain priviliges, as their performance will otherwise not be satisfactory.

Winkler gave me a report on the movie situation. A number of personnel questions have to be discussed. The Finance Ministry is trying to soak us with new taxes, so that it will hardly be possible to build up any capital reserves for tasks after the war. But Winkler is himself a pretty shrewd financier, who knows more about these things than the bureaucracy of the Finance Ministry. He has already found a way out that is extraordinarily clever and original and will no doubt bring him success.

[Dr. Hermann Winkler, a German industrialist, had been a democratic member of the Prussian diet, but in 1933 became a Nazi. He assisted in the Nazification of German newspapers, acting as a go-between for the publishers and the Propaganda Ministry. Later Goebbels entrusted him with many of the financial deals of his ministry, especially those having to do with the motion-picture industry which, it will be remembered, was taken over entirely by Goebbels on behalf of the Reich. See the diary of January 22, 1942. As this entry shows, Goebbels did not hesitate to cheat even the Finance Ministry when it was a question of saving his "empire."]

April 2, 1942

Fortunately the destruction of works of art in Luebeck has not quite reached the proportions we at first feared. St. Mary's Church has been destroyed completely, and with it also the great organ, the altars, and the famous painting, "Dance of Death." Only the little tabernacle and two paintings by Overbeck were salvaged from this church. Nothing could be saved from St. Peter's Church. The Cathedral has been destroyed; only the altar by Memling and the "Cross of Triumph" by Bern Notker could be saved. St. Jacob's Church, St. Catherine's Church, and St. Ann's Museum are unharmed, and the City Library and the Archives have been saved. The Hospital of the Holy Ghost also remained unscathed. The Burg Gate and the Holsten Gate are still standing. St. Aegidia Church is only slightly damaged. The most important big patrician houses have all been destroyed.

[Prewar Luebeck, especially the medieval central part, was one of the most interesting cities in northern Germany. It abounded in priceless artistic and historical monuments. Its wealth stemmed from the time of the Hanseatic League.]

We received a secret report from the United States to the effect that eyewitnesses claim an extraordinarily bad situation obtains in the Soviet Union. Stalin is hardly able to master the food problem. Morale has sunk far below zero. The Soviet system can continue to maintain itself only by terrorism. I don't believe this report is too pessimistic.

Roosevelt has thought up a new Christian propaganda for the Easter holidays. He compares the road of the vanquished peoples in Europe to the road to Golgotha, and claims that he of all people has been divinely ordained to protect Christianity against neo-paganism—this, of course, with the aid of the exceptionally Christian Soviets, who have distinguished themselves in the past by their religious fanaticism!

We must not place too great hopes on developments in France. I consider the French people sick and worm-eaten. Nothing noteworthy in the way of positive contributions for the reconstruction of Europe is to be expected from them. . . . Once more it has been proven that the Fuehrer's policy toward France has been absolutely right. One must put the Frenchmen on ice. As soon as one flatters them, they misinterpret it. The more you keep them on tenterhooks, the sooner they are inclined to come down a peg.

April 3, 1942

Observers in the United States report that there isn't the slightest enthusiasm for the war. Roosevelt has not succeeded in interesting the broad masses at all. . . . Roosevelt announced at a press conference that he intended to engender enthusiasm by military parades. He might just as well have elephants march through the streets.

The Ministry of Justice is extremely nonplused and offended that Freisler is to be eliminated from conducting the Grynzpan trial and that Thierack is to take his place. Gutterer so informed Schlegelberger, who immediately protested to the Fuehrer. But the Fuehrer's answer was "no." The Fuehrer stuck to his decision. This means we shall be in charge of the political side of the trial while Thierack is responsible for the legal. In normal times, of course, the two undersecretaries of the Ministry of Justice would have to resign in view of such a decision. It would be most desirable that they did, but they aren't thinking of it.

[Roland Freisler, a former Communist turned Nazi, developed into a pedantic bureaucrat as long as he held the office of undersecretary in the Ministry of Justice. That's why Hitler declined to appoint him special judge for the trial of Herschel Grynzpan, who in Paris shot and killed Herr vom Rath of the German Embassy (see diary entry of February 11, 1942). Instead, Hitler appointed Otto Georg Thierack, president of the star chamber People's Court (*Volksgerichtshof*). Later Thierack was appointed Minister of Justice (see March 20, 1942) and Freisler became president of the People's Court. He now became extremely radical again and not only railroaded his victims without even listening to them, but shouted and ranted at them in the most undignified manner. A newsreel of his behavior in court was shown in Nuremberg during the war crimes trial of major Nazis and generally disgusted the listeners from many countries who attended.]

April 4, 1942

The English claim they dropped one thousand-pound bombs on Luebeck. The damage done there is indeed enormous. I am shown a newsreel of the destruction. It is horrible. One can well imagine how such an awful bombardment affects the population. Thank God, it is a case of North German population, which, on the whole, is much tougher than the South German or the Southeast German population.

Nevertheless it can't be overlooked that English air raids have increased in scope and importance, and that if they can be continued for weeks along these lines, they might quite conceivably have a demoralizing effect on the German population.

April 5, 1942

The Foreign Office still opposes publishing an item about the torpedoing of Norwegian ships that tried to go from Sweden to England. The Foreign Office claims several things are cooking with Sweden. Negotiations are under way whose effect will be to make Swedish policy bind itself one way or the other. The Swedes seriously intend to resist actively in the event of a British attack on Sweden. It remains to be seen whether they will actually do it. In any case they are today trying to give us that impression. Consequently it is extraordinarily difficult to report officially on the insolence inherent in the fact that the Swedes want to surrender the Norwegian ships under their control to the English.

I now consider it necessary to let the German public know the reasons for the daily and nightly air raids on Malta. Otherwise they will get the wrong impression from the reports about them recurring in every OKW communiqué. We should frankly tell the German people that we aren't interested in conquering Malta, but merely in interfering as far as possible with the supply lines for North Africa. And that's the truth too.

[German radio listeners used to poke fun at the daily-recurring sentence in the military communiqué, "Malta was attacked from the air." No damage was ever indicated, and no explanation offered why the seemingly resultless bombardments continued.]

Dorothy Thompson delivered an absolutely insane speech against Hitler. It is humiliating and irritating that such foolish wenches [*so dumme Frauenzimmer*], whose brains can consist only of straw, have the right to speak at all in public against a historic figure of the greatness of the Fuehrer.

[Dorothy Thompson was a thorn in the flesh of the Nazis as she was one of very few American columnists who really knew Germany and the German language and mentality. She had studied at Vienna University and was chief of the Central European Service of the Philadelphia *Ledger* and New York *Evening Post*, with headquarters at Berlin, from 1924–28.]

I am having lots of work preparing the Grynzpan trial. The Ministry of Justice has deemed it proper to furnish the defendant, the Jew Grynzpan, the argument of Article 175. [See note under February 25, 1942.] Grynzpan until now had always claimed, and rightly so, that he had not even known the Counsellor of Legation whom he shot. Now there is in existence some sort of anonymous letter by a Jewish refugee, which leaves open the likelihood of homosexual intercourse between Grynzpan and vom Rath. It is an absurd, typically Jewish claim. The Ministry of Justice, however, did not hesitate to incorporate this claim in the indictment and to send the indictment to the defendant.

This shows again how foolishly our legal experts have acted in this case, and how shortsighted it is to entrust any political matter whatsoever to the jurists.

I proposed to the Fuehrer that he forbid visits of German soldiers to the Pope. This series of visits has really become a public danger. The Pope, of course, embraces every opportunity to receive German soldiers in order to impress them with the whole pomp of the Vatican's ceremony. Besides, the present Pope is clever enough to use these things for obvious propaganda. He speaks German fluently and his entire bearing naturally creates the desired impression with naïve soldiers, and especially officers. That's why this evil must be stopped.

My campaign against blackmarketeering is also very favorably received by the people. Here, too, the people demand that the proclamation of principles be brought into agreement with the behavior of the politically prominent.

[This is a jibe at such men as Goering, Frick, many of the Gauleiters, Raeder, Brauchitsch, and others who were living, or at least reported to be living, a life of luxury (chiefly due to black marketeering) while the whole nation was constantly pulling its belt tighter. Goebbels loved to pose as the friend of the common man, but in reality lived quite as well as other topnotchers of the regime.]

April 6, 1942

The propaganda by Bose, which is conducted and guided from here, is gradually getting on the nerves of the British. In their radio broadcasts they blame me especially for Bose's activity. It is evident that the English—and their history proves it—always look for a scapegoat when their imperial policies, founded as they are on cynicism and brutality, encounter difficulties. The Indians would be complete idiots if they allowed themselves to be influenced by empty British phrases. . . .

Gandhi has broken into print. He published an interview against British exploitation, but can offer nothing as a countermeasure except passive resistance, which naturally can't cause the English much trouble. Gandhi's policies have thus far brought nothing but misfortune to India. Had these four hundred and fifty millions of people been led by an energetic nationalist, Indian politics, and especially the Indian freedom movement, would undoubtedly be further along than they are today.

[Mahatma Mohandas K. Gandhi, born, 1869, devoted his life to achieving the independence of India, chiefly by passive resistance.]

The Americans and the British are trying hard to interpret my last article as a sign that I am alarmed about morale inside Germany. But they are not having much luck with it as far as the public is concerned. . . . Nations which survived World War I and are now at the point of pulling through the second don't care at all for diplomatic intrigues and misleading propaganda. They want to know exactly what's what and what's likely to be. That's the main reason why my articles are so fascinating both for the German and the international readers. They state bluntly what we mean and talk a language that isn't otherwise customary in political circles. All the more does such language have a right to be heard.

With Lieutenant Colonel Martin, who visited me for two days in my country home, I canvassed the possibilities of camouflaging our impending offensive. Unfortunately the eyes of all international observers are turned in the direction of the southern sector of our Eastern Front, in other words, to the very point where the first offensive action is to take place. The task of German propaganda will therefore consist of focusing international attention on either the central or northern front. It remains to be seen what chances we shall have for so doing. We have already published a number of articles in military periodicals pointing out that possession of the capital is always the determining factor in war, but the opposition thus far hasn't bitten.

I am now going to try to send Dr. Kriegk of the *Nachtausgabe*, a journalist well known in Germany, to the central Eastern Front for a

week and after that dispatch him to Portugal with exact instructions.
He is there to attempt to divert attention into another direction by
spreading rumors. I don't know yet whether he will succeed, but in
any case Kriegk is talkative enough to carry out a task of this kind with
a certain degree of virtuosity.

[Dr. Otto Kriegk, political commentator for Alfred Hugenberg's daily *Nachtaus-*
gabe (*Night Edition*), a boulevard sheet with conservative tendencies, was a
loud-mouthed, boisterous, bulky newsman whom most American correspondents
in Berlin knew but did not take seriously. He had been political adviser to Hugenberg when the latter was still chairman of the German-National party, but became an ardent Nazi after 1933. The sequel to this Goebbels venture in propaganda is recorded in the entries for May 20 and 21, 1942.]

April 7, 1942

From Lisbon we had news via Sweden that the internal situation in
the Soviet Union is desperate. Hunger is rampant to a degree that the
human imagination cannot conceive. If Stalin doesn't soon achieve
military successes on a huge scale, the Soviet system is doomed to collapse.

While I don't judge the situation to be so dramatic as it is here represented, there is no doubt some truth to this analysis.

April 8, 1942

I complained to the OKW about the OKM's exceptionally poor reporting on the British attack on St. Nazaire. The OKM missed the bus
here completely. . . . The OKM is laying down its own independent
news policy. Only Raeder knows everything that is happening within
the Navy. The Fuehrer gets to know only part of it and others only a
small part. That won't do. I am going to report on this to the Fuehrer
with the approval of the OKW.

[Grand Admiral Erich Raeder, born April 24, 1876, was a tar of the old school.
He did not believe in new-fangled publicity methods of the sort Goebbels favored.
Raeder received a sentence of life imprisonment from the International Military
Tribunal at Nuremberg in 1945.
The OKM (*Oberkommando der Marine*) was the Supreme Command of the
Navy.]

The news policy of the Foreign Office also leaves much to be desired. You can't base news policies on diplomatic viewpoints. It is
simply unbearable that one's own people alone in all the world know
nothing about the success of military undertakings carried out by their
soldiers. A drastic example of this is the sinking of Norwegian ships

in the service of the English, which left Sweden and had a great number torpedoed in the Skagerrak. The Foreign Office still sits on this news and won't even condescend to publish a perfectly neutral item. Meanwhile even the last Bantu Negro knows what really happened. The German people alone are not in the know. By that sort of policy we are fairly compelling the German public to listen to foreign and enemy broadcasts!

[Listening to foreign radio stations was punishable by death.]

I have received a report by General von Falkenhausen concerning conditions in Belgium. . . . In my opinion Falkenhausen is not quite up to his tasks. What we need there is an energetic and uncompromising National Socialist. The politico-military situation, however, for the moment forbids the conversion of the military administration of Belgium into a civilian commissariat.

[General Alexander von Falkenhausen, born, 1878, was Military Commander of Belgium, but was dismissed by Hitler in 1944. He was arrested by the Gestapo after the July 20, 1944, attempt on the Fuehrer's life, but was liberated at the end of the war. Until 1938 he had been military adviser to Generalissimo Chiang Kai-shek.]

[Lord] Halifax as former Viceroy of India spoke on the Indian question at a dinner in New York. He took up the various proposals hitherto made for the solution of this problem, turned against the parties, declared that there was hardly a possibility of solution left, and voiced the opinion that England should establish direct connection with the Indian people, bypassing the parties. As is customary with him, he clothed this rigorous and brutal plan in humane and religious phrases. It is quite clear what he intends. He wants to subdue the Indian people and at the same time make himself the mouthpiece for the Indian cause.

The Japanese Ambassador, who is about to go from Kuibyshev to Japan on leave, has given an interview about conditions in the Soviet Union. The picture drawn by him seems to be quite true. He declared that the Russians are living under the most primitive conditions, are feeding solely on bread and pickles, but are nevertheless remaining firm and tough and confident of victory. All difficulties of daily life were overcome with the centuries-old philosophy of *nichevo*.

[The name of the Japanese Ambassador to Russia was General Yoshitsugu Tatekawa, born, 1880, and educated at the Japanese Military Staff College. In 1932 he had been military representative at the League of Nations in Geneva. He had also been chief of staff of the Japanese General Staff Office.]

According to a report by Lippert, a pretty desperate situation exists in Greece. The food situation has developed into a real catastrophe. Untold men and women are dying of hunger. The Italians have taken rigorous possession of the country and the Germans are only running about as fifth wheels to the cart. We are surely making great sacrifices for the Axis friendship of our southern ally. The Greeks can hardly understand why we Germans are so liberal. They meet the Italians with open disgust and even contempt, and are more and more disposed to transfer that contempt also to us as the allies of the Italians. We are in no position at present to make any moral conquests in Greece.

[Julius Lippert was formerly mayor of Berlin but had a row with Albert Speer about Berlin's building program and was deposed by Hitler. Later he became an officer in the Army.]

Prostitution in Berlin is causing us many a headache these days. During a raid we found that 15 per cent of all women arrested had VD, most of them even syphilis. We must certainly do something now about it. In the long run we cannot possibly avoid setting up a "red-light district" in the Reich capital similar to those in Hamburg, Nuremberg, and other large cities. You simply cannot organize and administer a city of four millions in accordance with conceptions of bourgeois morals.

I spend the evening making a first draft of my speech for the Fuehrer's birthday. I work on it with special care, because I believe it will be especially important this year. . . . It will surely help to strengthen love and confidence in the Fuehrer throughout the entire nation.

The Fuehrer is and always will be the central and focal point of our national life. Around him are centered the hopes of the entire people. As long as he is in our midst in good health, nobody need worry about Germany's fate.

[Hitler was born April 20, 1889, at Braunau-on-the-Inn, Austria.]

April 9, 1942

American Secretary of the Navy Knox who, it will be remembered, before the outbreak of the conflict opened his trap rather widely [*der ja das Maul ein bischen sehr voll nahm*], has now suddenly become extraordinarily reserved and modest. In general one can note that the Americans are trying hard gradually to prepare their people for the seriousness of the war and the consequences resulting therefrom.

Public opinion in the United States has become essentially more skeptical. The masses of the people have become greatly disillusioned.

I find it necessary to start a new campaign for greater politeness in public life. Our propaganda thus far has not had the desired result. On the streets, in the busses and streetcars, in restaurants and theaters, extremely coarse language [*ein Sauherdenton*] has gradually become a habit. It jars the nerves and cannot be tolerated any longer.

April 11, 1942

A black day for the enemy side. The Americans must admit they have evacuated Bataan. They now have nothing more to defend in the Philippines except Corregidor. . . .

The whole United States is in a dither. The hero's halo they gave MacArthur is fading. We are naturally going to seize upon this opportunity. This big shot, whom New York only a few days ago still tried to sell as the outstanding genius of the century, will now be unmasked completely by our propaganda.

I have received confidential information to the effect that the Pope has appealed to the Spanish bishops under all circumstances to see to it that Spain stays out of the war. He supports his argument with humanitarian phrases. In reality he thereby gives expression to his enmity for the Axis. It is clear nonsense for a spiritual and ecclesiastical power to meddle so much in political and military questions. After the war we shall have to see to it that as far as our country is concerned at least, such attempts at interference are rendered impossible.

A new, heavy conflict with the OKH has started. The successor of Colonel Hesse, Lieutenant Colonel Schwadtlo-Gesterding, had Lieutenant Mansfeldt, in private life public-relations man for I.G. Farben, deliver a speech to the PK men which is just about the limit. According to that speech, the army reporters may report only about the Army. If they see anything in any theater of war that has been done or carried out by some other element of the Wehrmacht, they are shamefully to be silent about it. . . .

[Colonel Hesse, Lieutenant Colonel Schwadtlo-Gesterding, and Lieutenant Mansfeldt were in the public-relations department of the Supreme Army Command.

PK stands for *Propaganda-Kompagnie*. The PKs (*Propaganda-Kompagnien*) were military companies of newsmen. That is, men with journalistic training, instead of becoming combat soldiers, were drafted as soldiers of the pen, and as such were under the same commands as the rest of the Army. They could be sent to any combat area on orders, unlike the American war correspondent who decided for himself to what extent he was willing to risk his life. Many publishing houses—most of them belonged to the Nazi party—welcomed the arrangement because they had to pay no salaries to the PKs and because civilian pensions were not due the widows and next of kin in the event of death. Such families merely received the regular military pensions.]

I shall now become energetic and demand that the OKH remove the two officers at once, because I have no intention of bothering with nitwits in the difficult task of collaboration between the Propaganda Ministry and the various departments of the Wehrmacht. I shall require that hereafter only specially selected propagandists be placed in key positions since otherwise I cannot guarantee success for our common endeavor.

April 12, 1942

Before his departure, he [Cripps] admonished the Indian population to hold itself in readiness for its fight for liberation—a thing that it will undoubtedly do, but in quite a different sense from what Mr. Cripps had in mind. . . .

Taken by and large, the failure of British diplomacy in India is an eloquent sign of the increasingly critical developments within the empire itself. As a result pessimism in England is growing from hour to hour. One even has the impression of a Parliamentary and Party "Daemmerung."

[This refers to the *Goetterdaemmerung*, or twilight of the gods, which plays such a role in Wagnerian opera.]

April 13, 1942

India is still in the forefront of the international situation. The British are now making an earnest attempt to unload the blame for the breakdown of negotiations on the Indians themselves. That is childish and ludicrous, but corresponds exactly to the British character, which never finds fault with itself but always with others. London declares pompously that the mission of Cripps has not been a failure. The gods only know where one can find any success.

In the United States they still haven't got over the heavy loss of matériel and prestige occasioned by the fall of Bataan. American pride and national sensitiveness received a heavy blow. The Jews acted somewhat prematurely when they inflated movie hero MacArthur into a great general. You don't get to be a great general by letting pedestrians wear your picture in their buttonholes—you have to achieve a couple of victories. MacArthur can hardly produce any.

The Fuehrer approved my speech for his birthday without a single change and feels very happy about it. He especially liked the parallel I drew with the critical times of the Seven Years' War. My article against the "War of Paper" also received his complete approval.

[The Seven Years' War was fought by Prussia and Austria from 1756-63. Prussia under Frederick the Great won, and Austria under Maria Theresa had to cede Silesia.]

I am of the opinion that existing evils within the Reich cannot be removed merely by propaganda and enlightenment. We must put more blood into our propaganda. I am going to try that for the first time in connection with our campaign for greater politeness. This propaganda venture is to be given real substance by calling upon the public to help actively. I shall offer prizes, for instance, for the most polite traffic officer, the most polite official at the ration centers, the most polite waiter, et cetera. I shall make larger sums of money available for this campaign. Possibly the first prize will be a present of 1,000 marks cash. The public itself is to be the judge. By this method I hope to achieve more tangible results than by mere exhortations.

April 14, 1942

In the near future we intend to offer the Eastern Front a large amount of mosquito netting. The mosquito plague was simply unbearable for the soldiers during the past summer. The OKW has already made some preparations along that line, but after my experiences in connection with supplying the troops with winter clothing I don't pay much attention to that. I am therefore having this matter looked into carefully, and if, as far as any human being can foresee, the measures undertaken are not sufficient, we shall help once again by a popular campaign. The Wehrmacht is not in a position to carry through such improvisations.

The Grynzpan trial is now to start in the middle of May. I still have a few preparations to make. Preparations by the Department of Justice are in some respects not very clever psychologically. Thus, for instance, the problem of homosexuality, which really isn't under discussion, has been drawn into the trial procedure, and the question of Jewish evacuations is also to be dealt with publicly. I think this is about as bungling as possible. . . . I shall see to it that these two sets of questions are not raised in court at all. All the other preparations were made in accordance with my directives and, if carried out, will undoubtedly make the trial a perfect success.

Gluttony in foreign missions is creating a lot of bad blood. Thus a reception was recently held in the Croatian Legation during which a thousand of our people prominent in state, Party, and Wehrmacht filled their bellies. This is such an unworthy and shameless behavior that something has to be done against it. I demanded of the Foreign Office that it reduce the rations for the diplomats, and especially cut the allocation of gasoline down drastically, since a situation has developed whereby certain diplomats get themselves "gasoline sweethearts" with whom they go on excursions on Sundays out into God's free nature. That naturally causes severe criticism by the public. The diplomats should adjust themselves to the general usages of the country. They have no right to live the lives of drones at our expense, especially not when they are diplomats representing powers that are on terms of friendship with us and are fighting the war on our side.

[Diplomats at the German capital were given much better gasoline, food, clothing, and liquor rations than German citizens.]

The Americans launched a naval building program via the neutral press that is nothing short of grotesque. But we know what we are to think of American statistics. The Americans are trying to impress world public opinion by their fantastic figures. The course of the war thus far has shown convincingly what there is behind it!

Churchill delivered his speech in the House in the course of the afternoon. . . . His language is exceptionally modest. After all, he has nothing outstanding to report in the way of successes, but plenty of setbacks, defeats, and reverses. Nevertheless I don't believe that English morale is in any way rotten at the core. The English can stand a lot of beating before they become rebellious and notice things. Churchill certainly is the mouthpiece of the English people in so far as his imperturbability and his bragging are concerned.

The Japanese Ambassador in Kuibyshev, Tatekawa, who has returned to Tokyo, has made very favorable statements about internal conditions within the Soviet Union. These reports have been written for a definite purpose and therefore don't offend us. The Japanese have a couple of things under their hat for the coming summer. They must create an alibi for themselves. They are following a very logical policy and diplomacy. That was proven by the example of America. One need have no doubts whatsoever concerning the fidelity of Japan toward her allies. If once in a while they make detours, this is done for tactical reasons only.

April 15, 1942

The Japanese Ambassador in Kuibyshev, Tatekawa, . . . made too much noise about conditions inside the Soviet Union. Our Ambassador Ott objected, and as a result the Japanese Foreign Office censured him and called him to order.

[The Nazis were always very quick in protesting through their envoys against anything that did not meet with their pleasure. In this case the task of making the protest devolved upon General Eugen Ott, the German Ambassador in Tokyo.]

Almost no hopes are entertained [by the United States] regarding Corregidor. The Americans, too, admit they can hold out for only a few days more. The situation there must be simply horrible. Meanwhile General MacArthur sits in Australia and issues fervent appeals to his troops—a thing that is possible only in America. With us stones would be thrown at a general of that sort.

Interrogations of English prisoners of war at St. Nazaire indicate that our propaganda in England has been more effective than we imagined. The English pay more attention, however, to news than to argument. I conclude from this that all our foreign-language broadcasts, but especially those beamed to England, must be changed fundamentally. Times are no longer suited for long discussions. Just as during the fight of the National Socialist movement against the Republic there was a stage when the handbill was no longer effective because it was outmoded, so there is a stage now when argumentation is no longer effective. I slant our foreign-language broadcasting services chiefly in the direction of news, but see to it that the proper tendency is mixed into the news items.

I have received an exhaustive report about internal conditions in Sweden. Sentiment for the Reich has decreased rather than improved. I believe the chief reason for this is our weak diplomacy. Of course it can't be denied that events in Norway are having considerable effect upon Swedish sentiment. The Church fight started by Terboven and Quisling seems as superfluous to me as a goiter.

The English intended establishing a connection with the eastern theater of war via Sweden. But the Swedes are determined to oppose by force of arms anybody who attacks their territory. At least that's what they say today. It would have been better if we had also taken Sweden during our campaign in the north. This state has no right to national existence anyway.

The situation in Vichy has now been clarified so far as to show that in all likelihood Laval will enter the government in a few days as Prime Minister. This is a tremendous advantage for us, and for that reason it causes alarm in London and in Washington. . . . In any case a France under Laval, even though this French politician is personally most unsympathetic, is far more acceptable than a France of *attentisme*, with which you never know where you are at.

[Pétain followed a policy of what the French call *attentisme*—something like the American "watchful waiting."]

Herr von Neurath visited me and told me how he is now living. He feels rather shelved at a time when he enjoys the best of health. His attitude toward the Fuehrer is most loyal. All in all Herr von Neurath is a gentleman, who has never been guilty of any incorrectness or disloyalty toward the Fuehrer. The next time I report to the Fuehrer I shall tell him about this visit. Maybe the Fuehrer will see a new possibility for making use of Herr von Neurath.

[Baron Konstantin von Neurath and especially his wife were exceedingly ambitious to play a top role. After Hitler deposed Von Neurath as Foreign Minister to make room for the more robust Joachim von Ribbentrop, Von Neurath accepted the post of Protector of Bohemia-Moravia. Here, too, he proved ineffective and was replaced by Reinhard Heydrich, "The Hangman." (See diary entry for February 15, 1942.) But apparently Von Neurath was still hankering after office.]

Viktor Lutze visited me and did a lot of complaining. He is an unfortunate character. Everywhere he offends, everywhere he criticizes and gripes. The work nearest at hand he doesn't do; instead he is busy with all sorts of nonsense that has no relation to the war at all. Everywhere he senses filth and treachery, everywhere he feels that his SA has been put in the shade, and that he, personally, is out in the cold. But meanwhile he arranges for meeting Gauleiter Wagner, whom we have fired, keeps up his personal contact with Brauchitsch, et cetera. I hardly think he can be helped.

Naturally I once more appealed most emphatically to him. He realizes that the course he is pursuing is the wrong one; but heaven alone knows how long the effect of my admonitions will last. It is too bad about this old, doughty Party comrade and disciple of the Fuehrer. He has got into the wrong hands, and doesn't possess sufficient intelligence and strength of character to withstand baleful suggestions. I shall keep him under further observation.

[Josef Wagner (1899–1945) was Gauleiter and governor of Silesia until 1942, when he was dismissed by Hitler. He was at that time also Price Commissioner. He was not regarded as radical enough by the Fuehrer. Wagner was executed early in 1945 for complicity in the plot to remove Hitler. Von Hassell speaks favorably of him in his *Diaries*. Wagner, incidentally, was the only former Gauleiter who was purged with thousands of others, chiefly Wehrmacht people and noblemen and their families, after the unsuccessful attempt on Hitler's life on July 20, 1944.]

April 16, 1942

Laval's appointment as Prime Minister is the principal theme of the Anglo-American press. Our enemies realize that important consequences may result from this change in the course of French politics. That's why Laval is being insulted and called the worst possible names. He is called the Quisling of France, traitor to the Anglo-American cause, and the like. Anger in the United States and England is very great.

Roosevelt delivered a speech in which he said the war was likely to last two or three years. Nevertheless he still believes firmly in victory. His arguments to prove it are very thin and without substance.

Easter transportation is described as nothing short of horrible. My decree had no real effect because the railway administration did everything possible to annul it quietly. Conditions in the trains simply baffled description. It is high time that the top man in the Transportation Ministry be changed. Old Mr. Dorpmueller has neither the technical nor personal qualifications to master the problems of our communications and transportation.

[Dr. Julius Dorpmueller, Minister of Communications and Transportation (*Reichsverkehrsminister*), was retained by Hitler even though he was not a Nazi, because of his unusual knowledge of railroading. It is therefore surprising for Goebbels to claim that Dorpmueller lacked the technical qualifications for his job. What probably irked Goebbels much more was the fact that a key position like this was not in the hands of a dyed-in-the-wool Party member.
Dorpmueller was a holdover from the Bruening and Papen cabinets. At private parties he often made fun of Nazi leaders. Early in the Nazi regime a gang of radical Nazis, at the instigation of Goebbels, made a protest march to Dorpmueller's offices, demanding his resignation. Hitler, however, stepped in and insisted on retaining his Transportation Minister, who, as head of the German railways, could boast of being the largest single employer of labor in Europe.]

April 17, 1942

Our arms and munitions situation is exceptionally strained. Undoubtedly, however, the same thing prevails on the other side. Nevertheless there is cause for some alarm. Unfortunately much was neglected on this sector. We took the matter of arms and munitions production far too lightly and now have to pay for it.

The United States has already cut off its charities for France. There are pious Christians for you! They sing anthems when they want to subjugate small peoples, but the moment something doesn't quite suit them they throw their Christianity and their Bible overboard, and revert to their aboriginal instincts of a hyena-like greed for booty.

I had a long talk with the director of the Ministry of Justice, to whom I made clear that Justice has the task, especially during a war, to serve the leaders of the people and not vice versa. The Ministry of Justice regrets very much not having closer contact with the political leaders during the war, especially with the Fuehrer. I indicated my willingness to establish this contact. I shall now direct my attention more to the administration of law. Criticism alone won't change anything; one must attempt to get along with the existing forces, as they cannot be changed anyway. . . . In any case the gentlemen of the Ministry of Justice are quite willing and ready to follow a legal course that will tie them in more with the people; they must merely be told what is wanted, and I shall certainly do this aplenty.

[By a "legal course that will tie them in more with the people" Goebbels really means mob justice. He consistently advocated a justice based on the "healthy common sense" (*gesunden Menschenverstand*) of the people. Instigated by Party headquarters, Nazis would often march to a courthouse and demand "justice."]

I also had a long talk with Dr. Ley. He reported about his impressions on sentiment among the people and showed he had pretty strong illusions of which I cured him effectively. Dr. Ley hasn't the faintest inkling of what's happening among the people, although he is constantly on the go traveling around among plants and factories. He pursues a policy of self-deception which, if it became general, would someday bitterly avenge itself. I consider it my duty to open his eyes, and do this very successfully.

He also told me a lot of details about Party happenings, especially the case of the demoted Gauleiter Josef Wagner, which was handled entirely wrong when it reached the Reich Investigation and Arbitration Committee. Reich Justice Buch judges matters of this kind accord-

ing to purely juridical viewpoints. This, however, was an eminently
political question. No wonder the Fuehrer was in a rage about the
verdict and expressed his determination not to take it into account in
any way! That's right. Why should the Fuehrer, as the Party's leader
of the German people, bother about the Investigation and Arbitration
Committee! Judges are everywhere the same, whether they are active
in the state or in Party life! A jurist seems predestined to falsify and
channel in the wrong direction every case that is perfectly clear and
open and shut.

[The Reich Investigation and Arbitration Committee was an organization of
the Party and handled cases of Party members only. It had a presiding judge,
Walter Buch, like any other court. Ordinarily Hitler respected its findings, but not
in the case of Gauleiter Wagner, whose exact offense is not revealed by Goebbels. Goebbels had no respect for law of any kind, as this day's entry clearly
shows.]

April 18, 1942

The guessing game in London and Washington concerning the pending appointment of Laval continues. Laval is developing into the most
sensational and mysterious personality of present-day international
politics. The enemy powers worry more and more about him. They
already have visions of the French Fleet operating in the Mediterranean with the Italian and the German fleets. They see Malta and
Alexandria lost, et cetera. Also, the appointment of Rundstedt as supreme commander in the West elicits great interest. It has become
known to the enemy only now.

[The name of Field Marshal Gerd von Rundstedt will always be associated
with the "Battle of the Bulge," also known as the "Rundstedt offensive," in December 1944. It was one of the greatest surprise movements of World War II.
In an interview with American and British war correspondents in May 1945, the
captured field marshal denied that he was the author of the offensive. He said
he acted on higher orders and tried to make the best of it. Lack of gasoline for
the tanks, he said, was one principal reason for its collapse.]

I received a report written by the former United States Ambassador
in Moscow Davies, entitled, "What we did not know about Russia."
This report is extraordinarily favorable to the Soviet Union. Davies
has a very high opinion of the ability of the Bolsheviks to resist. The
Bolshevik leaders, headed by Stalin, are described as true friends of the
people. Obviously Potemkin villages were shown this gentleman.

[Joseph E. Davies, former chairman of the United States Federal Trade Commission, was Ambassador to the U.S.S.R. from 1936–38, from where he was transferred
to Belgium, and later to the State Department. At this time he was charged with

carrying a special letter to Stalin from President Roosevelt. This episode was dramatized in the much-discussed motion picture, *Mission to Moscow*.

The expression, "to show a Potemkin village," refers to an episode during the reign of Czarina Catherine II. When she visited the Crimea in 1787, the governor general for the southern Russian provinces, Prince Gregory Potemkin, had fake villages, complete with happy dancing villagers, erected along the way, thereby greatly impressing the Empress as to his achievements.]

The *Daily Express* has published a report on sentiment in the United States. According to it, people in the United States are at present anything but friendly to England. England is blamed for having let the United States slide into this war. The British correspondent states with resignation that one can hardly discover a single friend of England in the United States. I believe, on the whole, that is true. The Americans will be hopping mad at the British who concocted this soup and now ask the Americans to eat it. I am taking no notice in the German propaganda of these controversies between England and America. They should develop of themselves.

Magda [Goebbels] visited a hospital in the course of the afternoon. Unfortunately conditions in this hospital are none too good. The head physician seems not to be able to handle the wounded right, so their morale is pretty low. I am going to take a hand there and see that things are changed. The wounded have a right to proper treatment not only in a physical but also a psychological way.

April 19, 1942

At the northern end of the central Eastern Front we have noted a curious Bolshevik loud-speaker propaganda: The Bolsheviks announced that they would attack in four days. Once before the enemy made known his intentions in a similar manner and then actually launched the attack. One just doesn't know what to make of this queer conception of propaganda. For the enemy the net result was that his losses were all the greater.

Lieutenant Colonel Martin reported information reaching him from officer levels on the Eastern Front. It appears that my articles in the *Reich* are at present the most desired material for discussion on the entire front. Officers and soldiers agree that my articles point up the situation with rare realism and that the impression is as though I were there among the soldiers to record their sentiments so accurately and clearly. This is very encouraging proof to me of the close contact existing between our ministry and the front. It shows that we are not surrounded by a Chinese wall but, on the contrary, know exactly what's what, where the shoe pinches our soldiers, and what must be said to them so that they won't lose confidence in the leadership of the Reich and the state.

From the interior of the country I have received similar reports. It fills one with joy at so critical a time still to have the ear of the people.

Americans are insolent toward the French. They declare that Leahy will be withdrawn for good. [Sumner] Welles has handed the press representatives a communiqué that fairly bristles with insults and threatens the French in so provocative a manner that he himself must realize only little can be achieved thereby. The Frenchmen would have to be real eunuchs if they even considered such hold-up threats.

[Admiral Wm. D. Leahy was at that time American Ambassador to the Vichy Government.]

A merry fight has broken out in Australia about MacArthur's jurisdiction. The Americans would like to give him the supreme command without any strings attached, but the Australians don't seem very much inclined to approve. It appears they have seen through this American general with his somewhat unmilitary propaganda methods. Anyway, the political and military prestige of the Americans has sunk very low. You just can't conduct war with nice words alone. You must be able to record victories, and the Americans at present have exceptionally little to offer.

I had a little set-to with Gauleiter Buerckel who is again trying to push his plan for creating a new cultural office and not to place it under the jurisdiction of the Reich propaganda office. I won't permit that. Such a procedure is absolutely senseless, especially now in wartime, when there is such a chronic lack of man power.

[Joseph Buerckel was Gauleiter for the Saar region, which the Nazis renamed Gau Westmark.]

Mutschmann is having a fight with the mayor of Dresden, who is pursuing plans of his own about the theater. I am going to order him and Mayor Nieland to come to me and will give both a piece of my mind.

[Martin Mutschmann was Gauleiter of Saxony.]

Thank God, it now develops that the OKH has made proper preparations for mosquito netting and scarves for the coming summer period in the East. At least in this matter they have learned something from their failures last winter.

April 20, 1942

All signs indicate that the American public is extremely disappointed at the course of the war thus far. It had expected much more from what Mr. Knox advertised a few months ago as the "beginning of the shooting war." The Americans are therefore bragging about millions of soldiers whom they are training by all rules of the book for every theater of war. It would be better if some tens of thousands of these soldiers were already in the theaters of war where the war is actually being waged, and not on alleged training fields where you merely practice playing at war.

The French Cabinet shift still elicits great interest in the world. We continue to maintain reservations. The Americans have come somewhat to their senses. They are going to leave Leahy in Vichy after all. The reason assigned is that his wife has fallen ill. Plutocratic governments must have an excuse for everything; be it ever so rotten, it is advanced anyway.

[As a matter of fact Admiral Leahy's wife was gravely ill at the time and died soon thereafter. The admiral returned to America June 1, 1942.]

The most recent act of sabotage [in France] against a German military train which resulted in several deaths will be punished with severe reprisals. The number of people to be shot will be doubled, and over a thousand Communists and Jews will be put into freight cars and shipped East. There they will soon cease to see any fun in disturbing Germany's policies for order in Europe.

Gandhi gave an interview in which he once again urged non-resistance. He is a fool whose policies seem merely calculated to drag India further and further into misfortune.

The birthday of the Fuehrer . . . was celebrated in the late afternoon by an impressive demonstration in Berlin Philharmonic Hall. All who have rank or power in the state, the Party, and the Wehrmacht, were assembled there. The remainder of Philharmonic Hall was reserved for soldiers, the wounded, and munitions workers. It was a very dignified and solemn occasion. The celebration began with the air from the suite in D-Major by Bach. My speech . . . met with great approval. . . .

In the evening Goering, too, issued a birthday proclamation to the German people in which he paid tribute to the personality of the Fuehrer in very dignified language.

Unfortunately my health at present is none too good. The eczema caused by nerves is giving me a good deal of trouble. I shall have to relax for two or three weeks to recover.

How happy we may all be that winter is now finally over! The worst worries it brought are now past. That doesn't mean that we are without worries, but the sun is brightening up the approaches sufficiently so that we can again consider where we are standing and whither we are going. Soon we shall have to move into new land in our military activity. For a moment we shrink back and once more calculate the dangers and risks involved. But experience teaches that once the first step—which is always the hardest—has been taken, the second and third follow automatically and after that the march into the future develops automatically.

April 21, 1942

The military commander in France has adopted more stringent measures on account of the railway sabotage of the sixteenth instant. Thirty hostages (Jews and persons close to the perpetrators) are to be shot instead of the twenty originally intended. If the perpetrators are not caught within three days, an additional eighty are to be shot and a thousand Jews and Communists (instead of the five hundred originally intended) are to be deported eastward.

The English are at present in a very difficult position from a military viewpoint. The Bolsheviks are demanding more of them than they are at present ready or even able to give. So they must do a lot of bragging. They thereby cause us a certain embarrassment since we consider it more purposeful not to deny the crazily exaggerated successes of the British air raids. The German people, of course, are quite aware of the "efficacy" of these air attacks. When, for example, the English claim they destroyed and ruined the Ruhr region almost completely, everybody knows this is a stupid and obvious lie with which to impress the Bolsheviks. When, on the other hand, our exceedingly heavy air raids on Malta are represented by the English as fun for the Maltese population, that merely bears evidence to the cynicism with which the London plutocrats fight their war.

We have received the report of a deserter from Leningrad, according to which conditions there must be simply catastrophic. Even though there may be some exaggerations, it seems, nevertheless, that the food situation in this city of millions cries to high heaven. The deserter claimed more than a million people had already died of hunger. That may not be true, but nevertheless tens and hundreds of thousands of human beings are living there in direst and most unbearable distress. The deserter claimed that a great part of the population was now feeding on so-called human flesh jelly made of the flesh of dead or fallen citizens and soldiers. The whole report is so revolting that it makes one's stomach turn to read it.

April 22, 1942

The DeGaullists and Communists claim—and they aren't entirely wrong either—that Laval was involved in former French corruption scandals and is not qualified to represent France in the New Europe. But that is a matter of indifference to us. We could hardly find a better man than Laval for our policies. . . . We shall probably have to pay Laval something in case he fulfills the hopes we placed in him. But first it is up to him to show what he can do.

During the night a new and fatal attempt was made on the life of a German soldier in Paris. The reprisals are very severe. Ten hostages are shot, five hundred Communists, DeGaullists and Jews are shipped to an eastern labor camp, the curfew hour is set much earlier, and theaters, places of amusement, and movie houses are closed altogether. I am insistent that at last we publish in advance the names of all hostages who are to be shot (*die schussreif sind*). By doing so we will at least ensure that the relatives and friends who usually stem from the same circles as the perpetrators get busy and try at least to find the perpetrator. The military commander in Paris is quite ready to adopt my suggestion. For the present, however, he has no hostages, and will first have to look around for some.

Marshall and Hopkins, who have returned to the United States, fairly outdo each other bragging. They issue insane figures about production, and claim that within three months activities will have begun on the continent. The only thing they were still worried about was the scarcity of shipping space. I see in these Anglo-American threats nothing but an attempt to frighten us. By telling such tall tales they would like to induce us to leave as many troops as possible in the West. They think they are thereby making an effective contribution to the Bolshevik war. That, of course, is a calculation which they made without consulting us. We shall determine for ourselves what we need for the

West; indeed the Fuehrer has already determined this long since. No changes need be made in this respect. Enough is concentrated there to beat back immediately any Anglo-American attempts to gain a foothold on the continent.

Willkie wants to take control of the Republican party. For the present he has been given the bum's rush [*Vorlaeufig wird er mit Glanz und Glorie abgeblitzt*]. No doubt this corruptible character has lost all credit with the Republican voters.

[The fact that Wendell Willkie stemmed from German origins but nevertheless fought the Nazis meant but one thing to a man of Goebbels's character: Willkie must be a "corruptible character" whom the Allies bought!]

April 23, 1942

Neutral reporters indicate that London is full of rumors about invasions in both directions. Churchill is certainly thinking up measures of desperation in order to stir up the English public.

All reports from the United States agree that there isn't a spark of enthusiasm for war discernible there. That explains why Willkie in the Republican committee meeting demanded a more aggressive policy.

We have received amazing reports about conditions in Kuibyshev. Hell has broken loose there. One can understand, of course, that Stalin is having most serious difficulties about food. The loss of the Ukraine cannot be dismissed simply with a wave of the hand. While the disaster resulting from this loss will have its full impact only later, it is nevertheless inescapable.

It is reported from the United States that the Americans have declared our patents void [*fuer vogelfrei erklaert haben*]. That fits their mentality exactly. I have the impression anyway that the Americans participate in a European war every quarter century in order to be able to take for themselves as cheaply and easily as possible whatever cultural work has been done in Europe. The American continent is hardly in a position to bring forth anything of its own in the cultural realm. It is dependent upon imports from Europe, and as the Americans are so crazy about money they naturally like to take possession of the results of our creative and inventive labors as far as possible without paying for them.

The Metropolitan Opera has been closed. And that happens in a country that has only a single opera and whose leadership is insolent enough to wage war on behalf of a European culture allegedly threatened by us! It surely is a crazy world in which we are living.

That a man like Willkie today has the possibility in America of inciting to war even more violently than Roosevelt is a further sign of the moral decadence of America. I suppose it is chiefly due to Jewish leadership.

Former Democratic Reichstag Deputy Lemmer, who is now a foreign correspondent in Berlin, accompanied Oshima on a trip to the southeast. He gave us a detailed report from which we gather that Oshima spoke extremely eloquently in favor of the Axis policies. He behaved very cleverly and tactfully. He made no bones about his opinions, especially not about being pro-German, and thereby achieved great successes both in Bucharest and Budapest. At the moment Oshima is engaged in clearing away a large number of misunderstandings prevalent in Tokyo about conditions inside Germany. Oshima is really one of the most successful champions of Axis policies. A monument ought later to be erected in his honor in Germany. To this man we chiefly owe the fact that Japan took a hand in the present conflict.

[Ernst Lemmer during the Nazi regime was correspondent for Hungarian and Swiss newspapers. He is now co-chairman with Jakob Kaiser of the Christian-Democratic Union party of Berlin.]

My articles are described as being exceptionally effective. The article about the "War of Paper" has indeed wrought a veritable miracle. My definition of griping as the "bowel movement of the soul"—so I am informed by the SD service—has already become a household word in the entire nation.

Sweden and Switzerland still haven't formally joined the International Moving Picture Association. I am now having these two states boycotted by not supplying them with raw material. They will soon begin to feel the effects of their acting in such an aloof way.

Italian films in Germany are netting the Italians much more money than our German films net us in Italy. That fact is gradually causing us some foreign-exchange difficulties. The UFA has worked up a new export plan whereby we can gradually lay our hands on the entire Italian movie export in Europe. I hope the Italians fall for it.

[The UFA, Germany's largest motion-picture concern, is fully explained in a note in entry of March 5, 1943.]

Gauleiter Grohé of Cologne reported to me about the sentiment in the western provinces. He has taken over his new duties as Reich Defense Commissar and with them a great responsibility. Sentiment, he says, is absolutely consolidated and unified. Even the British air raids were unable to change the attitude of the population much. Grohé declared—and undoubtedly he is absolutely right in this—that the unfavorable reports on morale sent to Berlin do not correspond to the facts. People who wrote them did not have the ability to estimate sentiment correctly. His estimate of morale there just about corresponds to my own experience.

[Joseph Grohé, Gauleiter of Cologne, was a loud-mouthed Old Guard Nazi who placarded all Cologne only a few days before the victorious entry of the American troops with posters, admonishing every inhabitant of the ancient city on the Rhine to remain at his post, come what might. This appeal to heroism did not hinder him from leading the procession of Nazi officeholders who crossed the Rhine in a panic as the Americans drew near, thus abandoning the city to its fate and leaving it without an administration.]

April 24, 1942

The number of [Russian] deserters is on the increase although the Bolsheviks have heard from the population and escaped prisoners about executions, exposure to freezing, and bad treatment in the PW camps and are therefore afraid of German imprisonment. The Bolsheviks made clever use of such information. For instance, they gathered together soldiers who had returned from German imprisonment in schools where they were briefly indoctrinated and then divided among various troop elements to deliver lectures about the cruel treatment of prisoners by the Germans. Instructions have now been issued by us for better treatment of Soviet prisoners and for differentiation in the treatment of deserters and of real prisoners.

It is clear that Churchill is once again playing an extraordinarily insolent and impudent game. He can dare play it only with the English population. We would have to beware of doing anything like it to the German people. For instance, if in the autumn of 1940 we had advertised an invasion of the British Isles with so much noise and publicity even though it was not planned and could not be executed, without afterward starting it, that would have been nothing short of disastrous for our propaganda. The British can do a thing like that. The British people are like children and in addition have the limitless patience of sheep. They stand for having the invasion theme played again and again without compelling Churchill to make good.

Unfortunately we were somewhat behind the times in connection with the English undertaking at Boulogne. The reason, of course, was because the motorcycle rider who was to bring the report to the Army Group command point had an accident. As a result the English had a few hours' handicap, and experience shows that whoever speaks the first word to the world is always right.

[British Commandos on April 22 raided Boulogne, withdrawing after a two-hour foray. It was intended as a foray only, but the Goebbels Ministry tried to blow it up into a major defeat—the repressing of an attempted major invasion.]

I have received statistics about the number of Jews in the American radio, movies, and press. The percentage is truly terrifying. The Jews are 100 per cent in control of the film, and 90 to 95 per cent of the press and radio.

That fact explains the confused spiritual conduct of the war by the enemy. The Jews aren't always so clever as they would like themselves to believe. Whenever they are in danger they prove to be the stupidest devils.

To put a damper on public indignation Roosevelt has announced he intended to tax war profits very highly. On the other hand dividends are declared by the American munitions industry that simply make your hair stand on end. Our prognosis regarding this war is surely right. It is being conducted by the capitalists of all countries against the German social commonwealth. Were the latter—as is not to be presumed—to lose the war, the world would relapse into darkest social reaction.

Dorpmueller during his conversation with Gutterer was insolent about me. This old man, to whom we owe the fact that transport difficulties during the past winter almost got the better of us and who in 1933 was accepted into our regime only as a gesture of grace and charity, now dares to get fresh [pampig] shortly before reaching retirement age. But I shall finish him off all right.

The Fuehrer telephoned me from GHQ. He has now at last decided to deliver a speech, already planned for some time, before the Reichstag concerning the situation and all the conclusions which he must draw from it.

We deliberate as to which day would be most suitable for this session of the Reichstag and agree that it is to be called for 3 P.M. next Sunday.

I immediately made the necessary preparations and am very happy that the Fuehrer is now to come to Berlin for a few days. He gave me an exceptionally optimistic picture of the situation along the various fronts. He himself is in the best of health. Naturally we cannot go into details over the telephone because there is always the danger of someone listening in. I am always happy when the Fuehrer is in Berlin because I can then have several long talks with him.

The evening brought me a lot of work accumulated during the afternoon. All you need to do is to leave your desk a few hours and when you return you find it snowed under. I hope at the end of the coming week to be able to go to Lanke to relax for a short time. That is absolutely necessary. The condition of my health leaves much to be desired at present, and I believe I shall need health more than anything else during the difficult months ahead.

April 25, 1942

The Japanese Ambassador in Kuibyshev, General Tatekawa, now reports somewhat differently about internal conditions in the Soviet Union. It appears that rose-tinted spectacles were put on him in Kuibyshev and have now been taken off again in Tokyo.

In the United States they are continuing to bore at the British world empire. Roosevelt makes no bones about his appetite for India. The Indians in a bellicose declaration turn against these American attempts at penetration.

Our Admiralty has energetically denied the allegation that the air defense had not functioned properly during the last raid on Kiel, in the course of which several battleships and the *Monte Sarmiento* were seriously damaged. This denial by the naval command is not very convincing. The leadership of the German Navy isn't what it ought to be. There is too much praying going on there and too little work.

[This is a jibe at Grand Admiral Erich Raeder ("Papa Erich") who was a stanch Protestant.]

Field Marshal General von Mackensen again pleaded with me that I lift the ban on the Christian weekly, *The Best Friend*. I have sent repeated warnings to this weekly, but in view of the delicate character of this request I shall refer the whole matter to the Fuehrer at the next possible opportunity.

I had a long talk with Governor General Dr. Frank. He described conditions in the General Government. These are extremely complicated. Dr. Frank and his collaborators have succeeded absolutely in

balancing the budget of the General Government. He is already squeezing all sorts of money out of there. The food situation, too, has been
brought into equilibrium. . . . Frank is convinced that much more
could be got out of the General Government. Unfortunately we lack
man power everywhere for carrying out tasks like these. He must get
along with a minimum of help.

[Hanns Frank, Governor General of Occupied Poland, was another of Hitler's
earliest adherents. In fact, he defended Hitler during the numerous political trials
in which the Nazi chieftain became involved in the days of the Weimar Republic.
Hitler at first rewarded him by making him Reich's Leader of the Legal Profession
and president of a newly founded Academy of Law. While Governor General of
Poland he acted like an oriental potentate. He wrote some sixty volumes of diary
which proved most incriminating for him during the Nuremberg War Criminals
Trial. He was hanged for his atrocities committed on Jews.]

An article appeared in the *Nationalzeitung* of Bern [Switzerland]
written by the publisher . . . in which he pointed out that it is owing
chiefly to the arguments which I have kept repeating over and over
again that of all nations the German people has the most realistic attitude toward the war. He is quite right about that!

The inhabitants of the Ukraine were more than inclined at the beginning to regard the Fuehrer as the savior of Europe and to welcome
the German Wehrmacht most cordially. This attitude has changed
completely in the course of months. We have hit the Russians, and
especially the Ukrainians, too hard on the head with our manner of
dealing with them. A clout on the head is not always a convincing
argument—and that goes, too, for the Ukrainians and Russians.

In the course of the evening we had a little party at home and I had
an opportunity to speak at length and alone to the daughter of the
Duce and wife of the Italian Foreign Minister, Countess Ciano. In
contrast to previous visits, she impressed me this time as exceptionally
serious and earnest. She is extremely intelligent and when one talks
to her at length, she reveals herself as the real daughter of her father.
I explained our standpoint in appraising the over-all situation. From
her replies I gathered that the Italians are placing all their hopes in
the success of our impending summer offensive. As things stand, the
Italians cannot be expected to last through an endless continuation
of the war. Not that they have become tired of the war, but the difficulties and worries of war naturally grow at a much faster pace with
them than with us.

April 26, 1942

The British are publicizing their last air raid on Rostock in the grand manner. It has been, it must be admitted, pretty disastrous. The anti-aircraft didn't function properly so that the damage to public buildings was more extensive than in all other English air raids since Luebeck.

I sent a couple of robust journalists into occupied France with an assignment to give proper journalistic treatment to undertakings similar to that of Boulogne. Our reporting hitherto has been too dry and therefore could not compete with the flowery reports of Reuters. To impress the English you must represent an undertaking like that more like a sports event. You must not limit yourself to a mere rehearsal of facts but must complement the data by details to which the English and especially the Americans are known to be very susceptible.

It appears that British air raids on German cities are not taken so seriously by the Bolsheviks as the English would like. They have now chosen the expression "to luebeck" in place of the expression "to coventrize" invented by us. We are going to do everything possible to prevent this expression from being used in international terminology.

An English periodical, *The Empire Review*, has given expression to deepest pessimism on the part of the British Empire politicians. The low morale and even the actual collapse of the British world empire are described in so drastic a manner as to leave nothing to be desired. We ourselves could not give better expression to it. One almost has the impression that the writer of the article cleverly put together the ideas laid down in my *Reich* articles.

All Reich departments affected are now in favor of new regulations for the employment of labor from the East. In the long run we cannot solicit additional workers from the East if we treat them like animals within the Reich. They must, after all, receive enough food and clothing so that they will at least retain their capacity for work. Everybody is now in complete agreement about this.

The Fuehrer arrived in Berlin at noon. I immediately had a talk with him. He looks wonderfully healthy and is in the best spiritual and physical condition. However, he is in extremely bad humor about the poor anti-aircraft defense at Rostock which caused him no end of worry. The Luftwaffe wasn't adequately prepared and for this reason alone the damage to the Heinkel works was made possible.

[The Heinkel factories at Rostock and Travemuende were among the most important airplane producers in Germany.]

In addition, the Fuehrer is in a black rage about the escape of the French General Giraud, whom we still haven't succeeded in recapturing. He agrees that the press take a hand in the search for him, and offers a reward of 100,000 marks for his capture. Anybody who extends aid and protection to him is to be punished by death. Giraud is an extraordinarily dangerous French general.

[General Henri Giraud fooled the Germans twice. During World War I he managed to escape, and he duplicated this feat in 1942. He had been captured rather by accident in 1940, and had refused to give his word of honor that he would not try to make his getaway. After his escape he was appointed Commander in Chief of the French forces in North Africa. He and General de Gaulle did not get along very well, however, and he later resigned, delivering a farewell message to his troops on April 15, 1944. President Roosevelt and Prime Minister Churchill tried hard to bring about a reconciliation of the two French leaders, but failed.]

If he succeeds in fleeing to England, he will surely replace General de Gaulle, who is of weak spiritual and moral caliber. This would be very embarrassing, for the French émigré movement suffers at present, thank God, from not having any real head. General Giraud succeeded in escaping from German imprisonment once before, in World War I. He refused to give his word of honor not to escape. That ought to have been double reason for the guards to keep a most careful eye on him, but this seems not to have been the case, for otherwise he could not have escaped. That's what put the Fuehrer in such a bad temper, and rightly so. Let's hope that Giraud will yet be recaptured. One report via Vichy claims that he has already escaped over the Swiss border. This report, however, is as yet unconfirmed.

The building activities of the Navy do not meet with the approval of the Fuehrer. For a long time he has demanded that the "Strength-through-Joy" steamers be converted into airplane carriers. The Navy declined, claiming this was impossible, whereas the Americans and English are now carrying out such rebuilding with playful ease. Anyway, the Navy is about as unmodern as can be. It has no leadership of any caliber, and therefore does not exhaust the possibilities that present themselves. The inventions, too, that are offered the Navy are used only sparingly.

[The "Strength-through-Joy" movement was a subdivision of Dr. Robert Ley's German Labor Front. It tried to provide cheap summer and winter vacations for the industrial population, and built a series of one-class steamers for this purpose. There were regular excursions to Norway in summer, and to Madeira in the winter.]

In this connection the Fuehrer expressed the opinion that the state should buy up every invention even though it cannot be used for the moment. Inventions must never be sold to foreign countries. Bad experiences in World War I ought really to deter us from irresponsible treatment of German inventive genius. The tank was invented by a German-Austrian, but was then sold to England because there was no interest in it in Germany. The state must be much more careful in this matter. But just as you cannot expect a cow to lay eggs, so you cannot expect a bureaucrat to look after the interests of the state properly in such matters.

In judging our possibilities [for an offensive in the East] the Fuehrer is exceptionally optimistic. He has received reports about internal conditions in the Soviet Union that are said to be very depressing. They have nothing to eat, they live from hand to mouth, and the population feeds on bread and pickles. The equipment of the soldiers is said to be the poorest imaginable. There are heaps of examples and proofs of widespread eating of human flesh not only by the Bolshevik Army, but also by the civilian population. . . .

As things now stand the offensive can begin in the not-too-far-distant future. Possibly the weather god is anxious to make amends for some of the things he did to us.

An extended chapter of our talk is devoted by the Fuehrer to the vegetarian question. He believes more than ever that meat-eating is harmful to humanity. Of course he knows that during the war we cannot completely upset our food system. After the war, however, he intends to tackle this problem also. Maybe he is right. Certainly the arguments that he adduces in favor of his standpoint are very compelling. It is actually true that the great majority of humanity is living a vegetarian life and that the animals that live on plants have much greater powers of resistance than those that feed on meat. It is furthermore a very characteristic thing that the human being, generally speaking, eats only the meat of such animals as themselves feed on plants and not on such as feed on meat.

The dominating thought with the Fuehrer is his joy at the majestic coming of spring. He tells me that never before in all his life has he awaited it with such fervor. During the coming years he doesn't want to see any snow at all; snow has become physically repulsive to him—which I can well understand.

As regards the French the Fuehrer is of the opinion, now as before, that we shall never come to a friendly agreement with them. The talk about collaboration is intended for the moment only. He wants to see deeds first and not words. However the war ends, France will have to pay dearly, for she caused and started it. She is now being thrown back to her borders of A.D. 1500. This means that Burgundy will again become part of the Reich. We shall thereby win a province that so far as beauty and wealth are concerned compares more than favorably with any other German province.

[Hitler was one of those pan-Germans who regarded it as axiomatic that France and Germany were "hereditary enemies" (*Erbfeinde*) and who despised the Briand-Stresemann policy of *rapprochement*. The plan for annexing Burgundy will probably be news for most readers. This editor does not recall seeing any reference to it elsewhere.]

April 27, 1942

Last night the heaviest air attack hitherto launched again had the seaport of Rostock as its objective. Tremendous damage is reported. During the morning hours no exact estimate can be made, as all long-distance communication with Rostock has been interrupted. But reports from all sides agree that Gauleiter Hildebrandt initiated rescue measures in a model manner and is master of the situation. . . . Seventy per cent of all houses in the center of Rostock are said to have been destroyed.

[Friedrich Hildebrandt was Gauleiter for Mecklenburg.]

I now consider it absolutely essential that we continue with our rigorous reprisal raids. I also agree that not much is to be accomplished with raids on munitions centers. Like the English, we must attack centers of culture, especially such as have only little anti-aircraft. Such centers should be attacked two or three times in succession and leveled to the ground; then the English probably will no longer find pleasure in trying to frighten us by their terror attacks.

London continues to harp on the theme of invasion, but no longer with the same pep and enthusiasm as last week. Our reaction to it has already taken effect. The English have got cold feet. We continue to act insolently and arrogantly and thereby spoil for the English their intended effect of a war of nerves.

It is reported that the English have already stationed demolition squads in the Caucasus. That's exactly like them! They have proven themselves throughout the world as great destroyers of other people's property. History would lose its meaning if the Englishmen were not beaten decisively in this war.

At noon I had lunch with the Fuehrer. He is very angry about the latest English attack on Rostock. But he also gave me a few figures about our attack on Bath, according to which ours on Bath must have been much more extensive than the English raid on Rostock. The Fuehrer declared that he would repeat these raids night after night until the English were sick and tired of terror attacks. He shares my opinion absolutely that cultural centers, bathing resorts, and civilian cities must be attacked now; there the psychological effect is much stronger, and at the present moment psychological effect is the most important thing.

The munitions industry, he said, cannot be interfered with effectively by air raids. We learned that lesson during our raids on English armament centers in the autumn of 1940, and had a similar experience when, vice versa, the English attacked German munitions plants. Usually the prescribed targets are not hit; often the fliers unload their bombs on fields camouflaged as plants; and in both countries the armaments industry is so decentralized that the armament potential cannot really be interfered with. Our task now must be to reply to terror with terror and to respond to the attempted destruction of German centers of culture by razing English cultural shrines to the ground. That is now to be done on the biggest scale possible. The Fuehrer has already given orders for preparing and working out such a plan of attack on a long-range schedule. The English, I suppose, will have occasion to be surprised when this undertaking is launched on a big scale. There is no other way of bringing the English to their senses. They belong to a class of human beings with whom you can talk only after you have first knocked out their teeth.

In that connection the Fuehrer talked in favor of a much more radical conduct of the war and politics. That will also be the main theme of his speech before the Reichstag this afternoon. He complained bitterly that French General Giraud had succeeded in escaping. It was possible only because of the negligence and carelessness of the guards. The old reserve officers who are in command of the prisoner-of-war camps have a wrong feeling of humanitarianism [*eine falsche Humanitaetsduselei*] for which we are now paying dearly, as for example in this case. . . .

I talked to the Fuehrer once more in detail about the Jewish question. His attitude is unrelenting. He wants, under all circumstances, to push the Jews out of Europe. That is right. The Jews have brought so much misery to our continent that the severest punishment meted out to them is still too mild. . . .

Our military commander [in Paris], even since the new man has been installed there, is proving quite inadequate and especially unapproachable regarding my work. In the long run it makes me tired always to have to bother with the same problem, the ABC, so to speak, of propaganda, without finding the necessary understanding for it with the authorities in question. I shall now attain my goal via Jodl, who seems quite amenable about these problems. We will now simply have to do things by command that cannot be put through by friendly suggestion.

[Colonel General Alfred Jodl was Hitler's personal military Chief of Staff. When he was taken prisoner at Flensburg in May 1945, he carefully carried the last top-secret military orders of Adolf Hitler in his brief case, saying they should be preserved for posterity. This editor on reading them was convinced that they were the orders of a paranoiac. Jodl was hanged at Nuremberg as a major war criminal.]

The Reichstag convened at 3 P.M. It presented the familiar old picture. Many uniforms; also several wounded among the deputies. There was an atmosphere of great tension.

Shortly before the session began I got hold of Dorpmueller once more and gave him a good tongue-lashing. [*Ich kaufe mir noch einmal Dorpmueller und stauche ihn nach allen Regeln der Kunst zusammen.*] He became very modest. He will be quite surprised at what the Fuehrer will have to say about the "beneficial" activity of his Ministry.

After a brief introduction by Goering the Fuehrer spoke. He was in good form, even though he spoke somewhat haltingly at first. He told me after his speech that he was rather numb. The terrific exertions both of a physical and spiritual nature which he had to make during the winter have taken their toll after all.

Soon, however, he is fired with enthusiasm. His initial hesitation is overcome. His somewhat rapid manner of speaking, which makes him rather hard to understand during the first passages, soon ceases, and now he gives the German people and the world a report on the past winter that has a truly shattering effect. . . .

He began with the origins of the war and made an analysis of the British Empire and the reasons for its progressive collapse. He criticized Churchill in a superior and extraordinarily ingenious manner. The Fuehrer contrasted what the English consider as encouraging in their defeats with what we believe to be encouraging in our victories.

To this contrast the Reichstag replied with stormy expressions of hilarity. . . .

The generals are put in their place, but one can only read this between the lines. He speaks also of individuals who failed at critical moments and lost their nerve. In this connection the Fuehrer demanded absolute plenary powers for himself to do during wartime, even with reference to individuals, whatever he considers necessary, without having to take into consideration any so-called well-earned rights. This demand is approved enthusiastically and noisily by the Reichstag. . . .

In the speech of the Fuehrer I see nothing but complete vindication of the psychological line I took through the entire winter. . . . All in all, the Fuehrer delivered one of his best speeches. . . .

Goering then introduced the new bill whereby the Fuehrer is given full powers to remove even officials and judges whenever he considers this necessary and when this is demanded by the exigencies of our war effort. The new law is passed unanimously by the Reichstag amid stormy salvos of applause.

After the speech I had another long conversation with the Fuehrer. He was very happy to have talked himself out. I reported to him what effect his speech had had as I could judge it sitting in the Reichstag. He is now determined to proceed very drastically, especially in the administration of justice, which he regards as being out of contact with the people. He won't take anything more from that quarter. I cited several examples of their way of administering justice, which are merely a corroboration of the correctness of his course. The Fuehrer is determined also to invoke sharper measures against certain types of swivel-chair generals and against the whole bureaucracy.

We entered upon a long discussion of the importance and value of a well-conducted propaganda. So far as propaganda is concerned, the Fuehrer has no criticism whatever to offer.

The Fuehrer told me that the condition of his health was such that he simply must take three months' leave sometime. But when, how, and where can he go on vacation? He realizes himself that it can't be done. And yet he is pretty much overworked. Thank God, at least he will now go to the Obersalzberg for a few days, even though it be for important talks with the Duce. The Obersalzberg always has a quieting effect on him. The Fuehrer must now be very careful about his health. That's why we had no spotlights built into the Reichstag. There is always the danger that he might suffer a dangerous collapse during a very severe strain.

It is touching to hear the Fuehrer express his wish that he may be privileged to live to see the day of victory. The visions he has of the coming peace are truly intoxicating. God grant that we may be permitted to enter upon that period! Then the restrictions under which we live and work today will, for the most part, disappear like a nightmare. But for the present we don't want to think about it.

April 28, 1942

The air raid last night on Rostock was even more devastating than those which preceded it. Community life in the city is practically no longer possible. . . . The situation in the city is in some sections catastrophic.

I gave orders to have handbills printed with pictures of the damage done by the English in Luebeck and Rostock, and under them the Fuehrer's announcement of his Reichstag speech that reprisal raids are coming. These handbills are to be dropped in great quantities over the English cities that are to be attacked. I expect quite a psychological effect from this stunt.

The Fuehrer's speech is in the foreground of world discussion. The English and Americans are now making convulsive attempts to deny that it has any importance. In so far as they express any opinion about it at all, they infer a far-reaching internal crisis, owing to differences partly between the people and the leadership, and partly between the Fuehrer and the generals. . . . The charge that the Fuehrer was nervous is absolute nonsense. Unfortunately Goering, in his opening and closing remarks, spoke very indistinctly and haltingly and thereby showed a certain lack of assurance. . . .

In the United States astrologists are at work to prophesy an early end for the Fuehrer. We know that type of work as we have often done it ourselves. We shall take up our astrological propaganda again as soon as possible. I expect quite a little of it, especially in the United States and England.

The latest SD report does not yet deal with the Fuehrer's speech. But it does speak of the exceptionally deep impression created among the German people by our celebration of the Fuehrer's birthday in Philharmonic Hall. The speech I delivered there was received exceptionally well and favorably everywhere.

Ministerialrat Seiffert and the liaison officer from the Research Office, Severith, reported to me about the work of the Research Office. This work is very extensive, uses all modern technical gadgets, and manages to pick all sorts of secret information from the enemy news services. Above all it has proven possible to break down most of the enemy codes, so that we can today spy to a certain extent on the telegraphic communications between Ankara and London or between Moscow and London. The results of this work are to be laid before me regularly hereafter. One can draw a number of important conclusions from it. Naturally the work must be kept exceptionally secret, as its effectiveness will otherwise be wasted. The English, incidentally, are exceedingly careless in these matters. I hope that isn't true also of our secret communications. For if the English know as much about us as we know about them that might have very serious consequences.

[Seiffert and Severith were minor officials in the higher German bureaucracy.]

In the course of the day we learn that the effect of the Fuehrer's speech at home was much more favorable than we had at first supposed. Latest reports from the Reich propaganda offices are unanimous in conveying that impression. Unfortunately the opening and closing words of Goering were rather badly received. Their tone was too careless and too little adapted to the seriousness of the situation. I shall tell Goering about this when the occasion presents itself.

April 29, 1942

Thirty demolition and one thousand incendiary bombs (according to other reports fifty demolition and several thousand incendiary bombs) were dropped on Cologne. . . . The fires started within the municipal area of Cologne, and spread rapidly because of the strong wind. Some residential sections were burned out completely. About one hundred fires were started, among them twenty of great magnitude. They included fires in the Finance Office in the old part of the city, in the harbor, the city hall, a bank, five churches, two hospitals, and one chassis factory. One factory was completely destroyed.

The political scene is still dominated by the Fuehrer's Reichstag speech. . . . All lies of the past, dating back to times of peace and war, are warmed up again and adorned with new arabesques. The conclusion arrived at is that the Fuehrer's speech represents, as it were, the cry of a drowning man. To think what the enemy countries can make of a turn of speech that in itself is harmless! For instance, the dressing down which Justice received is exaggerated into a gigantic internal revolution. As though the judges had the ambition and the ability to start a revolution in the Reich! Ten per cent of the lowest officials of the NSV would be sufficient to quell it.

[The *National-Sozialistische Volkswohlfahrt* (NSV), or National Socialist People's Welfare, was an institution which collected vast sums of money for welfare purposes, a large part of which, however, was diverted to war purposes.]

Molotov issued a new atrocity note to the world powers. In it there has been gathered together about everything that can be said about us in the way of lies. It is very comprehensive and is intended especially for the populations in the areas occupied by us.

I received a report on the situation in Finland. Things there are anything but satisfactory. But the fighting morale of the Finns is entirely unbroken. The Finns are determined, under all circumstances, to continue the war with their accustomed vigor.

Their losses of men are enormous. It is especially regrettable that, when an entire Finnish regiment is liquidated, this usually means that the entire male population of villages or even cities is eliminated. The Finns are a very courageous and heroic people.

Roosevelt addressed a message to Congress. It is rather colorless and deals mainly with economic problems. But in contrast to his pompous speeches before the entry of the United States into the war he, too, must now admit the seriousness of the situation. There is no longer any indication of rosy optimism.

The SD gave me a police report on conditions in the East. The danger of the Partisans continues to exist in unmitigated intensity in the occupied areas. The Partisans have, after all, caused us very great difficulties during the winter, and these difficulties have by no means ceased with the beginning of spring. Short shrift is made of the Jews in all eastern occupied areas. Tens of thousands of them are liquidated.

The new slogan, "Land for the Peasants!" appealed especially strongly to the rural population. We could have achieved this success much earlier if we had been cleverer and more farsighted. But we were geared altogether too much to a brief campaign and saw victory so close to our very eyes that we thought it unnecessary to bother about psychological questions of this sort. What we then missed we must now attempt to catch up with the hard way.

I received a new report about the effect of the Fuehrer's speech on the German people. There has, after all, been some objection. Although the trust in the Fuehrer continues undiminished, nevertheless the German people are asking, surprised, why new plenary powers had to be granted to the Fuehrer and what reasons might have guided him to castigate and criticize domestic conditions thus publicly. Unfortunately one cannot very well explain these reasons in public.

There is also some skepticism in judging the military situation. Above all, since the Fuehrer spoke of a second winter campaign in the East, people believe that he, too, is not convinced that the war against the Soviet Union can be finished during the coming summer.

The questions raised by the Fuehrer's speech are very numerous. In a certain sense the address has spread a feeling of insecurity. The people want especially to know what the Fuehrer now intends to do in order to improve the conditions he criticized and to call to account the people responsible for them. Undoubtedly speeches frequently draw such psychological consequences in their wake. The main thing is that the people have been alerted to the seriousness of the situation and on the whole are aware that it is now a question of to be or not to be.

A report from the Reich Health Office goes into elaborate detail to prove that the food rations authorized at present are not sufficient for maintaining a normal state of health. We know that! I notice it in my own case. But there is no other choice. If we lost the war the rations at our disposal would suffice even less to keep up the health of the German people.

During the Ministerial Conference I objected strenuously to the increasing craze for the primitive in some departments of my ministry. It is nonsense, without any compelling reasons, to want to cut out things belonging to normal civilian life. Thus, for instance, the *Schwarze Korps* recently wrote an article against the barbers. Now, after all, we cannot run about with apostles' hair! Nor is it a crime if the ladies have their fingernails attended to so long as there is sufficient personnel for that purpose!

Waechter presented his plans for a great anti-Soviet exposition in the Berlin Lustgarten. It promises to become an exhibition event of first magnitude and to show the justification for our war against the Soviet Union. Of course I am going to see to it that nothing is exhibited that might in any way be an advertisement for Bolshevism.

[The Lustgarten was a gigantic square at the eastern end of the Avenue Unter den Linden.]

April 30, 1942

Of thirty-five airplanes flying into the Reich, twenty attacked the city of Kiel and dropped fifty demolition and two thousand incendiary bombs. According to latest reports seven persons were killed, twenty-one wounded seriously, and nine lightly. Strong winds again spread the fire considerably, setting many houses in about thirty streets aflame. Thirty houses were totally destroyed, thirty-two damaged heavily, and ninety lightly. The patients were immediately carried from two burning [private] hospitals into the city hospital.

Apparently opinion about air warfare is by no means unified in England. An American officer has reported that the English have poor, over-aged machines; that they can hope to accomplish something only with American matériel.

In recent air raids on Germany the English have used some extraordinarily dangerous phosphorous incendiary bombs which they drop over rural areas. As a result cattle have already been set on fire in various places. Although this method of fighting has not yet assumed large proportions, it is nevertheless a cause for worry.

The English have appealed once more to Vichy France. They have still not given up the hope of possibly winning Laval over to their cause.

Roosevelt addressed his people in a fireside chat. He also appealed to the French people. His speech fairly dripped with hypocrisy. That he also turned to the German and the Italian people deserves only to be recorded in the margin. He evidently intends to make good what British propaganda has missed and to prove himself a clever pupil of Wilson.

I received a detailed report from Hildebrandt concerning the situation in Rostock. The city is 70 per cent gone. More than 100,000 people had to be evacuated. It is now also becoming evident that the great successes of the English with their air raids are due to sabotage on the part of foreign workers. A detailed inquiry by the police is being conducted about this and the result is awaited with some curiosity. It cannot be denied that the presence of such large contingents of foreign workers has an element of danger in it. In the event of a panic these elements must be watched closely. The panic that started in Rostock, for instance, is in all likelihood because of inciting remarks made by Poles.

Vichy would very much like to conclude a separate peace with us. But the Fuehrer is undoubtedly right in declining this. France would not think of considering such a separate peace as binding in case we were defeated; but France would insist upon this separate peace in case we were victorious. The amputation of France would be practically out of the question. At best the French would be ready to cede Alsace to us; even in the case of Lorraine they would create the greatest difficulties. One might well ask in such a case why we had a war with France at all. If the French knew what the Fuehrer is one day going to demand of them their eyes would in all likelihood brim over. It is good for the present not to say anything about this and to try to get out of French *attentism* as much as we can.

The Fuehrer wants to break off his vacation on the Obersalzberg. Nature has very thoughtfully covered it with snow. That, of course, is exactly the right milieu for the Fuehrer to have during a few days of rest! He told me again during his last visit in Berlin that it would be simply impossible for him physically to look at snow for the next couple of years. Unfortunately he must pull up stakes again for that reason. It is, so to speak, a case of flight from the snow.

May 1942

JAPANESE SEIZE MANDALAY. FIFTY-FIVE FRENCH HOSTAGES EXECUTED BY NAZIS AT LILLE. SEVENTY-TWO NETHERLANDERS EXECUTED BY NAZIS. ROSTOCK BLASTED BY R.A.F. BRITISH LAND ON MADAGASCAR. UNITED STATES GARRISON AT CORREGIDOR SURRENDERS. CARDINAL FAULHABER ACCUSES NAZIS OF "WAR ON CHRISTIANITY." GERMANS LAUNCH EASTERN OFFENSIVE IN KERCH PENINSULA AND CAPTURE KERCH. NAZI SUBMARINE SINKS TWO FREIGHTERS AT MOUTH OF ST. LAWRENCE; ALSO CARGO BOAT NEAR MOUTH OF MISSISSIPPI RIVER. RUSSIANS IN DONETZ BASIN LAUNCH COUNTER-OFFENSIVE ON KHARKOV AND RELIEVE PRESSURE ON KERCH. RUSSIAN TROOPS EVACUATE KERCH PENINSULA. ROMMEL HURLS AFRIKA KORPS INTO LIBYA IN NEW OFFENSIVE. HEYDRICH CRITICALLY WOUNDED BY BOMB.

May 1, 1942

Several MP's have demanded that an arrangement, possibly a gentleman's agreement, be made with the Reich to the effect that cultural monuments are no longer to be attacked [in air raids]. The British Deputy Premier, Attlee, declined such a proposal. We had really not expected that the British Government would entertain such an idea. But it is very significant that the British people consider this question much more realistically now than they did eight days ago. Suddenly it begins to dawn on them that it is not a defenseless Germany they are attacking, but that this country, despite the severe strain on our Luftwaffe in the East as well as in the Mediterranean, still has reserve power enough left to pay the English back aplenty for what they are doing.

The American craze for figures is meeting with greatest distrust in London, as is indicated in a whole series of confidential reports. They don't think much of the Yankees, who are regarded as people who open their big mouths but hardly ever do anything.

Significantly enough, the stock market in London is on the rise, whereas in the United States it is falling. The rise in stocks in London is owing to the fact that actually they hope there for an Italian collapse, whereas the drop in stocks in the United States is owing to the fact that the Jews of the New York Stock Exchange know exactly how to differentiate between truth and propaganda in the American war effort.

For the present we won't discuss Giraud's escape into unoccupied France. Our Ambassador, Abetz, has been ordered to demand of Laval that he exert pressure upon Giraud to return to German captivity of his own volition.

This attempt must be made, but I don't expect very much of it. Giraud certainly won't think of returning voluntarily into our hands.

The commander of the fortress of Koenigstein really deserved to be shot. Through his neglect the German Reich has been so seriously harmed that he ought by rights to be punished with death. This commander may consider himself lucky that I am not the one to decide about his fate.

The Fuehrer has approved my draft of his telegram to the German people for the first of May. It is an exceptionally binding and farreaching declaration in favor of a social people's state and will be excellent for our propaganda at home. For the first time we can record the fact that the Fuehrer commits himself so completely on the aims of the National Socialist state of the future.

May 2, 1942

I have ordered official censorship to be exercised on foreign correspondents' reports on the air situation. The English are naturally making frantic efforts to obtain information about the results of their air raids. We cannot be expected to support their efforts. . . .

The phrase, "Baedeker attacks," is playing an important role in English commentary. Unfortunately, one of the gentlemen of our Foreign Office himself invented this phrase and thereby did us tremendous damage. I censured this in the sharpest terms and took measures for preventing the repetition of such folly.

[The Foreign Office functionary to whom Goebbels referred was Baron Braun von Stumm of the press department, who obviously meant that, in mapping out its retaliation campaign against the British Isles, the Luftwaffe consulted the "Baedeker" to determine just where the cultural monuments were located.]

Incidentally, London now admits that the worst kind of damage has been done in Bath, Norwich, and other English cities attacked by us. There is talk about scenes like those in Coventry. That's the sort of music we like to hear. The German Luftwaffe and German propaganda surely have succeeded within scarcely two weeks in changing the entire situation.

Burma has been written off completely by the English. Both in London and in the United States there is great pessimism because of this fact. Communications between the English and the Chinese have been broken off. That is a loss for Chiang Kai-shek which simply cannot be made up again. Some English critics even claim that this is the decisive event of the war in East Asia. They may be right.

Stalin has turned to his janissaries with a first-of-May appeal. His arguments can be described as nothing short of insane. He makes the claim that we are neither Socialists nor Nationalists but solely aggressors. Our fight was being conducted only in the interests of our bankers. The German people had to see the war through in order that the plutocrats might become richer. The whole appeal is so frothy that nothing can be done with it. It is hardly worth the effort to argue against it.

Paltzo presented me with a report on conditions in the Ukraine. In this report Koch complained bitterly about the ineptitude of the Ministry for Eastern Affairs. In that Ministry plans are being hatched for future decades, when in reality the problems of the day are so urgent that they cannot be postponed. The ineptitude of the Ministry is owing to the fact that there are too many theoreticians there and too few practical men. Every sectional chief builds up his department according to his personal taste. Rosenberg himself is by nature a theoretician, and it is quite evident that he must have constant conflicts with so pronounced a man of action and brute force as Koch.

[Joachim Paltzo was head of the propaganda section of the gau office for East Prussia. When Erich Koch, whose identification follows immediately, became Ukrainian Commissioner, he took his tried and trusted co-worker with him to his new job. Paltzo at this time was thirty years old.

Erich Koch, Gauleiter for East Prussia and nicknamed Czar of East Prussia because of his rigorous absolutist methods, was appointed Reich Commissioner for the occupied Ukraine by Adolf Hitler. As such he was responsible to Alfred Rosenberg, whom Hitler appointed Minister for the Eastern Areas. Rosenberg the theoretician and Koch the brutal and smart practical operator never got along well.]

Koch asked me to give him substantial support in matters of propaganda and stated that our work alone had thus far been of assistance in his difficult tasks in the Ukraine.

As regards food, we are not to expect too much in the immediate future. German troops have devoured everything there. There are no cattle left and there is a dearth of horses and other draft animals, so that the plows must again be drawn by human beings. It is not hard to imagine what the results will be. As one can see here, it isn't sufficient to possess land, one must also be in a position to work it.

I received a report about the present position of [German] agriculture which is anything but encouraging. There is a dearth of seeds, of man power, of gasoline, of horses, of cattle, of good weather—in short of just about everything essential to guarantee sufficient food. It may be necessary next autumn to take in our belts a few more notches.

We are much worried about the fact that an exceptionally high percentage of doctors has fallen on the Eastern Front. It is imperative that measures be taken to prevent this in future. I appealed to the Fuehrer. It simply won't do to let our quota of doctors, which is already very small indeed, and hardly sufficient to insure our health, shrink still further.

The Fuehrer was very angry about the draft of Ley's appeal for May 1. He was especially annoyed that the style was like that of a high-school sophomore. The Fuehrer sent word to me that he has no intention of becoming a schoolmaster now; I would please hereafter take a hand and see to it that such exercises be submitted to him only after they complied with the most elementary rules of style.

I received detailed information about the Fuehrer's meeting with the Duce. The Fuehrer is exceedingly happy about it. Nothing unfavorable transpired. The meeting came off in perfect harmony.

In the afternoon I was able to go out to Lanke. The weather has become very cool again. Spring just doesn't seem to want to come. That is nothing short of catastrophic for our harvest prospects. What we need is warm rain followed by sunshine. Instead of that it won't rain and the sun doesn't shine either. Sometimes one is tempted to despair.

May 3, 1942

The commentary in London on the meeting of the Fuehrer and the Duce proves that English mentality concerning German-Italian relations is completely wrong. Once again the Duce, as has been the custom for years, is described as the Gauleiter of the Fuehrer. An attempt is made to sow discord between the Reich and Italy. But it is done in such a stupid and childish manner that each line reveals the uncertainty of present-day English policy.

The English now admit heavy destruction at Norwich. It is as I thought from the beginning—they can't hold their tongues in such a difficult question. Two or three days later they talk anyway, as this example shows.

Great mass demonstrations for neutrality have taken place in Argentina. We shall have to handle Argentina very, very carefully in our commentary. It may become extremely important for further developments in South America.

There have been two more attempts to kill German soldiers in France; also a large-scale attempt on a railway train which resulted in almost twenty dead among the soldiers who were in the leave train. Severe reprisals were taken. But again our military commander didn't have the initiative to publish the names of the Communists, Jews, and DeGaullists who were to be shot. That means that our countermeasure is again rather meaningless and purposeless. I am now going to appeal personally to the Fuehrer to insist upon my viewpoint.

Otherwise nothing of consequence happened on May 2, which was set aside as a national holiday in lieu of May 1. Ley delivered a pretty unfortunate speech on the present position of Labor in the Mosaic Hall of the Reich Chancellery. The minute he opens his mouth he gets his foot into it.

All motion-picture producers visited me. In the evening we see the American technicolor picture "Swanee River," which affords me an opportunity for making a number of observations on the creation of a new German film based on folk songs. The fact of the matter is that the Americans have the ability of taking their relatively small stock of culture and by a modernized version to make of it something that is very *à propos* for the present time. We are loaded down altogether too much with tradition and piety. We hesitate to clothe our cultural heritage in a modern dress. It therefore remains purely historical or museum-like and is at best understood by groups within the Party, the Hitler Youth, or the Labor Service. The cultural heritage of our past can be rendered fruitful for the present on a large scale only if we present it with modern means. The Americans are masters at this sort of thing, I suppose, because they are not weighed down as much as we are with historical ballast. Nevertheless we shall have to do something about it. The Americans have only a few Negro songs, but they present them in such a modern way that they conquer large parts of the modern world which is, of course, very fond of such melodies. We have a much greater fund of cultural goods, but we have neither the artistry nor the will to modernize them. That will have to be changed.

May 4, 1942

The [Japanese] government garnered 81 per cent of all votes cast. That means, practically, that [political] parties in Japan have ceased to exist. Tojo's tactics were exceptionally clever. Even the fact that he called the Japanese people to the polls at this time was very smart. By a skillful move on the chessboard he eliminated the very thing that always stood in Konoye's way—the paramount supremacy of the parties, behind which stood the industrial concerns and the trusts. Japan is on the direct road toward an authoritarian regime camouflaged as parliamentary. Every state creates that sort of regime after its own fashion. This form is suited to the Japanese mentality.

Rostock . . . is a gruesome picture of destruction. I am informed that its center is more than 70 per cent destroyed. Incidentally, I deem it exceedingly unwise that the Foreign Office lent a hand to make it possible for Countess Ciano to visit Luebeck and Rostock, of all places. Anything more foolish can hardly be imagined. The effect, of course, was as might be expected. Countess Ciano visited us in Schwanenwerder on Saturday afternoon and reported about her experiences on that trip. It was obvious she received a good deal of a shock. Her wish to see areas destroyed by air action should have been side-stepped cleverly and her trip limited, say, to Hamburg and Bremen. She did visit these cities also and there, of course, received the best possible impression. One can never entrust tasks of this kind to our diplomats. The gentlemen of the Foreign Office busy themselves a lot with propaganda, but have no faculty whatsoever for calculating psychological effects in advance. To aggravate matters, the Italian Ambassador's wife and a number of ladies in waiting at the Italian court accompanied Countess Ciano. They will, of course, not hesitate to spread their observations around in every manner possible among the aristocratic and monarchist circles in Rome. Then it won't be long before it comes to the attention of the English. I am having a thorough investigation made of this case and am going to protest to the Fuehrer that such embarrassing happenings must not recur.

Naturally the effects of bomb warfare are horrible when one looks at individual cases. But they must be put up with. Besides, these women meddling in politics haven't the necessary imagination to envisage the other side of this type of warfare. More particularly, they don't see the English cities that were raided by us. Nor have they enough brains to take into account the general situation in the world and by so doing to regard bomb warfare as a mere episode. Women dabbling in politics are always a pain in the neck. One should not encourage them in their ambition to do their share of political talking.

Negotiations with the French Government about the fate of General Giraud have got nowhere. An attempt will now be made either to persuade Giraud to return to German imprisonment, or else to obtain his word of honor that he will not place himself at the disposal of de Gaulle. No progress has been made on this until now. I view the probable results of this procedure with a certain amount of skepticism. In my opinion Giraud isn't thinking of binding himself in any way for the future by any word of honor. Were he to do so, it would almost have to be considered a miracle.

The weather is still terrible, and truly poisonous for our harvest. Rain won't come, and sun won't come either. The temperature has sunk again. If that continues, we shall have to count on a complete crop failure.

Lieutenant Colonel Scherff of GHQ has sent me a compilation of quotations on the nature of genius by great Germans. It is put together exceedingly cleverly. Scherff presented it to the Fuehrer for his birthday. These quotations are very comforting in judging the present situation. Taken as a whole they almost give one the impression of an apotheosis of the Fuehrer. One cannot imagine a better justification of his nature, his personality, and his actions.

[Lieutenant Colonel Walter Scherff was attached to Hitler's GHQ to write the official history of World War II. It is not difficult to imagine what a one-sided history, blowing Hitler up into a superman, that history would have been had the Nazi regime survived.]

May 5, 1942

Reports from East Asia give us more details about Japanese victories in Burma. Mandalay, unfortunately, has been completely destroyed.

The English even brag about it. They are always quick about destroying other people's property. This time that is London's sole consolation, for from an operational or strategic standpoint the setback suffered in Burma is nothing short of fatal.

Cripps delivered a speech about his mission in India on the occasion of the Polish national holiday. It is disarmingly harmless and naïve. I consider this man insanely overestimated. That's an added indication of the chronic lack of leadership from which England is at present suffering. Among the blind, the one-eyed man is king.

The English report that they almost captured Rommel. Unfortunately this report is true. Rommel is altogether too careless about his life and security. It would be a terrible national misfortune if he were captured by the English. He ought to be advised to move about more circumspectly. In any case I am seeing to it that the German people learn absolutely nothing about this possibility [of his capture]; they would otherwise be very much disquieted.

In Norway eighteen spies and "England runners" were shot. These executions had a very sobering effect on the Norwegian people. The Norwegians imagined that for all time to come we would do nothing but threaten. Now they have experienced that in wartime there isn't much consideration for the life of the individual, especially not if he belongs to the enemy. I hope these executions will yield favorable results in changing the attitude of the Norwegian population. If they don't want to learn to love us they must at least fear us.

["England runners" were Norwegian patriots who kept up direct communications between the Norwegian government-in-exile headed by King Haakon and the loyal Norwegians at home who refused to follow Vidkun Quisling.]

May 6, 1942

Molotov's atrocity note was distributed in large quantities both within Soviet territory as well as in the areas occupied by us. While it was not clever at all for foreign consumption, it will nevertheless not be without effect domestically. We shall reply to it in a massive flood of handbills of our own and attempt to neutralize any unfavorable effect the Molotov note might have.

If we had to do with a civilized people in our eastern campaign, it would long ago have collapsed, but the Russians are quite unpredictable in this and other matters. They show a capacity for suffering that is simply impossible with other peoples. The men at present in control of the Soviet Union of course know that very definitely and base their plans for the coming summer on this mentality.

In the Netherlands, too, seventy-nine executions have now taken place. They were cases of spies and "England runners" who thought the patience of the German occupation troops and of the Reich Commissariat was such that they could play their nefarious game with impunity. These circles have now been taught an energetic lesson.

[The Dutch, like the Norwegians, had messengers (England runners) plying back and forth between their occupied native land and their government-in-exile in London.]

General Giraud, it develops, traveled to the Swiss border with an ordinary railroad ticket and while en route even talked at length with a German officer about the condition of our tank army in North Africa. It has been a real *Schildbuergerstreich*, which certainly doesn't redound to the honor of those guilty [of letting him escape].

[What Podunk is to the American, the little Saxon town of Schilda was to the Germans. Hence, when some particularly stupid thing was done anywhere, it was often called a *"Streich"* or prank or mischievous act by a *Schildbuerger;* i.e., a burgher or citizen of Schilda.]

The food situation is becoming constantly more critical on account of the continuing bad weather. We are going to have to put up with an exceedingly dangerous shortage in fats. It will probably be necessary soon to reduce the fat rations again considerably. In my opinion that will lead to a tremendous lowering of morale. It won't help matters either that we may possibly be able to increase the meat rations slightly. Our present reserves of meat are owing to the fact that we have had to slaughter a lot of cattle because of the lack of fodder.

May 7, 1942

The English in long, tedious sentences are trying to show how and why they have a right to occupy Madagascar. It is a veritable witches' Sabbath of democratic logic. The enemy hardly makes an effort in any way to gloss over this flagrant violation of international law.

Corregidor has capitulated. The Japanese so report, and the Americans admit it. The loss of this island fortress has come as a shock to the United States. There is deep mourning throughout the country. As a marginal note it should be recorded that General MacArthur, who is a sort of national hero in the United States, took a hand in this debate in a most loud-mouthed way from Australia—he who ought to have every reason to be quiet and modestly shut up. He declared that under his leadership Corregidor would be recaptured. Of course he doesn't divulge how he intends to do that.

Again a whole series of attempted assassinations has been made in France. I propose most urgently to the Military Commander that he requisition all or at least a large number of bicycles in the cities in which such attempts occur. In most cases the men who carry out an attempt sneak up to their victim on a bicycle. Besides, the bicycle is now an indispensable means of communication in France. Punishment of this sort would strike the population with extraordinary severity. But as my proposal is so good, I take it for granted that the military commander won't show any understanding of it. I therefore turn to General Jodl as a precautionary measure, so that my proposal may be passed on to the Military Commander in the form of an order.

Switzerland has recalled her representative in the International Motion Picture Association. It looks as though this stinking little state [dieser kleine Dreckstaat] is trying to provoke the International Motion Picture Association. I am going to insist that the association respond with a general boycott.

The Fuehrer did not accept my proposal to reduce appreciably the rations for the diplomats. He believes the good rations [for the diplomats] are partly the reason for their reporting so favorably on Germany. I can't quite believe this and am going to try once more to present my viewpoint to the Fuehrer.

At Lanke I must pay a great deal of attention to my ailment. It gives me a lot of bother. The itch has become almost unbearable. The cure is most annoying. I can hardly sleep. My health is pretty poor. The doctors tell me, however, that I must go through this period and that then things will be better. Let's hope so.

May 8, 1942

Churchill himself took the floor concerning Madagascar. He spoke in the House of Commons and issued pompous reports on the war like a victorious field marshal. This man is a real ogre. He is brimful of bumptiousness. The British Empire will owe its collapse to him.

Vichy already admits the retreat of the French troops [in Madagascar]. I feared from the very beginning that the French troops could and possibly would not offer any notable resistance. The French world empire is at the point of collapse. Democracies are simply not in a position to hold vast empires together. For so doing there is needed authoritary, determined, and definite leadership, such as is discernible neither in England nor in France.

Exceptionally happy news came during the night about a great naval victory of the Japanese in a battle in the Coral Sea which still continues. That, of course, means that the Anglo-Saxon East Asiatic fleet sustained an irreparable loss.

The Foreign Office had intended permitting Belgian children to be sent to Switzerland. I forbade this. The Swiss are doing this merely to advertise themselves and to influence the children along their lines. Anyway, it is a question of only five hundred children. If the Swiss really want to do something they should send food to the Belgians.

The Giraud case has been taken out of the hands of diplomacy and placed back in the hands of the military. The Fuehrer has given orders that proper reprisals be taken against French prisoners of war in Germany. They will have to accept decisive restrictions on their habits of life.

I proposed to the OKW that Giraud, who got out of German imprisonment illegally, be brought back into our possession again illegally. This could be done very easily. A half-dozen picked SD men could be sent into unoccupied France, there observe Giraud for a few days, shove him head over heels into an automobile, and drive him across into the occupied area. We will then have him again. A big noise will be made for forty-eight hours in the enemy press, but that happens anyway, no matter what we do.

My proposal to seize, let us say, 10,000 bicycles in occupied France as a reprisal for every attempt at assassination has been given a very favorable reception in the OKW. On the one hand we thereby inflict heavy punishment on the French, and on the other hand we can use those bicycles excellently for our troops. I take it that this reprisal will soon be effective. It shows once again that punishment must be thought up and meted out with intelligence, but our military authorities lack this intelligence. Their ailment is complete lack of imagination.

The churches continue to raise a stink. They must be punished by not noticing them; that's the best way to handle them. . . .

Roever issued a circular letter stating that he would not become an honorary godfather of children whose parents are still church members.

Roever is a boor [*ein Tolpatsch*]; he sometimes acts like a bull in a china shop.

[Carl Roever, one of the oldest Party members, was Gauleiter for Oldenburg. This "boor" became "one of the most faithful fighting companions of the Fuehrer —always very comradely and friendly" to Goebbels when he received notice of his death on May 17, 1942.]

May 9, 1942

I am having much trouble with the lack of discipline in Berlin. That's what happens when I am not on the spot. Nevertheless, I must now carry through my cure to rid myself of that infernal itch at last. I hope that I can accomplish this in fourteen days. The healing process, thank God, is going on nicely.

May 10, 1942

Fear about Australia is tremendous in the enemy camp. It is expected that the Japanese may attempt an invasion of Australia on the completion of this battle [Coral Sea]. Personally, I don't believe this will happen.

News policy is a weapon of war. Its purpose is to wage war and not to give out information.

Eden insolently declared that England has the intention and the mission of leading the Europe of the future. He indulges in most impudent insults to National Socialism and the Fuehrer. Eden is a hollow brain and need not be taken seriously. England, he claims, intends to form police troops for keeping Europe in order. There can be no question whatever, he said, of peace with Hitler. The question really is whether Hitler is willing to conclude peace with him.

[Anthony Eden, born, 1897, and educated at Eton and Oxford, has held many political and diplomatic posts, but is best remembered as Secretary for League of Nations Affairs (1935) and as Secretary of State for Foreign Affairs (1935–38 and 1940–45).]

Australian stocks are going down in all exchanges—a proof of the fact that not much confidence is set in Australia's future.

May 11, 1942

The Americans are trying to get their cut of the swag and to equalize the English rape of Madagascar by sneaking up to the French possessions on Martinique. They give the windiest of arguments for their procedure. But we are used to that in the case of the Anglo-Saxon governments. They are once again humane, liberal, and desirous of taking the possessions into custody solely on behalf of the real France, and the like. Behind all these resounding phrases there is the naked greed of imperialistic robber nations to try to get themselves the proper equivalent for their losses.

[Martinique was restored to liberated France. It was given the status of a department of France effective January 1, 1947.]

The Bolsheviks are now dropping forged handbills over the German front. Thus, for instance, handbills are distributed allegedly issued by the Party or the Propaganda Ministry. They are phrased exceedingly cleverly, in that they imitate our slang and contain only two or three dangerous points. I have taken measures for having the OKW explain the danger of these leaflets to the troops.

Schach reported to me on questions regarding the gau of Berlin. We must deal again with the Jewish problem. There are still 40,000 Jews in Berlin and despite the heavy blows dealt them they are still insolent and aggressive. It is exceedingly difficult to shove them off to the East because a large part of them are at work in the munitions industry and because the Jews are to be evacuated only by families.

[Gerhard Schach was one of Goebbels's personal aides in his capacity of Gauleiter of Berlin. Schach was chief of Goebbels's gau staff and liaison officer from the gau to the Propaganda Ministry.]

Confidential information indicates that Mussolini had a talk with the Indian nationalist leader Bose, in the course of which he pleaded for Bose to appear more conspicuously and especially to set up a countergovernment. We don't like this idea very much, because we don't think the time has come for such a political maneuver. It does appear, though, that the Japanese are very eager for such a measure. However, émigré governments must not live too long in a vacuum. They must have something solid behind them. Otherwise the whole idea remains in the realm of theory.

May 12, 1942

Our progress near Kerch is extraordinary. The Fuehrer is very well satisfied with the present state of things. These operations afford us an interesting insight into the power of resistance still available to the

Bolsheviks. According to our experiences at Kerch it must be evaluated, after all, more highly than had generally been supposed.

The most extreme reports of successes [regarding the Eastern Front] are sent out by London, whereas the Bolsheviks are significantly silent. It must be said that the Bolshevik news policy, despite everything, is more decent than the Anglo-American. In the democracies the lie has become unavoidable. It is a principle of democracy to spread false reports under the guise of free speech.

In Paris an assault was made on our short-wave radio station "Alois." Unfortunately it was successful. Two transmission plants were destroyed. As a result very serious reprisals are necessary. The Military Commander asked me whether he ought to requisition all radio sets in the entire occupied area of France. I don't regard this as a happy thought, for thereby we shall lose our own possibilities for propaganda. He accepted my proposal to requisition radio sets individually, that is, to take them, to begin with, from the enemies of the state. In that connection I urged him most seriously to prepare dependable lists of England runners and enemies of our policies, so that we may always have hostages on hand whom we can seize.

The weather is still exceptionally fine. But that doesn't bring any joy, since we need rain so badly. Our harvest prospects are the worst imaginable. Unless a radical change comes, we shall have to figure on an absolute crop failure. That would, indeed, carry disastrous consequences with it.

May 13, 1942

The Japanese Foreign Minister, Tojo, delivered a speech in which he came out strongly for the independence of India. The Japanese are showing exceptional wisdom in their approach to the peoples suppressed by the English. We could learn a lot from them; this applies especially to our political leadership in the occupied areas of the East. Unfortunately Rosenberg has again failed to take this topic up with the Fuehrer. There is nothing left for me to do except to take up this theme the next time I speak with the Fuehrer.

The SD report indicates that the Fuehrer's speech is still the chief topic of discussion among the people. The officials and the jurists simply won't quiet down. They feel they have taken a beating by this speech. Perhaps it would now be timely to give them a little pill to soothe their nerves. There is no purpose in humiliating two professions so deeply that they lose all interest in the war and in their work. I shall await a favorable moment to inaugurate such a policy.

I took a look at another French movie, *Annette et la Dame Blonde*. It is of the same levity and elegance as the Darrieux movie, *Caprices*. We shall have to be careful about the French so that they won't build up a new moving-picture art under our leadership that will give us too serious competition in the European market. I shall see to it that especially talented French film actors are gradually engaged for the German movie.

[Goebbels, as many entries in his diary indicate, was determined to give Germany a virtual European monopoly in motion pictures, and to subordinate Italian and French production to German. His handy man Winkler, as shown by the entry under date of April 23, 1942, had some crafty plan for cheating the Italians out of the fruits of their labors; Goebbels here revealed his plan for hoodwinking the French by buying off their best actors.]

May 14, 1942

Our attack on the peninsula of Kerch is completely successful. We are able to issue a special news bulletin. The question arises whether we should publicize this news over the radio with great ceremony. I finally decided to do so. We must accustom our people to the idea that such special bulletins deal only with individual incidents.

[During the first part of the war special news bulletins were read over the radio networks only to mark the victorious close of a whole series of operations. Now, in the fourth year of the war, large-scale victories were few and far between, and Goebbels thought it advisable that morale be stimulated from time to time by special bulletins even though, as he here explains, they now "deal only with individual incidents."]

Most appalling conditions are reported from Iran under Bolshevik-English rule. A terrible famine is said to have started there. Englishmen don't know how to organize a country. At best they know only how to exploit it in the most rigorous manner for their war effort.

In agreement with Ribbentrop the Grynzpan trial is postponed until next autumn. It isn't in the interests of German foreign policy to have the former French Foreign Minister [Georges] Bonnet advertised so much.

Franco is sitting on bayonets. His regime is actually not in a position to permit his entry into the great European event; namely, the war.

May 15, 1942

For certain reasons we launched an "unauthorized" article in the *Frankfurter Zeitung* which discusses the economic and operational possibilities of an attack on Moscow. With this article we are trying to divert the attention of the enemy to a different sector from the one on which we actually intend to attack. Whether we shall succeed in getting the Bolsheviks to fall for this [*auf diesen Leim zu locken*] is very doubtful.

[The *Frankfurter Zeitung* was chosen as the medium for this Goebbels swindle because it was still considered abroad to be somewhat liberal. Until the advent of Nazism it had been truly liberal and was read all over the world. The Nazis, realizing its importance as a possible medium for veiled propaganda, continued to give it an appearance of liberalism when in fact it was regimented, as was every other newspaper in Germany. Under date of May 20 Goebbels described what he did when the article appeared.]

Our victory at Kerch has impressed the neutral press very much. As a matter of fact, more is expected of it than we intended for the moment.

The Fuehrer has now given orders for stern measures to be applied in the treatment of French prisoners of war as an answer to the escape of General Giraud. The French PWs may thank their general for having all joy taken out of life. They are no longer to be allowed to leave their compound, they are to be placed under strong guard, and the French generals who are in our hands are to be put into solitary confinement.

A report from Paris informs me that a number of those who staged the last acts of terror have been found. About 99 per cent of them are eastern Jews [*Ostjuden*]. A more rigorous regime is now to be applied to these Jews. As far as I am concerned, it would be best if we either evacuated or liquidated all eastern Jews still remaining in Paris. By nature and race they will always be our natural enemies anyway.

[By eastern Jews (*Ostjuden*) are chiefly meant the Jews from Galicia and Poland.]

The situation in the East, according to reports of men on furlough and letters from the front, is being interpreted very favorably by the people. Of course all the elements of hope in our military position are somewhat neutralized by the extraordinarily strained food situation. Most people can't satisfy their hunger any longer, and a hungry stomach always inclines somewhat toward subversiveness. Unfortunately the prospects for an improvement of the food position are very unfavorable for the moment. The weather is about as bad as one could have it for a good harvest.

In the evening we viewed a new motion picture produced by our Continental-Gesellschaft in Paris after a scenario written around the life and activity of Hector Berlioz. The film is of excellent quality and amounts to a first-class national fanfare. I shall unfortunately not be able to release it for public showing.

I am very angry to think that our own offices in Paris are teaching the French how to represent nationalism in pictures. This lack of political instinct can hardly be beaten. But that's the way we Germans are. Whenever we go into another country, be it ever so strange to us or even an enemy, our first task seems to consist in getting order into that country regardless of the fact that perhaps in several years or decades it may go to war against us. The lack of political instinct among the Germans is the result of their passion for work and of their idealistic enthusiasm. You have to put on the brakes constantly so that evil and damaging consequences may not result.

I ordered Greven to come to Berlin from Paris, to give him absolutely clear and unmistakable directives to the effect that for the moment, so far as the French are concerned, only light, frothy, and, if possible, corny pictures are desired. No doubt the French people will be satisfied with that too. There is no reason why we should cultivate their nationalism.

[Herr Greven was the Paris representative for movie matters of the Propaganda Ministry.]

All actors of more than average talent in the French movies should, so far as possible, be hired by us for German film production. I see no other possibility of achieving a satisfactory result in this matter. We might well worry about the consequences that might result if we did not take a hand.

As citizens of the world, we Germans have as yet no vision. We grew up as the product of many little states and that's why we lack the necessary political practice and experience. We shall now have to catch up in a very few years on what we missed in centuries.

[One of the many shortcomings of National Socialism was the ignorance of their own country's history. To the Nazis, worth-while history began only with Adolf Hitler. Even Goebbels ignores the fact that Germany produced great citizens of the world in men such as Goethe, Schiller, Kant, Lessing, Von Humboldt, Beethoven, Brahms, Schumann, Mendelssohn, Schopenhauer, Duerer, Luther, or, in our own time, Eckener, Busch, Einstein, Strauss, Stresemann, Planck, Haber, and many others. Besides, the idea that world citizens can emerge only from large and powerful states is on a level with other Nazi doctrines.]

May 16, 1942

We issued a special communiqué about the sinking of an American heavy cruiser by the Luftwaffe near Spitzbergen. Special communiqués are again becoming more numerous. They have to do especially with the Americans. On the one hand that gives the German people extraordinary pleasure, because they would like to treat the Americans with special love; on the other hand it also awakens certain reactions in the United States.

[Goebbels propaganda always represented the United States as having declared war on Germany and made the people forget that Hitler, to the surprise of even some of his close collaborators, declared war on America at the request of the Japanese.]

It is a pity that our great operational success on Kerch Peninsula can be discounted by the opposing side through the successes of the Bolsheviks at Kharkov. I issued instructions to our news services to other countries to argue strongly against regarding these operations as on the same level.

The English report that they have had one thousand fatal casualties because of air action. The number killed on our side was not even one half this number. This shows once again how grossly the Englishmen exaggerate and that I was right in giving more publicity to our successes in the air than has hitherto been the case. Without a doubt our raids on English centers of culture and plutocracy will prove at least as effective as those of the English on Rostock, Luebeck, Kiel, et cetera.

The Research Office sent me background material on a number of political matters that are of some interest. Relations between Turkey and the Soviet Union have worsened very much. In his private talks the Turkish Foreign Minister, Saracoglu, used strong expressions of antagonism to the policies of the Soviets. The English are trying to calm him down. But Moscow has certainly provoked the Turkish Government.

May 17, 1942

The Bolsheviks suffered heavy losses at Kharkov, but of course our own losses in men and matériel are also considerable. The important thing is that the German troops succeeded in capturing Kerch.

The reports reaching London from the English-Burmese troops are simply hopeless. A debacle occurred there that baffles all description. This example shows clearly how cynical and mendacious Churchill is when he declares the situation improved. It is a sign of the moral decay of English public opinion that London boasts the British troops were able to accomplish their withdrawal without having contacted the enemy. Wavell characterized this withdrawal as a notable military achievement.

Churchill delivered an impromptu speech in which he declared that while England had not yet climbed over the mountain ridge and the final height [*freies Land*] was not yet in sight, nevertheless the ridge itself was already visible. That reminds one very much of the dictum of the former German Reich Chancellor, Bruening, who berated the National Socialists for their opposing the argument that he was only one hundred yards from his goal. In reality he was never farther from his goal than then. And anyway, even the wanderer through deep valleys sees the top of Mont Blanc without ever being able to reach it. The argument, therefore, that Churchill produces is anything but convincing.

[Former Chancellor Heinrich Bruening had virtually succeeded in convincing the statesmen of the major European powers of Germany's inability to continue to pay reparations. For this purpose in the summer of 1931 he had traveled to Chequers, Paris, and Rome and, instead of presenting German requests or even demands, had merely laid his cards on the table and asked his opposite numbers, "What would you do if you were in my place?" He could truly tell the members of the Reichstag sometime after his return that he was "only one hundred yards from his goal," for arrangements were then underway for Germany to make one more token payment, after which reparations were to be a thing of the past. That was precisely, however, what the Nazis did not want, since Bruening's success would have taken the wind out of their sails. They therefore managed to force his resignation in May 1932, before the reparations issue was finally settled.]

Our old party member, Roever, the Gauleiter and Governor of Oldenburg, has passed on. We have thus lost one of the oldest and most faithful fighting companions of the Fuehrer. Another member of the Old Guard has left us. One has the depressing feeling that those closest to the Fuehrer are gradually beginning to thin out.

The Fuehrer commissioned me to prepare a state funeral in the Mosaic Hall of the Reich Chancellery. The plans which Gutterer handed me for it are quite inadequate. Gutterer's proposal for this funeral is a ceremony of an essentially civilian character. I consider that quite unsuitable. While the Wehrmacht always carried its important men to the grave with great pomp and highest military honors, the Party is to have a solemn ceremony like this conducted, as it were, by any old funeral director. That won't do. That would set a bad example for later funerals and reduce the Party to the importance of a mere civilian administrative organization. I telephoned the Fuehrer, who agreed completely with me and gave orders that the funeral obsequies include highest honors.

[The Nazis always considered themselves the elite of the German people. It galled men like Goebbels that military funerals were brilliant and ceremonious, while funerals for Party members until now had lacked luster. By an irony of fate none of the top leaders who lived until the end of the war were buried with pomp and circumstance.]

Personally I feel the loss of Roever strongly. He was always very comradely and friendly. He was a good, dyed-in-the-wool National Socialist. It will hardly be possible to replace him in Oldenburg.

At noon Magda and the children came out here [to Lanke]. That is always a festive occasion for me. Magda is to deliver a speech before a thousand Berlin women on Mother's Day in Friedrichshain Hall. She is scared almost out of her wits.

May 18, 1942

It is relatively easy now to manage a German news service and conduct German propaganda with the necessary spirit. We again have material aplenty. Every second or third day there is either a special communiqué from the East or about our war against shipping.

Our diplomats and journalists have now arrived in Portugal [from America]. They gave exceptionally good interviews to the German and the foreign press and described conditions in the United States in terms suited to our propaganda line. We helped a little in that respect, but in this way we can once again make a relatively deep impression on international opinion concerning internal conditions in the United States. Our old DNB representative, Sell from Washington, made extremely clever psychological observations that will not fail to be effective.

[Kurt Sell was for many years DNB chief of bureau in Washington and broadcast to Germany on American conditions once a week.]

Spieler sent me a letter from occupied France. He complains bitterly about the provocative attitude of the French, who continue to live exactly as in peacetime and have everything in the way of food that their hearts desire. Even though this is true only of the plutocratic circles, it nevertheless angers our soldiers, who have but meager rations. We Germans are too good-natured in every respect. We don't yet know how to behave like a victorious people. We have no real tradition. On all this we must catch up during the coming decades.

[Spieler is not identified in the Goebbels diaries.]

The SD report calls attention to extraordinary transportation difficulties. This situation is indeed more than serious. The Transport Ministry is in no way capable of overcoming these difficulties. As a result there has been large-scale stoppage of production in munitions factories. In addition, the army draft has thinned out the ranks of skilled workers. Although one need not take this development too tragically, as it most certainly has its counterpart in the enemy countries, it is nevertheless a sign that we are in the third year of war.

May 19, 1942

Partisans blasted the railroad tracks in the central front between Brjansk and Rosslawl at five points—a further proof of the extremely discomfiting activity of the Partisans. To the south of this region Hungarian elements are fighting under great difficulties. They must now capture one village after another and pacify it, a thing that has not proved any too constructive. For when the Hungarians report that they have "pacified" a village, this usually means that not a single inhabitant is left. That means, in turn, that we can hardly get any agricultural work done in such regions.

In East Asia the French positions are further endangered. The Americans can hardly satisfy their appetites and no longer make any effort to camouflage their imperialistic aims with democratic phrases. It is a sign that the time of liberal slogans is coming to an end.

The declarations issued at Lisbon by our diplomats on their return from America are extremely clever and are actually getting good publicity in the world. But the American diplomats and journalists returning from Germany have also issued statements that make exactly the same claims about the Axis countries that our diplomats make about America. On the whole, therefore, there isn't much to be expected of these interviews from both sides. I was especially on the lookout that all sentimental remarks be taken out of the interviews given by our representatives. It wouldn't make much of an impression on the German people, for instance, to have our spokesmen deplore the fact that they were allowed only one newspaper per day during their intern-ment. You have to report something more serious than that [*man muss schon schwereres Geschuetz auffahren*] in order to make an impression on a people who have already gone through three years of war.

[The German, Italian, and Japanese correspondents in America were interned from December 1941 to May 1942 at White Sulphur Springs, West Virginia, while the American correspondents in Germany and Paris were interned during the same time at Bad Nauheim, Germany. Both sets of correspondents were given diplo-matic status for purposes of exchange and were placed in the same hotels with the diplomatic and consular officials and the military and naval attachés.

It was next to impossible for the Axis newsmen to find fault with White Sul-phur Springs, as they enjoyed every comfort and luxury, even the use of golf courses, whereas the Americans at Bad Nauheim were virtual prisoners in the Grand Hotel and could go for a walk only twice a week under Gestapo guard. Inside the hotel, however, they were free to do pretty much as they pleased. They had to get along on scant German rations and do many of the services themselves that are usually associated with the idea of a first-class hotel. The man-power shortage in Germany was already serious.]

As regards the American journalists, the representative of the United [*sic*] Press, Lochner, is behaving in an especially contemptible way. His attacks are directed above all against German propaganda and he aims at me personally [*nimmt mich persoenlich aufs Korn*]. I have never thought much of Lochner. We made too much fuss about him. We can now see what happens in time of crisis [*im Ernstfall*].

[For the record this editor is proud to say that he devoted himself for almost a quarter century to The Associated Press, but that, no doubt, he would have been equally happy to serve so distinguished a news association as the United Press. But Goebbels was a little mixed.]

Darré is completely discredited with the Fuehrer. He deserved it. In these serious times he occupied himself with writing "think-pieces" and books instead of getting order into the food situation, even though his means are limited. The Fuehrer deals only with Backe. Darré is a great flop and nowise equal to the tasks of war.

[Argentine-born Walther Darré belonged to the Old Guard but was so incom-petent that even the fact of long service in the Party did not help to save him. His successor, Herbert Backe, as Secretary of State for Food and Agriculture, had been running the Ministry for years.]

Berndt handed in a plan for occultist propaganda to be carried on by us. We are really getting somewhere. The Americans and English fall easily for that type of propaganda. We are therefore pressing into our service all star witnesses for occult prophecy. Nostradamus must once again submit to being quoted.

[Alfred Ingomar Berndt was a rather stupid young newspaperman who en-joyed a meteoric career under Goebbels as a typical "yes-man." He was attached to Rommel's army as a sort of personal spy for the little doctor. He was one of Goebbels's most trusted lieutenants. He was nicknamed *Roes'chen* (Rosie).

Nostradamus was the Latin name for Michel de Notredame, a French astrologer who lived from 1503 to 1566 and was court physician to Charles IX. His astrological prophecies attracted great attention.]

In the afternoon I had a long argument with Hippler and with Greven about the aims to be pursued in our French film production. Greven has an entirely wrong technique in that he has regarded it as his task to raise the level of the French movie. That is wrong. It isn't our job to supply the Frenchmen with good pictures and it is especially not our task to give them movies that are beyond reproach in their nationalistic tendency.

[Hippler, who is not identified more closely anywhere in the diaries was evidently an employee in the moving-picture section of the Propaganda Ministry.]

If the French people on the whole are satisfied with light, corny stuff, we ought to make it our business to produce such cheap trash. It would be a case of lunacy for us to promote competition against ourselves. We must proceed in our movie policies as the Americans do in their policies toward the North and South American continents. We must become the dominating movie power on the European continent. In so far as pictures are produced in other countries they must be only of a local or limited character. It must be our aim to prevent so far as possible the founding of any new national film industry, and if necessary to hire for Berlin, Vienna, or Munich such stars and technicians as might be in a position to help in this. After I talked to him for a long time Greven realized the wisdom of this course and will pursue it in future.

May 20, 1942

Meanwhile the article in the *Frankfurter Zeitung,* which was inspired by us and is intended to divert the attention of the observing enemy public from the southern front, has appeared. It is officially suppressed and denounced in the press conference.

[In his entry for May 15 Goebbels told of his intention to launch an "unauthorized" article in the *Frankfurter Zeitung.* By that he meant that, when it appeared, the writer would be publicly denounced (privately praised) for "lack of discipline" in "revealing" German war plans, and further circulation of the issue forbidden. By that time, of course, the copies for foreign countries had already left—and that was where Goebbels really wanted the "unauthorized" article to be read.]

Things have advanced to the point where I can send the journalist Dr. Kriegk, now that he has made a trip to the Eastern Front, to Lisbon to commit several indiscretions on orders from me. He is to get tipsy and, with his own impressions as a background, is to spread the assertion that the German attack is planned not for the south, but for the center. I hope it will be possible in that way to launch this canard as a rumor in the world organs of publicity. The coming weeks will have to show how far it is possible actually to mislead the enemy. I suppose one must not count on too great a success. But one must always try whatever one can do.

In the evening it was possible for us to issue a lengthy special bulletin on the complete conquest of the peninsula of Kerch. Our booty is tremendous. The number of prisoners has meanwhile risen to about 150,000. The first great victory of the year against the Soviet armies! We take a deep breath and feel as though all the people were taking a deep breath.

The American journalists who were transported from Germany and Italy to Lisbon have issued the funniest reports about internal conditions in the Axis countries. They are completely harmless for the simple reason that of course all promptly disagree with each other.

[Had Goebbels been able to see the smash front-page "spreads" which these accounts were given by the newspapers throughout America, he would probably not have spoken so derisively.]

May 21, 1942

New American units have arrived in Ireland. The purpose of this isn't quite clear for the moment. Americans seem determined by demonstrations of this kind to put the English gradually under moral compulsion to create a second front. But the English are merely standing by their guns for the present. They especially lament their heavy shipping losses and believe that in view of the catastrophic tonnage position an invasion of the European continent can scarcely be attempted.

Churchill's conduct of the war is attacked with exceptional vehemence during the debate in the House of Commons. He is standing in the cross fire of criticism by all parties. It is nothing short of a riddle how this man can still be so popular.

From Madrid student riots are reported, partly directed against the Franco regime. These riots, however, originated with the Falange movement and are explained on the grounds that, under pressure of the clericals, Franco has put the nationalistic sources of popular power pretty much on ice. Never has a revolution yielded so few spiritual and political results as that carried through by Franco. He is today practically the pacemaker for political reaction.

In Rumania measures are being taken against the German elements there—of all people. They have been forbidden to wear uniforms and have had to suffer all sorts of other humiliations. The situation has become so bad that Killinger for a while thought of resigning. Thereupon the Rumanians yielded on a number of unimportant points. Antonescu further promised, as a result of a protest by Von Ribbentrop, to call the deputy premier, Mihai Antonescu, to order for constantly interfering with Axis policies in the Balkans. I don't suppose much will come of it, however.

[Manfred Freiherr von Killinger, an Old Guard Nazi SA leader, of the beer-cellar fighter type, was appointed Minister to Rumania when Ribbentrop "Nazi-fied" the Foreign Office more and more. Until March 1935 he had been Saxon Premier, but did not get along with Martin Mutschmann, Nazi Statthalter or Governor for Saxony.]

I received Kriegk, the chief editor of the *Scherl Verlag*, who had made a trip to the central [eastern] front on my orders and is now to report about it in the *Nachtausgabe* and the *Lokalanzeiger*. These articles are to continue until next Tuesday. After that he is to fly to Portugal at my request, there to commit several indiscretions along the lines that our coming offensive is not planned for the south, but for the center. He is to say that he has exact information on this matter and that he has been able to convince himself of its accuracy by a personal visit. These remarks are to be made at some bar where he is to give the appearance of being drunk. I hope that they will then quickly reach the ears of neutral and even enemy journalists. These will report them with lightning speed to London and Moscow. Whether we shall succeed thereby in diverting attention from the south is not yet clear. But one does what one can.

[The Scherl Publishing House (*Scherl Verlag*) was the largest conservative newspaper and magazine concern in Germany, and was controlled by Alfred Hugenberg, chairman of the German National party, whom Hitler took into his first cabinet in 1933 for a while as Minister of Economic Affairs, but gradually eased out later. Hugenberg was also heavily interested in the leading German motion-picture concern, the UFA. (See note in entry of March 5, 1943.)]

The food situation is causing us great worry. According to a report by the Food Ministry the question of seed is especially depressing. During the next autumn, we shall lack the necessary grain so that we shall again be compelled to revise the bread rations considerably downward. That is a reduction that hits the broad masses of the people hardest. It would help matters if we at least had an abundance of potatoes, but if this swinish weather continues, as at present, there isn't a ghost of a chance of this either.

As regards bread, we won't be able to avoid mixing barley into it to a large extent. That will further reduce both the quality and the nutritive value of the bread. In short, we are faced with a problem which human intelligence and talent for organization are powerless to solve. Every day we look to heaven with fear and trembling to see whether the right mixture of rain and sunshine will come. We are surely a poor people, and if we continue to exist at all as a nation this is owing solely to our industry and intelligence.

The Fuehrer has at last decided to boot out Darré. Backe is to be his successor. I begged the Fuehrer urgently, however, not to make a public front-page announcement, because that would carry with it the danger that all mistakes made in our food policies and all curtailments of rations would be blamed on Darré and thereby on the National Socialist regime, for Darré, after all, is a National Socialist minister. The Fuehrer agreed to this and was willing merely to have an item published about Darré's illness which, for the present, prevents him from attending to the duties of his office; meanwhile he is to be replaced by Backe.

Backe does his job in an exemplary manner. You can depend upon him. He is not a pale theoretician like Darré, but a real, first-class man of practice. I never thought much of Darré. His theories are pure fiction. He doesn't understand much of practical farm life. His slogan, too, of blood and soil has been so ridden to death by himself and his henchmen that you can hardly even tempt a dog away from behind the stove with it.

[For background to the Walther Darré episode see the diary entry for May 19. It was typical for Goebbels to hush up anything unfavorable to an Old Guard Nazi. Although he had no use for Darré and was glad that he was dismissed, Goebbels did not want the public to know that there was any nincompoop in the Nazi hierarchy.

The "blood and soil" slogan refers to the Nazi teaching, especially by Darré, that man's position in the scale of human values is determined by the blood in his veins and the soil from which he stems. Nordic blood—this was axiomatic for the Nazi—was the best blood in the world, and there could be nothing more perfect than to have been born on hallowed German soil.]

May 22, 1942

In Ankara nobody believes in a second front. It is claimed that England merely wants to bluff the Axis Powers. I am not quite clear as to whether it is a case of actual camouflage in this question or in the threats of massive RAF attacks on the Reich. In any case it is extremely curious—without wanting to draw premature conclusions—that the air raids of the English have ceased along the whole line.

We have finally had the good sense to issue a decree which guarantees absolute religious tolerance in the eastern [occupied] areas. The Fuehrer decided that this decree is not to be signed by Rosenberg himself but by the commissars for the different sections. Rosenberg's signature in this matter would not mean very much to the world.

Personally, I believe we must change our policies essentially as regards the peoples of the East. We could reduce the danger of the Partisans considerably if we succeeded in at least winning a certain measure of confidence with these peoples. A clear peasant and church policy would work wonders there. It might also be useful to set up sham governments in the various sectors which would then have to be responsible for unpleasant and unpopular measures. Undoubtedly it would be easy to set up such sham governments, and we would then always have a façade behind which to camouflage our policies. I shall talk to the Fuehrer about this problem in the near future. I consider it one of the most vital in the present situation in the East.

The differences between the American and the English conception of how the war is to be waged are becoming more pronounced from week to week, at least judging by press commentary. The Chicago *Tribune* for the first time launched a very heavy attack against the English war leadership and especially against the meddling of the London press with internal American affairs. This newspaper, which was always isolationist and would have nothing to do with the war, has exploded in a manner hitherto unknown. As we have no interest in causing the little plant of Anglo-American enmity to wither by turning our sun lamps of publicity on it too officiously, we shall take no notice of this editorial in our news and propaganda services.

I received a report about the present food situation in Berlin. It gives cause for the greatest worry. Again there is a shortage of potatoes. What we have accumulated in the way of reserves must now be given out as seed potatoes. The early harvest will keep us waiting a good many weeks more, and we can hardly expect anything from Italy. We must therefore attempt to bridge over a whole series of weeks. There are no possibilities of getting extra bread or flour; in short, here again is a precarious situation that without a doubt may become the normal condition for the coming months of autumn and winter.

The letters arriving from various parts of the country indicate that the masses of the people are getting increasingly angry about the food situation. For this reason I think that the dismissal of Darré at this moment was more than dangerous psychologically.

May 23, 1942

Relatively exact figures going back to March now prove that during that month there was a record expenditure of all important types of munitions, so that even the reserve supplies lying behind the front were completely exhausted. Inasmuch as, on the whole, there are no reserves of these types of munitions back home, this means that the front in future will always use up whatever has just been finished back home.

We can be exceptionally well satisfied with the way things stand in the East. I have induced the OKW to have a camouflaged article written to divert attention to the central front. I am going to try to have this article placed through middlemen either in the Turkish or the Portuguese press. That will be quite difficult, as the authorship of this article will probably become evident, in which case the article would cause harm rather than do good. But one must now try everything possible to cover the whole situation with a veil of secrecy until the big assaults begin.

The opinion is voiced at Ankara that the Bolsheviks would in all likelihood throw up the sponge if we gained possession of the Caucasus and the city of Moscow. I consider this possible but not probable. The men who govern Russia today are hard-boiled sinners, who fully realize that they have a choice only between victory and complete destruction.

The American soldiers who landed in Ireland gave interviews to the big news agencies. These are of a strange and disarming naïveté. One might wish that the Yankees could sometime come in contact with tried and proven front-line soldiers. Their illusions about the European war would surely disappear very quickly.

Our English radio broadcasts are, after all, very effective, as I have been able to determine from a dependable source. However, an aggressive, superior, and insulting tone gets us nowhere. I have so often said so to our various departments and shall now insist that this nonsense be eliminated immediately. At present you can get somewhere with the English only by talking to them in a friendly and modest way.

The English speaker, Lord Haw Haw, is especially great at biting criticism, but in my opinion the time for spicy debate is past. During the third year of war you must carry on a different type of warfare from that of the first year. During the first year of war the people still listen to the delivery; they admire the wit and the spiritual qualities of the presentation. Today they want nothing but facts. The more cleverly, therefore, the facts are put together and the more psychologically and sensitively they are brought to the knowledge of the listening public, the stronger is the effect.

[Lord Haw Haw was the radio name for William B. Joyce, an unsuccessful Irish actor who left the British Isles and went to Germany, where the Nazis hired him to broadcast in English to the British Isles each night. He was seized by the British when Germany collapsed, taken to England, tried for treason, found guilty, and hanged, as W. L. White described it in his *Report on the Germans,* "with considerable pomp and judicial ceremony as a traitor to the British Crown."]

In the British House of Lords an interesting debate was staged, dealing chiefly with the manner in which the German people are to be treated after the war. There were some voices urging that a difference be made between the Nazis and the German people, as the English propaganda could not otherwise reach the German people. Criticism turned especially against Vansittart, who is known to favor not only the destruction of National Socialism but also the destruction of the German people. Vansittart's speech has not yet come into our hands. I am moving heaven and earth to obtain the text, for undoubtedly it will be of tremendous value for our domestic propaganda.

The English are very foolish to insult the German people thus brusquely. If they were to make a difference between the people and ourselves they could undoubtedly gain more thereby than they now achieve. I sense a certain danger in the tendencies aired in the House of Lords and forbid the German press to make any mention of such utterances. The less we talk about them, the less easily will these political germs become virulent.

I allocated a large sum from our Winter Relief fund for developing obstetrical service in the newly acquired eastern provinces. It is becoming more and more evident that repopulation is the cardinal problem of the European situation. He alone who has more full cradles than full coffins will be victorious in the end.

Gauleiter Florian of Duesseldorf paid me a visit and presented me with a folder of photos showing how Rheydt Castle in my home town is being renovated and made livable. The renovation is in excellent taste. The castle is to be placed at my disposal to live in. I shall be glad after the war to spend a few days there now and then so as to be in my home town.

[Friedrich Karl Florian was Gauleiter of the Duesseldorf area in which Rheydt, the home town of Goebbels, is located. The little doctor certainly did not dream in his youth that the ancient castle of his native town would be fixed up for him to live in!]

The Fuehrer has returned to Berlin from his GHQ. He wants to take part in the state funeral for Gauleiter Roever and also to speak to all the Reich- and Gauleiters. He called me immediately and had a talk about the general situation.

The Fuehrer has a very favorable opinion of the situation in the East. He is convinced that the battle near Kharkov is going to prove a victory of most far-reaching consequences. Our overrunning of the Bolshevik divisions on the Kerch Peninsula also gives occasion for great hopes regarding further military operations. It is true that we still have a hard road to travel, but this can be done.

I report to the Fuehrer about my attempts to divert general attention from the southern to the central front. He approves absolutely.

The Fuehrer places great hopes in the war on shipping. It seems to be absolutely true that an American battleship was sunk by an Italian submarine. That means that the Americans have once again lost a unit they simply won't be able to replace.

In the course of the next month we are going to put into service one and a half times as many submarines as are at present on the firing line. That means that the curve of sinkings will rise rapidly again. In the Fuehrer's opinion we shall here strike at an especially sensitive nerve of the enemy. If Churchill and Roosevelt a few months ago were hopeful that the German submarine danger was eliminated, the hard facts of the situation will convince them of the opposite. They are going to get so many unexpected blows in this submarine war that all their loud-mouthed boasts of being able to cover the losses easily by new construction will be relegated to the realm of fantasy.

The Fuehrer once more explained his standpoint with regard to the administration of justice in wartime. He said a people always consists of three parts: a small negative part, made up of criminal elements, a small positive part consisting of idealists, and then the broad masses that are in a constant doubt whether they should swing to the left or to the right. War, by a natural process, alarmingly thins out the ranks of the small minority of idealists. The idealists grow fewer, but the criminal elements, on the whole, maintain themselves. Justice must be administered rigorously and one must strive for an equilibrium. It won't do for the best sons of the people to fall at the front and for the criminals at home to be preserved, as it were, thanks to lax justice. All they need to do to be locked up in prison or the penitentiary for two or three years is to commit some criminal act, and when the war is ended they emerge in liberty, fresh and unused, whereas the counterweight of idealists who will always vigorously oppose them no longer exists. That's why one should not shrink from brutal punishment in wartime. If the soldier must risk his life because of idealism, the criminal should at least know that he must forfeit his life for his criminal attitude or his criminal deeds. Our Ministry of Justice is unable to understand a line of reasoning that is so obvious. It still moves in formal grooves. That's why it is necessary to watch Justice constantly, and the Fuehrer is grateful for every suggestion. After his last speech in the Reichstag, it will be remembered, he received full powers, even in the opinion of judges bound by formal conceptions, to do what he considers necessary. . . . I now proposed to the Fuehrer that bicycles be requisitioned in France as a punishment for attempts at assassination and that they be placed at the disposal of German soldiers. The Fuehrer regarded this proposal as wonderful and immediately ordered Jodl to see to its practical execution.

With Amann and Wagner I discussed the sorry policy of our Reich Investigation and Arbitration Committee. Buch has too little brains and is in no way equal to his tasks. But the more foolish a man is, the more insolent he becomes. That is the case here too. He seriously defends the view that he is a judge even of the Fuehrer. One simply cannot think of a more childish conception. Buch is nothing but a laughing stock among the circles of old Party members; he is a male governess.

[Adolf Wagner was Gauleiter for Munich.
Walter Buch was Chief Justice of the Nazi Party Court.]

I talked with Schmundt about the tasks devolving upon Colonel Scherff at the Fuehrer's GHQ. Colonel Scherff is outstanding for his exceptionally clear and plastic style. He is to write the history of the war, and it is a good thing that the chronicler of the war is living at the point where the real decisions are made. It is already noticeable today that attempts are under way here and there to falsify the history of certain military events. It is all the better that there is someone at GHQ whose task it is to keep an exact score and whose documentary material will in future serve to guarantee a correct historical evaluation of the war. It is simply impossible to write the history of our war solely from dry official papers.

I had a telephone conversation with the Reich Marshal who complained about the OKW because it protested against the new Leander motion picture. This picture shows an aviator spending a night with a famous singer. The OKW considers itself insulted morally and insists that an aviation lieutenant wouldn't act that way. Opposed to this is the correct view of Goering that if an aviation lieutenant didn't make use of such an opportunity, he simply wouldn't be an aviation lieutenant. Goering pokes great fun at the sensitiveness of the OKW. That's fine grist for my mill, since the OKW creates a lot of difficulties for me anyway in my movie work. In this case we can depend upon Goering as the better expert on the Luftwaffe and won't have to fear any jurisdictional difficulties.

[Zarah Leander was a German favorite of the screen.]

The Fuehrer is still in Berlin. He wants to talk to the Reich- and Gauleiters on Saturday and give them a picture of the situation. The fact that he is able to leave his GHQ for two days during the battle of Kharkov is a sign of how favorable the situation now is and with what great hope we can face the future.

Recapitulation of events between
May 23 and December 7, 1942

There is a gap of more than half a year in the diaries. It is to be feared that the entries for these six and one half months were destroyed and thus an important series of observations on dramatic world events, as seen by the highest official chronicler of the Nazi movement, lost to posterity.

Before even the month of May was ended, the incident occurred which made the Czech town of Lidice a synonym for Nazi barbarity; "Hangman" Heydrich was assassinated at Prague on May 25. Thereupon on June 10 Lidice was "wiped out." Also, Great Britain and the Soviet Union signed a twenty-year treaty which provided that neither party would make a separate peace with Germany or seek territorial aggrandizement.

In North Africa, Field Marshal Erwin Rommel, the "Desert Fox," at first still seemed invincible and not only captured the important fortress of Tobruk, but chased the British all the way back to the Egyptian frontier. Then, however, his luck turned. At El Alamein the British forces rallied under Field Marshal Montgomery, and slowly but surely, beginning in the latter half of October, the Axis forces were driven westward under the supreme command of Field Marshal Alexander and with Montgomery in charge of the famed British Eighth Army.

Meanwhile, as early as June 25, announcement had been made in Washington of the creation of a European Theater of War (ETO) under the supreme command of Major General Dwight Eisenhower. On November 8 the American armies landed on the Mediterranean and Atlantic coasts of French North Africa. From now on it was evident to every objective observer that the fate of the Axis forces in North Africa was sealed.

Oran was captured November 9, Casablanca surrendered two days later. Darlan appeared on the scene and was placed "temporarily" in charge of French interests, despite protests by General de Gaulle in London.

Hitler, however, apparently refused to see the writing on the wall, for in an address at Munich on November 8 he promised counterblows against the Allies in North Africa "in due time."

Stalin, on the other hand, on November 13 asserted that the Anglo-American operations in Africa had turned the tide of the war in Europe and had opened the way for the early collapse of the Axis.

During this gap in the Goebbels diaries there also began, on August 24, the ill-fated siege of Stalingrad, ordered by Hitler against the advice of some of his more far-sighted generals. The German rout at Stalingrad proved one of the major turning points of the war, at least in its effect upon the German population, which from then on regarded the struggle as lost.

On other sectors of the Russian front the fortunes of war favored the Nazis. The Russians had to retreat on the Kharkov front on June 23, after having started an offensive there. They had to evacuate Rostov on July 27. They had to destroy the important Maikop oil fields in the Caucasus as the German steam roller advanced in mid-August. On September 11, they admitted the loss of the Black Sea base of Novorossiisk. Even the appointment of Field Marshal Zhukov late in August as first vice-commissar of defense brought no immediate relief. Nor did the abolition of the political commissar system in Stalin's armies, announced October 10, change events in Russia's favor.

The heroic defense of Stalingrad, however, with its dogged house-to-house fighting even by civilians and the ultimate German rout compensated for these temporary reverses and had a tremendously favorable effect on Russian morale.

During these six and a half months the Western Allies started their non-stop, round-the-clock air raids on important German industrial centers, among them Cologne, Wilhelmshaven, Essen, Danzig, Flensburg, Munich, Nuremberg, Bremen, Duesseldorf (which experienced its fiftieth raid on September 11), and Berlin.

The German Luftwaffe, already visibly weaker, could retaliate only by raids on Canterbury on May 31 and October 31.

Other high lights of this half year were the Roosevelt-Molotov agreement of June 11 on Lend-Lease; Winston Churchill's visit to Moscow on August 12 after a previous journey to Washington announced June 18; the ill-starred Dieppe raid of August 19, in the course of which the Canadians lost 67 per cent of their men; Franco's ouster of Serrano

Suñer as Foreign Minister and his replacement by Francisco Jordana on September 3; Pétain's severance of diplomatic relations with the United States on November 8 in protest against the landing of American troops in French North Africa; and the French scuttling of their fleet at Toulon on November 27.

December 1942

MUSSOLINI ASSURES ITALIANS VICTORY IS CERTAIN. FLIERS OF EIGHT ALLIED NATIONS RAZE MILITARY OBJECTIVES IN NAZI-OCCUPIED FRANCE AND HOLLAND. HITLER APPOINTS GENERAL KURT ZEITZLER CHIEF OF GENERAL STAFF. ANTON MUSSERT IS MADE "LEADER OF THE DUTCH" BY HITLER. DARLAN DENIES PERSONAL AMBITIONS. HITLER HOLDS TWO-DAY CONFERENCE WITH CIANO AND LAVAL. DARLAN IS ASSASSINATED. TEN FLYING FORTRESSES RAID WAKE ISLAND. GIRAUD SUCCEEDS DARLAN. POPE PIUS DENOUNCES "GODLESS TOTALITARIANISM."

December 7, 1942

Kalinin delivered a pretty gloomy and pessimistic speech. But one must not draw wrong conclusions from it. The Bolshevik leaders are doing everything possible to keep up the spirit of resistance of the Soviet peoples during this winter.

[Michael Ivanovich Kalinin was president of the Presidium of the Supreme Council of the U.S.S.R.]

The newspaper *Madrid* has created a sensation by misrepresenting a speech in Tokyo as indicating separate peace negotiations were under way between Berlin and Moscow via Tokyo. I am now going to take energetic steps against this newspaper and its Berlin representative. It simply won't do for papers friendly to us to misrepresent our political intentions just to support untrustworthy and sensational reports by their correspondents.

De Gaulle has again spoken over a British network and turned vehemently against Darlan and the French opportunists. He said French territory would forever belong to France and French soldiers were fighting only for the honor of France and her possessions. This speech is undoubtedly a shaft poisoned in Churchill's laboratory. Churchill is detouring via de Gaulle to oppose American imperialistic and pluto-cratic demands in French North Africa. The fight between the City and Wall Street for the French colonies continues with unabated sever-ity.

In Paris, Doriot has again spoken in very sharp opposition to Laval. His speech teemed with insults against the present French Premier. I think it will be necessary for us to gag Doriot sooner or later, as he is beginning to be quite a terror.

[Jacques Doriot was a French politician who collaborated with the Nazis.]

My address in the Sports Palace attracted unusual attention in the domestic and foreign press. We ought really to deliver speeches more frequently than hitherto. The English are better than we in that re-spect. They attack the public of the world at regular intervals with ministerial speeches and in that way insure tremendous publicity for their arguments.

December 8, 1942

Practically all our troops have been supplied with excellent winter clothing. A catastrophe such as we faced last winter is simply out of the question this winter. The northern and central fronts are equipped 100 per cent with this winter dress; the southern front at the present only eighty per cent, but the remaining twenty per cent are in process of manufacture.

I wish experienced German combat troops could tangle with the Americans. The formations which made the Americans flee in Tunisia were not even a select body. Some were thrown together in a haphaz-ard way; nevertheless we achieved an outstanding success. How much greater would our triumph be if the Yankees, who have big mouths but no combat experience, were to clash, let us say, with the *Leibstandarte!* We would not even have to be curious about the result—everybody could figure it out for himself.

The Japanese have issued a balance sheet on one year of naval war-fare against the United States and England. The figures are truly im-pressive. Possibly some of these figures are exaggerated, but on the whole one can see that the war in the Pacific has gone completely in favor of the Japanese.

A big espionage trial against Germans has been started in Buenos Aires. A number of stool pigeons were paid to admit they took part in the espionage. Naturally they hasten to reveal the names of others allegedly implicated. The whole procedure has undoubtedly been initiated on orders from Roosevelt and is intended to worsen our relations with Argentina.

The publication of a part of my Sports Palace address by Radio London five hours after I spoke is explained in a way that makes me think I'm in a madhouse. This passage of my speech was not transmitted to London by a group of spies, but by our own Transocean Bureau! It's incredible how such a thing could happen. But that's how life is. There is always only one possibility of doing the right thing but there are thousands of possibilities of doing the wrong thing. You simply cannot protect yourself against all these possibilities of doing the wrong thing. There will always be some one among us who finds out a possibility not yet foreseen in our directives and makes use of it.

[Transocean (*Transozean*) was a German wireless news service owned by the German Government and distributed widely in every part of the world. A subscription fee was asked, but rather than lose the opportunity for propaganda which this biased news service afforded, papers were supplied with it free of charge if they indicated a willingness to use it but objected to the price.]

Thierack reported to me about the administration of the law. He has already introduced a number of innovations which augur well for the triumph of the National Socialist conception of justice.

The Fuehrer, he said, agrees with me about dealing with certain moral aberrations on the part of women. In the fourth year of war one can't be too strict about morals and must take into account the conditions from which laxity results. But the Fuehrer won't permit any change in the law about intercourse of German women with prisoners of war. That is undoubtedly right. A line must be drawn somewhere.

December 11, 1942

The Darlan case is still the *cause célèbre* for our adversaries. Roosevelt does not seem to be willing to yield to the covert or open threats of the English. He continues to support Darlan, no doubt because he regards him as reliable since he is dependent upon him.

I read a detailed report from our Research Office on the Darlan case. The treachery of this French admiral is traced from its very beginning. The report proves convincingly that Darlan started for North Africa to desert us and that his son's illness was only an excuse. One might even suspect from the data that Pétain was in cahoots with him. But it can't be proven.

Italy has published a new list of casualties. It is nothing to be proud of. During November 300 Italians were killed in action in Africa but 23,000 were missing. The ratio is more than devastating. While it is true that Mussolini's speech made a good impression on the German people, the ratio of Italian casualties [to surrenders] has had a very bad effect. I ordered that no notice be taken in the German press of this latest Italian casualty list.

The English have again made a massive air raid on Turin. The Italian Army communiqué speaks of very heavy losses. I have the impression that these Italian reports are somewhat exaggerated. A couple of days ago they spoke of an exceptionally heavy air raid, yet it resulted in only sixty-five fatalities.

The Fascist periodical, *Gerarchia,* which is edited by Mussolini himself, discussed at length the question of religion in Europe after the war. Christianity is pointedly placed in the foreground. Obviously the Duce feels that he must somewhat neutralize the work of the Church. He has always been dependent on many domestic factors that we need not be much concerned about in the Reich. One can well imagine why he is now taking a stand in favor of Christianity. But that is all the more reason for us not to say anything about these utterances of his.

[The Nazis were determined to eliminate Christianity altogether from Germany after the war. Alfred Rosenberg had already prepared a decree for Hitler's signature by which even the lowest-paid menial worker on the public pay roll was to lose his job if he continued church membership.]

The question of compulsory women's labor has now become acute. The *Reichsbahn* [Federal Railway] opposes the new decree, not because it provides for compulsory women's labor but because the women drafted are to be used for the Luftwaffe only. The Reichsbahn wants to have its share. I expected that and am glad of it. Once the question of compulsory women's labor has passed the theoretical stage, nothing can stop it—a development that I welcome heartily.

[Goebbels, one of the earliest and most uncompromising sponsors of total war, had long favored the drafting of women for war work.]

The Swedes have recently become very reserved toward us and very insolent. We are in no position at present to put pressure on them. The better we hold our own at the Eastern Front, the more impudent the

Swedish press becomes. It believes it need not fear us for the moment. Also, it feels safe under the protection of England. If the Anglo-Saxon nations achieve only mediocre victories, the Swedes regard themselves as on top of the world.

December 12, 1942

We started for Dresden early in the morning. The weather was so wonderful that it made this trip a pleasure. For the first time in a long while we can move freely along the road. We drove on the *Autobahn* [super highway]. The scenery was one of wonderful calm and austerity. I felt happy as in times of peace. . . . We arrived in Dresden shortly before 11 A.M. Even from a distance the city conveyed the impression of being stately, wonderfully bright, and clean. Just imagine what one could make of Dresden if it had farsighted cultural leadership! But this famous art city has become a Sleeping Beauty under Mutschmann; more than that, it has slowly drifted in a direction that is absolutely devoid of culture. I felt this development all the more keenly during my present visit since I had not been to Dresden for so long a time.

The funeral ceremony took place in the Great Hall of the Exposition Palace. It was very impressive. I addressed exceptionally warmhearted and affectionate words to the memory of Director Posse. I did it purposely because Posse deserved it. He had no easy time in Dresden under the aegis of Mutschmann; his memory should at least be honored. . . .

[Hans Posse had been director of the Saxon State Art Galleries.]

Frau Raubal visited me at the hotel. She had a lot of family news to tell me. Her husband has been at the Eastern Front for more than a year, and that, too, at an age of almost sixty-five years. Frau Raubal has developed very favorably and appealingly. I chat with her and refresh memories of days gone by. She, too, complained very much about Mutschmann's fizzling out. He has recently become exceedingly headstrong. His entourage, which is composed only of fellow sportsmen, eggs him on. His wife, too, has an exceedingly bad influence on him.

[Angela Raubal was Hitler's half-sister, who kept house for him during all the years of his struggle for power. The world learned of a disagreement between the two only when a news item announced on February 29, 1936, that the Fuehrer was too busy to attend his sister's wedding in Berlin to Dr. Martin Hammzsch of Dresden.]

Before starting for home I learned of the death of Director von Stauss. That means that the German Academy now also loses its vice-president in addition to its president. Stauss fell ill after attending Siebert's funeral. The way men in public life are dying almost frightens one. . . .

[Emil Georg von Stauss was one of the best-known financiers of Germany, a director of the Deutsche Bank and of many German industrial undertakings.]

The latest reports of the SD and the Reich Propaganda offices were presented to me. In both of these, as well as in the reports of the Gauleiters, there is very sharp criticism of our news policy regarding the situation at the front. I feel absolutely not guilty of this obvious fizzle. I have always urged greater frankness in news.

The Duce's speech has been given an excellent reception by the German people. The Duce is looked upon as an outstanding historical personality. Of course the casualty figures announced by the Duce have raised grave doubts as to the fighting qualities of the Italian Army.

My article about "Political Passion" has drawn a large number of letters which, without exception, agree with my ideas and in part are even very enthusiastic about them.

In Tunisia a terrible winter rain has started quite suddenly. That is unpleasant for the enemy but pleasant for us. The more time we gain, the better it is. That enables us to transport a lot of matériel and many troops there and strengthens our position more every day. The American-English airports are completely flooded. They can't start any air operations from there.

Mrs. Roosevelt has rendered her husband a poor service. She informed a mayor on the West coast that not five but six battleships were lost at Pearl Harbor. So now, a year later, and after much hemming and hawing, the whole truth will out; namely, that the Japanese reports were quite accurate and the Americans have always lied. . . . If in future the Americans dare to deny Japanese figures we shall simply refer to the events of Pearl Harbor to prove that the Americans like to pose as being serious about news, but actually are anything but truth-loving.

The English have meanwhile taken the fetters off the German prisoners in Canada. The English papers unite in the slogan, "Never again!" The whole affair has been exceedingly unpopular in England. We hope that by December 15 we can also unshackle the English prisoners. Then we, too, will be out of this loathsome affair.

[The British and German governments each charged the other with having shackled their prisoners of war. Whoever may have started, the fact is that both sides indulged in the practice. Goebbels here records that an agreement was reached for unshackling.]

It is interesting to note that the General Government [of Poland] is furnishing food far beyond the figures imposed upon it after I made my demand. In other words, the occupied areas are in a position to supply the Reich to a much greater degree than they hitherto admitted. They must be held to it energetically, and those in charge must be held to account. If they know they'll lose their jobs if they can't meet the most elementary requirements for their offices they will naturally work with all the greater energy at the solution of tasks important to the war.

In the evening quite a number of Gauleiters paid me a visit. They had been at the Reich Ministry of the Interior for a meeting of the Reich Defense Commissars. The meeting must have been nothing short of catastrophic. Frick told them about things they knew ages ago. Besides, the meeting merely skimmed the surface.

Among my guests may be especially mentioned all the Gauleiters of Austria, also Grohé from Cologne, Greiser from Posen, Giesler from Munich, Koch from the Ukraine, in short, a cross-section of our old top-notch leadership. I reviewed the whole political and military situation for them. They were most grateful. Many questions regarding economics, politics, and war morale were discussed. Among these men I feel as though I were with my own family. Here one can speak quite openly. Problems need merely to be hinted at. All are of one mind, and all are perfectly clear about everything. The evening was one of unadulterated joy for me. We sat reminiscing till the wee hours of the morning. . . .

I am now going to seek a closer and more personal contact with the Gauleiters. A leadership corps that represents the cream of the German people has developed here. When one can get the Gauleiters to support one's work, one can always be sure of success. And there is no place where co-operation with the Party is more necessary than in my work!

December 13, 1942

Submarine warfare is our great ace. Both the English and the Americans are at last admitting it. . . . We still have a lot on the ball in our submarine warfare. Doenitz is a superior brass hat who knows how to use his weapon in a dashing and imaginative way. . . . At any rate the submarine is just as effective an instrument of war for us as the air force is for the English; it enables us to strike at the enemy at his weakest point.

[Grand Admiral Karl Doenitz, born, 1891, an ardent Nazi, succeeded Grand Admiral Erich Raeder in 1943 as Commander in Chief of the German Navy. Just before he committed suicide in his bunker late in April 1945 Hitler appointed Doenitz as Reich President to succeed himself as chief executive of Germany. Doenitz was the first in a radio broadcast to the German people to announce Germany's unconditional surrender. He was taken prisoner at Flensburg, indicted as a major criminal, and sentenced to ten years' imprisonment at Nuremberg.]

The question of Jewish persecution in Europe is being given top news priority by the English and the Americans. . . . At bottom, however, I believe both the English and the Americans are happy that we are exterminating the Jewish riff-raff. But the Jews will go on and on and turn the heat on the British-American press. We won't even discuss this theme publicly, but instead I gave orders to start an atrocity campaign against the English on their treatment of Colonials.

Efforts are under way to declare Rome an open city, so that it won't be bombarded. The Pope is studying the question of air raids on Italian cities and seems to be exerting pressure on the English to spare at least certain districts. The declarations issued by the Vatican on this question are extremely clever and cannot but win favor for the Pope, at least in Italy. But the Italians are willing to accept any help offered them in this painful situation.

The Italians are extremely lax in the treatment of Jews. They protect the Italian Jews both in Tunis and in occupied France and won't permit their being drafted for work or compelled to wear the Star of David. This shows once again that Fascism does not really dare to get down to fundamentals, but is very superficial regarding most important problems. The Jewish question is causing us a lot of trouble. Everywhere, even among our allies, the Jews have friends to help them, which is a proof that they are still playing an important role even in the Axis camp. All the more are they shorn of power within Germany itself.

[Throughout Germany and the countries occupied by the Nazi Wehrmacht, the Jews had to wear a yellow band with a Star of David and the word "Jew" in the language of the country. The Nazis expected their allies to treat their Jews similarly.]

Another matter causing us difficulties with our Axis partners is the treatment of foreign labor. In the gau of Lower Silesia a handbill was issued on this question by the gau leadership which really must stir up and embitter our Axis partners most deeply. They are there very definitely characterized as second-rate, especially in discussing the relationship of foreign workers to German women. Protests are flooding the Foreign Office because of this handbill and the general treatment of foreign workers. I contacted the gau leaders of Lower Silesia and insisted upon the withdrawal of the handbill. The new Europe is posing many a question to us that cannot be answered at present. We must try so to balance the problems as to enable us to wind our way through the underbrush of the present. Regarding many of these questions you cannot, as Bismarck put it, go through the forest holding your pole horizontally; you must carry it vertically to get through.

The supply train from the Ukraine that Koch placed at my disposal has arrived in Berlin. It brought great quantities of high-grade food, especially butter. I have given orders that this food be distributed only to the wounded, the families with many children, and old people.

Distribution is to take place on a somewhat smaller scale than originally planned, so that every beneficiary may receive a really decent portion. One must not thin out an operation of this kind too much, because that does not impress the public. This food from the Ukraine does not have only intrinsic value; it is also to serve a propaganda purpose.

It is especially desirable that the Party be credited with this operation. The Party has so many unpleasant things to tell the citizens and has so many demands to make upon them, that it is no more than right and just that it should now, for once, bring them something pleasant. It is, for example, very disagreeable for the Party that the local group leader must inform the bereaved of the hero's death of a son, brother, or husband. Formerly the Church did this. Now the Party has been charged with it, with the result that in little villages people are scared to death whenever the local group leader comes to their home. The local leader is frequently looked upon as a funereal character and in some parts of our country has been given the nickname of "Bird of Death." Before this innovation was introduced I gave an impressive warning as I foresaw the results. But certain sections in the Party in their shortsightedness and in their blind hatred of the Church insisted upon driving out the devil with Beelzebub. The results now are anything but pleasant.

December 14, 1942

The city of Hanover looked almost as it did in peacetime. Almost no trace is left of past air raids. . . . I immediately drove to the *Kuppelhalle* (Hall of the Cupola), and addressed the representatives of the gau. There was an attendance of about five thousand. I was in very good form and evoked storms of applause. No one can say that morale in this section is not good. The Party has given an excellent account of itself despite the blows of recent weeks, and again carries our banner on high. I am exceedingly well satisfied with the spirit prevailing at this meeting. It is the old fighting spirit of the National Socialist movement, comparable with that which existed in our ranks during the second half of 1932. The present situation impresses me as bearing a striking similarity to those six months preceding our seizure of power [in 1933].

[One of the most striking buildings of Hanover was the New City Hall, a Renaissance structure built in 1910–13, whose vast gilded cupola is visible from afar.]

We were back in Berlin at 6 P.M. Nothing of importance had happened meanwhile. Gutterer called for me at the railway station and reported. I was free in the evening and could devote it to my own purposes.

Willkie has attacked Darlan violently in a speech, but opposition papers report that large portions of the address were struck out by the United States censor. The theme of Darlan has become a *cause célèbre* in the enemy camp. We keep adding fuel to the fire.

Willkie is being spotlighted by certain circles because they want him to be the next presidential candidate for the Republicans. Willkie as President would possibly be even more dangerous to us than Roosevelt, for he is an opportunist, a politician without character and firm convictions, with whom nothing can be done. He would certainly be the man to intensify the United States war effort.

Jewish rabbis in London have held a great protest meeting. The theme was "England, Awake." It is just too funny for words that the Jews are now compelled, after fifteen years, to steal our slogans and to call upon the pro-Semitic world to fight us, using the same battle-cry with which we once called upon the anti-Semitic world to fight Jewry. But all this won't avail the Jews anything. The Jewish race has prepared this war; it is the spiritual originator of the whole misfortune that has overtaken humanity. Jewry must pay for its crime just as our

Fuehrer prophesied in his speech in the Reichstag; namely, by the wiping out of the Jewish race in Europe and possibly in the entire world.

[The battle cry of the Nazis in the time of their struggle for power was "*Deutschland, erwache*" ("Germany, Awake"). Goebbels took sardonic delight in seeing the Jewish rabbis of London adopt as their slogan, "England, Awake."]

December 15, 1942

Montgomery had the American and English correspondents routed out of their beds to tell them that Rommel slipped through his fingers. That certainly isn't a very proud occasion for making so sensational an announcement!

Pétain wrote the Fuehrer a letter in which he asked for a new army and indulged in generalities about collaboration. But he must admit, even though with a heavy heart, that the actions of the Reich in recent weeks are justified. The letter is somewhat cooler in tone than the two letters which the Fuehrer addressed to Pétain. But that need not worry us. The main thing is that we are now talking turkey to the French and are approaching our goal step by step.

The Jews are making a terrible rumpus about the revival of the Mosley Fascist party. Generally speaking, the Jewish propaganda has become extraordinarily active of late. The Jews in London proclaimed a day of mourning for the atrocities allegedly committed on Jews in Poland by us.

Sentiment has turned very much against us in Sweden and in Switzerland. I learn from the Foreign Office that there has been a great change. My articles in the *Reich* are for the present about the only source of information on which the elements friendly to Germany in the neutral countries can depend for their moral uplift.

I talked about the Party's Reich Propaganda Office with Hadamovsky. He is on the wrong track at present since he has no real connection with me. He is trying to set up his own movie production and radio broadcasts in the Reich Propaganda Office. I consider that quite wrong. While the war is on we just can't afford to have both, a production looked after by the Reich and on top of it a production looked after by the Party. We lack the necessary personnel and also the material. Hadamovsky just wouldn't see the point and I had to be pretty tough to bring him to his senses. I must draw Hadamovsky over to my side to get him back on the right track.

My work keeps me busy until far after midnight. Now, during the Christmas season, a great number of yuletide chores must be attended to in addition to the regular daily work. I'll be glad when this whole Christmas racket is over. One can then devote oneself quietly again to real tasks.

December 16, 1942

The English are exceedingly angry about Rommel and are personally offended that he did not offer battle. They cannot refrain, however, from admitting that he retreated of his own volition and not under pressure by them. They complain movingly that they are now more than a thousand kilometers away from Cairo and that half of their transportation must be devoted merely to carrying water. Montgomery talks nonsense in claiming it is now a battle of wits. That, of course, is an alibi for letting himself be fooled by Rommel. . . .

That reminds me: I saw Rommel in a documentary movie put together by our Archives for Contemporary Events. He talked for more than three quarters of an hour about his successes at the beginning of this year. Without making any gesture he talked in a classic style, practically without correcting himself a single time. What he said and the way he said it, the play of his features and his whole appearance—all gave evidence of the greatness of an outstanding personality. It is not hard to imagine why the English don't trust him and feel their way with the greatest of caution. He has already put so many riddles to them that they don't want to let themselves be surprised a second time.

Gienanth, who interrogated prisoners of war in the transient camp at Oberursel, has sent me a report about present morale among English and American prisoners. The Americans are behaving exceedingly badly. They are quite inexperienced in battle. The fliers are still under the shock of their crash. They cry from homesickness and are ready for any unpatriotic misdeed. From all this one can see that the United States is in no manner of speaking a nation.

[Although Gienanth is not identified, he may well have been the Baron Ulrich von Gienanth who was listed as Second Secretary of the German Embassy in Washington.]

The people are simply a hodge-podge who have not attained unified expression of their consciousness of nationality. The English, of course, are behaving much better. They are in the main experienced combat soldiers who have already gone through a lot. But all are fearful—fearful of things to come, fearful of further developments in the war, fearful especially of the German soldiers. There is no one who believes in the absolute victory of the Anglo-Saxon powers and the Soviet Union, but also no one who believes in a decisive German victory. Without exception they are convinced the war will end in a peace of compromise. Characteristic of both the English and the American prisoners is their wholly unpolitical attitude. They are without knowledge of even the most elementary causes of this war. Almost all of them talk anti-Semitic, but that is owing more to a certain emotional reaction than to any clear perception of the problem.

Churchill had to defend himself against charges about the poor quality of British tanks. In so doing he went back to the time after Dunkirk. From the figures he produced one can see how extraordinarily precarious the situation of England was at that time. It is an open question whether we might not have achieved success had we followed through energetically in the autumn of 1940.

Our military attaché at the Embassy in Rome, General von Rintelen, is quite "black." His policies correspond. He is surrounded by only clerical or aristocratic elements. Instead of looking after supplies for northern Africa he has been much too busy with church questions. Visits of German soldiers and officers to the Pope have by no means grown less in number despite his assurances to the contrary. These visits are subject to his approval. Of course he okays them most generously. It would be a good thing to bring about a change of personnel there. I am gathering data to take to the Fuehrer.

[When the Germans refer to some one as "black" they mean that he is an ardent Catholic. General Enno von Rintelen, born, 1891, was German military attaché in Rome.]

The Berlin Kreisleiter, Kehrein, is in charge of military propaganda for the Ukraine. He reported to me about conditions there. The Ukrainians are a very friendly people and quite ready to work; if they are treated right something can be done with them. Women are the predominating element. They are very clean and wholesome. The men loaf all day long and need firm and strict leadership to make them do any work at all. . . . We Germans just don't know the art of running a large people or a large country from a few key positions. We are much too thorough and are always in danger of administering instead of leading, and of installing a bureaucracy instead of building up a mere supervisory apparatus. This case proves it.

Leni Riefenstahl reported to me about her motion picture, *Tiefland*. It has become involved in innumerable complications. Already more than 5,000,000 marks have been wasted on this film and it will take another whole year before it is finished. Frau Riefenstahl has become very ill from overwork and worry, and I urged her earnestly to go on leave before taking up further work. I am glad I have nothing to do with the unfortunate case, and hence bear no responsibility.

[Leni Riefenstahl, glamorous artist of the ski, attracted Hitler's attention by her winter and mountain pictures. He placed her in charge of directing all pictures made for German propaganda during the 1936 Olympic Games. *Tiefland* was an opera by Eugen d'Albert which was very popular in Germany.]

December 17, 1942

For the first time German prisoners of war in Russia have been heard from. Some four to six hundred postcards have arrived in the Reich from Russian PW camps, all of them without any propaganda. Nevertheless the Bolsheviks no doubt have a propaganda purpose in mind with these tactics. Although they have not signed the Geneva convention, they are now trying to pose as civilized and cultured people. Undoubtedly they intend first to establish a connection between these prisoners and their homes with non-committal postcards and later to follow these up with open propaganda. We are handling this whole question very delicately. The postcards were delivered to the families, but an explanatory covering letter was added. In future the wishes of the prisoners expressed on such cards are to be met by the Reich, but the cards themselves are no longer to be handed out to those next of kin. Extreme caution must be exercised in this matter, otherwise a door is opened to Bolshevik propaganda in Germany.

Axmann reported to me about the status of work among the young people. He is very much worried lest the drafting of juveniles for anti-aircraft duty might strip his Hitler Youth leadership corps of its most promising members. About 40,000 well-trained young people are affected. While the anti-aircraft can ill afford to do without them, I believe, nevertheless, that the work of the Hitler Youth must be kept up under all circumstances, especially during the war. Juveniles must be guided by a firm hand as far as possible. If left to themselves, the mischief will be all the greater.

[Arthur Axmann succeeded Baldur von Schirach as Reich Youth Leader. He was also in charge of competitions among men and women in various callings and professions, which were encouraged by the Nazis.]

December 18, 1942

In the East developments have not been so favorable as we expected. . . . Apparently the ring around Stalingrad can't be broken up so easily as some of our people thought.

In Tunisia the situation was quite critical several weeks ago. We had the good fortune, however, of being opposed by the American General Anderson, an exceedingly careful tactician who always plays safe. Had a Rommel been in his place we might conceivably have fared very badly.

General Nehring has been recalled from his present assignment. As Berndt described him, he was an outspoken pessimist and did not believe we could win. He is being replaced by General von Arnim, who seems to be of better caliber. It is a pity that we failed to make room for able and dependable National Socialists in the Wehrmacht during the years before the war. Quite obviously in critical situations not military ability alone but also character plays a very decisive role. General staff officers do not lack superior military knowledge, but in certain situations they are without the necessary moral stamina. Much more depends on that at certain moments than on superior military knowledge.

[General Walter Nehring commanded troops in North Africa under Field Marshal Erwin Rommel. He was replaced by General Juergen von Arnim.]

We learn . . . that Churchill intends to go to Washington around Christmastime. The visit is to be concerned solely with the question of who is to be boss in the French colonial area, England or the United States. Roosevelt is obviously pressing for redemption of the promissory notes which Churchill so thoughtlessly signed. He proposes to the English that the French colonies be turned over unconditionally to the Americans to meet the debts incurred by lend-lease. That makes it obvious why Roosevelt went into the war. It has nothing whatever to do with humanity or civilization. Wall Street, whose exponent he is in his war policies, has persuaded him to take this step. The English will someday realize how dependent upon Washington they became through their alliance with the United States. . . .

People in the United States are none too happy about the practices in which Roosevelt is indulging. Opposition newspapers fear that his methods will lead more and more to a sort of Roosevelt dictatorship, and that by the end of the war the devil, to be sure, will have been driven out, but Beelzebub will remain. Roosevelt is a man without restraint. He is a very selfish and headstrong personality who shoots straight at his target.

The situation in the East has compelled the Fuehrer to remain at his GHQ, contrary to his original intentions. Developments at Stalingrad give cause for some worry; the situation isn't sufficiently under control for the Fuehrer to leave GHQ. It is a great pity that this year, too, the Fuehrer can't possibly go on leave, even on a brief one. . . .

Ciano instead of the Duce will visit the Fuehrer. The Duce is in poor health, and as the meeting can't take place on the Obersalzberg, Ciano is being sent to GHQ as substitute for the Duce. The French problem is to be talked over with Ciano first; after that Laval is to come.

[Galeazzo Ciano (1903–1944) was Count of Cortellazzo e de Buccari. His wife, Edda, was Mussolini's daughter. Ciano was Italian Foreign Minister of the Fascist regime and reputed to be one of the wealthiest men in Italy.]

The *Fascist Revolution,* a periodical belonging to a nephew of the Duce, Vito Mussolini, has published an article opposing our National Socialist conception of religion. This article deals with the same theme that was discussed recently in *Gerarchia,* its tenor being that Europe is a Christian continent and that the Christian leadership of the continent must continue. It is obvious that the Italians are trying by means of their periodicals to lay claim to the spiritual leadership of Europe, since the military and power-political leadership has slipped completely from their hands. I pay no attention to this article in our commentary. There is no point in replying to such provocations now, as we are not in a position at the moment to publish all our arguments. We shall have to wait for a more favorable opportunity. Most likely we can tackle the church question bluntly only after the war.

My latest article on "The Claims of the People" is being quoted very widely in the foreign press. My new book, *The Heart of Iron,* which has just appeared, is reviewed very favorably in the Italian press.

The Jewish question is receiving a big play both in the enemy and in the neutral news services. The Swedes protest hypocritically against our treatment of the Polish Jews, but are by no means willing to receive them in their country. The leading newspapers of Stockholm warn emphatically against having the Ghetto Jews from Warsaw forced upon them. It would probably be a good thing if the Swedes were to admit several thousand such Jews into their country. That would give them a practical lesson on the Jewish question. In all likelihood they would understand our measures much better than appears to be the case today.

The Jews of Jerusalem have held noisy demonstrations of protest against us. They had a day of fasting. At the Wailing Wall they invoked the Old Testament Jewish curse against the Fuehrer, Goering, Himmler, and me. Until now I haven't noticed any effect on me. One must know these Jews to be able to handle them right. They are now trying to stir up the entire world merely to incite public opinion against the National Socialist Reich and its anti-Semitic convictions. There's only one answer to this, viz., to continue as at present, rigorously and without compromise. You're sunk if you give the slightest indication of weakness.

Goering addressed the officer candidates in the Fuehrer's stead at the Sports Palace. Colonel Martin says the speech was not a very happy one. Delivery was poor, and some remarks about death on the field of battle were in rather poor taste. But I can't venture any opinion as I didn't hear the speech myself.

The Christmas program for radio and the press has been submitted for my okay. We are limiting ourselves to only a few broadcasts and editorials dealing exclusively with Christmas. It won't do for the people in these difficult times to fall too much for the sentimental magic of these festival days.

December 19, 1942

The enemy press describes the situation in the East as almost desperate for us. German counterblows for the relief of Stalingrad are said to have failed completely. In Moscow they lie about great victories without, however, going into painful details. The Don Basin, it is claimed, was the sepulcher of the German Wehrmacht.

While it is true that the Italians are under a terrific strain, they have until now been able to stand it. There's no truth whatever to the alleged heavy inroads upon our front, nor is it true that our attempts at relief have failed. On the contrary, they give promise of all sorts of success in the near future. Obviously the enemy is anxious to invent victories as incidental music to Churchill's trip to Washington at Christmas.

Churchill evidently intends to strengthen his position somewhat so as not to come to Roosevelt with empty hands. . . .

It is true that Rommel's position is actually anything but favorable. I have received a letter by courier from Berndt, who reports rather alarming details. According to him the situation of our tank army is simply awful. The real trouble is that Rommel has no gasoline. He did succeed in beating his way through the English pincers. He could undoubtedly have expanded this success into a strategic victory had his tanks been able to move. But the English are torpedoing almost all the tankers we send to North Africa. It's a real catastrophe that we can't supply Rommel with gasoline. If he had fuel, he would undoubtedly find ways and means once again to outwit the English. Now, however, that's impossible because of this fatal lack which naturally has a very depressing effect on Rommel and his entourage. What about our position in North Africa, anyway? It depends upon so many imponderables that I don't dare to prophesy. The fortunes of war always depend on the potential means at one's disposal. Rommel has been virtually cut off from all supplies. What is he to do with his tanks if he can send them neither forward nor back?

Donald Nelson has issued a report about American armament production. It exceeds all previous American exaggerations. We simply must do something to offset this American munitions propaganda. Unfortunately our own propaganda about armament production has had a serious setback because of the unfortunate news item about two German weapons that hadn't yet been put into actual use. At present all who had anything to do with this press release have cold feet and don't want to venture on this decidedly slippery pavement again. I shall do everything, however, to give a new impetus to our munitions propaganda, for after all we must not let the Americans ride roughshod over us merely because of propaganda dogmatism.

[Donald M. Nelson, born, 1888, and educated at the University of Missouri, became chairman of the War Production Board in 1942, after having previously been Co-ordinator of Purchases. In 1944–45 he served as a personal representative of President Roosevelt.]

Eden delivered a speech in the House of Commons on the Jewish problem and answered planted questions. Rothschild, the "venerable MP," as the English press calls him, took the floor and delivered a tearjerker bemoaning the fate of the Polish Jews. At the end of the session the Commons observed a minute of silence. All members of Parliament rose from their seats as a silent tribute to Jewry. That was quite appropriate for the British House of Commons, which is really a sort of Jewish exchange. The English, anyway, are the Jews among the Aryans. The perfumed British Foreign Minister, Eden, cuts a good figure among these characters from the synagogue. His whole education and his entire bearing can be characterized as thoroughly Jewish.

Schirmeister attended a session of the military court at my request. A traitor who planned an attempt on my life was condemned to death. A mine was planted under the bridge leading to Schwanenwerder, and the plan was to make it explode from a distance. Things did not come to that pass, however, thank God. The would-be murderer was arrested before he could carry out his plan.

[This is the only time mention is made in the Goebbels diary of any attempt on his life. M. A. von Schirmeister was one of his numerous aides in the Propaganda Ministry.]

December 20, 1942

We are having some trouble about Stalingrad. Air transport isn't functioning as it should, due to bad weather. Our troops are not getting enough to eat.

Rommel has again succeeded in forcing his way out of the English pincers. But even though London is very much disappointed and claims the battle was not decisive, we must realize that Rommel's situation is extraordinarily critical, not to say desperate. The English, to be sure, also have their difficulties about supplies, but these can be overcome. They are facing an opponent who they themselves admit fights very well. They expect some sort of surprise from Rommel and believe he still holds some trick up his sleeve. But those in the know see quite clearly that Rommel cannot do anything if he doesn't have gasoline. That is decisive.

I received another letter from Berndt informing me eloquently of his troubles. The people around Rommel have come to the point of taking everything with a sort of scaffold mirth [Galgenhumor]. They are doing everything possible. We on our part have also left nothing undone. But the forces of the elements are stronger than we. Our supplies sent across the sea are, for the most part, lost. The English, we learn, have stationed approximately fifteen submarines in this area. One can well imagine how they are lying in ambush, determined not to let anything through.

The situation in French Africa is also not exactly rosy. The Americans are quite obviously bent upon taking Morocco away from the Spaniards. Their newspapers are already beginning a transparent agitation against the Franco regime. The tendencies of such a press campaign are too obvious. The Spanish public is therefore in a state of great alarm and nervousness. Possibly Franco will now have to pay for having been so dilatory. Had he risked taking Gibraltar by storm at the time we suggested it, he would today be in an absolutely secure position. He certainly can't claim that now.

[There were many unconfirmable rumors of German pressure on Franco to seize Gibraltar. Goebbels here admits that such a "suggestion" (*Vorschlag*) had been made.]

Ciano has already arrived at the Fuehrer's GHQ. The Fuehrer is conducting the negotiations personally. At last there is no mincing of words. We are trying to persuade the Italians to assign larger naval units for carrying supplies to North Africa. Everything hinges on that. If the Italians believe they can keep their fleet intact as a trump card for future events, they are pursuing a strategy that is absolutely reprehensible and exceedingly harmful. A fleet must be put in service; only then is it of some use. The Italians can't alibi by claiming they have no gas and oil. So many fuel ships have been torpedoed by the English on their way to Rommel that it would have been an easy thing to take something out of each ship for provisionally supplying the Italian Fleet. Possibly the Fuehrer will even demand that we have a decisive word to say about the Italian Fleet. The situation in North Africa can be saved only by making use of all available reserves. That the Fuehrer himself is conducting the negotiations is very reassuring. The bitter pill can be sweetened for the Italians by making greater concessions to them about France.

The appointment of Zeitzler has done a lot of good. Zeitzler has introduced a new method of work at GHQ. It consists in clearing the desk of everything that he can dispose of. In that way the Fuehrer is relieved of a lot of detail, and everything doesn't depend upon his decision.

[General Kurt Zeitzler, a tried and trusted Nazi, succeeded Colonel General Franz Halder, a Bavarian monarchist whom Hitler never trusted, as Chief of the General Staff of the Army. Zeitzler had served in World War I as a lieutenant. After participating in the Polish campaign in 1939, the French campaign in 1940, and the Balkan campaigns in 1941, he was made chief of staff of General Ewald von Kleist's first Panzer group in South Russia.]

The Fuehrer had been tied down altogether too much by military details because the post of Chief of the General Staff of the Army was previously filled so badly. Ninety-nine per cent of the Fuehrer's energies are devoted to the military side of the war; that leaves but little for civilian affairs. If Zeitzler were to succeed in changing the ratio somewhat in favor of the civilian sector, that would indeed be a great achievement. For while the Fuehrer must sometimes be bothered with ludicrous trivialities in the military sector, the most important things in the civilian sector are often neglected.

Enemy propaganda is exceedingly aggressive. The Jews, too, are talking again. Emil Ludwig Cohn, in an interview in the American press, demands the complete destruction of the German economy and the German war potential. The Jewish campaign against us is growing in volume. What won't the Jews do to discredit the Reich! They are working arrogantly and on a large scale. But they won't reach their goal after all, just as they haven't attained it in the Reich.

[The Mr. Cohn here referred to is better known by his pen name of Emil Ludwig.]

Letters addressed to me are very much in favor of my work. All my writings are praised to the skies.

In the evening I am able to devote a little time to the children, with whom I'm having much fun. It is such a pity that one can be so little with one's children. . . . Once the war is over I shall be able to devote myself much more than hitherto to their upbringing. I could not think and wish for any more beautiful task for the coming peace.

1943

1943

Recapitulation of events between
December 21, 1942 and March 1, 1943

Three months of diary entries are missing—months crowded with highly significant events. On December 24, 1942, Darlan was assassinated, and General Henri Honoré Giraud, about whose escape from Germany Hitler had fumed in his talk with Goebbels, was appointed French High Commissioner.

The new year 1943 began with a flamboyant declaration by the Fuehrer to the effect that victory was still in sight for the Axis, while at the same time the Russians announced jubilantly that twenty-two Axis divisions had been trapped in Stalingrad. Thirty days later the Soviets announced the surrender of Field Marshal von Paulus and ten other generals and the taking of 330,000 German prisoners at Stalingrad.

Roosevelt and Churchill, meeting at Casablanca on January 24, gave their reply to Hitler's boasts: Unconditional Surrender of Germany and her allies.

Dame Fortune definitely began to smile upon Soviet Russia: the siege of Leningrad was considerably eased in mid-January; the German offensive in the Caucasus, which had necessitated the destruction by the Russians of their precious Maikop oil fields, came to a halt late in January; on February 8 and 9 the Soviets recaptured Kursk and Belgorod, on February 14 Rostov and Voroshilovgorod, on February 16 Kharkov, and on February 20 Krasnogorod and Pavlograd.

Flushed by these victories, the Russians now let it be known that, despite their avowal in the British-Russian twenty-year treaty of having no aggressive intentions they demanded the three Baltic States of Estonia, Latvia, and Lithuania, besides Rumanian Bessarabia, as their share in the spoils of war. And Stalin, on February 23, claimed that Russia's armies were alone bearing the whole weight of the war—this despite Stettinius's statement, four days earlier, that more than 2,900,000 tons of matériel had been shipped by the United States to Soviet Russia.

In Helsinki Risto Ryti was elected president of the Finnish Republic and, as Goebbels's diaries show, there was considerable anxiety in Berlin as to what his policies might be.

The seriousness of the African situation for the Axis was revealed dramatically by the Allied announcement of January 19 that fourteen vessels carrying supplies to Tripoli were sunk and three damaged, and by the further announcement, four days later, that Tripoli had fallen to the British Eighth Army. On the other hand, Rommel staged a temporary comeback with his monster Mark VI tanks by hurling the American and French troops back to the Algerian border. On February 25, however, American troops were able to occupy the Kasserine Pass in central Tunisia.

Mounting troubles for Hitler were indicated by the following occurrences: on January 30 Grand Admiral Erich Raeder was retired and Admiral Karl Doenitz, submarine specialist, put in his place. Two days earlier Hitler had mobilized the entire civilian population for the war effort. On February 2, more than 100,000 German restaurants and many amusement centers were closed to secure additional man power for Hitler's total war. The same fate was shared by the German department stores. On February 24 Hitler stated that he would not hesitate to force workers from occupied countries to help the Nazi war effort.

In Italy Mussolini removed his son-in-law Count Ciano and twelve other aides from their high posts and assumed the entire burden of conducting the war and the administration of Italy. Ciano was sent to the Vatican as Ambassador.

March 1943

NINE HUNDRED TONS OF BOMBS RAINED ON BERLIN BY R.A.F. TWICE DURING MONTH. RYTI EXPRESSES FINLAND'S LONGING FOR PEACE BUT URGES CONTINUANCE OF FIGHT ON GERMAN SIDE. RUSSIANS RECAPTURE DEMYANSK, RZLEV, GZHATSK, VYAZMA. GERMANS RECAPTURE KHARKOV AND BELGOROD. UNITED STATES AMBASSADOR STANDLEY COMPLAINS RUSSIANS DO NOT TELL THEIR PEOPLE ABOUT LEND-LEASE AID. EDEN ARRIVES IN WASHINGTON FOR CONFERENCE. GIRAUD RESTORES LAWS OF FRENCH REPUBLIC IN NORTH AFRICA. HITLER CLAIMS FRONT HAS BEEN STABILIZED.

March 1, 1943

Conditions in Finland are steadily becoming more complicated. Kivimaaki, the Finnish Minister in Berlin, has been called to Helsinki. In the course of the next week a new government is to be formed. But I don't believe that Finland is in a position to desert our front.

[Toivo Mikael Kivimaaki, who had been Finnish Prime Minister from December 1932 to October 1936, was sent to Berlin as minister plenipotentiary in 1940 to replace Aarne Wuorimaa, who had little love for the Nazis.]

Our anti-Bolshevik propaganda has achieved notable successes. Already all leading London papers warn against the dangerous Axis propaganda whose sole purpose is that of sowing discord between the allies. This discord has already become strikingly visible. The quarrel between the Soviet Union and Poland concerning the drawing of frontiers exceeds by far the bounds usually respected by allies in wartime. The English newspapers are striving hard to soft-pedal this discord, but the Polish émigré government naturally won't content itself with cheap promises.

Regarding the fear of Bolshevism—to return to this subject once more—it is significant that even Dorothy Thompson now comments on this. She is apprehensive lest the Soviet Union alone determine the peace in Europe unless the Allies create a second front.

There's a lot of commotion in and about the Vatican. The North American Archbishop Spellman has arrived and has had various talks with Vatican people who count, and also with the Pope. Even Reuters expresses the view that it must be a question of peace feelers. Our reaction is cold.

[Francis Cardinal Spellman (then Archbishop) was regarded by the Nazis as an envoy of the late President Roosevelt. They refused to believe that his visits to the Vatican had to do with church matters only.]

In the afternoon I visited Magda whose health, thank God, has improved a great deal. She is in pretty good shape again and takes an interest in everything that is happening in the outside world. I am very happy that she is absolutely uncompromising and radical on the question of total war. If all Nazi women thought as she does, total war would certainly be much more of a reality.

In the afternoon Speer called me from the Obersalzberg. He had two long talks with Goering. Goering was at first somewhat ill-humored and distrustful about a number of things on which he had been given the wrong slant. In the course of the afternoon, however, he agreed fully and wholeheartedly to my proposals as transmitted by Speer. He wishes urgently to talk to me before his trip to Italy. I have decided to fly to see him next Monday. I hope that this talk, which is scheduled to take several hours, will be of decisive importance for our entire war strategy. Speer is very expectant and hopeful. I believe he did excellent spadework. When I talk to Goering I shall merely be carrying coals to Newcastle. If I should succeed in winning Goering over 100 per cent to the new war policy, that would be a positive achievement, the importance of which cannot be exaggerated. I shall certainly do my best. . . .

Let's hope perfect solidarity among the men closest to the Fuehrer will result from our get-together. We shall then be able to place a personal guard of coworkers at the Fuehrer's service such as he had only in the greatest periods of our struggle for power.

March 2, 1943

While the new government in Finland has not yet been formed, it seems certain that the Foreign Minister, Witting, won't return. I believe we are worrying prematurely about Finland's attitude. It is true that the Agrarian party continues to oppose the government, but for the moment at least it has no real influence.

During the afternoon Ryti delivered his anxiously awaited speech in Parliament. It is pretty much in our favor and hardly differs from previous pronouncements. He declared Finland was compelled to continue its defensive war and must concentrate all efforts on it. Although Finland did not intervene in the fight of the Great Powers, it must nevertheless have its national security guaranteed for the time to come. That's something, and we can certainly be satisfied. I was right in presupposing that Finland's position does not permit the government's deserting us.

[Risto Ryti was at this time President of the Finnish Republic, after having previously been governor of the Bank of Finland from 1923 to 1945 and Prime Minister in 1939–40. He was a member of the Progressive party, and generally credited with pro-English leanings which, however, he laid aside when his country entered the war on the side of the Nazis. He was arrested and indicted for war activities in 1945.]

General Zeitzler wrote me a letter about my proposal for a proclamation for the East, saying it was not approved. This letter is anything but flattering for Rosenberg. Rosenberg double-crossed Zeitzler. He tried to influence Zeitzler to become a star witness against me, without telling him about the real purpose for his step. Zeitzler is very angry about it. What he wrote about me in the letter is very encouraging for my work. I believe I have found a good friend in Zeitzler. He said that in future he would support my work in every way possible, and that he was exceedingly happy to have established such friendly relations with me. He characterized his recent talk with me as the most delightful in many a month.

England and the United States are worried considerably about developments in Tunisia. Fear of Rommel is a sort of children's bugaboo. The English and Americans have suffered a new setback on Tunisian soil. If only our supply lines were better!

We are now definitely pushing the Jews out of Berlin. They were suddenly rounded up last Saturday, and are to be carted off to the East as quickly as possible. Unfortunately our better circles, especially the intellectuals, once again have failed to understand our policy about the Jews and in some cases have even taken their part. As a result our plans were tipped off prematurely, so that a lot of Jews slipped through our hands. But we will catch them yet. I certainly won't rest until the capital of the Reich, at least, has become free of Jews.

[To the casual reader this "premature tipping off" may not seem very surprising. It must be remembered, however, that every German who was caught giving shelter to a Jew or notifying him of pending measures was either executed or sent to a concentration camp.]

The drive up to the Obersalzberg awakens a multitude of nostalgic memories. How often and in what different moods have I covered this stretch! . . . There isn't much left to indicate the grand-scale life of days gone by. The Fuehrer's residence seems to be sleeping the sleep of Snow White.

Speer awaited me and we talked immediately about his discussions with Goering. Speer has done splendid spadework and has created an atmosphere that makes me hope my talk with Goering will not only go smoothly, but have positive results. . . . The great danger seems to be that Goering, as Speer described it, is in a somewhat resigned mood. It is all the more necessary that I make him see things more clearly by using the right arguments. . . .

At 4 P.M. I drove up to Goering's home. His house is high up on the mountain in almost wintry quiet. Goering received me most charmingly and is very open-hearted. His dress is somewhat baroque and would, if one did not know him, strike one as somewhat funny. But that's the way he is, and one must put up with his idiosyncrasies; they sometimes even have a charm about them. . . .

[Goering's alpine home was only a short distance from that of Adolf Hitler on the Obersalzberg towering above the tourist town of Berchtesgaden in Upper Bavaria. When the American troops entered the Goering home in May 1945, they found 25,000 bottles of champagne stored in his big wine cellar. Goering was known as a gourmet. He was also famous for his unusual clothes. At Karinhall, his hunting lodge some twenty-five miles outside of Berlin, he once received the diplomatic corps dressed like Wotan and armed with an enormous spear.]

After the exchange of a few pleasantries we immediately got down to brass tacks. He gave a general survey of the situation which seemed somewhat superficial to me, but which, on the whole, went to the core of things. He regards the situation in the East as essentially favorable, although he naturally realizes that we are still on somewhat uncertain ground there. He is also somewhat worried about our having pretty much stripped the West in order to bring things to a standstill in the East. One dreads to think what would happen if the English and the Americans were suddenly to attempt a landing.

Events in Tunisia have also not developed the way he expected. He wants to go to Italy for several days to look after the supply lines. The quartermasters' offices in the Army have again made a lot of mistakes, and in Goering's opinion Rommel, too, is not quite equal to his task. Goering does not think very much of Rommel; he believes that he is splendid when it comes to advancing, but unable to meet serious crises and setbacks. That may be true. Rommel has served in North Africa under terrific conditions far too long for these years not to have done something to him. But I suppose Goering bases his opinion partly on the judgment of Kesselring, who has always been opposed to Rommel. Be that as it may, Goering says we must either try to achieve a decisive success in Tunisia or else swallow the bitter pill of giving up North Africa. He believes we'll lose Africa to the Americans anyway. Should we succeed, however, in breaking through in the East, our loss of Africa would not be irreparable. Goering certainly still thinks very highly of the military power and war potential of the Anglo-Saxons. He has no illusions about those.

[Field Marshal Albert Kesselring of the German Luftwaffe was placed in supreme command of German operations in Italy. He was later tried by an Italian court for authorizing inhumane warfare and condemned to death, but his sentence was commuted to life imprisonment on July 4, 1947. He appeared as a witness in the Nuremberg War Crimes Trial on March 3, 1946.]

With regard to England he finds it difficult to understand how the British plutocracy can make as close an alliance with Bolshevism as was evidenced especially on the twenty-fifth anniversary of the Red Army. Goering looks at these things somewhat naïvely and is unable to differentiate between expediency and real conviction.

He seemed to me somewhat helpless about Soviet war potential. Again and again he asked in despair where Bolshevism still gets its weapons and soldiers. In my opinion this question is unimportant. The essential thing is that it still has them and always manages to get more. But Goering has learned a lot. He, too, now believes that we must expect our enemy in the East to remain strong and that it would be decidedly unwise to take things too lightly. That means—and this is the essence of my argument—that the German war potential must be used to the limit regardless.

We still have one great opportunity with our anti-Bolshevik propaganda. Its intensity should be increased as much as possible. Great results are expected from it. My description of what I intend to do along this line impresses him very much. He is amazed at what we have already achieved on this sector and what I have scheduled for the coming weeks and months.

With regard to the Soviet potential, he agrees that we can meet it effectively only with sweeping measures.

In that connection I described the situation to him as I interpret it. I went far afield and proved my case with much assurance and great skill. He was greatly impressed. After talking to him for an hour he was completely in accord.

It seems to me that Goering has been standing aside too long from the political factors that do the real driving. As a result he has wrong ideas about a number of things. But that can be corrected easily. His advantage consists in his possessing a healthy common sense which always enables him to pick his way through the thicket of a somewhat confused situation. As he is no longer closely connected with our political leaders, he has probably become somewhat tired and apathetic. It is therefore all the more necessary to get him straightened out. For he is a first-rate factor of authority. A determined leadership can't possibly be set up without him or even against him for long. . . .

The little dissensions that have crept into our work in the course of time were not even mentioned. They seem quite unimportant compared with the historic tasks that we have to discuss. Goering evidenced no inclination whatever even to touch upon them. He knew perfectly well that everything was at stake in this meeting, and that we must come to an agreement on a long-range program. I dismiss our misunderstandings with a wave of the hand and then return to the discussion of the absence of any clear leadership in our domestic and foreign politics. With him, too, the Committee of Three does not sit well at all. He doesn't have any regard for any of the three "Wise Men from the East," as he calls them.

[The "Three Wise Men from the East" were Hans Heinrich Lammers, chief of Adolf Hitler's chancellery for political affairs; Martin Bormann, chief of Hitler's chancellery for Nazi party affairs; and Field Marshal Wilhelm Keitel, chief of the Supreme Command of the Wehrmacht.]

He hates Lammers from the bottom of his soul. He regards him as a bureaucrat who is attempting to get the leadership of the Reich back into the hands of the ministerial bureaucracy. Unfortunately the Fuehrer does not yet quite see through him and considers this super-jurist to be a non-jurist and this super-bureaucrat a non-bureaucrat. The Fuehrer's eyes will have to be opened about him slowly. As regards Bormann, Goering is not quite certain about his true intentions. There seems to be no doubt that he is pursuing ambitious aims. Keitel, in

Goering's opinion, is an absolute zero who need not be taken seriously, but whom the other two use in order to make it look as though the Wehrmacht had a hand in their measures.

Goering judges GHQ very harshly. Jodl especially has got his goat. He tells me that Jodl has even begun to tell jokes on the Fuehrer. That certainly won't do. The Fuehrer trusts these people altogether too much. To his face they are naturally very friendly but in their hearts they think quite differently.

Goering considers the working methods of GHQ quite wrong, especially the fact that stenographers are always present during staff conferences and take down every word. In the long run this will of course put the Fuehrer at a disadvantage. For the Fuehrer never makes any bones about his opinions, while the generals—Zeitzler, of course, excluded—always talk for the stenographic record.

Goering sees clearly that events on the Eastern Front the past winter led to a serious crisis of confidence. The generals are doing everything possible to unload this crisis on the Fuehrer. They are now taking revenge for the previous winter, when the measures of the Fuehrer showed them up as having been wrong.

Goering considers General Schmundt as the only honest and trustworthy personality at GHQ. The rest of the generals, including those who are at the front, are taking advantage of the situation by creating difficulty after difficulty for the Fuehrer. For example, Manstein, as Goering told me, on one occasion was even prevailed upon to suggest to the Fuehrer that he lay down the Supreme Command. This didn't actually happen, as he was told off before he could carry out this intention, but the Fuehrer got to know of it anyway and has drawn the necessary conclusions about Manstein. The Fuehrer really intended to dismiss Manstein during his trip to the southern front, but refrained from so doing for the present.

[Field Marshal Fritz Erich von Manstein commanded the German troops in the Crimea and before Sebastopol in 1941, and in 1942 was placed in supreme command of the German front in southern Russia. Hitler dismissed him in 1944.]

We must certainly be on our guard about the old Wehrmacht and Reichswehr generals. We have very few good friends among them. They are trying to play us off one against the other. So far as I am concerned, I won't have any part in such questionable dealings.

We also spoke at length about Paulus, whom Goering criticizes severely. He tells me that the Fuehrer, too, is now convinced that Paulus acted in a cowardly way in surrendering to the Soviets. Goering expects this captured field marshal soon to appear as a speaker in a Moscow broadcast. That would be just about the limit.

[Field Marshal Friedrich von Paulus, commander in chief of the Sixth Army Corps, surrendered to the Russians at Stalingrad when the hopelessness of his position was evident to everybody. He afterward played a leading part in the Union of German Officers of Moscow and was a witness at the Nuremberg trial.]

Goering evidenced the greatest concern about the Fuehrer. To him, too, the Fuehrer seems to have aged fifteen years during three-and-a-half years of war. It is a tragic thing that the Fuehrer has become such a recluse and leads so unhealthy a life. He doesn't get out into the fresh air. He does not relax. He sits in his bunker, fusses and broods. If one could only transfer him to other surroundings! But he has made up his mind to conduct this war in his own Spartan manner, and I suppose nothing can be done about it.

But it is equally essential that we succeed somehow in making up for the lack of leadership in our domestic and foreign policy. One must not bother the Fuehrer with everything. The Fuehrer must be kept free for the military leadership. One can understand his present mood of sometimes being fed up with life and occasionally even saying that death holds no terrors for him; but for that very reason we must now become his strongest personal support. As was always the case during crises of the Party, the duty of the Fuehrer's closest friends in time of need consists in gathering about him and forming a solid phalanx around his person. What we must now suffer in the way of torture to our souls will pass; what we did to master our difficulties, however, will remain.

Goering realizes perfectly what is in store for all of us if we show any weakness in this war. He has no illusions about that. On the Jewish question, especially, we have taken a position from which there is no escape. That is a good thing. Experience teaches that a movement and a people who have burned their bridges fight with much greater determination than those who are still able to retreat.

I made it clear to Goering that war must be waged not only militarily but also politically. In this connection I spoke about the proposed proclamation for the East. Goering is as firmly convinced of its necessity as I am. He does not believe, however, that Rosenberg can be persuaded to issue it.

He has the worst possible opinion of Rosenberg. Like myself he is astonished that the Fuehrer continues to stick to him and clothes him with powers which he is incompetent to use. Rosenberg belongs in an ivory tower, not in a ministry that must look after almost a hundred

million people. The Fuehrer thought of the Ministry of the East as a
guiding and not an administrative instrument when he created it.
Rosenberg, following his old inclination of fussing with things which
he knows nothing about, has made a gigantic apparatus of it which he
is now unable to control.

Goering also doesn't think much of Ribbentrop. He referred very
critically to the complete and obvious lack of an active foreign policy.
He especially blames Ribbentrop for not succeeding in drawing Spain
over to our side. Franco is, to be sure, cowardly and irresolute; but
German foreign policy ought nevertheless to have found a way to bring
him into our camp. Ribbentrop also lacks the elegant touch in the
handling of people. Goering gave me several truly devastating examples by way of illustration. Goering consistently claims that this war is
Ribbentrop's war, and that he never made any earnest attempt to
achieve a *modus vivendi* with England, simply because he has an inferiority complex. But there's no point in brooding over this today. We
must deal with facts and not with the reasons for these facts. There
will be plenty of time for that after the war.

There's the same trouble about our domestic policy. Everybody does
and leaves undone what he pleases, because there's no strong authority anywhere. The Party goes its own way and won't have anybody
interfere.

Here's where I introduce my proposals. I express the opinion that
we'd be "over the hump" if we succeeded in transferring the political
leadership tasks of the Reich from the Committee of Three to the Ministerial Council for the Defense of the Reich. This Ministerial Council
would then have to be composed of the strong men who assisted the
Fuehrer in the Revolution. These will certainly also muster the strength
to bring this war to a victorious conclusion.

I blamed Goering very seriously for having permitted the Ministerial Council for the Defense of the Reich to become inactive. He
could excuse himself, however, with the fact that Lammers always
torpedoed his efforts by constantly butting in and reporting to the
Fuehrer. This chicanery must be stopped. If Goering can muster the
strength to surround himself with courageous, upright, and loyal men,
such a group would undoubtedly be able to relieve the Fuehrer of
most of the chores, thus setting him free again for his high mission of
leadership. The Fuehrer would certainly approve of such a solution as
it would make his historic tasks much easier for him.

Goering was very much impressed with my statement that I had
not come to get something from him but rather to bring something to

him. I talked at him with all the persuasiveness at my command and finally succeeded in bringing him completely over to our side.

The Party must again be put on its toes and its ranks straightened out. The bothersome church question must rest for the duration of the war. The petty chicaneries still practiced here and there in public life must be done away with. We must no longer waste time on side issues, but keep our eyes fixed upon the main issue, war itself. Only thus can we succeed in concentrating the strength of the nation on a single aim.

While talking I gained the spontaneous impression that my presentation visibly pepped up Goering. He became very enthusiastic about my proposals and immediately asked how we were to proceed specifically. I suggested that he make a number of nominations and I would try to win over the rest. We won't tell any of these about our real intentions; namely, of gradually putting the Committee of Three on ice and transferring its powers to the Ministerial Council. That would only create unnecessary trouble. . . .

We have no other ambition than that of supporting each other and of forming a solid phalanx around the Fuehrer. The Fuehrer sometimes wavers in his decisions if the same matter is brought to him from different sides. Nor does he always react to people as he should. That's where he needs help.

Goering is fully conscious of his somewhat weak position today. He knows that it is decidedly to his advantage for strong men to come to his side and take upon themselves the task of relieving the Fuehrer of his worst worries. We are all determined to make a new contribution to the war by our action.

Goering himself wants to win over Himmler. Funk and Ley have already been won over by me. Speer is entirely my man. Thus we already have a group that can be proud of itself. It certainly includes all those who today enjoy the greatest prestige and highest authority in our political life.

Goering wants to come to Berlin immediately after his trip to Italy and there meet with us again. Speer is to speak to the Fuehrer before then—and if possible I also. Questions of personnel and of division of work can, I believe, be disposed of relatively quickly. We want to show the greatest loyalty in forming this group. We shall pursue no other object save that of victory. We will stand for no intrigue whatever. The fidelity of these men to the Fuehrer is to be unparalleled.

I believe we shall render the Fuehrer the greatest possible service by our action. One just can't stand by any longer and see how he is so weighed down with worries big and small that he can hardly breathe. The cause is greater than any of us; that goes without saying. The men who helped the Fuehrer win the revolution will now have to help him win the war. They were not bureaucrats then; they must not be bureaucrats today.

We still have many an ace up our sleeves. It surely isn't true that we are playing an empty game. If we make use of every possibility, we shall be able, I believe, to effect a fundamental change in the war within a relatively short time. Our problem today is not the people but the leadership. That has been true, incidentally, nearly every war.

The Committee of Three was given a task with a time limit, as the Fuehrer's decree expressly stated. The Ministerial Council for the Defense of the Reich, on the other hand, was given a task for the entire duration.

This first talk with Goering lasted almost four hours. I then had Speer brought in so that Goering himself could reveal to him what we had agreed upon.

We improved the occasion to touch upon a number of specific questions and thus to round out the picture. At the end of our talk each of us had the feeling that all problems that in any way come within our wide radius of action had found a solution in principle. As Goering put it, we shall manage the "Three Wise Men from the East" in a jiffy, whereupon we shall go to work with a driving power and an enthusiasm that will put into the shade anything that ever existed.

I am very happy that a clear basis of mutual trust was established with Goering. I believe that the Fuehrer, too, will be very happy about this. I hope we shall render him the very greatest service possible.

March 3, 1943

I learned at Halle, on our trip to Berlin, that Berlin had gone through a bad air raid during the night. From the first report reaching me I could not realize the seriousness of this attack. I became conscious of it, however, when the train slowly pulled into Berlin. We were more than an hour late. The tracks were torn up. The report Schach gave me at the railroad station indicated it was the most serious air raid thus far experienced by the Reich capital.

A tremendous number of places have been damaged. Industrial plants and public buildings have been badly hit. St. Hedwig's Cathedral was burned to the ground, and besides four other churches and a number of hospitals, homes for the aged, et cetera.

I am told the morale of the population is exemplary, although the civilian anti-aircraft protection failed to a certain degree, in that the Berliners sat in their basements too long and let their houses burn meanwhile. The Party, too, failed in some respects. It is no longer fully conscious of its real task of leadership and no longer knows how to adjust itself to extraordinary circumstances.

I immediately took the necessary measures. The population must under no circumstances be given the impression that the Party is not equal to the tasks imposed by such heavy air raids.

Things look pretty bad in downtown Berlin, but suburban sections seem even more hopeless. The damage is extraordinarily heavy. We register about two hundred casualties, a number that is not very big compared with other raids, but which nevertheless is quite a factor.

A rumor made the rounds of all Berlin that this attack was launched because of Air Force Day, which had been given somewhat unfortunate publicity. On the whole it appears that the Luftwaffe has lost much of its popularity with the people. Goering is quite unjustifiably blamed for it. The situation is aggravated by the unfortunate circumstance that he is neither in Berlin nor in his GHQ, but up on the Obersalzberg.

I immediately took a trip through the city and viewed several damaged places. I began with St. Hedwig's Church, which looks absolutely hopeless. The priests of St. Hedwig's importuned me to have at least one of the small chapels restored and to let them use the *Singakademie* for divine services. I readily granted this request. Small gifts foster friendships!

[The *Singakademie* (Singing Academy), a music hall famed for its splendid acoustics, was built in 1825 according to the specifications of Karl Fasch, one of the court conductors of Frederick the Great. Fasch in 1792 founded the Berlin Singing Society, devoted to choral music, especially that of Bach.]

I also inspected a bombed-out hospital in Luetzow Street. Several corpses were just being carried out—a touching picture. One of the nurses killed was an air-raid warden. It drives one mad to think that any old Canadian boor, who probably can't even find Europe on the globe, flies to Europe from his super-rich country which his people don't know how to exploit, and here bombards a continent with a crowded population. But let's hope we can soon deliver the proper reply. . . .

I have ordered the *Kreisleiter* and the *Gauamtsleiter* to report tomorrow for a good dressing-down. I immediately dismissed two local leaders in western parts of the city who were altogether too lax in trying to cope with the damage.

[The *Kreisleiter* were the precinct bosses; the *Gauamtsleiter* the responsible executives at the *Gauamt,* or office for the whole gau of Berlin.]

Dr. Ley asked me quite excitedly about the results of my trip to the Obersalzberg and was exceedingly happy about what I told him. . . .

Tass has issued an exceptionally sharp official communiqué directed against the Polish Government-in-exile in London. It charges this government with imperialism because it insists upon the old borders of 1939.

[Tass is the official news agency of the U.S.S.R.]

The Bolsheviks are now throwing off the mask wherever they can. A blind man with his cane can feel what Europe would have to expect if they had the power. The official Russian declaration waves aside the Atlantic Charter with an elegant gesture of the hand. Roosevelt and Churchill would be astounded to know what would happen to their little paper if the Russians were in a position to tear it to pieces.

Tass also published a wild attack on my last article, "The Crisis of Europe." That shows that our anti-Bolshevik propaganda is slowly getting on Soviet nerves.

The Duce issued an exceedingly emphatic order of the day to the Italian troops returning home on leave from the Eastern Front. This order is historically untrue; nevertheless we must stand for it, as we need the Italians very much. . . . The Duce is really our only completely dependable support in Italy. As long as he is in control we need have no fear.

[The Nazis were always irritated at the flamboyant wording of Italian orders, which made claims the Nazis found grossly exaggerated.]

Through an undercover informant I learn that the Pope intends to enter upon negotiations with us. He would like to get into contact with us and would even be willing to send incognito to Germany one of the cardinals with whom he is intimate. Apparently he believes we are momentarily so badly off that we would be willing to make him essential concessions. There can, of course, be no thought of it.

March 4, 1943

Our anti-Bolshevik propaganda is achieving enormous success. It is now actually the main subject for discussion in our own camp, in the camp of the neutrals, and especially in the camp of our enemies.

The Polish Government-in-exile is very much distressed that the Soviets handle them in such a high-handed manner. Stalin has no thought of considering himself bound in any way by the Atlantic Charter, and the English are getting nowhere by importuning him. He is heading straight for his target, the Bolshevization of Europe, and wants to begin with former Polish territory.

Bohle handed me a report about propaganda abroad. This report criticizes the so-called foreign propaganda of the Foreign Office in the sharpest terms. Bohle is right—it is about as bad as can be imagined. Diplomats are not fitted to conduct propaganda abroad. I could undoubtedly draw up a wonderful system for foreign propaganda in conjunction with the AO, but our diplomats keep getting in my way. The harm that the present Foreign Office has already done to our propaganda is simply incalculable.

[Ernst Wilhelm Bohle held a number of important offices in the state and in the Party. He was an undersecretary in the Foreign Office directly under Ribbentrop, and as such charged with looking officially after the interests of Germans living outside the Reich. For the Party he was a Gauleiter, his gau, or province, however, being no special geographical section of Germany but rather the abode of all Germans outside of the Reich, no matter where they might live. Also, he was chief of the *Auslandsorganisation,* or Nazi party organization looking after Germans outside the Reich from an ideological point of view. AO was an abbreviation for *Auslandsorganisation.*]

In the evening I saw a Bolshevik propaganda picture, *One Day in the Soviet Union.* This movie is a first-class piece of agitation, although anyone who really knows conditions can easily contradict it. Undoubtedly it will be effective in neutral and enemy countries, as it was cleverly adapted to their mentality. It seems rather significant to me that this picture is running unchallenged in Sweden with Swedish captions. That's how low the so-called Nordic states have sunk!

This film, however, once more made it clear to me that we have to be exceptionally careful about Bolshevism. Russia is not a bourgeois but a proletarian Jewish state. If we don't exert every effort it may someday overrun us. Our slogan should be, now more than ever: "Total War Is the Imperative Need of the Hour."

March 5, 1943

The enemy represented events at Rshev as a great success. We say nothing as it is to our interest not to have the situation in the East presented as favorably as it actually is. The OKW distinguished itself by a couple of silly denials of our own news item concerning Rshev. It shows once again that officers are absolutely incompetent as newsmen.

The American Secretary of the Navy, Knox, delivered a speech in which he proclaimed that the United States wants to dominate all oceans of the world. The English will certainly be delighted. As a matter of fact the English have already lost the war. They have had to give up so much property and territory that the Americans can even now call themselves the victors.

According to American reports the Japanese suffered a major defeat in the Bismarck Sea. Until now the Japanese haven't said anything themselves. But the Japanese news reports have not been very dependable recently. The Japanese, too, are not so greatly blessed by the fortunes of war as they were in the first months. We believed they would accomplish much more late this winter than they really did. On the whole they limited themselves to defending the areas conquered the previous winter.

Gandhi has ended his fasting. I think he played a great comedy for the world. The English papers so characterize it and add their own derision and contumely. Gandhi is an awfully clever fellow. I think that he is anything but a man of God. This time, however, the English were not bluffed by his dramatic fasting.

Lots of fuss is still being made about the American Archbishop Spellman. He is in Seville and there talked to the British Ambassador, Hoare. The Vatican denies he engaged in any peace talks with the Pope. I believe that's right.

In the afternoon the twenty-fifth anniversary of UFA was celebrated. Klitzsch delivered a long but interesting speech about the history of UFA. He showed how exceedingly hard a few patriots had to fight against Jewish-American efforts at control of the German motion picture during System Time. I was able to announce a number of honors conferred by the Fuehrer. Hugenberg received the Eagle Shield, Klitzsch and Winkler the Goethe Medal, and Liebeneiner and Harlan appointments as professors. As these honors had been kept secret they made the men thus distinguished very happy. Hugenberg was simply flabbergasted at the public tribute paid him. I treated him with special friendliness and courtesy and made a deep impression on him.

[The UFA (*Universal Film Aktiengesellschaft*) was Germany's largest motion-picture concern. Its executive director was Dr. Ludwig Klitzsch; its principal stockholder Dr. Alfred Hugenberg (see May 21, 1942). Winkler was a go-between for Goebbels with the motion-picture industry and negotiator of contracts with foreign countries. Wolfgang Liebeneiner and Veit Harlan were two popular movie stars. The title of professor was a coveted one in Germany, and did not necessarily signify that its holder was engaged in academic activity. The Nazis always referred to the period of the Weimar Republic (1919–33) as "System Time" (*Systemszeit*).]

In the evening Speer paid me a brief call. He was about to leave for GHQ. I gave him exact directives for his report to the Fuehrer on the domestic situation and especially about my talk with Goering and the many conversations of our intimate group in my house. He is to clear the atmosphere.

Late at night I went for a short visit to Professor Froelich. All the big shots of the UFA were assembled there. They were very happy that I sat down with them for an hour. . . . People, on the whole, are of good will. That applies even to the intelligentsia. All you have to do is to handle them right and give them support in these difficult times. After all, they have a right to this. One would sometimes like to split oneself into a million parts to take a hand wherever necessary. But unfortunately one is always only a single person.

[Professor Carl Froelich was president of the Reich Film Chamber.]

March 6, 1943

The Soviets seem to be quite conscious of the effectiveness of our anti-Bolshevik propaganda. They have now issued a formal declaration in the German language disclaiming all territorial aims in this war. That, of course, is pure bunkum. Their territorial aims would become apparent very quickly if the Soviets could achieve them within a foreseeable time. They and even their Anglo-Saxon friends make no bones about their claim to the Baltic States, to a large part of what was formerly Poland, and to Bessarabia. As compensation, East Prussia, Silesia, and the Mark of Brandenburg are generously placed at Poland's disposal. The neutral countries are extraordinarily alarmed at these exorbitant territorial demands of the Bolsheviks.

Salazar delivered an exceptionally sharp anti-Bolshevik speech which, however, has not been released for general use. He delivered it to a small group. It sufficed, however, to enable us to conclude that as long as Salazar is in power in Portugal, nothing really hostile to us will be done.

[Antonio de Oliveira Salazar, born, 1889, Prime Minister of Portugal since 1932 and Minister of War throughout World War II, was responsible for the drafting of the new Portuguese Constitution in 1933. He is president of the National Union of Portugal.]

Reports from the Rhineland indicate that the people in some cities are gradually getting somewhat weak in the knees. That is understandable. For months the working population has had to go into air-raid shelters night after night, and when they leave they see a part of their city going up in flames and smoke. The enervating thing about it is that we are not in a position to reply in kind to the English. Through our war in the East we have lost air supremacy in essential sections of Europe and are completely at the mercy of the English.

In Tunisia affairs are in relatively good shape. I received a letter from Berndt telling me about Rommel's present condition. Rommel seems to have a new lease on life as a result of his most recent successes. He gives the impression of a very active person, even though one must expect that in the event of a setback he will again suffer quite a relapse in health. . . .

What Berndt wrote me about my speech in the Sports Palace is very flattering. He said it had reacted on the troops in Tunisia like a battle cry and was received by them with the greatest enthusiasm.

The worries of the English public about tonnage losses keep increasing from day to day. People are asking themselves what is to happen after the war in case they have lost their entire tonnage and the United States competes with them with shipping that on the whole is intact. The English will then lose a large part of their world trade. They know it perfectly well. If the English were to recall under what auspices they began the war, namely, to prevent Danzig from becoming German, and what they have already lost in this war, they would probably become somewhat skeptical about the expediency of their declaration of war.

Antonescu delivered a speech that fits exactly into our line. He throws down the gauntlet to aristocratic critics in the capital. On the whole Antonescu is behaving very well. If the Rumanian soldiers were as upstanding as their marshal, things at the Eastern Front would be better than they now are.

Our fight against Bolshevism has created a very great impression in Italy and with all friendly and neutral countries. Todenhofer showed me a number of diplomatic reports which are extremely flattering for this propaganda and for my personal activity. All missions report that my speech in the Sports Palace had the effect of a clarion call.

[Todenhofer was another of Goebbels's numerous handy men.]

I had a very lengthy talk with Seyss-Inquart. . . . He is an enthusiastic supporter of my policies and has great expectations for them in the occupied areas. He reported that our generals sometimes get weak in the knees. But that, after all, has always been the case with the generals! I can gather from this talk that the chances for the success of my political directives are everywhere on the increase.

This view is confirmed by a long talk with Colonel General Guderian, who paid me a call as the new deputy of the Fuehrer for tank warfare. We discussed the abuses prevalent in the Wehrmacht. Guderian is a very sharp critic of these obvious improprieties. . . .

Guderian gave me the impression of an exceptionally wide-awake and alert commander. His judgment is clear and sensible and he is blessed with a healthy common sense. Undoubtedly I can work well with him. I promised him my unstinted support.

[Colonel General Heinz Guderian, born, 1886, commanded an armored corps in 1940, was Commander in Chief of the Second German Panzer Army in 1941–42, was Inspector General of armored troops after 1943, and was promoted to Chief of the Army General Staff following the generals' putsch of July 20, 1944. He also took part in World War I, having entered the Army as early as 1906.]

Again hundreds of letters have reached me that are for the most part extremely flattering. . . . Confidence in me is happily on the increase everywhere.

I am continuing my fight with the Ministry of Justice for the simplification of our entire judicial system. It is very difficult for people there to get out of their old grooves. They don't think, for instance, that appeals in civilian litigation can be dispensed with. I consider that absolute nonsense.

Schach gave me a long report on the situation in Berlin as affected by the last air raid. It is extremely serious, after all. The damage done to the Reich capital is very heavy, and it will take us an estimated six or eight months to repair it even halfway.

Yet that's the very moment the SD thinks favorable for continuing with the evacuation of Jews! Unfortunately there have been a number of regrettable scenes at a Jewish home for the aged, where a large number of people gathered and in part even took sides with the Jews. I ordered the SD not to continue Jewish evacuation at so critical a moment. We want to save that up for a couple of weeks. We can then go after it all the more thoroughly.

In the evening Funk and Ley visited me. I gave them the details of my talk with Goering. They are very happy about the result. But they have certain misgivings as to whether it will be possible to arrange things without any friction as we thought. Goering is unfortunately somewhat inactive and resigned, and it will take a lot of work to gear him up again. . . . Ley weeps on my shoulder about the inactivity of the Party, which is a thorn in his flesh. No doubt that is chiefly owing to the somewhat bureaucratic conduct of Party affairs by Bormann. Bormann is not a man of the people. He has always been engaged in administrative work and therefore has not the proper qualifications for the real tasks of leadership.

We remained together until the wee hours of the morning and touched upon a thousand questions and a thousand problems. We shall certainly endeavor to be a real help to the Fuehrer and to relieve him of countless secondary problems. He really has that coming to him, for he is at this moment carrying a load of responsibility that would break an ordinary man.

March 7, 1943

My collaborator Dr. Splett wrote me from Tunisia about the strange war customs of the Americans. This letter, based entirely upon his own observations, indicates that the Americans are still in a sense a half-savage people. They have no clear political conception whatever. The American soldiers, for the most part, have no idea as to why this war is being fought. If we could face them with numbers and weapons equal to theirs, we could indulge in a regular rabbit chase.

MacArthur blew up the alleged victory of the Americans over the Japanese in the Bismarck Sea in a big way. It really looks, however, as though the Japanese suffered a severe setback there. Until now they haven't published anything about that defeat. But sometime or other they will have to say something!

During the night Essen suffered an exceptionally severe raid. The city of the Krupps has been hard hit. The number of dead, too, is considerable. If the English continue their raids on this scale, they will make things exceedingly difficult for us. The dangerous thing about this matter, looking at it psychologically, is the fact that the population can see no way of doing anything about it. Our anti-aircraft guns are inadequate. The successes of our night pursuit planes, though notable, are not sufficient to compel the English to desist from their night attacks. As we lack a weapon for attack, we cannot do anything noteworthy in the way of reprisal.

I attended the funeral exercises in Dahlem Forest Cemetery for six young men of the Luftwaffe, the youngest soldiers of the Reich to be killed during the last bomb attack. I witnessed very touching scenes. A young minister delivered an excellent speech. We ought really to requisition him for our movement.

The entire German people have serious doubts about the fidelity of the Italians to their alliance. The rank and file of the people surely show a very fine instinct. Although they have no proofs of their suspicions, these suspicions nevertheless exist.

March 8, 1943

The Dutch bishops have caused an exceptionally insolent pastoral letter to be read from the pulpits, in which they incite to open opposition against the measures of Reich Commissar Seyss-Inquart. Seyss-Inquart, however, took countermeasures in time and averted possible embarrassing effects of this pastoral letter.

This Sunday was very quiet, both politically and militarily. There was wonderful spring weather in Berlin. The whole population of the capital seemed to be on the move. Places where damage was done by the last terror attack were the main goals of the pedestrians. However, I had these damaged areas roped off. They are not to be exhibitions for the public out for a stroll.

March 9, 1943

I studied the material on the reduction of the meat ration by fifty grams [1¾ oz.] as proposed by the Food Ministry. I regard this as absolutely necessary to avoid having to slaughter the last cattle in the Ukraine. That would have a very bad psychological effect since even the Bolsheviks left at least one cow to a farmer. I shall speak earnestly about this to the Fuehrer since we cannot found our food policies on illusions. The occupied areas must of course do their part in feeding the Reich, but you can't expect a cow to give milk and let herself be eaten up at the same time.

About 1 P.M. we arrived at the airport of Winnyzja. A large number of combat planes were assembled there for overhauling. Already one sniffs something of the atmosphere of the front. The combat fliers, who were also being overhauled here, gave me a very friendly reception.

I could see that my recent oratorical and journalistic efforts had met with great approval at the front.

On to Winnyzja. The countryside is pretty awful. Everywhere there is poverty and neglect. The clothes and especially the shoes in which the natives present themselves are indescribable. People would not appear in Berlin as they do here even as an exception.

We arrived at the Fuehrer's GHQ about 1:30 P.M. Speer awaited me to give me a briefing on the talks he had had with the Fuehrer. As always he did wise and clever spadework. He told me the Fuehrer was in exceptionally good form, owing, undoubtedly, to the fact that our position on the Eastern Front has become completely stabilized and we have again achieved notable successes.

The Fuehrer is having lots of trouble, especially with war in the air. He is thoroughly dissatisfied with the measures taken by Goering. They lack system and are not carried out on an elaborate scale. Goering is often given entirely wrong information by his generals. . . .

Unfortunately the utter failure of the Luftwaffe has reduced Goering's prestige with the Fuehrer tremendously, not only in this but also in other respects. That somewhat upsets my plans for playing him up more conspicuously. The Fuehrer, according to what Speer reports to me, is rather unapproachable at the moment as regards Goering. Speer therefore did not continue his spadework on that matter. Nevertheless I am of the opinion that we must not give up our plan. Goering, after all, has strong political and military authority which was gained in the course of years and certainly cannot be made to vanish into thin air overnight.

The Fuehrer is very much prejudiced against Fromm. He, too, has noticed that Fromm is not able to put over the 800,000-man program in a large way. Also, he has already had difficulties with Guderian, a thing that makes the Fuehrer especially angry.

[Colonel General Fritz Fromm (1888–1945) was commander in chief of the Replacement Army at this time. For a while he played with the officers' group who plotted to assassinate Hitler, but got cold feet at the decisive moment and was arrested by his fellow officers. Shortly thereafter he was liberated, and had several of these brother officers executed. He was in turn executed on Hitler's orders in March 1945. Von Hassell in his *Diaries* describes Fromm as weak-kneed.]

The Fuehrer continues to be very well satisfied with Zeitzler, who is at present his most effective assistant in the conduct of the eastern campaign. Keitel plays only a very subordinate role. But the Fuehrer keeps him because he does not want to cause comment by changes of personnel, and also because just now he has nobody to put in his place. The lack of real leaders in the Wehrmacht is truly terrifying. That is no doubt chiefly because of the fact that the selection process has been entirely wrong, in that social position, wealth, and education counted for more than natural endowment and excellence of character. This system may be adequate in peacetime but will sooner or later bear bitter fruit in war. Now we have to pay for what we failed to do in the past.

At 2 P.M. the Fuehrer came away from his staff conference. His health, thank God, seemed to be excellent; that is, he did seem somewhat tired, but otherwise appeared very active. He was happy that I came to GHQ for a whole day. . . .

I first gave him a detailed report about the last air raid on Berlin. . . . He listened with great attention and concentration. I noticed immediately that he was very suspicious of Goering, claiming that he was not at all aware of the decisive importance of air warfare. He [Goering] was being thoroughly misled by the generals of the Luftwaffe and therefore took an altogether too optimistic, not to say unrealistic, view.

The Fuehrer's opinion about the generals was unfavorable. They cheated him, he said, wherever they could. Besides, they were uneducated and did not even understand their own profession of arms—the least one could expect of them. They could not be blamed for lacking culture, for that wasn't part of their upbringing, but the fact that they knew so little even about the purely material questions of war was absolutely against them. Their training had been wrong for generations. We could now see the results of such education in our corps of higher officers. I was able to give him some examples from my own experience to confirm the Fuehrer in his views.

I told the Fuehrer how worried I was about perfecting the 800,000-man program. The Fuehrer himself had also worried about it. He gave me a number of directives for activating this program and issued the necessary plenary powers.

The debacle of the past winter, the Fuehrer explained, was chiefly owing to the utter failure of our allies to do their part. Now the front was in order again. This was a military achievement of the first magnitude, and simply cannot be overestimated. The Fuehrer doesn't want to see any more allies at the Eastern Front. He has fully made up his mind that only our own soldiers can finish off the Bolsheviks.

My first talk with the Fuehrer took place in the presence of Speer. Then the Fuehrer invited me into his air-raid shelter where we had a four-hour discussion in private [*unter vier Augen*].

First I completed my report on the Berlin air raid and gave the Fuehrer a presentation of my views regarding air warfare in general. . . . The Fuehrer hardly let me finish talking but said quickly that that was the very thing that kept him awake worrying until the small hours of the morning. He then criticized Goering with extraordinary sharpness. He had let his generals transport him into the realm of illusions. While his optimism was no doubt extremely valuable in times of crisis, it also easily made him a victim of wishful dreaming. That, however, was very dangerous in wartime. He thought the influence of General Bodenschatz, whom he regards as a cold cynic, was especially harmful. Field Marshal General Sperrle, too, in France, was not equal to his tasks. Like all air-force generals he had withdrawn to a castle and was there leading a sybaritic life. Air warfare against England probably didn't interest him much more than, say, an excellent luncheon or dinner. The Fuehrer wants to recall him.

[General Karl Bodenschatz was Goering's personal aide and his liaison officer between the Fuehrer's GHQ and the air force GHQ.
Field Marshal Hugo Sperrle was the commander in chief of the Western Air Command.]

Of the Luftwaffe he now thinks well only of the chief of the general staff, Jeschonnek. Jeschonnek was an absolute fanatic for truth, he said; he saw the situation very clearly and had no illusions.

[General Hans Jeschonnek's rise was meteoric. He was devoted to Hitler.]

Naturally the Fuehrer will under no circumstances let air warfare continue in a slipshod way as hitherto. One need only to think six months ahead, then we would face ruin in many cities, sustain thousands of casualties, and find the morale of our people somewhat impaired. This must not be, come what may. The Fuehrer is going to see to it under all circumstances that British terror be answered by terror on our side. To make that possible, everything must be scraped together from the Luftwaffe that can possibly be collected. All new construction of the Luftwaffe is to serve this one purpose. In place of Sperrle he wants to send to France a young, capable officer who is to be given special powers exactly like those of Doenitz for submarine warfare. He is to have no other task save that of carrying on air warfare against England so systematically and unyieldingly that the English will no longer relish bothering us every night. Moreover, the

Luftwaffe command staffs must be taken out of Paris; in fact, not only these, but also other command staffs. Paris is a dangerous place. No occupation force has ever stuck it out in this city without harm to its soul. . . .

The Fuehrer is very angry at the Italians because they are actually doing nothing. They aren't any good for the Eastern Front; they aren't any good for North Africa; they aren't any good for submarine warfare; they aren't any good even for anti-aircraft at home. The Fuehrer is right in asking why they are in the war anyway!

Production for the Luftwaffe [according to Hitler] must again be reduced to simple principles. There has been too much experimentation; consequently really convincing results have not been obtained. Here, too, Goering's illusions have had evil results. Goering likes to hear things that are pleasant. That's why his boon companions won't tell him anything unpleasant. That refers not only to the Luftwaffe itself, but especially to the damage done by the English. This is always minimized to Goering and never presented in its full extent. The Fuehrer is mad as a wet hen [*hat eine Granatenwut*] at this conscienceless entourage of the Reich Marshal which is largely responsible for bringing us into this extremely embarrassing situation.

The Fuehrer's judgment of the moral qualities of the generals—and that applies to all arms of the service—is devastating. He doesn't believe any general a priori. They all cheat him, fawn upon him, furnish him statistics that any child can contradict, and thereby insult the Fuehrer's intelligence. . . . The Fuehrer certainly won't have anybody give him a wrong steer in questions of air warfare. He knows exactly how things are and won't rest satisfied until Goering, too, has a clear conception of air warfare.

I proposed to the Fuehrer a series of changes in the directives for civilian air-raid protection, along the lines proposed last Saturday to my Ministry. On the whole the Fuehrer approved, especially as regards the placing of fire wardens on the roofs, but not on every roof and only one per block, because otherwise we would mourn too many losses.

In view of his general state of mind I deem it inopportune to introduce the question of Goering's political leadership. This is not the proper moment. We must postpone this matter to a later date.

I reported to the Fuehrer about the severe punitive measures I took in cases of looting in Berlin. The Fuehrer approved. He is extremely satisfied with civilian defense in the Reich capital.

At my suggestion he will hereafter award the casualty ribbon for injuries sustained in air warfare. I think this is only just, and that it will prove extremely effective psychologically.

[The casualty ribbon (*Verwundeten-Abzeichen*) was a decoration similar to the American Purple Heart.]

In this connection I warned earnestly against the plan to create now, during the war, a medal in the form of a black mourning ribbon with an Iron Cross for the relatives of men who fell. It would then be easy to estimate our exact losses, a thing that would not be very fortunate just now.

I also pleaded earnestly with the Fuehrer about the lack of political leadership in Berlin. He realizes the importance of this problem and instructed me to intervene here and there with a helping hand. The Fuehrer is not yet well acquainted with the working methods of the Committee of Three. Since I can't discuss the problem of Goering, I prefer not to speak about this committee now. Bormann still has the Fuehrer's confidence to a considerable extent, whereas Keitel is already on ice.

The Fuehrer shares my worries about the carrying through of the 800,000-man program. He has now become somewhat distrustful of Sauckel. Sauckel does not have the ability to carry the necessary transition process for this program through in practice. He depends too much upon the labor offices, which are most unsuited to this purpose.

The Fuehrer would be quite ready to remove Fromm from office if he had a proper successor. He believes, however, that only Zeitzler would be equal to this job. However, he needs Zeitzler as chief of the General Staff of the Army. The Fuehrer justly blames Fromm for not being able to improvise; that's the crux of the whole matter.

I recited some incidents illustrating conditions in the occupied areas to the Fuehrer, but he already knew most of them. In this connection we happened to talk about the case of the Governor General [of Poland], Dr. Frank. The Fuehrer no longer has any respect for him. I argued with the Fuehrer, however, that he must either replace Frank or restore his authority, for a governor general—in other words, a vice-roy—of Poland without authority is of course unthinkable in these critical times. Added to everything else Frank has an unfortunate divorce matter on his hands in connection with which he is behaving in a way that is not exactly noble. The Fuehrer refused to let him get a divorce. This, too, serves to play havoc with the Fuehrer's relationship to Frank. Nevertheless he wants to receive him within the next few days to determine whether he can still be saved, and if so, to strengthen his authority once more. Frank is not acting properly in this whole situation. He vacillates between brusque outbursts of anger and a sort of spiritual self-mortification. That's no way, of course, to lead a people. One must possess the necessary self-assurance, as it alone can radiate assurance to others. . . .

My measures concerning total war meet with the Fuehrer's full approval. In that connection he referred to my last address in the Sports Palace in the most flattering terms and characterized it as a psychological and propaganda masterpiece. He said he had carefully studied it from beginning to end, had read of the echo it had awakened in foreign countries, and had arrived at the conclusion that we had hit the bull's-eye. He was full of enthusiasm about its effect.

The Fuehrer fully endorses my anti-Bolshevik propaganda. That is the best horse we now have in our stable. He also approves of my tactics in letting the Bolshevik reports of victories go out into the world unchallenged. Let Europe get the creeps; all the sooner will it become sensible. Besides, our anti-Bolshevik propaganda is the apple of discord in the enemy camp.

Nevertheless the Fuehrer does not want to consider a proclamation for the East at this time. The situation in the East does not yet seem to him sufficiently stabilized or sufficiently promising. He believes that Bolshevism is so hated and feared by the peoples of the East that the anti-Bolshevik tendency of our propaganda is quite sufficient. I try again to convince the Fuehrer of the opposite. I believe, however, the real reason [for his opposition] is the fact that he does not want to do anything that might be interpreted as readiness to yield at a moment of temporary weakness. Once the situation in the East has become more clarified, I shall approach him again.

[Goebbels was a consistent opponent of Rosenberg's policy of letting matters drift in the occupied sections of eastern Europe, and favored a proclamation of the East, promising land to the peasants and freedom of worship to the religious.]

The Fuehrer was more approachable on the question of broad outlines for a European program. Even though he does not want to go into details at this time—which was never my intention—he nevertheless gave me permission in my next address in the Sports Palace to allude to this theme and even to outline it to a certain extent. I can do something with this permission.

To my great satisfaction I can inform the Fuehrer that one million laborers have meanwhile been mobilized by our measures. Now would be the time for the Wehrmacht to draft. This, however, is not happening. I shall have to talk very energetically about this to Keitel and

Fromm, otherwise there is danger that our whole program may prove
a flash in the pan.

I discussed Doenitz and Guderian at length with the Fuehrer; both
enjoy his complete confidence.

I made complaint about a number of Reichsleiters and Gauleiters,
whose standard of living is very much out of tune with the times. The
Fuehrer had heard about this too. He is going to forbid hunting for
the duration of the war and the use of alcohol at any events sponsored
by the Party. In principle only a one-dish meal is to be served. That
would mean considerable progress. As the Fuehrer informed me, some
very unfortunate scenes took place in Munich on February 24, even
cases of complete drunkenness. The Fuehrer is fed up. I hope he will
take proper measures.

The Fuehrer, too, is absolutely in the dark concerning the number
of reserves the Bolsheviks still have at their disposal. They are already
calling in the class of 1926, which is proof that they have made extremely heavy inroads on their man power. The Fuehrer ventured the
opinion that it was no means beyond the realm of possibility that they
might collapse sooner or later. He does not want to build his policies
and his war strategy, however, on such an assumption. . . .

I also proposed to the Fuehrer to change the staffs more frequently
in the occupied areas, especially in the West. The dangers of the city
of Paris are very noticeable. The staffs in the Netherlands, according to
Seyss-Inquart, are also exceptionally defective. The Fuehrer is now
going to institute a system of guard replacements.

I reported to the Fueher about my visit to bombed-out St. Hedwig's
Church [in Berlin], about the feelers put forward by the Pope, and
about the question as to whether in breaking up a number of publishing houses we should retain a few Christian ones. He heartily approves
of my tactics in going easy in the church question at present. We must
proceed very smoothly and not get wedded to doctrinaire ideas.

There isn't much to be done with the Fuehrer about Bouhler, who
has permitted pretty serious corruption to gain a foothold in the
Fuehrer's private chancellery. The Fuehrer is quite angry about it.
Appeals for clemency have in part been taken care of by bribery, a
thing that led to heavy punishments. The Fuehrer blames Bouhler for
not having intervened in time. At any rate, one can't get a new job for
him at present.

[Adolf Hitler maintained four different chancelleries, each with a responsible
chief. There was, first, a chancellery charged with dealing with matters that came

to Hitler in his capacity of chief of state—questions of pardons, et cetera. At its head was Dr. Otto Meissner. Next there was a chancellery dealing with matters devolving upon Hitler in his capacity of chancellor. It was headed by Dr. Hans Lammers. Then there was a chancellery dealing with Nazi party affairs, for Hitler always remained top leader of his Party. It was originally headed by Rudolf Hess, and later by Martin Bormann. Finally, there was a chancellery for purely personal affairs, whose chief was Philip Bouhler.]

The Fuehrer then told me a few funny stories about Grand Admiral Raeder and his somewhat bigoted Christianity which—that I hadn't known before—is not anchored in the Church but rests on pure fantasy.

[Goebbels's impression of Grand Admiral Erich Raeder's lack of "churchliness" is not shared by United States Army Chaplain Henry F. Gerecke, who visited the Protestants among the defendants in the Nuremberg war crimes trial almost daily. He reported that Raeder was the best lay Bible student he had ever encountered anywhere, and said he was one of the most regular churchgoers throughout the trial. Raeder, it will be recalled, was sentenced to life imprisonment.]

The Fuehrer talked with a certain sadness about Von Blomberg, whose fidelity toward him personally he lauded very warmly. If all generals in important positions were as faithful to the Fuehrer as he is, things would be better with the Wehrmacht.

[Field Marshal Werner von Blomberg, born, 1878, was Hitler's first Minister of War. Through an intrigue of Himmler, a woman with a shady past was brought into his life whom he married in ignorance of her former profession. Also in ignorance were Hitler and Goering, who were witnesses at the wedding. When the facts became known accidentally, General von Fritsch, chief of the Army, protested to Hitler who "solved" the situation by discharging both Blomberg and Fritsch.]

Ribbentrop's conversations in Rome were a complete success. The Duce is now willing to take an energetic hand, both in the political and the military sector. The Fuehrer doubts, however, whether he will be successful. The Duce doesn't actually have so much power as it would appear. The aristocracy and the court sabotage all his decisions. The Duce wishes to hold Tunis under all circumstances, for reasons of domestic politics if for no other. But what is to happen if we are forced to give up Tunis for compelling reasons? That will be a heavy blow to Fascism.

That's the reason why the Fuehrer would like to leave our anti-aircraft in Italy, because he would then have a certain feeling of security as regards Italy. Also, he would like to propose to the Duce to have ten to fifteen divisions of blackshirts trained in the Reich in the methods of the Waffen-SS divisions. The Duce would then at least have a dependable guard in case the worst came to the worst. He can't depend upon his generals; they cheat him wherever possible.

The purpose of a change of guard in Italy is undoubtedly that of putting Ciano in a corner. The Duce made a big fuss about it so that Ciano's elimination would not draw so much attention. In any case, the Duce once more assured the Fuehrer most positively that he would go through thick and thin with us and never be unfaithful to the Axis. That is quite true. As long as the Duce is in control in Italy we can rest assured of the fidelity of Fascism.

As regards the military situation, too, the generals are cheating the Duce. He was given information about a number of painful facts. He immediately took very sharp measures. Whether he can prevail in the long run remains to be seen.

The last Rommel offensive was again betrayed by Italian prisoners of war. You just can't play ball with the Italians. They are undependable, both militarily and politically.

The Fuehrer became exceptionally open-hearted and personal at the end of our discussion. He hides absolutely nothing from me. Intimate talks like that really strengthen one's heart. The Fuehrer assured me again and again that he was not only extremely satisfied with my work, but that he had the greatest admiration for it. German war propaganda was a masterpiece from beginning to end. I can therefore feel very proud of the recognition given me.

His only worry at present, he said, was his health. He doesn't know whether he will come through the war completely intact physically. "Once this war is ended!"—this turn of speech keeps recurring more frequently now with the Fuehrer. With a certain bitterness he observes he must conduct it with the present corps of generals. But once the war is over he wants to withdraw more than ever from military affairs and again devote himself to things that suit him much more personally.

He is most deeply shocked at the infidelity of the generals. They are ungrateful, too, and there is no dependence on them.

The Fuehrer then withdrew for an hour as he had not gone to sleep until early in the morning.

Meanwhile I had a long talk with Speer on the results of my talk with the Fuehrer. He, too, believes that we should not touch the question of Goering at the moment for tactical reasons. We must wait a while with it.

Speer showed me an interesting exchange of letters with Zeitzler and Fromm. Speer certainly took these high military gentlemen for a real ride. Perhaps he even went a bit too far. But they make demands upon him that simply can't be met.

We talked about the new tank production. In point of numbers, we are of course far behind the Bolsheviks, English, and Americans taken together; with us the man and the quality of our material must decide the issue. Speer believes he can soon eliminate the mechanical defects of the "Tigers." The "Tiger" went through no real period of testing; it went, so to speak, from the factory directly into the battle. Naturally it must now get rid of some "bugs." Nevertheless we save more time that way than when we let the full testing time elapse that is otherwise customary. The enemy at present has nothing to equal the "Tiger." Nevertheless the enemy's tank production is exceedingly dangerous for us. When we take into consideration what a reservoir of men and weapons the enemy still has, and add to it his general war potential, we must envisage a very long war. But I don't want to prophesy, for sometimes fate takes an unexpected turn and gives an entirely new direction to developments.

In the evening I met with the Fuehrer and Speer at dinner. The Fuehrer again briefed us on the general war situation. He gave high praise to the courage and slugging ability of the SS divisions. Sepp Dietrich enjoys his unlimited confidence. He considers him one of our top troop commanders and expects miracles from him. He is, so to speak, the Bluecher of the National Socialist movement.

In case there were ever an attempt at a revolt in Berlin by foreign workers, the Fuehrer would send his *Leibstandarte* to the capital; it would make an example of them that would make every lover of such excesses lose all itch for them. After all, Sepp Dietrich once before beat down a revolt during the Stennes Revolution; how much better would he do now! There is, of course, the danger, as long as there are any Jews left in Berlin, that the Semitic intellectuals may combine with the foreign workers. That's why I shall have to get the Jews out of Berlin as quickly as possible, even though this involves some psychological problems.

[Walter Stennes was one of the most radical early adherents of Hitler. Finding the Fuehrer too conservative, he staged a rebellion which was put down chiefly by Dietrich. Hitler excommunicated him from the Party on April 4, 1931. Stennes and his adherents replied by clashing with Hitler's men in Berlin.]

The Fuehrer once more gave detailed expression to his opinion of the generals of the Army, for whom he has nothing but contempt. He, too, thinks you need but imagine these gentlemen in civilian clothes, and you'd lose all respect for them. About Keitel the Fuehrer can only laugh. The Fuehrer's experiences with the army generals have embittered him beyond measure. He even becomes unfair and condemns decent officers, also, in a lump. One must therefore soft-pedal rather than pull additional stops.

After the war he wants very cheerfully to put on his brown uniform again and have just as little as possible to do with the generals.

The Fuehrer is very angry about the behavior of Field Marshal General Paulus. He believes, exactly as I do, that Paulus acted as the enemy reporters describe him as having acted. After the war he is determined to make Paulus face a court-martial with all his generals since he acted contrary to the specific order to resist to the last round of ammunition. These types of generals hate the Fuehrer because they are uneducated, because they regard him as an upstart, and because they haven't the intuition to recognize his genius. That applies also to the generals of the Luftwaffe. The Fuehrer feels very hurt that Goering places such confidence in them.

The Fuehrer is making every effort to inject new blood into the officers' corps. Slowly but surely the basis of selection for officers is being changed in the Wehrmacht. Schmundt is making a clean sweep here just as Doenitz is doing in the Navy.

The Fuehrer is also very indignant about the lack of technical knowledge on the part of the Wehrmacht generals. They always pretend to know everything when in fact they don't know anything. Even their great heroes are of no exceptional quality. One need merely to think of Seeckt in that connection. But the Fuehrer won't let himself be influenced by any of these things. He sweeps clean wherever he finds dirt and doesn't hesitate about it. I do believe that at the moment he is giving expression to his ill-humor more in words than in deeds, but everybody knows that with him that is always only a prelude to action. . . .

[Colonel General Hans von Seeckt is generally credited with having been the father of the German postwar *Reichswehr,* a professional army of 100,000 men enlisted for a period of twelve years and staffed with officers from World War I. He took part in and spoke at the get-together of National Socialists, German Nationalists, and men unattached to any party, which met at Harzburg in 1932 and formulated plans for bringing the Weimar Republic to a fall. Dr. Hjalmar Schacht, the internationally famed banker, was also present and spoke. Goebbels was always more or less contemptuous of people like Von Seeckt or Schacht who were not dyed-in-the-wool Nazis.]

The Fuehrer showed the greatest understanding of the psychological questions raised by the war and spoke in sharp terms about the impudence of prominent people and their wives. He criticized especially the behavior of Frau Lutze and partly also of Von Ribbentrop who acted disgracefully during the last air raid in Berlin. He confirmed once more that in situations like that I am the supreme and sole commander of the capital. The ministries, too, are to obey my orders. The entire public life is subordinated to me. In times of catastrophe only one person can give orders.

[Paula Lutze was the wife of SA Chief of Staff Viktor Lutze.]

With regard to the Jewish question he approved of my measures and specifically ordered me to make Berlin entirely free of Jews. I shall see to it that there is no concubinage between Berlin Jews and foreign workers. . . .

After the war we want to give Berlin its new profile. At present, of course, its municipal edifices cannot compete with those of Vienna. That, in the long run, constitutes a great psychological danger. Not to speak of Paris. After the war, therefore, tasks are awaiting us of a magnitude that far exceed our imagination. . . .

In the course of the evening we received the news that Nuremberg had suffered a heavy air raid. The Fuehrer is very much worried about the fate of this city. I called Nuremberg twice and asked for reports. The damage was not so great as we at first thought. The old part of the city, especially, has not been seriously hit, only Maut Hall has burned down. The Fuehrer ordered General Bodenschatz, who had just returned from Rome, to be pulled out of bed and gave him a very serious talk about air war. He had been with Goering and on the Fuehrer's order had informed him of the grave anxiety that the development of air raids is causing the Fuehrer. Goering now knows that it is five minutes to twelve for him. . . .

The Fuehrer is certainly extremely dissatisfied with the present condition of things. He expressed his ill will in the bluntest fashion. He recapitulated how many orders he had given the Luftwaffe since the beginning of war and even before and how few of them were really carried out. Generals always knew better than the Fuehrer. That's what the German people now have to pay for.

This midnight discussion developed into a full-sized row. Speer and I had a hard time calming things down somewhat. Here's where our new friendship with Goering stood its first test. In spite of everything I considered it right to support him, for his authority must be preserved under all circumstances. Bodenschatz was very grateful to me. . . . He was very much alarmed by the Fuehrer's words. He wanted to telephone Goering in Rome that same night. . . .

There followed a long and intimate exchange of views that lasted until three in the morning. The Fuehrer was very open-minded and

talked about all questions raised with a frankness that one seldom experiences with him. I am very happy that the Fuehrer sees things so
clearly and so unvarnished, despite his seclusion at GHQ. That gives
me all sorts of hopes for the future.

He was very much touched when I bade him farewell. Once again I
gained a large measure of strength and know what I must do.

March 10, 1943

Naumann in the course of the evening spoke to Walter Hewel at
GHQ. Quite a number of the young men in the Foreign Office are enthusiastic supporters of my policies. They expect much of them for the
future and impatiently watch the results that I have already achieved
and am about to achieve.

[Walter Hewel was the Foreign Office liaison officer to the Fuehrer. One of his
predecessors was Hans Thomsen, German Chargé d'Affairs in Washington at the
time of Hitler's declaration of war on the United States on December 11, 1941.]

I had a lot of work to do in the plane. Long dictation about my talk
with the Fuehrer. Lots of other things. Hardly a chance to rest. I slept
for only a little more than an hour during the night.

Brief landing in Warsaw. But I take no notice of the city; I would
only get angry anyway.

On the way between Warsaw and Berlin we receive news of an air-
raid alert in Berlin. A couple of Mosquito planes managed to get
through to the capital. We have to land at Frankfurt-on-the-Oder on
account of the Berlin anti-aircraft guns. That delays us another half
hour, so that we do not arrive in Tempelhof until almost 2:30 P.M.

The alert had lasted for more than an hour. That shows how very
inferior we are to the English in the air. They are constantly sitting on
our necks. It is simply maddening that a great power that once enjoyed
air superiority over all Europe can now be annoyed by such pinpricks
of air warfare. This is an added proof that the measures indicated by
the Fuehrer for the conduct of war in the air must speedily be carried
out; otherwise the German people will become very impatient indeed.

Regarding Tunisia the English claim that Rommel has now been defeated completely. He had made an advance similar to El Alamein,
they say, and Montgomery is now ready to make a final break-through.
As a matter of fact the situation in Tunisia has become somewhat critical, especially along the Mareth line. We ought soon to make up our
minds whether we can and want actually to hold Tunis or not. Halfway

measures such as have hitherto been the order of the day simply won't do for us in the future.

The English plutocracy has turned against Cripps because of his pro-Bolshevik speeches. A series of letters by industrialists has been published in English papers that fits exactly into our line. Because of our well-planned campaign, anti-Bolshevism is the principal theme of discussion in the enemy camp today. English Government circles are afraid not only of the effects of our propaganda, but also of the allegedly energetic activity of German diplomacy in the neutral countries, of which I have until now observed but very little.

The United States seems at present to act even more anti-Bolshevik than England. The United Press, for instance, praises my propaganda very highly, although it also fears it.

Standley, the American Ambassador in Moscow, made the sensational statement before the press that the Soviets have said nothing in their papers about the extent of United States aid to the Soviet Union in this war. There is pretty deep disappointment about this in the United States. Some people agree with Standley, others criticize him for letting the cat out of the bag. When Standley claims that the Soviet Union is acting as though it waged the war single-handed, that is actually true. This is certainly added proof of the extent of the differences in the enemy camp.

[Admiral William H. Standley was a member of the Anglo-American Mission to Moscow in 1941 and Ambassador to the U.S.S.R. in 1942–43.]

The former Italian Minister of Education, Bottai, has published an article about which I haven't made up my mind whether it was inspired by Mussolini or directed against Mussolini. He declared that Italy's capacity for waging war must be drawn upon more completely than has hitherto been the case. The Fascist party must devote itself to service to the people more than before. Social justice was being demanded more and more insistently by the people. Now and then open criticism was quite permissible. Technical knowledge rather than mere good intentions was essential in the ministries. Politeness in public offices toward the public was urgently desired. All that, Bottai claimed, did not constitute criticism but was an indication of Fascist maturity!

[Giuseppe Bottai was Italian Minister of Education, 1936–43.]

March 11, 1943

My propaganda has now become the main theme of news and propaganda commentary with the enemy. A tremendous fuss is made about it—certainly a good thing for us. . . . The English newspapers state quite frankly that German propaganda is inspired and calculated to cause the greatest confusion in England and the United States.

The Research Office sent me a report commenting on a despatch from the Turkish Ambassador in the United States. This report reflects great fear and trembling about the growth of Bolshevism not only in the military field but also as regards propaganda and politics. From this report it can be inferred that the appetite of the Soviets has caused great consternation in Turkey. All this convinces me that our own greatest chance lies in anti-Bolshevik propaganda.

Sooner or later we must decide whether we can send greater reinforcements to our troops in Tunis, or whether we must give up our position there. Rommel has been to see the Duce about this. The Duce is naturally very much interested in continuing to hold Tunis. But there are other factors. Rommel will fly from Rome to the Fuehrer's GHQ to discuss the entire problem once more with him.

Last night's air raid on Munich was an exceedingly heavy one. Many cultural monuments were damaged and some even destroyed. Again the question presents itself: How is this to go on? If the English are in a position night after night to attack some German city, one can easily figure out how Germany will look after about three months of such bombardments unless we take effective countermeasures. . . .

I discussed the reorganization of our civilian air defense with Schach. We have abandoned the idea of putting a fire watcher on every roof during an air raid. That would cause too many casualties. We'll try out a compromise measure and merely have regular patrols of the houses under the direction of the air-raid warden. Unfortunately these wardens are not always tops, but that is mainly owing to the fact that all men who are worth anything are now at the front.

From a letter from Murr I gather that prominent army officers at home are criticizing the Fuehrer very much. That is low-down and disgusting. Naturally a man like Keitel hasn't the necessary authority to stop this sort of thing. One can only agree with the Fuehrer's opinion of the top officers. They aren't worth a hoot.

[Wilhelm Murr was Gauleiter for Wurttemberg-Hohenzollern.]

The evacuation of Jews from Berlin has led to a number of untoward happenings. Unfortunately a number of Jews and Jewesses from privileged marriages were also arrested, thereby causing fear and confusion. The scheduled arrest of all Jews on one day has proven a flash in the pan because of the shortsighted behavior of industrialists who warned the Jews in time. We therefore failed to lay our hands on about 4,000. They are now wandering about Berlin without homes, are not registered with the police and are naturally quite a public danger. I ordered the police, Wehrmacht, and the Party to do everything possible to round these Jews up as quickly as practicable.

[Jews married to Gentiles were registered by the Nazis as living in "privileged wedlock." That meant they were originally not slated for deportation and extermination. In the closing months of their regime the Nazis seized Jews thus married.]

The arrest of Jews and Jewesses living in privileged wedlock caused a terrific commotion, especially in artistic circles, since these privileged marriages are still prevalent among actors. But I can't be squeamish about them. If a German still finds it possible to live with a Jewess as his legal wife, that's a point against him, and it's out of place to be too sentimental about this question in wartime.

In the evening I learned from GHQ that the Fuehrer has started for the front. He wants to visit Manstein again to express his appreciation to him for the way he conducted operations in the south thus far. I don't like this at all. The Fuehrer doesn't seem to know how infamously Manstein behaved toward him, or, if he knows it, is too good-natured about the military leaders. Of course one must not forget that the Fuehrer is in a somewhat precarious position. At present his main interest naturally lies in quieting things down again at the front.

March 12, 1943

The Fuehrer has visited the southern front and was very favorably impressed. Morale of the officers and the soldiers is simply fantastic, compared with his last visit.

Roosevelt seems to be cleverer than the others in the enemy camp. He let it be known through the press that he would attempt to arrive at an agreement with Stalin about territorial aims. Stalin, of course, will be careful not to fall for such an obvious American trick. There's certainly great excitement and deep discord on the enemy side.

The last air raid on Munich gave the English great satisfaction. They talk about the damage caused there with real cynicism.

The Fuehrer has ordered Goering back from Rome because of the constant increase in the number of English air raids on the Reich. The meeting between the Fuehrer and Goering is to take place in the course of the day. The Fuehrer is determined to express all his misgivings about air warfare and to insist that we make every effort to regain the initiative.

It is a good thing that Rommel, too, is to be at GHQ during the Fuehrer's talk with Goering. He gave a report about Tunisia that pleased the Fuehrer no end. Rommel again holds all trump cards. His talk with the Fuehrer went off wonderfully. In the afternoon there was a conference between the Fuehrer, Goering, and Rommel during which the question of reinforcements for Tunis was also discussed. It was agreed for the present that Tunis is to be held under all circumstances out of special consideration for our Italian ally.

I went into the question of closing up publishing houses as a measure of total war. I shall permit two Catholic and two Protestant houses to continue and thereby make a conciliatory gesture toward the denominations.

Total war is still the principal theme of public discussion. The whole people have taken to it enthusiastically. Some measures are widely criticized, not because they are too stringent but rather because they are not radical enough. A number of specific questions are debated, especially that of beauty parlors for the ladies. These play a curiously important role, especially in the large cities. Perhaps one must not be too strict about them.

The Fuehrer spontaneously awarded Rommel the diamonds to his Oak-Leaf Cluster decoration after their talk. Rommel certainly deserved this, for he is not only a great troop commander but also a courageous man who has proven himself worthy of this high distinction by his personal courage.

[The highest military decoration awarded by the Nazis was the Knight's Cross of the Iron Cross. But even here there were grades. The next higher step after the mere Knight's Cross was the award of swords crossed over the center of the Iron Cross. Then came the Oak-Leaf Cluster. In very exceptional cases, Hitler awarded diamonds to be placed around the Oak-Leaf Cluster.]

March 13, 1943

The Bolshevik steam roller has been brought to a standstill, and the Germans have wrought another miracle. They have triumphed over the peril in the East. All those who during the past winter lived in the greatest anxiety and fear, even though they praised Bolshevik successes, now feel born anew.

Sinclair, the English Minister for Air, delivered a speech that put into the shade anything ever said. He proclaimed the British intention of causing a German migration of peoples in the big cities. The cynicism underlying such a statement simply cannot be beaten.

[The Sinclair here referred to is Sir Archibald Sinclair, born, 1890, and educated at Eton and Sandhurst. Among the many public offices he has held was that of Secretary of State for Air, 1940–45.]

I gave instructions for greater restraint in reporting on air raids. We reveal too much and thereby encourage the English to continue their attacks from the air. The English are very reserved about their own air warfare. We have to date not been able to make a halfway accurate estimate of the effect of our raids on England, whereas the English know almost everything about the results of their attacks on Germany.

Reports from France indicate that the people there are very depressed, owing especially to the carrying out of the Sauckel program. But we can't be squeamish now about French feelings and touchiness.

Goerlitzer has been my deputy as Gauleiter of Berlin for ten years. I invited the *Kreisleiter* and the *Gauamtsleiter* for a little celebration of this anniversary.

[Arthur Goerlitzer never measured up to Goebbels's expectations, but anniversaries are almost sacred in Germany.]

Following the ceremony, I addressed the Berlin party sub-leaders on the present military and political situation, with special emphasis on the duties now devolving on the Party in Berlin. . . . I discussed especially the theme of total war and its relation to a sort of proletarian cult of which there have been evidences here and there. It has happened, for instance, that well-dressed ladies were insulted on the streets or in public conveyances on the ground that they were not living up to the requirements of total war. That, of course, is arrant nonsense. We must not make total war unpopular by such excesses. Total war does not involve a conscious and planned cult of the primitive. We do not become more primitive because of hatred or envy, but because the exigencies of war necessitate it. . . . Under no circumstances must it become a habit to look upon everyone who wears a starched collar as a less dependable Party member or a poor representative of the idea of total war.

It won't do for total war to be interpreted in a lax manner in one province and very strictly in another. The fact that hair dyeing and hair-dos are forbidden to ladies in some provinces, but permitted in others, has resulted in the better-class ladies traveling from one gau to another for their beauty-treatments. That, of course, is not the meaning of total war.

In the evening Speer, Funk, and Ley visited me. I gave the gentlemen a brief survey of my last talk with the Fuehrer. They are well satisfied. All three are sad, however, that at present Goering's position with the Fuehrer is not a very strong one, so that I could not touch upon the real question at issue. They realize, however, that my approach was the right one.

Funk is alarmed lest the new tax decrees of Krosigk and Reinhardt lead to complete extinction of personal initiative. That must not be the effect of tax laws. If, after having earned a certain income, a person must give up 120 per cent of it in the form of taxes, as has actually happened in certain cases, nobody cares any longer to work hard and exert himself, but will do only what is absolutely necessary.

The question of families with many children was introduced by me in this connection. All agreed that parents of numerous children in circles with a higher social standard must be accorded greater tax exemption than has been the case hitherto. At present we protect only parents with many children who come from the lower social classes.

[Goebbels had a large family but drew a high salary. In advocating higher tax exemption for big families of the more wealthy, he was speaking *pro domo*.]

Later in the evening the news reached us of another exceedingly heavy air raid on Essen. This time the Krupp plant has been hard hit. I telephoned to the Deputy Gauleiter, Schlessmann, who gave me a rather depressing report. Twenty-five major fires were raging on the grounds of the Krupp plant alone. Air warfare is at present our greatest worry. . . . Things simply cannot go on like this. The Fuehrer told Goering what he thought, without mincing words. It is to be expected that Goering will now do something decisive.

[Fritz Schlessmann, although only deputy Gauleiter, was at this time in complete control of the Essen area, as Josef Terboven, the Gauleiter, was in Norway as Hitler's Reich Commissioner.]

At midnight Funk suddenly rose to extend his congratulations upon the tenth anniversary of my taking over the Propaganda Ministry. Yes indeed, ten years have passed since I created the Propaganda Ministry as a new instrument for leading the German people. I believe I needn't be ashamed of my ten years of labor. A ministry that then seemed something like a blank calling card has meanwhile become one on which have been written very legible and clear letters, easily readable both at home and abroad. I believe nobody in the world would deny the tremendous importance of the Propaganda Ministry to the German state in the shaping of its policies during the past ten years.

[Germany had no Reich Ministry for Public Enlightenment and Propaganda before the Nazis took over. There was merely a small press department of the Reich Government. Although Goebbels was appointed Minister of Public Enlightenment and Propaganda in March 1933 in order to "prevent political lethargy," the Ministry as such was not created until June 30, 1933.]

March 14, 1943

It is interesting to note from the letter of an important person at the front that the attitude of the German troops toward the Russian people and Bolshevism is occasionally quite different from what we conceive it to be. Here, for instance, the point is made that one can get along with the Russians only by being severe with them. There is no talk in that letter of any proclamation for the East. There is something to be said for this viewpoint, even though, on the other hand, it cannot be denied that more can be done with good propaganda than by no propaganda at all.

SS Group Leader Kaltenbrunner sent me an over-all report on enemy sabotage activity during the year 1942. It appears that it was rather overestimated. While it is true that a number of regrettable events occurred, they did not affect the situation seriously. We can be quite satisfied with developments thus far, considering that, after all, we are now in the fourth year of war.

[Ernst Kaltenbrunner succeeded Reinhard Heydrich as chief of the Security Service. He was convicted of crimes against humanity at Nuremberg in 1946 and hanged. Kaltenbrunner was born, 1901, in Austria. He took part in illegal Nazi activities in Austria until the Anschluss in 1938 and was appointed by Hitler as SS and police leader for the Ostmark, as Austria thereafter was called.

At noon I received the representatives of the foreign press accredited in Berlin to inform them in a question-and-answer period about the most important political, military, and personnel problems. Some very ticklish themes were touched upon, but I was easily able to outplay the questioners. I believe I have once again fought an important news battle by this reception. The echo in the foreign press will no doubt be very great, possibly even sensational.

During a war news should be given out mainly for instruction and not for information. Not every item of news should be published; rather must those who control news policies endeavor to make every item of news serve a certain purpose. Unfortunately we do not always keep this in mind.

March 15, 1943

Hardly has Eden arrived in Washington than he unburdens himself of a lot of pronouncements. He gathered the American press about him and in typical Yankee manner sounded off on the international situation. All commentaries on Eden's speech indicate that the Anglo-Saxon powers are more violently opposed to the Soviets than ever. Washington is even outdoing London. The principal gripe is that Moscow won't show its hand to anybody when it comes to either military or political questions. The Anglo-Saxon powers are quite angry that they have had to grope and still must grope absolutely in the dark regarding the military situation in the East.

My recent interview for the foreign press has had great repercussions in the neutral press. On the whole it was given splendid publicity and my arguments were reproduced pretty accurately. . . . Neutral papers praise my interview especially for its astounding frankness and assert that among all the warring powers there is probably no other statesman who talks about the general situation with such candor. I am gradually beginning to believe that that is a very good trick. In wartime one can achieve certain successes by silence, but one can also gain certain results by very frank and candid talk. Since silence is the rule, speech is something extraordinary. Its effect is all the more sensational and convincing.

Now that air raids on German cities are increasingly frequent we are naturally getting shorter and shorter on artisans and materials for even partly repairing the damage. We are already being forced to transfer to Essen or Munich companies of skilled workers whom we have sent, for example, to Duisburg. They can make only the most necessary repairs and must then immediately be put to work where the damage is even worse. . . . We should by no means believe that the worst is already over. The worst is yet to come!

The Bolsheviks have sustained terrible losses because of the wonderful preparations we made for our withdrawal [on the middle Eastern Front]. They ran into mine fields of ours laid out very trickily and lost quantities of tanks and men.

Late in the evening the Fuehrer called me to brief me on the over-all situation. He was exceptionally happy about the way the SS-Leib-standarte was led by Sepp Dietrich. This man has personally performed real deeds of heroism and has proven himself a great strategist in conducting his operations. The Fuehrer awarded him the Swords for his Knights Cross tonight.

You just can't trust the Jews across the street. I therefore told the Fuehrer emphatically once more that I deemed it essential to force the Jews out of the entire Reich as fast as possible. He approved, and ordered me not to cease or pause until no Jew is left anywhere in Germany.

The Fuehrer was in complete accord with my interview [for the foreign press]. He had read it with the greatest of interest. . . .

March 16, 1943

The Fuehrer has awarded the Oak-Leaf Cluster to ·Manstein. Perhaps he deserved it because of his military achievement, but certainly not because of his human qualities or the attributes of his character.

Giraud has again attracted attention by a speech. He praised democracy as desirable for the European states, prided himself on the fact that in Algiers he rescinded the anti-Semitic laws decreed by Vichy, and on the whole proved himself a devoted servant of the Anglo-Saxon powers. It is quite interesting to note that, wherever the English and the Americans ˙go, their first act is that of rescinding the restrictions for Jews. It proves that in London, as well as in Washington, the Jews play a decisive role, even though it be back-stage.

[Goebbels evidently could not conceive that the world was shocked at the injustices committed against the Jews, and for moral and humanitarian reasons was eager to right the wrong done them.]

There is a lot of movement by the English along the Mareth line, and it is only a question of time when they will launch their offensive. I doubt very much whether we shall be able to resist effectively. Rommel, incidentally, because of his impaired health has gone to his family at Wiener Neustadt. That means that he will be entirely out of the next great battle in North Africa.

Florian gave me a telephone report on the results of English air raids on his province. These are more than serious. The dropping of forged food-ration cards from English planes is causing a lot of trouble. I had a press notice published in the provinces affected, stating that the use of forged food-ration cards will be punished severely, in certain cases even by death.

A new decree by the Fuehrer gives Sauckel complete authority over the departments of the Ministry of Labor now under his jurisdiction. Here we have another case of a ministry being hollowed out bit by bit without the head being removed. That is a very dangerous procedure which in the long run is quite harmful to authority. We are living in a form of state in which jurisdictions are not clearly defined. From this fact stem most quarrels among leading personalities and in the departments. In my opinion it would be best if Sauckel or, better still, Ley were put in the place of Seldte. That isn't done, however. Seldte is left at his post but is gradually undermined. The same thing is true of many other departments. As a result German domestic policy completely lacks direction.

[Franz Seldte, who lost his right arm in World War I, was appointed Minister of Labor by Adolf Hitler as part of the deal by which the Steel Helmet, a German veterans' organization of which Franz Seldte was co-chairman with Colonel Theodor Duesterberg, agreed to support the Nazi regime. Duesterberg, who refused to collaborate with Hitler, was ousted from office and often persecuted. The Old Guard Nazis, such as Goebbels, Ley, and Sauckel, made no secret of their dislike of outsider Seldte. Dr. Ley, especially, was very eager to succeed Seldte.]

I turned the heat on Hunke because of his collaboration with the Foreign Office. The Foreign Office is creating a lot of difficulty for us in our foreign propaganda. Unfortunately the Foreign Office lacks clear and purposeful leadership. Ribbentrop . . . avoids decisions by simply not being where he can be found. . . . I demand of Hunke that he hold his own energetically with the gentlemen of the Foreign Office. Now is the best moment for us to take absolute and unlimited charge again of foreign propaganda.

[The Propaganda Ministry and the Foreign Office were always at loggerheads over the handling of foreign correspondents. Goebbels cleverly took advantage of the situation to ease out the Foreign Office.]

March 17, 1943

Inasmuch as the theme of invasion is again being given greater emphasis [abroad], I direct our news and propaganda services to beat the drum hard. We must under no circumstances give an impression of weakness, even though our troop reserves in the West are at present very weak and we are still taking a dangerous risk.

But I believe we shall sooner or later have to beat back the English and Americans anyway when they attempt to invade the European continent. We are therefore faced with the necessity of taking this question up with more assurance than the situation warrants. If, however, we were to give any indication of weakness, that would be nothing short of an invitation to the enemy to attempt such an invasion.

I am also convinced that a firm attitude on our part will somewhat spoil the appetite of the English for an invasion. Undoubtedly there are two schools of thought, one that favors and one that opposes the invasion. The firmer the attitude we take, the stronger will those who oppose an invasion become.

I issued instructions to be firmer on this question than hitherto. I am also having a trip to the occupied areas of the West organized for a number of journalists and radio commentators. They will there be shown defense lines that are tops. I hope thereby to neutralize the invasion theme somewhat. Every day we win is a clear gain. For if the English wait four or six more weeks their invasion, assuming they planned it, would have hardly any prospect of succeeding.

Unfortunately I didn't get any farther on the question of propaganda in the occupied areas of the East and the Soviet Union. Following Lammers's report on my jurisdictional conflict with Rosenberg, the Fuehrer made a compromise decision whereby my influence upon eastern propaganda is to be exerted exactly as my influence upon all propaganda abroad; namely, through the so-called attaché system. I don't expect very much from this system; nevertheless I shall try to work along these lines and see how far I get with it. When I report to the Fuehrer the next time I shall revert to this question. I can under no circumstances be satisfied with the decision as made. The matter has quite obviously been reported wrongly by Lammers, and the Fuehrer made a decision that does not do justice to the facts. But I hope before so very long to be able to have this remedied.

Berndt visited me and reported about the present situation in North Africa, which is more than troublesome. We have about 75,000 men in North Africa and the Italians about 200,000. That is quite a troop concentration, but it lacks weapons, gasoline, and in some places even food. Only 60 per cent of the supplies reach Tunis; 40 per cent must be written off as lost. What is being sent to the bottom of the ocean in the way of matériel almost baffles description; consequently we are short of this matériel at decisive points of the Eastern Front. Nevertheless the Fuehrer has decided that Tunis must be held as long as possible and has opposed every compromise proposal.

Rommel described in detail to the Fuehrer his difficulties with the Italians. Hearing his description one can understand why Rommel fell ill. In North Africa actually almost half-a-dozen different command points are functioning one against the other—Rommel, Kesselring, Arnim, the *Comando Supremo* in Rome, the local Italian commander, et al. It is simply terrible to wage war when authority and jurisdiction are in such a muddle.

The English have concentrated considerable troops along the Mareth line and Berndt does not expect German resistance to be great. Rommel opposed resistance at the Mareth line from the beginning and really wanted to withdraw to the Gabes line. But this, too, was prevented by the different command points. . . . I believe we are facing very serious days in North Africa.

If they [the Italians] were also to lose Tunis now, a very serious crisis might conceivably ensue at this critical moment. If it were to happen in the summer, however, that is, at a time when we again have greater freedom of movement on the Eastern Front, this crisis could be neutralized to a great extent.

Rommel is now in Wiener Neustadt on several weeks' leave. The Fuehrer ordered him to have himself overhauled. . . . It may be that he will give him a command in the East, possibly that of reorganizing the Sixth Army and taking over its leadership. That, of course, would be a task for Rommel that would in large measure meet his great talents and his ambitions.

As regards the general political situation, it is noteworthy that the Vatican issued an extraordinarily sharp declaration against the forgery of a Spellman speech. . . . The Vatican stated it had nothing whatever to do with the war aims of our enemies. This would indicate that the Pope is possibly closer to us than is generally assumed. Certainly there is no point in provoking him unnecessarily and offending him. He may eventually be very useful to us in a certain situation.

Neither Spain nor Portugal wants to become an area for the enemies of the Axis to march through. It is understandable that Spain has an appetite for Algiers, but for the present there seems to be no practical way of gaining possession of Algiers except by entering the war. But that is exactly what the Spaniards do not want to do.

The damage to Essen was very considerable. There the problem of the évacués has assumed great proportions. There isn't a room available. Possibly we shall have to embark upon a somewhat mild form of compulsory housing if we are to find any place at all for the homeless. I am informed that in Duisburg, for instance, certain families who were bombed out in mid-December of last year are still sleeping on straw. Of course conditions like that can't continue. . . .

From a report by Petzke I gather that the industrial damage done to Berlin during the last air raid, while pretty extensive, was nevertheless reparable within a short time. I have always regarded that as likely. Damage to industry is repaired more easily than damage to civilian objectives, for industry naturally can improvise much more easily than a private person. . . . Once again practical developments have proven that my prognosis has been the correct one.

[Petzke was a Nazi placed in charge of industrial production in Greater Berlin.]

The Committee of Three met in the afternoon. There were a number of heated debates. The administration of justice is being overhauled exactly according to my ideas. Appeals in civil trials will no longer be possible in future. That will save a lot of personnel and matériel.

The universities are not to be closed en masse, but wherever drafts into the Army have rendered systematic teaching impossible, such institutions are to be closed down. The students are to be investigated as to their importance to the state and their political dependability. Preference is to be given to disabled and discharged soldiers. In any case, in future, we shall see to it that the daughters of rich families do not go to college in order to get out of the labor draft.

Next a Fuehrer decree, drafted by Lammers, was read which admonishes the prominent men of the state and the Party to conduct themselves in accordance with the needs of wartime. This decree is quite inadequate, because it is drafted on the principle of "wash my skin but don't get me wet." I demanded a severer decree. Some present opposed it, but I was able to press home my argument pointedly on the basis of material supplied me by Helldorf in the matter of Noethling.

In this profiteering trial a number of prominent men both of the state and of the Party are involved, among them Dr. Frick, Rust, Darré, and even Hierl, besides Brauchitsch and Raeder. The material is very incriminating and I think I shall have to present it to the Fuehrer. It is simply scandalous that men prominent in the state, Party, and Wehrmacht behave in a way that sabotages our war effort. Now one can understand why the people are whispering so much about so-called diplomats' rations. For if it is possible to secure food in such great quantities without coupons, that fact certainly cannot remain a secret. I shall see to it that this evil is eradicated. I won't, under any circumstances, stand for a corruption that in the long run must endanger our war effort. This is especially true of my gau, for if failings by prominent people go unpunished, that will affect morale in the capital adversely.

[Count Wolf Heinrich von Helldorf was one of Hitler's earliest followers, who achieved notoriety by staging anti-Semitic brawls in Berlin. Soon after the Nazis came into power he was appointed chief of police in Potsdam and later in Berlin. During the closing years of the regime, however, he lost faith in Hitler and even became one of the conspirators involved in the attempt on Hitler's life on July 20, 1944. He was arrested and executed. At the time here referred to by Goebbels, Helldorf was still chief of police in Berlin.

Goebbels does not say who Noethling was, but it is clear that the man was involved in a profiteering case which came to the attention of the chief of police of Berlin, Count Helldorf. He was probably a dealer in food, for Goebbels mentions that men of the prominence of Dr. Wilhelm Frick, Reichs Minister of the Interior, Bernhard Rust, Minister of Education, Walther Darré, Minister of Agriculture, Konstantin Hierl, chief of the Nazi Compulsory Labor Service, Field Marshal von Brauchitsch, and Grand Admiral Erich Raeder were able to secure food without coupons.

The diplomatic corps was given special ration coupons that entitled them to much better and more food than that of the average German. In the language of the street, therefore, any German who engaged in black marketeering was said to have "diplomatic rations."]

Terboven called me late in the evening from Oslo. He had taken a trip to the northern front and was very favorably impressed. He is happy about the deep impression my Sports Palace address made on Dietl, his officers, and also his men.

March 18, 1943

The theme of a second front is being discussed more widely again. Our military men, too, have let themselves be influenced by the scope of these discussions and are expecting an attempt at invasion by the English during this summer. I don't believe it will happen. Be that as it may, the second front is the theme most discussed by the enemy. We use strong language and point out emphatically that we shall meet an invasion, no matter where attempted, with proper counterforces, so that it will most likely end as Dieppe did.

[The Dieppe raid of August 19, 1942, was the most elaborate of the experimental commando raids undertaken before D-Day. It was carried out by 5,000 Canadians with American, British, and French contingents. The Canadians lost 67 per cent of their men.]

The submarines have again become a grave threat to England. An anti-submarine conference is being held to combat it, but to date nothing concrete seems to have developed. The resolutions adopted lack punch. After all, you can't conquer submarines with resolutions! Our strongest counterweapon to English air warfare is our submarine. I believe it inflicts at least as heavy wounds on England as the RAF inflicts on us.

Dr. Dietrich made an excellent short-wave broadcast to America in answer to the most recent effusions of the American Vice-President Wallace. The address was well organized and contained a number of extraordinarily effective anti-Bolshevik arguments. It showed up the pseudo philosophy of the American plutocracy.

[Dr. Otto Dietrich, Hitler's personal press chief, was in the anomalous position of being, on the one hand, one of the Fuehrer's most trusted collaborators—one of the few men who could report to him at any time without previous appointment —and, on the other hand, an undersecretary in the Propaganda Ministry, hence a subordinate of Dr. Goebbels. In addition, Dietrich, like Goebbels, was a Reichsleiter of the Nazi party, which gave him the rank of a cabinet member. It was therefore not easy to press him into the Goebbels mold.]

During the afternoon Speer, Ley, Funk, and I talked with Goering for almost three hours. We agree on the course to be followed regarding domestic leadership.

Goering at first gave us a rather detailed exposé on his conception of the present division of power. On the whole he uses the very arguments that I presented on the Obersalzberg. It gives me great satisfaction to note that my arguments have made a deep impression on him. Next he analyzed the psychology of the Fuehrer, pointing out that it is all-important to handle him the right way and at the right time to support one's proposals with the right arguments. Unfortunately we were somewhat negligent in this, whereas Bormann, Lammers, and Keitel proceeded much more cleverly. That must be changed. Goering does not think very much of the three.

So far as their authority and powers are concerned, they rank in the order of Bormann, Lammers, and Keitel, with Keitel an absolute zero. He is a locomotive that has run out of fuel, puffs out the last steam, and then suddenly stands still. Unquestionably these three intend to establish a sort of kitchen cabinet and to put up a wall between the Fuehrer and his ministers. The Committee of Three is to be the organ for putting this scheme into effect. This is simply intolerable.

Goering made the serious mistake of letting the Council of Ministers for the Defense of the Reich fall into desuetude because it created so many difficulties for him with Lammers and the Fuehrer. Had he kept it active from the beginning of the war, German domestic policy would not have got into the mess it is in today. But Goering can say in self-defense that the right men with power, who have genuine and not delegated authority, were not at his disposal. The Council of Ministers for the Defense of the Reich ought to be revived with the essential proviso that it be supplemented by several strong men. We are thinking mainly of Speer, Ley, Himmler, and me. Funk is already a member, and we'll have to put up with Frick whether we like it or not, since he has been a member of it from the beginning in his capacity of plenipotentiary for the Reich Administration.

We agree to proceed by having Goering during his next report to the Fuehrer propose that German domestic leadership be made more definite and for this purpose the Council of Ministers for the Defense of the Reich be revived and supplemented. . . .

Goering wants to make an early appointment with the Fuehrer, if possible within the next few days, since the Fuehrer will be on the Obersalzberg, as will Goering, because of the Duce's visit. After that we want to go to work without much ado and not concern ourselves so much with negotiations and intrigues as with practical measures. Goering is extremely enthusiastic about my plans. He undoubtedly realizes clearly that things can't go on as they are at present and that something fundamental must be done if his authority and his position are to be saved and if domestic policies are to be redirected into the right channels.

Whenever Goering is not able to preside over the Council of Ministers for the Defense of the Reich, which is to meet every week, he wants me to be chairman. This is to develop into my becoming his permanent deputy. Lammers would thereby be relieved unostentatiously as deputy to Goering and pushed back into the secretarial position intended for him from the beginning. Bormann and Keitel, too, are really nothing but departmental secretaries to the Fuehrer and have no authority to act on their own. They are assuming authority at present because those who were given far-reaching powers by the Fuehrer failed to use them. I am thinking chiefly of Goering who, during the past three-and-a-half years of war, has committed very grave errors. He realizes that perfectly today. Lammers can of course continue to write up the minutes of the Council of Ministers for the Defense of the Reich, but he must not blow himself up into a sort of Reich chancellor who must act as a superior officer to other ministers.

Once we have a clear domestic leadership, it won't be difficult to put the bridle on the somewhat recalcitrant Gauleiters. We are thinking, for instance, of summoning a Gauleiter who refuses to obey before the Council of Ministers for the Defense of the Reich, where his eyes are to be opened. . . . Of course we must proceed very carefully so that the members of the Committee of Three won't catch on to our scheme prematurely.

We also talked at length about air warfare. Goering still isn't quite aware of the extent of the damage done to property and persons. For instance, he was absolutely flabbergasted when I told him almost seven hundred people were killed in Berlin. Nor did he know the full extent of the material damage to Berlin. . . . But he, too, now realizes that the English air raids can be stopped only by counterterror. There is no point in attacking English industrial cities and ports; one must strike the English where they are most easily inclined to defeatism; namely, in the residential sections and the homes of the plutocracy.

Goering can't understand why the English don't attack the Ruhr Valley without respite, for we have there a number of very dangerous bottlenecks. But English air strategy has never been anything but an imitation of the German. The English have never really invented anything original, but have always merely imitated what others did before them.

The whole tenor of our talk with Goering was excellent. I have the impression that the serious situation of the Reich has brought the responsible men together much more closely than seemed possible in peaceful and happy times. Goering seemed somewhat more positive than on the Obersalzberg. Obviously, the fact that I told him to wake up made a deep impression on him. Speer, Funk, and Ley are of one mind. They are working most energetically for me. I believe the group which is now getting together will have a determining influence on war and peace.

In the evening I received the latest news from the Fuehrer's GHQ about the present situation. In the East everything is okay. The SS formations, especially, are winning one victory after another. The Fuehrer desires that the achievements of Sepp Dietrich be given more publicity. He is not to be classed as a mere "also ran" among the generals. This wish of the Fuehrer's strikes me just right. I had already suggested of my own accord that the SS be given a bigger build-up than hitherto in the news releases.

The Fuehrer has arrived at a decision about the so-called Exhibition of Young Art in Vienna. He has expressed violent disagreement with the cultural policies of Schirach and has ordered Vienna's cultural affairs to be placed under my direct supervision. If the Viennese should object, all subsidies from the Reich are to be cut off. That would, of course, mean the ruin of Viennese cultural life. This shows again that the Fuehrer is quite amenable to strong arguments provided they are presented to him in the right way.

[Goebbels was extremely jealous of his prerogatives. He considered cultural matters to be exclusively under his jurisdiction, and when a younger leader like Baldur von Schirach, former Reichs Youth leader and now Gauleiter of Vienna, dared inaugurate policies of his own, Goebbels was quick to denounce such an upstart to the Fuehrer. In this case it was easy to get Hitler's ear, as the Fuehrer, himself a frustrated painter, had very positive ideas about art and thoroughly disapproved of modernism. Ruthless as Goebbels always was, he prevailed upon Hitler simply to cut Vienna off from all art subsidies in case anybody objected to his measures.]

Magda, unfortunately, is not well. She is having a hard time recovering from her illness. She hopes, nevertheless, to be able to come home for a few hours this week end. I'm quite worried about her illness. The war depresses her not only physically but also psychologically.

March 19, 1943

I have received a number of reports from the front about our retreats during the past winter. The events that transpired were nothing to be proud of. The road from Rostov to Taganrog looked very much like another Dunkirk. It is evident that enormous quantities of matériel, especially of the heavier kind, are lost during such retreats.

A number of regrettable incidents occurred in Kharkov. Courts-martial are still pending. The commandant of Kharkov had reported that all supplies were destroyed before retreating. When our troops regained possession of Kharkov, however, they found a large part of our supplies still undestroyed. The Fuehrer ought really to take severe and stern action. The localities lying back of the front lines have developed into real centers of corruption during these three-and-a-half years of war.

The Jews all over the world are trying hard to make Bolshevism look innocuous and to represent it as the lesser danger as compared with National Socialism. The present slogan of the Jewish circles of London and Washington is that the Soviet Union is destined to lead Europe. That, of course, is grist for our anti-Bolshevik propaganda mill.

The English are now making daylight raids more frequently, and it is surprising how few losses they sustain. I wonder whether they intend to attack Berlin with large formations on Memorial Day—who knows? We have, in any case, taken all precautionary measures. The people, too, seem to fear something of the sort.

The Turkish Foreign Minister delivered an exceptionally pro-British speech. We fared rather badly in it. We are releasing only a few lines of it in the German press. In this speech he emphasized the great friendship that binds Turkey and England together. That's about the last aftertaste of our great losses of the past winter. These losses are even now having very formidable political repercussions.

Franco, too, addressed the Cortes, the new sham parliament of Falangism. While he turned sharply against Bolshevism, he also expressed himself as very skeptical about the war. He suspects it may last another six years, and doubts that at the end of it there will be victors and vanquished. . . . Otherwise the speech contains nothing of importance. Franco is the typical bourgeois coward who is glib at bourgeois phrases but vanishes into thin air when action is necessary.

I received a report about the activities of the "Young French Revolutionaries" who have withdrawn into the mountains in order not to be drafted for work in the Reich. It is, so to say, a revolution of lazy people who want to defend the liberty of not having to work. It strikes one as small-town stuff.

Many rumors are afloat. Not even the Fuehrer is exempt. These rumors are concerned especially with the condition of the Fuehrer's health. It is essential that he speak next Sunday. This whole wave of rumors will then be calmed in a jiffy.

[The occasion of Hitler's Sunday speech was the *Heldengedenktag*, or Heroes' Memorial Day. On one occasion he used the Memorial Day exercises for a political coup. In 1936 his Minister of War, Field Marshal Werner von Blomberg, was "inspired" by Hitler to tell the assembled Army, Navy, and Air Force generals and admirals that the time had come to break with the Prussian tradition whereby Wehrmacht officers distinctly kept out of politics. All officers, Blomberg pontificated, must become active National Socialists. Many officers present stiffened visibly, but nobody objected, and service with the armed forces became identical with service to National Socialism. It was a sensational departure from the Prussian tradition.]

March 20, 1943

It remains to be seen whether an invasion will actually be attempted or not. Should the English and the Americans actually prepare for it, they will most assuredly look for a point where we are not very strong. I don't believe that the invasion will take place in the west, but more likely in the south or southeast. But these are mere conjectures without any basis of fact.

The North African question has top priority with all the enemy news services. We have evacuated Gafsa, and the Englishmen blow this up into a gigantic success. The Americans boast of their alleged victory. In reality it isn't a victory at all.

Gienanth has sent me a report about our psychological position in Tunisia. The French have proven exceptionally poor soldiers. They desert and are happy to be transported back to France. Nothing is to be expected of the French in a military way. The American soldiers, too, are considered by our troops to be the worst possible, not only because of the fact that the American soldiers have had no combat experience but also that they are not cut out to be soldiers.
Our propaganda in Tunisia is having excellent results. We are especially successful with the Arabs, who are absolutely hostile to the English and the Americans. The Americans, ignorant both of the situation and of the Arab mentality, have made a number of most serious psychological mistakes that now are making themselves felt.

In London as well as in Washington there is great disappointment about the lack of Soviet successes; at least a show of disappointment is put on. In reality I believe tons of rocks are falling off the hearts of Anglo-Saxon statesmen.

The Americans undertook a great daylight raid on Bremen and inflicted heavy industrial losses. It really gets your goat to think that the Anglo-Saxon air powers are now in a position to blast the Reich with such formidable day raids. We shall have to make a big effort to regain at least half of the lost ground.

Gauleiter Florian gave me a number of valuable suggestions during a long talk about air warfare. Florian has seen the damage in Essen and described it to me as exceptionally heavy. The English operated there with absolute precision, and even if the claim that Krupp has been 80 per cent destroyed is terribly exaggerated, we must nevertheless expect serious stoppages of production.

From a report by Fritzsche I gather that the English and the Americans have greatly expanded their radio broadcasts to the Axis countries and intend to step them up even more. If we don't want to be pushed completely into the defensive, we, too, will have to do more about this. It is very difficult, however, to make arrangements with the Postal Ministry, for the Post Office Department is mostly filled with bureaucrats who do not have the proper understanding for improvised intellectual warfare.

Both Moscow and London have turned vehemently against the Polish émigré clique, which is making exorbitant territorial demands. The Moscow jargon is absolutely Bolshevistic. It speaks only of derelict [Polish] landed nobility and reactionaries. The leaders of the neutral countries are here getting a little foretaste of what they would be fed in case the Soviets actually had the power to prescribe their diet.

I discussed the question of better propaganda for the German Navy with Commander Meckel. A lot has been left undone in this respect by Raeder. Doenitz, on the other hand, is very anxious that the Navy be given more publicity than hitherto.

The Minister of the Interior is a bureaucratic hydrocephalus entirely unsuited to political leadership.

I discussed with Schach how the women who have thus far volunteered for work can actually be integrated into the industrial process. The labor offices mostly are quite unable to cope with this situation. On the one hand industry lacks labor power, on the other hand the labor offices are not in a position to send the volunteer women to their jobs quickly. I am going to get the Party in on this in Berlin, so that the process of inducting women into the munitions industry will go a little faster.

The new taxes are almost ready to be announced. I prevailed in practically every instance, and my suggestions were accepted by the Finance Ministry. In other words, the tax on movie and theater tickets will be only 50 per cent, and the income tax for fathers with many children in the better-situated classes of society will also be reduced.

Colin Ross delivered a speech in Salzburg which is very open to challenge. He acted the part of a fanatic for truth and even criticized the German leadership quite unjustifiably. I am going to stop him in his tracks.

[Colin Ross frequently visited the United States and wrote many articles about America, as representative of the *Berliner Morgenpost* and other publications of the Ullstein Publishing House. The Dies Committee on December 28, 1939, recommended his expulsion from America. The German Embassy in Washington on August 30, 1940, protested against branding him as a Nazi spy. On the same day Ross himself issued a statement denying all these allegations. From the data available this editor was unable to determine just when Ross returned to Germany, but if his memory does not fail him, the return occurred sometime before Pearl Harbor.]

In the evening the Fuehrer arrived in Berlin. . . . He asked me to come to him to talk over a number of things. I was happy to find him so chipper and healthy. At the moment he is most concerned about air warfare. I reported about my experiences with Essen. For the most part he was already informed about all this. I am very happy that the Fuehrer accepted Schlessmann's suggestion and placed empty or sparsely inhabited villas at the disposal of the évacués. In that way the first inroad has been made upon the freedom of housing economy.

I proposed to the Fuehrer in future not to bombard slums but the residential sections of the plutocracy when making air raids on England. According to my experience this makes the deepest impression. The Fuehrer agrees with this. It doesn't pay to attack harbors or industrial cities. At present we haven't sufficient means for such attacks. The Fuehrer agrees that air warfare against England must at present be conducted according to psychological rather than military principles. It is of course very difficult to make this clear to the Luftwaffe since it has remained completely in its old rut. . . . Our air reprisals can begin only in five or six weeks. Then, however, they can be carried out on a pretty large scale. The Luftwaffe has accepted this new policy for air warfare only slowly and grudgingly. The Fuehrer continues to be deeply dissatisfied with the Luftwaffe generals.

As regards the situation in the East the Fuehrer is very happy that he has succeeded in completely closing the front again. The Soviets now run into German defense positions and suffer enormous losses of men and matériel. The Fuehrer, of course, doesn't know exactly how long the Soviet Union can still hold out, but he believes that, once this colossus has become groggy, it will suffer a historic collapse. The Fuehrer thinks the collapse of the Soviet Union will begin, not with a lack of matériel reserves, but of man power. The Soviets have sustained such bloody losses during the past winter that they simply cannot stand them for long, though of course nobody can say how long. We must continue to fight stubbornly and tenaciously until the enemy is knocked out. At that moment a decisive turn will have come in the war. Then we shall have a Wehrmacht that can be regarded as the best and the most experienced in the world, fitted with the best equipment, and made up of human material that is most confident of victory. Then we need no longer fear the Anglo-American invasion, which at present is still something of a nightmare with us.

The Fuehrer intends to give a comprehensive picture of the present situation on the Eastern Front in his [Memorial Day] speech which is comparatively short, running to only fifteen pages. . . . I am quite satisfied that the speech isn't too long, for if a British air raid were to take place during this address our nerves would be taxed severely. I discussed with the Fuehrer the damage thus far inflicted by air raids. In Munich the English made terrible ravages. The Fuehrer showed me a city map of Munich on which the places hit were indicated. The damage is exceedingly serious. Cultural monuments, especially, were irreparably destroyed.

The Fuehrer agrees on the whole with the measures for total war. He merely complains of the resistance that is always offered to our measures by the bureaucracy. In some cases this resistance is simply intolerable and, as I tried to impress the Fuehrer, can be broken only by severe punishment.

The Fuehrer is happy over my report that the Jews have for the most part been evacuated from Berlin. He is right in saying that the war has made possible for us the solution of a whole series of problems that could never have been solved in normal times. The Jews will certainly be the losers in this war, come what may.

The Fuehrer asked me a lot of questions about my health. Unfortunately what he tells me about his own health is none too good. He has stomach trouble, but Professor Morell has succeeded at least in freeing him of pain and bodily discomfort. Otherwise he is in good form. I am able to confirm that during our talk. At midnight the Fuehrer went to his private rooms.

[Professor Theodor Morell was Hitler's personal physician. Orthodox medical circles considered him a "phony." Trevor-Roper in his *Last Days of Hitler* describes him as a "quack . . . a gross but deflated old man, of cringing manners, inarticulate speech, and the hygienic habits of a pig—a charlatan."]

If the Wehrmacht were really combed out, we would not have to worry about a lack of man power at the front. The trouble is that the front usually doesn't get the men; they are simply swallowed up by the areas lying farther back.

In this connection it is interesting to note that the Wehrmacht demands food rations for thirteen million drafted soldiers, whereas actually only about nine million were inducted. I brought this matter up with the Fuehrer, because this may open up a possibility of avoiding a cut in meat rations. The Fuehrer is having these figures checked over. One can see from this incident how irresponsibly certain circles operate with figures. Statistics do not only prove, they also lie. Anybody who depends on statistics is sunk.

Recapitulation of events between
March 20 and April 9, 1943

There is a gap here of nearly three weeks in the Goebbels diaries. During this time de Gaulle and Giraud had their great clash which resulted in Giraud's withdrawal from the scene.

Montgomery, with his British Eighth Army, pierced the Mareth Line in North Africa and captured Gabes; and United States troops punched a twenty-mile hole into the enemy's lines in central Tunisia.

Trouble for the Nazis from occupied peoples was indicated by the blasting, by an act of sabotage, of the large bridge across the Oder River at Frankfurt-on-the-Oder on April 4, and by the announcement the following day that Daladier, Blum, Gamelin, and Reynaud, French statesmen, had been removed from France and put into German prisons.

On April 9 Hitler and Mussolini were still conferring. Their meeting had started April 7.

April 1943

R.A.F. AND U.S. AIR FORCE POUND NAPLES, KIEL, ANTWERP. PÉTAIN CALLS
ALLIED RAIDS UNJUSTIFIABLE. HITLER AND MUSSOLINI CONCLUDE FOUR-DAY
CONFERENCE. SPAIN READY TO MEDIATE FOR "JUST PEACE." POLISH GOVERN-
MENT-IN-EXILE INQUIRES INTO GERMAN CLAIMS THAT RUSSIANS MASSA-
CRED TEN THOUSAND POLISH OFFICERS AT KATYN. MOSCOW, IN ANGER,
SEVERS DIPLOMATIC RELATIONS WITH POLISH GOVERNMENT-IN-EXILE.
HORTHY PLEDGES HITLER ANEW HUNGARY WILL FIGHT. ROOSEVELT AN-
NOUNCES JAPANESE EXECUTED U.S. AIRMEN.

April 9, 1943

The situation in Tunis offers the enemy a welcome opportunity to
blow the trumpet of victory. Events there are represented as a complete
victory for the Anglo-Saxons. It is claimed that the English and Americans have meanwhile joined forces and that central Tunisia is completely in the hands of our enemies. Their only headache is what to
do with the numerous prisoners. Rather modestly they add that at
present it is only a question of Italian prisoners. Their triumphant cries
really get on one's nerves, but unfortunately they are not entirely without background and reason.

A report on interrogations of American prisoners is really gruesome.
These American boys are human material that can in no way stand
comparison with our people. One has the impression of dealing with a
herd of savages. The Americans are coming to Europe with a spiritual
emptiness that really makes you shake your head. They are uneducated
and don't know anything. For instance, they ask whether Bavaria belongs to Germany and similar things. One can imagine what would

happen to Europe if this dilettantism could spread unchallenged. But we, after all, will have something to say about that!

Eden made a statement in the House of Commons about his trip to the United States. It contained only general phrases—another proof that his journey was not very successful. Eden admits openly that England and the United States have different views regarding the postwar period. It may be supposed that this question was the main reason for Eden's visit. As Eden could produce no practical results he resorted to cheap phrases. So the House gave him a frosty reception and the Labor party urged an early debate on Eden's declaration.

Dependable reports by our espionage services indicate that the Soviets will after all be able to induct two and a half million soldiers during this summer and the ensuing autumn. However, these will certainly be of an inferior quality.

Polish mass graves have been found near Smolensk. The Bolsheviks simply shot down and then shoveled into mass graves some 10,000 Polish prisoners, among them civilian captives, bishops, intellectuals, artists, et cetera. Above these mass graves they built installations to cover up any possible traces of their dastardly deeds. The secret about these executions became known through hints given by the inhabitants. Gruesome aberrations of the human soul were thus revealed. I saw to it that the Polish mass graves be inspected by neutral journalists from Berlin. I also had Polish intellectuals taken there. They are to see for themselves what is in store for them should their wish that the Germans be defeated by the Bolsheviks actually be fulfilled.

[In connection with this episode, known as the "Katyn incident," it is interesting to compare with it Jan Ciechanowski's version as he describes it in his *Defeat in Victory*.]

I received Gauleiter Giesler of Munich. He told me about the extraordinary difficulties with which he must cope in the capital of our movement. He has made a number of psychological mistakes, and now everybody is trying to get back at him. Hermann Esser is especially active as he is speculating on getting the Munich Gauleiter post. Giesler did the cleverest thing he could possibly do—he went straight to the Fuehrer, reported the situation, and assured himself again of the Fuehrer's absolute confidence. Giesler is certainly having a very difficult time. . . . He complains a lot about the prima-donna behavior of Clemens Krauss, who is gradually getting on everybody's nerves. I am going to tell the Fuehrer about this.

[Paul Giesler, former Gauleiter for southern Westphalia, succeeded Adolf Wagner, one of Hitler's oldest associates, after Wagner's death in 1943.

Clemens Krauss was formerly conductor of the Vienna and Berlin state operas, and at this time was musical director general of the Munich State Opera.

Hermann Esser was one of Hitler's earliest followers and collaborators, but evidently not a man of outstanding ability. He held Nazi party membership card No. 2, and, as he looked somewhat like Hitler, tried in every way to copy his mannerisms and gestures. He was finally given a berth in Goebbels's Propaganda Ministry, where he held the high rank of undersecretary—second only to Goebbels—in charge of travel propaganda. Hitler dreamed of making Germany the greatest tourist country on the European continent.]

Admiral Canaris gave me a verbal report on the work of our counterespionage. I gather that it has done better than I assumed. Unfortunately the results of its work were not used properly. Thus, for instance, our counterespionage reported the North African undertaking of the English and Americans as well as the meeting at Casablanca well ahead of time, but these facts were not reported to the Fuehrer with sufficient clarity. Canaris told me a number of details about his work that were extremely interesting. . . .

Canaris also claims that our counterespionage predicted Russia's war potential correctly, especially heavy tank production for the Bolshevik Army. Unfortunately the necessary conclusions were not drawn from this report. I arranged with Canaris that we would work together more closely in the future. He wants to report to me at regular intervals so that, if necessary, I may use my influence with the Fuehrer. Canaris on the whole makes a good impression, certainly a better one than I expected.

Schloesser reported to me about his trip to Vienna. Schirach was given a harsh calling down by the Fuehrer on the Obersalzberg because of his art policies. I believe we won't have to worry about Viennese art in future. Schirach will no doubt be more careful and will refrain from delivering irresponsible and dilettante speeches about art.

[Rainer Schloesser, born, July 28, 1899, was Reich Dramatist in Goebbels's Propaganda Ministry. Before Hitler's advent to power he had been the *Kultur* editor of the Nazi official organ, the *Voelkischer Beobachter*.]

During the afternoon I worked on my speech for the Fuehrer's birthday. That job is especially difficult this time, because it calls for infinite tact in its presentation. But I believe I succeeded nevertheless in developing a convincing argument.

In the evening I started for Essen with a large entourage. . . . We had long discussions in our special car. Field Marshal General Milch spoke in terms of sharpest criticism about the Reich Marshal. He blames him for having let technical research in the German Luftwaffe run down completely. The Marshal, he said, had gone to sleep on the laurels that the Luftwaffe had won in 1939 and 1940. Most pernicious for him had been the activity of General Udet, whose work later caused his collapse. That fact explained his human and physical collapse. He had committed sins of omission of historic importance. As a result we were almost completely defenseless today against British air terror.

He then described in detail the various measures he has undertaken to remedy our defenselessness. In his opinion it will not be possible until the beginning of November to make any sort of showing against the English and not until next spring—in other words, not until a year later—to pay them back in kind. A number of new types [of planes] have been developed, but until large-scale production is under way much time will pass. Until then the English can lay a large part of the Reich in ruins if they go at it the right way. Milch regards our air-warfare situation as very serious. He is much worried about it. He, too, sees quite clearly that the Reich Marshal's prestige has suffered very much. One cannot say that Milch is a pessimist. While he sees the tremendous danger threatening us in Tunis, nevertheless he does not consider the situation there as lost. He claims that our Sixth Army in Stalingrad could have been saved and that, had he been in command, he would have retreated even in the face of the Fuehrer's orders to the contrary.

This led to a long debate about the right of a military leader to act in violation of orders by his supreme commander if he deems this in accordance with his duties. I opposed this view energetically. Possibly one can cite examples from history to prove that such action was successful now and then, but one must never establish it as a principle.

Milch confirmed reports that the Fuehrer was exceedingly angry about the development of the German Luftwaffe. He expressed himself in the most furious and unrestrained language before the generals of the Luftwaffe, not even sparing the Reich Marshal. For these reasons, again, it is urgently necessary to give Goering greater support. His authority must under no circumstances be lost. That would be worse than the harm done by the slovenliness of the air command.

[Field Marshal Erhard Milch did not show much gratitude or friendship in discussing Goering and Udet. Milch was one of the three head directors of the German *Lufthansa,* or civilian airways corporation, at the time the Nazis took over. Goering, who had known Milch as army pilot during World War I days, made him undersecretary in the Air Ministry as soon as that new department was organized by the Nazis in 1933 with Goering as minister. That placed Milch second in command. Later, when Goering defiantly announced to the world at a dinner of the Foreign Press Association in 1935 that the Nazis had rearmed in the air in violation of the Treaty of Versailles, Milch was given the high rank of lieutenant general of the air force, again second only to the then General Goering. His rapid rise continued—in 1936 he was made a full general, in 1938 chief of staff, and in 1940 field marshal. It must therefore be assumed that he had quite as much responsibility for the failure of the Luftwaffe as Goering had, all the more so since he could devote all his time and attention to air warfare, whereas Goering had many other duties.

Milch could usually be seen in Berlin dining in one of the capital's most swanky restaurants—Horcher's—with none other than General Ernst Udet, well known in America as a stunt flier. Goering had put his old fellow ace from World War I in charge of all technical inventions and developments in the Luftwaffe. There was nothing to indicate that Milch then thought of Udet as Goering's evil genius. Udet in 1941 committed suicide. The official version was that Udet had been killed while trying out a new weapon.]

April 10, 1943

The English have issued pompous communiqués about their air raids and the damage caused. Their claims on the whole are right. English espionage service in the Reich is functioning alarmingly well.

The world is full of rumors, such as, for instance, that King Boris has met Inonu near Constantinople and has had a number of talks with him. The English conjecture on a number of reasons for the Duce's trip to the Fuehrer. They claim the meeting took place on the Brenner and that the only question at issue was the defense of the southern Italian coast. The English don't know that the meeting is still going on, on the Obersalzberg. So we don't have to be ashamed of having known only about a meeting of Churchill and Roosevelt but not that it took place in Casablanca.

Kállay addressed the [Hungarian] Government party. His speech was only halfway firm. He blew a little incense in our direction, but only weakly. He talked much more enthusiastically about his trip to Italy. He declared tactfully that the Duce had assured him of his wholehearted support of the Hungarian policies. He forgot to add what these policies are and to what goal they are to lead. He also didn't say Hungary would fight until victory is won, but merely that he has the intention of continuing the war.

We arrived in Essen before 7 A.M. Deputy Gauleiter Schlessmann and a large staff called for us at the railway station. We go to the hotel on foot because driving is quite impossible in many parts of Essen. This walk enables us to make a first estimate of the damage inflicted by the last three air raids. It is colossal and indeed ghastly. This city must, for the most part, be written off completely. The building experts of the city administration have figured out that it will normally take twelve years to repair the damage. . . .

The top city officials reported to me on the extent of the present damage. A map on which total destruction is indicated in red gives an over-all picture of the extent of the damage. It is terrifying. I believe Essen today is the city hit hardest by English air raids.

At ten o'clock there was a meeting in the *Saalbau*, attended by the Gauleiters of all western provinces, the men who accompanied me, Dr. Ley, and a number of mayors from the cities which suffered most. . . .

[The *Saalbau* was a large municipal auditorium in the Essen City Park on the southern outskirts of the Krupp metropolis.]

The Gauleiters in their observations on the situation severely criticized the bureaucracy in Berlin. They exempt only the Propaganda Ministry and, surprisingly enough, also the Food Ministry. Backe, who is present and does some talking, is told expressly that the food situation in the various gaus is exemplary. . . .

On the question of evacuating women and children I spoke earnestly against exercising coercion. A little moral suasion can be applied, but I deem it absolutely not feasible to take the children away from their mothers by force and evacuate them. . . .

The construction of bunkers and bombproof shelters is the most urgent problem. In a number of cities the population is defenseless and completely at the mercy of English air raids. But there is a shortage of man power and materials for building bunkers. Here the rest of the Reich will have to lend a helping hand.

Anti-aircraft is partly praised, partly criticized. The main criticism is that there is too little of it. Quite right. All who take the floor criticize the Luftwaffe and Goering unsparingly. Milch replies to these charges.

In a concluding word I summarized all the questions raised. Our meeting lasted almost four hours and was one of the most useful that I have experienced in the history of the Party. Here real he men were talking man to man. They minced no words and the problems were tackled squarely. Nobody acted like a cat walking around a hot dish.

Then we all made a tour of Essen. Only by going on such a trip can

one really estimate the damage. It was terrible. One's heart shudders
on revisiting and seeing, in their present condition, the streets and
squares that were once so beautiful. I suffer almost physically at the
sight, for I have known the city of Essen well ever since my childhood.
I can draw comparisons between what was and what now is.

I paid a short visit to Krupp's to inspect the destruction there. I was
received by young Bohlen, who has taken over the management of the
plant in the place of his father. Old man Bohlen, now seventy-two and
a half years old, is already somewhat gaga. Young Bohlen does not
impress me as very active but is most charming. Only time will tell
whether he is equal to managing this gigantic undertaking employing
nearly two hundred thousand workers, including branch offices and
plants.

[Gustav Krupp von Bohlen und Halbach was born Gustav von Bohlen und
Halbach. His immediate predecessor at the head of the gigantic concern, Alfred
Krupp, a son of the founder, had but one child, Bertha, after whom the German
supergun of World War I, "Big Bertha," was named. When Herr von Bohlen,
then a young diplomat in the German Foreign Office, married Bertha Krupp, his
name was changed with Kaiser Wilhelm II's permission to Krupp von Bohlen und
Halbach. Thus the name of Krupp was perpetuated. Gustav Krupp von Bohlen
und Halbach was among the twenty-two top Nazis indicted for major crimes by
the International Military Tribunal of Nuremberg, but by the time the trial opened
his arteriosclerosis had developed to a point that made it impossible for him to
attend court sessions. The indictment was dropped.
  Krupp von Bohlen lived the life of a robot. His every minute was organized.
Entertainment at Villa Huegel, the Krupp estate overlooking Essen, was also ac-
counted for by the minute. The guests had to, arrive promptly. The host and
hostess entered the reception room at the exact moment scheduled. The meal was
served with clocklike precision. The guests were dismissed at the moment speci-
fied on the invitations.]

I argued in favor of a substantial increasing of anti-aircraft at
Krupp's. Milch tried energetically to defend the Luftwaffe. But he is
in a pretty hopeless position.

Nobody can tell just how Krupp's is to go on. Everybody wants to
avoid transplanting Krupp's from Essen. There'd be no purpose in
doing it, for the moment Essen is no longer an industrial center the
English will pounce upon the next city, say Bochum or Dortmund or
Duesseldorf. A position must be held as long as possible. It does seem
important to me, however, that we evacuate the women and children
from Essen so that only such inhabitants as are essential for work will
remain.

Finally we make a trip through the old part of the city. Sometimes
we walk, as vehicles can move only through some streets. Destruction

is complete in many places. Sometimes one would like to avert one's eyes and not see all this devastation. Now at last I have a real picture of what English air warfare means. My views on this problem are not only confirmed completely, but more than confirmed by the facts. I foresaw developments correctly and tried in time to draw the necessary conclusions.

April 11, 1943

Although the English and Americans have become somewhat more reserved in their boasts about the situation in Tunis, we must not deceive ourselves, but realize that our situation there has become almost hopeless. The enemy press is now getting after Rommel in an infamous and shameless way. That's too bad, especially since Rommel has had nothing whatever to do with Tunisia recently. The Fuehrer is keeping him in reserve for a greater task.

Our North African undertaking has cost us much matériel and blood. In reality the Italians are responsible when all is said and done. They ought at least to have prepared sufficiently to hold their overseas possessions. Worse than that, they can't even protect their homeland. Our allies are certainly the world's worst!

An imposing funeral has been arranged by the local authorities for the victims of an American bomb attack on Antwerp. The English and the Americans have as yet taken no notice whatever of our propaganda about Antwerp. That is proof of their bad conscience. It supports our idea of making a first-class propaganda matter of the Antwerp incident. . . .

[On April 5, 1943, United States planes convoyed by British and Canadian aircraft bombed the industrial area of Antwerp at a loss of nineteen planes. Berlin claimed 2,000 Belgians had been killed.]

The British are at present waging an intense war of nerves in Turkey. It looks as though the British Government were determined under all circumstances to draw Turkey into its military plans.

Further proof of this was brought to me by Admiral Canaris who came with several officers to brief me on the enemy's intentions about an invasion. It would appear that the invasion of the English and the Americans will have Sardinia and Sicily, possibly also the southeast, as the target, so as to come close to the Rumanian oil fields. In the West only diversionary maneuvers will in all likelihood take place, assuming the secret reports of our agents are correct. Personally I consider this quite plausible. I don't believe that the English and the Americans will attempt to break in on us in the West as they know only too well that they will bleed to death there.

Morale keeps changing constantly. All sorts of things are criticized, but what depresses the people most is the fact that they no longer have any over-all picture of what is happening. Nobody can picture to himself just how the war is to end and how we are to win the victory. Everybody is worried about the coming summer offensive on which great hopes are based. It is dangerous for the people to keep arguing that we may not last through a third winter of war in case we fail to smash the Soviet Union this summer. Of course that isn't true, but for the moment I won't do anything to counteract this sort of talk. The time will come when it can be discussed publicly.

Sauckel has delivered a lecture to the heads of his labor offices. He sounded off again about women's compulsory labor in a way that certainly does not help total war. Sauckel is one of the dullest of the dull. Unfortunately he has allowed the heads of his labor offices to take him completely in tow. These types are for the most part quite unregenerate. He still keeps a whole retinue of former Centrists and Social Democrats who naturally are having the time of their lives leading the dumb fool from Weimar around by the nose.

[Sauckel employed former members of the Catholic Center and the Social Democratic parties without realizing they were sabotaging his efforts.]

April 12, 1943

It is a curious fact that we shun the phrase "European co-operation" just as the devil shuns Holy Water. I can't quite understand why that is true. So obvious a political and propaganda slogan ought really to become a general theme for public discussion in Europe. Instead, we avoid it wherever possible.

But, after all, the English are making the same mistake, no doubt at the instigation of Churchill. They refrain in every way from saying anything tangible about their war aims. I can only add, thank God; for if they were to put up a peace program somewhat along the lines of Wilson's Fourteen Points they would undoubtedly create great difficulties for us.

My last article in the *Reich* caused a great commotion abroad. But my speech in Essen had an even greater repercussion, both in the neutral countries as well as among our allies.

In the evening I started for Berchtesgaden with Funk to take part in the conference called by Goering.

We are living in a leadership crisis and it is high time that the Fuehrer sweep with an iron broom. Funk told me a number of incidents about men around Goering that simply make one shudder. . . . Funk is very unhappy about these developments. He has every reason to be. The events in question are connected with the Reichsbank, and Funk naturally knows the exact details. The Fuehrer must be informed about this. I am going to do that next time I report to him, come what may.

[Goebbels evidently refers to corrupt financial practices, possibly involving black marketeering in foreign exchange, by leading Nazis.]

I remained with Funk until the small hours of the morning and had him brief me on all details. All in all they throw no favorable light on a part of our National Socialist leadership. Nevertheless one must not lose courage. Such phenomena will always occur. It isn't so important that they happen; what matters is that they are eradicated.

April 13, 1943

We arrived at Freilassing early in the morning. En route (shortly before Freilassing) I had a terrible kidney attack. I suppose a kidney stone got loose. The pain was so barbaric that I couldn't get up at all. I immediately had Professor Morell summoned from the Obersalzberg. He did not arrive until an hour later. During that hour I suffered almost unbearable pain. Professor Morell immediately gave me a big shot of morphine that relieved me somewhat.

Unfortunately it was totally impossible for me to take part in Goering's conference. I couldn't even move and had to spend the entire day in the private car. Professor Morell put me into a sort of narcotic sleep; only in that way was I able to bear the pain.

By evening there was slight relief. It was touching how the Fuehrer, Goering, Ley, Speer, and all the others were concerned and worried about my condition. On the way to the meeting Ley even picked flowers and sent them to my compartment. Funk was touching in his solicitude about me.

There were some very serious clashes between Sauckel on the one side and Speer and Milch on the other. The meeting was not particularly harmonious. Sauckel had prepared for this meeting whereas Speer and Milch unfortunately came totally unprepared. They had depended completely on my familiarity with the situation and on my professional knowledge, which alas was not available to them. As a result Sauckel had somewhat of an advantage and won the race by default.

But for the moment I can't think about these things. The state of my health so bothers me that I have neither the urge nor the desire to do anything. Added to my terrible pain continuous vomiting set in that almost makes me despair of life. I had a terrible night. To make it half-way possible for me to stand the pain, Naumann had to give me two additional shots. I was happy when I reached Berlin in the morning. On the way, at Leipzig, we took an army doctor on board who looked after my health after a fashion.

April 14, 1943

When I arrived in Berlin my condition had somewhat improved. We had the train stop outside the Anhalter Station, so that my getting off would not be noticed much, for, if it were, violent rumors would start. But I had to go to bed at once. I'm now going to try to cure my kidney ailment.

The chief editor of the *Deutsche Allgemeine Zeitung*, Silex, has written a report on the way the press conference is run. While the tone of this memorandum is very impudent, he does hit the nail on the head. Any decent journalist with any feeling of honor in his bones simply cannot stand for the way he is handled by the press department of the Reich Government. Journalists are sat on as though they were still in grade school. Naturally this will have very serious consequences for the future of journalism. Any man who still has a residue of honor will be very careful not to become a journalist.

[Dr. Karl Silex was married to an Englishwoman whom he divorced when foreign marriages were frowned upon. He had been London correspondent for his paper, 1925–33. On Hitler's seizure of power he was made editor in chief.

Goebbels earlier in the regime often addressed the press conference himself. Now he left it to his young men, some of whom had a decidedly exaggerated idea of their importance. Old newsmen, grown gray in the service, often complained at their arrogant attitude.]

Berndt presented me with a report as to how we are to inform the German people when the end has come for us in Tunis. Berndt put together a lot of wonderful arguments, stressing especially our constant inferiority in arms and man power. I don't want to consider this question for the moment; fortunately things have not yet advanced to the point that we must impart so sad a piece of news to the German people.

We are now using the discovery of 12,000 Polish officers, murdered by the GPU, for anti-Bolshevik propaganda on a grand style. We sent neutral journalists and Polish intellectuals to the spot where they were found. Their reports now reaching us from abroad are gruesome. The Fuehrer has also given permission for us to hand out a dramatic news item to the German press. I gave instructions to make the widest possible use of this propaganda material. We shall be able to live on it for a couple of weeks.

[The details of the Katyn incident are given under date of April 9, 1943. With characteristic cynicism Goebbels sees the Katyn atrocities only in terms of their value for propaganda.]

I received news from the General Commissariat at Kiev that the area under cultivation has receded by 130,000 hectares since the occupation. That is a very regrettable phenomenon, and is partly owing to the fact that the peasants are not being treated right by us. If they were treated better we would in all likelihood have more grain in our barns.

Quisling wrote a report about the campaign in the East and sent me a copy. This document, too, states clearly and decisively that Germany neglected to take advantage of political means of waging war in the East. The solution of the Russian problem depended upon a reconstruction program for the East. The very absence of a proclamation for the East was having a most deleterious effect on the whole conduct of the war. We would certainly be able to stir up many of the peoples of the USSR against Stalin if we knew how to wage war solely against Bolshevism but not against the Russian people. Therein lay our only opportunity for bringing the war in the East to a satisfactory end. Quisling knows eastern mentality very well, as he lived in Russia for many years.

I heard from the Obersalzberg that Antonescu's visit took place in a very cordial and frank atmosphere. The Fuehrer is well satisfied. A visit by Horthy is to follow; then the first series of visits will be over.

The Fuehrer wants nevertheless to remain on the Obersalzberg for several weeks more. I believe this is the very best thing he can do now. If the Fuehrer will use this opportunity to restore his health halfway, that will be advantageous for us all and especially for German politics and our war effort. We all spent ourselves too much last winter. There is a limit to our physical and spiritual strength. If you draw too long upon your reserves you face a vacuum after a while. I believe I, too, shall have to slow up a bit. Otherwise I am in danger of collapsing someday. . . . That would not only be purposeless, but also irrational, and so I won't let things come to that pass.

April 15, 1943

Naumann had a long talk with Field Marshal General Milch. Milch would like to see the entire civilian air defense united under one head. He wants to propose both to the Fuehrer and to Goering that I be made responsible. I don't know whether I can take on this additional job. It does seem to me, however, that unified handling would be best, for the wild mixup that exists today can't be tolerated longer. Civilian air defense is one of the most important problems to be solved at home. Possibly if it can't be done in any other way I might have to let go of a number of other jobs in order to devote myself to this task with greatest zeal. For the moment, however, I am in no position to do this. I spent a very difficult afternoon. My fever rose and I am afraid that my kidney trouble may be of a rather serious nature.

Our Luftwaffe has now discovered that something could be undertaken against the British-American air war by using all our short waves to North America. General Martini has had a brainstorm and thought up a scheme which is calculated to torpedo our entire war of the ether against the United States, but which can hardly force British-American air war into more modest channels. I am therefore opposing the idea with every means at my disposal. It is bad enough that General Martini has succeeded in compelling us to stop our local radio broadcasts every night. If he wants also to make our foreign propaganda impossible, he will have me for an enemy.

[Goebbels was a firm believer in the co-equal importance of propaganda with military strategy, and resisted every attempt of the military to interfere with his propaganda. Broadcasts for domestic consumption had to be broken off every time enemy planes approached, because they served as direction finders for the planes. General Martini tried also to stop all short-wave broadcasts to the United States.]

An American news agency declared that Roosevelt and Eden had decided to re-establish the old borders of prewar Poland. As though Roosevelt and Eden had anything to say in the matter! It is exclusively the Axis Powers and the Soviet Union that have the say, and as regards the Soviet Union we still have the decisive word in this matter.

Colonel Martin gave me a report about the measures the Bolsheviks took after the recapture of Kharkov. It made me realize that the Soviets are masters in the art of improvisation. They have been able to do things that our authorities behind the lines could never have accomplished. It is obvious that one can make even a lazy fellow over into an industrious one if organizations and measures of the state are backed by severe punishments.

From a number of statements by Bolshevik prisoners I gather that General Vlassov's appeal caused some discussion after all in the Soviet Army. The appeal will be even more effective if we get behind it more energetically. Of course this depends upon the issuance of a proclamation for the East which the Fuehrer can't as yet be persuaded to issue. We must not only wage war in the East, we must also do a political job there.

[Russian Lieutenant General Andrej Andrejevitch Vlassov, captured by the German Army, formed a Free Russian Army to fight alongside the Nazis. After VE-Day the Western Allies extradited him to Soviet Russia and it may be taken for granted that he was executed.]

April 16, 1943

The enemy regards the position in Tunis as much more favorable to him. As a matter of fact it has indeed become somewhat more serious for us. The enemy now asks whether we have the intention of evacuating. For the present, at least, there can be no question of it. We shall try to defend ourselves to the last ditch. The English claim that the Italians have already begun evacuating. There's not a word of truth in this, either. They are certainly sitting on a high horse in London and doing themselves well. They look upon Tunis as absolutely safe for them. We can't do very much about it in our propaganda; we must be content to divert attention from this theme to other matters.

Major Balzer reported to me about his visit to the headquarters of Field Marshal General Kluge. There they are placing great hopes in me and expect me to persuade the Fuehrer to issue a proclamation for the East. I don't know what to do. For the present I can't start on the subject again with the Fuehrer, as he has taken such a positive stand. I do believe, however, that sometime in the near future the moment for broaching the subject again will be more favorable. I am very much discouraged that so obvious a political matter cannot be discussed at present.

[Field Marshal Guenther von Kluge (1882–1944) committed suicide in August 1944 to escape arrest by the Gestapo.

The question of a proclamation for the East is obviously one of the few matters on which Hitler and Goebbels did not see eye to eye.]

An exchange of letters and decrees between Koch and Rosenberg is laid before me which demonstrates how complete is the chaos in the administration of the occupied eastern areas. Rosenberg favors a more moderate, Koch a more radical, course. Both act as though they were great experts on the East; Koch as a native of Elberfeld and Rosenberg as a Baltic emigrant have every reason to do so!

In Finland a nationalistic movement has started that is very sharply directed against the defeatist news policies of the Finnish press. The Finns think they can carry water on both shoulders. They are thereby gradually causing a breakdown of the home front that will bring about the greatest difficulties if they want to continue the war—and that they must. It is a fine thing that there are at least a few courageous men in Finland who are trying to prevent a collapse at home.

My kidney trouble is still bothering me. I had Professor Huetepohl X-ray me in St. Hedwig's Hospital. The X-ray examination, thank God, indicated nothing serious. It was simply a case of a small kidney stone that was extremely painful and made me lose a lot of weight, but will not otherwise impair my health. Naturally I would not like to have a repetition of this attack in the near future, but no doctor can give me any guarantee on that score.

In St. Hedwig's Hospital I have been able once again to observe the excellent order and splendid management of such a denominational hospital. I am very glad I forbade the closing of denominational hospitals in Berlin. They are very serviceable. The nuns should be allowed to continue their nursing. Here they can't do any harm; on the contrary, they are true benefactors of suffering humanity.

[It is interesting to note that Goebbels, when his personal health is involved, does not go to a Nazi hospital, with the so-called "Brown Sisters" in charge, but to a Catholic institution.]

In the evening Roellenbleg showed me the pictures of the mass graves at Katyn taken for the weekly newsreel. These shots are truly gruesome. One hardly dares to imagine what would happen to Germany and Europe if this Asiatic-Jewish flood were to inundate our country and our continent. All hands must be put to work to the last breath to prevent such a misfortune.

[Roellenbleg is not otherwise identified in the diaries. He was probably a staff photographer or a functionary of the picture section of the Propaganda Ministry.]

April 17, 1943

Tunis is slowly moving into the foreground again. The English express the hope that it may soon fall. They want to prepare a second Stalingrad for us there, and claim that evacuation is impossible. Apparently they have no conception of the resistance that we are determined to offer.

A number of English papers and periodicals have been laid before me which give evidence of great respect for my person and my work. *News Chronicle* calls me the most dangerous member of the Nazi gang. I can be very proud of this praise. If the English continue to respect my work so much, I believe I shall gradually also win the approval of the German people.

[Although Goebbels enjoyed a certain popularity in the city of Berlin, he was not at all a favorite of the German people at large. His extremely radical viewpoint did not suit the average middle-class German. This is the first indication, however, that Goebbels himself was aware that his policies were not always approved by his own people.]

The United States has published statistics according to which there are 5,000,000 orthodox Jews in the United States. The United States can certainly be described as a Class-1 Jew state. We are going to step up our anti-Semitic propaganda so much that the word "Jew" will again be pronounced in the derisive manner that it deserves, just as it was in the time of our struggle for power. It must come to pass that even an enemy statesman won't dare to be seen in the company of a Jew without immediately being suspected by his own people of being a stooge of the Jews.

The Katyn incident is developing into a gigantic political affair which may have wide repercussions. We are exploiting it in every manner possible. So long as ten to twelve thousand Polish victims have sacrificed their lives anyway—probably not entirely without their fault, for they were the real instigators of this war—they might as well now serve to open the eyes of the peoples of Europe about Bolshevism.

In the evening a Globe Reuter report reached us containing a declaration by the Polish Government-in-exile. This declaration changes the whole Katyn affair fundamentally in that the Polish Government-in-exile now demands that the International Red Cross take part in the investigation. That suits us perfectly. I immediately contacted the Fuehrer, who gave me permission to send a telegram to the International Red Cross, requesting it to collaborate to the greatest extent possible in identifying the corpses. This telegram is signed by the Duke of Coburg and Gotha, whose name is well known in England and who has many family connections there. In that way, in my opinion, something has been started the repercussions of which we simply can't imagine as yet.

[Duke Charles Edward of Coburg-Gotha was a grandson of Queen Victoria of England and father-in-law of the Swedish Crown Prince's son.]

I received secret reports from the Research Institute indicating that Roosevelt intends to meet Stalin somewhere. These reports are unconfirmed as yet. I deduce from statements made by diplomats that there is a certain reconciliation between the views of the Soviets and the United States. Eden's visit to the United States seems not to have been so unsuccessful as we at first assumed.

The Spanish Foreign Minister, Jordana, delivered a long speech in which he mentions the war only incidentally. It contains a great fanfare against Bolshevism. That, however, is mere theatrical thunder. He offers Spain as a mediator and places great hopes, as he put it, in the Holy Father in Rome. Of course we cannot use these passages of his speech in Germany.

[Francisco Gomez Jordana y Souza, 1876–1944, had been Minister for Foreign Affairs under Franco in 1938–40, but was then made President of the Council of State, and Ramón Serrano Suñer became Foreign Minister in his place. In September 1942, however, Franco dismissed Suñer and returned Jordana to his former post of Foreign Minister.]

One might almost think it would be a good thing if the English were to bomb the hell out of Paris and the other western European capitals, so that their inhabitants would at last come to their senses.

The SD report is full of mischief. Its recent issues displease me deeply. It is entirely unpolitical and is sent to the various offices unsifted. That involves a certain danger, for most readers of these SD reports haven't the faculty of political discernment to distinguish between side issues and main issues. Above all, these reports contain too many details. The leaders of the Reich certainly don't have to know about someone in a little hick town unburdening his anguished heart. Just as the Fuehrer need not know if somewhere in some company people complain about the way the war is run, just so the political leaders don't have to know if here or there someone damns the war or curses it or vents his spleen. The make-up of the SD report must be quickly changed. I ordered Berndt to effect collaboration between the SD and the Reich propaganda offices. If the material of the SD, which in itself is good, is sifted politically and brought into line with the political views of the Gauleiters and the Reich propaganda offices, it can develop into a good source of information.

April 18, 1943

The English and the Americans are again placing Tunis in the foreground. They emphasize, however, that the series of flashy victories is over and that the difficult finish is yet to come. Quite superfluously the Italians have issued a detailed report about the battle in North Africa in which they lavish great praise on the English. That wasn't exactly necessary! The English certainly fare better in this report than the Germans. It is quite obvious why the Italians are doing this. They are trying to make plausible their own disgraceful defeat and their cowardly behavior. The report is simply terrible.

One cannot spare the Italians the reproach that in their news reports, at least, they are rendering a service to the enemy and are thereby weakening our position very much. Of course one can understand that the Italians try to blow up their soldiers into heroes, although nobody in the whole world believes it. No matter what Rome may do, I believe the military reputation of the Italians is gone once and for all. There wasn't much left of it anyway; the emergence of Fascism alone gave the friends of the Italian people a hope that the earlier period of weakness of the Italian nation might be overcome. That, however, is not at all the case.

In the United States the guarded mediation offers of the Spanish Foreign Minister Jordana are declined brusquely. While the language used is not so strong as after the Casablanca conference, nevertheless there is unanimity of opinion in the United States that only unconditional surrender by the Axis Powers will be considered. They will have to wait a good long time for that!

It was an exceptionally good idea that we raised the Jewish problem again on orders of the Fuehrer. Anti-Semitism is growing rapidly even in the enemy states. Reports to that effect reach us, especially from England. If we continue to high-pressure the anti-Semitic question, the Jews, in the long run, will be much discredited. All one needs to do is to be tough and determined, for the Jewish problem has now been frozen so tight that it will be difficult to thaw it out again.

From a secret report of the Research Institute I learn that the Swedish newspapers did everything in their power to prevent the publication of the reports of their correspondents accredited in Berlin [concerning Katyn]. It shows again how unneutral Sweden really is.

In the evening photographs of Katyn were shown me. They are so terrible that only part of them are fit for publication. The documentary evidence offered in the form of photographic reproductions is drastic proof of the blood-guilt of the Bolsheviks which cannot be denied.

Horthy's visit on the Obersalzberg has come to an end. On the first day it was conducted in a very heated atmosphere. The Fuehrer minced no words and especially pointed out to Horthy how wrong were his policies both in general and especially with reference to the conduct of the war and the question of the Jews. The Fuehrer was very outspoken. He charged the Hungarians with having tried to contact the enemy via Spain and Portugal. Horthy denied this but that did not help him very much.

On the second day the conversations were more normal. A communiqué was drafted similar to the one on Antonescu's visit. On the insistence of the Hungarians, however, the passage about our fight against the Western plutocracies was eliminated. I suppose the Hungarians believe that in the house of a man who has been hanged one should not talk about rope!

I gave orders to investigate all Jews still left in Berlin. I don't want to see Jews with the Star of David running about in the capital. Either the Star must be taken from them and they be classed as privileged, or they must be evacuated altogether from the capital of the Reich. I believe I shall have completed one of the greatest political achievements of my career once Berlin is free of Jews. When I consider how Berlin looked in 1926 when I came here, and how it looks now in 1943 when the Jews are being evacuated completely, I get a feeling of what has been achieved in this sector.

The condition of my health is such that I find it difficult to continue to work with the intensity to which I have been accustomed. I am often exceedingly tired and must use every effort to overcome my sleepiness.

Here and there certain groups of Germans, especially the intellectuals, express the idea that Bolshevism really isn't so bad as the Nazis represent it to be. That is owing to the fact that our consideration for the families of men missing in action in the East has been such that we have not described the atrocities of Bolshevism as they actually happened. The Katyn case now offers a welcome opportunity to catch up on this. The families of our missing men in the East simply must accept this sacrifice so that the German people won't someday have to make a greater sacrifice, perhaps even that of their national existence.

April 19, 1943

The Jews in England now demand laws to protect them against anti-Semitism. We know those tactics from our own past when we were struggling for power. It didn't help much. We were always able to find loopholes in the law. Besides, anti-Semitism cannot be eradicated by law once it has taken root with the people. A law against hating Jews is usually the beginning of the end for the Jews.

The English are in no position to strike us in our vitals. When I look at the pictures of the Atlantic Wall, I have a feeling that we are sitting in Europe in an absolutely secure fortress.

[The Nazis were always convinced that their Atlantic Wall (known to Americans as the Siegfried Line), the opposite number to the Maginot Line, was invincible.]

The Poles continue to press for an investigation [of Katyn] by the International Red Cross, which has not yet given final reply. Their considerate excuse is that nobody works in Geneva on Saturday and Sunday! These neutrals are certainly sitting pretty! There they are—far away from the firing line, and then they are even invited to play the role of arbiter between the Great Powers.

[Nazi ideology maintained that no power has the right to be neutral in a world war.]

The communiqué issued about Horthy's visit on the Obersalzberg is very downright. According to it, the Hungarians will fight unwaveringly on our side until the final victory. Would to God it were true! [Dies Wort in Gottes Gehoergang—literally This Word into God's auditory passage!]

At 6 P.M. the demonstration in honor of the Fuehrer's [fifty-fourth] birthday took place in Philharmonic Hall. . . . My speech created a very deep impression.

April 20, 1943

The statements of the Red Cross in Geneva are really funny. The Red Cross is in continuous session. I can just imagine how they talk themselves into a blue funk as to whether they are to go to Katyn or not.

I received a report on the situation in Croatia. That country is certainly to be pitied. The Italians are putting the Croatians under such pressure that there is no semblance whatever left of a free state. It isn't quite clear what the Italians are really after. Possibly they are merely trying to prove that the Croatian state cannot live. But there's a much easier way of doing that than supplying arms to the opposition and thereby directly and indirectly supporting the Partisan movement. The reign of terror which the Italians have established in some sections of Croatia baffles all description. The Italians are obviously playing with fire. No matter what orders the Duce gives, his army officers do not dream of obeying them. The more the Italians extort from the Croatians the more will they be inclined to come over to our side. Unfortunately, we cannot help them as we should like to, because of our treaty obligations to the Italians.

Dr. Ley visited me. . . . It is touching how anxious and worried he is about my health. He told me about the meeting at Goering's on the Obersalzberg in which I could unfortunately not take part because of my kidney attack. . . .

Dr. Ley was not very happy about the whole atmosphere on the Obersalzberg. He doesn't believe that Goering has the stamina to take a leading part in the direction of the Reich's affairs. Besides, air war is making so many demands upon him—to say nothing of the fact that it almost knocked him groggy—that he really has no enthusiasm or strength left for other plans.

Dr. Naumann had quite a talk with Sepp Dietrich, who is setting up a new tank corps on the Fuehrer's orders. Many of his men are taken from among the leaders of the Hitler Youth. With this human material he is to organize an SS regiment that is to be called "Hitler Youth." I regard this name as very unfortunate. It certainly will not help our cause, for the simple reason that other nations will conclude we are already drafting youth to have sufficient man power for waging our war. Sepp Dietrich, however, is very happy about his new assignment. . . .

Dietrich told Naumann that the Fuehrer has expressed himself as extremely satisfied and pleased with my work. He told Dietrich I was one of the few people who knew how to do something constructive about the war. The Fuehrer is not too well satisfied with Goering. Nevertheless he as well as I believe Goering's authority is indispensable for the over-all leadership of the Reich. We must strengthen and support this authority, no matter how difficult it may be at times. It is decidedly important for the war effort and the Reich. The Fuehrer is glad that I have established a more intimate relationship with Goering. When his authority and mine are combined, something useful for the administration of the Reich is bound to result.

Sepp Dietrich is shocked at the Duce. The Duce has become an old man. He looked sick and frail, and gave the impression of being tired and washed-out. The Fuehrer could only pity him. His army is cheating him where it can and he has no one on whom he can absolutely rely.

Sepp Dietrich requested that expressions of his great admiration for my work be transmitted to me. He urges me under all circumstances to stick to my course and let no one crowd me off it. The Fuehrer—so he assured him—would support me in every way. Also, the front was united to a man behind my policies.

A number of deserving combat soldiers of the Waffen-SS troops that recaptured Kharkov were my guests. They told me about the fights for Kharkov. They have very clear and decided views concerning the greater ability of the Bolsheviks to improvise. They feel certain that a war cannot be waged without imposing punishments. That's what I, too, have often emphasized. What they told me about conditions behind the German lines, especially in Kharkov, baffles all description. Our Etappe organizations have been guilty of real war crimes. There ought really to be a lot of executions to re-establish order. Unfortunately the Fuehrer won't agree to this, at least not for the present. Sometime something must be done. The conditions prevailing during the German retreat make your hair stand on end. The Etappe abandoned tremendous quantities of food, weapons, and munitions without destroying them; on the other hand the Etappe organizations on retreating took with them carpets, desks, pictures, furniture, even Russian stenographers, claiming these were important war booty! One can imagine what an impression this made upon the Waffen-SS when they met these caravans on their forward march against the Bolsheviks.

[There is no precise English equivalent for the German Etappe. The Etappe comprises the troops behind the front lines which are not engaged in combat, either because they are just on their way to the fighting front, or because they have occupation or rear-guard duty to perform. The fighting soldier thought about as much of the Etappe as a combat officer does of a swivel-chair general.]

The SS men claim that it is possible to polish off the Bolshevik soldiers without much ado. Whenever they are confronted with troops that are their equal, imbued with a philosophy and given the proper military training, they immediately show the white feather and run. Some German divisions, they said, failed just as badly as did some elements of our allies. We therefore can't complain of them on that account. Of course I believe that the SS people are exaggerating somewhat for reasons of *esprit de corps.* Nevertheless the facts they reported are anything but pleasant.

April 21, 1943

The English, who have started a new attack in Tunis, are at present saying nothing about it. Apparently they are not any too sure of themselves. The closer the space into which we are crowded together, the better, naturally, we can defend ourselves. It all depends upon the security of our supply lines. Fortunately some more shipments have arrived, but English supremacy in artillery is enormous. Critical days are again ahead of us. It is simply impossible to make predictions.

The English are celebrating the Fuehrer's birthday . . . with unprincipled, vulgar insults. They aren't behaving at all like gentlemen. In the domestic press a proclamation by the Reich Marshal and my speech for the Fuehrer's birthday were the main features.

An incident embarrassing to us occurred when a German merchant ship fired on a Swedish submarine. The Swedes are blowing their tops about it. The Swedish press, especially the section hostile to the Axis, is indulging in language that it dares to use only because our military position is not very secure at the moment. But one day there will be a change—and then we can talk differently to the Swedes.

April 22, 1943

The *Times* [London] has suddenly discovered that our position is exceedingly weak and our propaganda equally so. As a matter of fact in recent weeks we have limited ourselves too much to a defensive propaganda. This must be changed at once. I have given suitable orders to the press and radio.

Again and again it is claimed that the Japanese intend to declare war on the Soviet Union. I don't believe it. The Japanese are at present engaged so fully that they can hardly afford still another theater of war, although most certainly everybody in the know in Tokyo is aware that

Japan cannot win the war against England and America if we are bled white in the East.

For the present we don't see clearly the significance of the cabinet change in Tokyo. Some believe that Shigemitsu, who is an expert on China, is to work for a closer relationship between Nanking and Tokyo; others are of the opinion that Shigemitsu is charged with attempting to mediate between Berlin and Moscow. For the moment I confess I can't imagine what such mediation would look like. Some facts, nevertheless, seem to point in that direction. The Japanese have always tried hard to end the conflict between the Reich and the Soviet Union in one way or another. If this were possible in some way the war would assume a totally different aspect. Of course I don't believe that such a possibility will arise in the foreseeable future.

[Mamoru Shigemitsu, born, 1887, became Minister for Foreign Affairs in 1943, after a long career as diplomat, in the course of which he held ambassadorships successively in Soviet Russia, Great Britain, France, and China.]

A tapped telephone revealed the fact that the wife of our Ambassador Abetz expressed herself in a very irresponsible manner to some French politicians. Well, she is a Frenchwoman. That's further proof that diplomats must marry only among their own people.

April 23, 1943

Roosevelt protested in an extraordinarily sharp note against the conviction by a Japanese court-martial and execution of the United States fliers who bombarded Tokyo last year. We are seizing upon this opportunity to join the Japanese in taking violent issue with the Anglo-Saxon powers on the question of air warfare. The Japanese aren't at all impressed by the Americans. They carried through the proceedings against the American aviators according to the established rules and are determined to continue to do so. Possibly air warfare will take a new turn as a result of this stand. The proofs against the English and American fliers are truly overwhelming. Undoubtedly very strong aversion against bombing would crystallize even in aviation circles if every captured flier were executed who bombarded residential quarters or was not sufficiently briefed on military targets that he was to hit. I'm very much tempted to propose that to the Fuehrer. Naturally it has its bright and its dark sides, but I believe in this case the bright side outweighs the dark, because the English and Americans probably would not have the nerve to reply with adequate reprisals, whereas we of course would.

The Fuehrer gave orders to play up the execution of the American fliers in the press. It will be the big spread for the Good Friday editions.

The Katyn incident continues to command attention. The Red Cross is still investigating. We can just see these little cantonal diplomats sitting in a sweat box.

From reports of the Research Office I learn that the Rumanians were by no means so enthusiastic about the meeting on the Obersalzberg as we imagined. They felt the want of a clear aim in our policy and war effort. Mihai Antonescu seems to be especially busy pointing this out. He is very unreliable. In a diplomatic report I read about a conversation of his in which he emphasized that the Italians knew all about his aims and plans. It looks as though Bastianini were playing a somewhat dubious game.

[Giuseppe Bastianini, Italian diplomat, born, 1899, was at this time Undersecretary for Foreign Affairs. He was sentenced to death by Fascists at Verona, but escaped to Switzerland in April 1944.]

Terboven passed through Berlin. He, too, has heard something about the somewhat ill-starred conference at Goering's on the Obersalzberg. He doesn't believe that Goering has the stamina to assume leadership at home. Terboven thinks an awful lot of Field Marshal General Milch. I think he is right about that.

April 24, 1943

Winkelnkemper reported to me on our broadcast radioed to foreign countries, which is exceptionally effective. Here my directives are being followed extremely well. Winkelnkemper is a faithful old disciple of mine with whom it is a matter of honor to put together and transmit the foreign broadcasts exactly in accordance with my intentions.

[Toni Winkelnkemper was a Goebbels employee from the beginning of his Ministry. His first position after Hitler came to power was that of propaganda leader in the Cologne-Aachen Gau. He was an inexhaustible talker.]

Speer came late in the afternoon. He remained until evening; that gave me a chance to discuss the general situation fully with him. He has had a long talk with Goering and what he reported to me about it was all to the good. Goering has thus far hewn to our line and intends to do so in future. Speer, however, also reported that he [Goering] still gives the impression of a rather tired man. . . .

For our next meeting I am going to arm myself with material to hit back at Sauckel. Speer informed me about a so-called manifesto that Sauckel addressed to his organization within the Reich and the occupied areas. This manifesto is written in a pompous, terribly overladen, baroque style. It smells from afar and gives me a pain. Sauckel is suffering from paranoia. When he signs the manifesto with the words, "Written on the Fuehrer's Birthday in a Plane above Russia," that has the smell of the corniest Weimar style. It is high time that his wings be clipped.

What Speer reported from the Obersalzberg was encouraging. The Fuehrer is more convinced than ever that total war is our salvation. He won't let anybody push him off the course on which he has started. Gauleiters Eigruber and Uiberreither and, as Speer reported, also Dr. Jury, deserve great credit in this connection. Schirach hasn't the faintest idea about total war and tries again and again to torpedo it. The Fuehrer, however, was not only not influenced by his mouthings, but spoke very disparagingly to Speer about Schirach. He fears Schirach has fallen into the clutches of the Viennese reactionaries and no longer sees the interests of the Reich clearly. That is too bad, for at bottom Schirach is a good boy, who merely lacks the necessary political experience. . . .

[August Eigruber was Gauleiter for Upper Danubia; Dr. Siegfried Uiberreither for Styria; Dr. Hugo Jury for Lower Danubia; and Baldur von Schirach for Vienna. Von Schirach was the youngest man to be appointed to such a top position, and earned the rapid promotion because of the zeal he showed in indoctrinating German youth with Nazism as Reichsjugendfuehrer. He was indicted as a major war criminal and sentenced to twenty years' imprisonment by the International Military Tribunal at Nuremberg in 1946.]

Otherwise everything is in apple-pie order on the Obersalzberg. The Fuehrer spoke to Speer in terms of the highest praise for my articles in the *Reich*. He told him he read them every time and had not once discovered a psychological error in them. He regards them as the best political prose now being written in Germany. . . .

He is somewhat worried, however, about my health. Speer, too, most urgently advised me to see to it that my health be restored at least to its old level, since I would not be worth very much for total war if I were a sick man. I shall heed this advice. Next week I hope to go to Dresden for a fortnight to have myself overhauled.

Vansittart has published a new book of hate containing a program that fits wonderfully into our propaganda line. I give orders to answer him in the German press with the most massive counterarguments. This fellow Vansittart is really worth his weight in gold to our propaganda.

After the war a monument ought to be erected to him somewhere in Germany with the inscription, "To the Englishman who rendered the greatest service to the German cause during the war."

The Red Cross has finally arrived at a decision. We received a telegram to the effect that it is ready to send experts, but only on condition that all parties concerned, in other words, the Soviets also, request this. That's exactly as though a man indicted for murder were not only to face the court as a defendant, but also to act as an expert while the verdict is under advisement. Naturally we cannot accept the condition proposed by the Red Cross. It is absolutely unacceptable. Nevertheless I don't deem it good policy to attack the Red Cross. We are so dependent upon it in the matter of prisoners of war that it does not seem opportune to start a fight. I am having this whole matter of the Red Cross put on ice for the time being. And anyway, I suppose it wouldn't be proper to send an answer without having previously asked the Fuehrer his opinion.

The news that the American Minister has left Helsinki is interesting. While a chargé d'affaires is to remain, nevertheless the departure of the Minister is evidently to serve as a means of bringing pressure upon the Finns to make a separate peace with the Soviet Union. Practically speaking, the Finns are in no position to conclude such a separate peace, as they are completely dependent upon us for food. They know only too well that, while the Americans would like to head them for disaster, they cannot help them with food, not to speak of other things. The fact that the Finns let the situation develop to the point where the American Minister departed is proof that our somewhat dictatorial attitude toward the Finns is gradually beginning to yield results. We certainly got after the Finns exceptionally hard these last weeks. But that was very necessary, for without our interference they might conceivably have deserted our front. That would, of course, have been a great misfortune for Finland. Democracy has always brought nothing but bad luck to the Finnish people. Finland is a football in the hands of the big powers. Were it ever to come under the domination of the Soviet Union, Finnish independence would be gone for good.

April 25, 1943

From a report from the occupied areas I gather that a truly grotesque situation obtains in Warsaw. The Jews tried to leave the Ghetto by subterranean passages. Thereupon these underground passages were flooded. The Ghetto is now under artillery fire. When such conditions prevail in an occupied city, it certainly can't be said to be pacified. It is high time that we evacuate the Jews just as quickly as possible from the General Government.

In Warsaw conditions are chaotic not only in the Ghetto, but also among sections of the Polish population. It would be a good thing if the post of governor general were filled by a new man—a person who could put an end to these difficulties. . . .

The SD has taken the so-called Clemens Chapel away from the Catholics of Berlin. Pape wrote me a letter about it and urged me to return the chapel to the Catholic congregation. I did this immediately and bawled out the SD for taking action in direct violation of my directives.

[Pape is nowhere identified more closely in the sources available to this editor.]

I learn that terrible conditions prevail in the airplane works of Messerschmitt. The designing offices there have a great deal to do and the production plants very little. The claim is made in the report that for one-and-a-half years no planes worth mentioning have been sent on to the front, because altogether too much work went into designing, and such samples as were produced proved to be failures. Truly charming prospects for the future! In general I have the impression that our Luftwaffe has lately had lots of bad luck. It is high time that it pull up its socks.

That explains why the Luftwaffe is urging the Fuehrer with all possible eloquence not to start an offensive in the East during this summer; the Luftwaffe needs a pause to rest up.

The Fuehrer would like to talk to me before I go on leave, especially to discuss the next measures in the Jewish question of which he has very great expectations.

The Sauckel manifesto mentioned previously, which he issued on April 20 while in a plane above Russia, a more careful reading reveals is pure nonsense. Sauckel must be told that he can't make such irresponsible use of words. The manifesto fairly bursts with superlatives; on every page there are seven to ten of them.

April 26, 1943

It is reported that the churches in Moscow were overcrowded [on Easter day]. The Soviets, to a certain extent, have restored freedom of religion. That's very sharp and clever tactics. It would be a good thing if we also were somewhat more elastic in these matters.

The Swedes sent us an exceedingly insolent reply to our last note. They claim the statements in our note are not true. They surprise us with the assertion that they found anchored German mines in Swedish waters. The tone of the note is exceptionally arrogant, and the commentaries which appeared in the Swedish press about it outdo each other in insolence. This shows that our military situation has become somewhat unstable. Two years ago the Swedes would not have dared to come to us with such a document. But this is not yet the end. Scores we can't settle with the Swedes today can be settled tomorrow.

My article about air-raid areas has attracted great attention at home and abroad. Without any pressure on my part it was reprinted verbatim in the western and northwestern provinces of the Reich. In a certain sense it is balm for the wounds caused the inhabitants there by air warfare.

April 27, 1943

The fact that our troops succeeded in restoring their position in Tunis strikes me as nothing short of miraculous. German steadfastness and German heroism can be appreciated only if it is known how little material we are able to send over to North Africa, how extremely precarious the food situation is for our soldiers, how little they must get along with, how meager their supply of munitions.

It is surprising . . . how openly and cynically the Americans reveal their war aims. Thus, for instance, a project was published in the American press, according to which the United States Government intends to install its own Gauleiters in every German province after Germany's defeat. That's certainly a good long while off! I am having our foreign-propaganda section give the Americans a reply to this plan that will knock them cold.

The Katyn incident has taken a really sensational turn through the fact that the Soviets have broken off diplomatic relations with the Poles, giving the attitude of the Polish Government-in-exile as the reason. Reuter issued a lugubrious and tragicomical report about it . . . I am withholding this sensational news item . . . for the present; I want to watch developments for another day, to see what I can do with it.

LaGuardia has inflicted himself upon the Italian people with a speech. His address is so dull and foolish that it doesn't even deserve mention. This Italian from the New York Ghetto [*sic*] seems to judge all Europe from the horizon of an American gangster. It staggers the imagination to envisage what would happen to the civilized nations of Europe if they were to fall into the hands of the Bolsheviks or the American gangster politicians.

[This obviously refers to the late Fiorello H. LaGuardia, 1882–1947, former mayor of New York.]

April 28, 1943

According to a report by an officer who has come from Rommel, the supply situation [in Africa] is very difficult because munitions have priority in shipping. During the last few days the troops received daily only two slices of bread per man.

The most important theme of all international discussion is naturally the break between Moscow and the Polish Émigré Government. . . . All enemy broadcasts and newspapers agree that this break represents a 100 per cent victory for German propaganda and especially for me personally. The commentators marvel at the extraordinary cleverness with which we have been able to convert the Katyn incident into a highly political question. There is grave apprehension in London about this success of German propaganda. Suddenly all sorts of rifts are noticed in the allied camp the existence of which nobody had hitherto admitted. . . . There is talk of a total victory by Goebbels! Even important American senators publish worried comments. . . . Alarm in London has reached its highest pitch. The Poles are given a perky talking to because of their precipitate action and are blamed for having played right into the hands of German propaganda. . . .
One can speak of a complete triumph of German propaganda. Throughout this whole war we have seldom been able to register such a success.

Field Marshals Manstein and Kleist have introduced somewhat more humane treatment of the inhabitants in the regions that have again come under military administration because of our retreat. The measures of Koch, which could not be executed anyway, were mollified considerably.

[Field Marshal Paul Ludwig Ewald von Kleist commanded the German armies in the Ukraine, serving on the Eastern Front from 1941–45, when he was captured by the Allies. At the outbreak of World War II he served in France and Belgium with the Panzer troops. He was born in 1881.]

The military men at the Fuehrer's GHQ have actually succeeded in eliminating the pictures of Katyn from the weekly newsreel. Unfortunately the Fuehrer did not have time to see the reel personally. He may possibly authorize their release next week. But by then they will be so old that they won't have any news value. The military rest their case on the morale of the families of our men missing in action. We have the choice of considering the feelings of these co-nationals of ours or the interests of the whole people. I regard the latter as higher and therefore advocate that we show up Bolshevism exactly as it is.

I have finished my article against the Jews. It is going to attract considerable attention. In my opinion it is necessary once more to speak with authority on the Jewish question. Public interest is still focused on it, but it is too frequently tackled from an entirely wrong angle, even in our circles.

April 29, 1943

The Polish conflict still holds the center of the stage. Seldom since the beginning of the war has any affair stirred up so much public discussion as this. The Poles are given a brush-off by the English and the Americans as though they were enemies. It is admitted that I succeeded in driving a deep wedge into the enemy, thereby provoking a much greater crisis than that between Darlan and de Gaulle some time ago.

The Americans insist upon denying categorically that the *Ranger* has been sunk. It is hard to believe that a German captain should be so greatly in error. It is also possible, however, that instead of an American, an English airplane carrier was sunk. I suppose we'll get fuller information after a time.

The Russian General Vlassov, who is fighting on our side in the Separatist Army, has been pretty much shelved by the Ministry for the East. He wrote a report that rather grips at one's heartstrings. One cannot but be astounded at the lack of political instinct in our Central Berlin Administration. If we were pursuing or had pursued a somewhat cleverer policy in the East, we would certainly be further along there than we are.

I received a report on the treatment of occupied areas by the Japanese. It makes one green with envy to realize how cleverly that sort of thing is done in East Asia. The Japanese attach the greatest importance to treating every area occupied by them in accordance with its own peculiarities. They have everywhere installed territorial governments which naturally are tied to the apron strings of the Japanese military commander, but which nevertheless keep up the semblance of national liberty. Why don't we do that in the East? The Japanese procedure might well be a model for us.

In Croatia things are at sixes and sevens. True, Pavelič has visited the Fuehrer, but such a visit can only strengthen his prestige abroad. In Croatia practically all German offices are working at cross-purposes. In addition the Italians are mixing in, whereas the Croatian Government itself is only a football in the hands of the Partisans. If an invasion were to take place in the southeast, there would be cause to fear that large parts of the population would immediately desert us. The Balkans are still the powder barrel of Europe. It is to be hoped that the English and Americans are not aware of the chances beckoning them there. I am more than ever convinced that if they attempt an invasion, that's where it will come.

April 30, 1943

Our propaganda is suspected everywhere of having blown up the Katyn incident to enable us to make a separate peace either with the English or the Soviets. That, of course, is not our intention, although such a possibility would naturally be very pleasing.

Christiansen, our military commander in the Netherlands, has found it necessary to issue a decree ordering all Dutch soldiers to return to captivity as prisoners of war. Groups inimical to the occupation have been at work among the former Dutch soldiers. These have caused us much trouble, consequently the mercy which the Fuehrer showed to the Dutch soldiers in 1940, after the campaign in the West, is now no longer deserved. The Dutch families who now lose their relatives can thank English propaganda for this.

[General Friedrich Christiansen is remembered by many Americans for having flown the *Do-X* to the United States in 1930. During World War I he was commander of the German naval base at Zeebrugge, Belgium. After World War I he became an expert on naval aviation for the Dornier works at Friedrichshafen. Goering appointed him leader of the Aviation and Sports Department of the Air Ministry. He was appointed Military Commander of the Netherlands in 1940.]

In the Union Club in Berlin a number of defamatory rumors have been spread about me personally, not one word of which is true. I am having the Gestapo investigate them. The men involved are almost exclusively higher ex-officers. At the next opportunity I am going to give these men a thorough piece of my mind.

May 1943

STALIN LAUDS ALLIED AIR RAIDS ON AXIS CENTERS. BRITISH AND U.S. FORCES CAPTURE TUNIS AND BIZERTE. U.S. PLANES RAID PALERMO. FRANCO URGES BOTH SIDES TO MAKE PEACE. CHURCHILL ARRIVES IN WASHINGTON. GERMAN HIGH COMMAND REVEALS ROMMEL ON LEAVE FOR TWO MONTHS. COLONEL GENERAL VON ARMIN SURRENDERS AT TUNIS. RUHR VALLEY FLOODED BY DESTRUCTION OF EDER, SORPE, AND MOEHNE DAMS, JOSEPH E. DAVIES PRESENTS STALIN WITH F.D.R. LETTER. HEAVY RAID ON DORTMUND.

May 1, 1943

The conflict between the Polish Émigré Government and the Soviets still holds the world's interest. The Soviets at the moment are extremely insolent and arrogant. They are quite conscious of the security of their position. They have no consideration whatever for their Anglo-Saxon allies, nor need they have, as they are under no obligation to them for military achievements. The men in power in the Kremlin know exactly how far they can go. There is great bitterness in London and Washington about it which nobody seeks to disguise. The Anglo-Saxon camp is in a blue funk about the fact that our propaganda has succeeded in driving so deep a wedge into the enemy coalition.

Unfortunately submarine warfare did not come up to our expectations this month. April has been our most unfavorable month in two years, owing chiefly to the fact that our submarines did not succeed in engaging enemy convoys in major battles. To do so you need an extraordinary amount of cleverness and luck, which, unfortunately, we failed to have during the month of April.

Reports from the occupied areas contain no sensational news. The only noteworthy item is the exceedingly serious fights in Warsaw be-

tween the police and even a part of our Wehrmacht on the one hand
and the rebellious Jews on the other. The Jews have actually succeeded
in making a defensive position of the Ghetto. Heavy engagements are
being fought there which led even to the Jewish Supreme Command's
issuing daily communiqués. Of course this fun won't last very long. But
it shows what is to be expected of the Jews when they are in possession
of arms. Unfortunately some of their weapons are good German ones,
especially machine guns. Heaven only knows how they got them.
Attempts at assassination and acts of sabotage are occurring in the
General Government at far beyond the normal rate.

My recent article about the general situation has had a most favorable reception in neutral countries. Its effectiveness is owing to the
conviction carried by my clear and realistic manner of presenting my
proof.

Recapitulation of events between May 2 and 7, 1943

There is a gap of five days in the diary of the little doctor. During
this period the 800-acre Krupp armament plant was bombarded from
the air for the fifty-fifth time; the heaviest raid since Cologne descended upon Dortmund; and American fliers flew a mission against St.
Nazaire.

Tunis was captured by British and Bizerte by American and French
troops, and Reggio Calabria and Taranto on the Italian mainland were
bombed.

The Germans boasted on May 3 of sinking 415,000 tons and on May
5 some 102,000 tons of enemy shipping.

Fierce battles were in progress in the Kuban and Novorissiisk sectors
of the Eastern front.

May 7, 1943

[Adolf Hitler arrived in Berlin May 7, 1943, to take part in the funeral of Viktor
Lutze, supreme commander of the brown-shirted SA, who met death in an automobile accident. Soon after his arrival the Fuehrer summoned Goebbels.]

We talked briefly about the military position. The Fuehrer, too, regards the situation in Tunis as pretty hopeless. It is simply impossible
to transport reinforcements there. If we could regularly deliver supplies in Tunis we might possibly hold on for a long time. But this is
prevented by the watchfulness of the English, who won't let our ships
get through. . . .

I explained my apprehension to the Fuehrer as to how we can make this clear to the German people. At any rate we ought to use language in our OKW reports that will give some intimation that the end is in sight. . . .

It will, of course, be very difficult to explain to the people that Rommel is no longer in North Africa. Rommel is put in a very painful position. He has received the diamonds to his Oak-Leaf Cluster and the people know nothing about it; he has been on the Semmering for several weeks and nobody has the faintest idea of it! Everybody thinks he is in Africa. If we now come out with the truth, when the catastrophe is so near, nobody will believe us. . . .

The Fuehrer told me that the Duce had been really brought back into form during the four days' discussions. The Fuehrer did everything he could, and by putting every ounce of nervous energy into the effort, succeeded in pushing Mussolini back on the rails. In those four days the Duce underwent a complete change at which his entourage was also amazed. When he got out of the train on his arrival, the Fuehrer thought, he looked like a broken old man; when he left again, he was a man in high fettle, ready for any deed. We can see by the policies he is now pursuing that his regeneration is continuing.

[This was the first occasion that Hitler had to tell Goebbels about his conference of April 7 to 10 with Mussolini.]

Horthy heard very little in the way of pleasant things from the Fuehrer. But he does not seem to have taken this very much to heart, for he has so far fulfilled none of the promises he made on the Obersalzberg. Possibly the Fuehrer was too brusque. . . .

The Duce understands clearly that there can be no other salvation for him except to win or die with us. The Fuehrer is very happy that he will now talk a tougher language in Italy. That has become absolutely necessary. Only the future will tell how long Italy can stand air raids if the English are able to launch incessant attacks from North African bases.

In the East the Fuehrer will soon start a limited offensive in the direction of Kursk. He may, however, delay it to see whether the Bolsheviks want to beat us to it. That might offer us an even more favorable chance than if we took the initiative. Be that as it may, we are prepared in every way. There are arms and soldiers aplenty, so that we need not worry very much.

It is quite a different question about air warfare. Here the Fuehrer

also is somewhat pessimistic. Goering has not succeeded in taking the
initiative. The Fuehrer regrets very much that Goering is rather ill and
hopes that a different Goering will emerge after his leave.

It is a pity that the Fuehrer must always do everything himself when
one of his principal lieutenants fails him. Gradually the task is becoming so heavy, even for him, that he can hardly carry the load alone.
He complained to me about his somewhat precarious state of health.
That, naturally, is something that can't go on forever. . . .

Events in the General Government have now progressed to the
point where Governor General Frank can no longer be kept in his position. The Fuehrer will in all likelihood put Greiser in his place. Recent
events in Warsaw finally broke Dr. Frank's neck.

[Arthur Greiser, who succeeded Hermann Rauschning as head of the Danzig
Government when Rauschning, realizing what a gangster Hitler was, resigned
and fled, was later appointed Gauleiter of Wartheland when the so-called Polish
Corridor and adjacent territory were incorporated with Germany. Greiser was
tried by the Poles and hanged.]

The Fuehrer is thinking of Giesler as successor to Lutze. . . . I can
only say: if the post of Gauleiter in Munich were offered to me, I would
rather be the lowliest Kreisleiter in Pomerania than rise to highest
honors there. . . .

The Fuehrer was awfully nice and obliging to me. I am happy to
enjoy such a cordial personal relationship with him. The state of his
health somewhat alarms me. But I hope that when the present crises
have passed his health, too, will change for the better.

I must also be careful about my own health. I consulted Professor
Morell again. He is quite happy to have succeeded in curing my skin
eczema, except for small scars, but gave me urgent advice to go to
Karlsbad for a few weeks. How am I to do that? In view of the extremely precarious situation in Tunis, which may possibly result in a
major defeat, I regard it as impossible for me to sit still in any watering
place. I suppose I shall once again have to forfeit my vacation.

May 8, 1943

The end is in sight in North Africa. Bizerte and Tunis are the next
targets for the Anglo-American troops. The battle for them has already
begun. In the end the Axis is to be thrown out of Africa entirely. There
is tremendous confidence of victory in London, and rightly so. I see
hardly any chance for us. The problem of North Africa is one of reinforcements, and as things now stand it cannot be solved.

Much to my surprise my article "The War and the Jews" has attracted

much attention, even in neutral countries. I should have thought the
Jews would try to give it the silent treatment. But that is not the case.
It is being quoted to an extent that is simply amazing. That shows the
Jews are either so foolish as to let my arguments get out into the world,
or else in every editorial office sit secret opponents of the Jews who
gladly identify themselves with my anti-Semitic arguments by publishing my article.

Unfortunately German munitions were found in the graves of Katyn.
The question of how they got there needs clarification. It is either a
case of munitions sold by us during the period of our friendly arrangement with the Soviet Russians, or of the Soviets themselves throwing
these munitions into the graves. In any case it is essential that this incident be kept top secret. If it were to come to the knowledge of the
enemy the whole Katyn affair would have to be dropped.

[The "friendly arrangement" referred to is the period of sham German-Soviet
friendship which began with Ribbentrop's signing a non-aggression pact with
Stalin in Moscow on August 22, 1939, and the Nazi invasion of Soviet Russia on
June 22, 1941.]

At noon the state funeral for Viktor Lutze was held in the new Reich
Chancellery. It developed into a huge demonstration of the solidarity
of the Party and especially of the SA. Never since the founding of our
Reich have such high honors been accorded to a man at his burial as
were accorded Viktor Lutze. The ceremony itself was a very dignified
one. My memorial address created a deep impression. The Fuehrer
himself then took the floor and in a brief tribute honored Lutze. He
concluded by conferring upon him the highest category of the German
order. Thereby an honor was accorded Lutze and the SA that far exceeds the customary. But I am glad Viktor Lutze received it. He was
such a decent and fine fellow that this decoration at least had to be
awarded to him posthumously. I escorted Paula Lutze and the other
members of the family out of Mosaic Hall. Outside, in the Wilhelmstrasse, a very impressive funeral parade was held.

In the afternoon . . . a meeting of the Reichsleiters and Gauleiters
was scheduled at the Fuehrer's. Everybody was invited to lunch. This
gave me a chance to talk to a number of people. Wegener told me about
the day raids on Bremen by American bombers. These were very hard
indeed. The Americans drop their bombs with extraordinary precision
from an altitude of eight to nine thousand meters. The population has
the paralyzing feeling that there really is no protection against such
daylight attacks. This again shows that we are purely on the defensive

in air warfare and that, too, in a wholly inadequate manner. It will be difficult to make up for what our air force failed to do.

[Paul Wegener was Nazi Gauleiter for the Weser-Ems area of Germany.]

After luncheon the Fuehrer called together the entire leadership of the Party, that is, the Party, the SA, the SS, and the HJ [Hitler Youth], to warn them in very impressive words against speeding such as has been the vogue within the Party. The Fuehrer was extremely outspoken and was not sparing in reproaches. The lesson he drew from Lutze's motor accident is that all cars of Party members must cut speed down to fifty miles. I consider this a very sensible measure. In no other way can the Party be brought to its senses.

The conference of the Reichsleiters and Gauleiters followed. The Fuehrer honored his Party sub-leaders by giving them a detailed survey of the situation. He began with the fact that in this war bourgeois and revolutionary states are facing each other. It has been an easy thing for us to knock out the bourgeois states, for they were quite inferior to us in their upbringing and attitude. Countries with an ideology have an edge on bourgeois states, in that they rest upon a firm spiritual foundation. The superiority resulting from this fact was of extraordinary advantage to us until we began the campaign in the East. There we met an opponent who also sponsors an ideology, even though a wrong one. The Fuehrer recalled the case of Tuchachevsky and expressed the opinion that we were entirely wrong then in believing that Stalin would ruin the Red Army by the way he handled it. The opposite was true: Stalin got rid of all opposition in the Red Army and thereby brought an end to defeatism. The introduction of political commissars, too, has greatly enhanced the striking power of the Red Army. When one takes into account that the primitive human material of the East can be taught discipline only by strictness, one can imagine what purpose Stalin had in mind when he introduced political commissars and what he has actually accomplished thereby. . . .

[Goebbels here refers to the great purge of the Soviet Army and Communist party leadership in 1936 and 1937, one of the most famous victims of which was the commander in chief himself, Marshal Tuchachevsky, who was always regarded as pro-German and hoped to bring about an alliance of the military leaders of Germany and Russia. Commentators the world over predicted that the Russian Army would not survive the purge; Hitler claimed it was a healthy cleansing process. Curiously enough Hitler began instituting a system of political commissars just about the time Stalin discarded it.]

Stalin enjoys the further advantage over us of being opposed by no "high society." He rid himself of this opposition by liquidations during the past twenty-five years. Although the opposition of our "high society" constitutes no danger, it can create all sorts of petty annoyances. It gripes and complains without having any knowledge of the facts and thereby greatly reduces our driving power. Bolshevism rid itself of this danger in time and can therefore devote all energy to fighting the enemy. There is virtually no opposition left within the country.

[Goebbels always distrusted German "high society." At the same time he, like other Nazis, liked to have blue bloods as personal aides. His adjutant was a scion of one of the minor German reigning houses, Prince Stephan of Schaumburg-Lippe.]

Opposition by the churches, which is giving us such an awful lot of trouble, no longer exists under Bolshevism. If there is talk today of a Metropolitan of Moscow, that is naturally just a Jewish swindle. The Fuehrer rightly points out that a few months ago this Metropolitan was possibly still a furniture mover. In that respect Stalin has a much easier time of it than we. His people have all been placed in one groove. They are subjected either to Bolshevik education or the Bolshevik whip; in any case no other opinion prevails in the Soviet Union save that of the bosses of the Kremlin. . . . It is evident [the Fuehrer said] that lasting resistance to the Soviet Union can be offered in Europe only by the Germans. Even our allies are not equal to the fight against Bolshevism. The Fuehrer drew the lesson from the past winter of having war waged in the East hereafter exclusively and solely with German troops. The Rumanians made the best showing; second best were the Italians, and poorest, the Hungarians. The Fuehrer regarded this as owing mainly to the fact that there has been no social adjustment in Hungary, not even an indication of it. As a result the troops just do not realize the necessity of the fight. Whenever officers here and there gave a good account of themselves they were left in the lurch by their men.

In the opinion of the Fuehrer—and I believe he is right in this—the SS formations did so magnificently because of their unified National Socialist indoctrination. Had we brought up the entire German Wehrmacht exactly as we did the SS formations, the struggle in the East would undoubtedly have taken a different course.

The Duce, too, is now in a jam because he commands no formations like our SS. He must depend upon his royalist army, which of course is not equal to such a brutal war of ideologies. The Fuehrer was absolutely right when he emphasized the fact that the essential condition for the successes of our SS formations consisted in the fact that they were set up by divisions and not battalions. Had they been distributed in battalions over other divisions of the Army, they would surely have been relegated to a very minor place by the divisional commanders. . . .

The Fuehrer argued that the anti-Semitism which formerly animated the Party and was advocated by it must again become the focal point of our spiritual struggle. He thinks a great deal of the anti-Semitic movement in England, although he is naturally aware that it lacks organization and therefore cannot constitute a political factor. Nevertheless this anti-Semitism is most embarrassing to the Churchill Government. It is comparable to the anti-Semitic endeavors of certain bourgeois organizations in Germany in the old days. These, too, would never have achieved their end had not the revolutionary National Socialist movement taken up the campaign. . . .

The Jewish question is being solved least satisfactorily by the Hungarians. The Hungarian state is permeated with Jews, and the Fuehrer did not succeed during his talk with Horthy in convincing the latter of the necessity of more stringent measures. Horthy himself, of course, is badly tangled up with the Jews through his family, and will continue to resist every effort to tackle the Jewish problem aggressively. He gave a number of humanitarian counterarguments which of course don't apply at all to this situation. You just cannot talk humanitarianism when dealing with Jews. Jews must be defeated. The Fuehrer made every effort to win Horthy over to his standpoint but succeeded only partially.

From all this the Fuehrer deduced that all the rubbish of small nations [Kleinstaaten-Geruempel] still existing in Europe must be liquidated as fast as possible. The aim of our struggle must be to create a unified Europe. The Germans alone can really organize Europe. There is practically no other leading power left. In this connection the Fuehrer re-emphasized how happy we can be that there are no Japanese on the European continent. Even though the Italians today give us many a headache and create many a difficulty, we must nevertheless consider ourselves lucky that they cannot be serious competitors in the future organization of Europe. If the Japanese were settled on the European continent the situation would be quite different. Today we are practically the only power on the European mainland with a capacity for leadership.

The Fuehrer sometimes asks himself in a worried sort of way whether the white man is going to be able in the long run to maintain his supremacy over the tremendous reservoir of human beings in the East. There have been developments in former times when he no longer could. In this connection the Fuehrer referred to the wars of the Turks and to the conquests of Genghis Khan, which led him far into the heart of Europe, since the Germans could not resist successfully. From all this we must learn that the main burden of this fight must be assumed by us. As long as we live our main task will be the attempt to solve this problem. We don't know how later generations will stand up in dealing with it. It is therefore desirable that we turn the Reich over to our successors in a condition that will make it immune to any serious damage.

In this connection the Fuehrer defended the politics of Charlemagne. His methods, too, had been right. It is entirely wrong to attack him as the "Butcher of the Saxons." Who will guarantee to the Fuehrer that at some later time he will not be attacked as the "Butcher of the Swiss"? Austria, after all, also had to be forced' into the Reich. We can be happy that it happened in such a peaceful and enthusiastic manner; but if Schuschnigg had offered resistance, it would have been necessary, of course, to overcome this resistance by force.

[This paragraph is interesting for two reasons. In the first place, Hitler disavowed Heinrich Himmler and his pro-Saxon cult completely. Himmler had always maintained that Charlemagne was really the enemy of Germany in that he ruthlessly butchered the Saxons when he created the Holy Roman Empire. The shrine of Henry I, King of the Saxons, at Quedlinburg in Lower Saxony, became as much of a shrine for SS pilgrimages as, say, the tomb of St. Boniface at Fulda is a shrine for the Roman Catholics.

In the second place, this Goebbels entry reveals that Hitler would in the event of victory have compelled Switzerland to become a part of Germany even though he might have to butcher the German element there which was quite as violently opposed to German domination as were the French and Italian elements.

Kurt von Schuschnigg was the last chancellor of the Austrian Republic. He was ousted in 1938 when Hitler brought about Austria's Anschluss' to the Reich. Schuschnigg was born in 1897, and imprisoned from 1938–47 by the Nazis.]

Charlemagne had the right idea when he pushed the Ostmark forward so far. What then happened in a limited area must now be repeated in an area of tremendous dimensions. Moving our boundaries forward so far in the East has proven of great advantage to the German Reich proper. Modern war can be conducted successfully only if you have operational freedom. This operational freedom, however, presupposes wide spaces. During certain military crises you must be able to retreat five, six, or even eight hundred kilometers. If this retreat, however, takes you back into the very heart of the Reich, you can no longer fight the war with any prospect of success. Last winter our own experience showed how correct this observation of the Fuehrer is. Had our troops stood near the borders of the German Reich, the Reich would have cracked up during this crisis.

The East will forever regard Europe as an attractive jewel. The East will again and again try to break into this continent in order to dominate it. Our constant, untiring effort must therefore center upon taking the necessary measures for our security. If it be true today that the Bolshevism of the East is mainly under Jewish leadership and that the Jews are also the dominant influence in the Western plutocracies, then our anti-Semitic propaganda must begin at this point. The Jews must therefore be thrown out of Europe. . . .

For the Fuehrer there is practically no possibility of a compromise with the Soviets. They must be knocked out, exactly as we formerly had to knock out the Communists to attain power. At that time we never thought of a compromise either. . . .

The Fuehrer once more traced in detail the parallel between 1932 and today. It is truly amazing and most convincing. Everything that happened then is being repeated today, and just as in 1932 we attained victory only by a stubbornness that sometimes looked like veritable madness, so, too, we shall achieve it today. . . .

The Fuehrer gave expression to his unshakable conviction that the Reich will be the master of all Europe. We shall yet have to engage in many fights, but these will undoubtedly lead to most wonderful victories. From there on the way to world domination is practically certain. Whoever dominates Europe will thereby assume the leadership of the world.

In this connection we naturally cannot accept questions of right and wrong even as a basis of discussion. The loss of this war would constitute the greatest wrong to the German people, victory would give us the greatest right. After all, only the victor will have the possibility of proving to the world the moral justification for his struggle.

As regards the war itself, the Fuehrer expressed the opinion that it is chiefly a problem of movement. We lost Stalingrad because of the impossibility of mastering this problem of movement. We are now passing through a serious military crisis in North Africa because of the impossibility of mastering this problem of movement. Whoever has the organizational power to solve the problem of movement will be victor in this war. From this viewpoint we have the advantage over our adversaries, for they must attack on exterior lines whereas we can defend ourselves on interior lines.

Besides, our submarine warfare is a dangerous weapon to cut the arteries of the enemy's war of movement. The Fuehrer is firmly convinced that submarine warfare has not reached the end of its development, but is only at its beginning. The Fuehrer thinks it still has tremendous possibilities. . . .

We still have so many chances in our hands that we can await further developments with a clear conscience. The Fuehrer rightly recalled that his prophecies in 1919, 1920, and 1921 seemed insolent and impudent. Today they are proven to have been the results of his realistic thinking and of his comprehensive view of the general situation. We must never have the slightest doubt of victory. The Fuehrer is firmly determined under all circumstances to fight this fight through to the end. He does not want to give it up before twelve o'clock [the last hour] but, come what may, only after twelve. . . .

There will never be any rebellion within the Reich against our leadership. The people would never think of such a thing. There isn't any Jewish leadership here for it. The criminals in such a serious crisis would not be turned loose on the people but stood up against the wall.

In the evening I had a lot of work to do at home. Events in Tunis cast a heavy shadow over the whole day. Special bulletins issued during the evening by the English portend evil. We shall have to prepare ourselves for extremely heavy blows. Nevertheless I believe we can and will survive them.

May 9, 1943

The capture of Tunis and Bizerte is naturally blown up by the English as a sensational event. They speak about a brief final struggle that they have yet to face, but after that, they believe, the whole of North Africa will fall into their hands. All London is drunk with victory, the English newspapers report. Italy is treated as a negligible quantity. . . . We are slowly informing the German people what North Africa was all about. Actually our soldiers there have written a hymn of heroism that will be graven eternally on the pages of German history. They retarded developments for half a year, thereby enabling us to complete the construction of the Atlantic Wall and to prepare ourselves all over Europe so that an invasion is out of the question. . . . We can certainly claim that on the whole the purpose of our operations in North Africa was achieved.

Of course, on the other hand we must realize that our losses there are enormous. We are indeed experiencing a sort of second Stalingrad, although under quite different psychological and material conditions. . . .

It is understandable that the English speak of a first-class victory. They have thus far never won any decisive victories. It is quite different, however, for the English to drive us out of the African continent, which is not our living space [*Lebensraum*], than for us to chase the English out of the European continent whose balance of power, as they always claimed, is a *conditio sine qua non* of English politics. We can therefore stand a comparison with Dunkirk without having to blush.

We must now tell the German people what has happened to Rommel. That isn't such a simple matter. Rommel is at present setting up a command staff that is to become active in case the English or Americans attempt an invasion in any part of Europe. Rommel is undoubtedly the proper man for such an operation. Even though he be given only a limited force, he will be able to deploy it at the right point at the right moment and invoke his pronounced talent for improvisation.

The question has been put to me whether the radio sets in the Netherlands should be seized. Undoubtedly British propaganda in the Netherlands was a decisive factor in the recent strike. I therefore favor taking the radio sets away from the Dutch as quickly as possible. Anyway, we can make good use of them in our air-raid areas.

The compulsory closing of businesses is gradually coming to an end. It has stirred up a terrible lot of dust and has undoubtedly had a somewhat bad effect on morale at home. But I hope we shall be able to overcome this.

Ley talked to me about his earnest wish to have charge of a gau again. He would like to get back his old gau of Cologne-Aachen, which was wrested from him by Strasser. I don't believe the Fuehrer will agree, as this would tax Ley's energies more than is good for him and have a bad effect upon his other duties.

[Gregor Strasser, Ley's rival in labor matters, was purged on June 30, 1934, for alleged complicity in the Roehm plot. Seeing that other men like, for instance, Goebbels retained their position of Gauleiter at the same time that they held national offices, Ley was eager to become a Gauleiter again. He was such a notorious drunkard, however, that Hitler hesitated to increase his responsibilities.]

Frick and Rust were guests with me at the Fuehrer's. Their comments and remarks were so idiotic as to reveal how completely out of the picture they really are. They delivered themselves of stupid phrases, acted as though they were really important, and merely showed that they know nothing about the actual state of affairs. Funk, who was also present, kidded them a lot.

[Bernhard Rust was Minister of Education.]

We talked about all sorts of problems. Unfortunately the Fuehrer is very tired from overwork. He ought to take better care of himself.

The Tunis affair naturally hit him hard. Our position there is very serious, not to say impossible. I don't believe that we have any chance there.

Our envoys in southeastern Europe who stem from the SA have, in the opinion of the Foreign Office, by no means proven themselves capable. That shows that diplomacy, too, must be learned. You cannot simply assign good SA goose-steppers to a diplomatic post, for problems cannot be solved merely by manly courage and insolence. It would certainly be better if representatives of the Party who enter upon diplomatic careers were first given a certain amount of training before being let loose on neutral or friendly states.

In this connection we talked at length with the Fuehrer about what is left for diplomacy to do today in the period of war. The Fuehrer believes that in this war diplomacy hasn't so much to say as in former wars. He certainly does not think that, once the war is ended, a personality like Talleyrand can attain any success. Talleyrand's achievements can be measured only by comparing him with his opposite numbers. His opposite numbers, however, were of poor caliber, and that's why Talleyrand's successes must be evaluated in their relation to others.

The Fuehrer was stirred to the very depths of his soul by the state ceremony for Lutze. Music from the *Goetterdaemmerung* quite upset him.

In the course of the afternoon the Fuehrer discussed the necessary official appointments with Bormann, Ley, and me. He would like to appoint the chief of staff of the SA either from the SA or from the Party. The appointment is contingent upon the guarantee the appointee can give that the SA will again have a clear and definite task to perform. Lutze somewhat muddled this task. The second prerequisite is that the rather strained relationship of the SA with the SS be improved. Unfortunately Lutze permitted his wife and the family's friendship with Brauchitsch to maneuver him into excessive opposition to the SS. It won't do for these two fighting organizations of the Party to be enemies of each other. . . .

The Fuehrer has a low opinion of Von Schirach. Schirach has become "Viennaed." He let the Vienna atmosphere infect him. He has not shown any political sense and is no grown-up Nazi. He now suddenly begins to speak with an American accent and to roll his "rs" like an actor. He consorts too much with artists. That isn't good for him. Certainly the Fuehrer has nothing big in mind for him. He would sooner or later

like to shove him off into the diplomatic career for which Schirach is
more suited. . . .

Terboven is out of the question. Terboven didn't measure up to
expectations in Norway. His actions were too drastic. He considered
the Norwegian problem so to speak an SA man's job. Instead it demanded tremendous political cleverness. This Terboven did not possess. Jagow cannot be considered for the SA job. The Fuehrer would
not like to see any more members of the nobility in important leadership positions of the Reich and the Party. No matter how favorable
their attitude toward the Party may be, the Fuehrer doesn't know how
things will develop further and he won't stand for those with any other
interests playing a role in public life. Men with either clerical or aristocratic ties will therefore no longer be considered for decisive positions
of leadership. They will slowly be retired and in no case will new ones
be appointed. For this reason the post of the Reich Sports Leader must
also be filled by a non-aristocrat. The Fuehrer regards it as significant
that Tschammer-Osten wanted to see Count von der Schulenburg
appointed as his successor. The Fuehrer isn't dreaming of fulfilling
that wish. . . .

[As long as the Nazi movement still had an inferiority complex, Hitler and his
sub-leaders were very eager to show that they had good connections with the
nobility. Hohenzollern Prince August Wilhelm, fourth son of the late Kaiser, was
given a high rank in the SA and had the title of *Reichsredner* (Reich Orator).
Goering loved to have blue bloods at his parties. Hitler appointed Duke Charles
Edward of Coburg and Gotha president of the German Red Cross. Joachim von
Ribbentrop, Konstantin von Neurath, Eltz von Ruebenach, and Lutz von Schwerin-
Krosigk were his cabinet ministers. Hans von Tschammer und Osten was Reich's
Sports Leader during the Olympic Games and later. Lieutenant Hans-Georg von
Jagow was *Regierungspraesident,* or provincial governor at Magdeburg.

After these men had served for window dressing, Hitler and his top followers
were eager to get rid of the nobility, as the blue bloods for the most part had a
better education and better manners than the typical Nazis. Anybody who had
close connections with the two Christian denominations was also anathema to the
dyed-in-the-wool Nazis.]

Schwede-Coburg has the Fuehrer's complete confidence. As an
administrator he would naturally succeed in Munich and Bavaria, but
he does not have the necessary artistic sensibilities to make him an
ideal appointee there. . . .

[Franz Schwede, so long identified with Nazi activities at Coburg that his
name became hyphenated, was one of the "original" pre-1923 Nazis.]

Munich, of course, is extremely difficult. I wouldn't want this post if
it were served me on a platter. The Fuehrer said if he had a dozen per-

sons like myself he would appoint me, but I don't even want to imagine such an assignment, thank you. . . .

During this discussion we did not arrive at any final decisions. The Fuehrer wants to sleep over the matter once more. At least we had an opportunity this afternoon to discuss all personalities in public life with him. To my great surprise I noticed how tremendously well the Fuehrer was posted on the so-called big shots. He knows all about them, even though he never makes public use of this knowledge. He sees more clearly than any of us. He notices with regret that there isn't a single leader of stature in the SA who might become Lutze's successor. Naturally he would very much like to have me in the Munich post, but of course there can be no question of that. This talk made us realize anew how extremely rare are men of real caliber. If you have to fill two posts of decisive importance in public life you can search with a lantern and won't find anybody. . . .

These two hours with the Fuehrer were very beautiful and engendered confidence. Bormann acted exceedingly loyally. I must say that the criticism leveled at him is for the most part unjustified. When you compare what he keeps in the way of promises and what Goering keeps, Goering is undoubtedly at a disadvantage. There is no longer any real dependence on Goering. He is tired and somewhat washed up.

Backe has reported to the Fuehrer. The Fuehrer simply won't approve a 100-gram reduction in the meat ration. Yet it is so necessary. If we don't put it through we are headed for a catastrophe.

I feel that my health has been pretty badly undermined. I really ought to go on leave. But in view of developments in Tunis I just can't go to Karlsbad now. The public would not understand it and I can't explain to every person that I have really earned a vacation.

May 10, 1943

I received a report from the Army Group Center [on the Russian front] about the absolute lack of unity in our political procedure in the occupied eastern areas. This report is quite remarkable. Our eastern policy lacks a clear basis. Everybody does what he likes. It must be very depressing for a soldier at the front to experience what lack of direction there is in German politics.

The fights in the Warsaw Ghetto have largely petered out. I received a secret report on the mysterious question as to how the Jews got hold of the large supplies of arms with which they defended themselves. For the most part they bought them from our brave allies as they were fleeing homeward and in Warsaw got rid of their weapons for good money. There are soldiers for you!

At noon I had a long talk with the Fuehrer. . . . He is very much opposed to centralization in the Food Ministry and especially in the Ministry of the Interior. The policy of the Reich ought to be such that everything that must be done from the center should be centralized, but that everything that can be done locally should be decentralized. . . . This is true also of the centralization of electric and water power. Speer is on the wrong track there. He is trying to bring all electric and water power under the control of the Reich. The Fuehrer in no wise approves of this. The conception of property must not be toyed with lightly. It won't do simply to take properties of the communes away from them by pressure exerted by the Reich. A contract is a contract; that is true not only in private but also in public life. . . .

The Wehrmacht and the centralized instruments of political leadership are an exception to this rule. There can be no thought, for instance, of giving radio and press into the hands of lower-ranking authorities. They are centralized instruments of political leadership which must be retained exclusively by the Reich. . . .

Frick, who was present at this talk, cut a very poor figure. The centralized administration that he built up is by no means approved or even appreciated by the Fuehrer. The Fuehrer criticized the Ministry of Interior so outspokenly that Frick ought to draw certain conclusions. But for this he is already too old and too fond of his office.

The painter, Gerhardinger, has refused to let the Munich Art Exposition have his canvases because he fears they might be destroyed by air raids. The Fuehrer ordered that he be punished very severely. It just won't do for an individual painter to arrogate to himself the right of avoiding part of the national risk. . . .

Gerhardinger was a poor and hungry painter who became a rich man only through National Socialism. Things would come to a pretty pass if behavior like this went unchallenged and the artists were allowed to shirk their national duty! The Fuehrer decreed exceptionally severe punishment in this case as an example to others. . . . The Fuehrer spoke in terms of highest praise of the Dresden painter, Kriegel, who was discovered by my wife.

[The absolutism of the Hitler regime is well illustrated here. Without indictment or trial a painter is sentenced because Hitler was angry at the artist's refusal to jeopardize his life's work.]

Next the Fuehrer discussed Frank of the General Government. He is now firmly determined to remove him and name Greiser as his successor. I don't know as yet whether he will really take this final step, but, judging by what the Fuehrer said, there can hardly be any doubt about it.

In the early afternoon the Fuehrer asked me to come to the chancellery for a private talk with no one else present. We sat in his study on the second floor and I had abundant opportunity to present all problems on my mind. . . .

The Fuehrer was very much impressed with the Katyn incident. It showed him what tremendous possibilities are still inherent in anti-Bolshevik propaganda. . . . The Wehrmacht has no business to interfere in this matter. It should concern itself with military questions only. Questions of psychology are exclusively the concern of the Propaganda Ministry. . . .

The Fuehrer attaches great importance to a powerful anti-Semitic propaganda. He, too, regards success as depending upon constant repetition. He is immensely pleased with our sharpening up the anti-Semitic propaganda in the press and radio. I informed him about the extent to which this anti-Semitic propaganda was being pushed in our foreign broadcasts. At present about 70 to 80 per cent of our broadcasts are devoted to it. The anti-Semitic bacilli naturally exist everywhere in all Europe; we must merely make them virulent. . . . Unfortunately we have too few journalists to do this job. The Fuehrer gave me permission to call back from the PKs a considerable number of young journalists and distribute them over the entire German press. . . .

The press section of the High Command, which has always created a lot of trouble for me, is now to be transferred to the Propaganda Ministry. Keitel and Jodl are opposing this with every means at their disposal but the Fuehrer asked me to send him a report on this question, whereupon he will issue the necessary decree. Propaganda, he said, is a function of the Propaganda Ministry and not of the Wehrmacht.

Our propaganda in the East, too, is to be joined more closely to the Propaganda Ministry. It isn't Rosenberg's business to engage in propaganda of which, as the Fuehrer rightly observes, he knows notoriously nothing. Here, too, the Fuehrer agrees completely with me.

Unfortunately my views did not prevail in the question of continuing the *Frankfurter Zeitung*. The Fuehrer gave a number of reasons why the *Frankfurter Zeitung* should be eliminated. . . . Personally I believe the reasons for retaining the *Frankfurter Zeitung* are stronger than the Fuehrer realizes, but he is stubbornly of the opinion that it would be better to do away with it. I shall now carry out his wish and bring about the liquidation of the newspaper. . . .

The Fuehrer has no intention of following the Japanese procedure of court-martialing aviators shot down over German soil and having them executed. He fears the English have too many possibilities for reprisals and that we may stumble into a situation about which we know where it begins but not where it is likely to end. I must see to it that, while we let our press mention the strong language employed by the Japanese and also more recently by the Italians, we do not suggest to the German public that we should indulge in similar practices.

Turning now to the theme of total war, on the whole the Fuehrer was satisfied with the measures hitherto taken. . . . During total war, however, war must not be conducted against women. Never yet has such a war been won by any government. Women, after all, constitute a tremendous power and as soon as you dare to touch their beauty parlors they are your enemies. . . .

The Fuehrer vigorously opposes high taxes on movie and theater tickets. After all, the movie house and the theater are all that is left for the little man to go to for his recreation. If we take that away from him also, where is he to turn to forget the war for a couple of hours? The Fuehrer would much rather have us establish more lotteries or expand the existing ones, because by that means the money gets into the hands of the state without offending or angering the little man. . . .

I then went over to personnel problems. The Fuehrer agreed that Voegler be appointed president of the German Academy. This decision is a happy solution of a difficult problem. The Fuehrer can't reconcile himself to the candidacy of Bouhler. He considers Bouhler to be a decent National Socialist but a man without self-assurance and self-confidence. If Bouhler were his wife and the wife were Bouhler, the Fuehrer would be ready to give him the German Academy. . . .

[Geheimrat Albert Voegler, head of the United Steel Works of Germany, was one of the industrialists who cast his lot with the Nazis. His rival candidate for the post of president of the *Deutsche Akademie* was Philip Bouhler, who had the title of Reichsleiter, hence enjoyed cabinet rank, but who really was only a glorified secretary to Hitler in his capacity of supreme leader of the Nazi party. Bouhler's official job was that of Chief of the Chancellery of the Leader of the National Socialist party.]

The Fuehrer shared my opinion about most of the leading men in public life. He is very critical of Frick. He doesn't think Seldte worth a hoot. Rosenberg is more of a theoretician than a man of practical affairs. . . .

The Fuehrer was very enthusiastic about what we have been doing in Linz. . . . It is touching how concerned the Fuehrer is to balance the pronounced industrialization of Linz with even stronger emphasis upon the cultural character of this city. . . . The Fuehrer wants to erect grandiose buildings in Linz with the aim of making the city over into a German Budapest. . . . Vienna, of course, is fascinating as a city. Von Schirach succumbed to its charm. The Fuehrer told me that even he was completely captivated by the architecture of Vienna when he visited it the first time in his youth. It will need a lot of effort to make Linz over as a real competitor to Vienna.

[Although born in the little village of Braunau on the Inn, Austria, Hitler regarded Linz on the Danube as his "home town," as he went to school and grew up there.]

The Fuehrer spoke in glowing terms about the days ahead of us once the war is ended. Nothing will make him happier than to exchange his gray uniform for the brown, to visit theaters and movies again, to go to the Wintergarten with me in the evening, or to drop in at the K.d.d.K. and be a human being again among humans.

[For purposes of World War II Hitler had a field-gray uniform designed in advance which was an exact counterpart to his brown Nazi party uniform. He and his entourage appeared dramatically in their brand-new gray regalia for the first time in the Reichstag session of September 2, 1939. Hitler then vowed he would not change back to his brown uniform until victory was won. Many foreigners erroneously believed Hitler wore a military uniform. That was not the case—it was the Party uniform in gray. The Wintergarten of Berlin was a famous vaudeville theater. K.d.d.K. stands for *Kameradschaft der deutschen Kuenstler*—a Berlin club for all types of artists.]

He is totally fed up with the generals. He can't imagine anything finer than having nothing to do with them. His opinion of all the generals is devastating. Indeed, at times it is so caustic as to seem prejudiced or unjust, although on the whole it no doubt fits the case. He also told me why he no longer eats at the generals' mess at GHQ. He just can't bear the sight of generals any longer. He has not become a misanthrope; on the contrary, his old friends are more welcome to him today than ever, but his new collaborators just don't enjoy his confidence and haven't known how to work their way into his heart. All generals lie, he says. All generals are faithless. All generals are opposed to National Socialism. All generals are reactionaries. While that is not true, he is nevertheless right in some respects. He just can't stand them. They have disappointed him too often. They have no spiritual or cultural outlook and therefore there is no basis of understanding with the Fuehrer. They are faithless, they are not loyal to him, for the most part they do not understand him. For example, at the home of Colonel General Schmidt's brother, who had to be arrested for treason, a number of letters from the colonel general were found which spoke very disparagingly of the Fuehrer. Now that is one of the generals of whom the Fuehrer thought especially well! So once again he suffered a great disappointment. He added, however, that a general just cannot insult him. That class of people seemed like total strangers to him and he would in future stay farther away from them than ever. . . .

The Fuehrer had a talk with Field Marshal Rommel. A communiqué is to be released to explain the Rommel case to the public and especially to point out that he has not been in North Africa for months. The Fuehrer is particularly concerned about the latter point because otherwise Rommel will be regarded as responsible for our defeat in North Africa and this would be damaging to his name. Rommel ought to be very happy about the communiqué that the Fuehrer dictated concerning him. Everything in it is calculated to reassure the German people, including the fact that the Fuehrer awarded the diamonds to the Oak-Leaf Cluster to Rommel months ago. Rommel is to remain in the immediate entourage of the Fuehrer for the present. The Fuehrer wants to save him for the first difficult task that may arise and to send him into action at points where improvised leadership is most needed.

I am happy the Fuehrer has such a high opinion of Rommel. Mussolini must pay dearly for being so insistent about Rommel's recall. He always claimed that his generals did a better job. Now he has the pay-off for his miscalculation. Thank God, he thereby brought it about that Rommel's name was saved. That is of great value to our further operations, for military authority such as Rommel enjoys just can't be created at will and then taken away at will.

The Fuehrer believes that our position in Tunis has become quite untenable. . . . One of the reasons for our collapse there is the fact that Mussolini got Rommel out of North Africa. The Duce no longer sticks to a clear line, either in his policies or in his war strategy. As a personality, to be sure, he is a man of genius, but his entourage isn't worth a damn. He can rely on nobody for help, either in waging the war or for carrying out his policies. If it be true that the Fuehrer, despite his tremendous powers, has nevertheless been lied to and cheated so often by the generals, how much more must that be the case with Mussolini! As for the rest, he has become an old and tired man. While the Fuehrer somewhat pepped him up on the Obersalzberg by giving him the works for several days, it remains to be seen whether the effect will be lasting. Mussolini arrived on the Obersalzberg completely gray and passive; he left the Obersalzberg like a new person.

His new Party secretary, Scorza, is exceptionally active. Nevertheless the Fuehrer is not at all convinced that the Italians will stay put when the heaviest strain comes. Should they fail, this would not amount to a catastrophe for us, but it would nevertheless be exceedingly embarrassing, not so much militarily, as politically and psychologically. But we would naturally survive even such a blow.

I then talked with the Fuehrer about many matters of general interest. He yearns for the day when he can end this war. He wants then to return to his old comrades in the Party and also to the families here in Berlin in whose company he always felt so much at home. We want then again to devote our energies chiefly to the fine arts, the theater, the films, literature, and music. We want to begin again to be human beings. The Fuehrer raves about the possibilities for giving festivals again and receptions, and for surrounding himself with people he likes. From all this I gather that the Fuehrer has not become a misanthrope, despite his long loneliness at GHQ. He just doesn't want to see generals any more; that's all. He has remained his own self toward the Party and especially toward his old friends. Times may now be difficult but they will be replaced by happier ones after we have brought the war to an end. Let us hope this will happen soon.

However much our misfortune in Tunis may depress the Fuehrer personally, he has never for one second lost his firm faith in our final victory. That was proven to me anew by these two beautiful hours during which I could talk to him quite alone and he opened his whole heart to me. Even though he gives the impression of being somewhat tired and overworked, he is still the old Fuehrer, albeit fatigued and somewhat groggy. But within him there lives a fiery spirit that takes all cares off our shoulders. The German people simply don't know what they owe to their Fuehrer.

May 11, 1943

It is interesting to note that many of the London papers printed my article against the Jews. I can't figure it out. Are the Jews so foolish as to believe this article would militate against us and not, on the contrary, strengthen the anti-Semitic feeling in England considerably?

The Foreign Department of my Ministry proposed that we pep up declining morale in Italy by German propaganda. I'm against it. That's the last thing we want—do the propaganda for the Italians! They wouldn't stand for it anyway; on this point they are exceedingly touchy.

At noon I went to see the Fuehrer. We discussed the situation in Tunis in detail. The Fuehrer, too, now regards it as hopeless.

I touched upon a number of domestic questions. The Fuehrer used sharp words in denouncing the centralization of administration in Berlin as pursued by the Ministry of the Interior, the result of which is that the provincial and communal authorities can hardly move. It requires great skill to centralize the Reich's leadership, and at the same time to decentralize its administration. The Ministry of the Interior has no conception of this art. It has created a tremendous bureaucratic apparatus that acts like a sponge on officialdom, sucking up all initiative.

The Fuehrer's idea is that the Reich offices should have only a few well-paid officials; good pay would guarantee capable collaborators. As laudable examples where this principle obtains he cited the Reich Chancellery and the Propaganda Ministry. . . . As warning examples of how not to do things he cited the Air Ministry, which is really nothing but an administrative factory.

In our discussion the Propaganda Ministry cut an exceptionally good figure. The Fuehrer endorsed my principle that there must never be more than 1,000 employees in the Propaganda Ministry. . . . The Fuehrer observed that it would be a good thing if my ideas were observed in the entire administration of the Reich. Our leadership at home would certainly be much better than it is at present.

I vehemently opposed the idea that the Reich Finance Minister or the Minister of the Interior have anything to say about appointing officials in my Ministry. I alone can determine who is qualified to carry out the work for which I am responsible. . . . I then talked with the Fuehrer about a number of questions of culture and art. He is well satisfied with the plans designed by Professor Kreis for monuments in honor of our heroes. Professor Kreis is at present one of our best architects. . . .

[Clearly a case of counting chickens before they are hatched. Monuments glorifying war have been specifically forbidden by the victorious Allies.

Wilhelm Kreis, born 1873, a Dresden architect and senator of the Reich Chamber of Culture, built the Augustus Bridge of Dresden, the Bismarck Hall of Stettin, the Art Museum of Duesseldorf, the German Hygiene Museum of Dresden, the Reich Ministry of War Building of Berlin, and many other public structures.]

This time the Fuehrer was exceptionally interested in personal questions. He inquired minutely about the welfare of my family, was sorry that he had not seen the children for so long, and yearned for the moment when he could again devote himself more to the families of his closest friends. . . .

It is nothing short of touching to observe the innate confidence of the Fuehrer during these days. No matter how much the military catastrophe in North Africa may gnaw at his heart, he lets no one notice it and it can in no way affect his determination.

In the afternoon Rommel visited me. He looked splendid and has recovered beautifully during his furlough; nevertheless he told me that he had spent many a sleepless night. Developments in North Africa are almost breaking his heart, but the Duce would not have it otherwise. He and his generals shoved Rommel out of the North African theater of war. Italy didn't have the courage to use such means as it had, especially its fleet, and must now pay for it. Rommel's opinion of the Italians is devastating. He doesn't think anything of them and is convinced that if the English or Americans were to land in southern Italy, the Italians neither would nor could offer effective resistance. . . .

Rommel doesn't think much of the Duce now either. He described him as an old and tired man who occasionally still had a political or military inspiration but who lacked the ability to issue clear military or political orders.

I improved upon this occasion to explain the over-all war situation to Rommel both from a political and military standpoint. He listened to me for more than an hour with intense interest. I think the confidence I displayed reassured him very much and strengthened his backbone. Certainly Rommel is one of the best officers we have today. . . .

We sat together until midnight. These were beautiful and interesting hours for me. If all our marshals were cut out of the same cloth as Rommel we would need to worry no longer about our military leadership. Unfortunately, however, Rommel is not the rule, but the exception to the rule.

May 12, 1943

Events in Tunisia overshadow all other happenings in the field of international news. The English, and especially the Americans, publish fantastic reports about capitulations by Axis troops which, however, have been put together so stupidly that they have hardly any value. Naturally the Americans are happy as children to be able for the first time to take German troops into custody. But I hope we will soon have an opportunity to pay them back for this. . . . Our generals are behaving somewhat better during interrogations than did those before Stalingrad.

The Bolsheviks have held a pan-Slav congress in Moscow, the purpose of which was to win the Slavic peoples of the Balkans over to the Bolshevik cause. I won't permit the propaganda slogans of the Moscow Congress to be quoted; the less attention paid to them, the better it is for our cause.

Total war is giving me a lot of work to do, but matters are progressing according to rule and program. I have received a great number of letters—more than 15,000 in but a few weeks. All of these letters testify to the unqualified agreement of public opinion with my views, as well as to the great confidence of the letter writers in me—a thing about which I am very happy. I must try to justify this confidence; in other words, in case errors are committed in the realm of total war, I simply cannot fade out of the picture. The people identify the idea and conception of total war with my person. I am therefore in a certain sense publicly responsible for the continuation of total war.

Naumann has had a long talk with Himmler. Himmler is now ready to have the SD report stopped, at least as far as supplying it to all sorts of ministers is concerned, as its effect is too defeatist. Himmler now wants to have a special report made up by the SD for me personally, which is to contain everything that hitherto was submitted to a larger circle of subscribers. Himmler spoke in most flattering terms about the work of the Propaganda Ministry and about myself. He told Naumann I was at present one of the few strong men who were fighting without compromise for the great aims of the war; that I had pursued the same tactics in 1932 with the greatest success, and that there was reason to hope that my present tactics would also lead to success. On the whole he didn't think much of Goering. He especially deplored the fact that we had no domestic policies, that the Ministry of the Interior had become nothing but a bureaucratic goiter [ein reiner Verwaltungskropf], and that it showed no ability to undertake leadership tasks.

[Heinrich Himmler long aspired to take the place of Minister of the Interior Dr. Wilhelm Frick. His ambition was realized somewhat later, when Frick was appointed Protector of Bohemia-Moravia. Himmler, as head of the German police, was technically under Frick, but as leader of the SS was responsible to Hitler only.]

Everybody is against Dr. Frick. I just can't understand why the Fuehrer still keeps him.

At noon I went to see the Fuehrer.

The Fuehrer has received a letter from Cardinal Bertram in which the latter complained bitterly about the alleged suppression of the churches. The Fuehrer intends to reply to this letter and to inform Bertram that a large number of the Catholic clergy were assuming so treasonable an attitude toward the war that the Cardinal had better look after these matters, rather than gripe about conditions that the Fuehrer, too, regrets and that he is constantly trying to remedy.

I took the position in talking with the Fuehrer that the old cardinals of the type of Faulhaber and Bertram are much less dangerous than the young reverends who are serving at the front as army chaplains and even wear the Iron Cross of the First Class. These give us much more trouble, for they rate high with the people. They are the fighting type and know how to talk with their war experience as background. The Fuehrer agreed with me. We must be somewhat on our guard about such clerics.

[Cardinal Michael von Faulhaber of Munich was internationally famed for his outspoken opposition to the Nazi regime. Many of his boldest sermons were circulated secretly. Several attempts on his life were made by Nazi rowdies. Cardinal Adolf Bertram of Breslau was the senior cardinal in Germany, and, as such, the presiding officer of the annual Fulda Bishops' Conference which, during the Nazi regime, issued pastoral letters that had to be taken to the individual parishes secretly for reading to the congregations.]

The churches have always played a dubious role during wars, at least with us. They won't tolerate a leader going his own way, especially if he has a private point of view on religious matters. The Fuehrer characterized it as nothing short of absurd that Frederick the Great, for instance, was buried under the cupola of the Potsdam Garrison Church, contrary to his wish to be interred beside his dogs in the park of Sans Souci. Thank God, English air raids have compelled us to end this condition. The coffin of Frederick the Great has been placed where it is safe from bombs. The Fuehrer will never restore it to the Potsdam Garrison Church. Either an imposing mausoleum in Greek style is to be built for Frederick the Great in the park of Sans Souci, or he is to be laid to rest in the great Soldiers' Hall of a new War Ministry yet to be constructed. Personally I should prefer that the wish of the great king be fulfilled and that he be given his last resting place in Sans Souci. The Fuehrer, too, rather inclines to this view. But these are problems that we shall have to face only on the morrow.

The Fuehrer spoke very derogatorily about the arrogance of the higher and lower clergy. The insanity of the Christian doctrine of redemption really doesn't fit at all into our time. Nevertheless there are learned, educated men, occupying high positions in public life, who cling to it with the faith of a child. It is simply incomprehensible how anybody can consider the Christian doctrine of redemption as a guide for the difficult life of today. The Fuehrer cited a number of exceptionally drastic and in part even grotesque examples. The opinionated "sky pilots" of course know exactly how the world is constituted. Whereas the most learned and wisest scientists struggle for a whole lifetime to study but one of the mysterious laws of nature, a little country priest from Bavaria is in a position to decide this matter on the basis of his religious knowledge. One can regard such a disgusting performance only with disdain. A church that does not keep step with modern scientific knowledge is doomed. It may take quite a while, but it is bound finally to happen. Anybody who is firmly rooted in daily life, and who can only faintly imagine the mystic secrets of nature, will naturally be extremely modest about the universe. The clerics, however, who have not caught a breath of such modesty, evidence a sovereign opinionated attitude toward questions of the universe. . . .

The Fuehrer showed that he had read about and studied all these problems. There is hardly a fact, hardly a theory, hardly a date, that he doesn't know and that he isn't able to cite from memory. I have the greatest respect for the Fuehrer's tremendous intellectual achievement in all fields of knowledge. It is a pity that such talks can't be made known to a lot of people. Their veneration for the Fuehrer could only be increased thereby.

The Fuehrer is an enthusiastic advocate of pure science. . . . It was a great mistake that we failed to win science over to support the new state. That men such as Planck are reserved, to put it mildly, in their attitude toward us, is the fault of Rust and is irremediable. It makes one sad to think that the Fuehrer is so tremendously interested in the tasks and researches of science, and yet our research men and scientists do not realize this because they don't know it. The mediocre talents in the Reich Government are a wall between the Fuehrer and many sectors of public life. That is true of science, it is true of administration, it is true of justice, and of many other things.

[Professor Max Planck, born, 1858, was one of Germany's greatest physicists and a special friend of Professor Albert Einstein. He was the originator of the Quantum theory. From 1912 on he was permanent secretary of the Prussian Academy of Science. He was also president of the Kaiser Wilhelm Society for the Advancement of Science.]

It is a characteristic thing that during the war almost nothing has been done with domestic politics by the Ministry of the Interior. Whatever there is in Germany in the way of domestic policy stems from me. Naturally I can be very well satisfied about this development. If a strong man were in Frick's place, he would naturally be in a position to cause me a lot of trouble; as things are, however, I have been able to have my way in domestic politics. According to an old principle of mine I never give up what I have once taken into my hands.

My thoughts often turn to North Africa and to our soldiers who are there engaged in their last heavy struggles. The only comforting thing is the fact that they are falling into the hands of a civilized opponent. If our entire tank army in Africa were compelled, as was our Sixth Army in Stalingrad, to face death to the last man, that would be a gruesome thought. Now, however, we may regard tens of thousands of soldiers as saved.

The fight for Tunisia may come to an end any day now. The comforting thing about it is that if the English want once more to measure their strength against us, they will have to step on European soil. We shall then give them the reception they deserve.

May 13, 1943

There is talk in London of 100,000 prisoners. It is a good thing that so many of our soldiers from North Africa are taken prisoner. It would be terrible if the drama of Stalingrad were repeated there.

Knox declared that Sicily would be occupied next. We pay no attention to these unfounded rumors and attempts at camouflage.

The situation in Croatia can by no means be regarded as having been settled by the last purge; it continues to be strained. More than 13,000 rebels were killed, among them a great many intellectuals. The fight against European unification through the Axis Powers is for the most part carried on by intellectuals. The broad masses of the people, on the whole, are uninterested in this struggle.

I have devoted exhaustive study to the *Protocols of Zion*. In the past the objection was always made that they were not suited to present-day propaganda. In reading them now I find that we can use them very well. The *Protocols of Zion* are as modern today as they were when published for the first time. . . .

[*The Protocols of the Elders of Zion* were a scurrilous publication of alleged Jewish aims for world conquest and of the existence of an occult Jewish Government which formed the basis of a celebrated libel suit at Berne, Switzerland, in 1935. Experts from a number of countries, including Germany, were summoned to testify. One claim was that the *Protocols* had been fabricated by the Russian Czarist police. The ruling of the court on May 14, 1935, was that the *Protocols of Zion* were forged and faked.]

At noon I mentioned this to the Fuehrer. He believed the *Protocols* were absolutely genuine. . . . The Jewish question, in the Fuehrer's opinion, will play a decisive role in England. . . . In all the world, he said, the Jews are alike. Whether they live in a ghetto of the East or in the bankers' palaces of the City or Wall Street, they will always pursue the same aims and without previous agreement even use the same means. One might well ask why are there any Jews in the world order? That would be exactly like asking why are there potato bugs? Nature is dominated by the law of struggle. There will always be parasites who will spur this struggle on and intensify the process of selection between the strong and the weak. The principle of struggle dominates also in human life. One must merely know the laws of this struggle to be able to face it. The intellectual does not have the natural means of resisting the Jewish peril because his instincts have been badly blunted. Because of this fact the nations with a high standard of civilization are exposed to this peril first and foremost. In nature life always takes measures against parasites; in the life of nations that is not always the case. From this fact the Jewish peril actually stems. There is therefore no other recourse left for modern nations except to exterminate the Jew. . . .

There is no hope of leading the Jews back into the fold of civilized humanity by exceptional punishments. They will forever remain Jews, just as we are forever members of the Aryan race.

The Jew was also the first to introduce the lie into politics as a weapon. Aboriginal man, the Fuehrer believes, did not know the lie. . . . The higher the human being developed intellectually, the more he acquired the ability of hiding his innermost thoughts and giving expression to something different from what he really felt. The Jew as an absolutely intellectual creature was the first to learn this art. He can therefore be regarded not only as the carrier but even the inventor of the lie among human beings. Because of their thoroughly materialistic attitude, the English act very much like the Jews. In fact, they are the Aryans who have acquired most of the Jewish characteristics. . . . The nations that have been the first to see through the Jew and have been the first to fight him are going to take his place in the domination of the world.

May 14, 1943

During the night there was another exceptionally heavy air raid on Duisburg. Even though it did not prove quite so disastrous as we had reason for assuming after the initial news, it was nevertheless an exceedingly heavy bombardment, and unspeakable sorrow and great distress have come to the sorely tried city.

In Tunis the fight is ended. I write this with a heavy heart. I just can't read the exaggerated Anglo-American accounts. They are full of insults to our soldiers, who fought with legendary heroism to their last round of ammunition. These Anglo-American emanations demonstrate how badly English public opinion has already been infected by Jewish conceptions. One would at least have thought the enemy would be clever enough not to speak in derogatory terms of the adversary because thereby the heroism of their own soldiers is depreciated. I can't stand having to go into a black rage every day about such reports and fairly tear myself to bits with anger. Therefore I don't even read those accounts, especially as we are saying nothing in reply. We stand aloof in hard and stubborn pride and simply take no notice of barking dogs. . . .

Naturally the English now speak of the greatest defeat in our military history. But one must not judge defeats by the size of the figures but only by the foreseeable consequences. . . .

Attlee gave a final report to a jubilant lower house. His basic note, too, is triumph. We must now swallow these bitter pills, disgusting though it may be.

The failure of our submarines to win victories is having regrettable consequences. The defense of the Anglo-American convoys is now so formidable that, if it continues, a new situation in submarine warfare will have arisen. . . . Our technical development both in the realm of submarines and of air war is far inferior to that of the English and the Americans. We are now getting the reward for our poor leadership on the scientific front, which did not show the necessary initiative to stimulate the willingness of scientists to co-operate. You just can't let an absolute nitwit head German science for years and not expect to be punished for such folly.

[Goebbels here refers to his fellow cabinet member Bernhard Rust, Minister of Education, who as a young man had been an inmate of an insane asylum.]

My collaborator Lapper sent me a summary on conditions in the Ukraine, which are very sad indeed. Our administrative and policy-directing offices there have not succeeded in spurring the Ukrainian people on to collaborate with us. Accordingly, the harvest will be poor. We shall barely be able to feed our soldiers from the grain surpluses there. There can be no thought of transporting food to Germany. We Germans are not very well fitted for administering occupied territory, as we lack experience. The English, who have done nothing else in all their history, are superior to us in this respect.

That the fight in Tunisia has ended is very depressing. I sometimes feel as though we lack the necessary initiative for fighting the war. During the past five months the enemy has had the upper hand almost everywhere. He is defeating us in the air, he has inflicted heavy wounds on us in the East, he is beating us in North Africa, and even our submarine warfare is not so successful as we really expected it to be. It is high time that we now attain tangible results in the East. That would naturally brighten the whole scene for us considerably.

The submarine command and the Luftwaffe have done everything in their power, but we were not adequately prepared for this military drama. The Luftwaffe especially is having a continuous streak of bad luck. That is not exactly an accident. We rested on our laurels. The essential thing to me, however, is that at last we are realizing our position clearly.

In the evening we issued a final communiqué about Tunisia. The Fuehrer issued an order not to put this on the air. I don't think that was necessary. We ought not suddenly to introduce new methods into our news policies. In a great military crisis like this they lead the people to think that the reason for it is our bad conscience!

May 15, 1943

Air raids are becoming more frequent again. During the night the Skoda works near Pilsen were hard hit. Among other targets the drafting room [*Konstruktions-Buero*] was destroyed. That is naturally quite a setback for us. However, the number of planes we shot down is colossal. Within forty-eight hours the English lost seventy-eight four-engine bombers.

[The Czechoslovak Skoda plant was one of the greatest munitions factories in Europe. It fell into German hands as a result of the appeasement agreement between Hitler, Mussolini, Chamberlain, and Daladier on September 30, 1938.]

Meanwhile Beneš has arrived in Washington. He is to attend the conferences there as an expert for the southeast. That is not at all good for morale in the Protectorate. The more Beneš's finger is in the pie of great power politics, the greater will be the hopes people there will place in him. Evidently Beneš is regarded as the proper person to bring about a reconciliation between the Poles and the Soviet Union. He is soon to travel to Moscow.

[Eduard Beneš was president of the Czechoslovak Government-in-exile.]

The United States is once again boasting of enormous production figures. I consider it necessary for us to publish at least a part of our production figures. It cannot be denied that the United States is making a deep impression on world public opinion by its production figures.

A lot of criticism is contained in the letters reaching us. Morale among the masses is so low as to be rather serious. Even people of good will are now worried about further developments. The man in the street no longer sees any way out of the military dilemma. As a result there is criticism of the leaders, in some cases even of the Fuehrer himself.

Rosenberg criticized our motion-picture production in a letter to me. I could give him a stiff answer by criticizing conditions in the East, but I won't do it because the whole matter seems too unimportant to me. At any rate I should have thought that Rosenberg would worry about other things than about this or that movie that did not turn out successfully.

The well-known physics expert, Professor Ramsauer, Director of the Research Institute of the German General Electric Company and chairman of the *Deutsche Physikalische Gesellschaft,* presented me with a report on the status of German and Anglo-Saxon physics. This report is very depressing for us. Anglo-Saxon physical science has completely eclipsed us, especially in research. As a result the Anglo-Saxon powers are very superior to us in the practical application to warfare of the results of research in physics. That is noticeable both in air and submarine warfare. Professor Ramsauer proposed a number of changes which I shall attempt to bring about to the extent of my ability. He, too, believes we can catch up with the Anglo-Saxon physics experts by concentrating our research facilities, by combining the various research institutes which are doing substantial work, by raising the standards of the profession, and by increasing the number of physical scientists, both students and teachers. Of course this will take considerable time. It is better, however, to make a beginning and to count on certain results for the future rather than to let things merely go on as they are now.

[Professor Karl Ramsauer is listed in *Minerva,* the standard German publication on men and institutions of culture and learning, as a leading physicist.]

May 16, 1943

The over-all military situation causes us some worry. War in the air is becoming more and more bitter from day to day. The day raids by American bombers are creating extraordinary difficulties. Thus, for instance, at Kiel, we counted more than one hundred dead and found very serious damage to military and technical installations of the Navy. If this condition continues and we find no proper antidote for these day raids we shall have to face exceptionally serious consequences which in the long run will prove unbearable.

Developments in the realm of submarine warfare are very disagreeable. Our submarines again took up contact with various convoys, but soon had to give up as the enemy's defense was exceptionally strong. In no case were worth-while ships sunk. If this continues, we shall have to accustom ourselves to the thought that submarine warfare, at least for the present, has taken a turn that is unfavorable to us. The enemy air force, especially, is causing our submarines much trouble and worry. Technical developments on the enemy side are further advanced than ours. Professor Ramsauer pointed this out convincingly in his report. Surely our technicians and physicists will in a relatively short time find the proper means for making our submarines again ready for attack. For the moment the situation does not seem to be very favorable.

News has reached us that Roosevelt intends to meet Stalin soon. . . . In any case it seems to be a fact that the Americans are very eager either to gloss over or iron out the differences that have arisen between the Soviet Union and the plutocratic powers.

The report from the occupied areas indicates no fundamental change in the situation. Our chances have decreased generally because of the events in Tunisia. These are having a very unfavorable influence on public opinion in the countries under our military administration.

I was handed an appeal signed by Cardinal Bertram, which the Catholic bishops had addressed to the Reich Government. The manner in which the complaint is made about the relationship between State and Church is absolutely unrestrained. Significantly enough this appeal was published in the American press shortly after it was written. The Catholic clergy is collaborating with the enemies of our country in a truly treasonable manner. I could just burst with rage when I think that we cannot possibly call the guilty ones to account now. We shall have to save our vengeance until later.

During the night we had an air alert of pretty long duration. Many provinces throughout the Reich were affected. In reality, however, only ten nuisance planes flew over these provinces. We must therefore record the absurd fact that ten nuisance planes could drive fifteen to eighteen million people out of their beds.

May 17, 1943

Judging by a number of reports, our captured soldiers in Tunis are being treated relatively well. The Fuehrer will now do something about the treatment of English prisoners of war. They are still fettered and the English will undoubtedly very shortly approach us via the power protecting its interests in Germany during the war and pose certain questions. The Fuehrer has therefore decided to remove the chains quite inconspicuously from the prisoners of war so that, when the English make inquiries, we can say it has already been done. We can no longer indulge in a prestige fight with the English in the matter of fettering, since the English hold many more German prisoners in custody than we do English.

[The British Government requested Switzerland to take over the protection of British interests in Germany.]

May 18, 1943

Air raids the past night inflicted heavy damage on us. The attacks of British bombers on the dams in our valleys [Talsperren] were very successful. The Fuehrer is exceedingly impatient and angry about the lack of preparedness on the part of our Luftwaffe. . . . Damage to production was more than normal. Naturally the Gauleiters in all gaus in which there are dams that have not yet been attacked are very much worried, since the anti-aircraft measures there are quite inadequate.

[The Ruhr Valley was flooded after RAF bombings breached the Eder, Sorpe, and Moehne dams.]

The United States is talking of a peace offer to Italy which the Anglo-Saxon powers want to make together with an ultimatum stating that air raids against Italian cities would be increased horribly in case of non-acceptance. None of these reports is based on fact, just as little as is the banner-line item in London papers claiming that the Fuehrer sent me to Italy. We must expect the English and Americans to continue to wage a war of nerves on Italy, but I assume that Mussolini and the Fascist party will be equal to it.

To intensify this war of nerves the allied GHQ in North Africa beamed a radio broadcast to the French people and kept repeating it, to the effect that Frenchmen were to sit at their radio sets until late into the night and wait for important news. I think this whole matter is a gigantic bluff. The English and Americans won't stage an invasion at this time. They haven't prepared sufficiently for it, and the whole matter is still too uncertain.

Herr von Gienanth, who has just returned from Tunisia, gave me a report on the last skirmishes there. This report is very dramatic. The German soldiers regard the fighting qualities of the Americans as very inferior and mediocre. Every German soldier is convinced that the Americans will be defeated without the slightest difficulty once we meet them on an equal basis on the European continent. . . . The crime that Roosevelt and his Jewish clique committed against these men is positively outrageous.

The Fuehrer has given instructions to start an anti-Bolshevik legion made up of English prisoners of war. These are to take part in the fight against the Soviet Union as volunteers. The propaganda to which these English PW's are to be subjected must be handled with exceptional care. I shall take a hand myself in this important matter.

The whole day brought nothing but work and worry. Alarming news kept piling in. One must certainly keep one's mental balance and hold one's nerves in check so as not to become jittery under the impact. But there can be no question about this in my case. I know that war is tough business; I also know that one must see it through; I also realize clearly that it involves an exceptionally severe strain; but when one tackles the job courageously and survives the crises, victory beckons in the end.

May 19, 1943

The English and Americans discuss practically nothing but air warfare. Their successful raid on the German dams created a great sensation both in London and in Washington. Of course they know exactly what they have achieved by this attack. The former Berlin Reuter correspondent, Bettany, claimed that the plan for the attack stemmed from a Jew who emigrated from Berlin. I had this claim written up as a short news item for papers in the Reich, especially in the areas that suffered the disaster. This shows once again how dangerous the Jews are and how right we are in putting them behind bars. . . .

I feel certain that treason was involved in this whole attack, for the English were so absolutely in the know, and after their attack had such exact knowledge of what damage was done, that it is hardly to be presumed they ascertained this solely by air reconnaissance.

The English and Americans claim they took 109,000 Germans and 63,000 Italians prisoner in Tunisia. It may therefore be presumed that most of our troops there are in captivity. In the last analysis that is a comforting thought. It certainly does not leave so bitter a taste as did the collapse of our defense in Stalingrad.

The psychological pressure which is being brought to bear upon the Italian public at the moment is extremely heavy, and, I suppose, also painful.

A Hollywood movie about the Soviet Union, based on the book, *Mission to Moscow*, by the former American Ambassador in Moscow Davies, has created a great sensation in the United States. It pleads for friendship with the Soviets in such an evil-smelling manner that even the American people are protesting.

The reduction of the meat ration by one hundred grams has, after all, had a very serious psychological effect. Criticism is directed especially at Goering's speech of last autumn in the Sports Palace, in which he claimed that from then on everything would be better.

Knut Hamsun has published an exceptionally favorable appeal in *Fritt Folk*, organ of the Nasjonal Samling. In the afternoon the great Norwegian author visited me with his wife in Hermann Goering Street.

[*Fritt Folk* literally means "Free People." The Nasjonal Samling was Vidkun Quisling's Norwegian Fascist organization. The words literally mean "National Gathering." The meeting took place in Hermann Goering Street because Goebbels's official residence was located there next to the American Embassy.]

I was deeply touched by this visit. When Hamsun saw me for the first time tears filled his eyes and he had to turn aside to hide his emotion. I saw before me an eighty-four-year-old gentleman with a wonderful head. The wisdom of old age was written on his brow. It was exceedingly difficult to converse with him, as he is so deaf that he does not understand a word and his wife must translate everything I say into Norwegian and shout it into his ear. Nevertheless I was overwhelmed at his visit. To me he is the ideal figure of an epic writer, and we may consider ourselves fortunate to be his contemporaries. Whatever he says makes sense. He speaks only a few words, but they reflect the experience of age and of a life rich in struggle. His faith in German victory is unshakable. From childhood on he has keenly disliked the English, for whom he has nothing but contempt. He has lived in the United States for a long time and describes the people there as completely devoid of culture. He is visiting the Reich in order to look after his daughter Ellinor. . . . I placed every facility at his service for his family mission. I am very happy that I came to know the famous author personally at this late period of his life. He is of a touching modesty that fittingly matches the luster of a great personality.

Again and again I gazed at the high brow behind which the figures of Victoria, of Lieutenant Glan, of August the Globe Trotter, and all the many other characters sprang into being that from my earliest childhood on became my companions for life. Hamsun is a poet who has already passed beyond good and evil [der bereits jenseits von Gut und Boese steht]. He does not describe people as they ought to be; he does not regard them through the spectacles either of optimism or pessimism, but exclusively through the glass of a fascinating realistic objectivity. Undoubtedly he will later be ranked among the great epic writers of the world. It is a disgrace for Sweden, Denmark, and especially his native country, Norway, that the Scandinavian countries no longer publish his books because of his friendship for Germany.

I gave immediate orders to print a new German edition of 100,000 copies of his works. Hamsun very modestly tried to decline. He said he was so near the grave, there was so little paper available, and his works were printed so much that he didn't know whether he deserved such an honor. This great personality is a new proof of the fact that real genius is always coupled with an almost touching modesty. When Hamsun and his wife left me after two hours I had the feeling of having experienced one of the most precious encounters of my life. I hope we shall see the poet at our home very often.

Magda, too, was deeply impressed by his visit, especially since Hamsun had always been one of the favorite writers of our family. Hereafter, when I read his books, I shall be able to conjure up the image of the author himself. May fate permit the great poet to live to see us win victory! If anybody deserved it because of his high-minded espousal of our cause, even under the most difficult circumstances, it is he.

May 20, 1943

The Americans have made another day raid on Flensburg and Kiel. First reports were to the effect that they had dropped fountain pens and other articles filled with explosives. After a few hours this report, which was issued by the naval command at Kiel, proved unfounded. . . . Such events show how nervous the Wehrmacht commands have gradually become under pressure of Anglo-American air raids.

The damage to the dams has not been quite so serious as we at first feared. . . . The reports by Berndt which caused me such a headache the first day are now proven to have been tremendously exaggerated. It is quite obvious that Berndt got his information from Radio London. This fact illustrates once more how impractical and irrational it is to forward alarming reports of this kind to the higher leadership.

I received eyewitness reports from Katyn, based on interrogations of Russian laborers, especially railroad workers, who witnessed some of the dreadful executions. These reports make one's flesh creep. I had them worked up as news items for our foreign service. I don't have to make any use of them for our domestic service, for the material thus far published has completely convinced the public.

At Goering's suggestion the Fuehrer issued an order to direct evacuées from the air-raid regions of the West into the occupied French areas, especially the province of Burgundy. Of course that is more easily said than done. If we stick bombed-out families into French surroundings they will very soon filter back to their old homes. It is hard enough to settle them in Bavaria, to say nothing of France. But the Fuehrer does not want to see compulsory housing introduced in the Reich until we have first exhausted the housing capacity of the occupied areas. I shall contact the Gauleiters of the threatened provinces to ask them for proposals for carrying out this somewhat curious measure.

Speer got in touch with the Reich Marshal to persuade him to speak on this theme [increased production in the munitions industry]. I don't know whether the Reich Marshal has any desire to do that at present, especially as the Fuehrer has issued an order that all speeches that are broadcast must be submitted to him beforehand in writing. This decree is directed especially at Goering, who, during recent months, has made a number of unfortunate public statements which have harmed not only him but also the whole regime.

May 21, 1943

The English at present are making a sport of driving as large sections of our population as possible out of their beds by air alerts. Recent damage, excepting that done to the dams, has been relatively small. In the daytime, too, we have more alerts now, even in Berlin. The English accomplish this with their small Mosquito machines which are exceedingly hard to hit.

I did my work in Lanke today. The weather was beautiful and I was able to work out of doors so that at least I breathed a little fresh air. I needed it urgently. Since my badly-needed vacation has again gone by the board because of recent events, I am confronted by the rather impossible situation that on the one hand my health is no longer quite equal to the constantly increasing demands, yet on the other hand I see no possibility of getting myself in shape. I shall therefore have to try to get a little recreation on the installment plan.

We just cannot stand air warfare indefinitely. We must try as fast as possible to develop counter measures, especially reprisal attacks. Milch has every reason to get up on his hind legs and create an aggressive Luftwaffe to attack England. Otherwise sooner or later air war will become unbearable for us.

During my absence Colonel Martin made certain statements in the [press] conference which I must challenge sharply. He declared that the people no longer believed German news reports. He said we were absolutely discredited, no matter how hard we tried; people no longer believed the government. Even though I must admit there is a somewhat critical news situation at the moment, Colonel Martin must not mistake the attitude of the OKW toward our news policies for that of the German people. The German people, as far as the broad masses are concerned, are quite uncontaminated. All they need is a little stimulant for their hearts. I am hoping that the coming offensive operations in the East will give them that stimulant.

May 22, 1943

The London public fears that the German air *Blitzkrieg* will suddenly break out again over night. Would to God that we were in a position to do it! Obviously the English people consider us to be better armed in the air than we actually are.

Brendan Bracken made a very excited statement in the House of Commons against the Polish émigrés. . . . He declared that wherever there is a single Pole anywhere a newspaper is launched. He isn't exactly wrong about this. I imagine the English are having very grave difficulties with those émigré governments. They have to pay them, they have to provide a certain setting for them, they have to cover up their political mistakes—and all that just to play "Europe in the Sandbox."

[The Rt. Hon. Brendan Bracken, born, 1901, was Parliamentary Private Secretary to the Prime Minister, 1940–41; Minister of Information, 1941–45; and First Lord of the Admiralty in 1945.]

It is a pity that we are issuing no final report on Tunis. My last article in the *Reich*, entitled, "With Sovereign Equanimity," was to some extent a substitute for it. The Italians issue one communiqué after another.

My article on Tunis made a deep impression on the public opinion of the whole world. The arguments developed in it are absolutely convincing. If in addition a final military report were issued, I believe we would get by the psychological low that we hit because of our misfortune in Tunisia.

The French bishops have issued a pastoral letter against the labor draft. After all we are used to that in the Reich as well as in the occupied areas. The high Catholic clergy always opposes National Socialism. Terboven made short shrift of the matter and simply arrested the [Protestant] bishops who protested to him. He is somewhat too rigorous in such matters. One can certainly not describe his policies as especially flexible and clever. On the whole he is acting like a lumberjack. It can't be denied that evil consquences resulted in Norway. Terboven is now the most hated man in all Scandinavia.

The battle of the Warsaw Ghetto continues. The Jews are still resisting. On the whole, however, resistance is no longer dangerous and has virtually been broken. Within the area of the General Government assassinations, acts of sabotage, and raids by bandits are on the increase. Conditions there are in some respects truly chaotic. Unfortunately the Fuehrer has refrained from a personnel change in the General Government as intended. Greiser returned to Posen without accomplishing anything. Frank is to be given one more chance to prove

his worth. I should have thought it better to kick Frank right out.
When you are once convinced that a man is in no way equal to his job,
the necessary conclusions should be drawn.

New reports on morale in the Reich have reached me. They are nothing to be happy about. . . . All agree about a drop in morale throughout Germany. . . . This drop is ascribed to Tunisia, to the increasing
severity of the air raids, to the temporary failure of submarine warfare,
and to the reduction of meat rations. It is quite natural that the people
look for a scapegoat [*Pruegelknabe*], since the facts themselves can't
be changed. That scapegoat, as has always happened in the past, is
the press and the radio. The smallest tactical mistakes that we chance
to make in press and radio are chalked up against us. It is high time
that one of my articles be devoted to this theme. The communiqué
about Rommel, too, has not absolutely convinced certain sections of
our people. Sharp criticism is made of Goering. He is blamed for having given a wrong picture of the German food situation in his speech
in the Sports Palace and for not having mastered air warfare in any
way. I regard this criticism of Goering as exaggerated. Nevertheless I
believe it is time for him to say something in public. He ought to speak
or at least pay a few visits to the threatened air-raid areas. The fact
that he has withdrawn to his lonely abode and is not saying anything
is, to a certain extent, grist for the mills of his critics. There are even
mumblings of a crisis developing about Goering. I regard these reports as exaggerated, but it does mean we shall have to be on the alert
about him. His authority simply cannot be replaced, and in wartime
it is exhausted faster than one might expect. The people are somewhat
impatient that they can't get a clear picture of the further progress of
the war. Again and again I am appealed to, urged to publish something
along these lines. But so long as we have not yet become active in the
East, that is very difficult. . . .

The strained domestic situation leads the common folk to watch very
closely how the so-called prominent people are living. Unfortunately
not all the prominent people care about this. Some are living a life that
can in nowise be regarded as conforming to our present position.

The letters which reached me are also full of criticism. . . . There is
nothing but praise, however, for my work. In the present situation it
seems to be of decisive value.

The discussions which my collaborators had with Director Menzel
of the Ministry of Education had but little success. Professor Ramsauer's report was handed him. Menzel corroborated the charges fully

but claimed that the failure of science was owing to poor pay and the continuous public attacks on science, especially by the Party. I don't regard his objections as well founded. It should have been the duty of the Ministry of Education to remedy this situation during the past ten years. It should have protected science against insults and have provided sufficient material means. That did not happen.

I discussed with Fritzsche and Winkelnkemper the question of commentary ["talks"] in the foreign broadcasts of the German radio. These talks are, if possible, to be eliminated altogether. I shall, however, permit very brief comments. In the main our broadcasts are to consist exclusively of news. It is much more difficult to invent argument-provoking news whose bias is not noticeable; it takes more brains to do this than to read tedious commentary. By forbidding talks I shall compel the collaborators in our foreign radio service to increase our stock of news.

I had a sharp conflict with Cerff about the present program of our broadcasting system. Cerff takes a somewhat super-national-socialistic attitude. If he had his way music, for instance, would be made only on lyres. You can't operate a radio service for the masses that way. Broadcasts must have diversified and manifold programs. . . . Cerff just won't see this. I strictly forbade him to criticize the broadcast in the bulletins of the Reich propaganda office. I regard it as simply impossible that one of my departments should attack another publicly. We haven't sunk that low in the National Socialist state! We still have enough power to remedy known defects. But under no circumstances will I tolerate bringing about changes by stirring up the mobs.

[Karl Cerff was taken into the Propaganda Ministry by Goebbels from the Hitler Youth Organization, where he had been chief of the radio section. He was one of the "Reich Orators" both for the *Hitler Jugend* and the Nazi party.]

In the evening I was visited by Speer, Ley, and Funk. Once again we talked over the entire situation. The three gentlemen agree that the most serious part of our problem is a sort of Goering crisis. Goering is letting things drift with a certain lethargy and takes no countermeasures against the diminution of his prestige. I think that the right thing for him to do would be to face the public. The people are not unjust, and they would immediately applaud him if he had the courage to step before them. Funk believed Goering couldn't do this now. I regard Funk's objections as grossly exaggerated. Anyway, Funk gave expression to a number of defeatist ideas that I rejected very sharply.

But in the case of Funk they aren't to be taken seriously. He always swings from one extreme to the other.

Naumann reported to me about his visit to the Arado factory in Brandenburg, where he received a very favorable impression. Our new bombers are now being tested there. As soon as the final test flights have been carried out, serial production will begin, in all likelihood early in August. While we must start again from small beginnings, it is always much better to begin rather than to do nothing whatever. The failure of our Luftwaffe in technical respects is owing chiefly to faulty construction. Far and away the greatest blame for this falls on Udet. He tried to atone for this by committing suicide, but of course that didn't change things. . . .

The people show a very healthy instinct when in their word-of-mouth propaganda they blame Goering personally for the failure of the Luftwaffe. Goering pushed his old comrades of World War I too much forward. They were obviously not equal to the heavy tasks imposed by war.

Our talk continued until 2 A.M. A vast number of personnel matters were discussed, and we found ourselves on the whole in agreement in evaluating them. Ley again proved to be a very wise observer. He is by no means so extreme in his views as his speeches would sometimes lead one to think; on the contrary, his opinions are remarkably realistic. He hasn't anything good to say about Thierack, whom he regards as not at all competent for his job. Nor does he think much of Backe. He believes that Backe's policies will gradually lead to the complete ruin of our stock of cattle. He deduces this from his own experiences with his farm in western Germany. . . . I believe he is more pessimistic than the situation warrants. Nevertheless I believe he is right in his contention that Backe is too much of a theoretician and therefore is getting to be more and more impractical. The whole Food Ministry—but this is more the fault of Darré than of Backe—is quite a dogmatic institution, totally unsuited to wartime.

May 23, 1943

The eastern offensive is now expected in some quarters and regarded as not coming in others. In London people believe that an eastern offensive is near but that it will fail and that a German catastrophe will follow. Both sides involved in the eastern offensive are sticking to the principle of "After you, my dear Alphonse." [Literally: "Hannemann, you go ahead; you have the longer boots."] For this reason the Fuehrer has postponed his trip to Winnitza and, changing his mind suddenly, returned to the Obersalzberg. He wants first to recuperate there so that his health may be equal to the tasks of the next weeks and months. That is the best thing he can do. . . . The Fuehrer intends to let the Bolsheviks start things.

My article about Tunis continues to be front-page stuff for the neutral press. It is a case of having hit the jackpot.

A report concerning Turkey claims that under no circumstances is there any danger of Ankara's jumping over to the enemy side before autumn. Leading Turkish circles, however, expect us to wage war not only in a military but also in a political sense. According to influential Turks we achieve wonderful military successes, but our enemies are superior to us in their political strategy. That is probably largely true. But I know that I am free from any blame in this matter. The report regards Papen as the great diplomatic authority in Ankara. He enjoys the confidence of all leading Turkish circles; in Turkey he is the best horse in our stable.

I issued instructions to the press to pay more attention to domestic than foreign questions during the coming weeks. The Foreign Office is always eager for questions of foreign policy to take precedence. The present period, however, is so critical that it seems more important to me that we concern ourselves with the worries of the man in the street rather than with foreign policy. The Foreign Office cannot see the point, but I regard myself as responsible for the morale of the German people. From that fact I derive the right to keep out of the German press everything that is harmful or even that fails to be useful.

Goering, together with Speer, intends to discuss the question of munitions in the Sports Palace. I welcome this. The fact that the Reich Marshal is at last to appear again in public will be of decisive importance not only to him personally but to our entire regime. I shall personally see to it that his speech has the right tactical approach.

May 24, 1943

Churchill addressed the personnel of the British Embassy in Washington. He predicted a long war without committing himself on its further progress. Otherwise the speech is marked only by nonsensical trivialities without any significance. . . . Generally speaking one can note that there is great fear among all warring nations of an undue prolongation of the war. After all, four years are enough to get people down. Everybody now endures it only because he knows that the loss of the war would mean the end of national life for his own people.

The Social Democratic parties in all countries, including England, fear they are now being gradually undermined by the Communist party. The Communist party of England has already given hints along that line and will undoubtedly present a motion at the next convention of the Labor party for amalgamation with the British Labor party.

May 25, 1943

The night raid of the English on Dortmund was extraordinarily heavy, probably the worst ever directed against a German city. . . . Reports from Dortmund are pretty horrible. The critical thing about it is that industrial and munitions plants have been hit very hard. One can only repeat about air warfare: we are in an almost helpless inferiority and must grin and bear it as we take the blows from the English and Americans. One can now see how very shortsighted was Goering's proposal to the Fuehrer to evacuate people who suffered bomb damage to Burgundy and other sections of occupied France. In Dortmund there are some eighty to one hundred thousand inhabitants without shelter. Let the Reich Marshal go to Dortmund himself and propose that they evacuate to France! Decisions of this kind can be made at the conference table, but they cannot be put into effect in practice.

The English naturally make a lot of propaganda about Dortmund. They have every reason. The one happy thing about all this misery and distress is the fact that at least a respectable number of planes was downed. If that, too, had failed to materialize, we would hardly know what to say about such a dilemma.

Schaub called from the Obersalzberg in great distress. He had received reports from Bochum and Dortmund indicating a new low in morale. The reports to Schaub are somewhat exaggerated, but we must recognize that the people in the West are gradually beginning to lose courage. Hell like that is hard to bear for any length of time, especially since the inhabitants along the Rhine and Ruhr see no prospect of improvement.

The Moscow decisions have created almost no impression whatever in the neutral countries. There isn't a single newspaper in Switzerland or Sweden or Turkey which takes the decisions seriously. Everywhere there is frosty rejection or at least the strongest distrust of them. A Swedish newspaper points out that the Comintern possesses a handy catchbasin in the Red Aid. That is true. In the Reich the Red Aid always served to absorb the Communist party when it was officially forbidden. Personally I regard Communist parties operating illegally as much more dangerous than those under official surveillance, unless one is ready to extirpate them completely.

[During the Weimar Republic the German Communists maintained an organization known as the *Rote Hilfe* (Red Aid), which claimed to be non-partisan and non-political. Whenever any section of the Communist party was forbidden in any German state the members continued their subversive activity in the Red Aid under the guise of political neutrality. At the head of the organization was Willy Muenzenberg, a member of the Reichstag who enjoyed parliamentary immunity.]

The [London] *Times* has once again sunk so low as to publish an almost pro-Bolshevik article. It praised the Bolshevik Revolution and used words that make one blush with shame. Otherwise, however, the English papers are rather depressed. The kowtow to Stalin is lacking in sincerity.

I had a long discussion with Admiral Canaris about the data available for figuring out English intentions. Canaris has gained possession of a letter written by the English General Staff to General Alexander. This letter is extremely informative and reveals English plans almost to the dotting of an "i." I don't know whether the letter is merely camouflage—Canaris denies this energetically—or whether it actually corresponds to the facts. In any case the general outline of English plans for this summer revealed here seems on the whole to tally. According to it, the English and Americans are planning several sham attacks during the coming months—one in the West, one on Sicily, and one on the islands of the Dodecanese. These attacks are to immobilize our troops stationed there and thereby make English forces available for other and more serious operations. These operations are to involve Sardinia and the Peloponnesus. On the whole this line of reasoning seems to be right. Hence, if the letter to General Alexander is the real thing, we shall have to prepare to repel a number of attacks which are partly serious and partly sham.

[Field Marshal Sir Harold Alexander, born, 1891, educated at Harrow and Sandhurst, was at this time deputy Commander in Chief in North Africa. He later became military governor in Sicily, and during 1944–45 was Commander in Chief of the Allied armies in Italy.]

Admiral Canaris also had data about the present situation in Italy, which is anything but encouraging. He believes the mood of the Italian people has become exceedingly critical, the reason being that the man in the street no longer has any clear picture of the progress of the war and that the Fascist party on the whole is letting things drift. I don't believe the Fascist party intends to surrender voluntarily at any point in this war. On the contrary, I am convinced the Italian people, once they defend their own soil, will fight much more bravely than they did in North Africa, not to mention the Eastern Front.

The English have assembled so great an invasion fleet in the Mediterannean that one must conclude they are preparing their operations with greatest care. For the scheduled undertakings they have at their disposal five completely fresh divisions, not counting the somewhat groggy ones that fought in North Africa. The coming summer will therefore be something of a strain on our nerves. Added to this—so Canaris reports—is the somewhat critical situation in Spain. The Franco Revolution has achieved no visible successes there. . . . One cannot crush a modern revolution merely by arresting the Red and Socialist elements; one must have positive ideas to support one's own action. That, apparently, is not the case there.

Personally I shall look upon our situation as critical only in case we do not succeed in replying to the English air raids with a series of reprisals. The English have now, for the first time, had a taste of our new bombs, which are attracting considerable attention among their people. They are apparently very much afraid of a recurrence of our blitz air raids. It we had only one thousand modern bombers, the question of air warfare would surely become a secondary problem within a short time. Of course we are hard at work to bring that condition about, but it will take several months more.

The correspondent of the *Daily Express,* on his return from Moscow, reports pretty gloomily about conditions inside the Soviet Union. He calculates that the Soviets have lost about 30,000,000 men [*sic*] by death, fatal injuries, hunger, and freezing. That is, of course, a steep figure. Although it looks somewhat exaggerated to me, the remarkable thing is that it is being discussed publicly by the English. According to this report, social and nutritional conditions inside the U.S.S.R. are such as to give you the creeps. Any other country would have collapsed long ago under such stress. The Soviet Union is alive only because it is peopled with Russians and because Bolshevism dominates it as its dictator. We must get accustomed to the fact that the Soviet Union is still alive and pretty energetically so.

Zoerner has resigned as governor of Lublin. He called on me to give
the reasons for his resignation.

[Ernst Zoerner was an Old Guard Nazi who in 1930 became the first member
of the Party to be elected president of any German Parliament, viz., that of the
state of Brunswick. In 1932 he was elected to the Reichstag, of which he became
a vice-president. Soon after Hitler took over in 1933 Zoerner was appointed mayor
of Dresden.]

He had succeeded on the whole in squeezing an unusual amount
of food out of the Lublin district. Understandably so, for this district
is the most fertile in the entire General Government. Suddenly, however, he received orders for resettlement that had a very bad effect
upon morale. Some 50,000 Poles were to be evacuated to begin with.
Our police were able to grab only 25,000; the other 25,000 joined the
Partisans. It is not hard to imagine what consequences that had for
the whole area. Now he was to evacuate about 190,000 more Poles.
This he refused to do, and in my opinion he was right. His district will
now be governed from Warsaw by Governor Dr. Fischer. Although Dr.
Frank, the Governor General, agreed with Zoerner's views he hasn't
sufficient authority to put his foot down on the encroachments of the
police and the SS. It makes you want to tear out your hair when you
encounter such appalling political ineptitude. At home we are waging
total war with all its consequences and are subordinating all philo-
sophical and ideological aims to the supreme aim of final victory; in
the occupied areas, however, our politicos act [eine Politik wird
betrieben] as though we were living in profound peace. I could spend
hours boxing the ears of the men responsible for this. They don't deserve anything else. This example, however, once again demonstrates
the need of leadership in the Reich and in the occupied areas. We are
suffering from a lack of clarity and logic in our policies that may someday have serious consequences.

Our propaganda within the Reich also doesn't seem to have the right
spark to it, as I gather from a number of reports of Gauleiters. Here
again the sad fact is that we are without a governing hand at home. I
should be quite willing to undertake to solve all these problems, provided I were given the necessary plenary powers. But at present one
can't do anything without running into opposition here, there, and
everywhere. There are reports, for instance, from the gaus that many
people are again listening to foreign radio stations. The reason for this,
of course, is our completely obscure news policy of no longer giving the
people any insight into the war situation. Also, our reticence regarding
Stalingrad and the fate of our missing soldiers there naturally leads the

families to listen to Bolshevik radio stations, as these always broadcast the names of German soldiers reported as prisoners.

In the evening I received a report on the extent of the damage in Dortmund. The fires were under control in the course of the afternoon. Destruction, however, is virtually total. Gauleiter Hoffmann informed me that hardly a house in Dortmund is habitable. He expressed the opinion that the other big cities on the Rhine and the Ruhr can just about figure out for themselves what fate is soon in store for them. The fact is that the Royal Air Force is taking on one industrial city after another and one need not be a great mathematician to prophesy when a large part of the industry of the Ruhr will be out of commission. We must now face the problem of evacuating the population. I believe we shall be the more easily able to keep our industry going if we settle in other parts of the Reich such sections of the population as are not necessary for industrial production and maintenance.

[Albert Hoffmann was Gauleiter for southern Westphalia.]

May 26, 1943

Churchill has issued a declaration to the press in which he stated, without being in the least ashamed, that he was ready to travel around the whole globe with Roosevelt just to bring about a meeting with Stalin. Politics in the British Empire have sunk so low that Bolshevism is being kowtowed to in a way that upsets one's stomach.

Monitored reports by our Research Office give me an insight into the mentality of Roosevelt's Ambassador Davies, who is at present staying in Kuibyshev. It appears that he is a convinced friend of the Soviets. That stinks all the more since he comes from big capitalist circles, has married a million-dollar heiress, and now has the one ambition of making a career. He is . . . a menace to clear, realistic politics. We must regard him as a sort of parlor Bolshevik. Parlor pinks of this type must be thought of in terms of the Bible; viz., that they should be forgiven, for they know not what they do. It is certainly naïve for Davies in his talks with diplomats in Kuibyshev to voice the opinion that Stalin is waging this war without any territorial designs. I suppose there is Homeric laughter in the Kremlin about this amateurish American diplomat. If Davies speaks of himself as an unqualified admirer of Marshal Stalin, this plutocratic diplomat thereby shows that he hasn't the faintest idea of the issues at stake in the world today.

An interesting report tells about the conference at Casablanca. According to this report it was decided that the Anglo-Saxon powers would create a national home for the Jews in Palestine after their eventual victory. This national home is to take care of 20,000,000 Jews. These Jews are to engage chiefly in intellectual and managerial tasks; the work is to be done, as decided in Casablanca, by middle European and especially German workers. For this a large-scale resettlement would be necessary that would, to a certain extent, depopulate Central Europe. It isn't hard to imagine what's going on in the brains of these plutocratic statesmen who are dependent upon the Jews; but we also know what we must do to protect the German people against such a fate.

A Communist hangout was raided in Berlin. As a starter some forty arrests were made, but additional ones are expected. This group has no political significance whatever, but it is a characteristic fact that resistance groups like this are gradually beginning to form. The group worked its mischief especially in workers' quarters. Its head was a seventy-three-year-old retired *rentier* who obviously had nothing to do and therefore indulged in activities hostile to the state. We will make him a head shorter.

The new undersecretary in the Foreign Office, Steengracht, paid me a visit. . . . Steengracht is a rather mediocre figure. At best he is only a high-grade private secretary. There can be no thought whatever of his having any influence on foreign policy.

[Baron Gustav Adolf Steengracht von Moyland, born, 1903, joined the SS in 1933, and was appointed to the staff of the "Bureau Ribbentrop," where he was liaison officer between Himmler and Ribbentrop, 1936–39. In 1938 he became a regular staff member of the German Foreign Office.]

As I predicted, there will be no final communiqué about Tunisia. I regret that exceedingly for the sake of our news and propaganda services.

[The prediction was wrong. There was a final communiqué.]

May 27, 1943

Churchill still claims that unconditional surrender is the war aim of the Anglo-Saxon powers. He will have to wait a good long time before he reaches this aim. He praised the superiority of English and especially American production over Axis production, but his estimates are absolutely wrong. We are taking occasion to prove it in our reply to his interview. His language is coarse and cynical as can be. He says he is planning a knockout blow against us. We are planning something quite different for him. Only it is essential that we succeed soon in overcoming England's nervewracking air supremacy. . . .

The English are giving sensational publicity to their successes in the air. They exaggerate a lot, but unfortunately much of what they claim is true. Their attack on Dortmund, especially, is praised as a great accomplishment of the Royal Air Force. As a matter of fact we do have extraordinary difficulties to overcome there. Even though the English admit that the Ruhr region is defended splendidly, and that we cause them serious losses when they attack at night, the estimates of today must not be compared to those of 1940. A single plane today does much greater damage than was possible in 1940, considering the state of technical development in air war at that time. Consequently good strategy does not demand that one count on as long a life for a plane today as had to be figured then. If a plane actually participates in inflicting disastrous blows four or five times on an average, it has undoubtedly done us much more serious damage than that suffered by the enemy through its loss. Important English military critics nevertheless believe that air raids are by no means substitutes for an invasion. They are right in that. You must conquer a country if you want to take possession of it unless, indeed, a people loses its morale and voluntarily surrenders to the enemy under the pressure of extraordinary events. That's what we did in 1918. We shall certainly not repeat it in 1943.

A lot of fuss is made in England, and, significantly, also in Italy, about our new bombs. These are not so new as the Italians claim them to be. Pavolini sang a veritable hymn of praise about the bombs in an editorial. Of course that is done more for domestic than military reasons. It is understandable that he wanted to awaken some hopes in the hard-hit Italian population by his evaluation of air warfare.

[Alessandro Pavolini, born, 1903, held a number of important posts under Fascism, including president of the Fascist Professions and Arts Confederation, president of the National Institute of Cultural Relations with Foreign Countries, and Minister of Education. He died with the Duce.]

Hadamovsky reported to me on his visit to Warsaw. Conditions in the General Government appear to be more than catastrophic. Every day there are attempts at assassination and acts of terror, without our authorities being able to do anything about it. The German popula-

tion and our administrative officialdom seem to yield, not to say capit
ulate, to these conditions. Unfortunately the jealousies between the
SD and the Wehrmacht are having a very unfortunate effect. I believe
a careful combing out of these bodies would work wonders.

One worry after another piles up on us and we hardly know how
to meet them. I avail myself of every help that the Reich can give. But
all that is only a drop in the bucket. I cannot but shudder as I wonder
what city is going to be hit next.

The Fuehrer has decided to confer a very special honor on Yama-
moto, chief of the Japanese Navy, who fell in action. He is going to
award him the Knight's Cross with Oak-Leaf Cluster and Swords.
This is the first time a foreign military officer is to be awarded such
high honors by us. Of course there are some formalities still to be
straightened out with the Emperor.

[There was only one decoration higher than that awarded Count Gombei
Yamomoto posthumously—the diamonds added, as in the case of Rommel, to the
Knight's Cross with Oak-Leaf Cluster and Swords.]

May 28, 1943

Our supremacy in the air was wrested from us by the English not
only by a tremendous expenditure of energy on the part of the RAF
and the British airplane industry, but also because of a number of unfortunate circumstances and negligence on our part. Why should it
not be possible for us to wrest air supremacy in turn from the English,
provided we abandon the thesis that the war in the East must be ended
first? It seems to me that air warfare ought to be regarded as one of
the most important phases of war and that it ought to be conducted
quite independently of developments in the East.

We hear occasionally that Roosevelt intends to mediate between
Moscow and the Vatican. Stalin is at present pursuing a very realistic
policy with reference to the church question, quite the opposite of ours.
Obviously he intends to play the role of a respectable gentleman
[honoriger Mann] in his dealings with a Europe filled with suspicion
about him.

Secretary of State Frank received the Government of the Protector-
ate and on this occasion revealed the background of the attempt on
Heydrich's life, stressing especially the directives issued by Beneš.
Undoubtedly this speech will attract great attention in the Protector-

ate. For obvious reasons we are devoting only a few lines to it in the German press.

[Karl Hermann Frank (not to be confused with Dr. Hanns Frank, Governor General of occupied Poland) was the power behind the throne in the Protectorate of Bohemia-Moravia. Baron Konstantin von Neurath, the first Protector, and his successor, former Minister of the Interior Dr. William Frick, were mere window dressing. The only exception was Reinhard Heydrich ("the Hangman"), who succeeded Neurath and was assassinated at Prague. Heydrich was quite as ruthless as Frank and had greater authority.

According to this entry, President Eduard Beneš had something to do with the plot on Heydrich.]

Goering is to speak June 6 in the Sports Palace on the occasion of the award of the Knight's Cross of the War Service Cross to workers and plant managers. I am trying to find out whether he is actually thinking of delivering a big political speech. If so, I should like to have a hand in the drafting and formulation of it. I would far prefer, however, that he did not talk. That would give me a chance to discuss the pressing problems of the present situation. I believe I could succeed in clarifying the most important issues. . . .

An interesting transformation is taking place among our people. Our adherents have become even more fanatical in their belief in victory; the doubters, especially the intellectuals, are outdoing each other with defeatist utterances. That is an added reason why the positive elements should have their backs stiffened by a great speech and the negative elements should be restrained. The citizens who are faithful to the state must be furnished with the necessary arguments for combating defeatism during discussions at their places of work and on the streets.

Recapitulation of events between
May 28 and July 25, 1943

During the two months elapsing between May 28 and July 25, for which no diary entries were found, the invasion of Sicily, beginning July 10, by the Western Allies was the major event—an event which Goebbels's Propaganda Ministry had always pictured as extremely unlikely to happen.

Accordingly, on July 19 there were hurried conferences in northern Italy between Hitler and Mussolini. The invasion of Italy, after all, caused quite a shock to these two men. Only three days before their get-together, on July 16, Italy was warned by President Roosevelt and Prime Minister Churchill that she must overthrow Fascism if she wished to survive.

On the very day they met Rome was raided for the first time by five hundred United States daylight bombers. Hardly had the two dictators finished their talks, when on July 22 the American Fifth Army captured Palermo and on July 24 Marsala.

The stage was thus set for the gripping story of Mussolini's forced resignation with which the Goebbels diaries resume.

To complete the fill in on this short gap in the entries it should be added that the French Committee of National Liberation was formed June 3; that a ten-day non-stop air raid descended upon Germany beginning June 18, with Cologne and Hamburg as principal targets; that the 101-day lull on the Russian front was broken July 5 by the Germans opening an offensive in the Orel-Kursk-Belgorod sector; and that Mikolajczyk succeeded General Sikorski as Premier of the Polish Government-in-exile in London, after the latter's death in an airplane accident. Also, Field Marshal Sir Archibald Wavell was appointed Viceroy of India June 18 and Eamon De Valera re-elected Prime Minister of Eire on July 1.

July 1943

July 25, 1943

In the course of the day we received confidential information that a certain change was taking place in Italian domestic politics. Led by Farinacci, the Old Guard Fascists have requested the Duce to call a meeting of the Fascist Grand Council. At this meeting, according to Mackensen, the Duce is to be requested to initiate more energetic policies. He is to be persuaded to get rid of the burden of holding so many offices so that he may regain his initiative and strength for guiding the over-all policies and the war effort of Italy. Farinacci seems to have assumed the leadership in this demonstrative action of the Old Guard. Possibly he will play a most important role as things develop further in Italy. If that were the case, we could only welcome it, for Farinacci is not only an energetic man, but also a pronounced friend of Germany. We can depend upon him blindly. His nerves would certainly last through any crisis, no matter how great.

[Hans Georg von Mackensen, son of the German Field Marshal August von Mackensen, was the German Ambassador to Italy.

Roberto Farinacci, journalist by profession, was one of the radicals of the Fascist party. He was a member of the Grand Council, and was shot with Mussolini.]

Developments in Sicily give the Italian war leaders every reason for being more energetic than hitherto. Thus far only the Germans have stood their ground in Sicily. Every time the Italians were involved in a more serious fight, they capitulated, sometimes a whole division at a time, headed by the divisional commander. Air warfare on Sicily, too, is being conducted almost exclusively by the Germans. . . .

Unfortunately that means our preparations for reprisals against England during the ensuing winter are once again interrupted. I don't believe we shall be able to make reprisal attacks in the foreseeable future.

In the *Sobranje* [Parliament] of Sofia the former Prime Minister, Mushanoff, criticized Bulgaria's foreign policy rather insultingly. He used somewhat disquieting language. But I believe King Boris is man enough to hold his own against these opposing elements.

[Nikola Mushanoff, leader of the democratic party of Bulgaria, was Prime Minister from October 1931 to May 1934 when he was deposed after a military coup d'état.]

The results of English air raids are gradually becoming evident. Our textile industry has been pretty badly hit. We are not in a position to meet our obligations about the Reich textile coupon card, that is, we can't call up the unused points. Whatever we still have in the way of reserves must be pumped into the distressed areas.

The letters addressed to me give me some worry. There's an unusual amount of criticism contained in them. . . . Above all, these letters keep asking why the Fuehrer does not visit the distressed air areas, why Goering isn't to be seen anywhere, and especially why the Fuehrer doesn't for once talk to the German people to explain the present situation. I consider it very necessary that the Fuehrer do this, despite the heavy burdens on the military sector. One cannot neglect the people too long; in the last analysis they are the very kernel of our war effort. If the people ever lost their will to resist and their faith in German leadership, the most serious crisis we ever faced would result.

The letters are full of praise for my work. My activity as a writer and speaker is especially appreciated and is contrasted with the activity of a number of prominent people who hardly ever face the public.

July 26, 1943

During the night an exceptionally heavy raid on Hamburg took place, with most serious consequences both for the civilian population and for armaments production. This attack definitely shatters the illusions that many have had about the continuation of air operations by the enemy. Unfortunately we shot down only very few planes—twelve, all told. That, of course, is wholly inadequate when you consider that about five hundred planes took part in the attack. Unfortunately only two days previously Colonel General Weise took the heavy anti-aircraft guns away from Hamburg to send them to Italy. That was the last straw! One can imagine what a field day the enemy planes must have had over Hamburg. The eastern section of Altona was particularly hard hit. It is a real catastrophe. Heavy damage was done to property of the civilian population. For the moment no one can estimate how many people were killed. It is believed that new quarters must be found for about 150,000 to 200,000. I don't know at this writing how we are going to solve that problem.

A serious crisis seems to be developing in Italy. That is perhaps the reason why the enemy is not particularly active in Sicily. Most likely he wants to await developments in the hope of attaining his objectives without high and bloody losses. The Pope is said to be playing an important role in the development of this crisis.

In the United States there is much dissatisfaction with the Committee for a Free Germany formed in Moscow. This committee has created a sensation in the enemy press. The deduction is made that the Soviets are determined that if anybody is to inherit authority in Europe, especially in Germany, it must be themselves.

Stalin has issued an order of the day to the Red Army claiming that this year's summer offensive of the German Wehrmacht failed. The German Wehrmacht had not been able to make a decisive breakthrough. The Soviets were again in the positions in which they were surprised by the German offensive. The German Wehrmacht no longer had the power, as in previous summers, to compel the Soviets to yield sizable territory. Unfortunately the theses expounded by Stalin in his order of the day are, for the most part, correct. His claim that we lost rather than gained ground near Kursk is also in keeping with the facts. This shows that we must make every effort on the Eastern Front to hold our own even halfway against the advancing Soviets. I suppose we can't possibly change the situation by offensive operations as has been the case the past two summers.

During the entire afternoon news kept pouring into Dresden. All of it was calculated to give us many a worry and headache. I was happy to return to Berlin again in the evening. . . . Gutterer awaited me at the railway station. He gave me a first report on Hamburg. Developments there have been very tragic. Air warfare is our most vulnerable point.

When I reached my home I was immediately called by telephone from the Fuehrer's GHQ. The news from there sounds almost unbelievable. It is to the effect that the Duce has resigned, and that Badoglio has taken over in Italy in his place. The whole situation, I was informed, was still very obscure; such news as we received had come over the radio and was given out by Reuter. At GHQ nobody can figure out just what has really happened. The Fuehrer wants me to proceed immediately to his headquarters. He wishes there to evaluate the situation with his closest collaborators. . . .

[Marshal Pietro Badoglio, born, 1881, was chief of the Italian armed forces (with interruptions) from 1919 to 1940. After the Ethiopian campaign he was awarded the title of Duke of Addis Ababa.]

We received news to the effect that there was violent opposition in the Fascist Grand Council to Mussolini, his policies, and his conduct of the war. The main figures in this fight were Ciano and Grandi. They criticized the Duce and his policies in an extremely bitter manner. Unfortunately Farinacci was also involved, but from quite another viewpoint. He had been prevailed upon to criticize Mussolini, but wanted to give the whole attack a Fascist trend. He failed to prevail and thereby did great harm to the Fascist cause.

[Dino Grandi was one of Mussolini's earliest adherents, and was successively Minister of Justice, Minister for Foreign Affairs, and Ambassador to Great Britain. He was also a member of the Fascist Grand Council and took a leading part in the rebellion against Mussolini's leadership which led to his arrest and dismissal by King Victor Emmanuel.]

The King, too, addressed an appeal to the public. The noteworthy thing in this appeal is a sentence stating that Italy remains true to her tradition and her word. You can't do much with that! There are reports of demonstrations of fidelity to the new government in Rome. Personally I believe that, for the present at least, the end of Fascism has come. By his lack of initiative and his too patient waiting, Mussolini has permitted the opposition to grow. His frequent "changes of guard" have robbed him of any real and loyal following.

We can't tell as yet how things will develop. In any case it is well for us to be prepared for anything and everything.

I tried to get one or two hours' sleep before starting on my trip.

July 27, 1943

I arrived at the Tempelhof airdrome early. Dr. Dietrich flew with me to GHQ. He, too, was tremendously distressed about events in Italy. He developed a series of theories that seemed somewhat far-fetched and unconvincing. As long as we have no more exact information about what actually happened in Rome than what has come through thus far, we can venture no opinion. At the moment we don't even know what the revolution was all about. In any case, following

my instinct and my sound common sense, I believe we may assume that
the Roman camarilla has the intention of getting out of the war in some
elegant manner.

Before I could speak to the Fuehrer I had a talk at GHQ with
Himmler and Bormann. They don't believe Mussolini resigned voluntarily. I, too, regard it as out of the question. I believe the crisis developed in the following manner: As a curtain raiser the radical Fascists
of the type of Farinacci were sent forward to criticize the Duce. That
started things rolling. Badoglio and his henchmen used this occasion
to trip up Mussolini. Presumably he was then called to the Quirinal,
where he was arrested *stante pede* and compelled to resign. It is simply
shocking to think that in this manner a revolutionary movement that
has been in power for twenty-one years could be liquidated.

But this isn't the end yet. I believe there are still some possibilities
left for directing things into a different channel. Both Himmler and
Bormann indulge in the most varied theories. But these are of no real
value, as they are based upon suppositions and not on facts. I look at
the situation somewhat more realistically. According to the reports thus
far available, I believe I can assume that the Duce actually had lost
most of his authority with the Italian people. It is always true that as
soon as a dictator has fallen, the man in the street is heard from. I suppose, therefore, we won't have to wait long before this happens in Italy.

At ten o'clock, together with Goering, I had my first talk with the
Fuehrer. The Fuehrer impressed us with his quiet self-assurance and
his sovereign superiority. Although the events in Italy made a deep
impression upon him, they in nowise succeeded in throwing him off his
equilibrium. On the contrary, his brain was already at work feverishly
formulating and preparing new decisions. Half an hour later Ribbentrop, who had come by plane from Fuschl, joined in this decisive discussion. He had just come through an attack of pneumonia and was
still in a very weakened condition.

The Fuehrer first gave us his analysis of the situation. He was convinced the Duce had not resigned voluntarily. He had been arrested.
Nobody could know whether he was still alive. Personally I don't
believe that Badoglio and his henchmen laid violent hands on him. The
Fuehrer, too, believes the crisis was provoked by the session of the
Fascist Grand Council. Farinacci had behaved there like a clumsy bear
and, possibly with the best of will and the noblest of intentions, had
played a role that proved fatal. Then, after the Fascist Grand Council
had hurled its criticism at the Duce, the Crown had entered the picture. The whole coup had undoubtedly been prepared for a long time,

and Farinacci had merely played a decidedly minor role [*Chargenrolle*] in this high drama. Undoubtedly the Duce was no longer a free man, nor could he make any decisions. That meant Fascism was in mortal danger. If there was any possibility for us to avert this danger, it must be seized upon. Italian Free Masonry undoubtedly stood in the background of the whole development; though dissolved it still exists clandestinely. The Masons wanted to wreak revenge on Mussolini and deliver a crushing blow to the authoritarian conception of the state. The Italian King was too foolish and shortsighted to understand this development. He was not only physically but spiritually and morally completely in Badoglio's hands. Badoglio was the head of the camarilla which was now bent upon bringing down Fascism and everything it had created in the way of historical values.

In the final analysis this crisis was of course directed against Germany. The idea was to take Italy out of the war in order thereby to create an exceptionally dangerous situation for the Reich. Undoubtedly the English and the Americans sponsored this crisis. The Fuehrer was firmly convinced that Badoglio had already negotiated with the enemy before he took these decisive steps. The assertion in his proclamation that the war would continue meant exactly nothing. There was nothing else he could say, for any statement to the contrary would immediately have called the German Wehrmacht into action, and Italy would then have become a theater of war after all—a thing she is now trying to avoid. The English would certainly try to land at the most opportune moment, possibly in Genoa, in order to cut off the German troops stationed in southern Italy. We must anticipate this, he said.

The Fuehrer intends to deliver a great coup. In this manner: A parachute division now stationed in southern France is to land all around Rome. This parachute division is to occupy Rome, arrest the King with his entire family, as well as Badoglio and his henchmen, and fly them to Germany. Once we have the King, Badoglio, and all the men behind the scenes in our hands, the whole situation will naturally be changed completely.

I don't think the Fuehrer is right in believing in the possibility that the Duce is already dead. My hunch is that the hostile camarilla in Rome has taken him into custody so that he can't make himself heard. In any case we believe we shall get more detailed news from Farinacci. Farinacci, on learning that he was to be arrested—incidentally the payoff for his clumsy behavior—is reported to have gone to the German Embassy where he was handed over to Kesselring. Early Monday morning he was then flown from Rome to Munich in a German plane and was now on his way to GHQ. The Fuehrer intends to use Farinacci for setting up an Italian countergovernment. This countergovernment is to be in power and supported by us so long as we can't get hold of the Duce. Personally I doubt whether the Duce would be willing to form a countergovernment against the King. Of course if the King were in our hands this possibility, too, could be envisaged.

In order to create immediate possibilities for publicity and propaganda, I had a number of broadcasting stations in southern France changed over into illegal stations on orders of the Fuehrer. The stations involved are Toulouse, Bordeaux, and Monte Carlo. Farinacci might use these broadcasting stations to address the Italian public in case he proves serviceable for our purposes. But we shall first have to wait and see what attitude Farinacci assumes.

According to the reports reaching us the Vatican is developing feverish diplomatic activity. Undoubtedly it is standing behind the revolt [against Mussolini] with its great world-embracing facilities. The Fuehrer at first intended, when arresting the responsible men in Rome, to seize the Vatican also, but Ribbentrop and I opposed the plan most emphatically. I don't believe it necessary to break into the Vatican, and, on the other hand, I would regard such a measure as exceptionally unfortunate because of the effect our measures would have on the whole of world opinion.

Despite the fact that every hour brings us additional news, often of a conflicting character, the whole crisis is still hard to understand.

News reports at noon stated that the scum of the streets is beginning to take a hand. That is understandable and was expected by us. The insignia of Fascism were publicly removed; a Mussolini Street was rechristened Matteotti Street. The masses moved through the streets of the Italian capital, hailed the King and Badoglio, and stormily demanded peace. That is a development we welcome heartily. The more things are at sixes and sevens in Italy, the better it is for the measures we are planning. The fact that the demonstrations are in favor of Badoglio is a sign that in all likelihood he himself arranged them. Of course he will have to see to it that they don't get out of hand and that he does not experience the truth of the proverb that spirits once called up often can't be recalled.

Undoubtedly the Italian people have a deep yearning for peace. It now depends on how you talk to them. If an austere and manly appeal were addressed to the Italian public, it would undoubtedly have the same effect as an appeal to defeatism and compromise. That the official insignia [*Liktorenbuendel*] have been torn down and that the mob is storming the Fascist party offices are proof that Badoglio intends to liquidate everything connected with the Fascist revolution.

Aside from his hostility to Fascism he is undoubtedly trying to curry favor with the enemy. That proves that one must not pay too much attention to his statement that the war will continue. This whole episode is the greatest example of perfidy in modern history. The Fuehrer is firmly determined to see to it that Italy does not betray the German Reich a second time.

[Hitler here refers to Italy's abandoning the Austro-German-Italian alliance during World War I and joining the Allies. Despite Hitler's efforts the Italians finally declared war on Germany again.]

In the morning Mackensen called on Badoglio. Badoglio once more underscored the contents of his appeal without, however, giving it special emphasis or making new pledges. To Mackensen, too, he declared that the war would continue, but said nothing as to how or in what form, and especially not in what relationship to the Reich and the German Wehrmacht.

In the late afternoon he received Kesselring. Kesselring was favorably impressed. He believes Badoglio actually intends to continue the war with all the military means at Italy's disposal. Very evidently Kesselring fell for a well-staged show. Generals are usually much too unpolitical to understand the background of such a scene. Kesselring is convinced there is no reason to worry much at present.

Again and again reports reached us that the Pope is feverishly at work during this entire crisis.

First of all we took stock of the troops we still have in Italy. There are none too many, but if we reinforce them energetically we can still expect some success, considering the weakness of the Italian armed forces. Difficulties would arise only if the Italians decided to take up their positions on the Brenner Pass and to defend them, to cut off bridges, streets, and tunnels, and thus prevent us from moving. The situation in southern Tyrol is very critical.

Quite gratuitously there was a day raid of two hundred enemy planes on Hanover with very damaging results, owing chiefly to the fact that the fire department had just been loaned to Hamburg. There was therefore almost nothing that could be done about the heavy conflagration that started. I ordered the Hanover fire department back from Hamburg immediately.

It is quite obvious that the German people are uneasy and deeply distressed because we can't tell them anything at present about the background of the Italian crisis. What are we to tell them, anyway? We can't say, much less write, what we think personally. Anything we can write will fail to explain the Italian crisis to our people. We must therefore be satisfied for the present with publishing the momentous news without telling the people that the question at issue in Rome is not only Mussolini's resignation but a very profound organic and ideological crisis of Fascism, perhaps even its liquidation. Knowledge of these events might conceivably encourage some subversive elements in Germany to think they could put over the same thing here that Badoglio and his henchmen accomplished in Rome. The Fuehrer ordered Himmler to see to it that most severe police measures be applied in case such a danger seemed imminent here. He doesn't believe, however, that much is to be expected along that line. The German people are much too hostile to the Italians to regard the crisis in Rome as a precedent. And anyway, the common people have long anticipated and expected what is now happening in Rome.

The big question during our conference in the Fuehrer's GHQ is whether the measures planned against the Badoglio clique and Italian treachery should be prepared with great care, which would certainly require a week, or whether it is necessary to act quickly and by improvisation. The Fuehrer would naturally like to act as quickly as possible. That is undoubtedly right. The situation in Italy is as yet not so consolidated that one might not reverse it by an improvised stroke. Rommel, on the other hand, as an experienced soldier is more conservative in estimating the possibilities. He would prefer that preparations be made on a more permanent basis, with a certain probability of success. The Fuehrer placed Rommel in supreme command of the operations of the OKW to be taken in Italy. Keitel and Jodl fought hard against his making Rommel at the same time also supreme commander of our troops in Sicily. They don't like to give him too much power and too many troops, as they are jealous of him. That, however, is no reason for not doing what's necessary, and the Fuehrer therefore decided to place Rommel in supreme command of our troops in Italy.

Until noon it wasn't possible to get a clear picture of the situation in Rome. The news reaching us was contradictory. . . .

After our conference with the Fuehrer I discussed the situation with a number of people. Speer views developments anything but lightly. While on the one hand he is rather glad that we shall now probably not have to deliver as much coal and iron to Italy as before, on the other hand he realizes quite clearly what a tremendous psychological effect the defection of Italy from our front will have. . . .

At noon I had to withdraw for a little rest. I had slept hardly at all during the night. I rather imagine the afternoon and evening are going to be very hot.

At lunch we were all gathered about the Fuehrer. Besides myself, Goering, Ribbentrop, Rommel, Doenitz, Speer, Keitel, and Bormann. The top political and military leaders of the Reich here had an opportunity to talk the entire situation over once more. This conference developed nothing unusual. Generally speaking the men present saw the situation as the Fuehrer analyzed it. . . . All agreed that something decisive must be done. If we were to succeed in changing the whole situation by a bold coup, our prestige would of course grow tremendously. We must, however, realize that the measures planned by the Fuehrer involve exceptional dangers and a unique risk. But our situation is such that it can be changed only by decisions fraught with danger.

The Fuehrer again expressed his conviction that the Duce had undoubtedly been arrested. I think there can hardly be any question about it. That, of course, poses the question whether Fascism still has enough vitality left to be saved by generous measures on the part of the Reich. According to the information thus far available this seems to be possible only to a limited degree. Be that as it may, the actions of the Italian royal house show what is to be expected of monarchs. The monarchs and the aristocrats are always conspicuous for their provoking ingratitude. Just to think of all the Italian King owes to the Duce and how he now kicks him out! [*Wie schickt er ihn nun in die Wueste!*]

From all over the country we receive reports reflecting the concern of the German people over the Italian crisis. Some sections of the population are almost in a state of panic. The people demand information, and wish the Fuehrer would speak. Naturally he can't do that at the moment. The people will have to wait exactly as we must wait for further developments in the crisis.

The most outlandish rumors have been spread about Goering. It is claimed he has fled, has committed suicide, and things like that. It would be a good thing if Goering undertook something that would at least make him visible to the public.

Farinacci has arrived. The Fuehrer first had Ribbentrop give him a treatment.

Prince Philip of Hesse, who happens to be at GHQ, is to be kept out of the picture as far as possible. The Fuehrer therefore instructed me to take charge of him personally. Prince Philip told me some intimate details about Italian society. I gather that the Roman aristocracy is absolutely opposed to Mussolini. Only five days before the crisis, the Italian Crown Prince told Prince Philip that Mussolini must really be regarded as a criminal. The whole Roman aristocracy blames the crisis on Mussolini's inactivity. It does indeed seem as though the Duce had made a number of fatal mistakes. He is reproached most for simply having let things drift. That, however, is no reason for casting to the winds a twenty-one-year-old revolutionary work of reconstruction of historical significance. The Roman aristocracy without a doubt seized upon this favorable moment to join with the Free Masons in getting rid of the hated dictator.

What Prince Philip of Hesse told me about Mussolini is more in the nature of court gossip than serious political criticism. But Prince Philip's account proves that in Germany we can't depend upon our princes either. Thank God the Fuehrer's view on this is the same as mine; in fact, much more radical.

[Prince Philip of Hesse was married in 1925 to Princess Mafalda, daughter of King Victor Emmanuel of Italy. He was the Nazi district governor for the province of Hesse-Nassau, and had the rank of an SA *Obergruppenfuehrer* (General).]

Farinacci was received by Ribbentrop and then by the Fuehrer. He behaved very unwisely during these talks. The Fuehrer expected he would express his profound regret at developments and at least stand unreservedly by the Duce. This, however, he did not do. His report to the Fuehrer consisted mainly in severe criticism of the personality and conduct of the Duce. As he described events, the Duce was violently attacked by Ciano, Grandi, and several other defeatists during the session of the Fascist Grand Council. Farinacci, as I have already pointed out, found fault with him more from the viewpoint of Fascist ideology. These criticisms upset the Duce terribly. Farinacci, together with Scorza, later that Sunday conferred at length with the Duce. The Duce was then called to the Quirinal but failed to return.

[Carlo Scorza, Italian journalist and politician, was at this time secretary of the Fascist party.]

This description by Farinacci proves that our interpretation is right. Farinacci still believes that the King acted loyally toward Mussolini, and that the Duce resigned voluntarily; but how then is one to explain that Mussolini, before driving to the Quirinal, knew and foresaw nothing of this whole development, gave not the slightest intimation of his decision to resign, and then failed to return? It looks to me as though that clumsy fool Farinacci had been coaxed into taking part in a knavish plot of the Italian aristocracy and Free Masonry, and now, of course, does not want to admit his guilt, even though it was involuntary.

From the Fuehrer's talk with Farinacci it is evident that this man cannot be used by us on any grand scale. Nevertheless we are making sure of keeping control of him. The Fuehrer handed him over to Himmler to look after for the present.

Farinacci is a completely broken man. It is gradually dawning on him that he managed to put his foot in it. He was to have been arrested immediately when the crisis broke out. But he saw the men who were to seize him standing before his house when he returned from swimming at Ostia, and hastened to the German Embassy. He came without a hat, dressed in the lightest of summer suits, and his brown face still reflected something of the sun of Ostia. . . .

His last talk with the Duce was exceedingly characteristic. The Duce had not given the slightest indication of expecting the development that was then in the making quite secretly, in typical Masonic fashion. The Duce was, however, deeply shaken by the scenes enacted at the Fascist Grand Council.

Meanwhile Badoglio took exceptionally severe measures. Martial law was declared throughout Italy. No more than three people may walk or stand together in public. Houses must be kept unlocked at night. The curfew hour begins at 8 P.M. and lasts until 5 A.M.

Badoglio's measures are typically bourgeois. They may do as a transition, but can't be kept up permanently. I imagine Badoglio is going to install a regime similar to that of Franco, or even of Primo de Rivera. Whether he can thereby avert the danger threatening the Italian people remains to be seen.

[Miguel Primo de Rivera was the founder of the Spanish *Falange Española Tradicionalista*.]

The new Cabinet was installed. We know only two men. First there is Guariglia, until now Italian Ambassador at Ankara. He is the man who most likely has already negotiated with the enemy.

[Raffaele Guariglia, born, 1889, was Italian Ambassador in Paris, 1938–40; Ambassador to the Vatican, 1942–43.]

Then there is Rocco, Minister of Education. I know him from my numerous meetings with the various Italian ministers of education.

[Guido Rocco, born, 1886, after a long diplomatic career became Mussolini's Director General of the Foreign Press Service from 1936–43.]

Rocco was always regarded as the "Gray Eminence"; I never trusted him across the street. The rest of the Cabinet consists only of bureaucrats and military officers. With a Cabinet like that you can of course do something, but it will certainly not prove equal to a grandiose and daring coup on our part. If I were to try to imagine the composition of the Cabinet in terms of German politics, I should say it was as if Ministerial Director Greiner were made Minister of Propaganda. We would have an easy time with him as an adversary.

[The "Gray Eminence" was the sobriquet for a German official named Baron Friedrich von Holstein who played a much-debated role in the days of Prince Buelow and his immediate successors from 1906 on. He was an able, hard-working high official of the German Foreign Office who shunned publicity but loved power. He was the moving spirit behind Kaiser Wilhelm II's Morocco policy, which headed Imperial Germany for war. In the Hitler regime Martin Bormann developed a similar lust for anonymity and power, and was nicknamed the "Gray Eminence" by Old Guard Nazis.
Greiner was one of Goebbels's many handy men, none of whom had brains enough ever to constitute a potential danger to their chief.]

The decisive thing, of course, is whether Fascism or the Duce has any intention whatever of doing anything about the situation that has now developed. Mackensen sent us a letter from the Duce in which he expresses his thanks to Badoglio for the courteous treatment accorded him. He was still as loyal to the royal house as he had been during his twenty-one years of service to it. He was happy about Badoglio's declaration that the war would continue on the side of Italy's allies. He would like to be taken to Rocca della Camminata to do nothing but rest.

It is hard to tell whether this letter is forged or genuine. If genuine, it would be an eloquent indication that the Duce no longer has any intention of interfering with developments. On the other hand one must, of course, realize that this can't be determined with certainty. Should a German coup create an entirely new set of circumstances in Italy, the Duce would surely be ready to take an active hand again.

I had a long talk with Guderian. He told me about his grave concern over the present status of the war. He pleaded for concentration at some point. We can't afford to be active on all fronts. He complained about the inactivity of the OKW. There wasn't a real leader anywhere there. . . . Guderian again made an excellent impression. He is certainly an ardent and unquestioning disciple of the Fuehrer.

The Fuehrer was extremely busy all evening. He received one of us after the other. He was therefore very tired by evening and dined alone. A large group of us dined together but without him. At this dinner table the wildest conjectures and illusions were aired about developments in Italy. I have an idea that the gentlemen don't yet quite realize the seriousness of the situation. . . .

At night there was another conference with the Fuehrer. He once more developed his view that action against Italy or against the rebellious camarilla must be undertaken as quickly as possible. Rommel thinks this action should be prepared adequately and upon mature reflection. The debate lasted until far after midnight. Unfortunately it led to no final result as the number of participants was too large; about thirty-five persons took part. I sided with the Fuehrer. I, too, believe that at present you can accomplish much more with a small force than will be possible a week later with greater forces and after more careful preparation. The Fuehrer is right in claiming that success is the more certain the sooner one acts. The measures proposed by the military seem to me to be faulty in that they don't take into account what the enemy is going to do. Undoubtedly the English won't wait a week while we consider and prepare for action.

All of us, including the Fuehrer, now agree that the Vatican is to be exempted from the measures we are contemplating. A coup by parachute troops would certainly be successful if carried out within the next twenty-four hours. Personally I doubt whether the Duce is willing to sponsor such a policy as we have in mind. But I suppose we will get more information on that during the next few days.

Our conferences lasted far beyond midnight. I was completely exhausted when they ended. Dead tired I fell into my bed and slept a dreamless sleep.

July 28, 1943

Official [Italian] communiqués already speak of the "dissolved" Fascist party—a proof that Badoglio and the Royal House intend to tear up Fascism by its very roots. The *Giornale d'Italia* which, like all important Italian newspapers, has an entirely new editorial staff, reports the last session of the Grand Council. According to this report Grandi and Ciano were especially severe in criticizing the Duce, his policies, and his conduct of the war. In the vote which followed only eight ballots were for the Duce, two were blank, and eighteen against him. I take it that this report just about corresponds to the facts. A resolution was adopted appealing to the solidarity of the Italian people and announcing the decision to return power to the Crown. It's difficult to imagine anything sillier and more unrevolutionary. I can hardly assume that this report is fully accurate. No doubt it has been falsified by Badoglio and his henchmen for home consumption.

In the morning news reached us that Churchill intends to speak in the House of Commons. This old rogue [*dieser alte Gauner*] will no doubt ride triumphantly on his high horse.

It is very regrettable indeed that Mussolini's resignation gave world Fascism such a heavy blow. After all it was his movement that gave a name to the doctrine of the authoritarian state. I can hardly imagine that Fascism has thereby ceased to be a fact.

The Italian editorials available at noon are downright malicious. They talk about twenty years of slavery, and the creatures who now occupy editorial chairs hasten to assert that at last they feel free again. This freedom consists in being able to offer capitulation to the enemy.

The building of the *Popolo d'Italia* in Milan has been stormed. The Fascist insignia are being removed throughout the country. The political prisoners are being liberated. It won't be long before the criminals, too, will be freed.

Franco has instructed his press to register events in Italy without commentary and to be strictly neutral. This would-be big shot and inflated peacock owes it to the Duce alone that he is sitting on his pretender's throne.

The last raid on Essen has brought about 100 per cent stoppage of production in the Krupp Works. Speer is much concerned and worried about it.

The idea in the heads of enemies of our regime, that an authoritarian state can be overthrown in this manner [i.e., as happened in Italy] is, of course, a very dangerous one. These shortsighted elements fail to consider that conditions in Italy simply cannot be compared with those in the Reich.

At noon I had another long talk with the Fuehrer. He is firmly determined to act, no matter what the cost, preferably by clever improvisation rather than by too systematic preparations that begin late and allow things to become consolidated in Italy. He is tremendously disappointed in Farinacci. He expected to see an enthusiastic follower of the Duce and in reality met a broken man, who tries to slander the Duce by criticizing him in a tearful voice. With a fellow like that you naturally can't do much. I fear the Fuehrer entertained grave illusions about Farinacci. Today he is still entertaining illusions about the Duce and the possibilities of a Fascist comeback. Let us hope military events will support these illusions.

The Fuehrer has the right slant on the King. He sees in him a weakling, who is senile and decrepit and easily won over by any group offering him support.

Alfieri's whereabouts is still in doubt. Most likely Alfieri, too, voted against the Duce. That fits his character exactly. He has always been a clerical and a royalist. I don't believe he remained loyal to the Duce.

The Italian yellow press is now bubbling over with froth and foam. It makes one red in the face with shame to read it. We shall at the proper moment have to do some house cleaning there and mete out severe justice. Anyway, we now know what we have to do in our own country to prevent such a contingency for all time.

I requested the Fuehrer to let me return to Berlin as I have the feeling that a man of authority should be there at this critical time. The Fuehrer agreed. He will keep me informed by telephone and if necessary call me back to GHQ.

People are clamoring more and more insistently for an authoritative person, preferably the Fuehrer himself, to speak. But what can one say in the present situation? Events in Italy are still in a state of flux and we naturally can't say anything about the steps we are taking. I am extremely happy over the equanimity with which the Fuehrer judges the situation and our possibilities for mastering it. I firmly believe he will master it. At our parting he was exceptionally friendly and charming to me. I believe I can be a very strong support for him in these critical times.

I am somewhat confused about the results of our conferences. We are doing too much on the military and too little on the political side of the war. At this moment, when our military successes are none too great, it would be a good thing if we knew how to make better use of the political instrument. We were so great and resourceful along that line at the time of our struggle for power; why shouldn't we achieve mastery in this art now? The English owe most of their successes to their virtuosity in handling political possibilities. I am sure we could prove equal to them if only we made use of the facilities available to us.

Himmler told me something about a question that is rather secondary; namely, that of the International Bible Students. These Bible Students are a queer mixture of contemporaries living outside our time. Their refusal to bear arms is usually not because of cowardice, but a matter of principle. That's why Himmler rightly takes this view: Objectors to military service who are beyond draft age should be put behind bars so that they cannot proselytize; objectors to military service, however, who are of draft age, should be condemned to death for cowardice and desertion. Some of them accept the death penalty with absolute stoicism. The older Bible Students are giving an excellent account of themselves in concentration camps and are exceptionally able and dependable workers; they give us the least trouble of anybody there.

[The International Bible Students were a small sect claiming to be serious searchers into the verities of Holy Script. The conception of the "conscientious objector" was unknown to the Nazis.]

After finishing my work I drove to the airport at Rastenburg. A wonderful day. I can only shake my head at the folly of human beings who wage war where nature is so beautiful. After a flight of almost three hours we returned to Berlin.

We are having a lot of trouble about the relationship between German and Italian workers. The German workers wouldn't think of fraternizing with the Italians; on the contrary, there have been frequent fist fights. In 1918 it would undoubtedly have been different.

July 29, 1943

During the night we had the heaviest raid yet made on Hamburg. The English appeared over the city with 800 to 1,000 bombers. Our anti-aircraft succeeded in shooting down only very few so that one cannot claim any serious losses by the enemy.

Kaufmann gave me a first report on the effect of the British air raid. He spoke of a catastrophe the extent of which simply staggers the imagination. A city of a million inhabitants has been destroyed in a manner unparalleled in history. We are faced with problems that are almost impossible of solution. Food must be found for this population of a million. Shelter must be secured. The people must be evacuated as far as possible. They must be given clothing. In short, we are facing problems there of which we had no conception even a few weeks ago. Kaufmann believes the entire city must be evacuated except for small patches. He spoke of about 800,000 homeless people who are wandering up and down the streets not knowing what to do. I believe Kaufmann has lost his nerve somewhat in the face of this undoubtedly exceptional situation. Maybe he is a bit too lyrical and romantic for so great a catastrophe. . . .

I immediately summoned Berndt. He has already started a number of measures, and has, for instance, in the course of the morning begun moving 300,000 loaves of bread to Hamburg.

In addition to our great concern about this catastrophe we have increasing worries about developments in Italy. The parties in power in Rome have now issued a declaration which is quite a retreat in our favor. It is declared that Italian foreign policy will remain absolutely unchanged; that Italy stands by her pledged word; that the resignation of the Duce is only of domestic significance. As Knight of the Order of Annunciata the Duce retains the privileges of his rank. No decision has as yet been made about the final fate of the Fascist party. . . .

I don't believe that the growing revolutionary sentiment in Italy can be checked with bourgeois-military declarations of this sort. Other measures would have to be taken to accomplish that. The fact is that the barrier that stood in the way of Italy's downfall has been demolished. Just as when a dam breaks down, we now see floods of dirt sweep into the open country.

The *Corriere della Sera* contained a detailed report about the session of the Fascist Grand Council from which stemmed the outbreak of the crisis. It reports that industrialists, intellectuals, and high royal officials waited in a well-known hotel while the Grand Council was in session to learn the results. At the same time troops were already set in motion in the Italian capital. Grandi was the leader of the opposition in the session. It was he who formulated the declaration against the Duce and insisted upon a vote. De Bono, De Vecchi, Bottai, and Federzoni had taken his side. I assume Alfieri was also on the side of the rebels; that would be in character for him. Undoubtedly he regretted that he could not deposit three ballots, one with "yes," one with "no," and one with "I abstain." Scorza and Polverelli are reputed as having stayed on the Duce's side to the end.

[Emilio Giuseppe Gaspari Giovanni de Bono was commander in chief of the Italian troops in Africa in 1935; Marshal of Italy and Minister of State; and Inspector of Italian overseas forces in 1939.

Count Cesare Maria de Vecchi was president of the first Fascist group in the Italian parliament of 1921–22 and a permanent member of the Fascist Grand Council. He was a lecturer on modern history at the University of Turin.

Giuseppe Bottai was Italian Minister of Education, 1936–43. He had previously been Minister of Corporations, Governor of Rome, and Civil Governor of Addis-Ababa.

Luigi Federzoni had been Italian Minister of Colonies, Minister of the Interior, President of the Senate, and President of the Royal Academy.

Gaetano Polverelli was president of the Journalists Insurance Institution, also Minister of Propaganda from February to July 1943.]

According to reports from Rome efforts are under way to bring back the Italian workers from the Reich. We suppressed the beginning of manifestations of unrest among these workers by suitable measures; that was not very difficult.

There has been a complete about-face in the Italian press. The Fascist journalists have been fired and in their places have been put half Jews and Free Masons—in short, all those old scoundrels whom we knew only too well in the period of our struggle. They will see to it that developments in Italy are headed for chaos.

The Japanese military mission in Berlin has given me a memorandum on our present military situation. The Japanese military men believe we ought, under no circumstances, to give up Sicily. The loss of Sicily would create a totally new military situation. The Japanese urge that extraordinary measures be taken. They declare that if they were in a similar situation, they would operate with suicide torpedoes and suicide fliers so as to deliver a devastating blow to the English Mediterranean fleet. I, too, believe that it is necessary to do something beyond the normal. You cannot master the present situation with normal measures.

A great deal of unrest has been created in Berlin by the manner in which the evacuating of certain Berlin public offices has been handled. By drawing thousands of people into discussion and consideration of this problem, not only have our real plans become known, but also mere suggestions. The Berliners therefore believe that in case more serious air raids were to occur, the government would be the first to run away. Naturally there can be no thought of that. I have therefore started propaganda by word of mouth to offset it.

Recapitulation of events between July 30 and September 8, 1943

Goebbels's diary entries for the last two days of July, the entire month of August, and the first seven days of September 1943 are missing. Here, briefly, is what happened during this period:

On July 30 President Roosevelt warned the neutrals not to give asylum to any "war criminals." Sweden reacted by canceling the permission to Germany to send troops in transit through Sweden on their way to Finland and Norway.

By August 17 the Allies could announce that all of Sicily was now in the hands of the Americans, the British, and the French, after thirty-eight days of fighting. The German troops had pulled out five days earlier.

Sweeping onward, the Western Allies established a bridgehead in Calabria on September 3, thereby for the first time gaining a permanent foothold on the European continent. The new Badoglio government realized on August 14 that further resistance was useless, and declared Rome an open city; on September 8 it surrendered unconditionally.

The German offensive in the Orel-Kursk-Belgorod region, started July 5, bogged down, with the result that the Soviet armies recaptured Orel and Belgorod on August 5. They also recaptured Kharkov on August 23, Taganrog on August 30, and Stalino in the Donetz Basin on September 8.

Winston Churchill arrived in Quebec, Canada, to meet President Roosevelt for further war conferences. The American President rather surprisingly turned up with Secretary of the Treasury Henry Morgenthau as his principal adviser, and the so-called "Morgenthau Plan" for Germany was agreed upon whereby Germany was to be reduced to a mere farming country—a plan that was discarded during the Truman administration as impractical and unworkable.

In their communiqué on the Quebec conference the two statesmen emphasized their hope for early Anglo-American-Russian parleys. British Minister of Information Brendan Bracken took occasion on August 29 to brand all rumors of a separate peace between the U.S.S.R. and Germany as "fifth-column propaganda."

During this short period occurred two American air raids of the first magnitude—one on the Ploesti oil fields of Rumania on August 1 and one on Berlin on August 23, of which it was claimed that the fires were visible two hundred miles away. The Nazi Government found it necessary during this period to evacuate from Berlin all persons not essential to the war effort of the capital.

To curb rising unrest within the Reich, Hitler, on August 24, supplanted the elderly Minister of the Interior, Wilhelm Frick, with the tough, stern, sadistic Heinrich Himmler, chief of the German police and the dreaded Gestapo, as well as *Reichsfuehrer* of the black-uniformed SS.

September 1943

BRITISH AND CANADIAN TROOPS INVADE ITALIAN MAINLAND. ITALY SURRENDERS UNCONDITIONALLY. ROME SHELLED AND OCCUPIED BY GERMAN TROOPS. MAJOR PART OF ITALIAN FLEET SURRENDERS TO ALLIES. ALLIED 5TH ARMY CAPTURES SALERNO. MUSSOLINI FREED BY PARACHUTE TROOPS. RUSSIANS RECAPTURE NOVOROSSIISK AND BRYANSK. MUSSOLINI IN RADIO ADDRESS DENOUNCES ITALIAN KING AND BADOGLIO. FRENCH LAND ON CORSICA. MUSSOLINI SETS UP NEW GOVERNMENT. SUMNER WELLES RESIGNS. FLYING FORTRESSES BLAST EMDEN. RUSSIANS RECAPTURE SMOLENSK AND ROSLAVL.

September 8, 1943

The air raids on Stuttgart and Strasbourg were not too bad. Besides, the number of planes downed was so large that the Americans most likely will once again be busy licking their wounds. The night attack on Munich, too, can be regarded as only moderate. . . .

In Berlin the situation has become completely normal. Transportation is functioning again, and the damage to industrial plants, while serious, can nevertheless be repaired slowly. While it is true that in some factories there is still a 50 to 80 per cent stoppage of production, Petzke nevertheless hopes to make up for it within a short time.

The situation in Rheydt is pretty hopeless. I telephoned to Doemens. He reported to me that the textile industry in Rheydt has almost completely ceased production. Eighty per cent of the downtown area was destroyed.

[Doemens is nowhere identified more closely in the Goebbels diaries, but was probably a gau functionary.]

Grohé told me that life in Cologne had again become halfway normal despite the ruins. . . . He had only favorable things to report about the morale of the population. Morale, of course, depends very much upon how quickly air raids succeed each other. When a city is forced into air-raid shelters night after night, nerves give way after a certain time.

Grohé again pleaded with me for two types of night alerts, but I am unable to prevail upon the Fuehrer in this matter. . . . Lack of sleep is sometimes more difficult to bear than the damage inflicted by the enemy. Fatigue, especially, affects productive capacity—a thing that is anything but pleasant for Speer.

Churchill is to be regarded as nothing but a muddlehead when it comes to questions of a future order and an international regime. On the other hand, he is undoubtedly the right man for England for the practical conduct of the war.

The Fuehrer is still convinced that the English and Americans are merely carrying out a camouflage maneuver in Calabria. He believes they will shortly try an invasion in the West. The increasing concentration of air attacks in the West and certain accumulations of shipping units in the harbors of the mother country [England] seem to point in this direction. . . . But the Fuehrer is on the lookout. He doesn't, under any circumstances, want to be surprised by Churchill and Roosevelt.

[The invasion did not come until nine months later.]

The Italian press hardly mentions the war any more, a fact which even the small neutral countries are commenting on with indignation. It is concerned with the fight against Fascism. The Italians can hardly offer a more degrading spectacle to the world than that. . . .

But all these lesser worries disappear in the face of our great anxiety about the Eastern Front. The Soviets have reported enormous successes because of the capture of Makejewka, Konstantinovka, Kramatorskaja, Slavyansk, and Konotop. While the reports are not quite accurate, there is much truth in all of them. Obviously Stalin still has the intention of going all out this summer, at least in the south and the center of the Eastern Front.

The fall of Konotop is hard for us to take. It may be necessary to engage in larger retreat operations than were originally planned, especially in the Donetz Bulge. The situation has become so critical that the Fuehrer may fly there himself to look after things. In any case, there's once again a full-grown crisis in the East. While I am firmly convinced that the Fuehrer will succeed in mastering it, the energies that must be expended to do so are enormous.

Gernant has reported to me about conditions in Denmark. From his report which he prepared at the request of Best, I gather a situation that must be characterized as critical has arisen because of the somewhat lax and feeble manner in which the Danes were handled by the Reich's Plenipotentiary, Dr. Best. The Danes put a wrong interpretation on the generous treatment accorded them. Especially in Copenhagen events occurred that are more than shocking. German soldiers could hardly appear on the streets; German girls had Swastikas branded on their bodies; acts of sabotage against Wehrmacht barracks and communication installations increased day by day; and the government was neither willing nor in a position to do anything about it. Best was ordered to the Fuehrer's GHQ and given an energetic dressing down. He thereupon had to transfer his powers to the military command. The Danes at first tried to oppose martial law by a few stupid tricks, but when German tanks appeared they quickly became subdued.

[Dr. Karl Rudolf Best, born, 1903, was an old Nazi who was sent to Copenhagen in 1943 to replace Dr. Renthe-Fink as Minister Plenipotentiary. One of Best's first acts, according to the *Von Hassell Diaries*, was to liquidate the "wholly impossible Danish Nazis." Best is credited with the doubtful achievement of having "only" two Danes shot in reprisal for acts of sabotage instead of the five demanded by Hitler.

Gernant, who is not otherwise identified, was probably a Propaganda Ministry official attached to the German Legation at Copenhagen.]

I have the impression that the treatment of populations in the occupied areas is being handled best in the Netherlands. Seyss-Inquart is a master in the art of alternating gingerbread with whippings, and of putting severe measures through with a light touch. One can tell that he had good Hapsburg schooling. The Austrians had to hold their multi-nation state together for centuries. That gave them great experience in the treatment of peoples even in times of crisis.

During the course of the evening critical reports reached us from the Eastern Front that were anything but pleasing. At this stage of developments we are thrown from one scare into another. We are living in a phase of the war in which strategy—to quote Schlieffen—is nothing but a system of substitutions.

[Count Alfred von Schlieffen (1883–1913) was a German field marshal who tried to impress upon his fellow countrymen the importance of General Staff training and the necessity of being prepared for a war on two fronts.]

September 9, 1943

A sensational development took place in Italy in the course of the day. In the morning the British and American papers were already able to report the news—which proves that the Italians have cheated us to beat the band. The Anglo-American press declared that Churchill remained in the United States because he wanted to await this development. It spoke of an Italian intention to capitulate unconditionally.

During the afternoon we received more detailed news, until the actual facts became apparent at 6 P.M., first via the London radio. Without telling us a single word about it in advance, Badoglio has offered unconditional surrender and concluded an armistice with the enemy powers. This armistice is to be effective immediately. Eisenhower, who concluded the armistice, urged the Italians to chase the German troops out of the country.

Toward seven o'clock the Fuehrer telephoned me and requested that I come to GHQ the same night. He is incensed about developments. Only a few hours before his unexampled treachery, Badoglio informed our Counsellor of Legation, Dr. Rudolf Rahn, that he wasn't thinking of leaving the fighting Axis front, and that we would still have occasion to see how an Italian general keeps his word. Well, now we certainly know how he does it!

The Fuehrer, thank God, can rightly claim that he suffered no disappointment on the human side regarding Badoglio. Ever since Mussolini's exit we have anticipated and expected this development. We therefore won't have to make essential changes in our measures. We can now set in motion what the Fuehrer really wanted to do immediately after Mussolini's fall.

The Italians are deserting us in our most critical hour. But I suppose they realize fully that they have thereby chosen the most disgraceful political fate that history can record. They have lost face. Certainly one cannot break one's word twice in the course of a quarter century without smirching one's political honor for all time to come.

In the course of the evening Badoglio addressed a radio appeal to the Italian people. He announced the conclusion of an armistice, declared that firing at the English and Americans must cease (a superfluous order, since all this time they haven't fired at them anyway), but that arms must speak in case Italy were attacked by any other power (doubtless meaning us). That need not scare us. I take it that the Italians who put up their hands in all theaters of war just as soon as they smelled powder will do this also when confronted by German soldiers. . . . Badoglio naturally cannot claim that he yielded to the superior power of the enemy's weapons and armed forces.

Is Stalin really ready to negotiate with Churchill and Roosevelt? The Americans seem exceptionally firm and sure of their ground in so reporting. I can hardly imagine it. A great change must have taken place in Moscow if it is the case. Until now not the slightest signs of it have been discernible anywhere.

The Spanish Government is trying to revise its foreign policy drastically. Franco and the Spanish people no longer believe in German victory and are therefore inclining more and more toward the Anglo-Saxons. The theory now advanced by official Spanish circles is nothing short of funny: They really earnestly believe that, assuming the Reich were no longer the outstanding bulwark against Bolshevism in Europe, the English would award this position to Spain, of all countries! Proceeding from this assumption, Franco thinks that his position vis-à-vis the European powers is a pretty secure one. There is no subterfuge that is too foolish for a cowardly person to use in rationalizing his cowardice! Franco would be surprised at what would happen to him if such a development actually occurred. Be that as it may, we haven't much influence in Spain at present. The Spanish Government has initiated a new press campaign with a twelve-point declaration that inclines more toward the English than the German side. The dirty thing about it is that the Franco Government has not even deemed it necessary to give us any detailed reasons for it. This shows once again that there is nothing worse in politics than weakness.

A Swiss report furnishes me further details about the Duce's fall. The Fascist sub-leaders themselves really brought on the downfall of Fascism. The proverb here applies that infidelity strikes back at its originator. Ciano was the ringleader against his own father-in-law. He is a scoundrel and a contemptible traitor, unique and unparalleled in all history. The King hasn't proven much better. But what else can you expect of a King? The Duce can at most be blamed only for his unsuspecting nature concerning the people around him. Thank God, all conditions obtain here to prevent an occurrence of that sort.

September 10, 1943

A gray day dawned. It rained buckets. Just the right weather, in keeping with this critical day of decision. The impression prevails that a deep resignation pervades the whole country. . . .

When we reached Rastenburg the weather was almost November-like. We drove immediately to GHQ. On the way I was able to discuss a few minor matters with Dr. Naumann. At GHQ there wasn't much life stirring. Everybody had been up until five in the morning. The Fuehrer, too, was still resting, since the exertions of yesterday and last night were naturally enormous.

I first talked over the military situation with General Schmundt. He was somewhat depressed. That is easily understandable. The situation in the East is none too good. The Italian treachery has upset many of our plans. In the field of foreign politics we shall have an extraordinarily big job on our hands to keep our allies in line and to quiet down the neutrals. . . .

The problem begins to present itself as to which side we ought to turn to first—the Muscovite or the Anglo-American. Somehow we must realize clearly that it will be very difficult to wage war successfully against both sides. First of all, of course, we must set our various fronts in order. That, in turn, involves the problem of shortening our fronts. Wherever we now stand, we are represented by weak formations only and it is no soothing thought to imagine the English attacking us at any point they please with relatively small forces. But all these problems can be tackled only after we have succeeded in stabilizing at least the Eastern Front, in re-establishing order in Italy, and in recapturing air supremacy. . . .

The Fuehrer anticipated Italian treason as something absolutely certain. He was really the only one who firmly counted on it. And yet, when it actually happened, it upset him pretty badly. He hadn't thought it possible that this treachery would be committed in such a dishonorable manner.

Hardly had the Fuehrer got up, when he summoned me for a first conference. Contrary to my expectations he looked exceptionally well. It is always to be noted that in times of crisis the Fuehrer rises above himself physically and spiritually. He had had hardly two hours' sleep and now looked as though he had just come from a vacation. He regards the whole Italian problem as a gigantic example of swinishness and realizes clearly that we must exert every effort to master it. But he is also of the opinion that one never knows what the consequences will be in the long run. Something that today looks like a great misfortune may possibly prove a great boon tomorrow. It always turned out during the struggle of our movement and of our state that crises and setbacks, seen historically, were for the best.

On the previous day the Fuehrer had been in Saporoše to restore a semblance of order in the southern sector of our Eastern Front. He was quite favorably impressed, although our situation there is critical and our troops have to fight very hard. But even in the course of the day the Fuehrer was seized with a queer feeling of unrest that drove him back immediately to his GHQ. Hardly had he arrived here and retired than the first distressing news came from Italy. He then went to work at once.

We now began to examine the situation in detail. In the foreground naturally stood the Italian problem. Our Counsellor of Embassy, Rahn, only a few hours before the Italian treachery had had a talk with the Italian King on the occasion of being presented to him. During this talk he posed a number of critical questions to the King to which the monarch replied either evasively or with absolute assurance. The tenor of their talk was that Italy would remain true to the Axis and under no circumstances desired to desert our ranks. Two days earlier Badoglio had confirmed this expressly to Rahn during a conversation. Badoglio even gave Rahn his word of honor as an officer and a general. Now we know what to think of the word of honor of an Italian officer and general!

The news of the Italian treachery reached us first via a London broadcast, an occurrence that undoubtedly is unique and without precedent in history. Exactly as we imagined and suspected, surrender negotiations had been going on for a long time and had been signed as early as September 3. The English had insisted upon postponing publication until such moment as promised best publicity and the greatest political effect. That explains why the Italian troops in Calabria offered almost no resistance.

The real traitor in the whole hostile clique in Italy is Badoglio. He had prepared both the fall of the Duce and the whole capitulation negotiations at long range with the evident intention of hoodwinking and cheating us. The King was his ready tool, a man without character and will and therefore most useful for Badoglio's ambitious plans.

The Fuehrer immediately drew the right conclusions as regards the royal family, and had Prince Philip of Hesse arrested in GHQ that very night. He was transferred to Gestapo headquarters at Koenigsberg. He was very much surprised at being put under arrest; he had not thought such a thing possible. He must be held in custody in any case for reasons of state policy, for during the weeks he has stayed at GHQ he has found out so much that he might become very dangerous to us.

Up to this hour the place of sojourn of the Duce is unknown. The Fuehrer fears the Italians may want to give him into the hands of the English and the Americans. Pavolini, Ricci, and the Duce's son are now at GHQ working up an appeal to the Italian people and the Italian armed forces. They have been selected to form a neo-Fascist government and to act in the name of the Duce. They are to take up residence in northern Italy as soon as conditions there have been consolidated. They are working very industriously and the appeals which they have composed are drafted quite effectively from a propaganda viewpoint; they make sense. Farinacci is to arrive in the course of the afternoon to complement the work of this triumvirate.

[Renato Ricci was Italian Minister of Corporations, 1939–43, and in 1943 became leader of the Republican Fascist Militia.
Vittorio Mussolini was the eldest of the Duce's three sons.]

The explanation that we have issued to the press was drafted personally by the Fuehrer. Its tone is extremely sharp and gives the German people full details concerning the background of the Italian treachery. . . .

For the present we won't say anything against the Italian people since we may need them, especially for our supply lines and communications. Nor is the Army to be defamed, no matter how much we may itch to do so, for we must at least prevail upon it not to offer resistance and to turn its weapons over to our troops.

The Poglavnik has issued a sharp declaration against Italy. He stated that at last he was in a position to create a free Croatian state together with Dalmatia; the Fuehrer had already promised him that. He now shook off Italian suzerainty. What a pity that one doesn't observe that kind of spirit and speedy work in other European nations! . . .

The resistance offered by the Italian troops is, for the most part, only a token resistance. The Italians simply don't want to fight, are happy when they can surrender their arms, and even happier if they can sell them. Best of all, our troops succeeded in getting the power plants on Lake Garda into their hands. That is important for the entire railway system in northern Italy, as it is fed by current from these plants. . . .

We have about eight divisions in northern Italy and also eight in southern Italy; in other words, a total of some sixteen divisions of the best of human material, splendidly equipped. The Fuehrer is firmly convinced that we shall succeed in getting the job done in Italy with these sixteen divisions. Among them are a number of tank divisions against which the Italians have nothing to pit. Unfortunately about

50,000 of our men are still on Sardinia and 4,000 on Corsica. The Fuehrer wants to try to get the troops at least back to northern Italy; the matériel must be regarded as lost. Nevertheless it would be a great piece of luck if at least the men were to return. We have lost so much man power during the past year because of Italian cowardice and Italian treachery that we can hardly afford a further heavy loss like that.

The Italian Fleet has partly left its moorings. The Fuehrer fears it may be on its way to the English. Unfortunately our submarines arrived in the port of Spezia too late. Their assignment was to torpedo a part of the fleet. Now the Luftwaffe has been given that task and will undoubtedly smash a few vessels.

The Fuehrer is firmly determined to wipe the slate clean in Italy.

The reasons for the treachery are now quite obvious. The Fuehrer was right in being suspicious from the first moment after the Duce's fall. Both our military men and our diplomats in Italy were fooled by Badoglio. That applies especially to Kesselring, Mackensen, and Rintelen. They actually believed that Badoglio had honest intentions toward us and that it would be easier to work militarily and politically with his regime than with Fascism, which was too heavily mortgaged by its friendship with us. Now they have had their reward. They approached the Italian problem with a naïveté that staggers the imagination. They therefore failed to make the indispensable preparations for the moment of treachery, because they did not want to believe such deceit possible.

Nevertheless the Fuehrer believes he will master this situation, albeit with some difficulty. Naturally we shall not be able to hold southern Italy. We must withdraw northward beyond Rome. We shall now establish ourselves in the defense line that the Fuehrer always envisaged; namely, the line of the Apennine Mountains. The Fuehrer hopes we can withdraw that far and at that point build up a first line of defense. It would of course be a fine thing if we could remain in Rome. But at Rome our flanks would be too long and too vulnerable. We would always be in danger there. Of course, if we permit the English and Americans to go into Italy as far as the Apennines, this will constitute a steady threat to the Balkans, for Italy is the best springboard for the southeast.

If the English and Americans don't attack Croatia directly, we shall master the situation there without difficulty. The Poglavnik will see to this. Naturally he has gained the upper hand by his declaration of independence of the Croatian state.

The Fuehrer does not want as yet to restore independence to Albania. The Albanian Government itself must proclaim it, and the Fuehrer can then do nothing but confirm it.

The aim of our military activity in Italy must consist in freeing a number of divisions for the Balkans. For without a doubt the spearhead of the Anglo-American invasion will be pointed in that direction in the immediate future.

We must now do everything possible to pacify the [Italian] regions of which we are taking possession. We naturally haven't sufficient police to set up a regime of force there. That's why, too, we must defer political changes in the Italian area for a while. For instance, we cannot seize southern Tyrol now, because that would absolutely flabbergast the Italian people and condemn every neo-Fascist government to political inactivity. For this reason Hofer cannot be sent to southern Tyrol as civilian governor. His appearance there would be like a red rag to a bull.

[Franz Hofer was Nazi Gauleiter of the Austrian Tyrol and Vorarlberg.]

The other Austrian Gauleiters immediately swung into action. Eigruber has already brought to their senses the Italian workers at Linz, who are very numerous there. They wanted to start a rumpus which, however, was put down in a hurry. I issued a decree that Italian laborers who are working in the Reich are not to be subjected to insults, for which there is considerable inclination in the factories.

Gauleiter Rainer was also heard from. Our Austrian Gauleiters certainly are tops at making territorial claims. There can naturally be no talk of that at present. But one can understand why the Austrian Gauleiters are now feeling their oats. As everywhere else in life, appetite comes with eating.

[Dr. Friedrich Rainer was Gauleiter for the Salzburg area.]

Things are in quite a ferment in the Balkans. The Hungarians don't know exactly what to do. While the Rumanians are firmly in favor of Axis policies and conduct of the war, their Mihai Antonescu is a very undependable chap. The situation in Bulgaria is absolutely insecure. The Fuehrer told me that it must now be regarded as certain that King Boris was poisoned. The German doctors have arrived at this conclusion. He was taken out of this world by snake poison. Who mixed the poison isn't known as yet. The German doctors wanted to perform an autopsy on the deceased King. The Bulgarian Government was agreeable to this but the royal family refused. I would not regard it beyond the range of possibility that the poisoning was engineered by the Italians. After their latest act of treachery I am ready to credit the Badoglio regime and the Italians generally with anything. I believe that in the entire course of history no people has ever humiliated itself and besmirched its honor as much as the Italians have done. For the present they are in favor with the English, but in their heart of hearts the English no doubt despise them. It will take several months, possibly even years, before the Italians will realize fully what they have done to themselves.

The Fuehrer is somewhat worried lest the English now attempt an invasion in the West. While we have very strong lines of fortifications, there is behind them nothing but a thin veil of reserves. Our endeavor must therefore be to beat back any invasion attempt of the English and the Americans by our very first blow. Under no circumstances must they gain a footing. The Fuehrer is pretty hopeful about our possibilities, even though he is naturally somewhat worried. . . .

The Fuehrer expects the Anglo-American invasion attempt to come in the Netherlands. We are weakest there, and the population would be most inclined to give the necessary local support to such an undertaking. As everybody knows, the Dutch are the most insolent and obstreperous people in the entire West.

The exceptionally heavy bombing attacks which the English have launched against the western lines of communication for some days are rather suspicious. Could it be that this is the prelude to an attempt at invasion? The fleet, too, has repeatedly come up close to the European western coast, has started some fireworks, but has always left again according to schedule. The time of the year is the best imaginable for an invasion in the West. But only a short time remains; after that the weather will again be less favorable for that sort of undertaking.

We must therefore wait and see. That gnaws at one's nerves, especially when one considers that we cannot face such a situation with absolute assurance and preparedness.

In addition, the situation in the East continues to be extremely critical. Nevertheless the Fuehrer believes that he will succeed in mastering it. It means, of course, that we shall have to withdraw to a line lying far back; namely, that of the Dnieper. The retreat is to take place in a very orderly manner. . . .

The depressing thing is that we haven't the faintest idea as to what Stalin has left in the way of reserves. I, for my part, doubt very much whether under these conditions we shall be able to transfer divisions from the East to the other European theaters of war. This fact is a new proof of the unexampled treachery committed by the Italians against our cause. The present crisis would never have arisen if the divisions that we had to send to Italy after the Duce's fall could have been assigned to the Eastern Front. For the superiority of the Bolsheviks over us is only a very slight one. One can see it from the tremendous difficulties they have in advancing. Well, there just isn't any reason to discuss the treachery of the Italians; the whole world recognizes it as unique in history.

I asked the Fuehrer whether anything might be done with Stalin sooner or later. He said not for the moment. That is right, of course, considering the critical situation in the East. And anyway, the Fuehrer believes it would be easier to make a deal with the English than with the Soviets. At a given moment, the Fuehrer believes, the English would come to their senses. But I can't see that for the present.

It is true, of course, that Churchill is absolutely anti-Bolshevik. Churchill is naturally pursuing imperialistic British aims in this war. The seizure of Sicily gives him a great advantage. Sicily will never be restored to the Italians, for Sicily, possibly with Calabria added, will absolutely guarantee English domination in the Mediterannean and render it secure for all time. Undoubtedly the English will also snatch Sardinia and Corsica. If they can make their exit from this war with all this as booty, they will of course have made somewhat of a gain. The Fuehrer believes they will then possibly be amenable to some sort of arrangement. I am rather inclined to regard Stalin as more approachable, for Stalin is more of a practical politician than Churchill. Churchill is a romantic adventurer, with whom one can't talk sensibly.

The Fuehrer also isn't at all clear as to how much the Soviets still have up their sleeve. If we had fifteen or twenty first-class divisions to throw into the East intact, we would undoubtedly be in a position to repulse the Russians. Unfortunately we must put these fifteen or twenty divisions into combat in the Italian theater of war. It is therefore nothing but a pious wish to imagine such a possibility. . . .

The Fuehrer is somewhat more hopeful about air warfare. He believes we shall regain mastery in two or three months. . . .

Our defensive power has increased extraordinarily in recent weeks. Added to this are our progressive preparations for reprisals. Unfortunately the English raids on Peenemuende and on our OT work in the West have thrown our preparations back four and even eight weeks, so that we can't possibly count on reprisals before the end of

January. The Fuehrer places great hopes in rocket bombs. He believes that through them the whole picture may possibly change as regards England. . . .

[Peenemuende was the top secret laboratory and experimental station for rocket bombs. It was located on the Baltic Sea, near Stettin. By OT work is meant the western fortifications built by the *Organisation Todt*, civilian engineering troops named after Dr. Fritz Todt, Nazi Minister of Munitions.]

I described to the Fuehrer my observations on the effect of air raids on the civilian population. I could claim truly and sincerely that the German people can take air warfare as at present conducted. The Fuehrer was profoundly stirred by my description of the air raids on Berlin. One cannot picture such an attack unless one has witnessed it oneself. . . .

The Fuehrer was very much pleased with my measures against air raids. He believes I shall succeed in so mitigating the worst effects of air warfare on civilians that they will be halfway bearable.

The Fuehrer placed great hopes in the fog season in England that is due soon. . . .

Submarine warfare seemed somewhat more promising to him. The new gadget for neutralizing English radar has proven its worth. Since its introduction there have been no more submarine losses. The submarines are once again about to sally forth in packs to attack convoys. There isn't sufficient anti-radar equipment as yet, so that returning ships must hand theirs over for installation in submarines about to depart. But the new equipment does seem to be okay. The English can no longer determine the position of our submarines. We gather that from intercepted radio messages which often state that a submarine was discovered but that contact with it was lost afterward.

The Fuehrer expects more impressive submarine successes soon. It would be wonderful if at least we could show greater submarine activity. The Fuehrer is, generally speaking, extraordinarily optimistic in many respects. To me he seems even a bit too optimistic. But he, of course, must look at things from an optimistic angle. If he were to let bad news get him down it would be a national calamity. The Fuehrer certainly diffuses a healthy optimism all about him with a tremendously heartening effect upon his collaborators. But in this case Doenitz, too, is hopeful, and Doenitz is a very cool and realistic calculator.

Sooner or later we shall have to face the question of inclining toward one enemy side or the other. Germany has never yet had luck with a two-front war; it won't be able to stand this one in the long run either.

I pointed out to the Fuehrer that in 1933, too, we did not attain power by making absolute demands. We did present absolute demands on August 13, 1932, but failed because of them. After that we had to suffer a whole series of defeats before we came into power on January 30, 1933, with more modest demands. Very soon thereafter, however, we forced all our demands through.

[Goebbels here refers to the fact that Adolf Hitler, accompanied by SA Chief Ernst Roehm, on August 13, 1932, visited President Paul von Hindenburg, demanding that the entire government be turned over to the Nazis. Hindenburg virtually threw the two men out. On January 30, 1933, Hitler was willing to head a coalition cabinet with non-Nazis such as Franz von Papen, Alfred Hugenberg, Konstantin von Neurath, Eltz von Ruebenach, et al. Gradually these men were eased out.]

Most likely similar circumstances prevail today. In the case of revolutionary or military developments one cannot anticipate with mathematical precision how matters are going to progress. Too many imponderables are involved.

So far as I am concerned, I am certainly convinced that the English don't want a Bolshevik Europe under any circumstances, and that if given the choice between a National Socialist and a Bolshevik Europe they would most certainly choose the National Socialist. At present they still entertain the hope of gaining the mastery of Europe themselves after both the National Socialist Reich and the Soviet Union have bled to death. Once they realize, however, that this is impossible, and that they have a choice only between Bolshevism or relaxing somewhat toward National Socialism, they will no doubt show an inclination toward a compromise with us. I'm not even sure that it would be a good thing for Churchill to be ousted in England. His successor would no doubt be Eden, but Eden is contaminated more by Bolshevik ideology than Churchill. Churchill himself is an old anti-Bolshevik and his collaboration with Moscow today is only a matter of expediency.

The only certain thing about this war is that Italy will lose it. Its pusillanimous treachery to its own leader was the prelude to a cowardly treachery toward its ally. The Duce will enter history as the last Roman, but behind his massive figure a gypsy people has gone to rot. We ought to have realized that sooner, but for ideological reasons we always were too accommodating to the Italians. Once again our old German inheritance, our sentimentality, has had evil consequences when applied to politics. Added to this was a totally inept German diplomacy which didn't have enough vision to foresee the developments that have now taken place in Italy.

All this must teach us a great deal. National Socialism must undergo a renovation. We must link ourselves more socialistically with the people than before. The people must always know that we are their just and generous guardians. The National Socialist leadership must have no ties whatsoever with the aristocracy or with so-called society. . . .

As regards the situation within the Reich I pleaded energetically with the Fuehrer to address the German people. I presented every argument I knew and succeeded in convincing him of the justice of my demand. He isn't very anxious to speak since he cannot yet make a clear estimate of developments in Italy. But we can't afford to wait. The people are entitled to a word of encouragement and solace from the Fuehrer in this difficult crisis. . . .

With reference to Italy our people were undoubtedly cleverer than their government. The German people never had their heart in the alliance with Italy. They always viewed it with strong doubts, an unspoken skepticism, and a restrained suspicion. This suspicion has now proven well founded. As a result the Italian treachery was no surprise to the German people, but nevertheless gave them a shock. We shall no doubt feel the effects of this shock within the next few days. . . .

During our dinner praise and blame are invoked indiscriminately for or against this or that Italian. I don't know how many curses were called down on the Italian people by German mouths in the course of this day!

Himmler naturally is very anxious that we should have at least a halfway effective Fascist government in northern Italy. He hasn't got enough police troops there to govern by force.

It seems somewhat suspicious to me that the English openly announced they would land in central Italy in order to cut off our forces in southern Italy. They aren't talking at all about the West. Some reports claim that the English have landed near Naples, but we can't tell whether that is right, since we are without Italian news. The Luftwaffe alone is in a position to make observations.

It has now been proven beyond a doubt that the negotiations looking to capitulation had been conducted between the enemy and Badoglio for a long time. That means that the Italians have long been collaborating with the enemy. Since Sunday the negotiations have even been conducted in Rome. One unconfirmed report is to the effect that the King now intends to dismiss Badoglio also. I regard this as quite possible. Now that Badoglio is compromised by his disgraceful act of treachery, the King would naturally be happy to get rid of him. . . .

The Finnish, Rumanian, and Hungarian press reported the Italian treachery practically without comment. It is quite evident that Finland, Rumania, and Hungary want to wait and see how things develop further. An official Japanese declaration criticized Italian treachery very sharply. The Japanese stated that it was a clear case of treason, that the Italians had lost their military honor, and that they didn't want to fight, but that Germany and Japan would continue the struggle with unmitigated vehemence. The Japanese must truly be held in very high esteem as allies. The press of Tokyo, too, has used language such as we have hitherto not been accustomed to from those quarters. Undoubtedly Italy is today nothing but an object of disdain in Japan. . . .

Badoglio wrote a letter to the Fuehrer, giving a number of sanctimonious and hypocritical arguments for his defection. Although the letter is very courteous in tone, it is nevertheless, as concerns the subject matter, the most shameless and treacherous document ever to issue from the pen of a statesman. One wants to throw up—so nauseated does one feel on reading those lines.

The neutral countries naturally feel they are on the top of the world. The Axis Powers have already been written off. But Italy gets a kick in the behind. . . .

The question still remains as to where the Duce is. Nobody knows the answer. I regard it as likely that the Italian Government is trying to hand him over to the English or the Americans. The English seem to have demanded this as one of their armistice conditions.

I was able to work for a few hours. In the evening I had a talk with Colonel General Dietl, who happened to spend a day at GHQ. He had just completed his furlough and was sorry not to be assigned to duty against the Italians. For him as a Styrian this, of course, would be an especially desirable task. He is therefore very reluctant to return to the Finnish front.

According to the picture he gave, we need have no fear about Finland for the moment. The Finns are not fighting much but they do fight well. They are doing what they can. They would not like to become too much involved in this war. The main thing, however, is that they do not desert us. . . . The Finns are dependent entirely upon our military support. Like all our allies they are taking advantage of us, but in their case there can be no question of deserting the fighting front, at least not for the present. . . .

Dietl complained bitterly that the Swedes were behaving very insolently in their personal relationships and in the press. The Swedish press is chiefly dependent on the English plutocracy and Jewry. . . .

Dietl doesn't think very much of Mannerheim. Mannerheim is pro-English at heart, and would naturally like to get out of the war just as soon as possible. This war demonstrates once again that, generally speaking, the military people are more cowardly than the politicians. In Finland, too, President Ryti is the strong man and not Generalissimo Mannerheim.

[Field Marshal Gustav Emil Mannerheim, born, 1867, showed his contempt of Nazism on many occasions. He alone of top allies of Germany failed to come personally to Germany to be awarded a high decoration. This decoration was then conferred on him in Finland.]

A small group of us had dinner with the Fuehrer; added to those who were present at noon were Goering and Dietl.

Goering is furious about the treachery of Italy. He, too, has seen it coming. There isn't anybody among us now who doesn't claim to have seen it coming! Only nobody prepared for it to the necessary extent! Goering gave voice to his conviction that the King himself bore the greatest responsibility for the Italian treachery. The royal family is scheduled to leave Rome this evening, no doubt for fear of being caught by the German troops. . . .

The war of nerves started by the English and Americans against us doesn't impress anybody here at GHQ. But Goering is energetically in favor of the Fuehrer now making a public utterance. People are not only fairly crying for it at home, but the entire Eastern Front calls for a speech by the Fuehrer. Goering's air commanders in the East telephoned him about it; they claimed that an address by the Fuehrer would at this moment be worth ten divisions.

Meanwhile the Fuehrer has already worked up his speech; all he has to do is to edit it. I can only hope before I leave to persuade him to deliver it.

Goering is now somewhat more optimistic about air warfare than he was; in fact, in my opinion somewhat too optimistic. But it is always a good thing if the responsible man views his situation optimistically. You cannot master so difficult a problem as air warfare with pessimism.

An animated debate started as to what kind of regime we should set up in the occupied sections of Italy. The Fuehrer is right in believing that we cannot afford to install immediately the sort of regime that we would really like to have. . . . Nor is this the moment to attack the King personally, for the King is still respected by all Italians. . . .

All of us feel sorry for the Duce. We fear that he has already been handed over to the English and is on a British man-of-war. The English stated in their press that if they got hold of him they would make him face an international court. But that will take some time. . . .

Goering believes that the Italian Fleet will in all likelihood head for Spanish harbors, but I agree with the Fuehrer that it will place itself in the enemy's hands.

Reports from northern Italy indicate that severe resistance was offered in a couple of places. But that is being broken up everywhere by our troops.

The military measures adopted during the past six weeks are a certain guarantee that the Italian treachery won't become a national misfortune for us. Military and political measures are in process of execution. The so-called provisional Fascist government is diligently at work in the Fuehrer's GHQ, even though one or the other of its members is getting cold feet because he does not agree with the general political tendencies that we advocate. But what else can these gentlemen do except work for us? . . . It is better for them, in any case, to work in the Fuehrer's GHQ for a new, albeit reduced, Fascist Italy, than to go to prison in Italy, or even to be shot.

Thank God the Fuehrer has finished writing his speech! It is about twenty typewritten pages. At my suggestion it is to be broadcast at 5 P.M. Friday afternoon from the Fuehrer's GHQ. I shall have it repeated a number of times by transcription so that everybody at the front and at home may hear it.

We got to talking about decorations. The Fuehrer regards it as very difficult, if not impossible, to distribute decorations and badges of honor justly. Even in the case of the Knight's Cross this is sometimes exceptionally difficult. The Luftwaffe has an advantage over the Army because its successes can be measured in numbers whereas this is not possible with the Army. Colonel General Dietl, who took part in these talks, spoke fervently on behalf of the infantry, but, as already observed, it is very difficult to measure the bravery of the infantry in statistics. As a matter of fact every brave infantryman who has faced the enemy for four years ought to receive the Knight's Cross. . . . The Fuehrer believes that the only decoration that is really being distributed justly is the Mother's Cross, since at least its lowest category, even though not the upper, is sharply defined. Here there are no shenanigans and no priorities.

[The Mother's Cross was awarded by the Nazis to mothers with more than three children. There were three categories, depending upon the number of offspring— the Bronze, Silver, and Golden Mother's Cross.]

We chatted until 4 A.M. The Fuehrer had great fun with his dog Blondi, who has become his faithful companion. It is surprising how much this animal has adjusted herself to him. It is a good thing that the Fuehrer has at least one living thing constantly about him.

September 11, 1943

The enemy hasn't the faintest idea as to the actual situation in northern and central Italy. Fantastic rumors persist that we are transporting our divisions over the Brenner back into the Reich. Now, suddenly, a colossal attack on Berlin is planned, to be started from Italian airports.

Here and there news reports claim that the Duce has been surrendered to the English or Americans. I can imagine that the Italians might let him fall into enemy hands, but to deliver him officially would be about the most low-down thing that ever happened in the history of any war. Some reports claim that he has already been taken to North Africa and will soon be brought before an international court-martial. The London newspapers are naïve, of course, when they claim that Badoglio intends to declare war on the Reich. Badoglio, as a matter of fact, has deserted Rome and entrusted the security of the Italian capital to an insignificant general.

An article in the *Economist* deserves mention because it claims that the raids on Berlin are costing the Allies too much. Their losses thus far have been so heavy that they could not afford them long. Would to God that were true! It would be a tremendous help to me if I could at least be relieved somewhat of the burden of air raids on the Reich's capital.

A new Regency Council has been constituted in Sofia, composed of Prince Kyrill, Premier Filoff, and War Minister Michoff. This Regency Council is positively on our side; we can go places with it. The Fuehrer intends to transmit to Prince Kyrill the findings of the German doctors on the poisoning of Czar Boris, which he believes was in all likelihood inspired by the Italian Court. For it is very suspicious that Princess Mafalda, the worst wench [*groesste Raabenaas*] in the entire Italian royal house, was on a visit in Sofia for weeks before King Boris's death. It will be remembered that she is a sister of the Bulgarian Queen.

[Princess Mafalda, daughter of King Victor Emmanuel, was married to Prince Philip of Hesse. She died in a Nazi prison on April 19, 1945.]

There can be no thought of any crisis in German morale. The German people are too politically minded not to draw the necessary conclusions from the events in Italy. What they do want is the publication of the names of the new Fascist Government whose members for the present are sleeping on the floor in Ambassador Hewel's room at GHQ. The trouble is we can't publish these names, as they are too unimportant.

Before my conversation with the Fuehrer I had a long talk with Dr. Dietrich about our propaganda and press departments in the occupied countries. He was agreeable to having his public-relations officers integrated into the propaganda sections. If he were to start a new organization for his public-relations officers, we would have two sets of machinery in the occupied countries with resulting confusion. At present Dr. Dietrich and I are collaborating splendidly. I suppose he realizes it's no fun to pick a fight with me.

The German people, as I have emphasized repeatedly, are waiting for a speech by the Fuehrer. . . . Everybody realizes that a totalitarian decision must be made. Nobody doubts any longer that this is a war to be or not to be. The Eastern Front is causing the German people considerably greater worry now than in past weeks. The state of depression because of air raids has increased as a result of the most recent heavy attacks. Very few are left who believe reprisals are likely to be carried out.

Naumann has had a lengthy talk with Himmler. The differences that have arisen between Himmler and me were cleared up. Himmler attaches the greatest importance to collaborating with me harmoniously. That's something that I, too, desire. He will surely be careful in the future not to send me insolent teletype messages like those he sent the last time.

[There is no indication in Goebbels's diary as to the nature of Heinrich Himmler's "insolent teletype messages."]

At noon I went to see the Fuehrer. A little group of us, including Doenitz, Ribbentrop, and Keitel lunched with him. He told us the latest news. Affairs in northern and central Italy have developed exceedingly favorably, and there is hope for their complete clarification by evening. In view of this development, however, the Fuehrer was again inclined to postpone his address to the German people. This time I would not be sidetracked. I insisted he speak that very evening. We must not let the right psychological moment slip by; it has already been missed so often that we must now really take advantage of it. . . .

The Vatican has inquired of our Ambassador whether its rights would be safeguarded in the event of our occupying Rome. The Fuehrer sent an affirmative reply.

Meanwhile Badoglio has left the Italian capital. The royal family, too, has scampered away—a proof of the fact that the circles responsible for the treachery don't think much of Rome's fate. The Italian Crown Prince has gone to an island. We monitored a telephone conversation between Churchill and Eden during which Eden complained bitterly that the Crown Prince was creating difficulties for the English. He was unwilling to accept an English officer as his adjutant. In other words, so low has the Italian monarchy already fallen that it is completely in the hands of the enemy.

Unbelievable conditions prevail in Italy. The Italian people are today experiencing what we lived through in the November days of 1918. They are being punished more quickly and terribly for the treason committed by their government than we could ever have expected or thought possible.

[The Nazis always maintained that Germany capitulated in 1918 although undefeated. The German people, they claimed, would have continued the struggle and Germany would finally have won, but a weak and corrupt monarchy showed the white feather and gave up the fight prematurely. One reason why Hitler now continued the struggle even when the entire world regarded Germany's doom as certain was his obsession with the idea that victory was "just around the corner" in 1918, and that the Reich should merely have held out a little longer. To him German victory now was a matter of holding out in the face of terrific odds.]

While we were lunching Jodl brought the latest news. The garrison at Rome, including its best Guards regiments, has surrendered to Kesselring. The German troops are marching on Rome. Most of the northern Italian cities are in our hands. Above all, contact with our troops in the south has been re-established and secured. Thus the main problems connected with our security in Italy have been solved. . . .

This is an added reason for me to appeal once more to the Fuehrer to deliver his address in the evening. The Fuehrer was not quite so much opposed to the idea now as he was in the early afternoon. I must see to it that the speech is in the bag before I leave. The Fuehrer would prefer to wait for further developments. I rightly counter, however, with the argument that a development never comes to a standstill at a certain point, but will continue on, and that undoubtedly the present moment is most suitable. The Fuehrer said he wanted to think it over until late in the afternoon.

A long discussion followed, with the Italian question as the main theme. The Fuehrer once more told the men present how often he had warned the Duce against the monarchy and the aristocracy, but the

Duce was too trustful. He must now pay for it dearly. The monarchy thanked him in a manner that he certainly had not expected.

The King can no longer be spared in our propaganda. The Fuehrer once more expressed his conviction that Princess Mafalda was the trickiest bitch [*geriebenste Aas*] in the Italian royal house. He thought her capable of having expedited her brother-in-law Boris to the hereafter. It was also possible that the plutocratic clique administered poison to Mussolini, for Mussolini's illness, too, was somewhat mysterious. No words need be wasted about the treacherous Italian generals, he said. They had so besmirched Italy's military honor that it could not be washed clean for a long time to come. The plot hatched against us in Rome was backed by the monarchy, aristocracy, society, higher officers, Free Masons, Jews, industrialists, and clerics. The Duce became the victim of this plot. We have no intention of going his way. We are going to prevail, come what may.

The Fuehrer invoked final measures to preclude similar developments with us once and for all. He ordered all German princes discharged from the German Wehrmacht. I proposed to the Fuehrer that all the estates of the former ruling families be seized as quickly as possible. Real estate is the foundation of economic independence, and economic independence always furnishes a basis for political influence. The Fuehrer was quite in accord with this point of view.

As regards the Duce himself, I believe that from a sentimental point of view it would naturally be most regrettable if we could not liberate him. From a political viewpoint, however, I wouldn't regret it much. We must assess all these questions with a cool opportunism. If the Duce were to lead a new Fascist Italy, we would undoubtedly owe him consideration in many matters on which we can now act without restraint. Even though he denies it, I don't believe the Fuehrer would have the courage to take, say, South Tyrol away from a Fascist Italy led by the Duce and behaving itself for the rest of the war. However, we must not only get back South Tyrol, but I envisage the boundary line as drawn south of Venetia. Whatever was once an Austrian possession we must get back into our hands. The Italians by their infidelity and treachery have lost every claim to a national state of the modern type. They must be punished most severely, as the laws of history demand.

I talked to General Schmundt about the question of making use of princes in the German Wehrmacht. Their elimination will create some difficulties because some have given an exceptionally good account of themselves as front-line fighters. We cannot remove them from the

Wehrmacht without being grossly tactless. Nevertheless it must be done. Here, too, reasons of state must prevail over all other considerations.

The Fuehrer later took a walk with me through the woods surrounding GHQ. I pleaded once more with all my energy for him to deliver his speech this same evening. We read it through once more after the last corrections had been made. It is about twenty typewritten pages long and has turned out to be excellent. In it the Fuehrer tells in detail about the Italian treachery. In very impressive words he testifies to his friendship with the Duce, which will continue beyond the present. He was not changeable in such matters, he said. The Duce was the greatest son of Italy since the collapse of antiquity. The clique that brought him to his downfall was properly characterized by the Fuehrer. Next he described the measures taken for securing our position in Italy. This part of the speech, together with the special bulletin about our successes in northern and central Italy, will undoubtedly create a deep impression in the entire world. The Fuehrer said a few words about air warfare and the struggle on the Eastern Front. His whole speech was filled with the spirit of Clausewitz.

[Carl von Clausewitz, who served as a general in both the Russian and Prussian armies in the second decade of the nineteenth century, was director of the Prussian War Academy beginning 1818, and wrote a work, *Concerning War*, which is still considered a classic by military men the world over.]

There followed an admonition to the Party and the assurance that the Italian precedent never can and never will be repeated in Germany, and that Germany will finally carry off the palm of victory despite all tribulations. The speech is bound to serve as a clarion call to the entire German people.

I then put the Fuehrer before the microphone and had the speech, which was read by the Fuehrer in an exceedingly impressive manner, transcribed on to a magnetophone band in Berlin over the direct wire. I was very happy when I heard from Berlin that the reception had been good. Thus I have at last succeeded in bringing the Fuehrer before the microphone for the first time since Memorial Day last March. I can now return to Berlin with my mind at ease. The main purpose of my trip to GHQ has been fulfilled. I believe Goering is right in telling me that we have won a battle. This speech will do the work of several divisions at the Eastern Front and in Italy.

I had a short final chat with the Fuehrer. He, too, seemed very happy to have the speech out of his system at last. He extended best wishes for my health and my work. . . .

He promised me to come to Berlin soon to speak in the Sports Palace at the opening of the Winter Relief Campaign. I shall see to it that he again gets the taste for establishing direct contact with the people.

Our parting was very cordial. I wished the Fuehrer every success. . . .

At 8 P.M. we heard the broadcast of the special bulletin concerning our successes in Italy. It seemed very effective. Following it came the speech of the Fuehrer which, thank God, went over all stations without interference. Not even the Bolsheviks pulled themselves together to interfere on our air waves. That means we really brought home the bacon.

Some additional work; some more palaver; after that I fell into my bed dead tired. A mountain of work will await me in Berlin.

September 12, 1943

Returning to Berlin I found a wonderful spirit prevailing. . . . The news of our heavy blows against Italy—especially the capture of Rome —as well as the Fuehrer's speech acted like champagne on the people. It was almost as though we were on a great and successful advance comparable to that of 1939 and 1940. The seizure of Rome, especially, has given great satisfaction to the German people, for their anger at the Italians is indescribable. I am very happy that this profound change in morale has taken place so quickly and radically. . . .

Since the last terrible catastrophe in Hamburg we had gone through a very obvious low in morale. This low is now behind us. The women are largely responsible for an essential improvement of our sentiments, owing chiefly to the fact that the arguments advanced in the Fuehrer's speech appealed particularly to women's feelings. The hatred of Italy is indescribable and is directed not only against the Badoglio regime but against the Italian people as such. The entire German people wish we might succeed in liberating the Duce—a proof that our politics are still based too much on sentiment and too little on intellect. If the King were to fall into our hands it would be difficult not to have him shot, for the German people would demand it.

During the days of the Italian treachery a few enemies of the state in public office and even in the Party indulged in loose talk. There were only a few cases of this kind, but I proceeded against them with unflinching determination. Hereafter I will have anybody who says anything whatever publicly against the war or the Fuehrer either beaten up, sentenced by the courts, or incarcerated in a concentration camp.

The whole world is pouring scorn and derision upon the Italians. The English have already informed them politely that they cannot supply them with any coal for general use; coal can be furnished only for munitions factories working for the Allies. The English press added that the Italian people might as well freeze during the coming winter; they deserved nothing better since they took part in the war. That's the treatment you get when you lay down your arms!

One can only smile at the intimation of the Badoglio Government that it intends to declare war on us. With what? The Italian Government has neither soldiers nor weapons.

Even England admits that it [the Fuehrer's speech] is one of the most powerful delivered by him during the entire war. . . . This speech came at the right moment for us and the wrong moment for our enemies. I am very happy that I prevailed upon the Fuehrer to deliver it. I believe it can be put down as the equivalent of a battle won. Its effect upon the German people simply cannot be overestimated.

The situation was such that I was able to take time off to go out to Lanke in the afternoon. The entire family, Magda and the children, awaited me and greeted me with great joy and enthusiasm. I was happy to be with my family again. Even though I had a lot of work to do, the relaxation did me good.

I had to deal with a number of questions; for example, as to how we can prevent the English and Americans from stealing Italian works of art. Undoubtedly they intend to do this, and the Italians won't have the strength to prevent it.

As already pointed out, we are continuing to retreat in the East. There is no question, however, of this retreat taking place in a disorderly manner. It is quite orderly and gives no indication of a rout. Nevertheless we must be clear in our own minds that the areas we are yielding are valuable and important militarily.

I am very happy that the Fuehrer has been so pepped up by developments. We are too. I believe the German people are gaining new strength as a result of the Italian crisis. Misfortune is beginning to turn slowly into good fortune.

September 13, 1943

The English have made public the thirteen points of the capitulation arranged with the Badoglio regime. No traitorous clique of generals has ever signed a more shameless document. The conditions of the armistice are dishonorable and humiliating. . . .

It makes my blood boil to think that the King and Badoglio have addressed the Italian people urging resistance to the Germans and stuttering hypocritical explanations for having deserted Rome. The King twaddled about manly decisions that must now be made. He was ready to do his duty as King to the last breath, and he hoped God would help him. One just can't have any other opinion about Italian dishonor—it is now nothing short of comical and ludicrous. There's a bad odor to it when one remembers the big words that Fascism emitted about the rebirth of Italy. All this is now proving to have been nothing but empty words.

Our Japanese allies are naturally of a different caliber. The Japanese press and government are adopting an attitude toward the Italian problem that does credit to their manly pride and deep sense of honor. . . .

The Swedish press has again become somewhat more insolent. Nevertheless it is not quite so arrogant as it was a fortnight ago. Obviously Italian behavior has had its beneficent effect upon Swedish mentality.

In the evening the happy news reached us that it had been possible to liberate the Duce by a tour de force. It was an act of heroism on the part of the SD, Student's parachute troops and the Waffen-SS. With the Duce was Caballero, who had not been executed after all. The Duce is already on his way to Vienna. His family is at present in Munich. Tassinari, the former Italian Minister of Agriculture, a man of some stature, is also in our custody.

[Colonel General Kurt Student was commanding officer of the German parachute troops.

By "Caballero" Goebbels probably means Count Ugo Cavallero, Italian senator, who helped Mussolini, 1925–28, to reorganize the Italian armed forces along Fascist lines.

Giuseppe Tassinari was an agricultural expert who, before becoming Italian Minister of Agriculture, was director of the Agricultural Economy Institute of Bologna.]

Added to this is the news that our position near Salerno is relatively favorable. We are sending reinforcement after reinforcement, but the English and the Americans are also doing that. It is therefore a race against time as to whose reinforcements will arrive first and who will thereby gain the upper hand.

Naturally on the human side we are all deeply touched that the liberation of the Duce has proven possible. No one can as yet foresee, however, that political consequences will follow. At any rate, I went back to Berlin [from Lanke] in the evening.

Toward midnight the Fuehrer called me on the telephone. Naturally he was exceedingly happy about the Duce's deliverance. The Duce had been held prisoner in a small mountain hostelry on the highest peak of the Apennines. The Badoglio regime had at first interned him on the Island of Maddalena, but his stay there was regarded as too insecure. The SD had trailed him and had already prepared an attempt at liberation which, however, could not be carried through because of the Duce's transfer.

The liberation in the Apennines was undertaken with gliders. One of these landed fifty feet in front of the hostelry in which the Duce was staying. Within a few minutes he was a free man. He was of course deeply touched at being rescued from captivity by German soldiers. Our soldiers proceeded pretty brutally and thereby kept the Italian Carabinieri guards in check. A few hours later the Duce was in Vienna. Just before calling me the Fuehrer had had a telephone conversation with him. He told me that the Duce was deeply shaken by developments. He informed the Fuehrer that he was tired and sick and would first of all like to have a long sleep. On Monday he wanted to visit his family in Munich. We shall soon see whether he is still capable of large-scale political activity. The Fuehrer thinks so. At any rate he will meet Mussolini at GHQ on Tuesday.

However much I may be touched on the human side by the liberation of the Duce, I am nevertheless skeptical as to its political advantages. As long as the Duce wasn't there we had a chance to wipe the slate clean in Italy. Without any restraint, and basing our action on the grandiose treachery of the Badoglio regime, we could force a solution of all our problems regarding Italy.

To me it had seemed that, besides South Tyrol, our boundary ought to include Venetia. That will hardly be possible in case the Duce enters politics again. We shall have the greatest difficulty even to put in our claim for South Tyrol. Under the leadership of the Duce, assuming he becomes active again, Italy will attempt to start a national rump government, toward which we shall have obligations in many respects. Both the English and ourselves could hack the Badoglio regime to pieces. A regime under the leadership of the Duce would presumably fall heir to all the rights and duties incident to the Three-Power Pact. A rather distressing prospect! But that's something to worry about later. For the present let us rejoice with all our hearts that the Duce has been restored to liberty. The news of his liberation will create the greatest sensation throughout the world. . . . In any case I now have the feeling that our lucky streak has set in again. But one hardly dares say this openly.

[The Three-Power Pact was an alliance between Germany, Italy, and Japan, concluded in Berlin on September 27, 1940. Among other things the high contracting parties guaranteed the integrity of one another's territory. Hence Goebbels's worry about South Tyrol and Venetia.]

September 14, 1943

The liberation of the Duce is the great sensation at home and abroad. Even upon the enemy the effect of the melodramatic deliverance is enormous. While I believe in weighing carefully the advantages and disadvantages of Mussolini's reappearance on the scene, the entire German people, on the other hand, are profoundly happy. The English admit resignedly that the Duce has eluded them. . . .

The fact that the Fuehrer proved his friendship for Mussolini so demonstratively by his deeds has gained much sympathy for him and the Wehrmacht. Friend and foe alike are full of admiration for the liberation. The Americans have made a sensational story of it. A news item by Reuters now admits that Badoglio had undertaken to deliver the Duce to the English and Americans.

Japan, especially, admires the heroic spirit of Germany, which found expression in this act of liberation.

It is interesting to note how Vichy tries to contrast the Italian capitulation with the French and to make moral capital of it. The French and Italians are fighting about who acted in the most cowardly and dishonorable manner. Undoubtedly the Italians will come out on top in that scuffle.

In northern Italy Fascism is taking a new lease on life. In Milan the German troops together with the Fascists established order. The Fascist party insignia are again to be seen on the streets. Many of the anti-Fascists have fled and many others have been put behind bars by the Fascists. Swiss agents have reported that great Fascist demonstrations of joy are taking place in northern Italian cities. But there is no reason for such manifestations as yet. The Italian Army seems to have collapsed completely. No great army has ever been disarmed more quickly than the Italian Army of today.

The Fascists are pinning all their hopes on the Duce, but I don't know whether these will be fulfilled. The Duce is sick and frail; whether he will be in a position to play a decisive political role will be revealed during the talk with the Fuehrer in GHQ next Tuesday.

The Fuehrer is very happy at being able to meet the Duce again soon. Talking to Gauleiters Hofer and Rainer he said, however, that our policies regarding Italy are not to be changed. I welcome this. I had already feared that the reappearance of the Duce might change our line of approach. It looks, however, as though the Fuehrer were determined to remain hard-boiled.

During the last air raid on Berlin our Ploetzensee penitentiary was hit; a number of people condemned to death escaped. Thierack therefore gave orders that clemency pleas be disposed of as quickly as possible and the executions take place during the days immediately following. It would be just about the limit if several hundred men condemned to death were let loose upon the population of the capital after every air raid!

September 15, 1943

The enemy press continues to treat the liberation of the Duce as a sensation. There has hardly been a military event during the entire war that has so deeply stirred the emotions and evoked such human interest. We are able to celebrate a first-class moral victory.

The English correspondents claim that German resistance near Salerno is the toughest the Allies have ever encountered. Resistance is really the wrong word, as our troops have meanwhile gone over to the offensive.

One thing is certain; namely, that the Allies have failed, at least for the present, to attain their objectives in Italy. They tried to be too clever about it and have accordingly been too dumb. That explains, too, why London public opinion criticizes Churchill so violently. The military and political situation in Italy has changed completely within a few days.

As regards the situation of the Soviets in the hinterland, statements by prisoners of war indicate that morale has improved considerably because of the [Soviet] military successes of the past two months. Nevertheless the desperate food situation is having a depressing effect. Anti-Semitism is said to be on the increase throughout the entire Soviet Union. It's a pity that we can't reach the people of the Soviet

Union by radio propaganda. We would have a great chance there. The Kremlin has been clever enough to exclude the Russian people from receiving the great world broadcasts and to limit them to their local stations.

The Fuehrer has signed the decree for an emergency housing scheme, with Dr. Ley in charge. That gives Dr. Ley a chance, for once, to do something with a big assignment. In the past he has always been concerned about being clothed with authority. He fought energetically for authority. Once obtained, however, he would fail to use it, but start another fight for new authority.

The Duce has arrived at the Fuehrer's GHQ. Mutual greetings were exceptionally cordial and friendly. The Fuehrer awaited him outside his bunker with his son Vittorio. Hitler and Mussolini embraced after their long separation. A deeply moving example of fidelity among men and comrades was here shown. I suppose there is nobody in the world who can fail to be impressed strongly by so touching a ceremony.

The Fuehrer then withdrew for a private talk with the Duce. No doubt I shall learn details about it soon. Obviously not only personal but also political matters have been discussed. The Duce will no doubt have to renounce certain things that he hitherto took for granted, for in the last analysis we must receive some sort of compensation for the gruesome treachery that Italy committed against the Axis.

I used all the eloquence at my command to obtain authorization to issue a communiqué about the rescue of Mussolini. At first the Fuehrer was against it, but finally he became convinced that such a report would have tremendous publicity value today. The item was then composed in a classical manner. The real secret of liberation, namely, that it was carried out by glider formations, was not divulged; beyond that, however, the account of the liberation was so interesting, so full of suspense, so touching and moving, that it will undoubtedly create a deep impression throughout the world.

September 16, 1943

How wrong the Anglo-Americans were about the situation in Italy can be seen from the fact that in New York the telephone books had already been torn and made into confetti to celebrate victory. Now they are sitting before the shreds of their telephone books and the situation in Italy is at present even more favorable for us than it was before the capitulation of the Badoglio gang. For the English and Americans at Salerno are in a bad spot. There is consternation about it in London and Washington. . . . Even that big mug, Knox, had to admit in a press conference that the American troops at Salerno were given a very hot reception and that the battles in North Africa and Sicily could not be compared with those for this bridgehead. . . .

The English papers spoke of the possibility that Churchill might meet severe criticism on his return from the United States. He expected a different kind of return! It is now admitted by the enemy that he wanted to return triumphantly, so to speak, with captured Italy as a present for the English people.

Five Orders of the Day have been issued by the Duce from the Fuehrer's GHQ over the Italian broadcasting systems. They state that the Duce has resumed the leadership of Fascism as of September 15. He has appointed Pavolini as temporary Secretary General of the Party. The Party is hereafter to be called the Republican-Fascist party. All who were removed from office by the Badoglio clique are immediately to resume their work. The Fascist party is undertaking the task of making all possible support available for the German Wehrmacht which is fighting against the common enemy. It is to give the common people essential moral and material aid. The members of the Party are to be investigated as to their attitude during the coup d'état, and the cowardly and unfaithful punished heavily. In addition, a national militia is to be created anew.

From these Orders of the Day one can gather that Mussolini is determined to take things into his hands again and that he has learned a lot from earlier events. Although the House of Savoy is not mentioned by name in these Orders of the Day, Mussolini is determined to do away with the monarchy. . . .

One cannot yet estimate the political consequences of the liberation of Mussolini. Certainly the Fuehrer will do all in his power to bring him back on the right road. . . . Jointly with us the Japanese have issued an exceptionally firm declaration concerning the Italian defection. They express their determination to continue the war with unabated fury until final victory.

A report was presented to me about the situation in our universities. It appears that there are almost exactly as many women studying as men. The percentage of students of medicine is exceptionally high. I regard that as a very bad sign for the future of our young intellectuals. Students of medicine are exempted for quite a period from service with the colors. The sudden rise in the number of medical students is therefore not only a sign of enthusiasm for the science of medicine, but largely also of lack of enthusiasm for fighting at the front. The decrease in the number of students in the technical and natural sciences is alarming. Although there is already a great scarcity of students of these sciences, the figures are decreasing rather than increasing. It would be a good thing to extend to students of the natural and technical sciences the same privileges as to those of medicine.

The Duce's visit with the Fuehrer is still on. The talks of the two are almost exclusively private. The Duce is in splendid physical and mental condition. One can see this by his Orders of the Day which certainly breathe the old Revolutionary-Fascist spirit. I will go to GHQ next week. The Fuehrer will give me details of his talks with Mussolini. The visit is certainly a very harmonious one. The Fuehrer is very well satisfied with the result of his conversations thus far.

September 17, 1943

At Salerno there is a race against time. Our General Staff still believes it can master the situation and hurl the English and Americans back into the ocean. In the course of the day, however, the situation changed somewhat in favor of our enemies. Every hour is of irredeemable value.

There is great bitterness in the enemy camp about the Duce's Orders of the Day. They now realize how much they lost by our liberation of Mussolini.

With the support of the German local commander, government commissars have been appointed in Rome who are to take over the work of the partly fugitive, partly arrested Badoglio Government. I learned confidentially that the super-profiteer, Volpi, married a Jewess a few weeks before the Badoglio treachery and was therefore expelled from the Fascist party. Obviously he wanted to provide himself with an alibi for the future by this marriage.

[Count Giuseppe Volpi di Misurata, born, 1877, was founder of the Adriatic Electric Company. He was in charge of the negotiations for the Treaty of Rapallo in 1920. Later he was president of the *Assicurazione Generale* of Trieste and Venice.]

In the evening the very distressing news reached us that we must give up Novorossiisk. We were unable to evacuate the city according to plan; the abandonment took place under tremendous pressure by the enemy. Let us hope that the seasonal rains will soon fall in the Ukraine. That would give us a certain amount of relief.

Many acts of sabotage are reported from every occupied section. According to reports from Norway even Nasjonal Samling has been somewhat obstreperous. The ministers of Nasjonal Samling are offering a lot of opposition, evidently with the intention of having themselves dismissed and thereby providing an alibi for themselves.

The quietest spot, relatively speaking, is the Protectorate. The Czechs evidently have no desire to burn their fingers. On the other hand acts of sabotage and terrorism have increased enormously in the General Government of Poland.

The Duce is still at the Fuehrer's GHQ. He intends to remain there a few days more. He has arranged with the Fuehrer not to return to Italy for the present. He wants to establish his temporary seat of government somewhere in southern Germany. A proper location is being looked for. All our political and military measures remain intact; the Fuehrer has insisted that no change be made. . . .

The Duce intends first to rebuild the Fascist party. Next, with its help, he wants to start rebuilding the state, beginning with the lower administrative echelons. As the crown of this work he then proposes to call a constitutional convention. Its task would be to eliminate the House of Savoy. The Duce is still somewhat hesitant about taking this action as he is of course aware of the strong ties between the Italian people and the royal house, and knows that these ties cannot be severed lightly. Besides, his measures will depend very much upon military developments.

In any case there will be news during the coming days and weeks. On the whole I am very happy that the Fuehrer has stuck to his original intentions. Obviously sentimental, emotional considerations no longer influence him. The Italian problem must be considered and solved anew.

September 18, 1943

The Eighth [British] Army is now only eighteen miles from the Salerno theater of war. We must therefore attempt to change the front radically with the aid of our reinforcements so that we won't fall into a trap. The declarations by General Clark, issued during the day, become more insolent from hour to hour. The Germans, he claims, will shortly face an entirely changed situation. No wonder that morale in London has been given a great fillip!

[General Mark Clark was in command of the Fifth American Army in Italy, and later became American Military Governor of liberated Austria.]

I realize once again that our military propaganda for foreign countries has failed completely. Despite my earnest warnings it stressed German victory in Salerno quite superfluously. The military news sources under General Jodl have been writing about a Dunkirk and a Gallipoli, and now the whole pack of enemy propagandists attacks me and makes me responsible for this totally faulty news policy! I can no longer accept such responsibility and am going to take the offensive against our discordant news policy. It won't do for my good name to be dragged in the dirt by the world and, when things have gone wrong, for those who are responsible to fade away into the background, leaving me to take it on the chin. . . .

I have always held that victories are to be announced only after they have actually been achieved and that the skin of the bear must not be distributed until the bear has been killed. Our military public-relations offices have again sinned grievously against this elementary principle of war-news policy.

The Italian defection has brought us a few advantages after all: Kaufmann reports that he has seized 400,000 tons of Italian commercial shipping. That's a real swig from the bottle!

I viewed some sensational newsreels dealing with the liberation of the Duce. These pictures show with what dash the undertaking was carried through. The Duce himself appears on the screen for quite a time. He is in civilian clothes and looks rather dashing. His expression, however, is that of a suffering and careworn man. He has grown thin of late, but his eyes still sparkle with the old lust for combat. Judging by that look one can imagine his staging a comeback in Italian politics.

I hear that the Duce has protested against some of the Italian broadcasts sent over our networks. After all, these emanate exclusively from his own collaborators, especially from Pavolini and his own son. It is obvious that the Duce is trying to get Italian radio propaganda back into the hands of the Fascist National Committee. We are soon to feel the adverse effects of the Duce's re-entry into Italian politics.

Stalin is playing politics with his popes. He is having a new Holy Synod convened. English bishops are on a visit in Moscow to underscore this sycophantic action of Stalin's with their propaganda speeches. It makes one sick in the stomach to think of this hypocrisy, but it has been launched not without cleverness.

[In the Greek Orthodox Church, a pope is any clergyman, even a village priest.]

To date we have evacuated about a million people from Berlin. That is a tremendous achievement in organization. In comparison the migration of peoples in the Middle Ages was only a small and modest movement.

September 19, 1943

The Anglo-American press attacked me violently because of my allegedly premature reports of victories. But these didn't come from me; on the contrary, as I have already emphasized, I protested energetically against them. At the Fuhrer's GHQ there were a couple of generals who could not wait. They distributed the skin of the bear before it had been killed and trumpeted to the world a victory that we hadn't achieved. Developments as a matter of fact have been just about the opposite. . . .

I have made it clear both to the responsible men in my Ministry as well as to the Fuehrer's GHQ that I won't stand any longer for such premature and unsubstantiated reports of victories. . . . No military news must hereafter be issued unless it has had my approval. I have also written an energetic letter to Keitel and have demanded an end to the mistakes made so often during this war by his collaborators.

Our military measures at Salerno are one big scandal. The exuberant reports of victory emanated from our supreme command for the south, and came almost directly from Kesselring.

The Italian press is now slowly veering over to the Duce in the sections of Italy occupied by us. The only dishonorable exception is the *Corriere della Sera*. It would be a good thing to eliminate this dirty sheet as quickly as possible.

In the evening the Duce spoke over the German and Italian broadcasting systems from Munich, where he is stopping at the Prince Karl Palace since his visit to the Fuehrer's GHQ. His speech was clear, determined, and of superior quality. He did not try in the least to be sentimental. He spoke quite coolly, realistically, and without exaggerated pathos. His arguments were effective and convincing. They will certainly not fail to impress the Italian public. The Italian Fascists will no doubt draw new hope and new fighting courage from this speech.

The Duce again described the events leading up to July 25. A new item in his presentation is the fact that his talk with the King lasted only twenty minutes. This was followed by sharp criticism of the King and of the Crown Prince. He fairly poured derision on the House of Savoy for its infidelity and ingratitude. He found words of warm praise for the Fuehrer's fidelity, which he said was typical of the attitude of the whole German people. . . .

Fascism, he said, would henceforth be socialist, nationalist, and anti-plutocratic. The Duce believes a new Italy can grow from such a kernel. I don't know whether his hopes will be realized. Be that as it may, this is the only possibility for Italy to get out of the present terrible dilemma. It remains to be seen whether the Duce himself will stage a comeback. Surely his speech was very dignified. It convinced more by its arguments than by any pathos of delivery.

At noon I had quite a chat with Dr. Ley. He wanted to be informed about latest developments. He has somewhat queer ideas regarding our intentions in the east and south. One can see that much of the material at my disposal is being withheld from him, else he would judge the situation more realistically and not let his imagination run wild. But it is a good thing that the men who frequently address the masses are free from any knowledge of unpleasant news. That gives them much more self-assurance when talking to the people.

A report from Essen is very impressive. The population, especially in the former Communist quarters of the city, has to a large extent made shift for itself. The same fanaticism with which the workers formerly sponsored Communism is now concentrated upon national tasks. The population isn't thinking of depending solely upon government help as is so often the case with bourgeois circles. The workers help themselves so far as possible.

There was lots of telephoning back and forth during the day between the Fuehrer's GHQ and myself about our news flop regarding Salerno. My protest was received with greatest uneasiness in the Fuehrer's GHQ. They feel guilty and have a bad conscience. Dr. Dietrich blames his military informers, these again blame the inter-information office. I shall certainly find out who was guilty. It can't be denied that in the last analysis Kesselring is really the guilty one, for it was he who radioed the premature reports to the Fuehrer's GHQ.

September 20, 1943

The English . . . seem to be very much embarrassed by the fact that the Duce spoke with such sovereign confidence. They would certainly prefer to have him in their hands rather than devoting himself to the political resurgence of the Italian people. I think he will give them some cause for worry.

Large quantities of weapons have fallen into our hands and gigantic columns of Italian prisoners are on their way into the Reich. They will be very welcome here as skilled workers.

The situation in Dalmatia has become somewhat difficult for us because of the increase of Partisan formations by Italian deserters and Italian supplies of weapons. I don't believe that we can master the crisis there by propaganda alone, as has often been urged. A sharp sword must always stand behind propaganda if it is to be really effective.

A new tabulation of losses in the East is available. . . . Our total losses in the East, exclusive of Lapland, from June 22, 1941, to August 31, 1943, were 548,480 dead, of whom 18,512 were officers; 1,998,991 wounded, of whom 51,670 were officers; 354,967 missing, of whom 11,597 were officers; total 2,902,438, of whom 81,779 were officers.

It is a curious thing that every individual soldier returning from the Eastern Front considers himself personally quite superior to the Bolshevik soldier, yet we are retreating and retreating. The Soviets are able to publish every day new and justified reports of victories. Nor will it do to alibi ourselves by claiming that we are shortening the front. As a matter of fact we are not shortening the front but are even extending it at some points. It is true that our front thus far has not broken down, nor was it torn up. But that is meager comfort considering the extremely valuable industrial and agricultural terrain and the tremendous quantities of supplies that we have had to abandon.

The neutral countries are asking themselves whether our retreat is really based on military considerations. They cannot imagine that our fighting spirit should have sunk so low in the course of one summer as to compel us thus to withdraw our front. Many regard it as a tactical move to enable us to arrive at a separate peace with the Soviets. Personally I cannot imagine how that could be arranged. . . .

They believe we intend to withdraw slowly from the East and to divert Stalin's attention to the Near East and India while we negotiate with him. We could certainly discuss such a development; unfortunately it in nowise corresponds to the facts.

Some English periodicals take quite a radical view of the political conduct of the war. They regard the situation with an amazing realism.

They are aware that, if the Reich were to suffer a military collapse in the East, the European balance of power would be disturbed in a much more aggravating manner than if Germany became the dominating power in central and western Europe.

I have little time for reading. Just now I am reading the English novel, *How Green Was My Valley*. It is very informative about English mentality. . . . I don't believe that England is now in danger of becoming Bolshevized. English mentality is anchored too much in British tradition.

The Fuehrer has invited me to come to his GHQ on Wednesday for a talk.

September 21, 1943

The Duce's speech has created a deep impression on the Italian people. That is owing chiefly to the fact that it was sensational and that the Duce is just now the only person who is talking to the Italians. Nothing whatever is being heard from the King and Badoglio. According to an official English news item they have gone to Sicily and placed themselves under the protection of the enemy.

The Japanese are now speaking of a successful evacuation of Salamaua. These "successful evacuations" are getting the upper hand with the Axis. I don't believe we shall be able to use the expression much longer; it is making us more and more of a laughing stock. The Axis Powers in the course of one year have done so much successful evacuating that a large part of their former war potential was lost thereby. We must begin at last to give a clear picture to our peoples and the world about our situation and our methods in this war.

In the East, too, this question is now a burning one. . . . It gives one the creeps to look at the map and compare what we had under our dominion about this time last year with how far we have now been thrown back. . . . Certainly the Soviet Union is in a much better position now than it was a year ago. At that time the Soviet Union was actually struggling with military and economic death. Now there can be no talk of that.

The Italian question has created great difficulties for us in the Balkans. The Slovenes are now in open rebellion and have gone almost entirely over into the camp of the Partisans. At the moment we lack the police powers to knock out this somewhat dangerous movement.

The fact that the percentages of planes shot down by us have decreased within one year from twenty to five makes us worry. While it is true that we shot down more planes each month than the one before, yet the number of enemy flights to Germany has increased four times as fast as has the number of planes downed. Naturally that makes one wonder.

Speer claims that the production deficit in the armament industry is not too great after an enemy air raid. The fact that bombed cities undergo pretty bad dislocations of public life, as a result of which the workers often stay away from their workbenches for weeks, is far more aggravating. Thus, for instance, the Lanz works at Mannheim have been completely ready for production for a fortnight, yet only 60 per cent of the workers have thus far returned. This explains the large production deficits that we record. That's why, too, the English are more interested in destroying cities than in destroying the munitions industry. Destruction in the munitions industry can be more easily repaired than is the case with the disorganization caused in cities and especially in residential sections.

Lammers has issued a decree by the Fuehrer according to which only he may submit disagreements between ministers of the Reich and chiefs of the highest administrations to the Fuehrer for decision. The Fuehrer desires that Lammers examine such disagreements and arbitrate them so far as possible. Lammers is operating very cleverly. One has the impression that he is heading for some such office as that of Reich Chancellor. But I shall find enough confederates to prevent that!

A huge stream of fugitives is moving from the southern Italian regions occupied by the English and Americans into central and northern Italy. We are increasing this stream by our radio propaganda, especially by our claim that the English and Americans will compel all men of draft age to enlist. Our intention is to send the whole male population into the Reich as workers.

I had a very serious clash with Dr. Dietrich and General Jodl about the news handouts concerning Salerno. The two gentlemen felt very compromised. They would like, under all circumstances, to prevent my reporting this questionable matter to the Fuehrer. I can refrain from this only, however, if given binding assurances that incidents of this sort won't be repeated. I have no mind to let my good name be discredited by the journalistic amateurishness of inferior officers.

September 22, 1943

At the moment it looks very messy on the Eastern Front. Our retreats are no longer orderly and the troops naturally lose a lot of matériel owing to the speed of their movement. Once again there is a serious crisis. The Soviets blow up their victories to impress the world and to put the British under pressure politically. They are doing it also by founding a so-called Association of German Officers which has published an appeal against the Fuehrer containing much propaganda criticizing our politics and conduct of the war. A lot of generals and high officers in captivity in Russia have signed this appeal. Naturally one cannot determine whether the signatures are genuine, and, if so, whether they were given under pressure or voluntarily. Nevertheless this declaration does exist, and it will not fail to have its effect upon public opinion. . . .

Criticism in this declaration is aimed chiefly at the catastrophe of Stalingrad. The real point to the appeal is to be found in the demand for a direct peace which these officers claim they want to prepare for the German people.

Badoglio has issued an appeal to the Italian public. This appeal is about the most shameless thing that has ever come from the pen of a marshal. He calls upon the Italian people to engage in guerrilla warfare; he places himself on the side of our enemies; he declares that we betrayed Italy and left the Italian divisions in the lurch on all battlefields; we are now plundering Italy; his aim is a strong and faithful Italy—in short, he commits to paper whatever the human tongue can fabricate in the way of lies and hypocricy.

Meanwhile someone close to the Duce has published further details about his imprisonment. These are very interesting and indeed sensational. They convey the impression that the Duce had really counted upon being delivered over to the English and Americans but that he intended to thwart this by suicide.

As a marginal note I may register the fact that the Negus has demanded the extradition of Badoglio. He wants to place him before an Abyssinian court as a war criminal. There is no species of madness that the human brain is not capable of thinking up in this war.

I had a long talk with Undersecretary Esser. He told me about his wish to get assigned to some sort of political job and begged me to communicate this request to the Fuehrer. Evidently he would like to be Gauleiter for the Bavarian Eastern Mark. I don't know whether the Fuehrer is ready just now to take this gau away from Gauleiter Waechtler and especially whether he wants to assign Esser, of all people, to this post. Esser told me many flattering things about the effect of my editorials in the *Reich* on Bavarian public opinion. He claimed that I had acquired a political reputation there in recent months that simply could not be surpassed.

September 23, 1943

Churchill indulges in orgies of hatred against the Reich, against National Socialism, against an alleged Prussian Junker clique that is to succeed National Socialism, et cetera. . . . Italy in future is again to enjoy the advantages and blessings of democracy as the English understand it. The Reich is to expect total destruction. There could be no question of mercy for us. England would fight to the end to eliminate the totalitarian states. . . .

He called the Italian front the third front, inasmuch as the second front was to be in the West and was, in fact, already practically in existence, since the divisions now in the British Isles were keeping a large number of German divisions immobilized in the West. . . .

The most important result of the Italian armistice was the seizure of the Italian Fleet. . . .

Churchill's speech is naturally accorded high praise in the English press. But one need not take that very seriously in wartime. Things like that can easily be made to order and are no real barometer of public opinion.

Eden speaking in the House of Commons denied that England intended to take possession of Sicily and Sardinia. I suppose they will make crown colonies of them as in the case of Malta. . . .

Eden gave a detailed statement about the Hess case. He described Hess's mysterious trip pretty much in accordance with the facts. . . . It is very surprising that such a statement is made at this stage. I wonder what the English have in mind?

I have received a report by Schwarz von Berk about the present situation in Finland. Naturally, like all other nations, the Finns would like to have the war brought to an end. But there is all the less possibility of their deserting our front since the Finns are practically no longer engaged in war. The Finnish people are living under relatively bearable conditions. The food situation has improved tremendously as compared with the first winter of war.

[Schwarz von Berk was editor in chief of *Das Schwarze Korps,* official organ of the SS.]

Group Leader Bormann, who met us on our arrival at the Fuehrer's GHQ, brought me the sad news that our regional commissar in Minsk, Kube, was killed by a bomb during the night. A mine with a time fuse had been placed under his bed; he was literally torn to pieces. This shows what dangers leading National Socialists must face, especially in the occupied countries in the East. To remain alive in the present crises one cannot be too careful.

In the occupied areas a number of other attempts were carried out last night, but on personalities of less high rank. They were pretty successful. It looks as if the Bolsheviks intend to start a new wave of assassinations.

I am exceedingly sorry to lose Kube. He was a courageous, decent fighter for the National Socialist movement to whom I owe much devotion and friendship. Even though I often had altercations with him in the old days of our fight for Berlin, these were always on a very honorable and decent plane. He certainly never did anything to hurt me, and that's why I, too, gave him a helping hand when he faced a very serious personal crisis at one time.

[Goebbels's reference to the "very serious personal crisis" in the life of Wilhelm Kube, one of Hitler's earliest disciples, refers to the following: When Hitler took over, Kube was awarded the political plum of the Gauleitership for the Mark of Brandenburg. His administration was so scandalous and he committed such flagrant embezzlements that Hitler was reluctantly compelled to throw him out of his job. Old-line Nazis such as Goebbels, however, who all had been more or less dishonest and whose records were no better than Kube's, kept interceding for him. When Germany became victorious, temporarily, in eastern Europe, and "tough" administrators seemed desirable, Kube was reinstated in Hitler's graces and given the rank of a regional commissar in the Ukraine, under Alfred Rosenberg, Minister of the Occupied Areas.]

Shortly after I arrived at GHQ the Fuehrer asked me to accompany him on his morning walk. The Fuehrer seemed to be in exceptionally good health. Apparently he has recuperated well in recent weeks. He told me his morning walks with his dog Blondi did him a lot of good. In contrast to last year he at least gets into the fresh air every morning and every afternoon. That is excellent for his health. His condition gives no hint of the difficult days through which we are now passing; on the contrary, he seems to be in the best of form. That, in my opinion, is the most important thing for our political and military situation.

Whenever the Fuehrer is in top form, things always move forward after a certain period of stress and strain.

The Fuehrer started right in with the happy news that submarine warfare is beginning to take a new large-scale lease on life. . . . Nevertheless one must not forget that the English and Americans have built three to four million tons of new commercial shipping during the period when our submarines could not be active. Also, the Mediterranean has been cleared by the enemy through their successes in North Africa and southern Italy. . . .

The Fuehrer was very happy that Doenitz pulled back our submarines at the right moment; namely, when we were technically inferior. Had he continued to leave them on duty the larger part of them would undoubtedly be lying at the bottom of the ocean today. . . .

Our new magnetic torpedo has proven its worth, in that the sinking of nine destroyers can be credited to it. The Fuehrer places great hopes in this torpedo. He believes that possibly we shall now have four months of continuing great successes on the high seas. If that were the case, the English position would be shaken considerably. . . .

As regards the West, we have seventeen divisions there at the moment. This, of course, is too little to ward off a large-scale enemy invasion. But the Fuehrer will earnestly press for the increase of these divisions. We have fourteen divisions in Italy at present. That is enough for our purposes there. There are seventeen divisions in the Balkans, some of them first class; but these have their hands full to keep things even halfway in order there. By the spring of 1944 the Fuehrer hopes to have thirty-five new divisions set up. These will have exceptional fighting value. He wants to station thirty-four of them in the Reich itself as an operational central reserve to throw east, west, south, or southeast as needed. . . .

The Serbian Prime Minister, Nedic, has paid a visit to the Fuehrer. He acted very obediently and loyally during this visit. The Fuehrer believes he can make good use of him in re-establishing order in Serbia.

[General Milutin Nedic, born, 1882, was Yugoslav Minister of War at the time the Nazis overran his country. He agreed to collaborate and became Serbian Prime Minister during the German occupation.]

As regards air raids, he is naturally happy that they have decreased appreciably. He attributes this chiefly to the weather but also to our growing measures of defense. As to a weapon of attack, the Fuehrer expects a great deal of our magnetic bombs which are soon to be put into service. Now, as before, he is unflinchingly determined to pay back to England by reprisal attacks what England has done to us. Rocket construction as a weapon of retaliation is under way.

The Fuehrer is determined to strip the Italian cities completely of their anti-aircraft defense. The Italians deserve nothing better than abandonment to their military fate. . . .

The Fuehrer believes that our great reprisal campaign by rockets can begin at the end of January or the beginning of February of next year. Things have been made considerably easier by the fact that we got away from electric rays in connection with our rockets. This leaves the English no technical possibility of interfering with the course of a rocket.

If submarine warfare develops as we hope and if in January or February of the coming year our retaliation weapon swings into action, both these German successes will hit the English hard at a time when they are tired of the war. Possibly a fundamental change can be effected in the British attitude toward the war.

The *nusskern* rocket also offers some prospects of success. It weighs 850 kilos [about 1,870 pounds, or nearly a ton], hence is by no means so harmless as is supposed. I learned for the first time from the Fuehrer that our big rocket weighs fourteen tons. That, of course, is a murderous tool. I believe that when the first of these missiles descends upon London a sort of panic will break out among the English people. . . .

As regards the worrying question of the Eastern Front, the Fuehrer takes a much more optimistic view than does the General Staff on the whole. Our present retreats merely mean that we are retiring to a line behind the Dnieper. . . . Of course we must leave behind large supplies, especially of food and munitions, but that is unavoidable in the case of such quick withdrawals.

If we should be hard pressed the Fuehrer is determined to give up the Desna also, and to withdraw behind Lake Peipus. That, of course, would be quite a serious thing, for we would then have to give up Leningrad too. The Fuehrer expects, however, to hold the line along the Dnieper through the winter. By this operation we would save about 350 kilometers [about 220 miles]. That would make available the divisions we need for the new central operational reserve. This central operational reserve, in my opinion, is the alpha and omega of our present strategy. . . .

The Fuehrer's standpoint in this matter is 100 per cent right. We must not allow the English and Americans to determine our course of action, and it would be wrong for us to keep our eyes fixed almost hypnotically upon our front lines everywhere in Europe with the thought that we must defend them all in the same manner. Just let the English or Americans enter at this or that point; if we possess a large central operational reserve, we shall be able to throw them out again at a convenient moment.

The Fuehrer does not believe that anything can be achieved at present by negotiation. England is not yet groggy enough nor sufficiently tired of war and would interpret every attempt at negotiation as a sign of weakness. In the East, naturally, the present moment is quite unfavorable for indicating any readiness to negotiate. At present Stalin has the advantage, and however easy it may be for someone in an advantageous situation to indicate his readiness for an arrangement, it is quite impossible for one who is at a temporary disadvantage to do so. We must therefore try to survive this crisis, whatever the cost. . . .

The Fuehrer, too, naturally does not see clearly what Stalin really is planning and what reserves he still has. One never can tell in the case of Bolshevism. His present combat troops certainly are in the worst condition imaginable and are very poorly equipped. On the other hand they enter the fray in such great masses that our troops can hardly resist their onslaught. Besides, our troops are naturally overtired and urgently need a rest. . . .

It is refreshing to note the Fuehrer's optimistic attitude regarding the entire situation at the front. Seldom throughout this whole war have I seen the Fuehrer so tough and aggressive. It proves what I have claimed so often: The more furious the storm, the more determined is the Fuehrer to face it.

The Fuehrer told me in detail about the Duce's visit, which made a deep impression on him. That is, the Duce's personality did not act so strongly on him this time as in their earlier meetings. The main reason may be that the Duce now came to the Fuehrer without any power and that the Fuehrer accordingly looked at him somewhat more critically. The Duce has not drawn the moral conclusions from Italy's catastrophe that the Fuehrer had expected of him. He was naturally overjoyed to see the Fuehrer and to be fully at liberty again. But the Fuehrer expected that the first thing the Duce would do would be to wreak full vengeance on his betrayers. But he gave no such indication, and thereby showed his real limitations. He is not a revolutionary like the Fuehrer or Stalin. He is so bound to his own Italian people that he lacks the broad qualities of a worldwide revolutionary and insurrectionist.

His daughter Edda and, through her, his son-in-law Ciano are exerting an unwholesome influence on him. Edda Mussolini succeeded in completely reversing the Duce's opinion about Ciano. Immediately upon her father's arrival in Munich she had a long talk with him, the result of which was a reconciliation between the Duce and Ciano. Ciano has again been accepted in the good graces of the Duce. That means this poisoned mushroom is again planted in the midst of the new Fascist Republican party. It is obvious that the Duce cannot start criminal proceedings against the traitors of Fascism if he is not willing to call his own son-in-law to account. His son-in-law should have been the first to be tried. If he were a man of really great revolutionary caliber, Mussolini would have asked the Fuehrer to hand Ciano over to him and would personally have called him to account. This he won't do, and that handicaps him seriously in proceeding against the other traitors to Fascism. The Fuehrer had the greatest difficulty convincing him that at least Grandi was a deliberate traitor to the Fascist party and the Duce. The Duce at first wouldn't believe that either. But punishment of the Fascist traitors is the condition precedent to a resurgence of Fascism. The little Fascist out in the country cannot believe in the honesty of a new beginning of Fascism if those who headed Fascism for this life-and-death crisis are not called to account. The Fuehrer was deeply disappointed at the Duce's attitude. I am more than happy about it. I feared the meeting of the Fuehrer and the Duce might again lead to a close friendship with embarrassing political difficulties for us. But that has by no means happened; on the contrary, I have never before seen the Fuehrer so disappointed in the Duce as this time. The Fuehrer now realizes that Italy never was a power, is no power today, and won't be a power in the future. Italy has abdicated as a people and as a nation. That's in accordance with the law of nature and the principles of justice in historical development.

Churchill's revelations to the effect that he demanded the extradition of the Duce and that the Carabinieri had orders to shoot him in the event of a German attempt at liberation, are worth their weight in gold to us. The Fuehrer is so happy about it because he believes the Duce now cannot, under any circumstances, make a deal with his adversaries. He would in such a case be playing with his own life.

Personally I am very sorry that the Duce is turning out as he is. Politically, however, I am content, for many a measure that we would otherwise have carried out only with a heavy heart or perhaps not at all is made easier for us.

The Fuehrer, too, is convinced that territorial guarantees alone can give us no security with reference to Italy, if after all his bad experiences the Duce again places himself in the hands of his daughter Edda.

Edda Mussolini's utterly unrestrained behavior would seem to indicate that the Fuehrer's suspicions about her are all too well founded. Be that as it may, in any case it is certain that the Duce has not lived up to political and personal expectations and has thereby spoiled his great future chance.

The Duce, incidentally, is not so sick as was generally assumed. Professor Morell has examined him thoroughly and found no symptoms of any acute or dangerous ailment. It is especially not true that the Duce is syphilitic. It may be that he was earlier, but he was undoubtedly cured completely. Morell diagnosed only a circulatory disturbance and overworked and disordered bowels—in other words, the typical ailment of a modern revolutionary politician from which all of us suffer somewhat. In the case of the Duce it is in an advanced state, but Morell believes that it can be cured absolutely. . . .

There was, of course, no actual quarrel between the Fuehrer and the Duce. . . . But even the Fuehrer's observation that the Duce has no great political future signifies a lot, considering his former admiration for him. . . .

The Duce told the Fuehrer the details of the entire drama of his personal and political crisis. On the whole we had the right slant on developments, with the exception of the King's behavior. It is not true that the Duce had a two-hour talk with the King on the decisive twenty-fifth of July; this conversation lasted only twenty minutes. It precluded discussion of even the most elementary questions of Italian politics and strategy. The King immediately reproached him most bitterly, told him that the war was lost, that there was no hope, and that he had already entrusted Badoglio with the government. . . . After his twenty minutes' talk Mussolini was arrested in the hall by Carabinieri and hustled into an ambulance. At first they tried to deceive him, saying he was being taken into custody because of a plot against his life from which he must be protected; but he was pretty soon aware that he was under arrest. The royal house and Badoglio then had the Duce dragged from one place to another. . . .

Churchill evidently wanted to await the liquidation of the Italian question, the English and American advance to the Brenner, the extradition of the Duce and his public exhibition in New York. This was prevented only by our stroke of genius. The Duce told the Fuehrer very happily that he had always believed in his liberation by the Germans and had firmly counted on it. On the other hand he had always been fully determined never to surrender to his enemies but rather to put an end to his life with a pistol. . . .

The days at GHQ passed in greatest harmony except that the Fuehrer was inwardly reserved toward the Duce. We may consider him absolutely disillusioned concerning the Duce's personality. That is extremely desirable for our further conduct of the war. The Fuehrer is no longer determined to make the personality of the Duce the corner stone of our relationship with Italy. He now demands territorial security to prevent any further crisis. . . .

The Duce intends to call a new Italian national army into being from the remnants of Fascism. I doubt whether he will succeed in this. The Italian people are not equal to grandly conceived revolutionary politics. They don't want to be a great power. That desire was injected into them artifically by the Duce and the Fascist party. The Duce will, therefore not have much luck in recruiting a new Italian national army. . . . Old man Hindenburg was undoubtedly right when he said of Mussolini that he, too, would not be able to make anything but Italians out of Italians.

The Duce is naturally very much handicapped by conditions in his family. His wife, Rachele, hates Edda from the bottom of her heart. One can easily understand that. The Duce, on the other hand, trusts Edda more than he does his wife. Edda visited the Fuehrer some days ago. On that occasion she created a very bad impression. All she asked for was permission to emigrate to South America via Spain. In this connection she tried to settle some money questions. Ciano has brought about 6,000,000 lire with him from Italy. She wanted to exchange these for pesetas and actually offered the Fuehrer the difference in the exchange rate, a tactlessness that nauseated the Fuehrer. Ciano intends to write his memoirs. The Fuehrer rightly suspects that such memoirs can only be written in a manner derogatory to us, for otherwise he could not dispose of them in the international market. There is therefore no thought of authorizing Ciano to leave the Reich; he will remain in our custody, at least for the present.

All these circumstances show by what vile elements the Duce is surrounded and how little trust can be put in him if he lets a rabble like that influence him. If the Duce were a man whose politics were uninfluenced by family considerations, he would have Ciano executed, instead of forgiving him, and would have his daughter whipped. But there is no thought of that; on the contrary, he is putting on an act of a loving family. The Fuehrer has a much better opinion of the Duce's son, Vittorio. He is modest, decent, industrious, and touchingly devoted to his father during the crisis.

Fascism seems still to show no political strength whatever. We must now proceed very coolly and realistically in all these matters. We must use Fascism as far as possible, but of course must not expect the impossible. In the Fuehrer's calculation, Italy used to be a factor of power. That is no longer the case. . . . Italy was just as poor an ace in this war as it was in the last. . . .

Just as soon as he sits a little more firmly in the saddle, the Duce wants to transfer his residence to Bellazzo. It is doubtful, however, whether he can feel halfway secure on Italian soil. He does not yet seem to have his personal bodyguard absolutely under control. The Fuehrer would very much like to place SS guards of his personal regiment at his disposal, but then the Duce would be regarded as being completely in German hands.

One happy thing about Mussolini is his obviously fine state of health. Everything would be all right if he had the same abysmal hatred for other traitors that he has for King Victor Emmanuel. With him, at least, he is through. He expects nothing more from him. He wants to overthrow and eliminate him. But I fear he will hardly succeed if he proceeds according to plans thus far made. His whole political conception is without real clarity because he is bound too much to his family. He is undoubtedly an exceptionally inspired thinker and a high-grade political strategist, but in the last analysis he is nothing but an Italian and can't get away from that heritage.

The Fuehrer criticized the Fascist Grand Council very severely. He is now happy that he never approved of Frick's proposals for creating a senate out of elements that were partly very undependable. Frick had suggested that he set up a senate composed of the presidents of German universities, the high clergy, et cetera. What a senate that would have been! It would rather have overthrown the Fuehrer today than tomorrow. . . .

Someday the Fuehrer will establish a senate made up according to entirely different principles. Men are to be called into it, not on the basis of their positions, but of their achievements. He wants, so to speak, to create a College of Cardinals whose only task will be to elect a fuehrer as occasion demands. That, of course, is the highest political function that can be exercised in the modern National Socialist state. Possibly a system may develop whereby several thousand families, the cream of the National Socialist leadership, will govern the Reich for centuries just as is the case today in England with several hundred families, except that these families will be chosen and selected on an entirely different basis. . . .

The College of Cardinals or Senate should naturally comprise only the very first men of the Reich, chosen on the basis of their attitude and character rather than only their intelligence. The Fuehrer explained to me that on the basis of this principle Frick would not belong to it, whereas Gauleiter Grohé would. The Fuehrer is very happy that he did not establish the Senate prematurely. Had he done so it would have been set up solely on the basis of revolutionary selection, whereas there is now the additional selection of war which is even more exacting than revolution.

In that connection I asked the Fuehrer what our marshals were doing now. He is quite satisfied with their attitude. He spoke very favorably about Guenther von Kluge, Georg von Kuechler, and even Fritz Erich von Manstein, although he regards him as somewhat excessively ambitious. Paul Ludwig Ewald von Kleist has made a very close approach to the Fuehrer and to the National Socialist movement. Fedor von Bock is leading more of a sickly pensioner's existence. Of Walther von Brauchitsch one hears hardly anything; I suppose he has a bad conscience. The Fuehrer spoke in great praise of Field Marshal General Ernst Busch. He has a higher opinion of Albert Kesselring's military abilities than I do. Unfortunately Erwin Rommel had to undergo an operation for appendicitis during the critical days in Italy; otherwise he would undoubtedly have been able to take a hand in Salerno. Here one misfortune followed another. Even of Wilhelm Walter List the Fuehrer now has a more favorable opinion than several months ago. List, too, is ill; he was not equal to the wear and tear of a war lasting four years. Taken as a whole our generals are simply not to be compared with the Italians. Treason such as the Italian generals committed against Mussolini is impossible considering the mentality of the German and especially the Prussian generals. . . .

I put the question to the Fuehrer whether his GHQ was sufficiently protected against possible attacks by parachutists. The liberation of Mussolini has shown how easily such a maneuver can be carried out if it is quite unexpected. The Fuehrer, thank God, could assure me that security measures at GHQ have been strengthened considerably; nevertheless there are certain eventualities against which one cannot prepare in advance.

It touches one's heart that the Duce again and again emphasized to the Fuehrer that he assumed full responsibility for developments in Italy. But in so doing he whitewashed a large number of traitors who are close to him personally. That makes no sense. The Fuehrer repeatedly pointed out to him that he had warned him in time. The Duce admitted this but had been unwilling to listen. He finally failed because of his excessive loyalty toward the King and the House of Savoy, although experience should have taught him that this King and his House simply don't know what fidelity means. Today the Duce admits that. . . .

The Fuehrer asked me what I imagined he would do about such treachery. I believe he wouldn't have hesitated for a moment to inflict a punishment that would have frightened off for all time anybody who thought about treason even in the remotest corner of his heart. Where, by the way, is the dividing line between treason and folly? It is very hard to draw it, especially since every traitor can always claim he was merely foolish if his treachery fails to succeed.

I then posed the very serious and important question to the Fuehrer as to how far he intends to extend the Reich. His idea is that we ought to advance as far as the Venetian border, and that Venetia should be included in the Reich in a sort of loose federation. Venetia would be all the more willing to accept this, since the Reich alone would be able after a successful war to supply it with tourist trade, to which Venice attaches the greatest importance. I regard such a boundary line as the only practical and right one. I only hope that the Fuehrer won't let anything, especially not his reawakening friendship for the Duce, divert him from this decision. . . .

I then talked to the Fuehrer about a lot of questions of personnel. I told him how unbearably indolent and sleepy Seldte behaved during the last session of the Committee on Air-Raid Damage. The Fuehrer had nothing but gracious pity for Seldte. Seldte, too, is a sick man. But the Fuehrer rightly pointed out that he could boot Seldte out at any time, whereas he could not do that with Ley.

I also told the Fuehrer of the critical attitude that Popitz assumed during this session. He is absolutely convinced that Popitz is our enemy. He is already having him watched so as to have incriminating material about him at his disposal; the minute Popitz gives himself away, he would have him in his hand. . . .

[Dr. Johannes Popitz was Prussian Minister of Finance, a holdover from the Von Papen cabinet of 1932. He was executed by the Nazis in February 1945 for being implicated in the plot against Hitler which culminated in the July 20, 1944, attempt on the Fuehrer's life.]

The Fuehrer is full of praise for Seyss-Inquart. He governs the Netherlands very cleverly; he alternates wisely between gentleness and severity, thereby indicating that he has had excellent Austrian schooling.

In contrast to him on the one hand is Terboven, who knows only the hard-fisted way, and on the other is Best in Denmark, who knows only the velvet glove. Incidentally our quick action in Denmark reestablished peace and order there very rapidly. . . .

The Fuehrer misses Heydrich very much when it comes to present-day personnel questions. He would be the proper man to establish law and order in the General Government. Frank is undoubtedly not equal in any way to his heavy task.

But who is to be put in his place? Frank, incidentally, has made it up with his wife, but in a typically legalistic way. Jurists will always be jurists. The Fuehrer has just found that out in the case of Thierack. However much of an improvement Thierack may be over Guertner, he is still not an ideal Minister of Justice. In the end he keeps sticking to his juridical eggshells. . . .

The Fuehrer has nothing in mind for Esser. I put in a good word for him but did not succeed in changing the Fuehrer's opinion of him. . . .

I could easily eliminate Dietrich as the Reich's press chief, if I had a position open for which I could recommend him. Unfortunately the Fuehrer does not think him capable of handling any important task. I'm therefore stuck with him.

The Fuehrer has great regard for the personality of Keitel, but doesn't think much of his ability. But at least he is satisfied that he is an honest, straightforward character. On the other hand the abilities of Jodl are much greater. He is in fact a very good and solid worker whose excellent general staff training is revealed time and again.

I told the Fuehrer in detail about my difficulties with the press section of the OKW. The Fuehrer is simply flabbergasted that I should be hindered thus in the development of my work. He had always been told by the gentlemen of the OKW that the press section had already been dissolved. He is now determined to wipe the slate clean. I proposed to him that he receive General von Wedel first of all and size him up personally.

[General Hasso von Wedel was chief of the Wehrmacht public-relations section.]

The Fuehrer was most ready to accept this suggestion. I believe Von Wedel's reception will constitute a great triumph for me. Just as soon as the Fuehrer sees who it is that is responsible for the propaganda at the OKW, he will undoubtedly and without reserve subordinate the propaganda of the Wehrmacht to me and my Ministry. I am very curious to see how this reception will come off. The Fuehrer is determined to put a number of very touchy and difficult questions to Wedel. There is no doubt that he will flunk.

The propaganda in the occupied areas is also to be subordinated to me, not only in those with civilian commissars, but also where military governors are in charge of the administration. The Fuehrer is totally opposed to the Wehrmacht engaging in tasks that are not germane to it. There are always too few officers available for the front, but a superfluity of them in the occupied areas and in various sectors of civilian life. These are usually third or fourth raters who were merely taken out of civilian life and stuck into uniform. On the one hand they hinder civilian officers in their work, and on the other hand are missing from civil life, thereby creating shortages. The Fuehrer wants not only to make changes in the propaganda, but also to take from the Wehrmacht all economic, legal, and social-security questions. The Wehrmacht is to limit itself to conducting the war in a military sense and to leave everything else to civilians. The Fuehrer complained very bitterly about the military administration in the occupied areas. Parasites have there gained a foothold to an extent that cannot continue unchallenged. . . .

I developed my ideas concerning the nature of propaganda for the Fuehrer. I believe that when a propaganda ministry is created, all matters affecting propaganda, news, and culture within the Reich and within the occupied areas must be subordinated to it. . . . I emphasized that I insist upon totalitarianism in carrying out the propaganda and news policies of the Reich. He agreed with me absolutely and unreservedly. . . .

I complained to the Fuehrer that subordinate officers again and again try to tell me their orders were issued by the Fuehrer's GHQ, especially when somewhat shady matters are involved. The Fuehrer empowered me to reject all such attempts categorically. All his wishes—in my case he will not speak of orders—are to be made known to me through the channels with which I am familiar. If anybody else should claim that he is speaking with the authority of the Fuehrer's GHQ I can be convinced that this isn't true. . . .

I told the Fuehrer about the impertinence of Paula Lutze who now lays claim to the house on the Wannsee which was abandoned by Alfieri. The Fuehrer authorized me to reject her demand categorically.

Frau Lutze has completely lost the Fuehrer's sympathies by her insolent behavior. . . .

[The "house on the Wannsee" was a beautiful property on Lake Wann, directly outside Berlin and adjacent to Potsdam. It is now in the American sector of occupation of Greater Berlin, and very popular for boating, sailing, and swimming.]

I am to have dinner alone with the Fuehrer tonight. . . .

In the course of the dinner I was able to discuss a number of personnel and art questions with the Fuehrer. News had just been received from England about the information that Eden gave the House concerning Hess. The Fuehrer keeps asking himself in vain why the English are discussing the Hess case now, without any apparent urgent reason. . . .

I asked the Fuehrer whether he would be ready to negotiate with Churchill or whether he declined this on principle. The Fuehrer replied that in politics principles simply do not exist when it comes to questions of personalities. He does not believe that negotiations with Churchill would lead to any result as he is too deeply wedded to his hostile views and, besides, is guided by hatred and not by reason. The Fuehrer would prefer negotiations with Stalin, but he does not believe they would be successful inasmuch as Stalin cannot cede what Hitler demands in the East.

Whatever may be the situation, I told the Fuehrer that we must come to an arrangement with one side or the other. The Reich has never yet won a two-front war. We must therefore see how we can somehow or other get out of a two-front war.

The Fuehrer once more conjured up before me what would have happened if on Hess's arrival the English had taken the initiative to exploit this incident to make our allies distrustful. The war might then possibly have taken a catastrophic turn for us. The Italians would probably have deserted us and the Japanese might have failed to join us. On this occasion the English missed their greatest political chance of the war. . . .

The question as to when England might be inclined toward peace is naturally difficult to answer at the moment. . . . The yearning for peace, widespread among the German people, is also to be discerned among other peoples. All peoples are human, and after four years of war nobody sees any fun in it. Personally, too, we are yearning for peace. The Fuehrer stressed this. He said he would be happy to have contact with artistic circles again, to go to the theater in the evening and to visit the Artists' Club. He praised the theaters of Berlin about

which he has been receiving reports from go-betweens and observers.
. . . He has great plans for Linz. On the other hand he wants to push
Vienna back artistically, as already emphasized to me a number of
times. . . .

The Fuehrer does not like Goering's ideas of art, and is especially
peevish that Frau Goering always butts in on theater questions, and
that she plays personal politics in a rather unfortunate manner. . . .

[Emmy Sonnemann-Goering was an actress in Weimar before Hitler became
Chancellor. She often interceded with her husband on behalf of Jewish stage
people, at least during the first years of the Nazi regime. Later she became more
aloof, had herself addressed as *hohe Frau* (Exalted Lady), wore jewels and furs
rather conspicuously, and had her only daughter, Edda, constantly attended by a
nurse, a governess, and a bodyguard. She was arrested by the Germans during
the spring of 1947, together with other top-ranking Nazi women.]

In the evening there was a tea in honor of Field Marshal General
Keitel who was celebrating his sixty-first birthday. Only generals took
part in this tea party; I was the only civilian in the group.

Just then an air raid occurred which we at first believed to be on
Berlin. I was naturally very much worried, especially since I could not
be in Berlin personally. In the course of the attack it developed, however, that Hanover had been singled out. . . . Although I am sorry that
Hanover was the victim, I was nevertheless quite elated that the attack was not launched against the Reich capital during my absence.
I am not ashamed to admit that on this point I agree with the saying,
"Holy Saint Florian, my house do spare; on other houses please drop
the flare." . . .

In this circle of generals the Fuehrer reverted to the theme of Russia; but he spoke much more reservedly before the generals than when
talking to me privately.

It is quite doubtful whether we can choose between Russia and
England. If we actually had a choice it would naturally be much more
pleasant to start talks with London than with Moscow. One can always
make a better deal with a democratic state, and once peace has been
concluded, such a state will not seize the sword for at least twenty
years to come. Psychologically the English would not be in a position
to make war, and besides the English people are too tired of war and
possibly also too washed up. It is different with the Bolsheviks. Because of their close-knit system they are naturally in a position to embark upon war at any time. . . .

We talked about the Italian question. . . . A new government is to
be installed in Rome on Thursday. The Duce agreed with us on the
members who are to compose it. Besides Graziani there is no person-

ality of importance in the lot. Graziani is naturally a first-class military man, but he is said to be not quite dependable politically. However, he sided immediately and unmistakably with the Duce on July 25 after Mussolini's fall.

[General Rodolfo Graziani, Marchese di Neghelli, born, 1882, was Viceroy of Ethiopia, 1936–37; honorary governor of Italian East Africa, 1938; chief of army staff, 1939–40; commander of the Italian forces in North Africa and Governor of Libya July 1940 to January 1941; commander in chief of the Republican Fascist Army in North Italy, 1943–45.]

Pavolini is in Rome to build up the Fascist party and the Fascist militia. He isn't having much luck. In response to his first appeal for re-creating the Fascist militia, exactly fifteen men in the Italian capital reported! That is a distressingly small number and carries no weight whatever. But one can see from it to what depths Fascism has already sunk in public esteem. . . .

The Fuehrer showed me a copy of a letter that Edda Mussolini addressed to her father, the Duce. This letter beats everything. Edda Mussolini is acting like a wildcat in her Bavarian villa. She smashes china and furniture on the slightest provocation. This time she complained to her father because she did not get a telephone connection with him on one occasion and because she was once denied an automobile. She uses ridiculous trivialities to threaten her father with blackmail. She states in the letter that if he does not help her immediately and take her along to Italy, she will create a gigantic scandal for him, so that curses and disgrace will be showered upon her father's head before the whole world. It is hard to imagine that the daughter of a great man dares to act thus toward her father.

Of course the Fuehrer and I ask ourselves whether possibly Edda Mussolini and especially Ciano know something about the Duce that might compromise him in public opinion; otherwise she would hardly be in a position to write that sort of blackmail letter. Should that actually be the case, most of the riddle concerning Fascism would be solved. One could then explain why the Duce always yielded to Ciano, even this time—a thing that would otherwise be completely ununderstandable. The letter certainly bears testimony not only against Edda Mussolini but against the Duce himself. What sort of upbringing must the Duce have given his daughter if she dares write him such a letter under such circumstances!

I urgently warned the Fuehrer against permitting Ciano to escape to Spain. Edda Mussolini had urged this upon him. She said she wanted a separation from her husband, while Ciano wanted to write his memoirs there. One can imagine what these memoirs will be like. Ciano has no special talent as a writer; he cannot, therefore, achieve literary success by his style or the good quality of his memoirs. He can do it solely because of their sensational make-up. This, however, will be determined by his hostility to Germany. I am firmly convinced that this dirty scoundrel [*Miststueck*] would begin to write against us, before he had been gone a month, and would intrigue against us in the most contemptible manner. Ciano is the satan of the Fascist movement and the curse of Italy. We must safeguard ourselves against him, now he is in our hands. The Fuehrer doesn't know just how that is to be done, but as a starter he wants to put strong pressure on the Duce to create order at least in his own family. Only then will he be able to establish order inside the Fascist party and, after that, in Italy.

Johst, who is a neighbor of the Cianos in Upper Bavaria, has written a series of letters to the Fuehrer about the behavior of the Cianos. These letters are literary tidbits. Johst described conditions at the Villa Ciano as simply grotesque.

[Hanns Johst was a Nazi novelist and dramatist whom Goebbels advanced rapidly, appointing him president of the Author's Academy and Reich Leader of German Writers.]

Be that as it may, all this is the greater reason for us to look to our military security in the south. . . . The Italian soldiers will be brought into the Reich as prisoners and will here be integrated into production. This Italian debacle has proven good business for us, both in seizing their weapons and taking over their man power.

As regards the possibilities of treachery by other satellite states, Horthy would like to desert us, but the Fuehrer has already taken the necessary precautions against this. . . . Kállay, his Premier, is certainly a swine. But he doesn't show his hand; he is too careful to expose himself. Consequently we must put up with him for the present. Antonescu is a dependable ally in so far as one can say that of any person from the Balkans. He too, however, is in the hands of the corrupt and pro-British Mihai Antonescu, who would rather desert us today than tomorrow.

Our security service succeeded in arresting the Princesses Mia and Mafalda of Savoy. They are acting exceptionally insolently and insultingly, but they are being taken into the school of hard knocks. . . .

After the generals had taken their leave, long after midnight, the Fuehrer asked me to come to him once more quite alone. For hours we walked up and down in his map room and discussed the Italian question from its most intimate angles. The Fuehrer told me that, while he had no proofs, he thought it quite possible that the Duce at one time may have had the personal intention of deserting us. Badoglio referred to this in his last appeal to the Italian people, declaring that the Duce, too, had entertained the idea of ending the coalition with us. The Fuehrer fears that that is the blackmail material which Ciano and his wife have in their hands. Only that could explain the daughter's letter to her father. I don't believe that is the reason. Neither Ciano nor Edda Mussolini is clever enough to realize what consequences such revelations would have. I believe we attribute more intelligence to our opposite numbers than they possess. Edda Mussolini has something on her father that is either of a criminal nature or compromises him socially and politically. It is either a question of love affairs or of money. I have heard on a previous occasion that Ciano helped the Duce to transfer large sums of money from Italy to Switzerland. Such a revelation would naturally be an almost mortal blow to the Duce. . . . The whole affair is certainly pretty strange and it is desirable that we hold on to the personalities involved so that no disaster may result. With Fascism we got ourselves into somewhat mixed company.

In any case we must begin slowly to write off the Duce politically. However much we may like him personally, and however valuable the services may be that he rendered to us, there must be a limit somewhere, especially when the interests of the Reich are involved. The Fuehrer is very loath to do this, for after all he owes it to the Duce that he could bring about rearmament of the Reich, annex Austria, and integrate the Protectorate into the Reich. All this was essential for re-establishing a strong German Reich authority both at home and abroad. The Fuehrer certainly won't forget this so far as the Duce is concerned. But now that things have come to the present pass, we are compelled to consider the Reich's interests without inhibitions and without consideration for anybody else. . . . The Duce was spoiled by Ciano. He is no longer his old self, and one can no longer count upon him firmly as a political factor, especially since he no longer has any power. . . .

If Edda Mussolini employed more than a mere literary turn of speech by her blackguard threat, and if there is actually an unfathomed secret behind it, that would probably also be the secret of Fascism itself. I suppose that at some time or other we shall somehow get on the trace of that secret. For the moment it is only right that we should assume such a secret to exist and that we make sure of guarantees which will prevent harming the political interests of the Reich. . . .

It was 4 A.M. when I bade farewell to the Fuehrer. He invited me to visit him at least one day each week. Even if I had nothing special to report it would be a great relaxation and comfort to him if he could talk to me a couple of hours. I was glad to promise that.

I drove back to Rastenburg with Naumann. . . . While I talked to the Fuehrer Naumann had conducted a whole series of discussions with the gentlemen at GHQ, especially with the generals. The reputation that I and my Ministry enjoy everywhere at GHQ is at present extraordinarily great.

September 24, 1943

The raid on Hanover last night was pretty extensive after all. While there was no heavy damage to industrial plants, residential quarters were hard hit.

Our rocket bombs are the subject of most sensational reporting and rumor mongering throughout the world. Churchill's remarks during his last House of Commons speech gave an impetus to this. Exact details aren't known, nevertheless several English newspapers published reports indicating that the British on the whole are aware of the nature of these rocket bombs.

Badoglio has again addressed the Italian people. Obviously the resurgence of the Fascist party is giving him some trouble. His latest declaration contains eight points for Italian conduct. These points are nothing but a heterogeneous collection of lies and malicious slander. He declared that we exploited Italy during the war, that we seized Italians and dragged them to the theaters of war in Greece and North Africa, that the King was the exponent of the Italian people's will, that it was the duty of the Italian people to drive us from Italian soil, that Fascism was dead and could never be resurrected, and that Italy would emerge from this war stronger and freer than ever. It is hardly possible to comment on this aggregation of empty phrases and cowardly alibis. Nobody in the world takes Badoglio seriously.

The situation in the East has become more critical. . . . We must try under all circumstances to hold the Dnieper line; in case we lose it I wouldn't know where we might gain a new foothold.

On Stalin's orders the Free German Officers' Committee in Moscow has gone in for propaganda in a large way. General Seydlitz has even made a broadcast. Certainly no general of old Prussian stock can sink lower.

[General Walter von Seydlitz was one of the officers who capitulated with Field Marshal Paulus at Stalingrad. One of his ancestors, General Friedrich Wilhelm von Seydlitz, was a hero of the Napoleonic Wars. His victory at Rossbach in 1757 was regarded as one of the greatest triumphs in the history of cavalry warfare. The family was one of the oldest and most prominent in Germany. General von Seydlitz became one of the leaders of the Free Germany Committee in Moscow.]

Rumors about alleged peace negotiations between Berlin and Moscow keep growing daily throughout the world. There naturally isn't a word of truth to them, but they show that Stalin is trying to intensify his war of nerves. Again and again it is claimed that Tokyo is negotiating between the Reich and the Soviets. This, too, in no way corresponds to the facts.

Late at night there was another heavy air raid on Mannheim and Darmstadt. Details were not available since telephone communications were interrupted.

Unfortunately our concentrated submarine attack on a convoy in the northern Atlantic did not really get under way. . . . Nevertheless our submarines succeeded in sinking twelve destroyers and 15,000 tons of shipping. . . . It would be wonderful if submarine warfare took a new lease on life. We must achieve success somewhere. A kingdom for a victory!

September 25, 1943

The English and Americans are boasting of having set Naples on fire. One ought really to be quite sad about the barbaric acts against culture that this war entails. Undoubtedly later generations will curse us for having brought such ruin upon the peoples of Europe.

The situation in the East is engaging public attention far beyond any other topic. Moscow claims our retreat was not orderly but developed into a wild rout. That is not in accordance with the facts, but it is true that we have had to abandon tremendous quantities of supplies which we could neither take along nor destroy; and of course it is impossible to dynamite all military installations. Their advance is giving the Bolsheviks tremendous material advantages which will cause us grave difficulties.

I have been shown a collection of letters written by captured or fallen Red Army men to their home folk. These letters indicate real fighting spirit. There is no hint whatever of dejection. The Soviets are living on their victories. The Red Army soldiers believe they can advance up to the German border by autumn. Of course our Wehrmacht will be a barrier to that ambition!

In the afternoon I spoke in Kroll Opera House to all the Reich orators, the heads of the Reich propaganda offices, and the local Nazi sub-leaders of Berlin. I called them together to give them a survey of the situation and to supply them with material for a gigantic propaganda campaign for the Party. I talked for almost two hours, was in good form and gave them a series of valuable suggestions. Their morale was excellent. Here are first-class people trained in politics. They will never fail in a crisis.

[The term "Reich orator" was an official title conferred by the Nazi party on spellbinders considered especially effective.]

My article about the Italian question has had a fine reception. People now understand why I had to keep quiet for a while, and heartily welcome the resumption of my literary activity. Quite a number of letters state that my weekly article is regarded as the political directive for the week.

A number of Catholic and Protestant ministers have been sentenced to death. They had offended the German armed forces in a most cowardly manner. I proposed to the Fuehrer that the verdicts, together with the opinion of the court, be published. The Fuehrer will decide about this soon.

My new book, *The Steep Ascent*, is being put together by Schirmeister. A number of articles and speeches of last year cannot be used because they contain wrong forecasts. I don't want to edit them but prefer simply to omit them. There is enough unchallengeable material available to fill more than a book.

I feel somewhat ill. I caught a bad cold on my trip to GHQ. I shall therefore have to take care of myself over the week end so as to be in top form again next week.

September 26, 1943

Churchill has had to reconstruct his Cabinet somewhat. Among others he has taken in Beaverbrook as Lord Privy Seal. The deeper significance of this appointment is not yet apparent. Beaverbrook is known to be a friend of the Americans and foe of the Bolsheviks.

Terrible news reaches us from India about the awful famine raging there. The English authorities are proving themselves totally unable, not to say unwilling, to do anything about it. They have put the leading Indian politicians behind the bars; the Indian people are quite unable to defend themselves against the English; the English therefore have an awfully easy and comfortable time of it putting the Four Freedoms of Roosevelt and the Atlantic Charter into practice there.

In the East the fight for the Dnieper has begun. . . . Quite understandably Moscow is in a state of jubilation as never before during this war. We evacuated Smolensk during the night. I question very much whether we can hold Kiev. Naturally we are losing enormous quantities of supplies during this overhasty retreat.

There's nothing special to note about air raids. I intend awarding a badge to all who have been totally bombed out. This will label them as such when they reach their new abodes. Practice has shown that many doubtful elements are using bomb warfare to secure unauthorized advantages for themselves. That makes the people in the gaus designated to receive bombed-out persons less willing to give.

September 27, 1943

Graziani is proving to be a valuable asset to the Duce's Government. He appealed to the Italian people in a very plucky broadcast in which he arrayed the best possible soldierly arguments. He told off the King, the Crown Prince, and Badoglio in bitter terms. Graziani does not mince words. He told the House of Savoy what it must hear whether it wants to or not.

Our public-relations policy dealing with the section of Italy occupied by the English and Americans is not very clever. We are doing too little, in fact, almost nothing, about it. When I think what the English are reporting in the way of news from the areas occupied by us and compare with it how little we do to meet it, I am all the more anxious to do something in a big way.

September 28, 1943

The Americans are trying to impress the Bolsheviks with a gigantic program of armament production for 1944. They are talking of 102,000 planes to be produced during that year. Well, the American trees certainly won't grow to the heavens!

[Goebbels, like all top Nazi leaders, always underestimated the potentialities of American industry. Americans who tried to warn Hitler about this before the shooting war with the Western Powers began often told this editor that Hitler had a "blind spot" when it came to American production capacity.]

Sumner Welles has definitely resigned. His place will be taken by Stettinius, who has thus far administered Lend-Lease. Stettinius is one of the most hard-boiled imperialistic capitalists in the Roosevelt entourage.

[Edward R. Stettinius, former United States Steel Corporation top executive, was American Lend-Lease Administrator at this time. He became Undersecretary of State and finally Secretary of State.]

The Duce has transferred his seat of government to Italy and is trying feverishly to obtain recognition by any government whatever. Naturally the German Reich Government has already extended recognition. The Japanese Government followed in Germany's wake.

Alarming rumors have come from Madrid, too, about separate peace negotiations by Moscow and Berlin of which naturally not a word is true but which throw a significant light on the general situation.

The French politician, Châteaubriant, sent me a long letter about the present situation in France. He complains of the fact that the Reich has not sent any man of stature to Paris and that the position of the collaborationists has become very difficult. Laval, he said, was forever stalling; he could be made to act only if a German diplomat of rank stood behind him and kept driving him. Châteaubriant is proceeding from the wrong assumption that the Fuehrer intends to do something special with France. That is not the case.

[Alphonse de Châteaubriant, born, 1882, was a French novelist and essayist who won the Concourt prize in 1911 and the Grand Prix of the Académie Française in 1923. He edited La Gerbe, a pro-Nazi review.]

The state funeral for Gauleiter Kube took place at noon. Rosenberg delivered the memorial address. It was characterized by unusual tactlessness. Rosenberg is not the man to touch the hearts of his listeners.

I had a long talk with Gauleiter Florian about conditions in Rheydt. He had talked to a big gathering there the day before and reported to my satisfaction that the morale of the Rheydt population is beyond all criticism. The city wishes me to visit it as soon as possible. I shall try to do so some time next week.

September 29, 1943

The daylight raid on Emden was played up sensationally in London. Actually the Americans did achieve a success in that they flew in with pursuit planes and therefore had no heavy losses.

The reports on interrogations of United States flying officers have been submitted to me. These reports don't speak very favorably for the United States Air Force. . . . The Americans want to get home as soon as possible. . . . European differences seem very remote to them and they therefore have no real enthusiasm for the war. They also complain of the exceptionally high losses sustained in day raids on the Reich. They describe every flight into Germany as a sort of suicide mission.

The Americans and English are making a lot of fuss about the capture of the south Italian airport of Foggia. They hope to use it as a jumping-off place for targets in southern Germany.

The Americans and English have become much more modest about the situation in southern Italy than they were at first. They speak of exceptionally heavy losses and of very tough and harassing fights with our troops there. The Germans, they say, defend themselves in hand-to-hand combat and when captured behave very arrogantly, like typical National Socialists. We can only be proud of our soldiers.

The neutral countries are naturally afraid of taking any stand regarding the Fascist Republican Government. Even Franco declines for the present to follow our procedure in this matter. That's the Spaniards' way of thanking the Duce for the great aid he gave them in their civil war for liberty!

Unfortunately we have had to give up Katyn. The Bolsheviks undoubtedly will soon "find" that we shot the 12,000 Polish officers. That episode is one that is going to cause us quite a little trouble in the future. The Soviets are undoubtedly going to make it their business to discover as many mass graves as possible and then blame them on us.

We have received news via Tokyo that public life in Moscow has become distinctly more normal. Soviet successes of this summer are naturally having a notable effect on their home front.

Churchill evidently took Beaverbrook into his Cabinet in order to dispatch him to Moscow on a special mission. Beaverbrook has always favored an Anglo-Soviet understanding. The fact that he has now been taken into the Cabinet I regard as proof that Churchill is determined under all circumstances to bring about an accord between London and Moscow, at least for the present.

Foreign countries are laughing at our observations concerning the Three-Power Pact. It must be admitted they are somewhat hysterical. Since the Italian treachery they lack the punch they used to have.

Ritter, the representative of Sauckel, was shot to death in the street in Paris. We shall have to take extremely severe measures to make the French DeGaullist population understand there is a limit to German patience even in our present military situation.

[The man referred to is Julius Ritter, Sauckel's deputy for French forced labor.]

I had a long talk with Speer. He now intends to carry out the idea of total war by a number of seemingly unsensational measures. By putting the brakes generally on civilian production he expects to make 800,000 workers available for the munitions industry and 300,000 men for the Wehrmacht during the next few months. In addition Sauckel will pull 500,000 men out of civilian production, so that we shall actually see the entire German civilian production come to a standstill in a few months. That will mean the total war which I have demanded for years will become a reality. . . .

[Americans often wonder at the tremendous dearth of consumers' goods in Germany today. This entry sheds interesting light on this question. German production for civilian needs stopped completely a year and a half before VE-Day.]

The Fuehrer wants me to speak at the Harvest Festival in place of Goering. He would rather have Goering attend the coming military talks. Obviously, however, he also fears that, as in previous speeches, Goering may make some oratorical blunders. I shall use this opportunity to deliver a big speech on the general situation to be broadcast over all networks. Since I don't believe the speech will be effective if given in the Mosaic Hall of the Reich Chancellery, where it was scheduled to be held, I am having the meeting transferred to the Sports Palace. The address will keep me awfully busy these next few days, but I believe the people want me to speak now, and that I shall succeed in giving a big boost to the morale and spirit of the German working people.

Worry after worry, both in my official and personal life. But that's war for you! Nevertheless we must never forget that, once these anxieties are a thing of the past, they will later constitute our most beautiful memories.

September 30, 1943

Churchill made an appearance in Albert Hall and delivered a completely meaningless speech to the women against war fatigue. Apparently in England, too, there is no longer that enthusiasm for war that we always read about in the English press.

The Soviets believe they will shortly be in possession of Kiev and thereby in a position to recapture the whole Ukraine. London confirms this hope. Neutral public opinion clings to the belief that negotiations between Berlin and Moscow are already under way. Evidently the wish is father to the thought.

Again many complaints by fine soldiers have been received here from the German Etappe, especially from the West. Conditions have developed there that baffle all description. I am going to send the data to Field Marshal General Keitel. At the last meeting of the Committee of Three he doubted their authenticity.

During the night several hundred airplanes again flew over the Reich. This time the Ruhr was on the program. Bochum especially was heavily attacked. Damage there was pretty substantial. Unfortunately the weather was such that our defense could not do much.

Recapitulation of events between
October 1 and October 31, 1943

The month of October 1943, which is missing in the diaries, was high lighted by two important events:

1. Badoglio's declaration of war on Germany on October 13.
2. The journeys of Secretary of State Cordell Hull and Foreign Minister Anthony Eden to Moscow to confer with Molotov, beginning October 18, and to meet with Stalin. The outcome of these parleys was not disclosed during this month.

The Russians continued to regain lost ground, and on October 9 announced that all German troops had been cleared from the Caucasus. Also, they crossed the Dnieper on October 7, and on October 14 broadcast the recapture of Zaporoše and on October 25 of Dnepropetovsk.

On the Italian mainland the Allies occupied Naples on October 1 and crossed the Volturno-Calore line on October 16. The Germans cleared out of the island of Corsica on October 5.

Portugal came to the aid of the Allies by permitting the British to use the Azores as anti-submarine bases as of October 12.

It was a month of terrific air raids on German industrial centers— Hagen, Frankfurt-on-the-Main, Bremen, Muenster, Schweinfurt, and Hanover.

Field Marshal Rommel was put in charge of the German forces in Yugoslavia on October 14.

On October 31 the veteran anti-Fascist leader, Carlo Sforza, demanded the abdication of the Italian King, Victor Emmanuel.

November 1943

MOSCOW PARLEY REITERATES DEMAND FOR UNCONDITIONAL SURRENDER. CREATES EUROPEAN ADVISORY COMMISSION. RUSSIAN ARMIES CAPTURE PEROKOP, CUTTING OFF GERMAN RETREAT IN CRIMEA. HEAVY RAIDS ON WILHELMSHAVEN, DUESSELDORF, GELSENKIRCHEN, MUENSTER, BERLIN, LUDWIGSHAFEN, BREMEN. RUSSIAN ARMIES RECAPTURE KIEV, ZHITOMIR. HITLER ASSURES PARTY LEADERS HE WILL NEVER CAPITULATE AND WILL EXACT RETRIBUTION FROM ENGLAND FOR BOMBINGS. FORTY-FOUR NATIONS ESTABLISH U.N.R.R.A. CHURCHILL WARNS 1944 WILL ENTAIL GREATEST SACRIFICE. U.S. FORCES RAID MARSHALL AND GILBERT ISLANDS. TOULON AND SOFIA RAIDED. ROOSEVELT, CHURCHILL, AND CHIANG KAI-SHEK CONFER FIVE DAYS AT CAIRO.

November 1, 1943

The Moscow conference is about to end. As was to be expected, the English and Americans were quite unable to get anywhere with their demand for fixing western Soviet boundaries; on the contrary, Moscow now energetically demands a second front. . . .

The neutral countries realize perfectly what went on in Moscow. Almost everywhere there is doubt and concern. Despite our military misfortunes our political position has seldom been so strong as at present.

London already concedes to the Soviets that the small states of Europe no longer have any right to existence. It makes one's hair stand on end to think how the British plutocracy plays on the gullibility of the people. This war was started because of a midget state but now, when it has reached the decisive culminating point, such states allegedly have no right to exist any more. All fundamental conceptions of how nations are to live together seem upside down in this wild spiritual and political confusion. Therein lies our great chance.

November 2, 1943

The closer the hour approaches for the publication of the Moscow communiqué, the greater is the skepticism of neutral countries regarding the results to be expected. It now seems certain that boundary questions were not discussed at the conference. That is no doubt owing to the fact that Stalin exerted tremendous pressure on the negotiations. . . .

The Moscow Conference is regarded more as a theatrical propaganda show than as a meeting of minds resulting in practical achievements. The fact that a committee is to be established in London for dealing with controversial questions reminds one devilishly of the practice of the League of Nations, which also used to appoint a committee or a sub-committee or a sub-sub-committee when agreement could not be reached on a debatable question.

News has reached us via Ankara that Maisky and Litvinov can be regarded as dethroned. They were overthrown by Vyshinsky, who, after Molotov, is now closest to Stalin in matters of foreign policy. Stalin's ouster of these Jews can be explained only on the ground that they were too friendly with capitalistic circles in the plutocratic countries. They were too obliging to Churchill and Roosevelt, and that, of course, did not suit Stalin at all.

[Ivan Michaelovich Maisky, born, 1884, was Ambassador to Great Britain, 1932–43, when he became assistant Commissar for Foreign Affairs in Moscow.
Maxim Maximovich Litvinov, born, 1876, was People's Commissar for Foreign Affairs, 1918–39 and Ambassador to the United States, 1941–43.
Andrey Januarievich Vyshinsky, born, 1883, first commanded world attention as Soviet prosecutor during the great purges of 1936 and 1937, but more recently became more famed for his vitriolic attack on the United States at the United Nations Assembly in September 1947. He is Deputy Commissar for Foreign Affairs.]

In the evening we received the preliminary draft of the final communiqué. . . . Stalin has agreed to unconditional surrender as demanded by Churchill and Roosevelt. The Reich and Italy must deliver up their so-called war criminals. Austria is to be independent again. Fascism is to be eliminated in Italy. In addition, an international organization for the safeguarding of peace must be called into being. In other words, this conference ended with a communiqué that is a mixture of Bolshevik and League of Nations phraseology. . . .

Casualty figures for the East covering the ten days of October 11 to 20 inclusive are now available. The number of killed in action during this period is 9,279, the number of wounded 39,540, and the number of missing, 5,225. We just cannot stand such a drain for long. When we consider that our eastern campaign has cost us 3,000,000 casualties —men killed, missing, or wounded—nobody can deny that we have paid exceedingly heavily for this campaign. Naturally the Soviets, too, have sustained tremendous losses, but they are in a much better position to stand them than we are. At some point or other we simply must try to get out of this desperate bloodletting. Otherwise we are in danger of slowly bleeding to death in the East.

Reports based on interrogations of prisoners of war concerning morale in the United States indicate that the American people are not so tired of war as the English. Nor have they any great difficulties about food. On the whole the United States is still living very much as in peacetime. Hatred of Japan is very great. Anti-Semitism is only beginning to sprout here and there. In short, morale in the United States may be described as being virtually untouched by the war. Only the strikes give some hope of an early change.

The English and Americans are again talking about a general's plot in the Reich which is to overthrow the Hitler regime. It is very suspicious that, whenever the enemy speaks of a domestic crisis in the Reich, he always thinks of the generals. That is hardly an accident.

I have had a long talk with Seyss-Inquart. I have chosen him as president of the German Academy, and the Fuehrer has given his approval to his candidacy. I informed him in detail about the work awaiting him in the Academy. He will no doubt jump into it with all energy. Seyss-Inquart told me what he thought about the general political situation. His ideas coincide exactly with mine. Seyss-Inquart is a clever politician who undoubtedly could accomplish greater tasks than that of administering the Netherlands.

A report from Kassel describes conditions in that city as pretty desolate. Weinrich has in no way proven equal to the demands made on him by the recent air raid. The number of people killed is at present estimated at 5,000; it may even increase to 6,000.

[Karl Weinrich was the inept Gauleiter of Hessen.]

The problem of reopening the Berlin schools keeps cropping up. So far I have said no. Once we reopen the schools, the stream of inhabitants returning from their evacuation quarters will become unmanageable. In a matter like this one must not yield to the wishes of the people, since the people naturally cannot foretell the future development of air warfare. Now, as Christmas approaches, people begin to yearn; so they just get on a train and travel home, especially if the schools have been reopened. But if air raids should be resumed on a large scale in February or March, these same people will be anxious to leave again for the evacuation gaus. Thus the railroads would have to cope with these gigantic transports two or three times. For that they are quite understandably not at all equipped. We shall therefore have to try to erect a dam against this backflow. If it can't be done by friendly talk, pressure will have to be exerted. It isn't true that compulsion achieves no results. Of course it attains results if the public has been clearly told that it is coming, and if it is then actually put into operation.

Late in the evening I got the Fuehrer's okay for our commentary on the Moscow communiqué. We shall chiefly stress the point that the English got nowhere with their wish for specifying the territorial aims of the Soviet Union. Stalin was victor all along the line. He is no doubt the man of the hour at present.

November 3, 1943

The final communiqué about the Moscow Conference has now been issued. . . . London rejoices in so striking a way that the neutral observer must grow suspicious. The United States, too, let itself be infected by this wave of enthusiasm. I think all this is a show put on to mislead and bluff us. Above all, however, it constitutes an attempt to quiet public opinion in the neutral countries. . . .

I am firmly convinced that the Moscow negotiations have gone very much in our favor, however little it may seem so at the moment. Discord between the Soviets and the Anglo-Americans has not been eliminated, but, on the contrary, has rather been aggravated. . . .

As regards the situation in the East, the advance of the Bolsheviks to Perokop and Armjansk of course is anything but pleasing to us. Judging by the map, the Crimea must be regarded as cut off. But things are not quite so bad as that. We can always retreat by sea. . . . Operations there are at present largely a question of nerves. We can be very happy that the Fuehrer has the fortitude and equanimity to stand so heavy a strain.

Air raids have started again. The Americans made a day raid on Wiener Neustadt. They flew in from southern Italian airports some 200 planes strong, and bombed the airplane factories. They did considerable damage there. Some of the factories were destroyed completely. For at least a month there will be a 70 to 90 per cent deficit in production.

We are now naturally waiting with strained nerves for the arrival of our relief forces in the East. Much will depend upon it. If we were to succeed, as the Fuehrer intends, in recapturing the whole Dnieper, we would face an entirely new situation in the East. Such a situation would offer us a whole series of incalculable military and political chances. But we must not be happy prematurely. Dame Fortune is a very fickle beauty in wartime.

November 4, 1943

Skepticism about the results of the Moscow Conference is still growing in neutral countries. . . . [They] are very much worried but fail to grasp the advantage of aligning themselves more firmly with Germany. The German Wehrmacht, after all, offers the only protection against a Bolshevik inundation of Europe. . . .

How much the Soviets dominated the Moscow Conference can be seen from the fact that Beneš now wants to visit Moscow. England's little satellite governments are now trying to orient themselves more and more in the direction of the great power.

The Soviets have sent a delegation to Bari to participate in the administration of the Italian areas occupied by the enemy. They are beginning to cash in.

The war of nerves is continuing against us with undiminished severity. The most impossible reports about conditions in the Reich are being distributed in the enemy countries; for example, that martial law has been declared in Berlin and about forty other major cities. Obviously the disappointed peoples of England and the United States are being fooled in that way. But lies like that usually have short legs.

Ciano has actually been arrested on orders of the Duce and put into a military prison. The Duce has sent his daughter Edda into a sanatorium. That's the best thing he could possibly do.

The London press urges King Victor Emmanuel to abdicate. This cowardly traitor is now getting the expected kick for his treachery. He didn't deserve anything better.

During the day Wilhelmshaven was attacked heavily by American planes. As the weather was very unfavorable for our anti-aircraft, our fighter planes were not able to do much. We shot down only a minimum number of planes, about seven to ten. With only small losses like that the Americans can cheerfully continue this form of warfare.

In the early evening there were very heavy air raids on Cologne and Duesseldorf. Cologne was hard hit. Grohé told me that even the Cologne Cathedral has been badly damaged. The air raid on Duesseldorf was even worse. All communication with Duesseldorf was interrupted until late into the night. I then finally had a telephone talk with Florian, who told me the English raid had struck parts of the city that had hitherto been spared destruction.

I was given a report about the corruption of German blood by foreign labor. Several thousand illegitimate children of foreign workers and German women or of foreign women and German men are recorded. The numbers, however, are not high enough to cause too much worry. In view of the happenings at the front and in air warfare this problem can be considered later.

November 6, 1943

During the night only a minor air raid took place on Leverkusen. The damage, however, has been considerable and is chiefly owing to the fact that the plant had a fog screen laid over the city, thereby greatly hampering the work of putting out fires.

Mihai Antonescu delivered a somewhat curious speech at Bucharest University. He pleaded, among other things, for a modern edition, as it were, of the Peace of Westphalia. I don't believe, however, that this is a case of premeditated villainy on his part, although he'd be equal to it. Apparently he just doesn't know what the Peace of Westphalia really meant.

[The Peace of Westphalia was signed at Muenster in 1648. It ended the Thirty Years' War. Germany was divided into a multitude of small states, and the treaty was therefore anathema to the Nazis.]

The English are now demanding that not only the Italian King but also Prince Umberto abdicate. Another kick for the traitors!

I arrived at Kassel early in the morning and was awaited at the railroad station by Weinrich. It was too cold for him to ride in an open car with me, and so Prince Waldeck accompained me during my trip through the damaged areas of Kassel.

[Hereditary Prince Josias of Waldeck and Pyrmont was an SS *Obergruppen-fuehrer* (General) in charge of the Fulda-Werra sector of the Kassel area.]

The impression is devastating. The entire center of the city and most of the outlying sections have been destroyed. A gruesome picture strikes the eye. The destruction here can be compared only to that in Hamburg. A catastrophic fire of vast extent has run its unhindered course.

I believe much might have been prevented or at least mitigated, if suitable preparations had been taken by the gau leadership. During a conference with the responsible authorities, in the course of which reports were made on each question involved, I learned how little had been done. Weinrich played a very sorry role. He hadn't the faintest idea of the actual facts, didn't even know who was to talk at the conference, and forever had to question others so as to be able to reply to me. I shall certainly report to the Fuehrer the pitiful role he played as Gauleiter and urge that he be quickly replaced.

Then I talked to the political leaders of the gau in the undestroyed city hall and surveyed the political and military situation. I created a profound impression with my speech. My impression of the population is excellent. It will endure this great trial. Of course better political leadership must be given.

On the way to Hanover Prince Waldeck gave me some details to illustrate how Weinrich has fizzled out. These were simply terrible. The situation cries for remedy.

Lauterbacher called for me at Kassel for the trip through his gau. Wonderful autumn weather for the first time in a long while made driving a pleasure. We stopped on the way at the state farm where the Lauterbacher family is living. Frau Lauterbacher was most hospitable. . . .

[Hartmann Lauterbacher, then only thirty-four years old, was Gauleiter for southern Hanover and Brunswick. He had had a meteoric career in the Hitler Youth.]

Then we arrived at Hanover. On my way I became conscious of the tremendous reserves still extant in the German countryside. The province was quite undestroyed. . . . One must remember these reserves of the country in order to make an objective estimate of the present situation.

I then spoke in the Great Hall of the city hall while thousands of people stood outside on the square. The impression created by my speech was even greater here than in Kassel. The population of Lower Saxony is determined not to bow before British air terror. The points I made in my speech were greeted with storms of approving applause. I had the impression of living, not in the fifth year of the war, but in the first year of our seizure of power. It is quite obvious that the political leadership is on top of the situation in Hanover. I heard nothing but praise for Lauterbacher.

Dr. Lapper gave me a report on the situation on the Adriatic coast. It is anything but encouraging. The Fascists are completely done for in all cities along the Adriatic. . . . Mussolini is building on sand. The Italian people are totally unsuited for a strong nationalistic leadership, and the Fascist party is no longer qualified to go before the people with any claim to such leadership.

November 7, 1943

The enemy has threatened an intensified continuation of the air offensive, and I believe will carry out this threat if at all possible. During yesterday's daylight raid alone we lost thirty pursuit planes. That is an enormous loss, and simply cannot be borne in the long run. The Americans are now accompanied by pursuit planes when they attack in daytime. These carry first-class equipment and our own pursuit planes are not equal to them. It is very humiliating to note how the enemy is leading us by the nose in air warfare. Every month he introduces a new method which it takes weeks and sometimes months for us to catch up with. Once handicapped by the enemy in any phase of warfare, it is exceedingly difficult to catch up with him. We have to pay very dearly for what we failed to do in air warfare in the past.

My articles in the *Reich* about the domestic situation in England drew angry rejoinders from the British press. That's a proof that I hit the bull's-eye. For if my arguments were not based on truth, the English wouldn't take the trouble to reply.

In the East a new crisis is under way near Kiev. We have had to evacuate the city. . . . Possession of Kiev naturally constitutes a great sensation for the Bolsheviks and the entire enemy camp. The English are boasting that the Soviets are now only 200 kilometers from the former Polish boundary.

Colonel General Model sent me a report about the present situation on the central front and about the morale of our troops. Model points out that, while the troops are still bearing up relatively well, the enemy is infinitely superior to our soldiers both in man power and in quantity of matériel. That, of course, has a depressing effect on the troops, especially when they realize how the Etappe is overstaffed.

[General Walther von Model—promoted to field marshal later—was at this time in command of the Second Tank Army. In February 1944 he was placed in charge of the northern Russian front. Later, in September of that year, he became commander in chief of the Western Front, and soon replaced Field Marshal von Rundstedt as Supreme Commander in the West.]

Speer's speech to the troops was a downright fiasco. One reason why the Bolsheviks crossed the Dnieper was because our soldiers simply had no more ammunition. They therefore ask in consternation where is the stepping up of production promised by Speer? Model also complained bitterly that the soldier no longer received any political material. Model has the best of intentions but lacks the necessary means for carrying them out. The propaganda department of the Wehrmacht has failed here completely. Oh, if only the Fuehrer would decide to subordinate it to me! I believe I could master this relatively difficult problem in a short time. But officers are not suited to propaganda, especially not if they judge the situation from Berlin.

The troops are naturally hopping mad that no Eastern Wall has been built along the Dnieper. That is the question officers as well as men keep repeating. No convincing answer can be given.

Air raids at home also cause deep concern to the troops. Hatred against England exceeds all bounds. For the present, however, it is an impotent hatred. The troops would naturally like to know something about our plans for retaliation. But we can't oblige them about that.

Model spoke in very appreciative terms about my articles in the *Reich* and claimed that at present they constitute the only political material available to officers and men. He pleaded that many more copies of the *Reich* be sent to the front. With those at least something could be done. I am very happy that my own writings are having such a great influence at the front.

The problem of letters from our prisoners in the Soviet Union is causing us many a headache. These letters now no longer number a few hundreds, but arrive by thousands and tens of thousands. It cannot be denied that they make a deep impression upon the people and that it is impossible in the long run to be silent about them officially or to hold them back. I shall present this matter once more to the Fuehrer and propose that the letters be delivered to the relatives by officials of the

Party. These Party wheel horses can always counteract their propaganda effect and warn the relatives not to accept every statement as God's truth.

We are very much worried about the question of reopening schools in Berlin and other evacuated cities. The subject has already been debated for days by the authorities concerned. . . . Beginning December 1 travel is to be strictly rationed. In addition certain compulsory food-allotment measures are to be carried through. We all agree that these must not be allowed to drift any longer, but that a regulating hand must take hold if we are not to face chaos in communications during the Christmas season.

Our German press is, generally speaking, not in top form. Our editors have somewhat lost courage or have gone stale writing about problems of the war so much in recent years. Perhaps some editors ought to be recalled from the front and others from home sent out in their place. In other words, a change of personnel should be brought about to inject fresh blood into German journalism.

The Fuehrer has the intention of possibly going to Munich November 8 to talk about the over-all situation. Although I don't believe he'll be able to do this, it would be wonderful if he could. In our present situation the people must be cheered up. They have been made somewhat lethargic by continuous alarming news and misfortune. If the Fuehrer could persuade himself to survey the situation in a big speech, this would almost be equal to winning a battle.

In the evening I started on a three-day trip to Munich. A meeting of the Reichsleiters and Gauleiters is to take place and a survey of the military situation given them. Personally I think it quite out of place that the entire political leadership of the Reich is to sit in Munich for three days. It really ought to have more important things to do. When one has in mind the general situation, especially the position at the front, one can find no end of more important work than sitting in Munich for three days. But for the present there is nothing to be done against this method of Party leadership. Possibly even harder blows must come before we are taught readiness for the necessary toughness in conducting the war. I have the impression that we sometimes take the war altogether too lightly. It has become a bitter life-and-death struggle. The sooner the German people, and especially our leadership, realize this, the better it will be for all of us. It would be tragic if at a certain point in this war we should have to say, "too little and too late."

November 8, 1943

Eden's negotiations with Menemencioglu are in the foreground of
public interest in Cairo. The English make quite a theatrical show of
this conference in their papers and act as if Turkey were to enter the
war tomorrow. I regard this as quite outside the realm of possibility.
There isn't the slightest reason for Turkey to abandon her neutral
position. The English will make every effort to persuade them, but the
Turkish statesmen are much too realistic to enter upon so daring an
adventure, especially at this moment. I am therefore firmly convinced
that Ankara is not thinking of yielding to English wishes.

[Numan Menemencioglu was Foreign Minister of Turkey, 1942–44. In 1944
he was appointed Ambassador to France.]

We have again achieved great military defensive successes in Italy.
The English and Americans are simply not advancing, and must pay
for every kilometer of ground with rivers of blood. But that's good.
That will put a damper on them and they will be better able to imagine
what awaits them in case they attempt an invasion in the West at a
moment favorable to us.

In Moscow there was a celebration of the anniversary of the Bolshevik Revolution. It just makes you want to throw up when you see
how hypocritically the plutocrats in England and the United States are
pretending to be interested in it. Stalin delivered a speech at the Bolshevik Congress characterized by a lack of the usual Bolshevik bom-
bast. He talked of a turning point in the war that had taken place this
summer. The English press has seized upon this expression and claims
jubilantly that the danger is now definitely over. Of course they won't
be quite so happy in England about Stalin's pointed demand for a real
second front. Stalin spoke of 4,000,000 casualties suffered by us this
year. We would be happy if we had so many soldiers to put into the
Eastern Front! On the whole Stalin is full of hope for victory. He
threatened the severest punishment to so-called German war criminals,
and sang the praises of the western allies in tones more resounding
than we have ever heard before from his mouth. It is obvious that the
Moscow Conference is still having its repercussions. The Bolsheviks
have evidently put so much pressure on the English and Americans
that they must now be somewhat more affable to them.

The Fuehrer has decided, after all, to speak in the Loewenbräu Beer
Cellar this afternoon and is already on his way to Munich. I think that
is excellent. It is high time the Fuehrer delivers a long speech in public

to instill courage in the German people, who are now somewhat confused as to their opinions, conceptions, and hopes.

During the morning meeting of the Reichsleiters and Gauleiters I had a long talk with Bormann. I told him about my experiences in Kassel. He agrees with me that Weinrich must be bounced out as quickly as possible. He wants to press the Fuehrer again about this.

I also had a talk with Schwarz and Amann. All responsible leaders of the Party now have a desire to get closer together. The critical situation is awakening a feeling of comradeship and solidarity in the Party.

It is a good thing that the Army was given the floor during this meeting of Reichsleiters and Gauleiters. At the last meeting in Posen the Army was not even mentioned, consequently such mention was also absent in the communiqué about the meeting. That created a lot of bad feeling. The Army is now to be satisfied by the communiqué about this meeting.

Late in the evening I had a long talk with Himmler about the general situation. I noted that our views agree absolutely. Himmler's judgment is very clear and realistic, and he knows very well that in this war we must avail ourselves not only of military but also of political methods if we are to be victorious. I developed my thesis about such possibilities for Himmler, who agreed with them 100 per cent. He, too, deplored the complete lack of an elastic foreign policy and sharply criticized Ribbentrop, whose views have lately become completely inflexible.

Himmler also told me about the existence of a group of enemies of the state, among whom are Halder and possibly also Popitz. This circle would like to contact England, bypassing the Fuehrer, and has already entered into relations with the former Reich Chancellor, Dr. Wirth, in Switzerland. I regard these amateurish attempts as innocuous in themselves, but naturally one must keep one's eye on them. Himmler will see to it that these gentlemen do no major damage with their cowardly defeatism. I certainly have the impression that the domestic security of the country is in good hands with Himmler.

[Colonel General Franz Halder was chief of staff of the German Army, and frequently clashed with Hitler on matters of strategy. Halder advised the Fuehrer, for instance, to follow the French debacle of June 1940 by an immediate invasion of England. Although opposed to Nazism, he was very lukewarm about any forcible overthrow of the regime, such as the ill-fated attempt of July 20, 1944.

Dr. Joseph Wirth was German Chancellor in the early days of the Weimar Republic. It was under his chancellorship that Walther von Rathenau, Germany's martyr Foreign Minister, negotiated the Treaty of Rapallo with Soviet Russia in the spring of 1922. Wirth fled from Germany when the Nazis came into power.]

As regards the Army, Himmler is naturally somewhat prejudiced. But his criticism of the army leadership is absolutely justified. The Fuehrer would do well to replace a number of our divisional and even several army group commanders. Himmler was especially opposed to Manstein, whom he regards as a first-class defeatist. The crisis in the southern sector of the Eastern Front would not have had to become so serious had a man of caliber stood there in Manstein's place. . . . As I learn from Berlin, the Fuehrer received Manstein at GHQ. Contrary to expectations the interview is said to have come off well, and it is assumed that Manstein is to return to his post. I regard this as a grave disaster. But one must wait and see what actually happened during that talk.

November 9, 1943

After the conclusion of the [Cairo] Conference a very frosty communiqué was issued, merely stating that Eden had informed Menemencioglu about the Moscow Conference. The Turkish newspapers are leaving no doubt that Turkey is not thinking of abandoning her position of neutrality. In other words, developments at the Cairo Conference were exactly as we anticipated and as Papen predicted.

The English are trying to launch a gigantic sensation by asserting that Papen has been called to GHQ. All that is intended to intensify the campaign of nerves for November 9. The Fuehrer will take occasion during his speech in the Loewenbräu Cellar to tear apart this whole structure of fantasy. I believe November 9 will turn into a heavy propaganda defeat for the enemy. The people were promised that the German nation would collapse on that day. There is not the slightest sign of a breakdown to be seen anywhere.

The dropping of some enemy bombs on Vatican City still creates a world sensation. Under the pressure of commentary in the neutral press the English have been compelled to deny any guilt and to attempt to blame us. They are doing that, however, in such a clumsy and transparent manner that nobody will believe them. Their lies are too brazenly foolish. . . .

Unfortunately the *Osservatore Romano* assumes only a very moderate attitude concerning this event. Obviously the Pope does not want to forego the possibility of acting as mediator between the Reich and the western enemy powers, at least not for the present, although there isn't the slightest occasion for such mediation at the moment.

The enemy continues to press the Italian royal house vigorously for

King Victor Emmanuel's abdication. It is impossible for the present to determine what the English really intend to do with the Italians. In any case they seem to pursue a plan for removing all who had anything whatever to do with Fascism; they believe things will take care of themselves after that. They are obviously toying with the idea of revolutionizing the whole of Italian political life. They are proving their lack of political instinct, however, by selecting the eighty-year-old Count Sforza for this purpose.

The situation in the East continues to be critical. The Bolsheviks have started an advance from Kiev that may possibly be dangerous to us. They have already taken possession of Fastov. This development is more than dastardly.

I spoke with Sepp Dietrich. . . . The *Leibstandarte* has assembled for an attack which is to start at 7 A.M. next Tuesday. It has been given orders to advance up to Melitopol. . . . Dietrich is very hopeful about the prospects for this assault. He will start out with more than 22,000 men and a total of 1,000 tanks. That surely is something worth while.

In Helsinki there have been deliberations about the possibility of a separate peace. These conferences have fortunately ended with complete success on our side. Even the Social-Democratic party published a declaration which emphasized once more that Finland had no part in the war among the Great Powers, that Nordic collaboration must be planned for the future, and that Finland has a feeling of solidarity with the peoples of Norway and Denmark; it insisted, nevertheless, nobody was playing with any thought of capitulation. . . .

I have a thousand and one things to do at the hotel. . . . A report by the leader of the medical profession about artificial insemination was handed to me. This artificial aid to procreation is now to be regulated by decree! I think this is absolutely impossible. This touchy proposal is about the one thing we have been waiting for! So far as I am concerned the draft will be tabled until the end of the war. We shall have enough time after the war to concern ourselves with these delicate problems.

This afternoon Goering delivered a two-and-a-half-hour address on aerial warfare. The address did not achieve the effect that Goering evidently expected. He repeated many things that Milch had already told us about during the meeting of Gauleiters in Posen. . . . Goering insisted especially that reprisals against England had already been taken in advance by our raids in the autumn of 1940. . . . That, of

course, is very cheap. . . . Goering also explained a whole series of
new weapons and new airplane models which, however, can't be produced in quantity until the dim and distant future. A certain lack of
assurance is noticeable in Goering during his address. That is quite
understandable. One cannot stand before this critical aggregation of
Reichsleiters and Gauleiters who know all the answers with declarations of so little substance. . . . Nevertheless I think it was a good
thing that Goering established contact again with the Reichsleiters and
Gauleiters. . . .

During dinner I had a long talk with Goering, who tried in every
way possible to renew his old connections. Personally he is an exceptionally lovable character. He is obviously suffering from the fact that
he did not find the right collaborators in the past and that he did not
keep the reins sufficiently firmly in his hands. . . .

The Fuehrer arrived from GHQ to talk to his old co-fighters. He
seemed vital and healthy, a fact that naturally has a very consoling and
comforting effect upon his old comrades and collaborators. During his
speech the Fuehrer was in his best form. . . . He had many sparkling
turns of phrase. His uncompromising obduracy in proclaiming our will
to resist was extremely convincing. This speech will undoubtedly have
a deep effect on the German people. Foreign countries, too, will be very
much impressed.

The Fuehrer devoted a great part of his address to the Eastern Front
and to enemy air warfare. Here, too, his presentation was brilliant. Especially when discussing air raids he told the German people how
much he was suffering with them during these weeks and months, but
how firmly he was determined to overcome the present crisis and how
gigantic was the reconstruction work throughout the Reich he was
planning for after the war. This speech had an unexpected fascination
for this gathering. That is a good thing, because it will be noticeable
in the radio broadcast also. With the Fuehrer's permission I struck out
a few clumsy turns of phrase when preparing the broadcast. I then had
it delivered at 8:15 P.M. over all networks.

I am very happy the Fuehrer has spoken again after so long an in-
terval. It was high time. It was, so to speak, a case of his speaking the
redeeming word. The Fuehrer, too, seemed deeply gratified to stand
among his fighting comrades again and talk to them.

In the evening we were assembled with the Fuehrer in the Fuehrerbau. . . .

[The Fuehrerbau was a gaudy edifice erected on the Koenigsplatz of Munich
as part of a series of structures intended to bear testimony to the grandeur of

Nazism. Next to it stood one of the two Greek temples containing sarcophagi of the men killed during the ill-fated beer-cellar *putsch* of November 9, 1923. The fate of Czechoslovakia was decided at the Fuehrerbau by Chamberlain, Daladier, Mussolini, and Hitler on September 30, 1938.]

Here I had an opportunity for a long talk with Hofer and Rainer, who told me miraculous things about the occupied Italian areas. According to these reports nothing is to be expected either of Fascism or the Duce. The Duce hasn't the faintest idea as to his real position. He overestimates the power of the Fascist party. He is living a life of make-believe and struts around in a heroic pose that has no place in a world of realities. He actually thinks he can persuade the Italian nation to re-enter the military struggle on our side. I think that is absolutely out of the question. One can measure his unrealistic attitude by the fact that he seriously intends to speak in public at Milan. Sepp Dietrich told me that if he really wanted to do this he could do so only under the protection of German arms, because he would otherwise be booed off the stage, or worse.

The personal conduct of the Duce with his girl friend, whom Sepp Dietrich had to bring to him, is cause for much misgiving. One can see from it that he has no clear understanding of the seriousness of his situation, and that, accordingly, the reconstruction of the Fascist party is also more a matter of theory than of practice. While he had his son-in-law arrested, all those in the know understand clearly that he won't have him condemned to death. It is assumed that the absent Count Grandi will be condemned to death only because he is absent, whereas the rest will get off with imprisonment or the penitentiary for life. Their sentences will then be commuted after a few weeks. One certainly can't begin reconstructing a great revolutionary movement that way! It is tragic to think how far the Duce has drifted away from his original ideals. Had he remained faithful to them he would never have lost Italy and the King would not have been able to fire him.

November 10, 1943

The Fuehrer's speech in the Loewenbräu Cellar has simply amazed the enemy. They had expected quite a different song. They thought the Fuehrer was sick, nervous, depressed, and devoid of all confidence in victory. Also, they had already joyfully anticipated that November 9 could be looked on as a day of great triumph for them. Now the English are sitting there like a sorry tanner whose pelts have swum away. Everything they prophesied in their propaganda has failed to happen.

. . . Now they suddenly say that the Fuehrer has spoken aggressively and boastfully, that he was a different Hitler from the one known the last few months. The significant thing is that his pronouncements are again being taken seriously. Nobody any longer pokes fun at the reprisals threatened by the Fuehrer. On the contrary, the enemy considers this very realistically and without skepticism. I have the impression that this eighth and ninth of November signified a great psychological achievement for us.

As in reply, Churchill delivered a speech at the banquet of the Lord Mayor of London that fitted like a fist in the eye. He praised the Soviet Union eloquently for its military contribution, which no other people could have made. . . . He designated 1944 as probably the most difficult year in English history, unless there was some extraordinary piece of luck. During that year the English people would have to make the heaviest and greatest sacrifices of blood. He talked of the fact that the battles to be fought during that year would put Waterloo far in the shade. He no longer made sarcastic remarks about retaliation, but considered it very earnestly, said he expected it under all circumstances, and emphasized that the English people would meet it manfully and courageously.

Roosevelt, too, delivered an address. He spoke of a world of decency that the plutocracies intended to create and promised the occupied areas large-scale help in the way of food and clothing after their liberation. The inhabitants of Sicily know what such help looks like in practice. It would be far more to the point if the English and the Americans were first to offer aid to the hungry peoples of India.

The situation in the East has become more complicated. It must indeed be admitted that the Soviets, as they themselves report, have achieved a great success near Kiev. Even though our losses were not so grave by far as was claimed in Moscow, the territory gained by the Soviets is considerable.

I received a detailed report about the latest developments in Hungary. It is anything but comforting. Influential circles in Hungary are at work for a direct break with us. The Regent is trying to create the impression that he is neutral about these efforts. That is, however, in no wise the case. I even regard him as the mainspring of this development. . . . If the English were to attempt an invasion of the Balkans, Hungary would be the first country to desert us. The Hungarians are also interested in keeping their Wehrmacht intact because they are still flirting with the idea of fighting the Rumanians. This attitude of Hungary is perfidious and shameless.

After three days' stay in Munich I have at last finished my work here. At 10 P.M. we started again for Berlin. I am happy in anticipation of the work that awaits me there.

November 11, 1943

There is no longer any talk in the English press of the possibility of a moral collapse of the Reich. On the contrary, we are credited with much greater military prowess than we enjoy at the moment. The theme of retaliation against England has struck home. The English people are in a state of great unrest, especially since they don't know in what manner this retaliation is to take place. The spreading of rumors is therefore the order of the day.

The American chief of production, Nelson, has delivered a pro-Bolshevik speech that contains just about everything. A layman would think there is hardly any difference left between capitalism and Communism.

The situation in the East is no longer so very critical, at least not in the south. On the other hand, our situation at Kiev and Smolensk is again very threatening.

I have at last reorganized my propaganda machinery in the occupied areas of the East. Unfortunately the decision in this matter came very late, almost too late. But I'll try, nevertheless, to save what I can.

I have received a detailed report about the situation in Portugal. From it the following can be gathered: Salazar is undoubtedly the master of Portugal. . . . But he relies on his armed forces. Unfortunately he has somewhat lost his faith in us and therefore keeps swaying back and forth between the two warring sides like a pendulum. That is also the case with Franco. The dictators would fare better if they openly took sides with us, for if our side doesn't win they are lost anyway. English influence predominates in Portugal. The English are carrying on a very clever propaganda, especially by word of mouth, not without success. Our diplomacy is evidently not equal to these practices. I shall now increase our propaganda in Portugal considerably. . . . As regards the placing of German movies in Portugal, we must try to purchase several motion-picture theaters, for the Jewish boycott among movie theater owners is so effective that a German picture cannot be shown there normally.

Immediately on reaching Berlin I learned that the Fuehrer's speech had made a tremendous impression upon the German people. . . . The effect has been simply amazing. The passage in the speech in which the Fuehrer assured the German people they might be at rest, for victory would be on our side, acted like balm on an open wound. The categorical threat of reprisals against England and the promise to reconstruct the destroyed cities in a very short time after the war also evoked great enthusiasm.

Naturally we have one worry on top of another and can hardly find a solution. For instance, the problem of a gas shortage has cropped up here in Berlin and has already led to some stoppages of work in the armaments industry.

The Fuehrer arrived safely at GHQ. His meeting with his old Party comrades acted on him like a refreshing bath. It was a very good thing he left the circle of generals surrounding him and took up direct contact with the Party. His contact with the people, too, did him much good.

November 12, 1943

From a very confidential source I learn via Lisbon that Stalin put forward the argument [at the Moscow Conference] that he had already lost 16,000,000 men, that he could not continue the war without a second front, and that he was determined to conclude a separate peace with the Reich, if England and the United States did not hasten to his aid. Impressed by this presentation both Eden and Hull naturally yielded all along the line. They had to make far-reaching concessions to Stalin on the Balkans, not to mention the fact that of course the Soviet western frontiers were not debated at all. One can therefore speak of an outright defeat of the English and Americans. They are now completely in the tow of Bolshevism. . . . If all Great Powers engaged in this war were able today to select their positions anew without any previous ties, the whole picture would most likely be changed completely in twenty-four hours.

The Leibstandarte has not yet entered the fray. That will take another two or three days. Their deployment did not function the way we thought it would. . . .

There is rain on the southern front, and the dreaded thaw for which we waited so anxiously in the past weeks has set in, but that won't help now.

Our series of meetings has proven a tremendous success. Thousands of them were held and they were overcrowded almost everywhere. The everlasting grumbling has also diminished considerably since death sentences against defeatists have been pronounced, executed, and published. That had a very sobering and deterrent effect on the defeatists. Our Reich propaganda officers claim that one single victory at any one front would completely change morale at home.

November 13, 1943

A new tendency is slowly developing in the English war policy. The Soviets seem to have overplayed their hand somewhat and as a result British plutocracy has been more than sobered up. The British Communist party, too, is beginning to get busy. Evidently Stalin is not satisfied with the results which he has been able to extort from England and America, or else he doesn't have complete faith in the present situation.

English periodicals for the first time have published reparations demands on the German Reich. They are so insane that one can vividly imagine the threat against us in that matter if we were to weaken. I am having these English demands published prominently in the German press. The German people should realize clearly what fate is in store for us in case of defeat.

I have received confidential information which enables me to appraise the Moscow Conference. I gather from it that Stalin categorically demanded the opening of a second front. The English and Americans were not in a position to comply with this demand at present. They had therefore to be satisfied with a promise by Stalin not to conclude a separate peace with the Reich. In return the English were to refrain from any action concerning the Balkans. No agreement was reached about Poland or the Baltic States and Finland because the Soviets permitted no discussion whatever on these topics. On the whole England and America got the short end of the deal at the Moscow Conference.

Eden negotiated in Cairo with Menemencioglu. He submitted the Soviet demand for military bases in Turkey. Menemencioglu refused and insisted that the constitutional authorities in Turkey, especially the Turkish People's party, would first have to be consulted. Eden presented the Soviet demand in only a half-hearted way and did not make it hard for the Turks to decline it. . . . There certainly can be no talk of Turkey being put under pressure.

My new article, entitled, "The Inevitable Conclusions," which deals with the Moscow Conference, has attracted the greatest attention, especially in the neutral press. It is very significant, though, that the English don't even take notice of it. That shows me they don't want to discuss in public the ideas contained therein. The arguments are too obvious and too strong for the British to believe they could gain anything by a discussion.

Glasmeier has gone to work in Paris. He is meeting with great difficulties there. The OKW had really intended to throw the Paris propaganda section into the lap of the Foreign Office. By sending Glasmeier I anticipated this move. Keitel has now hit on the typical way out by submitting the question to the Fuehrer's decision. I'm not worrying about that decision.

The Fuehrer's speech . . . is still being discussed everywhere by the people. Reports from all gaus state that this speech acted as a shot in the arm.

Vice-President Lange of the Reichsbank reported to me about the present state of our finances. It is relatively favorable. We shall certainly suffer no reverses for financial reasons. On the whole our war financing rests on firm ground. That is owing especially to the fact that we have a modern monetary system which is independent of the gold standard and is therefore quite untouched by monetary crises in enemy countries.

November 14, 1943

The enemy press is devoting more space to discussing reparations. The English are set on handling the problem on a commercial basis while the Bolsheviks are more concerned with man power. . . . There is no more terrible prospect for the German people than to fall into the hands of Bolshevism. That's why this news will frighten our people.

One can well imagine that international Jewry is behind all these machinations. It believes the moment has come for satisfying its hatred of Germany. On the other hand, anti-Semitism is growing in the entire world. I have news about that both from the United States and from England.

The situation in the East is very sad at present, although not as yet hopeless, as claimed in Moscow. But we shall have to work hard to overcome the present crisis. It is undoubtedly one of the most dangerous that we have thus far experienced in the entire war.

At noon about three hundred and fifty American bombers flew over northwestern Germany. Their formation was pretty well scattered by our anti-aircraft, so that the concentric attack on Bremen did not take place as planned. A considerable number of planes are said to have been shot down; the Luftwaffe spoke of more than forty. On the other hand we lost some twenty pursuit planes. The Americans are now flying in by day with pursuit-plane protection, a thing that is naturally very hard for our anti-aircraft to cope with.

I had a heavy set-to with Ribbentrop about our propaganda section in France. Ribbentrop claims that France must be regarded as a foreign country and not as a defeated state because it has a chief of state and a prime minister. Consequently, only the Foreign Office has a right to political activity there. I opposed this standpoint violently and Field Marshal General Keitel joined in my protest. For, after all, we have defeated France and there is a military occupation force in France. The Embassy in Paris is only, so to speak, an outside subbureau of the Foreign Office, but can in no way be considered a diplomatic representation of the Reich in a free and sovereign France. The argument went back and forth. Ribbentrop is trying to solve the situation by a *fait accompli* of bypassing the Fuehrer. But I shall under no circumstances agree to this. It is amazing with what fanaticism the Foreign Office and especially Ribbentrop deal with questions of such subsidiary importance, whereas they simply push aside questions of great moment. Our foreign policy today has become completely sterile and frozen. If it were more fluid, undoubtedly a different slant could be given through political means to a war that today has taken such an unfavorable turn on the military side.

Goering, thank God, is showing himself oftener in public. He has evidently recovered from his recent period of stagnation. I am very happy that he is again in evidence and that thereby his authority is gradually being strengthened.

November 15, 1943

The enemy press again endeavors to claim that the German generals intend to make peace. In this connection the same names keep cropping up again and again. That looks somewhat suspicious. Undoubtedly the men mentioned have said very indiscreet things on this or that occasion. Only generals of the Army are named. There is no talk of the Navy or the Luftwaffe, to say nothing of the Waffen-SS. Politically our Army is not as it should be. The reason for it, no doubt, is that it has had no political education.

The Lebanon crisis keeps growing. In their procedure against de Gaulle's France the English are making sure of the support of Moscow and Washington. The Lebanon crisis is a cleverly conceived maneuver of camouflage and intrigue on the part of London imperialism, for which de Gaulle evidently fell, as he hasn't the faintest understanding of politics. Now that de Gaulle has advanced in a very rude way, the London press is playing the role of an innocent angel. It pretends to be all stirred up, takes the side of the Arabs, and at the same time does a wonderful piece of propaganda. One cannot but admire this English policy of intrigue. It would be a fine thing if we understood a little more about this business than may be assumed from present achievements of our Foreign Office.

[The outbreak of rioting led French officials to arrest the Lebanon leaders who had proclaimed the independence of this French-mandated Arab state.]

Badoglio can't even form a cabinet. All men in Italian public life who were asked declined to enter his government. He must therefore content himself with a cabinet of so-called experts. Sforza declared that he would have nothing to do with any Italian government as long as the King had not abdicated. This eighty-three-year-old fogy pretends to act as representative of Italian youth!

The situation in the East is causing us great anxiety. What is it to lead to? The Soviets have reserves at their disposal of which we hadn't the faintest idea, despite our very realistic consideration of their possibilities.

A veritable hospital has been installed at Lanke. Almost the entire family is sick in bed. It is as though tons of misfortune hit us both in our general war situation and in our family.

There is no rest for me all day. One piece of bad news follows another. We are passing through weeks of extreme worry. Usually, however, weeks of this kind also mean that you are speedily approaching a decisive point in developments.

November 16, 1943

I have ordered all our propaganda services at home and abroad to start a great, new anti-Bolshevik campaign. This campaign will be based upon the military successes of the Soviets and is to give Europe and our enemies the creeps. I don't want them to stop being frightened about Bolshevism. I hope especially to stir up Anglo-American public opinion against the war with this campaign.

It is very sad that a number of German generals, especially aristocrats, have placed themselves at Stalin's disposal in the Free Germany Committee of Moscow. That does us a lot of harm. There is especially a certain Count Einsiedel, scion of one of the oldest German officer families, who is attracting attention to himself in a most obnoxious way. This proves again that our officers lack all political instinct. In their folly and amateurishness they haven't the faintest idea as to what they are being used for. Stalin's camouflage about the churches is a clincher to reconcile these bigoted officers to Bolshevism. Stalin picked up an exceedingly old Metropolitan and made him Patriarch of Moscow. He is using him for propaganda in the whole world, and the Anglican Church is acting as though it fell for this swindle. . . . Naturally nobody among the leaders of the Church of England really believes that Stalin has become a faithful servant of the Lord!

[Count Otto von Einsiedel, a grandson of the Iron Chancellor, Prince Otto von Bismarck, became a leader in the Free Germany Committee formed at Moscow with Field Marshal von Paulus and General von Seydlitz as the prime movers.]

The Vatican has issued a note about the minor bombardment of Vatican City. It is directed at all warring powers, accuses everybody and nobody. We can't do anything with such a note in our practical political fight.

Morale among our people at present is excellent. This is partly owing to our good propaganda, but partly also to the severe measures which we have taken against defeatists. . . .

After a meeting tonight I visited the new command point in the air-raid shelter of the Wilhelmplatz. It is now completely equipped and adequate for all emergencies. We shall be able to conduct our defense of the Reich capital from here. I hope very much, however, that we shall not have to make use of it too often.

[The Wilhelmplatz was a large square before the Reich Chancellery, the Propaganda Ministry, the Finance and Transportation ministries, and the Kaiserhof Hotel. One of the largest air-raid shelters (bunkers) in Berlin had been constructed under it, and the main command point for the defense of the capital installed there. It must have given Goebbels, a frustrated hero whose physical shortcomings precluded his becoming an officer and earning laurels on the field of battle, great satisfaction to have been placed in supreme charge of air-raid defense and consequently to be furnished a *Befehlsstand,* or place from which he could issue commands.]

November 17, 1943

The Soviets have taken a hand in Lebanon. Everything is at sixes and sevens there. Nobody knows who is opposing whom. Unfortunately the German press was infected by this confusion and rather ran amok on the Lebanon question. I have insisted upon clearer instructions for the press.

In this fifth year of the war Socialism has become a favorite theme, especially with those who don't want to have anything to do with it. The Fascist party, too, during its Milan convention came out with a new social program that contains just about everything. If this social program were really put through we would have reason to be ashamed of ourselves in face of the radicalism of the Fascists. But I deliberately say "if." At the decisive moment the Fascists will abandon their radicalism and neutralize everything by bourgeois respectability.

In Moscow there was a great celebration in honor of the Bolshevik party. It was hailed as the originator of the Red Army victories. It would be beautiful if the same thing could be said about the National Socialist movement in the Reich. I regard it as a cardinal error in the relationship between Party and Wehrmacht that the Party has not had the opportunity and possibility of injecting its ideas into the Army. As a result the Army today is not so dependable as it really ought to be in times of severe strain.

There is constant talk among Soviet prisoners about a joint war of Germany and the Soviet Union against England and the United States. Interestingly enough the English and American prisoners talk about a joint war of Germany and the Anglo-Americans against the Soviet Union. That means that although each warring side wants to destroy us, it would nevertheless like to use us as allies against the other side after such destruction. This circumstance, which now represents only the wishful thinking or the dream of individual soldiers and officers, may at some future time bring us to a decisive turning point of the war.

Rather disagreeable developments are observable in France. . . . Laval keeps hesitating. It's not quite clear whether he is stalling from apathy or intrigue. Certainly Pétain is very much dissatisfied and would like to get rid of him. That's why he has wanted to regulate the question of his succession anew and to announce the change in a radio speech. However, at the last moment German censorship prevented the broadcast. Now both Pétain and Laval have gone in for watchful waiting. Both, in their innermost hearts, are quite naturally opposed to the Reich and its interests. We therefore cannot trust them across the street. Pétain is nursing the wishful dream that France may be called upon to establish peace between Germany and the Western Powers!

Our representatives have negotiated with representatives of the Italian Government in Venice about German-Italian movie relations. The Italian Fascists are actually planning to start a new movie production in Venice. Obviously they still haven't learned anything. Instead of fighting a war they are taking time out for minor questions. I imagine that if we were in as desperate a situation as the Italians, we would have something else to do than build movie studios. I shall certainly see to it that Italian motion pictures don't enter Germany for the present.

I had a minor altercation with Rosenberg on account of my press agreement with Dr. Dietrich regarding the eastern areas. Rosenberg is constantly at work either to torpedo the decree of the Fuehrer about propaganda in the East or render it innocuous. It is hard for an outsider to realize what difficulties I have to face. These difficulties invariably stem from second-class personalities. Usually one can work well with personalities of real stature because they know their own limitations. The smaller the brain, the bigger the appetite.

Dr. Naumann received General [Heinrich] Scheuch, the last Prussian Minister of War during World War I, who wanted spontaneously to express the opinion that we would also have won World War I if I had been a member of the Government at that time. He regards our present moral power of resistance against the afflictions and adversities of the war as owing chiefly to the National Socialist movement and to National Socialist propaganda as conducted by the Party and the State. I can be very proud of this appraisal by an old and meritorious leader of World War I.

November 18, 1943

At noon . . . the news is reported that Leros has capitulated. Some 3,000 English and 5,000 Italians surrendered. Apparently the English depended quite as much upon the Italians as we used to do, and were disappointed exactly as we used to be by their lack of fighting qualities and their unwillingness to take any risks. Naturally London is very much dissatisfied about the quick fall of the island.

The Italian Minister of State, Preziosi, paid a visit to our Ministry. His report on the situation within Fascist Italy gave much food for thought. He even criticized the Duce very severely and blamed him for not having hewn to the line in his treatment of Jews and Masons. That, he said, was the reason for his fall.

[Gabriele Preziosi was an Italian diplomat who served as Ambassador to Belgium, 1936–39 and to Argentina, 1939–41.]

From many parts of the Eastern Front I receive letters from National Socialist soldiers who complain of a decided lack of political orientation. They always contrast it with the political education of the Red Army, which is something quite different. Often these letters end in the desperate cry, "Where are our political commissars?" . . . I sent a number of these letters to the Fuehrer for his information. I assume he will take proper measures for correcting the situation.

During the burial of victims of the last bomb attack on the Bulgarian capital, the Bishop of Sofia delivered a speech in which he attacked the Bulgarian Government rather severely. Barring exceptions in only a few countries, bishops are almost always opposed to the temporal power, not for reasons of Christian conviction but rather because of a yearning for power. Therefore their wings must be clipped as much as possible.

Major Gaza, who is a product of the Hitler Youth, also complained very much about the lack of political education in the Army. That is a complaint against the leadership of the Army which upright National Socialists voice again and again. . . .

[Major Gaza was one of Germany's best-known tank aces. He received one of the highest decorations, the Oak-Leaf Cluster to the Knight's Cross of the Iron Cross.]

There is also much complaint about the government section of Berlin as a rumor factory. No doubt that is owing to the fact that all bad news reaches this central point and that the higher officials stationed there are taking too little time out to strengthen their own morale by talking to the broad masses of the people. I believe I shall have to talk to a larger meeting of government officials to lace them up in moral corsets.

November 19, 1943

Papen visited the Fuehrer and reported about conditions in Turkey. He is very optimistic about our chances there. The Turks are not thinking of abandoning neutrality; there isn't the slightest prospect of their yielding to English-Soviet pressure within any foreseeable time.

There is some complaint about the attitude of certain classes of our population toward English prisoners of war. Their behavior must be characterized as lacking in dignity. I have given orders that people who are so unmindful of their honor as to behave thus be summoned into court and given heavy penitentiary sentences. I shall have these sentences published. They will certainly have an educational effect.

I had a long talk with Dr. Ley. . . . In Cologne various people earnestly proposed that carnival be celebrated during the coming winter. It is simply surprising what vitality our people manifest even in the fifth year of war.

[The Cologne carnival was famous throughout Germany for its jollity and abandon.]

The English appeared over the Reich with large formations. One formation of 200 to 250 bombers attacked Mannheim. The city took a pretty bad beating. Some 500 to 600 explosive bombs hit the northern part of the city. Damage to buildings and plants was considerable, but casualties very small.

November 20, 1943

A number of authentic reports confirm that during his Cairo negotiations Eden asked Ankara for air bases in Anatolia and for Turkey's early entry into the war. The Turkish Government called together the constitutional authorities, especially the People's party, and obtained a categorical veto on yielding to Eden's demands.

The English and the Americans are in for a lot of joy with the Italians. That serves them right. The Italians gave us so much trouble in the earlier years of war that it is no more than just that our enemies should also get their share.

The Fuehrer will in all likelihood go to Breslau next Saturday to speak to 10,000 young cadets in Century Hall. It's good for the Fuehrer to speak to a larger audience. He not only radiates strength, but himself becomes charged with it.

November 21, 1943

The Soviets have repeated their demand that Germany furnish 10,000,000 workers for five years for reconstruction purposes on the conclusion of peace. Demands like that are wonderful for our propaganda. They stir German public opinion deeply. The idea that our soldiers might not return home at all but might have to remain in the Soviet Union as forced labor is a terrible thought for every woman and every mother. The German people would prefer to fight to their last breath.

Although Pétain has thus far given no indication of any intention to resign he is nevertheless very much offended and blames the German occupation authorities for the failure of his plan. Laval, following his old tactics, has kept out of the conflict. His attitude toward Pétain and ourselves is less clear than ever.

Reports from the Ruhr Valley indicate that the women are determined to get back to their husbands, come what may. They would rather live in destroyed cities under the most primitive conditions than in the sections to which they have been evacuated where, incidentally, conditions are none too rosy either. Strange examples have been given me of the cleverness which women show in trying to get home despite all orders to the contrary.

November 22, 1943

To compensate for vanishing hopes of victory the London press now supplies its readers with tall stories about the damage alleged to have been done to Berlin during the last air raid. It is claimed, for instance, that even at this hour communications in Berlin are completely interrupted. As a matter of fact not a single tram, subway, or elevated has failed to run because of the raid. Nevertheless I shall refrain from denying these English reports. It is a good thing for the English to imagine that their new tactics achieved great successes; they will cling all the longer to these tactics, much to our advantage.

It seems grotesque and almost as though the devil had taken a hand to think that good weather prevails in all those areas along the front where the Soviets are becoming active and bad weather at points where we must attack.

The Fuehrer spoke to the cadets at Breslau. I am told that his speech was exceptionally good. The Fuehrer laid special stress on the political education of the officer corps. The young officers gave the Fuehrer a stormy ovation. He was very happy to speak before such a large gathering of men.

A sad piece of news reached us: Count Reventlow has died at Tegernsee. The National Socialist movement mourns the loss of a very unselfish, idealistic champion of its ideas. Even in the days of the Kaiser, Reventlow distinguished himself by an exhibition of highest civil courage. His articles in the *Reichswart*, which appeared week after week until the very last, were on an exceptionally high plane. Reventlow is one of the great spiritual phenomena of our movement. I requested the Fuehrer to have the Party take charge of the funeral. The Fuehrer agreed. It is to take place in the New Palace in Potsdam, and at my suggestion Dr. Frick, as floor leader of the Reichstag majority, is to deliver the commemorative address.

[Count Ernst von Reventlow was a stormy petrel in the Reichstag in the days of the Kaiser, his pet aversions being the Jews and the British. He joined the Nazis in 1927, after having previously been very active in the Deutsch-Voelkische party, an anti-Semitic movement.

The New Palace in Potsdam had been the regular residence of Kaiser Wilhelm II. Although the Nazis were in complete control of the Reichstag after 1933, they still went through the formality of maintaining a floor leader. He was called the *Fraktionsvorsitzende*, or chairman of the Nazi "fraction," an expression dating back to the empire and the Weimar Republic, when every political party had only a fraction of the seats. Each party floor leader was known as the *Fraktionsvorsitzende*. Until the Nazis took over, they, too, were only a "fraction," and Dr. Wilhelm Frick was their chairman. Hitler himself never stood for election before he became Chancellor.]

Unfortunately our radio, by its exceedingly sentimental programs, contributes to the depressed state of our morale. I shall have to take a hand. It won't do for sadness to be placed on the program in this saddest of all months. Once we have November behind us we shall all thank God.

November 24, 1943

Work began quite early this morning. First, Schach gave me an over-all picture of the situation in Berlin, which is a sad one indeed. I just can't understand how the English are able to do so much damage to the Reich's capital during one air raid. . . .

The picture that greeted my eye on the Wilhelmplatz was one of utter desolation. Blazing fires everywhere. The Propaganda Ministry was spared, for the most part, chiefly because of the courageous fire fighting of our own air-raid guards. Although damage in the Reich Chancellery is quite heavy, it is nothing compared with other ministries. . . . Schaub called on me and reported on destruction in the Reich Chancellery. Although he defended the private apartments of the Fuehrer with the fury of a bear, he could not prevent their suffering some damage. From the outside the chancellery looks almost unscathed. It is owing mainly to Schaub's intervention that it is standing at all. . . .

Transportation conditions are still quite hopeless but I trust we shall soon master our difficulties sufficiently at least to start an emergency service to all sections of the city. . . . Transportation is the heart of all public life. Once it no longer functions, business soon stops, supplies cease to move, and difficulties increase by the hour. . . . In our home in Hermann Goering Street things are pretty desperate. The top floor is burned out completely. The whole house is filled with water. It is practically impossible to live there; there is no heat, no water, and all rooms are filled with pungent smoke. Magda has come to Berlin to salvage what she can. The impressions she gained on her trip, especially driving through the Wedding district, were terrible. The poor people, who are the victims of these low-down methods of English warfare, are really to be pitied. But it would be even worse if they fell into enemy hands, especially the Bolsheviks. In this case sufferings which now can be limited to weeks or at least months would continue indefinitely. . . .

[The "home in Goering Street" was the official residence of Dr. Goebbels, but his wife and his six children did not live there much. They were usually in the suburban home at Schwanenwerder on beautiful Wannsee, or at Lanke.

The Wedding district of Berlin, named after a metallurgist, Gustav Friedrich Wedding, was one of the poorest in Berlin. In republican days it was known as a hotbed of Communism. It is now one of the *Verwaltungsbezirke* (administrative districts) of the American occupation sector of Greater Berlin.]

Ley has returned meanwhile. He had carried out a number of assignments I gave him. . . . He was fit to be tied because the pursuit planes did not take to the air during the unfortunate night. What if the weather was bad! After all, the English fly in bad weather from their southern English airports all the way to Berlin; but the German pursuit planes can't rise from the ground in Berlin because weather prevents! You can't simply surrender the capital of the Reich to the terror of the enemy. If we conduct war on such squeamish principles we won't get very far. Ley is undoubtedly right. . . .

In between I am able to sleep for half an hour. Then, however, duty again calls me. Large English formations are once more on their way, headed straight for the capital. It means we must stand a second blow. . . .

Meanwhile I learn that my mother and my mother-in-law were bombed out completely in Moabit. Their homes have simply vanished. The house in which they lived was transformed into one vast shambles. But what is that at a time of universal misfortune which has now fallen upon this city of four and a half millions!

[Moabit was a section of Berlin that is now part of the British sector of occupation. In this district was one of the largest jails of Berlin, so that to "go to Moabit" usually meant to go to jail.]

The attack began shortly after the alert had been sounded. This time more explosives than incendiary bombs were used. Again it was a major, grade-A attack. I was in the bunker on the Wilhelmplatz. It wasn't long before fires started all around. Bombs and land mines of notable size were dropped over the whole government quarter. They destroyed everything around the Potsdamer Platz. The pressure was so strong that even our bunker, though constructed deep underground, began to shake. Unfortunately the pursuit planes arrived twenty minutes late. That gave the English a big lead. During those twenty minutes the anti-aircraft guns were forbidden to shoot because it was believed the pursuit planes had already arrived.

[The Potsdamer Platz, several blocks from the Wilhelmplatz, was Berlin's busiest square.]

Devastation is again appalling in the government section as well as in the western and northern suburbs. The workers' quarters in the Wedding and the region along Wolgast Street are especially hard hit. The State Playhouse and the Reichstag are aflame, but fortunately we are able to localize these fires. People keep coming and going in our bunker just as at a command point. Well, after all we are living in a war and many a sector at the front would certainly not want to trade with us, so enormous is the strain. Hell itself seems to have broken loose over us. Mines and explosive bombs keep hurtling down upon the government quarter. One after another of the most important buildings begins to burn. As I look out on the Wilhelmplatz after the attack, the gruesome impression of the evening before is even heightened.

I go over to the Propaganda Ministry. It is burning at two points. . . . The air-raid wardens under the leadership of Gutterer are fighting these fires with the greatest energy, but sometimes things seem to hang by a silken thread. Only with the aid of large fire-fighting units are we able, after hours of fighting, to control the fire. Unfortunately I can't bother about these things myself, as I am too busy worrying about the city as a whole.

Meanwhile Ley returned to offer his aid. It is most touching the way he is concerned about me and my gau. But he can't help me very much. What I now need is not good advice but fire-fighting units. They are being requisitioned from nearby cities all the way to Hamburg. We must risk stripping other cities of their fire departments, as it can be taken for certain that Berlin will be the main target in future attacks. The enemy leaves no doubt about it!

The Kaiserhof was hit by countless incendiary bombs and was soon ablaze. Although the largest fire-fighting units were put to work there, the edifice could not be saved; it burned to the ground. Nothing but the outer walls remain standing.

[The destruction of the Kaiserhof Hotel must have been especially hard for Goebbels to take, because of its many historic associations for the Nazis. Throughout the years immediately preceding Hitler's appointment as Chancellor in 1933, the Nazi Fuehrer stopped at the Kaiserhof, within a stone's throw of the chancellery, whenever he was in Berlin. As he returned to the Kaiserhof after Hindenburg appointed him Chancellor on January 30, 1933, a huge crowd of adherents gathered before the hotel and cheered him. Describing the struggle for power in a book which appeared soon after Hitler's assumption of power, Goebbels significantly chose for its title, *"Vom Kaiserhof zur Reichskanzlei"* ("From the Kaiserhof to the Reich Chancellery").]

In the Reich Chancellery, too, a big fire started in the Hall of Models, but we were able to contain it pretty well. Everything is at sixes and sevens in the Reich Chancellery, but that's true also of my own home, where almost all windows and doors are gone because of the enormous air pressure of the explosive bombs and mines.

[The Hall of Models was a huge space in the top story of the chancellery. Hitler spent his leisure hours there making architectural plans for big public edifices. Models were then cast from his plans.]

The government quarter is nothing short of an inferno. One can hardly recognize the Wilhelmplatz. . . .

The gau is in flames. Unfortunately Goerlitzer gave us a somewhat too optimistic report on this fire so that we sent the fire-fighting units too late. As a result serious fire damage is done to the gau, so that it cannot be used for the present.

[By the gau, Goebbels evidently meant the office building at No. 14 Hermann Goering Street which housed the administrative headquarters of the gau or district of Greater Berlin. Greater Germany, it will be remembered, was divided by the Nazis into forty-three gaus, each with a Gauleiter, a deputy Gauleiter, and a large staff. Goebbels was Gauleiter for Berlin, but the daily routine was handled by his deputy, Arthur Goerlitzer.]

The work that has to be done around 3 A.M. is maddening. My head aches from pain and fatigue, but that can't be helped. We must now do our part; the decisive hour has come.

Toward 2 A.M., thank God, the Wehrmacht arrived from Potsdam. It is under the command of a first-class lieutenant colonel named Friedrichs, a son of General Friedrichs, the present mayor of Potsdam. He took steps that made sense. It was chiefly owing to him that the fires in the government section were got under control within a relatively short time, as far as it could still be done. The Kaiserhof, for instance, and large parts of the Finance Ministry could no longer be saved.

A cause for misrepresentation developed through the fact that the Wehrmacht units from Potsdam had no other vehicles except tanks. That meant that the Army showed up in the government section with very threatening-looking vehicles, so that an outsider could assume we needed them for our protection. To avoid such a bad impression I saw to it that the tanks were withdrawn to the Berlin barracks by morning, otherwise we would certainly have read in the enemy press the following day that the Nazis had to call upon the Wehrmacht to protect themselves from the furious people! And so one has to pay attention to a thousand big and a thousand small things. It is wise always to be at hand, for sometimes the most unimportant of happenings can cause great difficulties.

It was 4 A.M. when I finally enjoyed a little rest. There are but few opportunities now to rest one's weary head. This time I slept in the bunker in Hermann Goering Street where Magda, too, took up quarters for the night. The house is a sad sight. I would far prefer to close my eyes so as not to have to see anything. This is one of the worst nights of my entire life. But I believe we got the upper hand. Although flames are still soaring sky high and in a part of Berlin large surface fires are still burning, we hope to overcome the worst difficulties by noon, and then to get ready for the next night. It would be a wonderful thing if we had one day's rest so that the fire department and the Party formations could for once get a little sleep.

Before taking my nap I was able to read a few telegrams from abroad that I had neglected completely during the day. Naturally the raid on Berlin was the main theme of enemy propaganda. Cynical admission was made of the intention to ensure the same fate for Berlin as for Hamburg.

The initial communiqué issued by the Luftwaffe about the first air raid is very bad. Too much emphasis is laid on the damage done. That gave the enemy press the text for extensive comment. Malicious joy is expressed. But I'll stick to my course. I cast only a fleeting glance at the telegrams. I have more important things to do than to get angry at the English.

London expects a new German peace offensive. It is believed that Envoy Bismarck, who is at present visiting relatives in Sweden, and the former Secretary of State Kuehlmann have been selected to conduct these peace negotiations. In reality there isn't a word of truth to either.

[Prince Otto von Bismarck, grandson of the Iron Chancellor, entered politics in 1924 during the Weimar Republic as a Reichstag deputy for the German Nationalist party. He later joined the Foreign Office staff and held a number of diplomatic posts, among them that of secretary of the German Legation at Stockholm. Here he met a Swedish lady, the daughter of Architect Tengbom, whom he married in 1928.

Baron Richard von Kuehlmann was one of the last Secretaries of State for Foreign Affairs during the Imperial regime, after having previously been Minister to the Netherlands and Ambassador to Turkey during World War I. He negotiated the treaty of Brest-Litovsk in 1918. After his retirement he was a frequent contributor on foreign affairs to German newspapers, especially the *Deutsche Allgemeine Zeitung* of Berlin.]

I read the latest speech delivered over the Moscow Radio by General von Seydlitz. This high-born aristocrat is the greatest swine in the German officer corps. I'd like nothing better than to spit contemptuously in his face. An honest, decent German worker would never stoop to such cowardly treachery; for that you have to look for in an aristocrat, if possible a general.

The hatred of the English among the population of the Reich capital exceeds all bounds.

November 25, 1943

The [second] heavy air raid equaled the first in intensity. Though at first we thought it might be weaker, this hope was not realized. The damage was quite as extensive as that of the previous one. Its character, too, was similar to the other. It was mainly the inner city that was hit and also the working-class suburbs. Unfortunately only about twenty planes were shot down. The pursuit planes took a hand but arrived too late and meanwhile the anti-aircraft was forbidden to shoot. The English therefore got away pretty cheaply with this attack.

Conditions in the city are pretty hopeless. The air is filled with smoke and the smell of fires. The Wilhelmplatz and the Wilhelmstrasse offer a gruesome picture. There was nothing to be done except to press everybody available into service and wait for rain. Rain came in the course of the day.

Gradually we learn to accustom ourselves again to a primitive standard of living. In the morning in Goering Street there is no heat, no light, no water. One can neither shave nor wash. One must leave the bunker with a burning candle.

I got up at an ungodly hour with my head throbbing as never before. All day long headaches pursue me. What of it? I simply must go to work. I drive straight to the office to wash and shave. I am very much hampered in my work. All telephone lines are down; I can contact the outside world only with the help of couriers. Most of the Reich ministries have been bombed out. The ministers and departmental heads can be found only with difficulty. That makes my work more difficult in some respects, but easier in others.

I had the various gau authorities report to me in a conference about the over-all situation. Critical conflagrations are still raging in some sections of the city, but surface fires have stopped. . . .

Fire-fighting units have been summoned in large numbers from other cities as far away as Hamburg and Breslau. These are naturally a great help to us. Petzke has tried to bring order into the provisioning, but an extremely difficult problem arises from the fact that the streets have not yet been cleared and the supply trucks can't get into the destroyed quarters. I must therefore do everything to get communications started again. The streets must be cleared before repairing the worst damage. For this, however, the man power available is not sufficient. The Wehrmacht must therefore help, not only with troops stationed in this defense area, but also with troops from other areas. The Wehrmacht supported my plans willingly and promised within twenty-four hours to furnish me two-and-a-half divisions, or 50,000 men. These 50,000 men are to do nothing except to clear the main traffic arteries of the Reich capital so that motorized transportation may be resumed and we be enabled to convey the most necessary articles of food and necessities into the bombed-out sections. Communications are the foundation of public life, as is here demonstrated. . . .

I have received detailed reports from various sections. It appears that even more bombs were dropped on the workers' quarters, especially Wedding, than in the government section, although this looks like a heap of rubble.

We must now face the problem of evacuation to emergency quarters. About 400,000 people in Berlin are without shelter. Some are lodged in municipal emergency quarters, others must spend their nights in subway tunnels. But I hope in two or three days to solve this problem also.

The first trains of homeless people left the city. But the Berliners for the present refuse to make much use of them. Everybody wants to stay here to save the things most needed and to await further developments. This morning no papers appeared. I am doing everything possible to see to it that at least a few newspapers make their appearance on the streets. The papers with an out-of-town circulation, especially, must resume publication because of the effect on foreign countries. The Deutscher Verlag remained unhurt, thank God, so that we can have most of the Berlin dailies printed there. Papers appearing twice daily must be reorganized on a once-a-day basis. . . .

[The Deutscher Verlag was Berlin's largest publishing house and commercial printing plant. It was for generations the property of the Ullstein family and had the official name of Ullstein Verlag until the Nazis in pursuance of their anti-Semitic policies compelled the Ullstein Brothers to sell out for a song. The name was then changed to Deutscher Verlag.]

As I learned from an over-all report, the potato situation in the Reich is not so serious as to prevent us in an exceptional case like this from making a special allotment. I also ordered that the Berliners get fifty grams of meat additional per week. Ten cigarettes are distributed to everybody, also some other delicacies. If everybody gets something into his stomach, and is given something to stimulate nerves strained to the breaking point, that helps a lot all along the line.

On orders of the Fuehrer I am now to organize an air-raid inspection service based on my experience in Berlin. The inspectors are to travel to all regions in which air raids have not yet taken place and to test the anti-aircraft facilities. This air-raid inspection is to be under my chairmanship and is to have authority to issue orders. I consider this inspection extremely important. . . .

The noon news report pictures the situation in Berlin as still very serious. . . . Contrary to expectations the number of people killed is, thank God, quite low. During the first air raid we registered 1,500 and during the second about 1,200 dead. I attribute these low figures chiefly to my evacuation measures, to farsighted emergency measures, and to the circumspection of the Berlin population. . . .

There is no dearth of food, but for the present we are unable to deliver it. The problem of people without shelter is naturally a pressing one, for it is hard to manage a great mass of people without a roof over their heads. The Fuehrer ordered the Reich Chancellery to be opened to shelterless people. I issued similar instructions about my residence in the Hermann Goering Street. Of course this is hardly usable, as it is still partly filled with water, has no heating, and taps that give no water. For the present, therefore, we shall have to make a great number of people spend their nights in the subway. But the Berlin population is very patient about it. . . .

What the enemy press is writing about the raids on Berlin simply can't be beaten for impudence. Their triumphant tone is enough to make one go mad. . . . Joined to their reports is an ultimatum to the German people to the effect that the end of the Reich capital will have come unless it offers to capitulate. Churchill, Roosevelt, and Stalin allegedly are to meet soon to launch this ultimatum.

The enemy now places his hopes chiefly in the breakdown of our morale. In an appeal to the Berliners I call their attention to what is at stake and what must be proven these days. Not only the German people but all foreign countries are looking to developments in Berlin with bated breath. Some foreign newspapers have expressed undisguised approval of the morale shown by the Berliners during these exceedingly heavy air raids.

Compared with all these problems, of what importance is the speech that the English King delivered in Parliament? It is as inane as can be and bubbles over with childish phrases. England, he maintains, has won victory with the aid of God. He lavishes special praise on Stalin, the murderer of the Czars. He praises the successes attained by English arms, but forgets to add that it was the weapons of air pirates operating chiefly with block busters to destroy dwellings. He feigns hypocritical sympathy with hungry India, and for the rest entrusts England's cause to God. This cheap, bigoted hypocrisy really makes one's blood boil.

After a short alert in the evening which, however, was not followed by a raid, I was able at last to make a tour of some of the destroyed sections of the city.

I drove via the Tiergarten, Zoo, Knie, and Kaiserdamm. What I saw was truly shattering. The whole Tiergarten quarter is destroyed, likewise the section around the Zoo. While the outer façades of the great representative edifices are still standing, everything on the inside is burned to the ground. This is true especially of the buildings all about the Zoo—Ufa Palace, Gloria Palace, Kaiser Wilhelm Memorial Church, Romanisches Café, et cetera. The Kurfuerstendamm looks terrible, not to speak of the Knie. Here you see nothing but remnants of walls and debris. Along the Kaiserdamm everything is still on fire but the fire department hopes to master the situation in the course of the night. Groups of people scamper across the streets like veritable ghosts. Your heart turns in your body as you go through these parts. How beautiful Berlin was at one time and how run-down and woebegone it now looks! But of what avail are all sorrow and pain? They won't change conditions. This war must be seen through. It is better that our workers crawl into cellars than that they be sent to Siberia as slave labor. Every decent German realizes this. . . .

Arriving in Schwanenwerder about midnight, we seem to be transported into a paradise. Here everything seems as though we were at peace. The house is delightfully warm. I can wash again, take a bath; telephone and radio are functioning; in short, for a few hours I enjoy a happiness which I thought I no longer deserved. It is not hard to imagine what thoughts keep stirring.

I worked for one more hour and then fell into a deep, dreamless sleep. When I awoke, the whole tragedy of the hard-hit city was again on my mind. I shall leave nothing undone to insure a halfway decent life for the unfortunate people who were stricken by this catastrophe.

November 26, 1943

The English are achieving nothing with their attempts to unload the responsibility for air warfare on us. Everybody in Germany knows that the English started it and that the blood guilt falls on them. The English now openly admit the terroristic intentions underlying their air raids. They talk with brutal cynicism about the block busters that were at work on the capital and that will continue to come.

In the early afternoon I visited the Reich Chancellery. It looks terrible. All the rooms that were formerly so beautiful and so dear to us are now destroyed, either burned out or full of water. My heart turned in my body when I saw all that has been destroyed here by air raids.

During lunch in the Reich Chancellery I had a talk with Lammers. He wants to have his main headquarters in the Fuehrer's bunker in the Reich Chancellery. I think he's right. According to a directive by the Fuehrer, the ministries and other highest offices of the Reich are to remain in Berlin just as long as possible. I regard this directive as extremely effective psychologically. I have no intention of leaving Berlin anyway. I shall stay here as long as there is even the remnant of a wall. Difficulties have arisen over the fact that homeless people have been lodged in the bunkers of the chancellery, but I hope soon to transfer them to other quarters.

The aspect of the Wilhelmplatz has already undergone quite a change. The fires are out, the atmosphere is clear, smoke has disappeared. There is no blaze left to extinguish. In short, although one sees the bare ruins of buildings projecting into the air, the most serious catastrophe has already been overcome. It is remarkable how fast everything goes. I thought it would take weeks; in reality only two days were needed. I have now installed the air inspections for other air gaus, as ordered by the Fuehrer. The Fuehrer will give me extensive plenary powers, including the right to issue orders. Advice alone won't do.

At last I have got the Fuehrer to the point that we may give two types of air alert in Berlin: one, a genuine alert, when bomber formations are on their way here, the other a mere warning in the case of a few nuisance planes. That is necessary, for I don't want to throw a city of four-and-a-half millions into a panic every night merely because of two Mosquitoes. While the Fuehrer has given his permission for this differentiation between types of alerts for Berlin only, I hope this method can be applied soon in other gaus also. In future the broadcasting stations are no longer to interrupt their programs when nuisance planes appear; they are to do it only when large bomber formations fly into the Reich.

In the evening the situation at first appeared somewhat critical. . . . Fires have started again in many places, so that Berlin is ablaze. I instructed Helldorf to resume fire fighting energetically. As soon as phosphorus dries, it begins to ignite again. . . .

I arranged with Bormann and Ley for political leaders from other gaus to be placed at my disposal in large numbers, for I must now and then replace my own officials, especially the Kreisleiters, as they will otherwise collapse physically.

Again and again I receive reports about the increasing seriousness of the situation in France. Many people even claim an uprising will take place there sooner or later. I don't believe, however, that things are so critical as represented.

November 27, 1943

Last night it was Frankfurt's turn to suffer fairly heavy attacks. The damage is not too bad, except for cultural monuments. Thus, for instance, the Goethe House has been hit. One's feelings are already so blunted by air raids that this hardly seems like sacrilege. There's nothing one can do about it anyway! Air raids hang over us like fate.

As a marginal note it may be recorded that the Duce is suddenly singing a Socialist song. He has installed an Italian Social Republic, as he calls his new Fascist State. I don't believe much will result from it. Fascism is compromised too badly to put a social-revolutionary movement on its feet.

As regards our situation in the East, the enemy credits us with more than we really have. Our difficulties there are enormous, chiefly because of the weather. Our attack did not really get under way. It got stuck, as it were, in the mud. We had expected so much of it, and so little came of it. We are having a streak of bad luck this year that is simply unique. All one can do is to hope that it may before long change over into an equally enduring streak of good luck.

During the last ten days, thank God, our casualties have not been too high. They totaled 6,473 killed in action, among them 180 officers; 26,000 wounded; 3,800 missing. That is bearable. On the other hand sickness has increased, and above all the troops have reached a new low physically and spiritually because of our continuous retreats. They must be given a rest and an opportunity for recreation to recuperate.

In the morning I undertook an extended trip through the damaged areas of Berlin. Sometimes I'd like to close my eyes so as not to see all this horror. The diplomatic quarter along the Tiergarten looks like one gigantic heap of rubble. One can hardly pass through the streets, as they are covered with debris. The rubble of the Rheingold is just being blasted. I have to wait here because the streets were being roped off. The Berliners gather around my car. I am amazed at their excellent spirit. Nobody cries, nobody complains. People slap me on the back familiarly, give me good advice, prevent me from continuing because, as they put it, nothing must happen to me since I am still very much needed. In short, the morale shown here by the Berlin population is simply magnificent.

[Soon after the Nazis came into power they started a special section along the Tiergarten as a diplomatic quarter and gradually eased various foreign missions that had hitherto been scattered all over the city out of their buildings and persuaded them to go to the new section. That made it much simpler for the Gestapo to check on the coming and going of visitors.

The Rheingold was a famous wine restaurant near the Potsdamer Platz.]

Letters addressed to me breathe a very resolute and manly spirit. Berlin is appealed to with the slogan, "Persevere and don't give in!" That isn't necessary, for we won't do that anyway. My articles are praised most warmly, especially by soldiers at the front. Now it's the turn of the front to encourage the people at home. It does this very eloquently. Only the complaints about the Etappe continue. The Fuehrer is now determined to do some general housecleaning in the Etappe. He ordered the Wehrmacht to release at least a million soldiers from the Etappe for combat duty. I don't believe the Wehrmacht can do it, but it will nevertheless manage to squeeze out a certain number. If I were the Fuehrer, I would appoint a man of caliber and make him responsible for this work. I believe if he had full powers and were a real man, he would perform the miracle of getting the million combat soldiers out of the Wehrmacht itself.

At noon I had a long talk with Speer. The beating Berlin took has shaken Speer considerably. Even though industrial plants were not hit very badly, nevertheless irreplaceable values have been destroyed. He is somewhat skeptical about our prospects in air warfare, especially since reprisals can begin only in March. The zero hour is being postponed again and again. That's the terror of terrors. If we could at least strike at the English soon! But look where you will, no such possibility is discernible.

Schaub took me through the private apartments of the Fuehrer. These have been completely destroyed. It makes me sad to find these rooms, in which we enjoyed so many hours of spiritual uplift, in such a condition.

With Naumann and Schaub I then took another trip through the damaged areas. We also stopped at some soup kitchens. I inquired into even the smallest details. The people show a touching devotion. The misery that meets my eyes is indescribable. My heart is convulsed at the sights. But we must grit our teeth. Sometimes I have the impression that the Berliners are almost in a religious trance. Women come up to me and lay their hands on me in blessing, imploring God to preserve me. All that is very touching. But then I am doing everything I can for the people. The meals are everywhere praised as excellent. People without shelter are gradually being provided quarters. People are weighed down with sorrow about loved ones who fell, but they are getting over it. The attitude and morale of the population are exemplary. We shall never lose the war for reasons of morale.

I took several women from the soup kitchens with me and had them driven to the east side, where they could not get with normal transportation facilities. They are more than happy. Show these people small favors, and you can wrap them around your finger. I can hardly believe that this city started a revolution in November 1918. It would never have happened under my leadership.

Work and nothing but work is piled on me in my office. In addition I must write my speech for the Sunday demonstration of the Hitler Youth as quickly as possible. I am going to say some pointed things in it about England. This time I'm going to draw on my lexicon of abuse. I must use a hardboiled, invidious language in dealing with England. That's the kind of talk the people want to hear today.

The Ministry has become a bit more livable again. The windows have either been pasted over with paper, or cardboard has replaced glass. But at least the rooms are warm again so that one can work.

In the early evening attention was naturally focused on the question of a possible air raid. At first it looked as though everything was to be perfectly harmless, and as though only nuisance planes were to fly over us. Then a stronger formation started after all for Frankfurt-on-Main and we received news that this city would be attacked again. But that was merely a camouflage maneuver. The English turned off from Frankfurt unnoticed and sneaked over the Thuringian Forest toward Berlin. In Berlin the question was first raised whether any alert should be sounded at all, as it was thought mere nuisance planes were approaching. Suddenly, however, we noted that a major attack was again in the offing. It had merely been camouflaged cleverly to mislead our pursuit planes. The starry sky is clear so that the pursuit planes, if they were here, could take a hand splendidly. They did arrive at the last moment, thank God.

And then things started. Once again a major attack descended upon the Reich capital. This time it wasn't so much the center of the city that was the target as it was the suburbs of Wedding and Reinickendorf, and chiefly the large munitions plants in Reinickendorf. Some of the main traffic crossings in the center of the city also took a beating, among them the Spittelmarkt and the Gendarmenmarkt. But the important thing was the damage to industry. The news that the Alkett plant was on fire was especially depressing. Alkett is our most important factory for the production of fieldpieces. There we produce one half of our entire output of these guns, amounting to 200 pieces. That must not be lost. In agreement with the Fuehrer I order that the fire-department companies be concentrated on Alkett, but they arrive a bit too late. For hours we discuss the question as to whether the Alkett factory can be saved. I send Helldorf there. Companies of the fire department and of auxiliary troops are hurried out to Alkett. Nevertheless they cannot prevent the assembly hall from burning to the ground. That is a heavy blow. The Fuehrer, too, is very much depressed.

[Reinickendorf is a borough of Berlin now in the French sector of occupation.]

I then drove quickly to the Deutsches Theater and the Kammerspiele, which are also on fire. We did succeed in so localizing the fires that the theaters on the whole remain more or less intact. Unfortunately I had to withdraw the fire fighters from the theaters at a critical moment and send them to Alkett to the big industrial plants. Nevertheless we are able to save the theaters.

[The Deutsches Theater and the Kammerspiele were contiguous and before the Nazi regime belonged to Max Reinhardt.]

The scenes at the Gendarmenmarkt are gruesome. All around it whole rows of houses are ablaze. The State Playhouse alone is still undamaged. But how much longer? I fear its days, too, are numbered, if enemy air raids continue.

[The Gendarmenmarkt was one of the most artistic squares in Berlin. In the center stood the *Staatstheater,* or State Playhouse, a beautiful building constructed by the famous architect of Frederick the Great, Schinkel. It was flanked on one side by the Garrison Church and on the other by the French Church, erected by French Huguenots. Along its sides were chiefly the offices of the clothing trade.]

Back to the bunker at the Wilhelmplatz. The situation has become even more alarming in that one industrial plant after another has been set on fire. The main damage, however, is at Alkett. . . .

The sky above Berlin is bloody, deep red, and of an awesome beauty. I just can't stand looking at it. . . . It seems as though all the elements of fate and nature have conspired against us to create difficulties. If only frost were to set in, so that our tanks might move again in the East!

Profound peace prevails in Schwanenwerder. I had only a brief, restless sleep. What a life we are leading! Who could have prophesied that at our cradle! I don't believe anyone can lead a more dramatic and nerve-racking life. Nevertheless it has great and impelling impulses. One must throw oneself into this life with abandon both to taste it to the full and to help shape it. Later generations will not only admire us but be jealous that life entrusted us with such tremendous tasks.

November 28, 1943

The British are greatly overestimating the damage done to Berlin. Naturally it is terrible, but there is no question of 25 per cent of the capital no longer existing. The English naturally want to furnish their public a propaganda morsel. I have every reason to want them to believe this and therefore forbid any denial. The sooner London is convinced that there is nothing left of Berlin, the sooner will they stop their air offensive against the Reich capital. . . .

This time the munitions industry was especially hard hit. The Alkett works received a blow from which they won't recover easily. At Alkett 80 per cent of our fieldpieces were produced, of which there will now be a shortage. At Borsig's also tremendous destruction took place. It must be remembered that Borsig produces a large percentage of our gun output and has 18,000 employees. Naturally everything is being done to get munitions production started again. But that is more easily said than done. . . .

In the evening the so-called "Calais Soldiers Broadcast," which evidently originates in England and uses the same wave length as Radio Station Deutschland when the latter is cut out during air raids, gave us something to worry about. The station does a very clever job of propaganda and from what is put on the air one can gather that the English know exactly what they have destroyed in Berlin and what not.

Ellgerin was given special orders by me to find substitute quarters and shelters for the homeless. Ellgerin has had a vast amount of experience in this matter in the west. He promised to see to it that within twenty-four hours at the latest everybody would have at least a roof over his head. It's high time that the people get out of the subway tunnels, for that's no way to live. Communicable diseases start there; possibly they are even breeding places for political decadence. This won't do at all.

[Ellgerin is not identified more closely in the diaries.]

At noon I and my collaborators addressed the Reich Cabinet. . . .
The Cabinet was extremely interested and for the first time in its history broke into applause at the end of my talk.

London reports that more than a million people met their death in
Berlin. That, of course, is arrant nonsense, for the number of fatal
casualties owing to three heavy air raids totals between three and four
thousand. But I don't issue a denial of these exaggerations. The sooner
the English believe there's no life left in Berlin, the better for us.

The Soviets are outdoing themselves in their demand for unconditional German surrender. They ask us for 1,600,000,000 gold marks
as reparations and declare quite insolently that they don't want this
sum paid them in cash, but instead want all of Germany's production
facilities plus the workers surrendered to them. We would rather defend the last remnants of our walls than accede to such a mad demand.
The English are already giving hypocritical support to these insane
Soviet demands. They naturally would like to use this occasion to sell
out the entire German future. The English would then not have to
bother any longer about Europe, at least as they see it. The most surprising thing about the whole matter is that nobody in England seems
to recognize that once the Soviet Union is in Europe, it will be a much
more dangerous opponent of the British Empire.

There was a tempest in the teapot in the Hungarian Parliament.
The representative of the Small Peasants' party delivered a speech in
which he protested vigorously against Hungary's participation in the
war and berated the Reich. This speech is really the climax in meanness to an ally. But one must not take the Hungarians too seriously.
They have lost their nerve and are acting crazily.

November 29, 1943

We spent a quiet evening. That was balm for the wounds of the
Reich capital. I started early from Schwanenwerder for the Hitler
Youth demonstration in Steglitz. . . . Fortunately the Titania Palace is
undamaged, so that our meeting for the Hitler Youth and their parents
could be held there. Axmann awaited me.

As we enter the movie hall, earsplitting applause greets me. Never
before have I seen the Berlin public so receptive to a message as now.
. . . My address seemed as if made to order. The public broke into
stormy applause at every sentence with a punch. . . . I believe this

speech will make a very deep impression not only on the German people but on the entire world. I am very happy that I spoke, despite the objections that were raised. The right word spoken at the right time sometimes achieves miracles.

[Steglitz is a borough of Berlin now in the American occupation sector.
The Titania Palast, one of Berlin's largest motion-picture houses, is now a Red Cross recreation center for American occupation forces. Also, as Philharmonic Hall was burned to the ground, the concerts of the Berlin Philharmonic Orchestra are now given there.]

The Berlin munition industry is still in bad shape. Alkett is almost completely destroyed, and, worst of all, valuable and virtually irreplaceable tools and machines have been put out of commission. The English aimed so accurately that one might think spies had pointed their way. . . .

It's surprising that the theaters and movie houses have opened their doors again and that the people fairly stream into them. There are queues before all the motion-picture houses. People crave recreation after the grueling days and nights of the past week. They want solace for their souls. . . .

I drove to Reinickendorf and Wedding. At the Gartenplatz I took part in the feeding of the public. The men and women workers received me with an enthusiasm that is as unbelievable as it is indescribable. This section of Wedding, all around Acker Street, was at one time full of Reds. I should never have thought it possible that such a transformation of spirit and viewpoint could take place. . . .

I had to eat with the people and was lifted onto a box to talk to them. I delivered a very earthy and slangy speech which won the hearts of the workers. Everybody accosted me with "Du" and called me by my first name. The people wanted to carry me on their shoulders across the Platz and I had difficulty preventing it. Women embraced me. I had to give my autograph. Cigarettes were distributed and I smoked one with them. In short, people were in as high spirits as at a carnival.

Naturally the destruction is enormous, but in so far as the people themselves are involved, they take it with the best of humor. They are firmly convinced that we shall be able to overcome the difficulties. They have only praise for the measures thus far taken.

Wedding itself is for the most part a shambles. The same goes for Reinickendorf.

I took leave of the people. There were deeply touching scenes. One woman had given birth to a child during an air raid two or three days ago; nevertheless she insisted on getting up when she heard I had come, dressed, and hurried to the Platz. We can never lose this war because of defective morale.

I discussed at length with Dr. Ley how we can get back to work the men who have not yet returned to their factories. We shall have to do something to stimulate their return. We want especially to give cigarettes and liquor to workers who return on time, and beyond that to appeal to their sense of duty, which is by no means a thankless labor in the case of Berlin workers. Work must be resumed as quickly as possible. Also, the workers must help to clear away the rubble. They must not leave that to the soldiers, who know nothing whatever about the plants, and possibly are destroying more than they are putting in order. . . . The Berliner will stand on his head for a cigarette!

I was called by the Fuehrer's GHQ. The Fuehrer and all his collaborators are enthusiastic about my speech and in full agreement with it. They characterize Berlin as a combat company that is doing its duty with the finest *esprit de corps*.

The Fuehrer has issued a decree to the Wehrmacht for bringing order into conditions in the Etappe. I place this decree chiefly on the credit side of my ledger, for my incessant appeals to the Fuehrer contributed essentially to its being issued.

November 30, 1943

London replied to my speech in the Titania Palace with an outburst of anger. The fact, especially, that I described the English aviators as cowards has made the blood of the English propagandists boil.

A typically English thing is happening in London in that a prayer racket for India has been scheduled. The bishops and priests have been mobilized for it. They are to address fervent prayers to God to let the Indians have the food that the English have stolen from them!

Exposés about the Duce and his entourage written by Professor Preziosi were submitted to me. They are very depressing. Despite his grave debacle the Duce has learned nothing. He is still surrounded by traitors, former Free Masons and Jew-lovers who give him entirely wrong advice. His son Vittorio is playing a pretty loathsome role, not so much because of his lack of character as because of his stupidity. It is nauseating to read these reports. The Duce has learned nothing and forgotten nothing.

My visit to Wedding has had a tremendous effect on the working-class population there. Veritable legends about it are spread throughout the northern and eastern quarters of the city. We make no mention of it in the press; it is much better that propaganda by word of mouth do its work.

I discuss a number of personnel questions with Bormann. Bormann, too, is worried about German foreign policy. Ribbentrop is too rigid to be able to spin his web in this difficult war situation. But I don't believe the Fuehrer is ready to part company with his Foreign Minister. Yet Ribbentrop would not be able to negotiate either with London or with Moscow were such an eventuality to arise. Both sides consider him too heavily compromised.

Bormann expressed himself as very much concerned over the war in general. It is so hard to get the Fuehrer to make any decision, and of course we can't win the war with morale alone; we must have arms and man power. Our arms production, however, is being destroyed by enemy air raids to a very noticeable degree.

December 1943

ROOSEVELT, CHURCHILL, STALIN, CONFER FOUR DAYS AT TEHERAN. ALLIED RAIDS ON SOLINGEN, BERLIN, LEIPZIG, SOFIA, EMDEN, AUGSBURG, INNSBRUCK, BREMEN, FRANKFURT-ON-MAIN, MANNHEIM, LUDWIGSHAFEN, AND SOUTH-WEST GERMANY. YUGOSLAV PARTISANS FORBID KING PETER TO RETURN. TURKISH PRESIDENT INONU CONFERS THREE DAYS AT CAIRO WITH ROOSEVELT AND CHURCHILL. RUSSIANS HALT GERMAN COUNTEROFFENSIVE IN KIEV AREA. CHURCHILL ILL WITH PNEUMONIA. EISENHOWER NAMED SUPREME COMMANDER FOR INVASION OF WESTERN EUROPE. RUSSIANS CUT GERMAN SUPPLY LINE LINKING VITEBSK AND POLOTSK. BATTLESHIP SCHARNHORST SUNK OFF NORTH CAPE, NORWAY. RUSSIANS RECAPTURE ZHITOMIR. RUSSIAN ARMIES IN UKRAINE ROUT TWENTY-TWO GERMAN DIVISIONS.

Recapitulation of events between December 1 and 4, 1943

There is a gap of only three days at this point in the diaries, but for a proper understanding of what follows it is necessary to remember that on December 1, 1943, President Roosevelt, Generalissimo Stalin, and Prime Minister Churchill completed a four-day conference in Teheran.

Also, there was another terrific air raid on Berlin on December 2.

December 4, 1943

A speech delivered in London by Smuts is truly sensational. He declared that the Reich would disappear from the map for a long time. That's nothing new to us. Then, however, he continued with observations that must be taken more seriously, to the effect that the Soviets would become the masters of Europe. The Russian colossus would dominate the entire European continent. England would come out of this war with honor and glory but poor as a beggar. The United States would in large measure be the heir to the British Empire. England would no longer have much to say in Europe since the Soviet Union would take its place.

[Field Marshal Jan Christiaan Smuts, born, 1870, is Prime Minister of the Union of South Africa.]

I received a detailed report about the situation in the East from Major Voss, who for more than a year has been on duty on the Eastern Front at various command points. Passing over many things already known to me, the essential thing appeared to be Major Voss's emphasis on the fact that we made a big mistake in not evacuating the male population in time from regions about to be abandoned. During their advance the Soviets immediately recruited this male population for their troops. Most men were not even given uniforms but are merely wearing a red armband. In this way Stalin secured some 400,000 to 500,000 soldiers for himself in a very simple way. As long as we left the male population directly behind the front lines, the danger of Partisan formations could not be eliminated. Major Voss's report seemed so important to me that I shall send it as an item of information to the Fuehrer.

Incidentally, the information which I send to the Fuehrer always attracts extraordinary attention at GHQ and much use is made of it. Usually the Fuehrer takes the reports I send him to the staff conference to bring them to the knowledge of his generals.

Our hate propaganda against England is falling on most fertile soil with the German people. My speech in the Titania Palace is regarded as one of the most effective that ever issued from the mouth of a German during this war.

In Italy the enemy has started new assaults on our front. They have succeeded here and there in making inroads. But considerable reserves of ours are on the march, so that people in the Fuehrer's GHQ don't worry about further developments. The operations are chiefly under Jodl's command. But Jodl does not seem to me any too competent for evaluating a critical military situation. He has so often been wrong in his prognoses that personally I am unable to drop my worries about the southern Italian front.

December 5, 1943

We have received a valuable report via Lisbon about the domestic situation in England. According to it the fear of German retaliation is almost indescribable, especially in the English capital. The English have a bad conscience.

According to the English yellow press, the conference of the Big Three is to decide on military plans of great magnitude against Germany. The Anglo-Americans have asked Stalin for airports within the territory of the Soviet Union so as to be able to bombard Germany from the east also. Churchill again intends to cede all of eastern Germany to the Poles as an equivalent for the Soviets' laying claim to eastern Poland. I can hardly imagine that the leading English statesmen are so stupid and shortsighted as to put that sort of an estimate on Bolshevism. Stalin won't think of fulfilling obligations entered upon with England and America.

In the margin I may note that the French press took sharp issue with Smuts because he claimed that France has lost her position as a Great Power.

Rediess, head of the higher SS and police in Norway, has visited the Fuehrer to report on the Oslo students. The Fuehrer was somewhat put out—and rightly so—that this question was handled with a sledge hammer. The Fuehrer is also skeptical about the success to be expected. Undoubtedly it would have been possible to achieve an essentially greater effect with less effort, for there are only a couple of dozen rebels among the Oslo students who could have been arrested without the public noticing it. Most decidedly it was a big mistake to arrest all students of Oslo. Terboven is especially to be blamed for not having informed the Fuehrer before acting. The whole affair would have run an entirely different course had he done so.

The Swedish Government has protested to us because of the arrest of the Oslo students. At the Fuehrer's orders this protest is to be answered by Ribbentrop in the sharpest language. Naturally we can't beat a retreat on this Oslo student question now. But it would have been better to think matters over before rather than after.

Unfortunately the air raid on Leipzig last night was exceedingly severe and fateful. The city was not prepared for so massive an attempt at terrorization. The fire department was not adequate. As a result whole rows of houses went up in smoke. The center of the city was especially hard hit. Almost all public buildings, theaters, the university, the Supreme Court, exhibition halls, et cetera have either been completely destroyed or seriously damaged. . . . About 150,000 to 200,000 people are without shelter.

[Leipzig was the seat of the German *Reichsgericht,* or Supreme Court. It was famed the world over for its annual fairs, for which it had built an imposing series of exhibition halls. Johann Sebastian Bach was choirmaster and organist at the *Thomaskirche,* or Church of St. Thomas from 1723 to his death in 1750.]

December 6, 1943

The conference in Teheran has become quite mysterious. The enemy has so far refrained from issuing any sort of informative communiqué about it, so that we are still groping in the dark. . . . There are a number of conjectures, however, about the Teheran show which contradict each other and therefore have no political value. In the spring, after the German cities have been reduced to ruins, the English allegedly want to start the invasion. Of course chills run down their backs even at the use of this word. They want, above all, to intensify their air offensive against us during January because that is the coldest month and it is expected that air raids will then affect German morale more adversely.

In the evening it is claimed that an editorial committee has been appointed in Teheran to compose an appeal to the German people. But that appeal is not forthcoming! At any rate, we have already taken massive countermeasures in our propaganda against such an appeal. If it should actually come, it will find us by no means unprepared. The German people will surely treat it as a scrap of paper that has no political significance.

In Sweden and Finland the turmoil about the Oslo students continues. Ribbentrop received the Swedish Chargé d'Affaires in Berlin and gave him a very juicy and cutting reply to the Swedish *démarche*. His reply summarizes all the reasons why it ill becomes the Swedes to raise an accusing finger in this matter. Nevertheless the whole Oslo affair stinks. The Fuehrer, too, is quite angry about the way it was handled. He received two representatives of Terboven and gave them an energetic scolding. Terboven has once more behaved like a bull in a china shop. Himmler is furious about the effects of Terboven's action. He was going to enlist about 40,000 to 60,000 volunteers in Norway during the coming months. Prospects for this seemed to be excellent.

By Terboven's stupid action a good part of the plan has fallen in the water. Here you can see again what dire consequences result if everybody does as he pleases. It was Terboven's duty to seek the Fuehrer's advice in this matter; the Fuehrer would surely have absolutely forbidden the coup planned by him.

December 7, 1943

In the morning we were still ignorant of what happened at Teheran. . . . Everybody is tense and full of expectation. As a result there is very little news, because the entire world news machinery is geared to the Teheran communiqué. . . . In the evening the long-awaited communiqué was at last issued. It is neither flesh nor fowl. There is no talk whatever about any appeal to the German people. . . . One might expect that a little more would result from three days of conference, but apparently Stalin could not agree to the plans of Churchill and Roosevelt. Stalin was undoubtedly the guiding spirit of the Teheran Conference. It is like a fist in the eye when they talk of democracy, freedom of peoples, and elimination of intolerance and slavery in a document bearing his signature. . . . I believe that the plan for an appeal to the German people was dropped mainly because of our anticipatory propaganda. . . . I regard this communiqué as a complete German victory.

In the evening I telephoned my commentary on the Teheran Conference to the Fuehrer. He expressed complete agreement with it. He, too, is of the opinion that the communiqué reveals anything but success. We can publish it almost verbatim in the German press; it contains nothing dangerous to us. . . . I imagine that our seed is at last beginning to sprout. If things develop further like that, we may yet find ourselves facing undreamed-of changes in the general situation this winter.

Goering traveled west on orders of the Fuehrer to prepare a retaliatory blow against England. We need about 200 heavy four-motored planes for it. They are to fly to England twice in the course of one night and strike a heavy blow against the British capital. Naturally we cannot repeat such an assault as often as we would like, but it will give the English something to think about. I expect great psychological results from it.

I now hope to reach an agreement with Rosenberg about the question of press management in the occupied eastern areas. Rosenberg's collaborators complain bitterly that it is impossible to work with him because he is too rigid. They say he has an inferiority complex in regard to me, which leads to a number of differences for which there is no real reason.

Reuter reports that Count Ciano has been executed. Unfortunately this report does not correspond with the facts.

The great task of the hour is to see to it that law and order prevail in the occupied areas. In Copenhagen, for instance, a German soldier was shot. The military levied a penalty of two million marks on the city. That's an effective method of punishment. You have to grab the Danes by their purse strings. They are most touchy there.

The English are waging war in Italy very effectively. It is by no means true that they lack combat experience. On the contrary, they are making the cleverest use of every advantage. Their most striking advantage is their superiority in the air. Every day they lay a curtain of bombs on us in numbers hitherto unknown in this war. In southern Italy one can speak of matériel battles comparable to those of World War I in the west.

December 8, 1943

The enemy press naturally accompanies the conference of Teheran and the communiqué with the obligatory anthems of jubilation. . . . When Reuter declares that the communiqué is tantamount to a military death sentence for the Axis, the obvious reply is that military verdicts of death are written not in conferences but on the field of battle. . . .

It was to be expected that the communiqué would be characterized as the "Magna Carta of the Twentieth Century." The whole world is to be reorganized for centuries to come. But who still cares about these phrases and subterfuges? To me it seems much more important that even the English admit that Stalin undoubtedly dominated the conference. . . . The English journalists claim that Stalin had grown very gray and that there were deep furrows of worry on his brow. That is easily understandable.

The German press and radio go after the Teheran Conference communiqué in a big way. Our reply is biting and insolent; we empty buckets of irony and derision over the conference. Our sarcasm is superior and I must say German propaganda has reached the very heights of what can be achieved in publicity.

At noon I addressed a meeting in celebration of the Day of the German Railway Man at the People's Theater. . . . Even as I stepped on the stage a veritable hurricane of applause greeted me, such as I experienced only in the time of our struggle for power. Every point made by me evokes an enthusiastic echo from the railway workers. The spirit is an excellent one, and in no respect inferior to that of the recent Hitler Youth demonstration in the Titania Palace in Steglitz. The people were simply mad with enthusiasm when I pointed out what the enemy intended to do against German war morale in the way of propaganda.

December 9, 1943

A pompous, phrase-laden communiqué has been issued about Roosevelt's and Churchill's meeting with Inonu in Cairo. No doubt the Turks were willing to stand for this communiqué only because they wanted to camouflage somewhat their opposition to the Anglo-American demands. It is quite obvious Turkey shows no inclination whatever to enter the war in favor of England or the United States, not to speak of the Soviet Union. But the enemy is still not giving up hope.

[General Ismet Inonu succeeded the late Mustapha Kemal Ataturk, founder of the modern Turkish State, on November 11, 1938, as Chief of State.]

The second front has now been graciously announced as due within three months, and Churchill declared before his old regiment in North Africa that the year 1944 would bring the decision. We look forward to it with great confidence, for we shall beat the English and Americans back when they attempt an invasion.

A serious epidemic of influenza has broken out in England. The King, too, is ill. How wonderful if the epidemic were to prove fatal! That would suit us exactly. But that's too good to be true.

The Japanese celebrated the beginning of the third year of war. Tojo delivered a speech about Japanese successes to date and also predicted the decision for 1944. I can only warn him about fixing dates. We had some very bad experiences along that line during this war.

How badly we are doing our political job in the East can be seen from the fact that Rosenberg has still not carried out the Fuehrer's order to transfer the propaganda there to us. He is doing everything he can to sabotage and torpedo it. I don't understand how the Fuehrer can leave such an obstreperous nincompoop in his job. If I were in his place, I would clear the boards in a hurry. Rosenberg has done more harm than good, not only in the East but also in the realm of politics generally. It is high time for a showdown.

Lammers, at my request, reported the situation regarding the propaganda department in Paris to the Fuehrer and told him about Ribbentrop's attempt to take it out of my hands via the OKW. The Fuehrer was in a rage and turned against Ribbentrop, using very harsh and insulting expressions. The Fuehrer described the report given me by Ribbentrop through Minister Ritter as absolutely untrue and mendacious.

The Fuehrer was very much excited during this talk and told Von Ribbentrop he would not stand for his coming to him again in private on such matters. He decided that for the present everything should remain as it is until I've had an opportunity to present the case to the Fuehrer. One can see how unscrupulously Ribbentrop is wont to proceed in such matters and how little true comradeship he shows a colleague. If Ribbentrop is as clever in his foreign policy as he is toward his colleagues in matters of domestic politics, I can well understand why we don't achieve any notable successes in our dealings with foreign nations.

[The entry for December 9, 1943, was the last found among the Goebbels papers. It is a rather curious fact that the outstanding impression gained from this last entry is that of the jealousy and disunity among Hitler's top leaders.]

Index

Index

Index